The Anthology

Vettius Valens

―――― ✣ ――――

Translated by Mark T. Riley

Amor Fati Publications | Denver, Colorado
2022

© 2022 Amor Fati Publications
All rights reserved
First edition, published October 16, 2022.

ISBN-13: 978-0-9985889-1-9 (paper)

All rights reserved. No portion of this book may be reproduced without permission from the publisher, except as permitted under fair use by U.S. copyright law. Sales of this book help to support further publications in this field. Please support this work by purchasing only authorized editions, and by not participating in piracy of copyrighted materials. Thank you.

An errata sheet listing typos and corrections can be found at:
https://www.hellenisticastrology.com/valens

Names: Vettius Valens, author. | Riley, Mark T., translator, editor.
Title: The anthology / Vettius Valens ; translated by Mark T. Riley.
Other titles: Anthologiae. English
Description: First edition. | Denver, Colorado : Amor Fati Publications, [2022] | Includes bibliographical references and index.
Identifiers: ISBN: 978-0-9985889-1-9 (paperback) | LCCN: 2022916691
Subjects: LCSH: Vettius Valens. | Astrologers--Biography. | Astrology--Early works to 1800. | Astrology --History--To 1500. | Astronomy--History--To 1500. | Science, Ancient. | Science--History--To 1500. | History--Greco-Roman period, 332 B.C.-640 A.D. | Civilization, Greco-Roman. | Philosophy, Ancient. | BISAC: BODY, MIND & SPIRIT / Astrology / General.
Classification: LCC: BF1680 .V4713 2022 | DDC: 133.5--dc19

This book has been typeset in Arno Pro 12/15 pt.

Printed on acid-free paper.

The Ancients wrote about this topic, darkly and mysteriously. We have cast light on it.

—Vettius Valens

c. 175 CE

Table of Contents

Foreword, *by Chris Brennan*		*vii*
A Survey of Vettius Valens, *by Mark Riley*		*xiii*
1	BOOK I	1
2	BOOK II	49
3	BOOK III	119
4	BOOK IV	147
5	BOOK V	193
6	BOOK VI	229
7	BOOK VII	249
8	BOOK VIII	283
9	BOOK IX	325
10	A FIFTH-CENTURY ADDITION	355
Index		367

Foreword

Chris Brennan

Vettius Valens was an astrologer who lived in the middle of the second century. His *Anthology* is a collection of instructional texts on astrology that he wrote for his students in Greek. It is perhaps the single most important surviving source for understanding what the practice of astrology was like in ancient times, because Valens included more than a hundred examples in order to demonstrate how birth charts were interpreted in antiquity. Valens lived in the Roman Empire during the reigns of Hadrian, Antoninus Pius, and Marcus Aurelius. He wrote in Greek because that was the common language that was used for scientific and philosophical works in the Mediterranean region during that time. Valens' work became popular later during the medieval period with astrologers who wrote in Greek and Arabic, however he was largely forgotten in the subsequent eras, until recently. This publication marks the first time that the entirety of the *Anthology* has ever been translated into English.

Mark T. Riley is a retired Classics scholar who taught at California State University, in Sacramento. In the 1980s and '90s he spent a period of his career studying the surviving works of Greco-Roman astrologers, and authored several academic papers on Claudius Ptolemy and Vettius Valens. He was contracted to write an extensive survey of Valens' work for the series *Aufstieg und Niedergang der römischen Welt* (*Rise and Decline of the Roman World*), but the series stopped being published before his article appeared in print, so he instead he posted the survey online in the year 2000. In some ways the release of this survey online allowed it to circulate much more widely than it might have otherwise, and it was used by a number of subsequent scholars, such as Joanna Komorowska in her 2004 book *Vettius Valens of Antioch: An Intellectual Monography*.

In order to complete his *Survey*, Riley made a full English translation of Valens for his own private use, based on both the first critical edition of the Greek text of the *Anthology* produced by Wilhelm Kroll in 1908, as well as a later and more authoritative critical edition published by David Pingree in 1986. However, Riley did not think this translation would be comprehensive enough for publication without consulting the Arabic fragments of Valens that survived from the medieval tradition, and he also did not feel like he was at a stage in his life where he was prepared to learn Arabic in order to accomplish this task. Eventually he abandoned the project and returned to his previous interest in other areas of Latin and Greek classical studies.

On December 14, 2010 Mark posted a full PDF file of his translation of Valens online for free, after exchanging emails with another scholar named Roger Pearse who encouraged him to release it after learning of its existence. This marked the first time that the full text of the *Anthology* had appeared in English, as previously only a preliminary translation of the first seven books of the *Anthology* had been published by Robert Schmidt between 1993–2001. There was also a complete German translation of Valens by Otto Schönberger and Eberhard Knobloch that appeared in 2004, and a French translation of book 1 of the *Anthology* by Joëlle-Frédérique Bara in 1989. A publisher named David R. Roell began preparing a version of Riley's translation for print in 2011, but this project was cut short by his untimely death in 2014.

Over the past decade Riley's translation has become the main one used both by academics and astrologers when studying the *Anthology*, although the absence of diagrams to display the chart examples that Valens describes has made the text harder to follow than it should be. Over the past decade I have made excerpts of different chapters and inserted illustrations of the chart examples, for the purpose of teaching and making the text clearer to my students. More recently I realized that it was time to complete this work by releasing a full edition of Riley's translation that contains illustrations for every chart example that is described in the text. At the suggestion of my friend Jenn Zahrt, I asked Riley if I could publish an illustrated version of his translation, and he graciously agreed.

The first part of this book contains the full text of Mark Riley's 1996 *Survey of Vettius Valens*. The *Survey* has been included in this publication because I think it provides a nice introduction and overview of Valens' text, and I thought that it was an important enough contribution to the field that it should finally appear in print. While it was completed in 1996 and does not take account of any scholarship done since that time, it still provides a very thorough treatment of Valens' life and work. The text has only been edited lightly, and still reflects Mark's thoughts and work on Valens from that time. One particularly notable feature in the *Survey* is Mark's work on Valens' chronology, which extends some of the research that Otto Neugebauer did in the 1950s on establishing the timeline of Valens' life, based on chart examples that are used in the *Anthology*.

The second part of this book includes Mark's complete translation of all nine surviving books of the *Anthology*. Each time Valens introduces a chart example, we have placed a diagram next to it in the text which illustrates the placements in a round zodiac wheel. Both round and square chart wheels were used in antiquity, and so we opted for circular wheels here as a matter of convenience and familiarity for modern readers. I worked with Paula Belluomini to illustrate each of these diagrams, with assistance from Claire Rootjes. We took great pains to design these diagrams exactly as Valens describes them in the text, neither adding anything in nor leaving anything out. I assume that diagrams were originally included in the text but were lost at some point during the long transmission of the *Anthology*, just as many of the tables were either partially or entirely lost as well. Since Valens intended these examples to be used to help elucidate his techniques for readers, I think he would appreciate our having restored the illustrations.

I have tried to proofread and fix a number of typos and other errors in the translation, sometimes by consulting the underlying Greek text in Pingree's critical edition, and I feel like we have been able to make enough corrections that this edition represents a worthwhile improvement over the version of Riley's translation that was released online a decade ago. I would like to thank Leisa Schaim and Claire Rootjes for their help with proofreading the text and catching many typos, as well as one other anonymous proofreader whose assistance on this project was invaluable. Additionally, with Mark's help, we were able to translate and include a set of important tables from the end of book 8 of the *Anthology* that were not included in the previous release. Elsewhere, there were some additional chapters that were added to the end of the *Anthology* in the fifth century, but some of these chapters are not included in this publication because Mark decided not to translate them. Some of this omitted material just consists of interpolations of verbatim quotations from the texts of later astrologers who lived after Valens such as Hephaistion of Thebes, or in other instances summaries of different parts of the *Anthology*. Since Hephaistion's text has already been translated into English elsewhere, I did not feel the need to commission additional translations in order to include that material here.

While I did try to fix a number of typos in the process of preparing this translation for publication, I otherwise tried to be very sparing about making significant edits or changes to the translation, because the primary purpose of this book is simply to put Mark's translation into print and let it speak for itself. I think there is still plenty of room for additional work and scholarship on Valens' *Anthology*, and I have no doubt that we will see other translations of this important text in the future. In the meantime, I felt that it was important to try to finalize Mark's translation and put it into a more readable format, so that others can learn from and build on his scholarship.

All footnotes in the text are Riley's own, except when occasionally marked with a note from the editor, which I will designate with my initials CB. In the *Survey* you will see numbers that end with the letter K or the letter P, such as /160K/ or /152P/. These refer to the page numbers in the two different critical editions of the text by Kroll and Pingree, and Riley included them so that it is easy to look up the passages in the corresponding Greek text. These numbers were also originally included in the translation, although I have removed them from this publication for the sake of readability. There was a similar numbering scheme for the chapters in the original translation involving K and P numbers, since Kroll and Pingree numbered the chapters differently in their two critical editions, but for the purpose of this publication we have adopted the more recent chapter numbering scheme based on Pingree's edition.

I would like to thank Jenn Zahrt for doing the layout of the book and helping to shepherd this project to completion, Paula Belluomini for designing both the cover and diagrams used in the text, and Mikhail Medvid for compiling the index. Credit to Kenneth Hirst for designing the Astro font that we used to represent the planets and signs of the zodiac in the chart examples. The central image on the cover is an illustration by Camille Flammarion of a Greco-Roman coffin lid that depicts the Egyptian goddess of the sky Nut, surrounded by the twelve signs of the zodiac.

Finally, thanks to Vettius Valens and all of the other astrologers, scribes, and scholars who preserved and passed down this work so that we could gain some insight into the practice of astrology nearly two thousand years ago. May this publication carry that work forward for another two thousand years.

Chris Brennan
May 2022

SHORT BIBLIOGRAPHY OF WORKS AND SCHOLARSHIP ON ANCIENT ASTROLOGY

Barton, Tamsyn, *Ancient Astrology*, Routledge, London, 1994.

Beck, Roger, *A Brief History of Ancient Astrology*, Blackwell Publishing, Malden, MA, 2007.

Bouché-Leclercq, Auguste, *L'Astrologie grecque*, Leroux, Paris, 1899.

Brennan, Chris, *Hellenistic Astrology: The Study of Fate and Fortune*, Amor Fati Publications, Denver, CO, 2017.

Campion, Nicholas, *A History of Western Astrology. Volume 1: The Ancient and Classical Worlds*, Bloomsbury, London/New York, 2008 (repr. 2012).

Cumont, Franz, et al (eds.), *Catalogus Codicum Astrologorum Graecorum*, 12 vols. in 20 parts, Lamertin, Brussels, 1898–1953.

George, Demetra, *Ancient Astrology in Theory and Practice: A Manual of Traditional Techniques*, Volume I, Rubedo Press, Auckland, 2019.

George, Demetra, *Ancient Astrology in Theory and Practice: A Manual of Traditional Techniques*, Volume II, Rubedo Press, Auckland, 2022.

Heilen, Stephan, *Hadriani Genitura. Die astrologischen Fragmente des Antigonos von Nikaia*, 2 vols., De Gruyter, Berlin/Boston, 2015.

Hephaestion Thebanus, *Hephaestionis Thebani apotelesmaticorum libri tres*, ed. David Pingree, 2 vols., Teubner, Leipzig, 1973–74.

Holden, James H., *A History of Horoscopic Astrology*, American Federation of Astrologers, Tempe, AZ, 1996 (3rd rev. ed. 2013).

King, David A., "A Hellenistic Astrological Table Deemed Worthy of Being Penned in Gold Ink: The Arabic Tradition of Vettius Valens' Auxiliary Function for Finding the Length of Life," in: *Studies in the History of the Exact Sciences in Honour of David Pingree*, ed. Charles Burnett, Jan P. Hogendijk, Kim Plofker and Michio Yano, Brill, Leiden & Boston, 2004, pp. 666–714.

Komorowska, Joanna, *Vettius Valens of Antioch: An Intellectual Monography*, Ksiegarnia Akademicka, Kraków, 2004.

Kroll, Guilelmus, *Vettii Valentis Anthologiarum Libri*, Weidman, Berlin, 1908.

Neugebauer, Otto, "The Chronology of Vettius Valens' *Anthologiae*," *Harvard Theological Review*, 47 (1954), pp. 65–67.

Neugebauer, Otto, and H. B. van Hoesen, *Greek Horoscopes*, American Philosophical Society, Philadelphia, PA, 1959.

Pérez Jiménez, Aurelio, "Notas sobre la posición de Marte en tres horóscopos de Vetio Valente," *MHNH*, vol. 3 (2003), pp. 317–322.

Pingree, David, "The Byzantine Tradition of Vettius Valens' Anthologies," *Harvard Ukrainian Studies*, vol. 7 (1983), pp. 532–41.

Pingree, David, *Vettii Valentis Antiocheni anthologiarum libri novem*, B.G. Teubner, Leipzig, 1986.

Ptolemy, Claudius, *Tetrabiblos*, ed. and trans. F. E. Robbins, Loeb Classical Library, Harvard University Press, Cambridge, MA, 1940 (repr. 2001).

Ptolemy, Claudius, *Claudii Ptolemaei opera quae exstant omnia, vol. III, 1: ΑΠΟΤΕΛΕΣΜΑΤΙΚΑ, post F. Boll et Æ. Boer secundis curis*, ed. Wolfgang Hübner, Teubner, Stuttgart/Leipzig, 1998.

Riley, Mark, "Theoretical and Practical Astrology: Ptolemy and his Colleagues," *Transactions of the American Philological Association*, vol. 117 (1987), pp. 235–56.

Riley, Mark, "Ptolemy's Use of His Predecessor's Data," *Transactions of the American Philological Association*, vol. 125 (1995), pp. 221–250.

Riley, Mark, "Manilius," in *The Encyclopedia of Classical Philosophy*, ed. Donald Zeyl, Greenwood Press, Westport, CT, 1997.

Riley, Mark, *A Survey of Vettius Valens*, originally completed in 1996; published online in 2000; last accessed May 12, 2022: https://www.csus.edu/indiv/r/rileymt/PDF_folder/VettiusValens.PDF

Riley, Mark, "Science and Tradition in the *Tetrabiblos*," *Proceedings of the American Philosophical Society*, vol. 132.1 (1988), pp. 67–84.

Valens, Vettius, *Vettius Valens d'Antioche, Anthologies, Livre I: etablissement, traduction et commentaire*, ed. and trans. Joëlle-Frédérique Bara, Brill, Leiden/New York, 1989.

Valens, Vettius, *The Anthology, Book I*, trans. Robert Schmidt, ed. Robert Hand, The Golden Hind Press, Berkeley Springs, WV, 1993.

Valens, Vettius, *The Anthology, Book I, Part 1*, trans. Robert Schmidt, ed. Robert Hand, The Golden Hind Press, Berkeley Springs, WV, 1994.

Valens, Vettius, *The Anthology, Book II (concl.), & Book III*, trans. Robert Schmidt, ed. Robert Hand, The Golden Hind Press, Berkeley Springs, WV, 1994.

Valens, Vettius, *The Anthology, Book IV*, trans. Robert Schmidt, ed. Robert Hand, The Golden Hind Press, Berkeley Springs, WV, 1996.

Valens, Vettius, *The Anthology, Book V & VI*, trans. Robert Schmidt, ed. Robert Hand, The Golden Hind Press, Cumberland, MD, 1997.

Valens, Vettius, *The Anthology, Book VII*, trans. Robert Schmidt, The PHASER Foundation, Cumberland, MD, 2001.

Valens, Vettius, *Blütensträuße*, trans. Otto Schönberger und Eberhard Knobloch, Subsidia Classica, 7, Scripta Mercaturae Verlag, St. Katharinen, 2004.

Valens, Vettius, *Anthologies*, trans. Mark T. Riley, originally released online in December 2010; last accessed May 12, 2022. https://www.csus.edu/indiv/r/rileymt/vettius%20valens%20entire.pdf

A Survey of Vettius Valens

Mark Riley

The *Anthologiae* of Vettius Valens presents us with the longest, and at the same time the most difficult, text surviving from the astrological literature of antiquity. Valens's exotic methods, many unparalleled in other astrological works, and the vicissitudes of the text itself, which was written over a period of many years and which was thereafter in constant use from late antiquity to the Renaissance, make interpretation of this work difficult.[1] The *Anthologiae* is, however, important for the study of ancient astrology: it presents some 125 actual horoscopes whose interpretation illuminates ancient astrological doctrines during the first centuries of our era. These horoscopes also give brief life histories of the clients, from which some demographic information can be derived. The *Anthologiae* also illustrates astronomical calculation of the pre-Ptolemaic type and gives tables that predate the *Almagest* and the *Handy Tables*.[2]

One hundred years of research into the methods of ancient astrology, the fruits of which can be found in *CCAG*, and the labors of editors and

---

[1] The writing took place in the middle decades of the second century (see below); the table of kings in I 19 was extended into the fourth century; several long chapters were appended in the fifth century; titles and marginal notes were added at various times; in 1648 Claude Saumaise rewrote parts of the *Anthologiae* in his *De Annis Climacteris* (1648). For the use of the text in the thirteenth century see Pingree, "Byzantine Tradition," 540.

[2] Although Valens and Ptolemy were near contemporaries, Valens shows no signs of familiarity with Ptolemaic astronomical methods, which were based on precise calculations of arcs and radii and on the theorems of plane and spherical trigonometry. Valens' methods (illustrated in the note on I 20 below) were purely arithmetical, like those of their Babylonian predecessors. Ptolemy recognized the difference between his methods and those exemplified in the *Anthologiae* (*Alm.* IX 2; Heiberg I 2, p. 211).

commentators, particularly Kroll, Neugebauer, Pingree, and Bara, have illuminated many dark corners. This work has uncovered Valens's century, perhaps even his birthdate, and has gone far toward restoring his text to its state in the fifth century CE, the date of the archetype of the extant tradition. This paper will survey what can be learned of Valens' biography, will compare his methods and goals with those of the other surviving astrological writers, particularly Ptolemy, whose *Tetrabiblos* became this art's undisputed classic, and will outline what can be gained from the text with further research: information about astrologers whose works are lost but who are quoted in the *Anthologiae*; pre-Ptolemaic mathematical and graphical methods for astronomical calculations; and glimpses into the everyday world of the practicing astrologer.

Biography

The *Anthologiae* supplies our only accurate information about its author.[3] Vettius Valens (Οὐέττιος Οὐάλης, medieval Latin Balens, Arabic Wālīs) of Antioch was conceived on 13 May 119 CE and born nine months later on 8 Feb. 120 CE. His mother predeceased his father in the 140's. At age 34 he "worked abroad, was a friend of great men, was in mortal danger because of a woman, and suffered cuts and bleeding." At age 35 he took a sea voyage during which he was in danger from pirates and from a storm. He moved to Egypt in search of occult knowledge. There, according to his account, which matches other ancient tales of religious quests, he "suffered much, endured much…and spent money that seemed inexhaustible, because I was persuaded by mountebanks and greedy men" (301.16K; 288.15P). His teachers were avaricious, and, although he paid great sums, he did not attain the truth. He then withdrew into an ascetic life for a time, but was later drawn back by the lure of astrology, particularly the lure of determining which star rules a given period, i.e., the "chronocratorship" — see the note in Appendix B on Book IV 1-5 (172.9K; 163.6P).[4]

---

[3] There appear to be two distinct traditions about Valens: one consists of the *Anthologiae*; the other consists of stories and references to Wālīs al-Rūmī (as he is called in the *Fihrist* of Ibn al-Nadīm), who wrote treatises called *The Sultan, Rains, The Revolution of the Years of the World*, among others, and who had various colorful adventures, one of which is related in the section Manuscripts and Editions below. This paper is devoted solely to the author of the *Anthologiae*; a scholar at home in the Arabic tradition must sketch the career of this (other?) Wālīs.

[4] His name and home are given in the mss ascriptions. For the conjectured date of birth see Pingree in the introduction to his edition, p. v. The predecease of his mother is mentioned in the horoscope quoted at 101.32K; 96.28P (a passage written in the early 150's—see Appendix A), the work abroad at 227.21–27K; 216.10–12P, the adventure at sea

His dedication to astrology was total. He was never attracted by horse races, spectacles, art and music, or love (242.8-18K; 231.34-232.10P). He never came to desire command, high rank, wealth or possessions (355.9-15K; 340.22-27P). His astrology was a mystery and an ascetic art. Even kingship was insignificant compared to the god-like knowledge granted man by astrology/astronomy: "by means of it one can know the Sun's ordered paths… and the varying paths of the Moon… From all this we hope to understand everything on Earth, in the seas, in heaven, as well as the beginning and end of all created things" (241.20-29K; 231.16-24P). Astrology enabled him to bear all blows of Fortune:

> Fate has decreed for each person the immutable working out of events, surrounding him with many occasions for good or bad… Two self-begotten gods, Hope and Fortune, the assistants of Fate, control man's life and make him bear Fate's decrees by using their compulsion and deception… Fortune raises some high only to cast them down and degrades others only to raise them to glory… Hope moves everywhere in secret, smiling like a flatterer, and she displays many attractive prospects which cannot be attained. By deceiving men, she controls most of them… Those ignorant of the prognostic art are led away and enslaved by these gods. They endure all blows and suffer punishments with pleasure. Some partially attain what they hoped for; their confidence begins to increase, and they await a permanently favorable outcome—not realizing how precarious and slippery are these accidents of Fortune. Others are disappointed in their expectations, not just once, but always… But those who have trained themselves in the prognostic art and in the truth keep their minds free and out of bondage. They despise Fortune, do not persist in Hope, do not fear death, and live undisturbed… They are alien to all pleasure or flattery and stand firm as soldiers of Fate. (219.26-220.28K; 209.10-210.6P)[5]

---

in 287.35–288.3K; 274.22–29P, the move to Egypt at 172.4K; 163.1P. The horoscope for Hadrian year 4, Mechir 13 = 8 Feb. 120 is cited at least 21 times, 12 times in Book I alone. The date of conception (Hadrian year 3, Pachon 11 = 13 May 119) is cited at 51.32K; 51.5P. The gestation period, 278 days, is used as an example in the text. This birth on 8 Feb. 120 was an important date and his stock example; hence probably his own. The *Anthologiae* was completed around 175 CE; the birthdate of 13 May 120 would give Valens a lifespan of about 55 years. His disappointment with his teachers is parallel with that of Plotinus (Porphyry, *Vita Plot.* 3) and the unhappy student of P. Oxy. 2190, quoted in N. Lewis, *Life in Egypt* 63–64: "…my prayers would be answered if I could find some worthwhile tutors and never have to lay eyes on Didymos [his former tutor] even from a distance." Like Valens, Plotinus and the unhappy student lived in Egypt.

[5] A translation of this passage in G. Luck, *Arcana Mundi* 349–50. Similar expressions of faith throughout V 9. See Bara, *Anthologies* 14ff.

Astrology taught him his duty: in a revealing passage he compares himself to an intelligent slave of a harsh master (=life), a slave who does not contravene his master's orders and who thus avoids pain and suffering (355.15-21K; 340.27-33P). Astrology was his fortification against the inevitable fatalities of life. Such doctrines are of course not confined to Valens: Ptolemy defends astrology's usefulness by first declaring that the prognostic art tames and calms the soul and prepares it to meet whatever the future brings with steadfastness (*Tetr.* I 3.5).[6]

In short, astrology was the anchor of Valens' faith. The religious feelings expressed in the *Anthologiae* become more striking when Valens' phrases are compared with those from an obviously religious text like the *Hermetica*. These texts emphasize the need for secrecy, for maintaining the doctrine free from defilement at the ears of the vulgar. In maintaining this secrecy, the adepts separate themselves from the uninitiated. Just as Hermes tells Asclepius that his discourse should not be profaned by the presence of the crowd, so Valens likewise urges his students to conceal this work "from the unworthy or uninitiated" (359.24K; 344.27P).[7] Valens exacts oaths of secrecy from his students:

> I adjure them by the sacred circle of the Sun, by the varied paths of the Moon, by the powers of the five other stars, and by the circle of the twelve signs to keep these matters secret, never to share them with the ignorant or the uninitiated, and to remember and to honor the one who inducted them into this art. May it go well for those who keep this oath and may the aforesaid gods grant them what they wish; may the opposite happen to those who foreswear this oath. (263.19-24K; 251.18-23P)

Both texts emphasize the spiritual relationship between master and pupil, with the master handing on his doctrines as one link in a chain of succession: Valens' student received (παραλαμβάνων - 294.1K; 281.14P) the doctrines

---

[6] Ptolemy's second argument for astrology's utility is that foreknowledge can allow us to prepare such defenses as cures for diseases and remedies for evils (*Tetr.* I 3.10). Valens never uses this second argument.

[7] A.D. Nock and A.-J. Festugière, *CH* II 297. Many parallel examples could be cited from the *Hermetica*. Valens was steeped in Greco-Egyptian mysticism. See Garth Fowden, *The Egyptian Hermes* (Cambridge 1986) 155-95, for a description of the Hermetic milieu which presents many parallels to Valens' attitudes, if not doctrines. A.J. Festugière, *L'idéal religieux* 120-27 emphasizes Valens' view of astrology as a mystery, transmitted by tradition, through which the soul is raised to heaven, and becomes a participant in immortality. (Valens never mentions Hermes, a fact which would argue for a post second-century date for most of the *Hermetica*.)

and will pass them on, just as Hermes received (παραλαβών - *Poimandres* 1.26 in *CH* I, p. 19) doctrines from Poimandres and then becomes a guide to others who are worthy. Both Hermes' doctrines and Valens' are presented as an intellectual system (θεωρία, αἵρεσις; the philosophers and Hermes use γνῶσις) which brings with it a way of life characterized by secret knowledge and status as the elect of God. All this is popular Greco–Egyptian spirituality.

Also part of this popular spirituality is Valens' emphasis on astrology's ancient traditions, which he claims to be developing further. Besides consulting the astronomers Hipparchus and Apollonius, and the Babylonians, Soudines and Kidenas, whose data for the Sun and the Moon he claims to have used, Valens studied the "ancient astrologers," particularly King Nechepso and the sage Petosiris, legendary Egyptian astrologers, and Critodemus, who lived in the first century CE.[8] His comments on these earlier astrologers are of two types: he lauds their dedication and skill; at the same time he criticizes their grudging and stingy attitude towards other adepts or students. Nechepso is the divine King, who "made his explanations with mystic intelligence. His wisdom is shown by his willingness to confess his earlier errors. He despised his kingship and his power compared with the loftiness of mystic knowledge. No trickery caused by greed and the necessity for making a living affected him" (329.7–14K; 316.7–15P). Valens envied the King because he had lived in a time which "saw such a climate of free and ungrudging speech and inquiry," a time when men "left the earthy sphere and walked the heavens" (241.9–15K; 231.3–8P). The other astrologer, Critodemus, laid the basis for Valens' work (348.9K; 334.9P) and was very wise (329.18K; 316.16P).

Nevertheless, the Ancients laid themselves open to criticism: the wise Critodemus wrote in a "fantastical style, marvelous to the unlearned." He claimed that his work contained great powers and prodigious deeds, and he exacted fearsome oaths from his students, but he locked up the truth of his teachings in infinite verbiage and useless bombast. If Critodemus' reader could get through the bombast, the results were worthwhile (150.11–27K; 142.12–27P). The same cannot be said of other astrologers. Some waste the time of men and lead them astray, defrauding them (150.9–10K; 142.11P); they propound their art in a recondite fashion (301.21K; 288.20P); they perform a "concerto" of fine, enticing words and meter (260.27K; 249.18–19P). Even worse, some were "driven by envy to hide this art because of their vainglory," or perhaps they "had not in fact grasped what Nature had created, prescribed, and bestowed abundantly on mankind," but wrote nevertheless (272.7–11K; 260.3–7P). These rivals of Valens "bastardize this science with fancy words

---

[8] For these astrologers, see below in the section "Quotations."

and complicated schemes and they lead the uninitiated astray." They walk in the paths of deceit, not of truth (238.21–30K; 228.24–31P). Envy might even damage Valens' own treatise, and to forestall the evil effects of this envy, he has not shrunk from repeating and amplifying his earlier pages (242.26–32K; 232.17–22P).

As a corrective for these shortcomings of his predecessors and rivals, Valens claims to have written in a simple manner, to have tested what he propounded, and to have given worked-out examples, of which he was quite proud (301.30K; 288.27P). (Indeed, his examples make the *Anthologiae* unique in ancient astrology.) Furthermore, he claimed to have revised his work in the light of his later experience, and this claim can be supported. He had, for example, described how to calculate by signs alone the distribution of the chronocrators (in Book III). Later, in VI 1, he spoke of the "intervals and contacts using the degree-positions, a method which I had treated obscurely before" (243.6K; 232.27P). In the preface to Book VI, he says that when he previously had read of some new method, in his enthusiasm he simply copied it and appended it to his treatise—this statement certainly applies to the sections from Critodemus in Book V. Later, however, he returned and reworked those earlier appendices— and it is certainly true that the methods for critical periods are elaborated in Books VI-VIII (242.27–30K; 232.18–20P). The *Anthologiae* contain a record of his astrological researches.

Like any professional, Valens had students to carry on the tradition. One special student, Marcus, is named as the heir to his glory (293.24K; 281.2P, written in 163/4; cf. 359.13–20K; 344.16–22P). The death of a student (Marcus?) brought him great grief (157.28–33K; 149.23–27P, written in 169). His last horoscope is dated to 173. Presumably he died shortly thereafter in his mid-50's.

Valens was no creative genius; he was neither a systematizer like Ptolemy nor a scientist like Hipparchus nor a widely influential guru like Apollonius of Tyana—though he certainly would have liked to be all of these. Cumont's low opinion of him ("esprit borné, dépourvu de tout originalité" *L'Egypt* 18) has been repeated by Bara (*Anthologies* 16). His energy, however, cannot be faulted: he was able to write 300+ pages of astrological theory and practice over a period of more than 20 years, in addition to his professional work, whatever that was. Later astrologers had a more just appreciation of his talents. Salmasius in particular, who has been studied by Bara, thought it worthwhile to rewrite the *Anthologiae*. Moreover, even if we do not read him as a fellow professional, Valens embodies the popular spirituality of his age and is thus a valuable witness to his contemporaries and their concerns. He merits study for this reason, if for no other. But it is also for his mathematics, examples of which are given below, and for his usefulness as a source of earlier astrology that his works may be studied. No one can yet claim to have mined the *Anthologiae* for all its gold; this survey is only preliminary.

The Composition and Contents of the *Anthologiae*
Valens composed his *Anthologiae* over a period of at least 20 years. As mentioned above, internal evidence shows that he published the text in several sections or books: VI 5 (252.3K; 240.29P) refers to a book, αἱ Ἐπικρατήσεις, *The Controlling Points*, our present Book III 1–13. Book VII 3 (272.30–31K; 260.24P—one of the latest sections of the *Anthologiae*) and VII 5 (279.14K; 267.2P) refer to his book Περὶ χρόνων ζωῆς, *On The Length of Life*, the fragments of which are found in the present Books VI to IX. The many horoscopes cited as examples in the text, which make Valens' work so valuable to the historian of astrology, provide further information for dating. The dates of death (or of some other significant crisis) of the persons whose horoscopes are given allow us to give a *terminus post quem* for the chapters containing those horoscopes.[9]

Appendix A lists the chapters which cite horoscopes containing the date of birth <u>and</u> of death (or crisis) which is under investigation; horoscopes for adults which give only birthdates are useless for determining a precise *terminus post quem*. From this information the various sections of the *Anthologiae* can be dated:

> Books I-II – The early 150's or before. (I 5 is a later insertion.)[10]
> Book III 1-13 – early 150's.
> Book III 14-16 – 169/170 (an insertion).
> Book IV 1–10 – 156; an introduction the theory of chronocrators and critical times.
> Book IV 11–30 – slightly later than IV 1–10; a different system of chronocrators.
> Book V – 158; a continuation of the discussion of chronocrators and critical times.
> Book VI – A late book (170?) with the majority of the extended similes and poetic quotations found in the *Anthologiae*.
> Book VII 1–4 – 173; one of the latest sections, with the remaining poetic quotations.

---
[9] Statistics are cited in *GH* 176–79.
[10] The horoscope dated in *GH* 130–31 to 188 CE has been re-dated by Pingree to 70 CE (93.13K; 89.8P).

Book VII 5 – 164/5
Book VIII – 167
Book IX – Fragmentary, with sections of various dates assignable to earlier chapters.

The figures listed above and in Appendix A, and the purpose for which the horoscopes are cited, divide the *Anthologiae* into two sections: 1) a general introduction to astrological studies, Books I to III 13 from the early 150's, and 2) length of life and critical year calculations, to which most of his text is devoted; this is Book III 14 to VIII, compiled from 156 to the 170's. 1) Much of Books I and II contain standard astrological doctrine: the nature and influence of the stars, signs, and terms, the influence of the Places/Houses, exaltations, and the standard aspects of opposition, trine, square, and sextile. These doctrines are illustrated by horoscopes of living persons and can be paralleled in Ptolemy and Hephaistion, as indicated in Appendix B. These same books, along with Books VIII and IX, contain unique passages showing how the astrologer calculated the positions of the planets and the Ascendant, and what type of tables he had at his disposal (samples in Appendix B). 2) Valens, however, considered as his main contribution the doctrines and methods of calculating critical periods and the length of life, and of determining the planetary ruler of any given period (=the chronocrator). With some digressions, these two topics fill Book III 1–13, which contains an early sketch of the control (ἐπικράτησις) and of the influence of the days of the week. They also fill Books IV, different methods of determining the chronocrator; Book V, critical and "operative" (χρηματιστικός) years; Book VI and VII, critical periods and length of life calculations; and Books VIII and IX, in which various tables are used to calculate the length of life. In this second section, specific numbers had to be cited from specifically dated horoscopes of persons who had died or barely survived a crisis. These critical dates calculated from the horoscopes show that our present text of Books I–VIII, though certainly disarranged here and there, is roughly in the order of original composition. Book IX can be viewed as a collection of notes or fragments.

The reader should skim Appendix B to get an idea of the contents of the *Anthologiae*. The topic developed at greatest length and with the greatest mathematical elaboration—including tables—is the length of life calculation. The underlying principle is not difficult: the life of any individual is cast like a dart on the rim of the zodiac, viewed as a wheel rotating with the universe. The place where the dart hits, the point representing the birthdate, is the starting point (τόπος ἀφετικός). The place where the dart is knocked off, the day of death, is the destructive place (τόπος ἀναιρετικός). The starting point and the destructive place are no more than one-fourth of the circumference of the circle apart, usually the distance from the Ascendant to Midheaven. The number of degrees which the dart traverses, converted into degrees of right ascension, gives the length of life in years. Valens' elaboration of this scheme can best be seen in Books III 2–3 and VIII 1–7. (See the notes on these chapters in Appendix B.)[11]

The differences between the *Anthologiae* and Ptolemy's *Tetrabiblos*, the best known ancient survey of astrology, are striking. Ptolemy's text is systematic, outlining first the stars' and signs' physical nature, which influences the Earth's environment (Book I), then describing the effects of these influences on the Earth as a whole (Book II), on the birth and overall character of persons (Book III), and on the separate events of an individual's life, e.g., marriage, occupations, personality (Book IV). All of these influences are derived from the basic "astrophysical" nature of the stars and signs, e.g., Mars = heat, the Moon = moisture, Cancer (June/July) = heat, Capricorn (Dec/Jan) = cold, etc.

Nothing like this can be found in Valens, no physics, no systematic discussion of the causes of astrological influences, no description of the overall (καθόλου) influences on the Earth's environment. Valens concentrates on individual men and their diseases, their rise and fall, their personalities, and their lifespans.

In the *Tetrabiblos* Ptolemy rarely uses numbers. As mentioned, his doctrines are based on the physical nature of the stars and signs, and "physics" for him and for his colleagues meant "qualitative description" with no numerical values.[12] Valens on the other hand was a *mathematicus* and used numbers constantly: his procedures require the use of tables, calculations, and the numerical distance in degrees from one star, sign, or critical point to another.

Finally, Ptolemy's discussion is entirely theoretical—in this respect he is unique among ancient astrologers. Ptolemy never mentions individuals, never cites horoscopes, never describes what an astrologer really does in his everyday business. Valens, on the contrary, cites some 125 horoscopes or birth dates of real persons and takes pains to describe the procedures by which an astrologer

---

[11] The clearest description of this scheme in ancient texts is *Tetrabiblos* III 11; see *AG* 411.

[12] The *Tetrabiblos* is physics; the *Almagest*, which simply describes the positions of the planets, not their physical nature, is mathematics, but even there the structure of the Ptolemaic system is based on geometry, not on arithmetic. For the distinction between physics and mathematics see Simplicius in his commentary on Aristotle's *Physics: In Aris. Physicorum Comm.* ed. Diels (Berlin 1882) 291.23–292.26; also Aristotle, *Physics* 193b23ff, and M. Riley, "Theoretical and Practical Astrology."

may cast and interpret horoscopes with accuracy, advise his clients, and raise his standing in his profession. In short, Valens was writing for the practicing astrologer, and his contributions, his length of life calculations and the description of how to perform these calculations, are aimed at a professional audience. One can imagined that the astrologer's clients, the middle class of urban Egypt, would have been wonderfully baffled by the astrologer's explanations of his forecasts.

Quotations from Earlier Astrologers

Valens mentions and quotes from many earlier astrologers and astronomers, many of whose works have been lost. Following is a list:[13]

Abraham (Ἄβραμος) is quoted in Book II 28 and 29 on the factors which cause a nativity which is subject to travel—always an invitation to disaster. Valens considered Abraham's work to be an original contribution: ὁ δὲ θαυμασιώτατος Ἄβραμος ... δέδειχεν ἡμῖν ἄλλων δηλώσεις τε καὶ αὐτοῦ ἴδια - "The most amazing Abraham has opened to us the explanations of others and his own contributions" (96.9K; 91.27P). Book II 29 seems to be a summary of Abraham. His terminology is different from that of Valens: Abraham wrote ὁ κλῆρος ὁ περὶ... plus genitive case (δαίμονος, ἀποδημίας) instead of Valens' usual ὁ κλῆρος... plus genitive case; Abraham uses the unique word ἀφώτιστος – the Unlit Place (99.6K; 94.16P). Abraham used the system of chronocratorships (χρόνοι) which are held by certain stars which then transmit the year (ἐνιαυτός, ἔτος) to each other. Valens adopted this system in the *Anthologiae*.[14]

Apollinarius is mentioned in Books VI 11 and IX 12 as a compiler of astronomical tables. He correlated earlier observations and periodic intervals, but admitted that his tables were in error by 1° or 2° (250.26–29K; 239.24–27P). Valens claims to have used his tables with a correction factor of 8° (339.22P). An Apollinarius is cited for the length of the year (=365 8/45).[15]

---

[13] I have mentioned some of the special vocabulary used in the quotations, but more work is needed to demarcate one quotation from another and from Valens' own words. Astrological terminology was not fixed, as a cursory comparison between Valens and, for example, the nearly contemporary P. *Mich.* 145 will show.

[14] The book from which Valens quoted had been attributed to the patriarch, who was (according to Eusebius, *Praeparatio Evangelica* IX 16–17) the inventor of astronomy, who had studied in Phoenicia and in Egypt, and who had learned the science from Enoch (called Atlas by the Greeks). See AG 578; Gundel, *Astrologoumena* 52–54.

[15] See Gundel, *Astrologoumena* 159 and A. Jones, "248–Day Schemes" 30ff for Apollinarius. Jones suggests that Apollinarius developed pre-Ptolemaic lunar tables. Also see Jones *Ptolemy's First Commentator* 12ff. Apollinarius' distribution of the terms (see note on I 3 above) is mentioned in Porphyry's *Isagoge*, CCAG 5.4 (1940), 212 and in E. Maass, *Comm. in Aratum* 47.

Aristarchus is cited for the length of the year (353.11K; 339.7P).

Asclation, otherwise unknown, is mentioned as a bombastic writer. Cumont identified this Asclation with the 'Askletario' mentioned in Suetonius *Domitian* XV 3.[16] Accused before the emperor of practicing magic, he did not deny the charge, but boasted of his skillful predictions. When asked what his own end would be, he answered that he would soon be torn by dogs. Domitian then ordered him to be executed immediately and to be buried with care, in order to refute the forecast. However, when a storm came up and extinguished the pyre, the dogs did rend the body. The story disturbed Domitian, who was shortly thereafter to die. The implication is that the astrologer had foreseen—and was foolish enough to mention that he had foreseen—Domitian's end, and was for that reason denounced. The long sections in Valens describing the methods for forecasting the length of life indicate that Asclation/Askletario was simply practicing a well-known, if dangerous, art.

Asclepius is cited as a compiler of the system of the XII Places (334.13K; 321.7P).[17]

Critodemus is cited at least 10 times, and his work, the Ὅρασις *(Vision)* is mentioned twice. His style is called obscure and fantastic. Critodemus is cited for two doctrines: the determination of the starting point (ἀφέτης) of the vital sector (ἄφεσις), i.e., the point at which the quadrant representing the lifespan begins (III 7–8), and the determination of the length of life (χρόνοι ζωῆς) using the method outlined in the note on VIII 6–7 in Appendix B—at least he began the development of this method which Valens completed (348.10K; 334.9P). His contemporary Balbillus employed the same methods (*CCAG* 8.4 235–39). In addition, the "Forecasts of the Terms: from Critodemus" (*CCAG* 8.1 257–61), is similar to I 3 "Concerning Terms," and a partial table of contents of a book by Critodemus (*CCAG* 8.3, 102) roughly corresponds to *Anthologiae* IV 17–24. The frequency with which Critodemus is mentioned indicates his importance for Valens, who may have taken more from Critodemus than he explicitly acknowledges.[18] Nevertheless ii is difficult to see the differences between Valens' work and Critodemus'. Critodemus is mentioned as the author

---

[16] Cumont in *CCAG* V.1, 205; Gundel, *Astrologoumena* 158–59.

[17] A *De Horoscopo* of an Asclepius is known; *DSB* 11.245. *P. Mich.* 149 ix. 20 attributes a system of Places to Asclepius; this system matches Valens'. The name might be taken as a generic reference to Hermetic astrology, rather than to a specific individual; an Hermetic tractate *Asclepius* survives in Latin translation.

[18] For Critodemus, see Boll, *RE* 11.2 (1922) 1928–1930 and Cumont's notes at *CCAG* 8.1, 257 and *CCAG* 8.3, 102; *GH* 185–86, which dates Critodemus to the first century CE, using the horoscopes in Valens' quotations; Gundel, *Astrologoumena* 106–7 dates him in error to the third century BCE. A section from Critodemus begins at 117.21P.

of the Πίναξ in Hephaistion II 10.41.

Euctemon - see Meton.

Hermeias is cited in the title of IV 27 as an authority on the determination of the ruler of the day, month, and year, or the operative (χρηματιστικός) day, month or year (IV 27–29).[19] Hermeias is directly quoted: ...ὡς παρετηρησάμην ἐγὼ Ἑρμείας - "as I myself, Hermeias, observed" (205.13K; 195.14–15P) and thus it appears that IV 27-29 are verbatim quotations from him. Hermeias had his own terminology: περίπατον - "transmission" (205.10,15K) instead of ἄφεσις or ἐπιδιαίρεσις; κατὰ πάροδον - "in transit" for a star's position at the time of the inquiry. (Its position at the nativity is κατὰ γένεσιν). In a closely parallel passage in V 4 Valens uses the phrases ἀπὸ τοῦ παροδικοῦ Ἡλίου and ἡ κατ' ἐκτροπὴν Σελήνη (214.4–5K; 203.20–21P). Hermeias' methods are repeated in different words in V 4, and a similar procedure can be found in a horoscope from Rhetorius.[20] (This citation may be due to the fifth-century redactor, in which case this Hermeias may be the commentator who mentions Hermes Trismegistus—and thus may have dabbled in the occult—in his scholia on Plato's *Phaedrus*.[21]) An otherwise unknown Seuthes is mentioned in the title to IV 27.

Hermippos in cited in the title to II 29 "Concerning Travel, From Hermippos." The chapter is actually from Abraham (see above).[22]

Hipparchus - Valens claims to have used Hipparchus' figures for the Sun (354.4K; 339.20P). The important chapter concerning the methods for calculating lunar positions is called a *Hipparcheion* (I 19K; I 17P). Does this chapter represent Hipparchus' methods—at least in his calculations of the five planets?[23]

---

[19] The titles of each chapter are not necessarily Valens' own: the title to III 10 is ἐκ τῶν Βάλεντος περὶ ἀριθμίου κλήρου καὶ χρόνων ζωῆς... Other titles, hence other citations and indeed whole chapters, could have been added by later redactors, although the evidence for this is not strong. Hermeias then might be a later astrologer.

[20] *CCAG* 8.1, 232–34; *GH* 132–34. A geometrician Hermeias is a participant in Plutarch's *Quaes. convivialium* 9.2, 738, discussing the reasons for the number and order of the letters of the alphabet.

[21] Hermeias of Alexandria, *In Platonis Phaedrum scholia*. ed. P. Couvreur (Paris 1901), quoted in G. Fowden, *The Egyptian Hermes*. 184.

[22] Gundel, *Astrologoumena* 108–9 hypothesizes that this Hermippos is the student of Callimachus and librarian at Alexandria. I consider this unlikely. The name may be a book title, not a person: a dialogue Ἕρμιππος ἢ Περὶ ἀστρολογίας defends astrology from a Christian standpoint. See Kroll, *RE* 8.1 854–57.

[23] Ptolemy describes Hipparchus' methods for the Sun and Moon (*Alm*. IX.2; H 2.210), but states that Hipparchus had not begun to describe the motions of the five planets by means of uniform circular motions, i.e., by the means used in the *Almagest*. Hence the arithmetical methods of *Anthologiae* may indeed represent Hipparchus' approach.

Hypsicles, well-known as a geometrician, is cited for a table of erroneous rising times (157.12K; 149.8P). An *Anaphorikos*, or *Table of Rising Times*, which may be Hypsicles' work, is cited 8 times.[24]

Kidenas the Babylonian - Valens claims to have used Kidenas, Soudines, and Apollonius for the Moon (354.5K; 339.21P).[25]

Meton the Athenian, **Euctemon**, and **Philip** are cited for the length of the year (365 1/5 1/19 using Egyptian fractions) (353.10K; 339.6P).

Nechepso the King and **Petosiris** are frequently cited as the "Ancients" or as the "King." They were model astrologers: steeped in their art, they despised wealth and power when compared to mystic knowledge; they were inventive discoverers. Most of the fragments of their work, which dates to the late first century BCE, comes from Valens, who cites Petosiris' Ὅροι *(Terms)* and the thirteenth book of Nechepso, the King.[26] Thrasyllus (first century CE—see below) is the first witness to their existence (*CCAG* 8.3, 100.19–20).

An unknown **Orion** is cited in III 2 for the doctrine of the four angles: the Ascendant, Midheaven (MC), the Descendant (D), and Lower Midheaven (IC). One-third of the arc between, for example, the Ascendant and IC will be powerful, two-thirds will be inoperative (ἀχρημάτιστοι). Another system: of the same arc, the first third will be beneficial, the middle third will be of moderate influence, the final third will be harmful. This system is the origin of the values attributed to each of the XII Places. Orion is said to have published all this "in his book" (135.36K; 128.26P). An Orion is mentioned in E. Maass, *Comm. in Aratum* 47, as writing on eclipses and the seven klimata.

Philip - see Meton.

Seuthes - see Hermeias.

Soudines - see Kidenas.

---

[24] See *DSB* 6.616–67; Hypsicles' treatise is available: V. de Falco and M. Krause, *Hypsicles. Die Aufgangszeiten der Gestirne* (Göttingen 1966), with an introduction by Neugebauer.

[25] Kidenas is Kidennu in cuneiform texts; see *DSB* 15.678.

[26] Edition of the fragments in E. Riess, "Nechepsonis et Petosiridis Fragmenta Magica." Additional fragments can be collected from *CCAG*. The best study of Petosiris (and Nechepso by association) is Pingree's in *DSB* 10.547–49; a long discussion in Gundel, *Astrologoumena* 27–36. The fourth-century BCE tomb of a Petosiris ("gift of Osiris") is described in G. Lefebvre, *Le Tombeau de Petosiris*. Lefebvre reports the attractive conjecture that this tomb is that of the original Petosiris: the tomb's inmate is called a sage (Lefebvre 9), the inscriptions of the tomb present a series of philosophical/religious texts with parallels in the *Proverbs* and *Psalms of the Old Testament* (Lefebvre 37–41), and the tomb was a place of pilgrimage for Greek-speaking Egyptians (Lefebvre 21–27). *EAT* 3.216 rightly doubts a direct connection between this Petosiris and the first century BCE astrologer. I might suggest however that the astrologer owed his name to the earlier sage. Astronomers were known in fourth-century BCE Egypt; see the inscription on the statue of an astronomer and snake-charmer reported in G. Daressy, "La statue d'un astronome," and *EAT* III 214.

The *Sphaerica* (τὰ Σφαιρικά) is cited for the stars which rise at the same time (συνανατέλλει) as a given point on the ecliptic. The work cannot be identified with the treatises on the sphere written by Aratus, Eudoxus, or Hipparchus.[27]

Thrasyllos is cited as the discoverer of a method for forecasting the length of life: determine the distance in rising times from the Sun to the Moon; adjust the Ascendant of the nativity using this distance; then forecast the length of life (352.7–27K; 338.3–20P). This method is similar to that used throughout Book VIII (see note on VIII 6–7 above). Thrasyllus was Tiberius' astrologer, and his son predicted Nero's rise to power.[28]

Timaios is cited as an obscure and fantastic writer, along with Critodemus and Asclation (329.22K; 316.19P).[29] He is quoted for the interpretation of horoscopes relative to parents, a section which follows immediately upon the chapters on travel from Abram. Timaios' vocabulary is distinctive: ἐπιδεκατευόμενοι (102.27K; 97.23P) for καθυπερτηρούμενοι - "to be in superior aspect;" the unique ἐπιδεκατείαν - "superior aspect" (102.33K; 97.27P); φθοροποιοί (102.31K;97.26P *et al.*) for κακοποιοί - "malefic stars;" καταπονούμενος - "afflicted stars" (only at 103.6K; 97.34P); the unique οἰκοδοχεύς (102.24K; 97.20P) for οἰκοδεσπότης - "houseruler." Perhaps φθείρεσθαι "to be depressed" instead of the usual ταπεινοῦσθαι is Timaios also (119.13K; 113.24P), in which case most of II 37–38 would be from Timaios.

Zoroaster is cited as a riddling author of a method for finding the vital sector (ἄφεσις) from the zones of the stars. He assigned periods of 9 (years/months/days/hours) to each star in the order of its distance from the Earth: first the Moon, then Mercury, Venus, the Sun, Mars, Jupiter, and Saturn (337.3–8K; 323.18–22P).

Valens cited none of the earlier astrologers whose works have survived (Dorotheus, Manilius, Aratus, Eudoxus), nor does he cite his contemporary, Ptolemy.

The Astrologer's Clients

What can be learned about life in Greco-Roman antiquity from the astrologers, particularly from Vettius Valens? Many investigators have been optimistic in

---

[27] For details see F. Boll, *Sphaera* 59–72: "nach ihm (the writer of the *Sphaerica*) zu forschen würde keinen Sinn haben: es muß einer jener zahlreichen Schriftsteller gewesen sein die... populäre Traktate verfaßt haben."

[28] Gundel, *RE* 2er Ser. 6:1 581–84.

[29] Timaios wrote about "interrogations" (see note on II 29–41 in Appendix B) concerning runaway slaves and thieves; see Kroll in *RE* 2er Ser. 6:1 1228 and *CCAG* I 97; Gundel, *Astrologoumena* 111.

this regard. Franz Cumont, in *L'Egypt des Astrologues*, attempted to sketch the government, society, occupations, and spiritual world of Ptolemaic Egypt on the basis of the astrologers' testimony. Even before Cumont, Thorndike had used Firmicus Maternus as a historical source: "In trying to predict the future the astrologers really depict their own civilization."[30] More recently MacMullen has studied ancient society as reflected in astrology.[31]

Several considerations should forestall a naive view of the astrologers as reflectors of their own society. 1) The astrologers all borrowed from each other; their language is stereotyped and reflects an earlier period (see LANGUAGE AND STYLE below). The fact of this borrowing and the conservatism of the astrological tradition is the basis of Cumont's thesis that astrology reflects the realities of Ptolemaic Egypt, not of the Roman Egypt from which our texts really come. 2) On the other hand, the imaginative world of the astrologers has much in common with that of the novelists, the dream interpreters, and the declaimers, and while this world overlaps the real world, it is not identical to it.[32] For example, Although Egypt, the home of astrology, swarmed with peasants and small farmers, these people are never mentioned in astrological forecasts. In fact, references that can be localized in Egypt alone (metropolitan Greek office titles, local gods, even the Nile and its floods) are rare, or (in Valens) nonexistent. I would suggest that what might be references to Ptolemaic Egypt are really references to the world common to the novelists and declaimers, a world derived from the imaginative descriptions of Egypt written by Hecataeus, Hellanicus, Manetho, Timotheus, Phylarchus, and others.[33]

These texts are full of kings and magnates by whom the client will be benefited and raised to high status as the master of life and death or by whom he will be condemned to prison, exile, or a miserable death. The client thus lives his life subject to ἀνωμαλίαι, ups and downs, certainly not tied to a peasant's parcel of land. In this very point we can see the parallels between astrological forecasts and the ancient novels, with their heroes and heroines falling from high status to slavery, then back to nobility and happiness.[34] I suppose this

---

[30] L. Thordike, "A Roman Astrologer" 416.

[31] R. MacMullen, "Social History in Astrology" 105–16. Cumont was preceeded by W. Kroll, "Kulturhistorisches aus astrologischen Texten." Kroll dated Nechepso / Petosiris to the second century BCE and Hermetic astrology to the Ptolemaic period, as did Cumont. These conclusions have been revised by later work. The *Liber Hermetis* (ed. Gundel) in particular has been dated to the ninth or tenth century CE by Pingree "Indian Iconography" 227.

[32] MacMullen, "Social History," 105 recognized this problem.

[33] J. G. Griffiths, *Plutarch's De Iside et Osiride* 84–85 makes the point that even Plutarch's treatise seems to reflect early Ptolemaic Egypt, not the Roman Egypt of its composition date (second century CE).

[34] Chariton is an ideal example—and from the same milieu as the astrological forecasts!

is natural enough: people do not go to fortunetellers today in order to hear humdrum predictions that they will continue working in the post office until retirement, after which they will live 4.3 years, then die of a heart attack.

Nevertheless, many chapters of the *Anthologiae* present data from which to sketch ancient life: those chapters which contain lists of horoscopes as examples (see Appendix A; the horoscopes themselves are translated in *GH* 78–130) and those which outline the influences of the stars and signs are most important.[35] These two sources, the horoscopes and the theoretical chapters, were written for different purposes and only vaguely resemble each other. Some horoscopes in the *Anthologiae* were cast in order to make length of life predictions, and in these nothing is said about the events of the client's life. Other horoscopes were written to expose the factors which control the subject's way of life, his fate, his diseases, his misfortunes—and these horoscopes illuminate the astrologer's methods, if not his view of ancient life. Such horoscopes for the most part simply state the salient fact about the client: of low birth, he attained high rank, but fell into vicissitudes and trouble; afflicted with vice, he came to a bad end; and so on (complete translations in *GH*). In this reticence Valens' horoscopes are like those found in the papyri, which simply give planetary positions, with little interpretation or detail.[36] One may presume that the astrologer gave verbal, not written, forecasts. The details outlined in the theoretical passages (listed in footnote 35 above) are much more complete, much more circumstantial, and from them a sketch of the client's life can be made, as follows.[37]

For a similar world of adventure, see the portrait of "Sophistopolis," the city envisioned in ancient rhetorical exercises, in D. A. Russell, *Greek Declamation* (Cambridge 1983) 22–39. For an early astrological forecast involving pirates, adultery, ransom, and triumphant vengeance, see *P. Mich.* 148, from the first century CE.

[35] The latter include:

    I 1 - the stars (1.4–5.8P)

    I 2 - the signs (5.21–13.26P)

    I 3 - the terms, the degrees in each sign which are ruled by the individual stars (13.28–18.10P)

    I 21 - combinations of two stars (36.22–40.23P)

    I 22- combinations of three stars (40.26–48.29P)

    II 2 - the triangles (55.14–58.12P)

    II 22 - the Lots of Fortune and Daimon (83.12–86.14P)

    II 36 - diseases and injuries (103.30–106.15P)

    IV 17-25 - the transmissions of the stars to each other (179.10–192.34P).

Needless to say, other chapters contain theoretical data about the stars' and signs' influences.

[36] *GH* 162.

[37] The following sketch is derived from I 21, with some references to IV 17ff.

The client is a man of Greek culture, consulting Valens about what will happen to him.[38] He may be of average/mediocre (μέτριος) fortune: a small landowner, a steward or supervisor of another's property (37.16K; 36.24P), a secretary who receives pay (39.15K; 38.21P), or someone involved in buying and selling, a base occupation (40.8K; 39.20P). This person of moderate fortune will be concerned about employment possibilities (πράξεις) or how he will make a living (βίος). He may succeed through education, may become an accountant, a secretary, a teacher (39.13–14K; 38.18–20P). He may become a scholar and an initiate into the mystery religions (40.14K; 39.24–25P)—not that this promises happiness, because he may go too far and become a devotee of magic and the curious arts, a brazen and inquisitive person (42.32–34K; 42.9–11P). The most commonly foreseen method of gaining a livelihood is by winning the favor of the great. By these magnates he may be thought worthy of gifts and honors (189.14K; 179.18P), jewelry and slaves (189.27K; 180.1P), and other "unexpected" benefits (190.6K; 180.15P)—probably no one expected somebody of his status to win them. This favor, however, will not last; success will be fleeting (41.5K; 40.22P). The great have the nasty habit of elevating someone, only to ruin him later (45.14K; 44.22P). Indeed, hostility from the great is a constant worry (38.18K; 37.21P).

These men of moderate fortune may also make progress through legacies (37.15K; 36.23P—a common source of gain, even though they usually bring with them lawsuits—194.9K; 184.19P), from adoptions (37.15K; 36.23P), and from treasure troves (39.16K; 38.22P). These men, however, always meet obstacles and rebuffs (196.8K; 186.19P), setbacks and hostility from the great (189.8K; 179.12P). They may fall into debt, resort to forgery, and have to flee the law (40.30K; 40.12P).

Alternatively, Valens' client may be of high rank, and his opportunities are greater: he may become a tyrant, founding cities and sacking them, looting and pillaging (63.25K; 62.10P). He may live with great spectacle and show (φαντασία), even if he is in reduced circumstances (38.26K; 37.29P). His high status is visible in his insignia of office (crowns and garlands) and in his preeminence and dignity, his slaves and his jewelry (194.17K; 184.28P). He becomes a governor or a high official in the royal court.

---

[38] Women are only occasionally the subject of forecasts: "When forecasting for women, daughters, or female individuals, start from Venus..." (205.16K; 195.19P); other forecasts for women at 71.5K; 68.24P (a queen) and 197.27K; 188.8P. Only two horoscopes are those of women (281.24K; 269.8P. 282.16K; 270.1P). A section on marriage prospects for women begins on 121.9K; 115.17P.

Do not be envious of this person's high rank. Like the Dallas oilman's, his wealth and power is accompanied by public scandal (49.2K; 48.10P), by popular envy and hatred (48.17K; 47.25P), and by upset in the family. In fact, high rank and family happiness seem inversely related (39.24, 30K; 38.29, 39.5P). His family is riven by quarrels (37.20K; 36.28P), divorce (38.11K; 37.14P), and instability of all kinds (39.10, 23K; 38.14, 29P). Entanglements with base-born women bring harm and scandal (38.4K; 37.9–10P). Indeed, women are a constant source of trouble, disorder, and scandal to men, and men are trouble for women (197.24–27K; 188.6–7P). In short, the client's happiness consists of wealth and the visible symbols of office and rank, but he is plagued by annoyance, trouble, and mental and physical anguish.

The client is surrounded by villains; he may be robbed or swindled (200.17–18K; 190.28–29P). He may suffer betrayal, an ever-present danger (45.21K; 44.28P). He also faces dangers arising from his own villainy: ambition may lead him to abandon his own family and to consort with strangers (43.4K; 42.14–15P); he may become a poisoner (if he is not poisoned himself), a homosexual, a fickle person (39.35K; 39.10P. 43.28K; 43.3P). He may repent (48.28–29K; 47.34P), if he does not first commit suicide or go insane from his many troubles (201.15–16K; 191.25–26P). His actions may lead him into lawsuits, trials, and imprisonment (43.16K; 42.25P).

Sometimes the client must travel: he may fail at home but succeed abroad. He may also fail abroad, be abused there, suffer shipwreck and typhoons (200.4–5K; 190.19P). Generally speaking, travel is to be avoided (see II 29 *passim*).

The gods are no consolation. A client may be a scholar devoted to the mystery religions. He may also worship the gods with a bad conscience (37.28–29K; 37.4–5P). He may even curse the gods because of his miseries (44.4K; 43.9P), sometimes with justification, having fallen into debt because of religion (43.31K; 43.6P).

Love is no consolation either. The client's disturbed family life was mentioned above. Women trouble him because of their jealousy and their constant illnesses (196.21K; 186.30P. 197.9K; 186.23P), although they may be of great help when they are of high rank. Indeed, many men are helped by high-born women (38.32K; 38.4P). They fall in love with the client, and their love may even be reciprocated (201.28K; 192.5–6P). The astrologer, however, says little about the client's feelings. His reading of the chart concerns what happens to the client, not what he does to others or what he feels about others. Rarely does the astrologer mention that the client may accuse others of the villainy which he has committed himself (200.19K; 190.31P).

Language and Style

The *Anthologiae*, rich in poetic terms, astrological vocabulary, and religio-philosophical bombast, combines utilitarian language—the literary *koine*—with frequent purple patches. What follows is a small selection of examples; for extended studies see Warning, *De Sermone* and Kroll, "Mantissa" 143–54.[39]

His language is the popular *koine* with variants and with the poetic touches common in popular texts:

He writes ἀρσενικός and ἀρρενικός, θαρσελέος and θαρραλέαν, περισσότερος and περιττός. For the earlier forms in -αρχος, Valens writes -αρχης: δεκαδάρχης, ἑκατοντάρχης, πολεμάρχης. For the earlier ἡ νίκη, he writes τὸ νῖκος, as in the LXX and N.T.

Valens adds μᾶλλον to a comparative form: μᾶλλον φυσικοτέραν, μᾶλλον ἀπρακτότερος (Rydbeck 80–85).

He uses many perfect participles as adverbs: πεφυλαγμένως, ἐφθονημένως, ἐπισταμένως.

In verb forms, Valens often substitutes first aorist for second aorist endings, as is common in the koine: εὕραμεν and εὕρομεν; προείπαμεν and προείπομεν; ἀφείλαμεν. The older contract futures are rare: Valens usually writes ἀποτελέσει, not ἀποτελεῖ; ἀπολέσει, not ἀπολεῖ. The four main -μι verbs usually maintain their old forms, but ὄλλυμι, and δείκνυμι compounds have become -ω verbs: ἀπολλύουσι, παραδεικνύει.

In syntax, Valens uses ἕως and ὅτε + subjunctive, as well as ὅς ἐάν, both features of pre–atticist prose (Rydbeck 182–83).

However, the most striking feature of Valens' style is his large vocabulary. Even omitting the technical terms of astrology, his contribution to the Greek lexicon is large. One reason for this is his listing of occupations, social activities, and individual syndromes, much like those in the medical writers and physiognomists. His lists of diseases and injuries also add new words. Warning, *De sermone,* lists Valens' unique words.

A number of Valens' words and poetic phrases seem to be common to all astrological writers:[40]

ἀνώμαλος, ἀνωμαλία, ἀνωμαλίζω - "(to be) subject to ups and downs" are frequent in the *Anthologiae* (more than 60x) and occur in Manetho I 270 and

---

[39] *Indices verborum* can be found in both Kroll's and Pingree's editions, the latter of which is very comprehensive. On levels of style see L. Rydbeck, *Fachprose*. For an extensive treatment of Valens' astrological vocabulary see Bara, "Apotélesmatique et intitiatives."

[40] See W. Kroll, "Mantissa" in *CCAG* 5.2 143–46. Firmicus Maternus is cited according to the volume (I, II) and page number in the edition by Kroll-Skutsch-Ziegler; Manetho from *Manethonis Apotelesmaticorum* ed. Koechly.

Firmicus Maternus, "inaequalitatem vitae" I 103.16, 119.2.

The phrase συνοχῶν καὶ καταιτιασμῶν πεῖραν λαμβάνοντες- "experiencing prison and accusations" (43.16K; 42.25P) can be compared to Manetho II 283 (ἐν συνοχῇσι γένοντο), III 203, IV 486, and to Ptolemy *Tetr.* II 9.5.

Valens says men may be ἀλλοτρίων ἀγαθῶν ἐπιθυμηταί - "covetous of others' goods" (10.23K; 10.14–15P). Manetho says ὄλβου τε ποθήτορας ἀλλοτρίοιο (IV 120); Firmicus "Alienas res...desiderabit" (I 115.32).

Valens' clients encounter ἀπειλὰς μυστικῶν καὶ παλαιῶν πραγμάτων ἔνεκα - "threats due to religious and old matters" (163.20K; 155.2P). Manetho says Νείκεα καὶ κρισίας γραπτῶν χάριν ἠὲ παλαιῶν ἔργων ἴσχουσιν (III 161).

The client's appetites may lead him astray: οἱ δὲ καὶ ταῖς τῶν ἀδελφῶν ἢ ἐπιστατῶν ἢ ταῖς τῶν πατέρων ἢ καὶ μητρυιαῖς τὰς ἐπιμιξίας ποιοῦνται - "Some lie with the wives of brothers, guardians, or fathers, or with their stepmothers" (75.14K; 72.22P, also 115.18–29K; 109.29–30P). Manetho has ἢ καὶ μητρυιῇσιν ἑαῖς ἢ παλλακίδεσσιν σφωιτέρου γενετῆρος ὁμὸν λέχος εἰσανέβησαν (II 189); Firmicus "Aut enim cum sororibus aut filiabus aut fratrum uxoribus coire coguntur" (I 153.8).

The noble client may experience ὄχλων ἐπαναστάσεις - "revolts of the masses" (59.8K; 58.3P *et al*; cp. *Tetr.* II 9.11; Firmicus I 111.10) and ψύχεις or καταψύχεις τῶν πράξεων - "chilling of activities" (42.17K; 41.26P; cp. *Tetr.* IV 4.12; Firmicus II 46.23 "tempus frigidum").

These examples of common phrasing and matter, which could be multiplied at length, show that many of the forecasts associated in all ancient astrologers with given planetary configurations have been borrowed from earlier texts and perhaps go back ultimately to the lost work of Nechepso and Petosiris.[41]

Like St. Paul, with his "Bad companions corrupt good morals," Valens had had the usual school education with its tags of poetry influencing his writing:[42]

ἀκάματος - "untiring," epic and tragic (331.21K; 318.18P)
ἀοίδομος - "Sung of," Pindaric (3x)
ἄτη - "delusion," epic (285.28K; 273.15K)
εὐσταθής - "tranquil," epic (3x)
λυσσώδης - "raging," epic and tragic (356.5K; 341.16P)

---

[41] For these astrologers see "Quotations" above.

[42] Many (all?) of the earliest astrological works are in verse: Dorotheus, Nechepso / Petosiris (?), Manetho's *Apotelesmatica*, Anubion (in P. Oxy. 464 and P. Berlin 7508), and the original text from which the *Ars Eudoxi* was derived (*HAMA* 686). Poetic words may derive from this tradition. Note, for example, βαστάζει (10.1K; 9.24P) in the Homeric sense "carry," not used in Attic prose; Valens elsewhere uses διαβαστάζει (2x). The passage containing βαστάζει must come from a poetic text.

ὀλετής - "a destroyer," epic (303.17K; 290.11P)
τρυχηρός - "tormenting," tragic (109.1K; 103.22P)
ὑφηγητής - "a guide," Sophoclean (222.12K; 11.16P)

He also adds a poetic/literary color to his text with quotations from the poets and philosophers, and with extended similes. Homer is quoted nine times.[43] Fragment 527 of Cleanthes is quoted several times, once wrongly attributed to Euripides (VI 9; 250.14P). An anecdote about Euripides and a youthful critic is related (276.25–30K; 264.18–23P). Orpheus is quoted on the nature of the soul (330.24–30K; 317.19–26P). Valens confesses that he has a collection of such passages (347.28–29K; 333.29–30P); indeed, Manetho V 18 quotes the same verse about Fate (*Iliad* 6.488). His extended similes are perhaps more original and seem to have become more elaborate as his magnum opus progressed. Two are particularly worthy of note because of their reference to contemporary life. In VI 1 he compares man's life and the stars' influence on that life to the game of *latrunculi*, a chess-like game played on a board with black and white pieces.[44]

> The [celestial] system might be compared to the game of white and black pieces—for life is a game, a pilgrimage, and a fair. Competitive men devise wicked traps for each other, move their pieces along the many straight rows, and put their pieces down in certain places when summoned to a skirmish. As long as the place happens to be unguarded, the piece moves unchecked according to the will of the player: it flees, stays, pursues, attacks, wins, and loses in turn. If it is surrounded by the opposing pieces (as if caught in a net) and finds the straight rows to be blocked, it is intercepted and captured. In this way, of the two players, one finds momentary pleasure and enjoyment for himself, the other momentary mockery and pain—momentary because the one who had been in despair suddenly comes back into the game by means of some stratagem and gives back the burden of despair to the [other player] who had just now laid it on him. The stars' effects should be viewed in the same way... (245.34–246.13K; 235.16–29P)

---

[43] *Iliad* 6.488 (272.4K; 259.27P), 8.19 (347.9K; 333.12P), 13.730-3 (221.15–18K; 210.23–26P), 15.605 (347.18K; 333.20P), 19.128 (272.2K; 259.25P), and 22.213 (347.21K; 333.23P). *Odyssey* 4.73 (263.15K; 251.15P), 4.379 (257.17K; 246.24P), and 24.1-2 (346.22–23K; 332.28–29P).

[44] See *RE*, 23er Halbband (1924) 980–84 for the few details known of this game. It may have been played on a 9 x 9 board.

Immediately following the simile just quoted, he compares the quality and influence of each star to the colors used by painters (VI 2; 237.21P). In V 9 he compares the two types of astrology students, the diligent and the careless, to two vintages of wine or to the fruit from different trees of the same species:

> A distinction is made among those who encounter this art: some are true, some insubstantial, some uncomprehending. It is like this: several earthenware amphoras receive a single crop of precious wine from one farm. After a time, some of the amphoras give the wine back perfect, filled with flavor and enjoyment for those who entrusted the wine to their keeping. Other amphoras, however, allow the measure of the wine's volume to diminish, are not able to contain the new wine, and allow it to foam over—these amphoras did not entirely alter the flavor or cause the savor of the wine crop to disappear, but they do cheat the vintner in both respects, for the taste does not last any time nor does it keep its real nature, but immediately changes. (We can see the same thing occur in other plant growths: from one tree the fruit is sweet and ripe when it is gathered; the fruit from another tree is hard and wild; of another the fruit is bitter and rotten or harmful to its consumers.) Just so are the minds of those who encounter this art: one student does his lessons to the end with eagerness and determination and has pleasure in it. The unscientific and ignorant students get only a taste of the introductory portions, spend no time on these studies because of their lack of diligence, study with no legitimate teachers, and bring the charge of ignorance on themselves and reproaches upon the instructors of this art. (221.26–222.14K; 210.32–211.17P)[45]

Other comparisons: Valens passes on his last words like a dying father (257.11K; 246.9P); the searcher for truth is like a man who hikes through the valley and up the mountain to come upon a temple adorned with gold and silver and ivory, and he worships the gods in great splendor (263.13K; 251.12P); those who expect a great future are sometimes disappointed, like the heirs of a (supposedly) rich man, who find that his wealth is tied up in litigation (270.31K; 258.20P); the stars' influence continues through the years like the echo from a sounding gong (275.3K; 262.29P—these four comparisons come from the latest sections of the *Anthologiae*); the searcher for truth is like a man walking unknowing on the spot where treasure is buried (352.3K; 337.31P).

---

[45] The comparison of the mind to a jar is a commonplace in popular philosophy: Cic. *Tusc.* I 61, Plato, *Phaedrus* 235C, Plutarch *de Aud.* 39A, 48C. See Hillyard, *Plutarch: De Audiendo* 259.

Mathematical Expressions

Valens offers some unusual mathematical expressions. Like all Greek mathematical writers, he never uses formulas or equations, but describes his operations, even the simplest, in words.[46]

ἀναλύω εἰς - "to transform into": [τὸν χρόνον] εἰς ἡμέρας ἀνέλυσα - "I transform [the remaining period of months] into days" (253.32K; 242.27-8P). ταῦτα [ρπ'] ἀναλύω ἕως τῶν ξ' - "I transform this [180] into sixtieths" (296.24K; 283.22P). Compare P. Mich. 145 III v.2: ἀνάλυσον τὰς β' ἥμισυ εἰς ἥμισυ, ε' - "Reduce 2 1/2 to halves, = 5." A similar expression in Ptolemy's Handy Tables: ἐὰν...τὰς καιρικὰς ὥρας ἀναλύειν θέλομεν εἰς ἰσημερινάς - "If we want to transform seasonal hours into equinoctial hours" (Ptolemy, Opera Minora 161.20).

ἀνατρέχω - "to count back" (cp. ἐκβάλλω below): ἀναδραμὼν ἀπὸ τῆς γεννητικῆς ἡμέρας - "counting this [amount] back from the date of birth..." (51.36K; 51.9P).

ἀπολύω - "to count off," usually with καταλήγω - "to end": ταύτας [νη'] ἀπέλυσα ἀπὸ Ἡλίου· κατέληξε Παρθένῳ - "I counted this amount [58] off from the Sun's position; [the count] ended in Virgo" (19.25K; 18.30P).

ἀφαιρέω - see under ἐκκρούω.

γίνεται- "equals" followed by the answer, *passim*.

διεκβάλλω - "to begin, then continue, counting": δεήσει ἀπὸ Ἡλίου καὶ Σελήνης καὶ ὡροσκόπου διεκβάλλειν τοὺς ἐνιαυτούς - "It will be necessary to count off the years from the Sun, the Moon, and the Ascendant" (174.23K; 165.14-15P). P. Ryl. 27.11 and Ptolemy (Op. Min. 165.17, 166.5 et al.) use διεκβάλλω in the same sense.

εἰσέρχομαι εἰς ὄργανον - "to consult the astronomical table": εἰσῆλθον εἰς τὸ προκείμενον ὄργανον εἰς τὰς ιδ' μοίρας τὰς ἐν τῷ πρώτῳ στίχῳ... – "I consulted the attached table at 14° in the first column..." (20.12K; 19.17P).

---

[46] For interesting parallels to Valens' mathematical vocabulary, see F. E. Robbin's commentary to P. Mich. 145 in *Papyri in the University of Michigan Collection*, vol. 3 *Miscellaneous Papyri*.

ἐκβάλλω - "to count off": τὰ καταλειφθέντα ἔκβαλλε ἀπὸ τῆς Σελήνης τῆς κατὰ γενέσιν - "Count off the remainder from the Moon's position at the nativity" (204.25–26K; 194.29–30P). The astrologer of *P. Mich.* 149 used ἐνψηφίζω in the same sense: ἐνψήφιζε δὲ τὰς μοίρας ἕως ἔλθῃς… - "Count off the degrees until you come to…" (vii 6–7). ἐκβάλλω and διεκβάλλω are confused in the manuscripts; δεῖ ἐκβάλλειν is written for διεκβάλλειν several times in Book IV 11.

ἐκκρούω ἀνά - his usual word for "divide by": τὰ ἔτη πλήρη ἀναλαβὼν ἔκκρουε ὁσάκις δύνῃ ἀνὰ λ΄ - "taking the full years, divide them by 30," literally "cast out as many 30's as you can" (33.31–2K; 33.4–5P). Occasionally he uses ἀφαιρέω in the sense "to cast out": ἀφαίρει τοὺς κύκλους ἀνὰ τξ΄ - "Cast out/subtract 360° circles." (28.27–28P) Note ἀνά meaning "at the rate of" as in commercial language (*P. Mich.* 145 III iv.1) and ἆρον ἀνὰ κε΄ - "divide by 25" (*P. Ryl.* 27.1).[47]

λοιπογραφέω - Two senses: "to discard the remainder" (i.e., to use integer division) and "to deduct." μερίσεις εἰς τὸν γ΄, μὴ λοιπογραφῶν τὸν ἀριθμὸν ἀλλὰ κατέχειν - "divide by 3; do not discard the remainder but keep it" (31.16K; 30.16–17P; the remainder is the important factor for the succeeding calculation). "This will happen…καὶ μηδεὶς τῶν ἀναιρετῶν… λοιπογραφήσῃ τὸ πλῆθος τῶν ἐτῶν" - "if…none of the destructive stars deducts from the number of years [in the client's lifespan]" (136.19K; 129.9P).

ὅρος - "a factor," "a coefficient": τριῶν ὅρων ὑπαρχόντων - ἐλαχίστου τε καὶ μέσου καὶ μεγίστου - "There are three factors: the minimum, the mean, and the maximum…" (50.8K; 49.16P; the figures referred to here are the coefficients for calculating the date of conception: 258, 273, 288.) For a similar use of this word, see Ptolemy, *Op. Min.* 181.18.

πολυπλασιάζω (38x) and πολλαπλασιάζω (5x) – "to multiply" *passim*.

προσβάλλω - "to add a factor": τὴν πρόθεσιν τῷ ζητουμένῳ ἔτει προσβάλλων - "adding the addition–factor to the year in question" (31.15K; 30.16P).

---

[47] Valens rarely uses the customary word for "divide by" - μερίζω εἰς/παρά; ἐμέρισα εἰς τὸν γ΄ - "I divided by 3" (32.7K; 31.8P). μερίζω usually has the sense "allot": ὁ τοιοῦτος εὐδαιμονήσει περὶ τῆς ὑπὸ Κρόνου μεριζομένης πράξεως - "This type of native will be fortunate in the occupation[s] allotted by Saturn" (60.8K; 58.28P).

προσλαμβάνω - once meaning "to assign for each month": ἑκάτου μηνὸς προσλαβὼν ἀνὰ β΄ ἥμισυ – "Assign 2 1/2 for each month" (33.19P; different reading in K). For ἀνά see under ἐκκρούω above.

προστίθημι - "to add" *passim*. Occasionally συντίθημι is used in the sense "to combine" = "to add together more than two numbers": ἑκάστου μηνὸς Αἰγυπτίου ἀνὰ μοῖραν α΄ λεπτὰ λε΄. ἑκάστης δὲ ἡμέρας λεπτὰ γ΄ συνθείς - "having combined 1° 35' for each Egyptian month and 3' for each day [with the previous number]" (28.26–27P)

σύνδεσμος - in addition to the usual sense "lunar node," σύνδεσμος also means "a sequence" of planetary positions or of figures in a table: τὸν Ἥλιον εὑρίσκομεν ἀπὸ Κριοῦ τὴν ἀρχὴν ποιούμενον...καὶ...τὸ μέγεθος τῆς ἡμέρας ἐπαύξοντα, ἐν δὲ τῷ διαμέτρῳ Ζυγῷ τὸν σύνδεσμον λύοντα καὶ εἰς τὸ μειωτικὸν χωροῦντα - "We find the Sun to be beginning in Aries and increasing the length of the day [from that date], but in the opposite sign, Libra, breaking the sequence and turning to a reduction [in daylength]" (163.5-9K; 154.22–25P). In IV 5 συνδέσμου λύσις "breaking the sequence" refers to the moment when one chronocrator (a star which rules for a given period) passes the rule to another star (163.28,31K; 155.9,12P). With reference to tables: Valens describes a table (now found at the end of Book VIII) with the figure 2 entered at Libra 1°, 4 at Libra 2°, 6 at Libra 3°, 8 at Libra 4°, 10 at Libra 5°, and 12 at Libra 6°. He continues: τουτέστι παραύξησις [μοιρῶν] β΄ · εἶτα ἀπὸ τῆς ζ΄ μοίρας συνδέσμου λύσις. παραύξησις προσθέσεως [μοιρῶν] ιδ΄ - "i.e., a progressive increase of 2; then [at Libra] 7° the sequence is broken and an additional factor of 14 is added" (295.6–7K; 282.6–7P).[48] Perhaps the same meaning in *P. Ryl.* 27.8: ἐπὶ τῶν συνδέσμων - "If a connection is made."

Manuscripts and Editions

The *Anthologiae*, like most astrological texts, was used and consulted by later astrologers. Pingree has emphasized the importance of this fact for establishing the history of our present text.[49] As our study of the chronology of the *Anthologiae* has shown, the text, with the exception of Book IX, is in its approximate order

---

[48] μοιρῶν is an error in the text; these figures are not degrees but factors (ἀριθμοί) used in length of life calculations. See *GH* 174–75 for the construction of the table on 321–24K; 308–11P. Part of this table is reproduced on p. 38 below. Σύνδεσμος once refers to the star α Piscium, the "link" between the two fish in Pisces (14.9K; 13.24P).

[49] Pingree "Antiochus and Rhetorius" 203.

of composition, but with many short insertions and glosses. It also has several sections appended in antiquity, with horoscopes dating to 431 (365.3K; 350.9P) and 419 (365.29K; 351.4P). The fifth-century version of the *Anthologiae* was the archetype of all later Greek mss, and it was used by Rhetorius and the Byzantine astrologers of the tenth through the twelfth centuries, who tried to make sense of Valens' rules and procedures.[50]

Valens' posthumous fame was great. To him was attributed the horoscope for the city of Constantinople.[51] He also had quite a vogue among Arab astrologers. Māshā'allāh (died ca. 815 CE) knew ten books of his (*CCAG* I 82). The *Fihrist* of Ibn al-Nadīm reports the titles of nine books of "Wālīs." This Wālīs has long been identified with Vettius Valens, and the supposition has been that his *Anthologiae* were translated into Arabic, possibly from an intermediate Persian translation, with additional stories about the author and additional works ascribed to him.[52] From this Arabic tradition anecdotes about Valens re-entered the Greek tradition. At the request of the king of Persia, Valens interpreted a horoscope: "This man will be exalted, will rule lands, and will be called blessed by many men." Little did Valens know that he was interpreting the horoscope of the very man, Mohammed, who was then threatening Persia. The Persian king became angry and threw Valens in jail, from which he was saved by God's mercy.[53]

The renaissance scholar Claude Saumaise (Salmasius) rewrote much of the *Anthologiae* in his *De annis climactericis* (1648), but the first modern edition of the complete text was by W. Kroll (1908), the second by D. Pingree (1986). An edition with French translation and extensive commentary on Book I has been published by Bara. This edition presents the best introduction to the topics, terminology, and methods of the astrology of Book I; unfortunately Valens' main interest, length of life calculations, is not discussed in that book. All modern editions are based on very few manuscripts: *Vaticanus graecus* 191 (V, written ca. 1300) and its copy, *Arch. Selden* B. 19 (S, ca. 1520), in the Bodleian Library. S supplies the text for the quires lost from V after S was copied. Another manuscript, *Marcianus graecus* 314 (M, ca. 1300) supplies much of the text for *Anthologiae* I and II. V and M are descended from a common Byzantine archetype.[54]

---

[50] Pingree "Byzantine Tradition" 537–40.

[51] Details in *CCAG* 5.1, 118. See *RE* VIII A,2 1872.

[52] See F. Sezgin 38–41, and the references there to earlier studies. The *Fihrist* is available in English in *The Fihrist of al-Nadim*. ed. B. Dodge; Walis is on p. 641. Apomasar attributed to Valens a work on the paranatellonta (simultaneously rising stars) for each degree of the zodiac (*CCAG* I 84). An example of Valens in Arabic in King (1989).

[53] The anecdote is in *CCAG* 5.3, 110, dated in Pingree "Byzantine Tradition" 537 to 939 CE, a date which does not fit the story.

[54] For details of the fairly simple manuscript tradition see Kroll's preface ix–xii, Pingree's

Pingree's text differs relatively little from Kroll's: both are editions of the Byzantine Greek manuscripts only. As mentioned in footnote 3 above, there seems to be another tradition for Valens' work, the traces of which can be found in the *Fihrist*, in the Arab complers al-Qasrānī and al-Saymarī, and in several late Greek texts. This Eastern tradition of the *Anthologiae* is kin to the mass of Arabic texts derived from Dorotheus, Rhetorius, and Antiochus, and must be discussed in conjunction with them.[55] This tradition, however, has not significantly influenced the current text, although parts of it appear in the lengthy appendices to Pingree's edition (369–455P). Pingree's improvements to Kroll's text are due to his detailed studies of the mss and to a half-century's work on the techniques of ancient astronomy carried out by O. Neugebauer and his collaborators, the immediately relevant parts of which were published in *GH*. Thanks to this work, the horoscopes of the *Anthologiae* can be dated and many of Valens' procedures can be explained.[56]

There is still much to do in reconstructing the text: the mss omit tables which may be reconstructible;[57] the text may be restored to its original order, with the fragments of Book IX assigned to their proper places; many glosses and lacunae remain to be identified. Particular techniques remain obscure, especially the use of lunar and solar gnomons in Book VIII. The study of the vocabulary and techniques of the different sections of the *Anthologiae* may allow the recovery of fragments from other astrological writers.

---

preface vii–xiii, and Pingree "Byzantine Tradition" 532–41.

[55] Pingree "The Indian Iconography" 227 and his review in *Gnomon* 40(1968) 276–80 of Wilhelm and Hans Georg Gundel, *Astrologoumena*.

[56] See especially *HAMA* 793-801 on the planetary calculations in I 20 and *GH* 174–75 on Valens' astronomical tables.

[57] Tables omitted in III 6 (145.22K), V 7 (233.23K), V 11 (restored by Pingree at 222.1–13P), VIII 5 (303.32K).

Appendix A

Chapters which contain horoscopes whose time of *casting*, as opposed to time of *birth*, is dateable. All dates are CE.

Book I: no horoscopes are cited.

Books II–III: these early chapters are a general introduction to astrology. Valens had not yet developed his special interest in the topic, length of life, and no dates other than birth dates can be calculated. Some horoscopes were reused at later dates which can be calculated.

Book II 21: this chapter cites examples of horoscopes for living people and describes the astrological reason for their fortunes. No dates of death are given—hence the date of casting cannot be determined; no date can be assigned to this chapter. Later, however, three of the horoscopes were reinterpreted after the subjects had died or had suffered a crisis. The years were 143/4, 152, and 153 for the later reuse. This chapter must antedate 143/4.

Book II 26: no final dates can be determined.

Book II 30: Valens' own horoscope, interpreted to show why his mother had predeceased his father. Valens was born (if the surmise is correct) in 120; this passage must have been written or revised after his mother had died in 155.

Book II 37: these horoscopes concerning disease mention no deaths or critical times. One (112.5K; 106.24P) is cited again in 287.22K; 256.16P, with a critical date of 154. Presumably II 37 was written before that time.

Book II 41: all of this chapter's horoscopes are for violent death, but no dates can be calculated.

The following Books contain the horoscopes with dateable deaths or crises.

	Date of Birth	Date of Death or Crisis
Book III 6:	75	144 (134.9P)
	110	161 (134.21P)
Book III 10:	114	143 (139.22P)
	127	139 (140.1P)
Book III 13:	74	144 (146.1P)

	115	147 (146.10P)
Book III 14:	75	151 (148.1P)
	135	169 (148.8P)
Book III 16:	82	152 (149.11P)
	102	169 (149.15P)
	102	169 (149.19P)

This chapter is to be dated to 169/170. The horoscope of birth date 82 is cited from earlier records (Book II 21).

Book IV 8:	75	145 (154.19P)
Book IV 10:	152	156 (161.13P)
Book IV 11:	120	155 (165.1P)
Book V 1:	121	156 (200.3P)
Book V 10:	120	154 (216.6P)
	134	157 (216.16P)
	111	157 (216.33P)
	107	158 (217.15P)
	135	157 (217.22P)
	112	157 (217.29P)
	110	157 (218.22P)
	153	157 (218.26P)
	102	154 (218.29P)
	120	156 (218.33P)
	122	157 (219.4P)
	114	158 (219.13P)
	123	155 (219.22P)
	113	133 (220.12P)

This horoscope is cited later for the date 161. This chapter was completed by 158.

Book V 11: 37   68 (222.15P) This horoscope is cited from Critodemus, an astrologer of the first century. The date 11 June 68 is being investigated for a client who was born 15 Dec 37.

Book V 12: 104   158 (227.25P)

Book VI 5: 132   184 (242.3P) The latest horoscope in *Anthologiae* I-IX; ten years subsequent to any other investigation date, this must have been misdated or added by a later investigator.

Book VII 2:   120   162 (255.17P)
              114   153 (255.30P)
              122   159 (256.4P)
              118   138 (256.16P) From II 36; also in VII 5
              117   157 (257.1P)
              74   143 (257.29P)
Book VII 3:   173   173 (261.5P)
              159   169 (261.16P)
              162   173 (261.25P)
              122   172 (261.34P)
Book VII 4:   122   166 (263.5P) This is one of the latest sections of the *Anthologiae*, completed in 173.

Book VII 5:
              124   159 (268.18P)
              134   161 (269.8P)
              108   160 (269.22P)
              110   164 (270.1P)
              113   162 (270.12P)
              129   159 (27024P)
              102   142 (271.3P)
              105   153 (271.23P)
              158   161 (271.31P)
              111   158 (272.26P)
              114   155* (274.14P)
              120   155* (274.22P)
              118   155* (274.30P)
              127   155* (275.3P)
              122   155* (275.9P)
              133   155* (275.14P)
              142   165** (276.7P)
              120   160 (277.28P) The single-starred nativities were almost shipwrecked in 155. This is the critical date under investigation. The double-starred nativity is interpreted in the text up to the subject's 23rd year (164/5), with a brief forecast for the future: "There will be troubles and expenses, or there will be independence…" (277.17–18P). I judge from these comments that this passage, and perhaps the whole chapter, was written in 164/5.

Book VIII 7: this chapter and the one following explicitly gives the date of birth and the length of life, from which the dates of death have been "calculated":

54	127 (291.23P)
79	151 (292.14P)
114	156 (292.28P)
115	155 (293.12P)
127	154 (293.22P)
69	150 (293.32P)
113	114 (294.10P)
142	145 (294.18P)
152	152/3 (294.27P)
157	158 (295.4P)
105	127 (295.13P)
125	156 (295.27P)
131	151 (296.11P)
67	153 (296.26P)
109	154 (297.7P)
83	154 (297.28P)
85	150 (298.6P)
79	157 (298.20P)
151	157 (299.1P)
121	153 (299.12P)
119	152 (300.1P) Several fragmentary, undatable

horoscopes follow.

A slightly later section of Book VIII 7 continues:

	102	167 (303.17P)
	75	144 (304.9P)
	134	168 (304.24P)
	151	163/4 (305.3P)
Book IX: 19	118	(not cited here)

Appendix B: Astrological Topics

I append notes describing Valens' own procedures when these have no obvious parallel in Ptolemy or Hephaistion, as well as sample translations.[58]

Books I and II present a general introduction to astrological forecasting:

I 1: The influence of each star.[59] A sample passage:

> Saturn makes those born under him petty, malignant, care-worn, self-depreciating, solitary, deceitful, secretive in their trickery, strict, downcast, with a hypocritical air, squalid, black-clad, importunate, sad-looking, miserable, with a nautical bent, plying waterside trades. Saturn also causes humblings, sluggishness, unemployment, obstacles in business, interminable lawsuits, subversion of business, secrets, imprisonment, chains, griefs, accusations, tears, bereavement, capture, exposures [of children]. Saturn makes serfs and farmers because of its rule over the land, and it causes men to be renters of property, tax farmers, and violent in action. It puts into one's hands great ranks and distinguished positions, supervisions, management of others' property, and the fathership of others' children. Of materials, it rules lead, wood, and stone. Of the parts of the body, it rules the legs, the knees, the tendons, the lymph, the phlegm, the bladder, the kidneys, and the internal, hidden organs. Saturn is indicative of diseases and injuries arising from cold and moisture, such as dropsy, neuralgia, gout, cough, dysentery, hernia, spasms. Of syndromes, it rules possession, homosexuality, and depravity. Saturn makes bachelors and widows, bereavements, and childlessness. It causes violent deaths by water, strangulation, imprisonment, or dysentery. It also causes falling on the face. It is the star of Nemesis; it is of the day sect. It is like castor in color and astringent in taste. (1.24–2.20P)

The parallel chapters of the *Tetrabiblos* specify the physical nature of the stars: Saturn is cool and dry, Mars hot and dry, etc. In these chapters Ptolemy mentions none of the stars' influences on occupations, character, and fate.[60]

---

[58] A useful table of contents in Kroll's edition. In the following translations, brackets surround explanatory additions to the text; the parentheses are in Valens. The chapter numbers are those of Kroll's edition. The *Tetrabiblos* is cited from the edition by Boll-Boer (Leipzig 1940). A complete translation of Book I is found in Bara, *Anthologies*.

[59] *AG* 124–57; French translation in Bara, *Anthologies*, 27-29.

[60] *AG* 88–123. M. Riley, "Science and Tradition."

I 2: The nature of the 12 signs, the fixed stars to be found in each sign, and the geographical areas ruled by each sign (this is the science of *chorography* -cp. *Tetr.* II 2–4). Close parallels in Hephaistion I 1.[61]

I 3: The terms, the degrees in a sign ruled by each planet. Compare *Tetr.* I 20–21.[62]

> The first 6° of Gemini belong to Mercury: temperate, with fine weather, intelligent, versatile, skilled, effective in his work, poetic, prolific. The next 6° belong to Jupiter: competitive, temperate, with fine weather, prolific, luxuriant, beneficent. The third term, 5°, belongs to Venus: blossoming, artistic, addicted to plays and mimes, poetic, much-honored, popular, cheerful, prolific. The fourth term, 7°, belongs to Mars: much-burdened, with no brothers, having few children, a wanderer, with a good income, destructive, bloody, inquisitive. The last 6° belong to Saturn: temperate, a procurator, having possessions, intellectual, with a wide knowledge, distinguished, noted for intelligence, an arranger of great matters, most famous. (14.15-23P)

I 4–20 covers various methods for calculating important zodiacal or planetary positions: the Ascendant (I 4),[63] Midheaven (I 5), rising times (I 7), new and full Moons (I 9), the week (I 10), the Moon's phases and its astrologically significant positions on the third, seventh, and fortieth days after the birth (I 13–15), the nodes (I 16–18), and the planetary positions on any given date (I 19–20). Valens' procedures for calculating Saturn, Jupiter, and Mars are translated here:

> **Saturn** is to be calculated as follows: take the full years since Augustus and cast out as many 30's as possible [=divide by 30]. Multiply the remainder of the division by 12°. Multiply the result of the division by 30 (=cycles of Saturn) by 5°. For each month from Thoth to the date of birth add 1°, and for each day 1/30°. Having totaled all this, count from Cancer in the direction of diurnal motion, giving 30° to each sign. The star will be wherever the count stops.

---

[61] *AG* 124–57. The most thorough description of the values attributed to the signs is in W. Hübner, *Die Eigenschaften*.

[62] *AG* 180–240, *GH* 12; translation in Bara, *Anthologies*, 79. A completely different system of terms in *P. Mich.* 149 vii 28–40. Valens never mentions the decans.

[63] See A. Jones, "248-Day Schemes" 28–29 for a discussion of this chapter.

Jupiter as follows: divide the full years since Caesar by 12. Multiply the remainder by 12° and add this number to the result of the previous division by 12, one for each cycle of Jupiter plus 1° for each month and 2' for each day. Add them together and count the sum from Taurus, giving 12 to each sign.

Mars as follows: take the number of years from Augustus to the year in question, divide by 30, and note whether the remainder is odd or even. If it is even, start counting from Aries; if it is odd, start from Libra. Having found this number, double it and add to it 2 1/2 for each month after Thoth. If the result is more than 60, count off the amount over 60 from Libra or Aries, giving 5 to each sign. Wherever the count stops, make note of the sign and examine which sign the Sun is in. If the Sun is found to be west of the star, the star will be behind [=to the west] its calculated sign; if the Sun is found to be east of the star, the star will be ahead [=to the east] of its calculated sign. In other words, in each case, place the star nearer the Sun than the sign in which you have calculated it to be. The rest of the stars, especially Venus, show the same peculiarity when they are moving near the mean position of the Sun. (33.31–34.25K; 33.4–27P)[64]

I 21–22: The astrological influence of the stars in combination, first by two's, then by three's, e.g., Saturn, Jupiter, and the Sun together:[65]

Saturn, Jupiter, and the Sun are unsteady and insecure with respect to possessions, friendships, and other business enterprises. They cause loss of possessions. They cause some to fall into invidious accusations. These stars, having indicated help from unexpected sources or from the deceased, and having increased someone's reputation, bring ruin and accusation, along with sudden danger and plots. They do cause preeminence, guardianship of others' business, tribute, and salaries, for the sake of which men endure disturbance and crises, but these stars make the basis [of the preeminence] insecure and worrisome. (41.8–16K; 40.26–41.6P)

---

[64] Translation in Bara, *Anthologies*, 169–71. Valens' methods in this chapter have been explained in *HAMA* 793–801 and in A. Tihon "la longitude de Vénus" 71–81 and A. Tihon "la longitude des planètes" 16–22. Their purely arithmetic character differentiates Valens, the older Babylonian texts, and even Hipparchus (in his description of the motions of the five planets) from Ptolemy's system, which was based on trigonometry and mean motions. For a discussion of Valens' procedures for the moon see Jones "248–Day Schemes" 27–30.

[65] Translation in Bara, *Anthologies*, 197. A similar description organized in groups of two and three stars is found in *Anonymi de Planetis* (*CCAG* 2.159–80), a section derived from Valens, who is named there.

The information in these chapters can be used to sketch a client's career. See the section of this chapter The Astrologer's Clients.

I 23–24: Determining the date of conception and the length of the gestation period. Compare Hephaistion II 1.

Book II describes the system of the XII Places ("Houses" in modern terminology) and of the Lots, astrologically significant points on the zodiac.[66]

II 1–2: The four triangles (Aries Leo Sagittarius; Taurus Virgo Capricorn; Gemini Libra Aquarius; Cancer Scorpio Pisces) and their influence. Cp. *Tetr.* I 18, Hephaistion I 6.

II 3–4, 17, 19, 20, 27: the Lot of Fortune. It is found by determining the distance from the Sun to the Moon, then measuring an equal distance from the Ascendant and is mentioned in most horoscopes. The other Lots are found by measuring to and from the other stars in much the same fashion. See *Tetr.* III 11.5.[67]

II 5–15: The system of the XII Places. Each chapter describes the influence of each Place. Ptolemy, for whom the Places are not important, mentions only five of them (Tetr. III 11.3–4).[68] Valens also uses a scheme of Places relative to the Lot of Fortune, where for example the 8th Place from the Lot is called the Place of Death.

II 16: The influence of the geometric configurations of opposition, trine, square, and sextile; a long section transcribed from earlier astrologers, with sources common to Firmicus Maternus. See *Tetr.* I 13.

II 18: The Lot of Fortune and its astrological significance. See *Tetr.* I 19.[69]

II 23-25: Other Lots: of Debt, Deceit, Rank.

II 29–41: Standard methods of answering traditional astrological questions: travel (29), parents (30–33), free or slave nativities (34), injuries and diseases (36; this long chapter includes a *melothesia*, the assignment of the parts of the

---

[66] *AG* 276–88.
[67] *AG* 288–310, *GH* 8.
[68] *AG* 256–87, *GH* 7–8.
[69] *AG* 193–99, *GH* 7.

body to the signs and planets with illustrative horoscopes[70]), marriage (37–38), childlessness (39), brothers (40), violent death (41). Similar interrogations are covered in Hephaistion II 1–25 and *Tetr*. III–IV.[71]

Book III begins the elaboration of Valens' specialty, the determination of the critical periods (κλιμακτῆρες), years during which the client will suffer a crisis, and the determination of the client's length of life (χρόνοι ζωῆς):

III 1: the Control (ἐπικράτησις), the point of the zodiac which controls the length of life. Various configurations at the nativity change the Control. This chapter contains an early discussion of a method as yet undeveloped.

III 2-3: The vital sector (ἄφεσις), the arc of the zodiac which determines the length of life. One point is fixed as the "starter" (ἀφέτης), usually the Sun, the Moon, or the Ascendant; another is fixed as the "destroyer" (ἀναιρέτης), and the distance between them (not more than 90°) represents the length of life. In the following sample passage, the destroyer is the point 90° from the starter:

> Therefore in casting a nativity, it will be necessary to determine if it does or does not have a houseruler, and if the Sun, the Moon, or the Ascendant is the ἀφέτης. If the Sun or Moon are in the aphetic place, then it will be necessary to figure the total rising times (in the klima of the nativity) from the position of the apheta to the point square with it. Having found the total time, you can forecast that the native will live as many years. This forecast will be accurate if the houseruler is in its own terms or is configured appropriately, has contact or is in aspect with the apheta, and if no ἀναιρέτης applies its rays and deducts from the number of years. If the houseruler is not in aspect with the controller, but is otherwise found to be favorably configured (i.e., in the Ascendant, at the Midheaven while rising), it will allot the full span of years. If it is not at one of the other angles, it will deduct a segment of the arc proportional to its relationship with the rest of the horoscope, but will allot the remainder as the length of life. (129.1–14P)

A similar passage in Book V 11:

> The aphetic points of the years are operative when starting from any star, but the following aphetic points are most effective: for day births the Sun,

---

[70] W. Hübner, "Eine unbeachtete Zodiakale Melothesia," *AG* 319–26.
[71] *AG* 458–86, *GH* 7.

for night births the Moon, especially when they are at the angles. Next in effectiveness is the Ascendant. If the vital sector beginning at the Ascendant, the Moon, or the Sun passes to one of the stars in the nativity, then use it for forecasting. (220.21–26P)

This procedure is also described in *Tetr.* III 11.[72] Valens went on to develop more complex methods.

III 4–5: The exaltations, depressions, and sects of the stars. Cp. *Tetr.* I 12, 19.

III 7, 10: The vital sector and length of life. (See note on III 2–3 above.)

III 8–9: The terms, an interpolation. (See note on I 3 above.)

III 11: The critical periods determined according to the day of the week and the ruler of the day. This chapter uses a 7-day week and 9-day week. The purpose of these weeks is to enable the astrologer to determine the planetary ruler of the day, and hence the particular influences operative on that day (explanatory matter in [ ]):

> Saturn will be the beginning of the 7-day-week because of the Sun and Moon; Mars will be the beginning of the 9-day-week because Capricorn and Aquarius (which are Saturn's houses) are in opposition, in the seventh place, to Cancer and Leo [houses of the Sun and Moon], and Aries [Mars' house] is the ninth sign from Leo [=Sun], and Cancer [=Moon] is the ninth sign from Scorpio [Mars' house]. But it would be more scientific to derive these from the exaltation of the Moon in Taurus: the beginning of the 7-day-week would be Mars, because of Scorpio; the beginning of the 9-day-week would be Saturn, because of Capricorn.
> An example: the nativity was in Hadrian year 3, Athyr 27 in the Alexandrian calendar [23 Nov. 118]. I wish to investigate the subsequent date Antoninus year 17, Phamenoth 11 [7 March 154]. I take the full years, 35, plus the 3 remaining days in the birth month [Athyr 27 to 30], plus 2 days for each month from Choiak to Mechir, [3 months. The total is 44.] With the 5 whole weeks [=35 days] subtracted, the remainder is 9. Now add the 11 days of Phamenoth (total 20), plus the 8 intercalary days. The grand total is 28. Therefore Phamenoth 11 will be a critical day in the

---

[72] See Robbins' note in his Loeb edition of the *Tetrabiblos* (Cambridge, MA, 1940) 286–89, and *AG* 404–22.

7-day-week system. [4x7=28, so Phamenoth 11 begins a week.] According to the sequence of days, Phamenoth falls in Scorpio [a sign of Mars, the ruler of the first day of the week]. Examine which stars are in aspect with this sign and with the Moon.

The 9-day-week is found as follows: I multiply the full years by 5 1/4, since each year contains forty 9-day-weeks with 5 1/4 days left over. For each month I add 3, since each month has three 9-day-weeks with 3 days left over. Then I divide the number of days remaining until the day in question by as many 9's as possible [=divide by 9]. I make sure that the remainder is less than 9. Now the result will be the number of the critical day, just as in the 7-day-week system. (141.11–31P)

These periods of seven and nine are also mentioned in Firmicus Maternus as the "ebdomaticis et enneaticis annis" (II 41.18).[73]

III 12–14: The length of life with methods for determining the Ascendant (see note on VI 9 below). III 14, with an introduction claiming independent discovery, was written several years after III 13.

III 15: Critical years. (See note on V 2 below.)

III 16: The period of each star. In standard astrology each star had a certain period associated with it: Saturn 30, Jupiter 12, Mars 15, Venus 8, Mercury 20, Sun 19, Moon 25.[74] Valens uses these figures as well as several others. Various schemes for adding these figures to the rising times of the signs yield the length of life for the client. Two sample horoscopes:

> Another example: Sun in Taurus, Mercury in Taurus, Moon in Pisces, Saturn in Scorpio, Jupiter, Mars, Venus in Aries, Ascendant in Gemini. The rising time [of Gemini] in the second klima is 28. Mercury in Taurus adds its [Taurus'] rising time, 24, plus Mars in Aries, 15. He died in his 67th year.
>
> Another example: the same configuration of stars [as in the preceding horoscope] for a different nativity, except that the Ascendant was in

---

[73] For the astrological week see *AG* 476–86 and Boll, "Hebdomas" *RE* 7.2 (1912) 2556–78, especially 2557–58 and 2572. Claude Saumaise devoted many pages of his *De annis climactericis* to the value of the numbers 7 and 9 for determining critical points. The 63rd year (= 7 x 9) is especially dangerous.

[74] For the origin and use of these periods, which have little astronomical meaning, see *AG* 408–10 and *GH* 10–11.

Capricorn, the Lot of Fortune in Pisces. The rising time [of Pisces] in the second klima is 20, plus the period of Jupiter, 12. Since Jupiter is in Aries, we add its rising time, 20, plus the period of Mars, 15. The total is 67. He lived that long. (149.15–22P)[75]

Rising times are added to rising times, periods to periods, periods to rising times, anything required to derive the correct length of life.

From Book IV to Book IX the exposition is not systematic. These books were written over a period of 20 years and deal with a variety of topics centered on the determination of the length of life, with some attention to the related topic of critical periods.

Book IV 1–5: This section, written at one time, describes how each star rules for a given period, then transmits (παραδίδωσι) its control, or chronocratorship (χρόνοι = years), to another.[76] As a result each period of time will show the predominant influence of the star which is its chronocrator and the influence of the various transmissions from and to other stars. The Lots may be considered as transmitters also. Sample passages:[77]

> For new-Moon nativities, the star located immediately after the new Moon begins the vital sector [=is the first chronocrator], then the other stars as they come in order. For full-Moon nativities, the star following the full Moon serves in the the same capacity. It is necessary to examine how the star is configured and which stars are in aspect. Also determine if the other stars that receive the chronocratorship are at angles or precede angles, or are rising or setting. Determine the sequence of their transits and their sympathies and antipathies. After the 32 year 3 month period is completed, the second cycle is begun starting with the next aphetic star [=chronocrator] of the one-fourth period.
>
> Make the distribution of days as follows: if Saturn is found to be the overall ἀφέτης [=the first chronocrator], it assigns 7 1/2 years. Now since it is necessary to include all the stars in this 7 1/2 year period, we will

---

[75] For these two horoscopes see *GH* 100.
[76] *AG* 491–506.
[77] In this section ἄφεσις - "vital sector" means the series of transmissions from the first star (the ἀφέτης) to the others in their order in the natal chart, i.e the sequence of chronocrators. In II 2-4, ἄφεσις had quite a different meaning: it was the quadrant of the zodiac which represents the length of life. The figures 7 1/2 and 6 1/4 are taken from a table in IV 1 (150.4–16P).

> make the allotment as follows: multiply the 85 days of Saturn by 7 1/2 to get a total of 637 1/2. This is the amount Saturn will allot to itself from its 7 1/2 years. Now let us find Jupiter: since it governs 34 days, multiply this 34 by 7 1/2 (since Saturn is the ἀφέτης), for a total of 255. Jupiter will have this number [of days] after Saturn's chronocratorship. Next in order Venus receives the chronocratorship: since it controls 22 2/3 days, we will multiply this amount by 7 1/2, and we will find the total to be 170. Venus will control this amount after Saturn's chronocratorship. And so on with each star; if we multiply its days by 7 1/2, we will find its allotment. If the Moon, on the other hand, controls the vital sector, we multiply each star's days by 6 1/4 to find its distribution. Similarly for the rest. (150.18–151.15P)

Valens then suggests another method in which the vital sector is counted from the Lots of Fortune or Daimon:

> Let's say that the Lot of Fortune or Daimon is located in Aries. The overall houseruler of Aries is Mars. Let Mars' successors be determined, then see if they are or are not configured properly. Mars itself allots 15 years first, and from this period it assigns itself 15 months. Next (because of Taurus [the next sign]) it assigns 8 months to Venus, next (because of Gemini) 20 months to Mercury, next (because of Leo) 19 months to the Sun, next 20 months to Mercury, next 8 months to Venus, next (because of Scorpio) Mars assigns itself [again] 15, next (because of Sagittarius) 12 to Jupiter, next (because of Capricorn) 2 years 3 months to Saturn. Next it assigns to Aquarius the remaining 11 months to fill out the 15 years. Now Venus receives from Mars the overall chronocratorship for 8 years and assigns years to each signs as already illustrated. Because of Gemini, Mercury receives 20 years after Venus and assigns the years to each sign. Next is the Moon with its 25 years, then the Sun with its 19. It is necessary to assign the years in the order [of the stars] to whatever date the nativity extends [i.e., to the date of the casting of the horoscope or to the date of death]. (153.8–22P)

IV 6-10: The same topic with examples.

IV 11-25: A new section with an autobiographical introduction. In IV 11, after the introduction, a new method is described for determining which star is chronocrator: given a year (e.g., age 35), divide by 12 and note the remainder (35/12=2, remainder 11). The stars which are 11 signs apart will be transmitting the chronocratorship to each other. For this nativity, the same results will occur at age 23, 47, 59, and 71. In general, similar things will happen in a 12-year rotation: "The same transmissions are indicated every 12 years, but they will not have the same causative influences" (168.1–2P).

IV 12-25: Various transmissions: in the XII Places (12), in the exaltations (13), at phases (14), in the III or the IX Place (15), to or from each star and Lot (16–25). A sample will give the tone of these chapters:

> An example: if Saturn or Mars is in the Ascendant and is either transmitting or receiving, we can say that during this year there will be bodily troubles, danger, or bleeding. If these stars are in the VII Place from the Ascendant, there will be a turn to the worse because of a wife, or danger to a wife, or an upsetting crisis because of marriage. If they are in the IX Place from the Ascendant, there will be hazardous travel, trouble abroad, or betrayal at the hands of foreigners. If they are in the XII Place, there will be grief because of slaves or enemy revolts. In other words, the star will activate those matters which each Place influences. (170.24–171.1P)

IV 26-30: Miscellaneous methods quoted from other astrologers, including Critodemus and Hermes.

Book V continues the topics of chronocrators and critical times:

V 1: The Crisis-Producing Lot.

V 2: The critical years (κλιμακτῆρες). These are dangerous periods, in later astrology at 7- and 9-year intervals, with the sixty-third year (=7 x 9) being particularly fatal. Such intervals are not important in the *Anthologiae*.

> The critical year is found from the transmission or reception of malefics in relation to the luminaries, the Ascendant, and each other—in general it is found thus. In specific cases, it is necessary to count off the years from the sign in the Ascendant. If the current year is found to be in the sign of the new or full Moon, or in the sign in square or opposition [unfavorable aspects] to the new or full Moon sign, the year will be critical and troublesome, especially if (under these circumstances) Saturn [a malefic planet] is found to be passing through the four places which just preceded the angles at the nativity, and if the basis of the nativity is in accord: death will follow,

bodily weakness, bleeding, dangerous diseases, hidden troubles, falls, sudden dangers. Sometimes the critical point affects matters of livelihood and rank, if the bodily state is helped by an aspect of benefics.

In addition, determine the distance from Saturn's position at the nativity to the ruler of the new or full Moon, then count that distance from the Ascendant. When Saturn is at that position, or in opposition or square with that position, death will occur, or a grave crisis to health or business. Likewise the critical year will occur if Saturn is at the ascending or the descending node, or the points square with these. If someone takes to his bed ill while the Sun is passing through the ascending or descending node, or through the points square with them, and if a malefic beholds the Sun, then the bout of disease will be dangerous and hazardous. (200.14–201.3P)

V 3: Initiatives (κατάρχαι), whether to begin an action or activity.[78] Valens has only a brief discussion of this topic to which Hephaistion devoted Book III, Περὶ καταρχῶν, of his *Apotelesmatica*. Of course Valens' methods for determining the critical periods would apply to Initiatives as well.

V 4-7: The operative (χρηματιστικός) day, month, and year; "operative" seems to be equivalent to "critical."

V 8: The inclinations (πρόσνευσις) of the Moon, i.e., the sign of the zodiac to which the Moon "inclines" at its phases. The significance of the inclination is not discussed here. The inclination of the Moon at eclipses is part of Ptolemaic theory (*Alm.* VI 11, the *Handy Tables* in *Op. Min.* 178.24–181.9), but I see little similarity between Valens' doctrine and Ptolemy's. See *HAMA* 141–44, 997.

V 9-10: Reflections on the value of astrology. A review of the method for the chronocratorship described in IV 11, with examples. The following chapters outline similar, purely numerological, methods.

V 11: A review of the vital sector, the transmission of the chronocrators.

V 12: Another method for the vital sector, using the distance (in signs) between stars. If, for example, the astrologer is investigating the client's twentieth year, he factors 20, for a result of 4 and 5. He investigates the stars that are 4 or 5 signs from the Moon, and he interprets the events of that year in light of that

---

[78] AG 458–86.

transmission. This method is similar to the method of IV 11 and can also be found in the *Liber Hermetis* (ed. Gundel, 1935).

Book VI begins a new section with an introduction describing Valens' personal devotion to astrology. The topics covered in this book are again the critical periods and the length of life.

VI 1, 4–6: Propitious and impropitious periods and the distribution (=transmissions) of the chronocrators. Valens claims to be simply refining his earlier methods, transforming them from a sign-basis to a degree-basis. Book VI 6 includes a table of factors for each star.

VI 2–3: The qualities (=colors) of the stars.

VI 7: The ruler of the current day.

VI 8: A new section begins with reflections on the necessity for combining different astrological systems. Valens prided himself on his eclecticism: "Every method (ἀγωγή), when combined and critically compared with every other, brings forth the scientific (φυσικήν), precise system (θεωρίαν)" (257.23–25K; 246.19–21P). A review of the vital sector follows.

VI 9: How to determine the Ascendant and the Moon's position retroactively after birth. This was necessary in order to fix the beginning of the vital sector. The Ascendants reported in the horoscopes were calculated, not observed, and several methods for such calculations are described in the *Anthologiae*:

> After we calculate precisely the positions of the stars on the birth date in the current year, we will find the Ascendant as follows: while the Sun is still in the natal sign, we examine when, at what hour, the [Moon] will come to the exact same degree where it was at the nativity, and we call that point the Ascendant. (213.23–28K; 203.10–14P)

> The sign in the Ascendant is found (for day births) by counting the number of the Sun's degree-position from the Sun's sign, giving 1° to each sign. The sign where the count stops is in the Ascendant. (340.18–20K; 326.31–327.2P)

> The appended table [not extant] is constructed so as to give the sign in the Ascendant and the required, scientific time of day. It resembles the roughly

accurate table which was constructed (in a puzzling manner) by the King, and used by him starting with the Sun at conception. I have constructed a precise table, starting with the month Thoth (which is odd because it is month #1), then with Phaophi (which is even because it is month #2), then Athyr (likewise odd), then Choiak (even). Then in sequence you must examine the remaining months one by one. Enter the appended table at the day or night in question and at the operative month, and we will find for day or night births the hour of the nativity on that line. (361.9–18K; 346.9–19P)

As is clear from this last example, the astrologer had tables at his disposal to make his task easier. For these methods of calculating the Ascendant, see *Tetr.* III 3.

Book VII starts a new section devoted to the same topics: critical periods and length of life.

VII 1–5: Propitious and impropitious times using the periods of the stars and the rising times of the signs, or a fraction (1/2, 1/3, 2/3) thereof:

> Now if, as we have already said, the chronocratorship of a configuration coincides with the time under investigation, when calculated from the total of the rising time of the sign and period of the star, then use the preceding rules. Then, because these combined chronocratorships coincide to produce what will be predicted, attend to and determine the outcome using the positions of the angles and the stars preceding or following the angles, the positions of the Lots, and the new and full Moons, considering all of these according to the proper aspects or oppositions of the stars. If the chronocratorships of the aspects are combined, the results will come to pass in one-half, one-third, or two-thirds of the time, provided each one does not hold the chronocratorship alone. (267.25–268.6P)

A sample horoscope as an illustration:

> Another example: Sun, Mercury in Capricorn, Moon, Mars, Ascendant in Taurus, Saturn in Scorpio, Jupiter in Cancer, Venus in Pisces, klima 6. In his thirtieth year he escaped slavery, committed many robberies, avoided capture for a short time, but was caught in the same year. Both sets of signs in opposition were operative [Taurus/Scorpio, Cancer/Capricorn]: they

both total 60, one-half of which is 30. Also 28 for Capricorn, 20 for Mercury, plus 12 for Jupiter total 60, one-half of which is 30. Also 30 for Saturn plus 15 for Mars, two-thirds of which is 30. Also 25 for Cancer [=Moon], 12 for Jupiter, plus 8 for Venus (which is trine) total 45, two-thirds of which is 30. Because of the benefics, he seemed destined to escape danger for a short time and to live comfortably from the takings of his robberies, but because of the malefics, he fell. (270.24–271.2P)

Book VIII starts a new section which uses two tables found at the end of Book VIII to find the length of life.

VIII 1: The construction of table 1. Following is the column for Libra:[79]

Degrees	Star	Factors	Years	Months	Days
1	Sun	2	6	1	15
2		4	12	3	
3		6	18	3	
4		8	24	4	
5		10	30	3	15
6	Mars	12	36	7	
7		26	78	0	
8		28	84	0	
9		30	89	11	
10		2	6	0	
11	Jupiter	4	11	9	

---

[79] For the structure of these two tables, see GH 136–38, 174–75. The factors (ἀριθμοί) increment by 2, with a jump of 14 every 6 degrees, returning to 1 when 30 is reached (e.g., 28 + 6 = 4). The years/months/days increment by 6 years 1 month 15 days, with a jump every 6 degrees. The degree calculated to be the Ascendant (using the method described below in the note on VIII 6–7) is associated with the length of life given in the years/months/days columns according to the following scheme: the years/months/days figure, when divided by the factor in the same row, yield the length of daylight at the solar longitude in the same row. For example, Libra 8° is the autumn equinox in this system; 84 (the figure in the years column) divided by 0;28 (from the factors column) =180°, the length of daylight at the autumn equinox, when the day and night are equal. (In decimal notation this is 84 divided by 0.466 = 180°. A similar calculation yields the same result for Aries 8°, the spring equinox.) Several obscurities remain: the significance of the star column and the accuracy of the figures in the months column, which could easily be corrected, but which might then not be what Valens wrote.

Degrees	Star	Factors	Years	Months	Days
12		6	17	1	
13		20	59	1	
14		22	64	5	15
15		24	70	6	
16	Saturn	26	76	8	
17		28	81	3	
18		30	87	4	
19		14	40	11	
20		16	46	9	
21	Mercury	18	51	5	
22		20	57	11	
23		22	62	5	15
24		24	68	8	
25		8	22	9	
26	Venus	10	28	5	15
27		12	33	11	
28		14	39	5	
29		16	44	10	15
30		18	50	4	

VIII 2: The construction of table 2.

VIII 3–4: How to determine the Ascendant retroactively after birth. (See the note on VI 9 above.)

VIII 5: How to use tables 1 and 2 (this translation refers to the portion of the table printed above):

> For example: the number 2 is entered next to Libra 1°. Two is one-thirtieth of 60. One-thirtieth of 180, the magnitude of Libra 1° [=total rising time of the arc beginning with Libra 1°], is 6. Now Libra comprises 30°. If we calculate with this many years, the 30° [of Libra] will allot 180 years, an impossible length of life for a person. So if we take one-sixtieth of 180, we will get 3 as the amount which 1° of Libra will allot. Three times 30° is 90: we can say that Libra allots a maximum of 90 years, according to the applicable degree of its magnitude.
> Likewise for the rest of the signs: we multiply the magnitude entered next to each degree by 12, then take 1/60 [=one-half of the original factor]

of it to find the minimum or the maximum years. Each degree of each sign has a different time in the table's progressive increase, and for this reason the seconds and the minutes of the hours and the rotation of the degrees have great effect. (300.25–301.2K; 287.23–288.3P)

VIII 6–7: The calculation of the lunar and solar gnomons and their use in forecasting the length of life. In these chapters Valens used the rising times of the signs. If, for example, Aries (rising time 20) is in the Ascendant, the astrologer assigns 0;40 (=2/3, or 20 rising times allotted to 30°) to each degree of Aries. The number of degrees in Aries is the first factor. The second factor is in Taurus, the next sign. Taurus rises in 24, so each degree of Taurus will have 0;48 (=48/60, or 24 rising times allotted to 30°), and the number of degrees in Taurus will be added to the 20 of Aries. If the vital sector extends from Aries 1° to Taurus 1°, the length of life would be 20;48 years (=20 years 8 months). If the vital sector extends to Taurus 30°, the length of life would be 20 in Aries plus 24 in Taurus = 44 years. If the vital sector extends into the third sign, then the astrologer calculates a third factor, in Gemini. Gemini rises in 28, so each degree has 0;56. If the vital sector extends from Aries 1° to Gemini 1°, the length of life would be 44;56 years; if to Gemini 30°, 72 years, the maximum, since the vital sector extends over no more than 3 signs (290.28–291.11P).

As a corollary to this, a native born in signs of long rising time (e.g., Leo, Virgo, Libra) will theoretically live longer than one born in signs of short rising time (e.g., Aquarius, Pisces, Aries), although Valens admits this is rarely possible (315.28K; 302.21P).[80]

In the cited horoscopes, Valens used either the "first factor" (=one sign), or the "second factor" (=all of one sign plus part of another), or the "third factor" (=all of two signs plus part of a third). Occasionally he adds two of the factors to arrive at the length of life, which—it must be remembered—he already knew; these are retrospective calculations.

In order to use this method the Ascendant must be known to the degree, which cannot be done from observation alone. To determine the Ascendant, the astrologer consults a table (not extant) of sign equivalents. If, for example, the Sun is in Scorpio 10°, the Moon in Aquarius 30°, and the Ascendant in Sagittarius (no degree-position), the astrologer searches for some equivalent

---

[80] The text has δυνατὸν in error for ἀδυνατὸν. The calculation of lifespans from the rising times in different klimas is found elsewhere. Pliny (*N. H.* 7.160) reports that Nechepso and Petosiris fixed the maximum length of life at 124 years in the latitude of Italy (*in Italiae tractu*), Epigenes at 112, Berossus at 116. These figures are the rising times of Leo, Virgo, and Libra (the signs of long rising time) in Italy, Alexandria, and Babylon respectively. See O. Neugebauer, "On Some Astronomical Papyri" 260.

of Scorpio 10° and finds it in Libra. He finds Libra entered in his table at Sagittarius 14°/15°. These degrees will be the *solar gnomon*. He carries out the same procedure for the Moon, and finds that Sagittarius 1°/2°/3° is the *lunar gnomon*. In his table there are four rows between Sagittarius 1°/2°/3° and Sagittarius 14°/15°, and so he adds 4° to the solar gnomon, for a result of Sagittarius 18° as the Ascendant to the degree (305.3–20K; 291.23–292.8P). Having determined the Ascendant, he then looks at the table of *apogonia* for Sagittarius 18°, and for the third factor he finds a total of 73 years. The subject of this horoscope died at age 73 (305.20–22K; 292.9–11P).[81] This method of gnomons and factors fills most of Book VIII and seems to be the culmination of Valens' ingenuity. A similar method is used in the fifth-century addition (365.29K; 351.4P).[82]

VIII 8: The terms. The end of Book VIII is fragmentary. VIII 6–8 is the latest section of the *Anthologiae* (see Appendix A); VIII 7 is the utmost elaboration of Valens' pet scheme.

Book IX begins a new section. This Book is fragmentary; many sections belong with earlier chapters. The chief topic is again the length of life calculations.

IX 1: A general review of astrological forecasting.

IX 2: A review of the XII Places.

IX 3: Propitious and impropitious periods.

IX 4. The critical years derived from the factors of numbers. For example, Jupiter's period is 12 years. The factors of 12 are 3 plus 4 plus 5. A period controlled by Jupiter will come every 3 years: "Jupiter acts as a benefic and brings high rank every 3 years: 3 plus 4 plus 5 total 12" (338.28K; 325.10–11P).

IX 5: Initiatives. (See note on V 3.)

IX 6, 10, 18: How to determine the Ascendant retroactively. (See note on VI 9.)

---

[81] The lost table of *apogonia* contained the three factors for each degree, but they can readily be calculated: take the rising time for all of Sagittarius (34;10) plus all of Capricorn (25;50) plus 18° of Aquarius (12;54 = 21;40 rising time x 18/30), which totals 72;54, or very nearly 73. The rising times are for klima 6, as specified in this example.

[82] For a discussion see *GH* 136–38.

IX 7: Miscellaneous topics: malformed births, determining the Ascendant.

IX 8: A new section begins with an introduction on the value of astrology. The use of a table of *apogonia* (see note on VIII 6–7) to make forecasts. The method is similar to that in VIII 6-7.

IX 9, 13, 15, 17: Fragmentary methods for the length of life using the Sun and the Moon.

IX 11: The source of Valens' astronomical knowledge. He "used Hipparchus for the Sun, Soudines, Kidenas, and Apollonius for the Moon" (354.4–5K; 339.20–21P). Astrology makes men submissive to Fate.

IX 14: Conception (a fragment).

IX 19: How to determine the Moon's exact position using two appended tables, now lost. Valens describes a graphical method for finding the Moon's longitude and phase:[83]

> Both tables indicate the longitude of the Moon and its phase. If we want to know the Moon's longitude at a nativity with reference to its hourly motion, we calculate in this way: first it is necessary to enter the table of klimata, holding the compass with legs apart. Having determined the length of the hours in the night hemisphere (at the current longitude of the Sun), we place one leg of the compass right there. Then we open the compass until the other leg reaches the hour in question. The 12 hours of the night are so arranged as to allow this. If the nativity was during the day, note the extension of the compass legs in the night hemisphere and extend it to the hour in question of the day.
>
> Now, having measured out the total number of hours in the way described, move the compass [viz. without changing the extension of the legs] to the lunar table. Set one leg of the compass at the number in the chart approximately equal to its daily motion, then see what longitude the

---

[83] For roughly similar graphical (γραμμικῶς – the mathematical procedures are ἀριθμητικῶς) procedures in Ptolemy's *Handy Tables* (*Op. Min.* 165.13–166.18, 167.23–169.5) see *HAMA* 990 and A. Jones "248-Day Schemes" 29–30. Ptolemy was using an instrument like an equatory. Valens' two grids, lined out with red ink (361.31K; 347.1P), must have been drawn to a common scale in order for his procedure to work. A papyrus in the Brooklyn museum is also lined in red; see O. Neugebauer, "Astronomical Papyri and Ostraca" 385.

other leg touches. The degrees will be evident from the chart of its motion, and these must be added (if the nativity is after Sunset) to the degrees previously determined for the Moon; add the difference due to klima as well. Having done so, consider this to be the Moon's longitude. (362.13–31K; 347.16–33P)

The fifth-century addition to the *Anthologiae* gives examples of critical period and length of life calculations, using the methods and tables of Book VIII.

Abbreviations

AG - A. Bouché–Leclercq, *L'astrologie Grecque* (Paris 1899)

CCAG - *Catalogus Codicum Astrologorum Graecorum* (Brussels 1898–1953).

CH - A.D. Nock and A.–J. Festugière, *Corpus Hermeticum* (Paris 1983).

DSB - *Dictionary of Scientific Biography*

EAT - O. Neugebauer and R. A. Parker, *Egyptian Astronomical Texts* I–III (Providence R.I. 1960–69)

GH - O. Neugebauer and H.B.Van Hoesen, *Greek Horoscopes* (Philadelphia 1959)

HAMA - O. Neugebauer, *History of Ancient Mathematical Astronomy* (Berlin and New York 1975)

RE - Pauly–Wissowa, *Realencyclopädie der Klassischen Altertumswissenschaft*.

The *Anthologiae* is cited either by the book and chapter number of Kroll's edition, followed by the page number in Pingree's edition—e.g., Book III.5 (133.31P), or by the page number in Kroll's edition followed by the page number in Pingree's edition—e.g., 141.17K; 133.31P. All chapter and page references in the scholarly work on Valens since 1906 refer to Kroll's edition.

Several passages contain fractions expressed in sexagesimal notation: 0;30 = 1/2, 0;40 = 2/3, 0;50 = 5/6, 2;30 = 2 1/2, etc.

Bibliography

Bara, Joëlle-Frédérique. "Apotélesmatique et Initiatives." In *Documents pour L'histoire du vocabulaire scientifique* 1 (Publications de l'institut de la langue française 1980): 49–90.

———. *Vettius Valens d'Antioche Anthologies, Livre I (Études Préliminaires aux Religions Orientales dans L'Empire Romain* vol. 111). Brill: Leiden, 1989.

Boll, Franz. *Sphaera*. Leipzig, 1903.

Cumont, Franz. *L'Egypt des Astrologues*. Brussels, 1937.

Daressy, G. "La statue d'un astronome." *Annales du Service des antiquités de l'Égypte* 16 (1916): 1–5.

Darmstadt, Karl *De Nechepsonis-Petosiridis Isagoge Quaestiones Selectae*. Leipzig: Teubner, 1916.

Festugière, A.J. *L'idéal religieux des grecs et L'Evangile*. reprint Paris, 1981.

Firmicus Maternus, *Mathesis*. ed. Kroll-Skutsch-Ziegler. Leipzig, 1896, 1913. repr. Stuttgart 1968.

Fowden, Garth. *The Egyptian Hermes*. Cambridge, 1986.

Griffiths, J. G. *Plutarch's De Iside et Osiride*. University of Wales Press, 1970.

Gundel, Wilhelm. *Neue astrologische Texte des Hermes Trismegistos*. Munich: Bayerischen Akademie der Wissenschaften, 1936.

——— and Hans Georg Gundel. *Astrologoumena*. Wiesbaden, 1966.

Hillyard, Brian. *Plutarch: De Audiendo*. New York: Arno, 1981.

Wolfgang Hübner, *Die Eigenschafter der Tierkreiszeichen in der Antike*. Wiesbaden, 1982.

———. "Eine unbeachtete Zodiakale Melothesie bei Vettius Valens." *Rheinisches Museum* 120 (1977): 247-54.

Jones, Alexander. "The Development and Transmission of 248-Day Schemes for Lunar Motion in Ancient Astronomy." *Archive for History of Exact Sciences* 29 (1983/4): 1-36.

———. "Ptolemy's First Commentator." *Transactions of the American Philosophical Society* 80.7 (1990).

Lefebvre, Gustave. *Le Tombeau de Petosiris*. Cairo: L'Institute français d'archéologie orientale, 1924.

Lewis, N. *Life in Egypt Under Roman Rule*. Oxford, 1983.

Luck, Georg. *Arcana Mundi*. Baltimore: Johns Hopkins, 1985.

King, David. "Some Arabic copies of Vettius Valens' Table for Finding the Length of Life." *Symposium Graeco-Arabicum II/Akten des Zweiten Symposium Graeco-Arabicum* ed. Gerhard Endress (1989) 25-28.

Kroll, Wilhelm. "Kulturhistoriches aus astrologischen Texten." *Klio* 18.3/4 (1923): 213-25.

———."Mantissa Observationum Vettianarum." in *CCAG* 5.2 (1906): 143-54.

MacMullen, Ramsay. "Social History in Astrology." *Ancient Society* 2 (1971): 105-16.

Manetho, *Apotelesmatica* ed. Koechly. Leipzig, 1883.

Maass, E. *Commentaria in Aratum*. Berlin, 1958.

al-Nadim, Ibn. *The Fihrist of al-Nadim*, trans. B. Dodge. New York, 1970.

Neugebauer, O. "The Chronology of Vettius Valens' *Anthologiae*." *Harvard Theological Review* 47 (1954): 65-67.

———. "Astronomical Papyri and Ostraca." *Proc. Am. Philos. Soc.* 106 (1962): 383-91.

———. "On Some Astronomical Papyri and Related Problems of Ancient Geography." *Trans. Am. Phil. Assoc.* 32 (1942): 251-63.

——— and R. A. Parker, *Egyptian Astronomical Texts* I-III. Providence, RI 1960-69).

Nock, A.D. and A.-J. Festugière, *Corpus Hermeticum* I-IV. Paris, 1983.

Papyri in the University of Michigan Collection, vol. 3 *Miscellaneous Papyri.* ed. J. G. Winter and others. Ann Arbor, 1936.

Pingree, David. "The Indian Iconography of the Decans and Horas." *Journal of the Warburg and Courtald Institute* 26 (1963): 227.

———. "The Byzantine Tradition of Vettius Valens's *Anthologies.*" *Harvard Ukranian Studies* 7 (1983): 532–41.

———. "Antiochus and Rhetorius." *Classical Philology* 72 (1977): 203–23.

Porphyry, Εἰσαγωγὴ εἰς τὴν Ἀποτελεσματικὴν τοῦ Πτολεμαίου in *CCAG* 5.4 (1940): 190–228.

Riess, Ernst. "Nechepsonis et Petosiridis Fragmenta Magica." *Philologus Suppl.* 6 (1892): 325–94.

Riley, Mark. "Science and Tradition in the *Tetrabiblos.*" *Proc. Am. Philos. Assoc.* 132.1 (1988): 67–84.

———. "Theoretical and Practical Astrology." *TAPA* 117 (1987): 235–56.

Russell, D. A. *Greek Declamation.* Cambridge, 1983.

Rydbeck, L. *Fachprose, vermeintliche volksprache und Neues Testament.* Zur Beurteilung der spr. Niveauunterschiede im nachklassischen Griechisch. *Acta Universitatis Upsaliensis* 5. Uppsala, 1967.

Salmasius, Cl. (Claude Saumaise). *De Annis Climactericis.* Leiden, 1648.

Sezgin, Fuat. *Geschichte des Arabischen Schrifttums: Band VII, Astrologie.* Leiden: Brill, 1979.

Thorndike, Lynn. "A Roman Astrologer as a Historical Source: Julius Firmicus Maternus." *Classical Philology* 8 (1913): 415–35.

Tihon, Anne. "Le calcul de la longitude de Vénus d'après un texte anonyme du Vat. gr. 184." *Bull. Inst. Hist. Belge de Rome* 39 (1968): 51–82.

———."Le calcul de la longitude des planètes d'après un text anonyme du Vat. gr. 184." *Bull. Inst. Hist. Belge de Rome* 52 (1982): 5–30.

Warning, Wilhelm. *De Vettii Valentis sermone.* diss. (Münster, 1909).

The Anthology

Book I

<1. The Nature of the Stars>
In a nativity the all-seeing Sun, nature's fire and intellectual light, the organ of mental perception, indicates kingship, rule, intellect, intelligence, beauty, motion, loftiness of fortune, the ordinance of the gods, judgement, public reputation, action, authority over the masses, the father, the master, friendship, noble personages, honors consisting of pictures, statues, and garlands, high priesthoods, <rule over> one's country <and over> other places. Of the parts of the body, the Sun rules the head; of the sense organs, it rules the right eye; of the trunk, it rules the heart; of the spiritual (i.e., the perceptive) faculties, the nerves. Of materials, it rules gold; of fruits, it rules wheat and barley. It is of the day sect, yellowish, bitter in taste.

The Moon, lit by the reflection of the Sun's light and possessing a borrowed light, in a nativity indicates man's life, body, the mother, conception, <beauty>, appearance, sight, living together (i.e., legitimate marriage), nurture, the older brother, housekeeping, the queen, the mistress of the house, possessions, fortune, the city, the assembly of the people, gains, expenses, the household, voyages, travel and wanderings (it does not provide straight pathways because of Cancer). The Moon rules the parts of the body as follows: the left eye, the stomach, the breasts, the breath, the spleen, the dura mater, the marrow (as a result it causes dropsy/moist syndromes). Of materials it rules silver and glass. It is of the night sect, green in color and salty in taste.

Saturn makes those born under him petty, malignant, care-worn, self-depreciating, solitary, deceitful, secretive in their trickery, strict, downcast, with a hypocritical air, squalid, black-clad, importunate, sad-looking, miserable, with a nautical bent, plying waterside trades. Saturn also causes humblings, sluggishness, unemployment, obstacles in business, interminable lawsuits, subversion of business, secrets, imprisonment, chains, griefs, accusations, tears, bereavement, capture, exposures of children. Saturn makes serfs and farmers because of its rule over the land, and it causes men to be renters of property, tax farmers, and violent in action. It puts into one's hands great ranks and distinguished positions, supervisions, management of others' property, and the fathership of others' children. Of materials, it rules lead, wood, and stone. Of the limbs of the body, it rules the legs, the knees, the tendons, the lymph, the phlegm, the bladder, the kidneys, and the internal, hidden organs. Saturn is indicative of injuries arising from cold and moisture, such as dropsy, neuralgia, gout, cough, dysentery, hernia, spasms. It is indicative of these syndromes: possession, homosexuality, and depravity. Saturn makes bachelors and widows, bereavements, and childlessness. It causes violent deaths by water, strangulation, imprisonment, or dysentery. It also causes falling on the face. It is the star of Nemesis; it is of the day sect. It is like castor in color and astringent in taste.

Jupiter indicates childbearing, engendering, desire, loves, political ties, acquaintance, friendships with great men, prosperity, salaries, great gifts, an abundance of crops, justice, offices, officeholding, ranks, authority over temples, arbitrations, trusts, inheritance, brotherhood, fellowship, beneficence, the secure possession of goods, relief from troubles, release from bonds, freedom, deposits in trust, money, stewardships. Of the external body parts it rules the thighs and the feet. (Consequently in the games Jupiter governs the race.) Of the internal parts it rules the sperm, the uterus, the liver, the parts of the right side. Of materials, it rules tin. It is of the day sect. In color it is grey verging on white and is sweet in taste.

Mars indicates force, wars, plunderings, screams, violence, whoring, the loss of property, banishment, exile, alienation from parents, capture, the deaths of wives, abortions, love affairs, marriages, the loss of goods, lies, vain hopes, strong-armed robbery, banditry, looting, quarrels among friends, anger, fighting, verbal abuse, hatreds, lawsuits. Mars brings violent murders, slashings and bloodshed, attacks of fever, ulceration, boils, burns, chains, torture, masculinity, false oaths, wandering, embassies under difficult circumstances, actions involving fire or iron, craftwork, masonry. In addition Mars causes commands, campaigns and leadership, infantrymen, governorships, hunting, wild game, falls from heights or from animals, weak vision, strokes. Of the body parts, Mars rules the head, the seat, the genitals; of the internal parts, it rules the blood, the sperm ducts, the bile, the elimination of excrement, the parts in the rear, the back, and the underside. It controls the hard and the abrupt. Of materials, it rules iron, decoration of clothing (because of Aries), as well as wine and beans. It is of the night sect, red in color and acid in taste.

Venus is desire and love. It indicates the mother and nurture. It makes priesthoods, school superintendencies, high offices with the right to wear a gold ring or a crown, cheerfulness, friendship, companionship, the acquisition of property, the purchase of ornaments, agreements on favorable terms, marriages, pure trades, fine voices, a taste for music, sweet singing, beauty, painting, mixing of colors both in embroidery, dyeing, and unguent making. <Venus makes> the inventors and masters of these crafts, as well as craftsmanship or trade, and work in emeralds, precious stones, and ivory. Within its terms and degrees in the zodiac, Venus causes men to be gold-spinners, gold workers, barbers, and people fond of cleanliness and toys. It bestows the office of supervisor of weights and measures, the standards of weights and measures, markets, factories, the giving and receiving <of gifts>, laughter, good cheer, ornamentation, and hunting in moist places. Venus gives benefits from royal women or from one's own, and it brings very high rank when it operates in such affairs. Of the parts of the body, it rules the neck, the face, the lips, the sense of smell, the front parts from the feet to the head, the parts of intercourse; of the inner parts it rules the lungs. It is a recipient of support from others and of pleasure. Of materials it rules precious stones and fancy jewelry. Of fruits it rules the olive. It is of the night sect, white in color, very greasy in taste.

Mercury indicates education, letters, disputation, reasoning, brotherhood, interpretation, embassies, number, accounts, geometry, markets, youth, games, theft, association, communication, service, gain, discoveries, obedience, sport, wrestling, declamation, certification, supervision, weighing and measuring, the testing of coinage, hearing, versatility. It is the bestower of forethought and intelligence, the lord of brothers and of younger children, and the creator of all marketing and banking. In its own character, it makes temple builders, modelers, sculptors, doctors, secretaries, legal advisors, orators, philosophers, architects, musicians, prophets, diviners, augurs, dream interpreters, braiders, weavers, systematic physicians, those in charge of war and strategy, and those undertaking any unusual, systematic work in accounting or with reasoning. Mercury makes weight lifters and mimes, those making their livelihood with displays of skill, deception, gambling, or sleight of hand. It also rules those skilled interpreters of the heavens, those who by using pleasure or winning charm, earn fame for their amazing feats—all for the sake of gain. This star's effects go in many directions, depending on the changes of the zodiac and the interactions of the stars, and yields quite varied results: knowledge for some, selling for others, service for others, trade or teaching for others, farming or temple service or public <employment> for still others. To some it grants authority, rentals, labor contracting, rhythmical performance, the display of public service, the acquisition of personal attendants or the right of wearing temple-linen, robed in the luxury appropriate to gods or rulers. As for the end result—Mercury will make everything capricious in outcome and quite disturbed. Even more, it causes those having this star in malefic signs or degrees to become even worse. Of the parts of the body, it rules the hands, the shoulders, the fingers, the joints, the belly, the sense of hearing, the arteries, the intestines, the tongue. Of materials, it rules copper and all coins used in buying and selling—for the god makes exchanges. ...<It is blue in color, sharp in taste.>

The benefic stars which are appropriately and favorably situated bring about their proper effects according to their own nature and the nature of their sign, with the aspects and conjunctions of each star being blended. If however they are unfavorably situated, they are indicative of reversals. In the same way even the malefic stars, when they are operative in appropriate places in their own sect, are bestowers of good and indicative of the greatest positions and success; when they are inoperative, they bring about disasters and accusations.

...Each star is the ruler of its own "element" in the universe with reference to <the stars'> sympathy or antipathy or mutual influence. Their <aspects> are blended according to their "applications" or "separations," their "superior aspects" or "blockages," their "attendance," their "ray-shooting," or the "approach" of their masters. The Moon becomes the ruler of foresight, the Sun the ruler of light, Saturn the ruler of ignorance and necessity, Jupiter the ruler of rank, crowns and zeal. Mars becomes the ruler of action and effort, Venus the ruler of love, desire, and beauty, Mercury the ruler of law, friendship, and trust. These stars have their own effects…

Now that these matters have been settled, the nature of the twelve signs must be mentioned.

<2. The Nature of the Twelve Zodiacal Signs>
Aries is the house of Mars, a masculine sign, tropic, terrestrial, governing, fiery, free, upward-trending, semi-vocal, noble, changeable, procuratorial, public, civic, with few offspring, servile, the Midheaven of the universe and the cause of rank, two-toned (since the Sun and the Moon make white lichen). It is also unaspected and ecliptic. Depending on its relationship with the houseruler,

men born under this sign will be brilliant, distinguished, authoritarian, just, hard on offenders, free, governing, bold in thought, boastful, great-hearted, restless, unstable, haughty, inflated, intimidating, quickly changing, wealthy. When the houserulers are favorably situated and have benefics in aspect, kings and powerful men are born, those having the say over life and death.

Aries is by nature watery, with thunder and hail. From its first degree to the equinox, it is stormy, full of hail, windy, destructive. The middle degrees up to 15° are mild <and fruitful; the following degrees are hot and cause plagues> of animals. This sign has 19 bright stars. On the belt are 14 bright stars, 27 dim, 28 somewhat bright, and 48 faint. The constellations that rise at the same time as Aries are (in the north) the first part of Perseus, and the rear and the left parts of Auriga, and (in the south) the fin and tail of Cetus. <When Aries is rising,> the feet of Bootes (in the north) and the hind parts of Lupus (in the south) are setting.

The following zones are subject to Aries: to the front parts, Babylon; to the head, Elymais; to the right side, Persis; to the left, Palestine and the neighboring areas; to the turn of its head, Babylonia; to its breast, Armenia; to its shoulders, Thrace; to its belly, Cappadocia, Susa, the Red Sea and the Dead Sea; to its hind parts, Egypt and the Indian Ocean.

Taurus is feminine, solid, lying in the Sun's spring tropic, full of bones, with some limbs missing, rising backwards, setting straight down. This sign lies for the most part in the invisible sky. It is calm. From its first degree to 6° (the section of the Pleiades) it is worthless, even destructive, disease-producing, thundering, causing earthquakes and lightning flashes. The next two degrees are fiery and smokey. The right part (toward Auriga) is temperate and cool. The left parts are worthless and changeable, sometimes chilling, at other times heating. The head (to 23°) is in a temperate atmosphere, but it causes disease and death for living things. The rest is destructive, worthless, disease-ridden.

It has 27 stars. The constellations that rise with it are (in the north) the rear of Auriga and (in the south) the rear of Cetus and the first section of Eridanus. Venus, the Moon, Ceres, <Vesta,> Mars, and Mercury. The constellations that set <when Taurus is rising> are (in the north) Bootes up to the belt and the leg of Ophiouchus up to the knees. In the south Orion rises with Taurus; he is belted around the waist, extends his sword in his right hand, and holds in his left hand the so-called caduceus.

This sign is productive of order, earthy, rustic, related to farming, a freedman, downward-trending, with few offspring, semi-vocal or mute, noble, invariable, energetic, unfinished, indicative of estates and possessions. The ecliptic lies to the north, rising in line with its <Taurus'> highest point. Men born under this sign are noble, energetic, toilsome, good at keeping things, pleasure-loving, music-loving, generous. Some are laborers, propagators, planters. If benefics incline toward this place or if the houseruler is favorably situated, men become priests and school superintendants, as well as those judged worthy of crowns and of the purple, of monuments and statues; also supervisors of temples and distinguished and brilliant individuals.

The following zones are subject to Taurus: to its head, Media and the adjoining areas; <to its breast, Babylon; to the right side toward Auriga, Scythia;> to the Pleiades, Cyprus; to the left side, Arabia and the surrounding areas; to its shoulders, Persis and the Caucasus mountains; to its truncated portion, <Sarmatia>; to its loin, Africa; to its torso, Elymais; to its horns, Carthage; to its midparts, Armenia, India, Germany.

Gemini is male, bicorporeal, articulate, the house of Mercury, upward-trending, celestial, feminizing, a freedman, sterile, public. Under it are born scholars, those working in education and letters, poets, music-lovers, declaimers, stewards, those who receive trusts; also translators, merchants, judges of good and evil, sensible people, practitioners of the curious arts, and seekers after mystic lore. In general, whatever the houseruler usually produces according to its own nature, whether good or bad, greater or lesser, this it produces in each of the signs according to the operative or inoperative configuration of the houseruler. (I mention this so that we will not seem to be constantly writing the same thing.)

This sign is calm. Its first 3° are worthless and destructive; from 3° to 7° it is well-watered; good weather from 7° to 15°. The southern parts are well-watered. The last degrees are a combination of traits. It has 21 stars. It lies toward the west wind. According to the *Sphaerica*, the tail of Cetus lies touching Gemini at one of its southern points; also at its southern point, on the due-south line, is the Satyr <=Orion> touching it with its club, and it rises after the north part of Satyr, where the spear is. Lyra lies to the south; it lies on the due-south line, being midway between north and south. Under Gemini's feet on the due-south line (in the hemisphere visible to us) is the so-called Canis in front of its right foot; Canis is cut by a line running from the south pole through Gemini's head straight to the north pole. Gemini rises with the rest of Eridanus and Orion in the south. The gods Apollo, Hercules, Vulcan, Juno, Saturn are associated with it. To the north, Bootes, Ophiouchus (except the head), and half of the Crown set <when Gemini rises>. The following zones are subject to Gemini: to the front part, India and the adjoining areas and Celtica; to the breast, Cilicia, Galatia, Thrace, and Boeotia; to the midparts, Egypt, Libya, Rome, Arabia, Syria.

Cancer is calm. The parts are as follows: under the two initial stars to the southeast, it is worthless, destructive, stifling, productive of earthquakes. From that point to 10° it makes the air damp and hot, having heavy rains and constant thunderstorms. The right parts are worthless and destructive. In the north the Hare, the front part of Canis Major, and Procyon rise with Cancer. It has 4 stars. Mars, Mercury, Jupiter, <Neptune>, Venus. To the north, the head of Bootes sets as Cancer rises, as well as Hercules, Aquila, and half of the Crown.

It is the house of the Moon, feminine, solstitial, the Ascendant to the universe, slavish, downward-trending, mute, watery, noble, changeable, public, popular, civic, prolific, amphibious. Men born under this sign are ambitious, popular, constantly changing, theatrical, cheerful, easily downcast, pleasure-loving, party-giving, public. Unsteady of mind, they say one thing but think another, and not sticking to one activity or (at the most) two, they become wanderers and travelers.

The following zones are subject to Cancer: to the front, Bactria; to the left, Zakynthus and Acarnania; to the back, Ethiopia and Schina; under the head are the Crimean Gulf and the tribes surrounding it, the Red Sea, the Caspian Sea, the Hellespont, the Libyan Sea, Britain, and Thule. Under the feet are Armenia, Cappadocia, Rhodes, Kos. Under the tip of Cancer (i.e., at the mouth) are Troglodytia, <Lydia>, Ionia, and the Hellespont.

Leo is masculine, the house of the Sun, free, fiery, temperate, intellectual, kingly, stable, noble, upward-trending, changeable, solid, governing, civic, imperious, irascible. Men born under this sign are distinguished, noble, steady, just, haters of evil, independent, haters of flattery, beneficent, inflated with their lofty thoughts. If the houseruler is at an angle or in aspect with benefics, then brilliant, glorious individuals are born, tyrants and kings.

Leo is hot: the bright star in its breast <Regulus> is fiery and stifling. The parts are as follows: to 20° it is stifling, causing diseases of animals in the zones and places subject to it. The right side is moveable, fiery; the south part is wet; the lower parts are destructive to everything; the middle and the left are temperate.

Leo has … stars. According to the *Sphaerica*, in the north the left arm of Bootes rises with Leo; in the south the prow of Argo, the rest of the Dog, and Hydra, whose tail stretches to the claws of Scorpio <=Libra> and its head to the claws of Cancer as far as the Crater. Above Leo lies the Little Bear, and on line with it lies the head of Draco, which Ophiouchus touches. On the north are the Dolphin, Lyra, Zeugma, Cygnus (except for the bright star in its tail) and the head of Pegasus.

The following zones are subject to Leo: to the head, Gaul and the adjoining areas; to the fore parts, Bithynia; to the right side, Macedonia and the neighboring areas; to the left side, Propontus; to the feet, Galatia; to the belly, Gaul; to the shoulders, Thrace; to the flanks, Phoenicia, the Adriatic, and Lybia; to the midparts, Phrygia and Syria; to the tail, Pessinus.

Virgo is the house of Mercury, feminine, winged, anthropomorphic, luxurious, standing like the figure of Justice, bicorporeal, barren, a freedman, with no offspring, downward-trending, earthy, common, semi-vocal or mute, concerned with the body, incomplete, changeable, industrious, two-natured. Men born under this sign are noble, modest, religious, burdened with care, leading a quite varied life, administrators of others' goods, trusted, good stewards, secretaries, accountants, actors, practitioners of curious arts and seekers after mystic lore, spendthrifts in their early years but prosperous later in life…[1]

Libra is the house of Venus, masculine, equinoctial, anthropomorphic, upward-trending, airy, feminizing, vocal, noble, changeable, a diminisher of estates, the Lower Midheaven of the universe, public, ecliptic, the supervisor of crops, vineyards, olive groves, aromatics, homesteads, measures, and artisans. Men born under this sign are noble and just, but malicious, covetous of others' goods, average in fortune, losing their original possessions and falling into vicissitudes, living through ups and downs of fortune, being in charge of measures, posts, and the grain supply…[2]

Scorpio is the house of Mars, feminine, solid, rainy, fecund, destructive, downward-trending, mute, servile, unchangeable, the cause of stenches, a destroyer of property, ecliptic, having many feet. Men born under this sign are tricky, base, thieves, murderers, traitors, incorrigible, destroyers of property, connivers, burglars, perjurers, covetous of others' property, accomplices in murder, poisonings, and other crimes, haters of their own family…[3]

---

[1] <*A later supplement from Ms Laurentianus 86.18*> As a whole Virgo is soaking wet and stormy. By part it is as follows: its first decan is hot and destructive, the second temperate, the third rainy. Its northern parts are windy, the southern temperate. The following regions are subject to it: Mesopotamia, Babylonia, Greece, Achaea, Crete, the Cyclades, the Peloponnesus, Arcadia, Cyrene, Doris, Sicily, Persis. Of the parts of the body it rules the belly and all the internal and hidden parts.

[2] <*A later supplement from Ms Laurentianus 86.18*> As mentioned, as a whole Libra is tropic and changeable. By part it is as follows: its first and second decans are temperate, the third rainy. Its northern parts are windy, the southern dry and disease–ridden. The following regions are subject to it: Bactria, China, the Caspian area, Thebais, the Oasis, Troglodytia, Italy, Libya, Arabia, Egypt, Ethiopia, Carthage, Smyrna, the Taurus mountains, Cilicia, Sinope. Of the parts of the body, it rules the hips and buttocks, the groin and intestines, the hind parts and rump.

[3] <*A later supplement from Ms Laurentianus 86.18*> As a whole, Scorpio is stormy and fiery. By part it is as follows: its first decan is cloudy, the second temperate, the third indicative of earthquakes. Its northern parts are burning hot, the southern dry. The following regions

Sagittarius is the house of Jupiter, masculine, fiery, upward-trending, vocal, moist because of the constellation Argo, noble, winged, changeable, bicorporeal, two-natured, mysterious, with few offspring, half-finished <=childless?>, governing, kingly. Men born under this sign are noble, just, great-hearted, judges, generous, loving their brothers and their friends. They lose much of their original possessions but gain them back. They are superior to their enemies, seek a noble reputation, are benefactors, prominent, and act mysteriously...[4]

Capricorn is the house of Saturn, feminine, tropic, earthy, destructive, barren, downward-trending, chilling, mute, servile, the cause of troubles, brutal, lurking, mysterious, two-natured, moist, half–finished <=childless?>, a hunchback, lame, the Descendant of the universe, indicative of misfortune and toil, a sculptor, a farmer. Men born under this sign are bad, warped. They pretend goodness and sincerity. They are toilsome, burdened with care, insomniac, fond of jokes, plotters of great deeds, prone to make unfortunate mistakes, fickle, criminal, lying, always criticizing, shameful.

Capricorn is temperate on both sides. By parts it is as follows: the first parts are destructive, the second moist, stormy, changeable; the middle parts are fiery; the last destructive. It has ... stars. According to the *Sphaerica*, Casseiopeia and the right part of Pegasus rise with it in the north. In the south the rear of Centaurus and the legs of Hydra (up to the Crater) set <while Capricorn is rising>. These are the gods: Venus, the Moon, Ceres, Mercury. On the north there is nothing.

The following zones are subject to Capricorn, all of them to the west and south: to the flanks, the Aegean Sea, the inhabitants of its coastline, and Corinth; to its waist, Sicyon; to its back, the Mediterranean; to its tail, Spain; to its head, the Tyrrhenian Sea; to its belly, mid-Egypt, Syria, <and Caria>.

---

are subject to it: Metagonitis, Mauretania, Gaetulia, Syria, Commagene, Cappadocia, Italy, Carthage, Libya, Ammon, Sicily, Spain, Rome. Of the parts of the body, it rules the unmentionable parts and the rump, the groin and seat. Because of its sting, it causes blindness, dimming of vision, attacks of the stone, strangury, ruptures and strangulated hernias, unmentionable vices and promiscuity, fistulas, cancers, and hemorrages.

[4] <*A later supplement from Ms Laurentianus 86.18*> As a whole, it is windy. By part, it is as follows: its first decan is quite wet, the second temperate, the third fiery. Its northern parts are windy, the southern moist and variable. The following regions are subject to it: Etruria, Gaul, Spain, Arabia Felix, Cilicia, Crete, Sicily, Gaul, Italy, Spain, Cyprus, the Red Sea, Casperia and the nations along the Euphrates, Mesopotamia, Carthage, the Libyan Sea, the Adriatic, the Atlantic, the Triballi, Bactria, Egypt and the nearby places. It is masculine and autumn. Of the parts of the body, it rules the thighs and groin. Because of its point, it often causes births with extra limbs, baldness, epilepsy, troubles of the eyes, or blindness. It always causes danger from animals, the loss of limbs, or dangers from wild beasts.

Aquarius is the celestial sign which is masculine, solid, anthropomorphic, somewhat damp, single. It is mute, quite cold, free, upward-trending, feminizing, unchanging, base, with few offspring, the cause of troubles arising from athletic training, carrying burdens, or work in hard materials, an artisan, public. Men born under this sign are malicious, haters of their own families, incorrigible, self-willed, deceitful, tricky, concealing everything, misanthropic, godless, accusers, betrayers of reputations and the truth, envious, petty, occasionally generous (because of <this sign's> flow of water), uncontrollable.

As a whole this sign is wet. By parts it is as follows: the first parts are wet, the upper parts fiery, the lower worthless and useless. It has …stars. According to the *Sphaerica* the right parts of Andromeda rise in the north with Aquarius, as well as the rest of Pegasus; in the south, the southern one of the <two> Fish, except for the head. Juno, Hercules, Vulcan, Saturn. In the north nothing sets. In the south the rest of Centaurus and of Hydra (up to Corvus) set <when Aquarius rises>. This sign lies toward the west wind. In addition it faces toward the zone of Egypt and the surrounding cities, i.e., from Egypt's southern parts up to Pselchos, Dodecaschoinos, and Sykaminos; from its western parts to the oasis of Ammon and the surrounding cities; from its eastern part to the Red Sea which touches Egypt; and from its northern parts to Sebennytos and the Heracleotic mouth of the Nile.

According to the *Sphaerica*, Eridanus and the Great Fish lie next to Aquarius in the south, touching the tail of Capricorn. In the north, around the north pole, is the so–called Cygnus, above which is Sagitta, where the Bear (called Cynosura) looks to the north. The following zones are subject to Aquarius: to the front parts, Syria; to the middle, the Euphrates and Tigris, Egypt, Libya, the interconnected Egyptian rivers, and the Indus. Under the middle of the Water Jug are the Tanais and the rest of the rivers which flow from the Hyperboreans to the north and west.

Pisces is the celestial sign which is feminine, moist, quite wet, bicorporeal, with many offspring, mossy, scaley, sinewy, humpbacked, leprous, two-formed, mute, motile, with rough skin, in conflict with itself because one Fish is northern, the other southern. It is moist, downward-trending, servile, changeable, with many offspring, bicorporeal, sociable/lewd, with some limbs missing, the cause of wandering, varied. Men born under this sign are unsteady, unreliable, changing from bad fortune to good, sexy, theivish, shameless, prolific, popular.

As a whole, Pisces is cool and breezy. By parts it is as follows: the first parts are temperate, the middle moist, the last destructive and worthless. It has…stars. In the north the rest of Andromeda rises with Pisces, as well as the rest of Perseus—

the parts on the right—and Triangulum in Aries. In the south the head of the Southern Fish rises. Neptune, Mars, Mercury, Venus, Jupiter. In the south Ara and the rest of Hydra set <when Pisces is rising>; in the north, nothing.

Pisces lies toward the north wind. It also lies toward the zone of the Red Sea, having not a few islands under its control, above which lie India and the so-called Indian Ocean. In its eastern parts Pisces touches Parthia, the land of the Indies, and the Eastern Ocean; in its northern parts, Scythia. In its western parts it washes with its waves Myosormos, Orthosormos, and the surrounding cities.

According to the *Sphaerica*, Aquila, cut off by the north pole, and part of Sagitta lie to the north of Pisces, not far away from the north pole. The so-called Pegasus is within the Arctic pole. (The Arctic Circle, lying in the middle of the universe, stands apart from the other divisions <of the sky>. It has in it the Great Bear (called Cynosura) stretching from the north toward the east, and from the south the other Bear, called the Lesser, which rises at midnight, and which the so–called Bearguard <Bootes> controls, having a rein on both Bears. He is invisible depending on the elevation of the two Bears. One looks north, the other south.)

The following zones are subject to Pisces: to the front, the Euphrates and the Tigris; to the middle, Syria and the Red Sea, India, mid-Persis and the neighboring lands; to the tail, the Arabian Sea, the Red Sea, and the Borysthenes river; to the tie of the Northern Fish, Thrace; to that of the Southern Fish, Asia, Sardinia.

<3.> The 60 <Terms>

The first 6° of **Aries** belong to Jupiter: temperate, robust, prolific, beneficent. The next 6° belong to Venus: cheerful, clever, radiant, even, pure, handsome. The following 8° fall under the ambiguous influence of Mercury: changeable, clever, idle, windy, stormy, full of thunder and lightning. The next 5° belong to Mars: baneful, fiery, unsteady, characteristic of rash, wicked men. The next 5° belong to Saturn: cold, barren, malicious, injured.

The first 8° of **Taurus** belong to Venus: prolific, with many children, moist, downward-trending, convicted, hating their children <?>. The next 6° belong to Mercury: intelligent, sensible, criminal, with few offspring, sinister, fatal. The next 8° belong to Jupiter: great-hearted, bold, lucky, ruling and beneficent, magnanimous, temperate, loving modesty. The fourth term, the next 5°, belong to Saturn: sterile, barren, a eunuch, a vagabond, censorious, theatrical, gloomy, toilsome. The final 3° belong to Mars: masculine, tyrannical, fiery, harsh, murderous, a looter of temples and a criminal—not an unknown one, rather destructive and short-lived.

The first 6° of **Gemini** belong to Mercury: temperate, with fine weather, intelligent, versatile, skilled, active, poetic, prolific. The next 6° belong to Jupiter: competitive, temperate, with fine weather, prolific, luxuriant, beneficent. The third term, 5°, belongs to Venus: blossoming, artistic, addicted to plays and mimes, poetic, a contest winner, popular, cheerful, prolific. The fourth term, 7° belong to Mars: much-burdened, with no brothers, having few children, a wanderer, with a good income, destructive, bloody, inquisitive. The last 6° belong to Saturn: temperate, a procurator, having possessions, intellectual, with a wide knowledge, distinguished, noted for intelligence, an arranger of great matters, most famous.

The first 7° of **Cancer** belong to Mars: hurling thunderbolts, moved in different directions, uneven, contradictory in his wishes, manic, prolific, poor, destructive, and in the end, base. The next 6° belong to Venus: prolific, censorius, moist, changeable, skilled, popular, promiscuous. The following 6° belong to Mercury: precise, a robber, a leader in public matters, a tax gatherer, in the public eye, rich, wealth-producing. The fourth term, 7°, belongs to Jupiter: kingly, imperious, glorious, judging, great-hearted, temperate, ruling, entirely noble. The final 4° belong to Saturn. In this term everything is water, moist, poor in personal property, and in the end quite needy.

The first 6° of **Leo** belong to Jupiter: experienced, masculine, imperious and in general having leadership qualities, active, eminent, with no mean traits. The next 5° belong to Venus: very temperate, yielding, talented, luxurious. The third term, 7°, belongs to Saturn: having much experience, fearful, scientific, naturally clever, narrow, religious, with many children, searching out secret lore, barren, without offspring. The next 6° belong to Mercury: addicted to plays and mimes, popular, scholastic, guiding, prescribing, intelligent. This term is barren and characteristic of long-lived men. The final 6° belong to Mars: very base and monstrous, destructive, injured, torpid, censured, unlucky.

The first 7° of **Virgo** belong to Mercury: lofty, procuratorial, an arranger, handsome, organizing great affairs, most intelligent, entirely noble and eminent. This term is not, however, lucky in love. This misfortune is generally true of Virgo, especially in this term and in that of Venus. This term causes men who are open to criticism; the term of Venus causes those who err constantly. They fall conspicuously short in regard to boys. The next 10° belong to Venus: censured, wronging their marriage and falling into difficulty because of this, lucky in theatrical matters. They are most unnatural in their passions, especially when Saturn is in aspect; when Mercury is in aspect, they commit adultery; when Jupiter is in aspect, they commit a great number of sins which are forgivable—but still there are condemnations. When the Sun is in aspect, they commit hidden actions; when the Moon is in aspect, they meet with reverses and political opposition. If this term is beheld by malefics, it causes prostitution. The third term, 4°, belongs to Jupiter: agricultural, proper, reclusive but not ignorant. Men born under this term are trustees, fruitful, upright. The fourth term, 7°, belongs to Mars: masculine, harsh, public, demagogues, night prowlers, <hired men>, counterfeiters, imposters. These degrees assault men and lead them to chains, mutilation, tortures, and imprisonment. The last 2° belong to Saturn: monstrous, chilled, destructive, short-lived, the term of deluded men.

The first 6° of **Libra** belong to Saturn: kingly, lofty, effective—especially for day births, but <disturbed> for night births. These degrees are also barren, moist, destructive. The next 5° belong to Mercury: businesslike, craftworking, marketing, the term of instruments of exchange and numbers, collecting; in general, just and intelligent. The third term, 8°, belongs to Jupiter: wealth-producing, but despite that, this term is characteristic of unlucky men, cheerlessly hoarding their possessions, living without ostentation, with a sordid lifestyle, with no appreciation of beauty, censorious—and not, of course, blessed with children. The fourth term, 7°, belongs to Venus: loving beauty, loving crafts, craftsmen themselves, e.g., sculptors, painters, engravers. In general this term is rhythmic, pious, mild and slow, fortunate, making progress without effort, exceedingly fortunate in marriage, and lucky in everything. The remaining 4° belong to Mars: ruling, leading, lucky in all martial affairs, optimistic/spirited, steady, successful, great-hearted; not, however, with many brothers or lucky with those he has.

The first 7° of **Scorpio** belong to Mars: easily upset and disturbed, unsteady, irascible, frank-speaking, arrogant, with few children but many brothers, uneven in fortune, inflamed, very appropriate for nativities which promise campaigns and travel abroad. The next 4° belong to Venus: lucky in marriage, pious, loved by everyone, loving children, wealthy, selected for every office, living graciously. The third term, 8°, belongs to Mercury: military, competitive, prizewinning, and, where words are concerned, bitter, contentious, not to be despised. These degrees are also prolific and fecund. In general they plan mischief, especially against those who attempt evil or do it. The fourth term, 5°, belongs to Jupiter: talented, lucky, high-priestly, glorified in gold, purple, and the high offices appropriate to the inherent greatness of the nativity. This term is beneficent and as a whole loves men and gods. The last 6° belong to Saturn: punitive, with few children or brothers, haters of their own relatives, poisoners, melancholic, and misogynists, having secret wounds, and in general very punitive and cursing fate. They are hated by both gods and men; they resist their superiors and are despised by their inferiors.

The first 12° of **Sagittarius** belong to Jupiter: active men. These degrees are damp but temperate, dabbling in all crafts and skills, prolific, with many children and brothers, yet poor. The next 5° belong to Venus: temperate, prominent, victorious, prizewinning, pious, honored both by the masses and by the rulers, blessed with children and brothers, living with many women. The third term, 4°, belongs to Mercury: verbal, subtle, active, producing eternal verities, philosophical, and in general prominent in science and wisdom; fond of learning if Mercury inclines, but if Mars inclines, loving weapons and tactics. The next 5° fall to Saturn: sterile and baneful, cold, harmful, characteristic of base and completely unlucky men. The next 4° belong to Mars: hot, rash, violent, shameless, destructive—except that this term is restless in all things. All the terms in Sagittarius indicate varied possibilities in all matters.

The first 7° in **Capricorn** belong to Mercury: theatrical, comic, on the stage, lying, whoring, seducing, covetous of others' things, of no reputation, <talented> in everything, blessed, wealthy, but not of high rank. The next 7° belong to Jupiter: it brings vicissitudes of glory and infamy, wealth and poverty, largess and public ridicule. This term is barren, having female or deformed children, of low rank, vulgar. The next 8° belong to Venus: profligate, lecherous, downward-trending, thoughtless, censured, having their ends very much in doubt, not dying well, nor steady in marriage. The fourth term, 4°, belongs to Saturn: severe, cheerless, alien, unlucky with their children and brothers, bloody and destructive, cold, pitiless/stand-offish, malicious, slow to act, but tricky. The last 4° belong to Mars: lofty, prosperous, dictatorial, aiming at rule in everything, poor, destructive of their own relatives and of <brothers>, wandering, loving solitude, quarrelsome to the end.

The first 7° of **Aquarius** belong to Mercury: rich, miserly, gladly hoarding wealth up to the measure of the nativity, intelligent, learned in the law, precisely defining everything, imperious, petty, careworn, loving education and all disciplines, supervisory, overseeing, philanthropic. The next 6° belong to Venus: loving well, pious, wealthy without effort, profiting by sudden and unexpected good fortune, prosperous, seafaring. These are prolific degrees. It is beneficial for anyone born under these degrees to unite with old women, the feeble, or with eunuchs, and to gain advantage from the barren or the aged. The next 7° belong to Jupiter: lucky, petty, lurking at home, careless of his reputation, living in obscurity, fortunate in his children, misanthropic. The next 5° belong to Mars: diseased (particularly in the internal organs), troubled by lawsuits; this term is characteristic of wicked, intractable, and incapable men—except that these men readily attempt evil deeds. The remaining degrees, 5°, belong to Saturn: barren, moist, conceiving with difficulty, enfeebled, especially in the dura mater and the internal organs, afflicted with dropsy and fits, poor, with few brothers or children, envious, unlucky in their ends.

The first 12° of **Pisces** belong to Venus: cheery, fecund, downward-trending, luxurious, living graciously, with a friendly greeting, celebrating, loving, making progress without effort, dear to the gods. The next 4° belong to Jupiter: literary, learned, preeminent among the masses and victorious over everyone because of his words, with many brothers, prolific, with many children, having too many associates and brothers. The next 3° belong to Mercury: fecund, ruling, those of high rank, with many friends, bounteous, loving their parents, charitable, pious, temperate. The next 9° belong to Mars: active, naval warriors, bold guides, attaining success in mystic lore, plundering but then restoring, varied, not dying a natural death. The last 2° belong to Saturn: enfeebled, moist, subject to fits, entirely unlucky.

We have given instruction about what effect each degree produces. <We add that> if the houseruler is located in a given term, the houseruler will produce its proper effect as well, whether good or bad. Now I will explain the Ascendant.

<4. Finding the Ascendant>

Having determined accurately the Sun's degree-position at the nativity, note where the dodekatemorion falls. The sign in trine to the left of this position will be the Ascendant, or the equivalent sign (i.e., either masculine or feminine), providing you take into account the distinction between night and day births. For example: let the Sun be in Aquarius 22°. The dodekatemorion of this point is in Scorpio; the sign in trine to the left is Pisces. If the birth was in the day, either Pisces or Taurus or Cancer must be the Ascendant. If the birth was at night, one of the diametrically opposite signs <must be>. Virgo would be in the Ascendant in the first hour <of the night>.

Having determined accurately the degree-position of the Sun, for day births add to this position the rising time of the sign in which the Sun is; then begin to count from the Moon's position at the nativity, giving each sign one degree. The Ascendant will be <in the sign> where the count stops, or (as mentioned above) in the equivalent sign. For night births add the rising time of the Moon's sign and count from the Sun's position at the nativity. Using the previous example again: the Sun in Aquarius <22°>, the Moon in Scorpio. I add the rising time <of Scorpio>, 37, to 22° <the Sun's position>, for a result of 59. I count this off from the Sun and stop at Virgo. The Ascendant is there.

Find the number <of days> from Thoth to the day of birth; multiply the hour/time <of birth> by 15 and add the result to the first number. For day births count from Virgo, giving 30 to each sign. For night births, count from Pisces.

Alternatively, multiply the hour/time <of birth> by 15 [and add the degree-position of the Sun]. Then for day births, count from the Sun with reference to the rising time <of the sign> in the klima of birth; for night births, count from the point opposite the Sun with reference to the rising time. In this way, the mystical, compelling Ascendant will be found. For day births the point of conception will be trine or sextile to the Sun and in the Ascendant; for night births the signs in opposition <to these places> will be the point of conception. As a result, for whatever hour you observe, night or day, you will find the Ascending sign.

To find the Ascendant precisely to the degree, do this: multiply the hour/time of birth by the motion of the Moon. For day births count from the Sun's degree-position; for night births count from the point in opposition <to the Sun>. The degree where the count stops will be considered the Ascendant. For example: Hadrian year 4, Mechir 13, the first hour of the night. The Sun was in Aquarius 22°, the Moon is Scorpio 7°, the motion of the Moon in its <204th> day from epoch was 13;52°. I consulted the appended table under 14 in the first row and I found below in the first column of hours, 16. I then counted from the degree in opposition to the Sun, Leo 22°. I stopped in Virgo 8°. If more or fewer degrees are found in the table

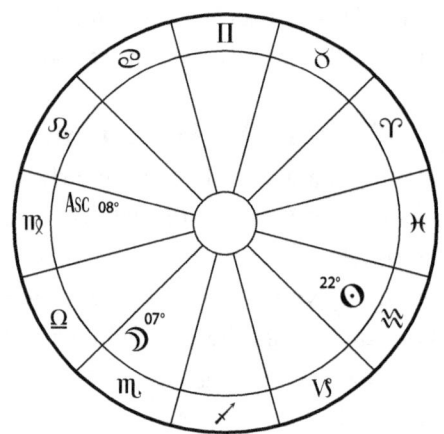

of rising times, it can be ascertained from the aforementioned procedure whether the hour requires an added or a subtracted factor.

For those born during the day, add the remaining degrees in the Sun's <sign> to the Moon's degree-position and divide by 30. The remainder will be the <degree in> the Ascendant. For those born at night: add the remaining degrees in the Moon's <sign> to the Sun's degree-position. If the resulting number is greater than the calculated hour/time <of birth>, the amount by which it exceeds either 30 or the number of the hour will be the Ascendant.

Count the days (including the intercalary days) from Epiphi 25 to the day of birth, and add 22 to this number. Count the result off by 30s, starting at Cancer for day births, at Capricorn for night births. The Ascendant will be where the count stops, and the degree thus determined will be the degree in the Ascendant.

The Gnomon of the Ascendant

Take the degree-position of the Sun with reference to its "Ascending time," and multiply it by ten. (Do this for day births; for night births take the point in opposition <to the Sun>.) Then multiply the result by the given hour/time <of birth>, whether day or night, whether given in whole hours or including fractions. Then divide by 360, and treat the remainder as the "gnomon of the Ascendant." For example: klima <2>, second hour of the day; Sun in Cancer 21°, Moon in Aries 22°. The "Ascending time" of the Sun's degree-position is 22;24. Multiply this by ten for a result of 224. This figure multiplied by two, then divided by 360°, gives 88. This is the gnomon of the Ascendant.

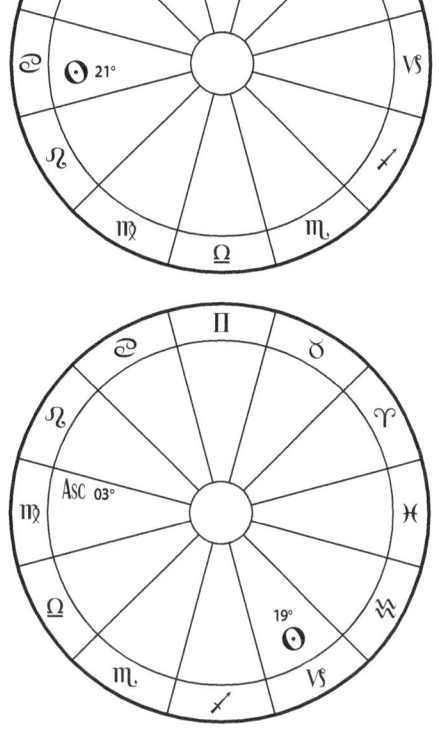

Another example: the Sun in Capricorn 19°. The birth was in the third hour of the night. The Moon's motion was 12 17/30°. I enter the column of the table under the third hour, where I find at 12 of motion, 41 ½, and at 13 of motion 44 ½. The difference between 44 ½ and 41 ½ is 3, and 17/30° times 3 equals 1 7/10°. I add this figure to 41 ½ because the Moon's motion was 12 17/30°. All together the degrees total 43 1/5. Now add to this figure the Sun's degree-position, 19°. The total is 62 1/5°. I count this off from Cancer, since the birth was at night, and the Ascendant is in Virgo 2° 12′. According to the table, the Ascendant was Virgo 3°.

For new-Moon births, it will be necessary to look carefully at the term of the new Moon and the ruler of the sign. Whichever of them controls the degree which just precedes the hour, that degree will be the Ascendant. For full-Moon births, it will be necessary to determine the term of the full Moon and the ruler of its sign.

For day births, it is necessary to take the Sun's <degree-position> and the remaining degrees of the Moon and to divide by 30. Find the remainder in the table of rising times and multiply the figure entered there at the Sun's sign by the degrees of the sign. Then, having added the Sun's degree-position, divide by 30. Whatever is left will be the solar gnomon. We note this figure carefully and make it the lunar gnomon as follows. Double the Moon's degree-position; divide by 30; multiply the remainder by 12 and add the Moon's degree-position. Then divide by 30 and the remainder will be the lunar gnomon. For night births, add the remaining degrees of the Moon to the Sun's degree-position, divide by 30 in the table of rising times. We add the remainder to the Sun's sign and note the "horary magnitude." We multiply the Sun's degree-position. We add the Sun's degree-position and divide by 30. The remainder will be the solar gnomon. If the solar gnomon is greater than the lunar, then subtract from the Ascendant. If the lunar is greater, then add whatever the excess is. If they are equal, do not add or subtract. Likewise if the remainder is 15 or less, there will be addition or subtraction.

Having determined by <u>sign</u> the sign in the Ascendant, we will find the <u>degree</u> in this way: note the year of the quadrennium as it is given below. Add the hours entered there to the hour/time <of birth>. Calculate the Moon's degree-position <for the new time>. We will consider the Ascendant to have that position.

First Year	1 Hour
Second Year	6 Hours
Third Year	12 Hours
Fourth Year	6 Hours

The year of the quadrennium is associated with the rising of the Dog Star <Sirius>:

First Year	Sirius rises with Cancer in the first day hour
Second Year	It rises with Libra in the sixth day hour
Third Year	It rises with Capricorn in the twelfth day hour
Fourth Year	It rises with Aries in the sixth night hour

Calculated in this way, the Ascendant is useful in casting horoscopes in later years <after birth>, the hours from the quadrennium table being added (depending on the year in question), then counted from the hour of birth. Put the Ascendant in whichever hemisphere of the sky—day or night—the count ends, and interpret the nativity with respect to the stars which are occupying an angle at that time.

5. Midheaven

The Midheaven <MC> can be handily found in this way: using the rising times for the <appropriate> klima, add the rising times from the Descendant to the point in opposition, then take half of the sum. Count this off from the Descendant. The Midheaven will be where the count stops. For example: the Ascendant is Capricorn 15° in the second klima. I take the rising times from the Descendant, Cancer 15°, to Capricorn 15°; the total is 214. Half of this is 107. Adding to this the 15° of Cancer, I count from that same point. The count stops at Scorpio 2°, which is the Midheaven. Similarly for the other <degree-positions>.

If you wish to know the length of the hours of the day, in all cases add the rising times from the Sun's degree-position to the point in opposition. Take ¹⁄₁₅ of that and you will know the length of the hour. For example: assume the previous Descendant, Cancer 15°, is the Sun's position. The rising times from there to the point in opposition total 214; ¹⁄₁₅ of 214 equals 14 [remainder 4] with ⁴⁄₁₅ parts of an hour left over. Therefore the day in the klima of Syria, with the Sun in Cancer 15°, will be 14 ⁴⁄₁₅ hours. If you want to know the length of the night, work out the calculation by adding the rising times from the point opposite the Sun to <the Sun's> position. Similarly with the rest of the signs.

6. The Rising Times of the Signs

How many hours each <u>sign</u> takes to rise can be figured from the rising times of each sign. For example: Aries rises in 20 <equatorial times>; now an hour has 15 equatorial times. If you take 15 from 20, the result is 5, which is ⅓ of 15. Therefore Aries will rise in 1 ⅓ hour.

You can discover how long each <u>degree</u> takes to rise thus: double the rising time of each sign; multiply this by six—the result <for Aries> is 240. The degree is 8 "months" <=⁸⁄₁₂ of an equinoctial time>.

For each sign the amount its rising time is more or less <than another sign's> can be found as follows: Aries rises in 20; Libra in 40, for a total of 60. The rising time of a sign plus the rising time of the sign in opposition will total 60. The hours of a sign plus the hours of the sign in opposition will total 4 hours. The "days" and "months" of each sign plus those of the sign in opposition will total two "years." By however much one sign exceeds the half, by so much the sign in opposition will fall short, and vice–versa. So—in the previous example—subtract the lesser from the greater, 20 from 40; the remainder is 20. One-fifth of this is 4, so the addition/subtraction factor for each sign is 4. If to the 20 of Aries we add 4, the result is 24. In this time Taurus will rise. Then Gemini in 28, Cancer in 32, Leo in 36, Virgo in 40, Libra in 40. From Scorpio to Pisces subtract in the same manner. By investigating in this way, you will find <the rising times> for each klima.

Another method: assume Leo rises in 36; the same for Scorpio, but Taurus and Aquarius in 24. <When subtracted> the result is 12, of which the third part is 4. This is the addition/subtraction factor. And so by investigating in this way, you will find the rising times for each klima.

The difference between klimata and the progressive increase <of the rising times> are calculated as follows: in the first klima the rising times from Cancer to Sagittarius total 210; ⅙ of this is 35. In this amount Leo rises. Continuing with the procedure at hand, if you subtract the 25 of Aquarius and take one-third of the remainder, you will know the rising times of the signs.

Given that there are 7 klimata, in the seventh, from Cancer to Sagittarius, the rising times total 234. If you subtract the 210 of the first klima from 234, 24 are left. One-sixth (since there are 6 klimata between) of this is 4. Thus 4 is the increase needed for each klima in the construction of the table of rising times. So in the first klima the rising time from Cancer to Sagittarius is 210. In the second klima, 214; in the third, 218; in the fourth, 222; in the fifth, 226; in the sixth, 230; in the seventh, 234.

7. Listening and Beholding Signs

Similarly the listening and the beholding signs (the sextile signs) must be calculated from their rising times as follows: Pisces beholds Taurus; in the second klima the rising times of the six signs from Pisces <to Leo> total 160 and from Taurus to Libra total 200. Pisces is less than Taurus and therefore listens to it. The rising times of the two groups total 360. Likewise from Gemini to Scorpio there are 212 and from Leo to Capricorn 212; therefore Gemini and Leo are of equal rising time and listen to each other. Again from Virgo to Aquarius is 200, from Scorpio to Aries 160. They behold each other and <Scorpio listens to Virgo . From Leo to Capricorn is 212>, and from Libra to Pisces is 180... From Sagittarius to Taurus is 148, and from Aquarius to Cancer is 148. They listen to each other and are of equal rising times. Similarly for the rest <of the signs>.

Some astrologers consider the sympathy of the sextile signs to be as follows: they add the rising times of the two <sextile> signs and divide the sum in half. Then they see if the intervening sign actually rises in that time. For example: Aries 20 plus Gemini 28 totals 48, half of which is 24. Taurus actually does rise in that time. Therefore Aries will have sympathy with Gemini. Likewise Taurus with Cancer, since their rising times total 56, half of which is 28. In this time Gemini actually does rise. Likewise Gemini with Leo and Cancer with Virgo. Leo however does not have sympathy with Libra because their rising times total 78, half of which is 39—but Virgo actually rises in 40. Likewise for the rest of the signs.

8. A Handy Method for New and Full Moons

To find new and full Moons handily: take the distance from the Sun's degree-position to the Moon's, and determine how many dodekatemoria there are between. Count this amount off from the Sun's degree-position and you will find the new Moon there. The Moon will be as many degrees from conjunction as there are dodekatemoria which have been determined. For full-Moon nativities, take the distance from the point opposite the Sun to the Moon, and determine how many dodekatemoria there are <in this distance>. Subtract that amount from the position of the point opposite the Sun. The full Moon will be there. Also, if you add 15° to the degree-position of the full Moon, you will find the position of the next new Moon. If you add 15° to the position of the new Moon, you will find the next full Moon.

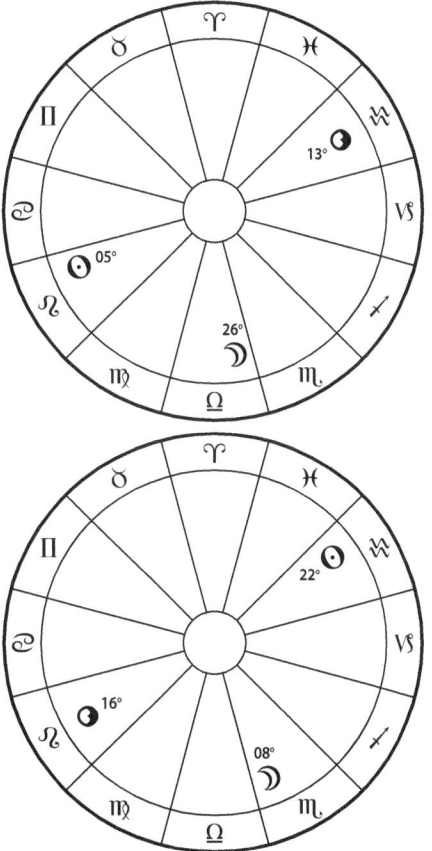

For example: Mesori 2, the Sun in Leo 5°, the Moon in Libra 26°. The distance from the Sun to the Moon is 81°, which is very nearly 7 dodekatemoria. Therefore the Moon is seven days past the conjunction. Next I deduct the 7 from the Sun's position and arrive at Cancer 28°. The previous new Moon occurred there. From Mesori 2 I subtract 7; the result is Epiphi 25. If we add 15 to Cancer 28° the result is Leo 13°. The full Moon will be at Aquarius 13°.

Calculate the full Moon as follows: assume Mechir 13, the Sun in Aquarius 22°, the Moon in Scorpio 7°. I take the distance from the point opposite the Sun, Leo 22°, to the Moon's position; this is 75°, which equals 6 dodekatemoria. I subtract this from Leo 22°. The result is Leo 16°, where the full Moon occurred. Again I subtract the 6 dodekatemoria from Mechir 13, for a result of Mechir 7. Since from the conjunction to the full Moon there are 15 days, I add the 8 <days from Mechir 7 to Mechir 13> to this 13, and get 21. Therefore the Moon is that many days <21> from new.

9. A Handy Method for the Seven-Zone System [or the Sabbatical Day]

For the week [and the Sabbatical day] proceed as follows: take the full years of the Augustan era and the leap years, and add to that sum the days from Thoth 1 to the birth date. Then subtract as many 7's as possible <=divide by 7>. Count the result off from the Sun's day, and the birth date will belong to the star at which the count stops. The order of the stars with respect to the days is

Sun, Moon, Mars, Mercury, Jupiter, Venus, Saturn.

The arrangement of their spheres is

Saturn, Jupiter, Mars, Sun, Venus, Mercury, Moon.

It is from this latter arrangement that the hours are named, and from the hours, the day of the next star in sequence.

For example: Hadrian year 4, Mechir 13 (in the Alexandrian calendar), the first hour of the night. The full years of the Augustan era are 148, the leap years are 36, and from Thoth 1 to Mechir 13 are 163 days. The total is 347. I divide by 7 for a result of 49, remainder 4. Starting from the Sun's day, the count <4> comes to Mercury's day. The first hour of that day belongs to Mercury.

Hours of the Day <of Mechir 13>	Hours of the Night
1 Mercury	1 Sun
2 Moon	2 Venus
3 Saturn	3 Mercury
4 Jupiter	4 Moon
5 Mars	5 Saturn
6 Sun	6 Jupiter
7 Venus	7 Mars
8 Mercury	8 Sun
9 Moon	9 Venus
10 Saturn	10 Mercury
11 Jupiter	11 Moon
12 Mars	12 Saturn

The next day, Mechir 14, continues in this pattern: the first hour belongs to Jupiter.

10. The Houseruler of the Year

If you want to know the houseruler of the year, calculate in the same way. To continue with the previous example: the full years of the Augustan era are 148, the leap years are 36, plus the one day of Thoth 1, for a total of 185. I divide by 7 for a result of 26, remainder 3. Count this <3> from the Sun's <day>. The year goes to Mars. Now that you have found the ruler of the year, you can find the ruler of the month as follows, applying the arrangement of the spheres in ascending order: Thoth <1> is Mars'. Since Thoth 29 goes to Mars again, the 30th is Mercury's. Phaophi 1 is Jupiter's, Phaophi 30 is Venus', Athyr 1 is Saturn's, Choiak 1 is the Moon's, Tybi <1> is Mercury's, and Mechir <1> is Venus'. Since the ruler of the year is Mars, of the month, Venus, of the day, Mercury, and of the hour, the Sun, it will be necessary to examine how these stars are situated at the nativity. If they are in their proper places and proper sect, they indicate activity/occupation, especially when the ruler of the year happens to be transiting the current year, the ruler of the month transiting the current month, and the ruler of the day transiting the current day. If however they are unfavorably situated and have malefics in aspect, they indicate reversals and upsets.

To me it seems more scientific to take the full years of the Augustan era plus the leap years (as was just stated), plus the days from Thoth 1 to the birth date, then to divide by 7 and count the remainder from the Sun<'s day>. Then consider that <day's star>, where the count stops, the ruler of the year. The first day of the month of each nativity will control the birth day. It does not seem reasonable for everyone born in the same year to have the same houseruler <=ruler of the year>. In general, the old astrologers took the ruler of the year and of the universal rotation from the first day of Thoth (where they put the start of the new year), but it is more scientific to take it from the rising of Sirius.

11. Masculine and Feminine Degrees

The masculine and feminine degrees are as follows: the first 2 ½ degrees of the masculine signs are masculine, the next 2 ½ degrees are feminine. The first 2 ½ degrees of feminine signs are feminine, the next <2 ½ degrees> are masculine, the next <2 ½> are feminine. The degree of the new Moon will be indicative for new-Moon births; the degree of the full Moon will be indicative for full-Moon births. Others say that the degree in which the Ascendant or the Moon falls…

12. The Visibility Periods of the Moon

The visibility periods of the Moon are as follows: in its first day it appears ⅘ of an hour. In its second day it appears 1 ⅗ of an hour. Forecast the time <of its visibility> by multiplying the days <since new Moon> by 4, then dividing by 5. For example: it is 15 days since new Moon; 4 times this equals 60, of which ⅕ is 12; the Moon, being full, will be visible 12 hours.

Day	Visibility Period	Day	Visibility Period
1	⅘ hour	9	7 ⅕
2	1 ⅗	10	8
3	2 ⅖	11	8 ⅘
4	3 ⅕	12	<9 ⅗>
5	4	13	<10 ⅖>
6	4 ⅘	14	11 ⅕
7	<5 ⅗>	15	12
8	<6 ⅖>	Similarly <from> 16 <to 30> as from 1 to 15, but subtracting.	

The month is 29 ½ days; the year 354 days.

13. The Invisibility Period of the Moon

The Moon becomes invisible as it approaches conjunction with the Sun. The calculation of this in each sign is as follows: take one-half of the rising time of the sign in which the Sun is located, and at that point the Moon will be invisible. For example: the Sun in Aries in the second klima. The rising time of this sign is 20, half of which is 10. Subtract 10 from 30° <Aries 1° = Pisces 30°>. The Moon will become invisible at Pisces 20°.

The Sun In:	Half of Rising Time	The Moon Becomes Invisible In:
Taurus	12	Aries 18°
Gemini	14	Taurus 16°
Cancer	16	Gemini 14°
Leo	18	Cancer 12°
Virgo	20	Leo 10°

Similarly for the rest of the signs.

14. The Third, Seventh, and Fortieth Days of the Moon

The third, seventh, and fortieth days of the Moon as follows: assume the

Moon is in Scorpio 7°; the third day will be in Sagittarius 7°. [It is necessary to investigate the day in this way. Sagittarius 7° has become the third day.] In the nativity chart the seventh will be found in square, at Aquarius 7°. The fortieth will be at Taurus 7°. (Some add 160° to the Moon's position at birth and count off this amount from the Moon's sign. Others add to the Moon's position at birth <its positions> on the third and seventh and fortieth days, then after calculating, they interpret the Moon at those places.)

In general they note the fortunate, unfortunate, and average nativities according to the third, seventh, and fortieth days: if these locations are beheld by benefics in operative places, and not by malefics, then you can predict exceedingly great good fortune. If two of these locations are beheld by benefics and one by malefics, then you can predict average fortune. If three are beheld by malefics, with the benefics turned away, then predict misfortune. If the situation is mixed, say "average."

15. A Handy Method for Finding the Ascending Node

A handy method for finding the ascending node: take the full years of the Augustan era and multiply them by 19 ⅓. Add for each Egyptian month 1° 35' and for each day 3'. Divide by 360° circles. Now count off the remainder <of the division> from Cancer in the direction of diurnal motion <=east to west>, giving 30 to each sign. The ascending node will be where the count stops. For example: Hadrian year 4, Phamenoth 19. The full years from Augustus are 148; this figure times 19 ⅓ equals 2862. From Thoth to Phamenoth there are 10°, for a total of 2872. I divide this by 360° for a result of 7; a remainder of 352 is left. This remainder is counted in the direction of diurnal motion from Cancer and comes to Leo 8°. The desired ecliptic point will be there, the descending node at the point in opposition.

It will be necessary to examine if benefics are in aspect with these positions, especially with the ascending node. If so, the nativity will be prosperous and effective. Even if the nativity is found to be average or inclined toward diminution, the native will ascend and rise to a high rank. Malefics portend upsets and accusation.

From the <tables of> lunar epochs and daily motions the ascending node and the sign of its latitude will be found as follows: for example, take the previous nativity, Hadrian year 4, Phamenoth 19. From the epoch to the nativity date is 204. Next to the epoch is entered 12;18 of latitude. Next to 204 is entered 11;37 of latitude. The total is 23;55. Multiply this times 15° and the result is 358° 45'. This is counted from Leo in the direction of proper motion <=west to east> and comes to Cancer 28° 45'.

[Another more concise method: the 23;55 is counted from Leo, 2 given to each sign. The count stops at Gemini, having allotted 22, with 1;55 remaining. This I multiply by 15°, and the result is 28° 45' of Cancer.)

Next in every case I take the degrees from Taurus to the previously determined degree; the distance is very nearly 89°. I subtract this amount from the Moon's degree-position (which is Scorpio 7°), and come to Leo 8°, the ascending node. It will be necessary to do the same calculation for the rest of the nativities.

If I wish to know the sign of the latitude, I will calculate as follows: the latitude entered next to the epoch is 12;18. I multiply only this by 15° and the result is 184° 30'. I count this off from Leo and stop at Aquarius 4° 30'. Next the "degrees of latitude" entered next to 204 is 11;37. I multiply this figure by 15°, and the result is 174° 15'. I add Aquarius 4° 30' to this and count the sum off from the same place. The result is Cancer 28° 45'. By using this method for the rest of the epochs we will find the sign of the latitude.]

16. The Determination of the Steps and the Winds of the Moon

We will find the step and wind as follows: from Leo to Libra the Moon declines northwards; from Scorpio to Capricorn it declines southwards; from Aquarius to Aries it ascends southwards; and from Taurus to Cancer it ascends northwards.

The steps are found as follows: since each step is 15°, and since a sign contains 30°, each sign comprises two steps. We can find the step of the latitude by starting at Leo. Since the latitude in the previous nativity was found to be 23;55, I count this off from Leo, giving 2 to each sign. The count stops at Cancer 1;55 <step>. We now know that the Moon is ascending northwards at the sixth step of this wind.

17. A Hipparcheion Concerning the Calculation of the Sign of the Moon

I handily find the sign of the Moon as follows: add the <correct> factor for the year in question from the table of kings below. Divide the factor by three, not discarding the remainder, but keeping it. If the remainder is one, add 10 to the number; if the remainder is 2, add 20; if the remainder is 3, add nothing—the number divides evenly. Next take one-half of the months from Thoth until the birth date, and add the number of days <in the month of birth> to the first number. Divide by 30 (if possible) and count off the remainder from the Sun's sign. If it was in the beginning <of the sign>, give 2 ½ <to each sign>; if it is towards the end, give the appropriate amount. The Moon is wherever the count stops.

Use the same method to find the date of a given nativity: add the factor to the year in question and divide (as explained) by 3. Then add one-half of the months, note the number. Next estimate the distance from the Sun to the Moon by assigning 2 ½ <days> to each sign. Now determine which is the larger number. If <the number derived from> the distance from the Sun to the Moon is larger, subtract from it the previously calculated number and the result will show the date. If the distance is less, add 30 to it, then subtract the previously calculated number. If the two numbers are both divisible by 30, the Moon is in conjunction with the Sun.

For example: Hadrian year 3, Athyr 28. I add 2 (the customary factor for this king) to year 3, for a total of 5. I divide by 3, the remainder is 2; therefore I add 20, for a total of 25. One-half of the months <from Thoth to Athyr> is 1 ½, plus the 28 <days in Athyr> make the total so far 54 ½. I divide by 30, for an answer of 1, remainder 24 ½. The Moon will be this many days from conjunction with the Sun. This number I count off from the Sun's position in Sagittarius, giving 2 ½ to each sign. The Moon is in Virgo on the aforesaid day.

To find the date as follows: again to year 3 I add 2, then divide by 3, for a remainder of 2. Therefore I add 20, for a total of 25, then one-half of the months, 1 ½, to get the total 26 ½. Then I estimate the distance from the Sun to the Moon (i.e., from Sagittarius to Virgo) to be 24 ½ days. Since it is not possible to subtract 26 ½, the previous total, from 24 ½, I add 30 to it and get 54 ½. Now from this I subtract 26 ½, with 28 as the result. This indicates the date of birth.

The customarily added factors for each king is appended, in chronological order as follows:

King	Years of	<Running Total>	Subtract	Remainder
Augustus 1	43	44	30	14 I add this figure to Tiberius.

The years of Tiberius are:

Tiberius	22 for a total of 36. I subtract 30 with a remainder of 6:			
Gaius	4	10	—	10
Claudius	14	24	19	5
Nero	14	19	The 19-year period is full. Since this period is operative, we add (in order to complete 30) 11 years to Vespasian's reign:	
Vespasian	10	21	19	2
Titus	3	5	—	5
Domitian	15	20	19	1
Nerva	1	2	—	2

Trajan	19	21	19	2
Hadrian	21	23	19	4
Antoninus	23	27	19	8
Antoninus & Lucius Commodus	32	40	30	10
Severus & Antoninus	25	35	30	5
Antoninus	4	9	—	9
Alexander	13	22	19	4
Maximianus	3	7	—	7
Gordianus	6	—	—	—
Philip	6	The 19-year period is full.		

<18. The Reckoning of the Sun and the Five Planets>

You will discover the Sun's degree-position as follows: in every case, to a birth date which falls in the months from Thoth to Phamenoth add 8°; you will find the total to be the Sun's position. To <birth dates in> Pharmouthi add 7°, to Pachon 6°, to Payni 5°, to Epiphi 4°, to Mesori 3°. For example: in Phaophi 6, I add 8°, total 14; the Sun will be in Libra 14°. In Pachon 6, I add 6°, total 12. The Sun will be at Taurus 12°.

Since some students have become very enthusiastic about the derivation of numerical data, for them I must append the handy methods for the rest of the stars, so that through such studies they may gain delightful and precise-to-the-degree methods. They can now make an examination of the more important procedures with the greatest enthusiasm.

Now then, **Saturn** is to be calculated as follows: take the full years since Augustus and divide by 30, if possible. Multiply the remainder <of the division> by 12°. Multiply the result of the division by 30 (=the synodic period <of Saturn>) by 5°. For each month from Thoth <to the date of birth> add 1°, and for each day 2'. Having totaled all this, count from Cancer in the direction of proper motion, giving 30° to each sign. The star will be where the count stops.

Jupiter as follows: divide the full years from Caesar by 12. Multiply the remainder by 12° and add this to the result of the previous division by 12 (=the synodic period <of Jupiter>). Total this, plus 1° for each month and 2' for each day. Having added, count the sum from Taurus, giving 12 to each sign.

Mars as follows: take the number of years from Augustus to the year in question, divide by 30, and note whether the remainder is odd or even. If it is even, start counting from Aries; if it is odd, start from Libra. Having found this number, double it and add to it 2 ½ for each month <after Thoth>. If the result is more than 60, count off the amount over 60 from Libra or Aries, giving 5 to each sign. Wherever the count stops, make note of the sign and examine which sign the Sun is in. If the Sun is found to be west of the star, the star will be behind <=to the west> its calculated position; if the Sun is found to be east of the star, the star will be ahead <=to the east> of its calculated position. In other words, in each case, place the star nearer the Sun than the sign in which you have calculated it to be. The rest of the stars, especially Venus, show the same peculiarity when they are moving near the mean position of the Sun.

Venus as follows: take the years from Augustus to the year in question and divide by 8. Examine the remainder (which will be less than 8) to see if Venus is at a point of maximum eastern elongation <during that year>. If it is, use this point and add the number of days from that point to the day in question; if not, use the number right above it <in the table>, just as with the Moon. In other words, if the point of maximum eastern elongation is found to be before the nativity, use it; if it is after the nativity, use the number right above it. Add together the days, then subtract the elongation factor of the sign. Subtract 120° [for each sign[5]]. Count off the remaining degrees from the adjoining sign [from the sign of the elongation], giving each sign 25°. Venus will be where the count stops. The point of maximum eastern elongation will be clear from the remainders in the calculation of years above. If the remainders in our first calculation are 1, 3, 4, 6, or 7, then Venus is at maximum eastern elongation <during that year>. If the remainders are 2 or 5, it is in motion <during that year>.

<Remainder	Date	Sign of the Elongation>
1	Phamenoth 10	Taurus
<2 No maximum eastern elongation occurs in this year.>		
3	Phaophi 10	Sagittarius
4	Payni 22	Leo
<5 No maximum eastern elongation occurs in this year.>		
6	Tybi 8	Pisces
7	Mesori 14	Libra

In the eighth year Venus has a point of maximum eastern elongation.

Mercury is calculated as follows: take the days from Thoth to the birth date and add to these in every case an additional 162. Find the total, and if the sum is more than 360, divide by 360 (a circle) and count the remainder off from Aries, giving 30 to each sign. The star is where the count stops. In every

---

[5] *Marginal note from the manuscripts:* [i.e., for the sign of the elongation.]

case make it very near the Sun. For example: if the Sun was in the beginning of its sign, Mercury can be found at the end of the sign. If the Sun is in the end of its sign, Mercury can be found in the next sign.

An example: Trajan year 13, Phamenoth 18. The full years from Augustus are 138. I divide by 30, for a result of 4, <remainder 18>. I multiply 5 times the 4 cycles, and the result is 20. I multiply the remainder <of the original division>, 18, by 12, and the result is 216. From Thoth to Phamenoth I count 1 for each month—total 7. All together this is 243. Now I count this sum off from Cancer giving 30 to each sign, and I arrive at Pisces. Saturn is there.

Next I divide 138 by 12, for a result of 11, remainder 6. This <remainder> times 12 is 72. To each 12 which I divided <into 138> I assign 1, for a total of 11. Also to each month <from Thoth to Phamenoth I assign 1>, for a total of 7. The grand total is 90. I count this off from Taurus, giving 12 to each sign. The count stops in Sagittarius. Jupiter is there.

Next Mars as follows: from Caesar to the year in question is 139 <!>. I divide this by 30, for a result of 4, remainder 11 <!>. (Since the remainder is odd, I know that I must start counting from Libra.) I double this figure and get 22. For the months from Thoth to Phamenoth the total is 17 <=7 months × 2 ½>. The grand total is 39. I count this sum off from Libra, giving 5 to each sign. I stop at Taurus. Mars is there.

Venus as follows: I divide the 139 years by 8 and the remainder is 3. This indicates a point of maximum eastern elongation during that year on Phaophi 10 in Sagittarius. I add the rest of the days in Phaophi, 20, plus the days from Athyr to Mechir, 120, plus those in Phamenoth, 18, for a total of 158. I subtract 120 for the maximum elongation and for Sagittarius. The result is 38, which I count from Capricorn, giving 25 to each sign. The count stops in Aquarius. Venus is there.

Since there seems to be great <difficulty> about calculating Venus in nativities, I will explain it with another example. Hadrian year 4, Athyr 30: the years from Augustus are 148, which I divide by 8, giving a remainder 4. This indicates a point of maximum eastern elongation on Payni 22 in Leo. Since this point is not applicable because of its being after the date of the nativity, I go to the one right above it <in the table>, in the third line, Phaophi 10 in Sagittarius. So I add the remaining 20 days of Phaophi, the days from Athyr to Mesori, 300, and the 5 intercalary days. The total is 325 of the previous year, plus 90 days from Thoth <1> to Athyr 30 of the current year, for a grand total of 415. From this sum I subtract 120 for the maximum elongation and for Sagittarius, for a result of 295. I count this off from Capricorn, giving 25 to each sign and stop at Sagittarius 20. The star is there.

Another example: Hadrian year 4, Mechir 13: the years from Augustus are 149, which I divide by 8, giving a remainder of 5. This indicates no point of maximum eastern elongation. I go to the point above, which is Payni 22 in Leo. I add the remaining 8 <days> in Payni, plus Epiphi and Mesori <60>, plus the 5 intercalary days. The total is 73. Then I add to this the days from Thoth <1> to Mechir 13, 163. The grand total is 236. From this sum I subtract 120 for the maximum elongation and for the sign Leo. The result is 116. I count this from Virgo, giving 25 to each sign. The count stops at Capricorn 16°. Venus is there.

I calculate Mercury for the same nativity as follows: I add the days from Thoth <1> to Mechir 13 for a total of 163; then I add 162 for a grand total of 325. I count this off from Aries, giving 30 to each sign and stop at Aquarius 25°. Mercury is there.

[**Transits**

The Sun: the second, the sixth, and the twelfth are good; the seventh and the fourth are rotten.

The Moon: the third, the eighth, and the ninth are rotten; the fifth, the eleventh, and the twelfth are good.

Saturn: the fourth and the tenth are rotten; the sixth, the eighth, and the twelfth are good.

Jupiter: the third, the ninth, the tenth, and the eleventh are good; the fourth and the seventh are rotten.

Mars: the third, the fourth, and the ninth are good; the seventh and the tenth are rotten.

Venus: the third, the seventh, and the eighth are good; the fifth is rotten.

Mercury: the second, the fifth, and the eleventh are rotten; the seventh, the eighth, and the ninth are good.

The other <numbers> of each star are variable in effect.

If the stars are in the previously mentioned places in their transits, particularly when they hold the chronocratorship in operative places, with benefics or malefics in aspect, then they are bestowers of good or evil depending on whichever aspect prevails. If the <benefics and malefics> are together, a mixture of good and bad will ensue according to the quality of each person's nativity. Therefore it is always necessary to observe the places with respect to <the stars'> transits in order to evaluate the chronocratorships.]

19. The Combinations of the Stars

Let us append the associations and combinations of each star.

When Saturn and Jupiter are together, they are in agreement with each other, and they bring about benefits from legacies and adoptions, and they cause men to be masters of property consisting of land, to be guardians, managers of others' property, stewards, and tax gatherers.

Saturn and Mars are hostile, productive of reversals and ruin. They bring family quarrels, disharmony, and hatred, along with treachery, plots, malevolence, and trials. However, if these stars are in their own or in operative signs, and if they have benefics in aspect, they produce distinguished and noble nativities, although unsteady in their happiness and prone to unexpected dangers and treachery.

Saturn and Mercury are allies and productive of activities/employment. They do, however, bring slanders about religion, lawsuits, and debts, as well as disturbances about written matters and money. On the other hand, these stars make men who are not without resources and not unintelligent, with much experience and awareness, and who are curious, far-seeing scholars, seekers after mystic lore, revering the gods, but with much on their consciences.

Saturn and Venus act harmoniously with respect to activities/employment: they promote success with respect to entanglements and marriage, agreeing and beneficial only for a time, not to the end. Indeed they cause abuse, divorces, inconstancy, and death, often entangling men with the base-born and the lowly, and causing them to fall into harm and lawsuits.

Saturn and the Moon are beneficial, productive of money, estates, ship ownership, and profits from the deceased, especially if the Moon happens to be in the part of its orbit just following first visibility and has benefics in aspect. Then it causes association with the great, gifts, and the discomfiture of enemies. This combination, however, is unsteady with respect to possession, and with respect to women it is insecure and painful because of separations, hatred, and grief. It also produces bodily suffering, sudden fits, pains of the governing faculties and nerves, as well as the deaths of important figures.

Saturn and the Sun are at odds, giving and taking away possessions and friendships maliciously. Therefore those born under such a juncture suffer secret enmities and threats from great persons and are plotted against by some and live hated to the end. Playing their part well, they outlive most <of their enemies>. They are, however, not without resources, but are disturbed and long-suffering. They are self-controlled in this onslaught of reversals.

When Jupiter and the Sun are together, they produce noble and distinguished men, rulers, governors, dictators, vigorous men, honored and blessed by the crowd. These men are wealthy, rich, living with much spectacle. Sometimes however they are involved in uncertainties and hostility. Especially if the star <Jupiter> is found to be setting, they resort to greater showiness and make a pretense of the truth.

Jupiter and the Moon are good, acquisitive: they cause men to be masters of adornments and slaves, and they bestow distinguished offices and ranks. They cause men to benefit from women and distinguished individuals, to be treated well by family and children, and to be thought worthy of gifts and honors. They make treasurers, men who lend much, who are trusted, and who find treasures and become wealthy.

Jupiter and Mars make glorious and showy characters, friends of the great or of kings, distinguished governors and receivers of stipends, those making a career in public affairs or in campaigns, and those considered worthy of honor and status, but uncertain in their livelihoods and habits, tossing away their possessions.

Jupiter and Venus are good, in harmony, productive of rank and profits, bringing new acquisitions, gifts, adornments, control over slaves, rulerships, the begetting of children, high priesthoods, preeminence among the masses, honors of garlands and gold crowns. These stars make men who are worthy of statues and images, but they also make them subject to ups and downs with respect to marriages and children.

Jupiter and Mercury are good, in harmony, and supervisory. They make men who are managers, overseers of affairs, in posts of trust and administration. They make men who are successful as secretaries and accountants and who are respected in education. These are approachable people with many friends, judged worthy of pay and stipends. If Jupiter and Mercury are found in operative signs, they make men discoverers of treasures, or moneylenders who profit from cash deposits.

Venus and the Sun are in harmony, glorious, bestowers of good. They cause the association of male and female, they bring gifts and conveyances, and make men successful in their enterprises. Occasionally they make those men who take on popular leadership or trusts, those who are in charge of foreign/secure places, those thought worthy of stipends. These men, however, are not without grief with respect to wife and children, especially if Venus is setting.

Venus and the Moon are good with respect to rank, acquisitions, and the inception of business, but they are unsteady with respect to living together, friendships, and marriage, bringing rivalry and hostility, as well as ill-treatment and upset from relatives and friends. Likewise with respect to children and slaves, these stars are not good: they cause possessions to be fleeting and bring mental anguish.

Venus and Mars are at odds. They make men unsteady and weak of mind; they cause rivalry and murder; they cause men to have many friends, but to be blameworthy, shameless, fickle, and equally prone to intercourse with men or women; to be malicious, and plotters of murder by poison. These stars cause men to remain with neither the good nor the bad, to be slandered and reviled because of their friendships, to be spendthrift, flitting from one occupation to another, to be eager for many things, to be wronged by women and because of them to suffer crises, upsets, and debts.

Venus and Mercury are in harmony. They make men sociable and gracious, gregarious and hedonistic, paying attention to education and sensibility, receiving honors and gifts. For those of mediocre fortune, these stars bring about the receiving of goods, selling, and exchanges, and they bring a base livelihood. These stars make men unsteady and fickle with respect to women, changeable in their agreements <with them>.

Mercury and the Sun make adaptable men with many friends, those flexible and self-controlled men who spend their careers in public places. These stars make pure, sensible men, men of good judgement, lovers of beauty, learned men, initiates into divine matters, beneficent, fond of their associates, independent, braggarts. These men endure reversals nobly, but are ineffective, suffering ups and downs in their livelihoods, experiencing vicissitudes. They are not poverty-stricken, but find a success proportional to the basis of their nativities.

Mercury and the Moon are good with respect to the union and status of men and women, with respect to the power of speech and education, and concerning commerce and other enterprises. They make men who act in common, who are resourceful, experienced, inquisitive. They also cause men to advance by great expenditures, to be very changeable, not persevering in their activities or intentions for the future. <These men are> noble in the face of adversity, but are subject to ups and downs in their livelihood.

Mercury and Mars are not good. They cause hostility, lawsuits, reversals, malice, betrayals, wrongs from superiors or inferiors. These stars make some men athletic, martial, commanding, beneficent, inquisitive <of the occult>, getting a livelihood in a varied manner. They resort to forgery in order to embezzle, steal, and loot, and having fallen into debt and expenses, they bring on themselves infamy and hot pursuit. If the configuration is afflicted, men meet with accusations and imprisonment, and they suffer loss or confiscation of goods.

The Sun and the Moon are good. They are productive of associations with the great and of high rank, as well as possession of estates, property, money, and adornment. These stars cause men to be successful in business enterprises and to receive profit. If the basis <of the nativity> is found to be great, men become leaders of cities, in charge of affairs, preeminent among the masses, gifted with a very high public image, munificent, governing, ruling, unsurpassed, and possessing a kingly property and spirit. Those starting with a moderate/average fortune become lucky and are called blessed. The good, however, does not last for this type of person, because of the waning configuration of the Moon.

...

20. The Combination of Three Stars

Saturn, Jupiter, and the Sun are unsteady and insecure. <They bring failure> with respect to possessions, friendships, and other business enterprises. They cause loss of possessions, and they cause some to fall into invidious accusations. These stars, having indicated help from unexpected sources or from legacies, and having increased someone's reputation, bring ruin and accusation, along with sudden danger and plots. They do cause preeminence, guardianship of others' business, tax gathering, and salaries, for the sake of which men endure disturbance and crises, but these stars make the basis <of the nativity> insecure and worrisome.

Saturn, Jupiter, and the Moon are in harmony, bringing rank and profit, associations with the great, and gifts. Men travel abroad; they succeed in foreign lands or because of foreigners, not only in their own business, but also in others'. Men also derive benefits from women, and coming into possession of estates and land, they become lords. Some become shipowners and thus increase their livelihood, or they manage their livelihood by getting hold of whatever is involved with water.

Saturn, Jupiter, and Mars bring about mixtures of good things. They make some men famous, high-priestly, governing, influential, in charge of the masses, of villages, or of military matters, commanding and obeyed. These men are not adorned with great show of wealth; they are involved in reversals, accusations, and violent affrays; and they lead worried lives. <These stars cause> others to be graced with the possession of an income, to be masters of estates and property, and to profit from the deceased, but their reputation is low. Therefore matters must be interpreted according to the configuration of the heavenly bodies and the effects of the signs.

Saturn, Jupiter, and Venus are good, helpful in occupations, bringing possessions. They cause associations of male and female, as well as friendships, advancement, and benefits from legacies. However in their associations men are slandered and envied; they are unsteady in their marriages, suffering embarrassments, hostility, and judgements. On the other hand, they are fond of their associates and easy to live with, enjoying many new friendships. They are not entirely tranquil, nor do they lack grief with respect to children and slaves.

Saturn, Jupiter, and Mercury when configured together produce vigorous men, stewards, trustworthy, preeminent among the masses, commanding and obeyed, handlers of money and directors of documents and accounts. Such men have an independent and adaptable nature: sometimes they appear malevolent and wicked, and they will become covetous of others' property, thievish, and greedy, because of which they will endure upsets and crises, debts and public infamy. Sometimes these men advance because of their success in action and because of their trustworthiness. Then they gain support and are thought worthy of gifts from the great and of honors. Since they have a generous disposition, they will benefit their own family and even others'. They, however, will take part in the mysteries and in esoteric affairs, and in other respects they will inquire into the curious arts and be subtle, pretending that their character is straightforward.

Saturn, Mars, and the Sun are indicative of forcible, outré, and dangerous matters. These stars make bold men, men of great ambition, wicked atheists, traitors, insubordinate, men who hate their own families, who abandon their own relatives to go with strangers. They are involved in contumely and dangers. They suffer falls from high places or from animals. They are afraid of burns, and are toilsome in their activities. They do not guard what they already have, but desire others' goods. They profit from crime. If, however, the configuration happens to be military or athletic, they are toilsome, but not unsuccessful.

Saturn, Mars, and the Moon cause men to be venturesome in their business enterprises and noble, but ineffective, meeting with reversals and violence. They become in turn violent, reclusive, wicked: they have a plundering and thievish disposition, and become defendants in trials. They experience detention and criminal charges, unless of course the nativity happens to be fond of wrestling or of weapons, in which case the "detention" configuration is fulfilled by the holds <of wrestling>. Some become injured or diseased and will suffer a violent end.

Saturn, Mars, and Venus are favorable at the start of actions, friendships, associations. These stars bring profit, high rank, and political associations. Later, however, men are put into a disturbed state, liable to lawsuits arising from some envy/hatred and treachery. Because of this, such men make accusations and they endure hostility from men and women. They are involved in shameful faults and adultery, and are the object of scandal and denunciation. Some are inclined to unnatural, bisexual vices, and they become accomplices or participants in crime or murder by poison. Then they suffer no ordinary anxiety.

Saturn, Mars, and Mercury cause crime, treachery, judgements, and alarms. Men go into debts and expenses for the sake of scriptures or mystic lore, and they suffer no ordinary tribulations and ruin. In other cases these stars make men keen and intelligent in business, leading a varied life, maligned by some because of violent and illegal activities. Occasionally they become involved in toilsome and dangerous business and fall into poverty. Then they blame their own Fortune, blaspheme the gods, and become oath-breakers and atheists. If the stars are not in their proper domicile, they bring criminal charges and imprisonment. If the stars do happen to be in their proper, operative places, these men will undertake struggles of behalf of others and will generally prevail, or they will profit from documents, from accounts, or from public office, and will increase their livelihood.

Saturn, Venus, and the Sun are indicative of lofty associations, honors, and deeds, and they are the cause of high rank, distinction, and preeminence among the masses. They are unstable with respect to property or other matters, and they involve men in ups and downs: they dissolve friendships, effect the reduction of livelihood, and bring public exposure or punishments arising from the betrayal of females or of religious matters. <They cause men to be> unstable and bisexual in their intercourse and other relationships.

Saturn, Venus, and the Moon bring vicissitudes and instability of life, especially with respect to wife, mother, and children. They impose bad manners, ingratitude, as well as jealousy and quarrels, divorces, censure, public exposure, unnatural vices. But in business these men are not without resource, sharp, full of accomplishment, profiting from legacies. They do not however retain this wealth, since they are plotted against by many, and are themselves accomplices in crime and murder by poison, as well as seducers of women.

Saturn, Venus, and Mercury make intelligent, clever individuals, shrewd and designing in their business enterprises. These men, however, are unsteady and frozen in their first enterprises. They become covetous of others' goods, accomplices in many crimes, seekers of curious lore, flexible, healing, enjoying newness, change, and travel. If, under these conditions, the configuration is afflicted, or if Mars is in aspect from the right, these men fall into disturbances and trials because of poisonings, of females, or because of legacies, or they suffer a loss of livelihood or an afflicting accusation after being wronged by women. In general they will be insecure and pained with respect to women, children, and slaves.

Jupiter, the Sun, and the Moon cause distinguished, brilliant, prominent men, supervisors of public, civic, and royal affairs, governors, generals, men without peer, dictators, as well as men who are envied, maligned, and betrayed by some, men who hate their own families, men who change their minds.

These men are fickle and mentally unstable, arrogant, planning for their own advantage and falling into vicissitudes. They are adorned with all the pomp of wealth, but do not continue happy to the end; they falter in some things and ultimately come to grief.

Jupiter, Mars, and the Sun are indicative of men involved in disturbances and dangers, but enthusiastic and effective in their business enterprises. These men have a share of glory: they are leaders, governors, supervisors of public matters, but are prone to fall because the hatred of the great follows them, along with threats, betrayals, plots from their families, and criminal charges. A few, lifted from average fortune by the favor of the great, have later been ruined.

Jupiter, Mars, and the Moon produce shrewd men, bold, public men with many friends, men advancing to high place from humble fortune and thought worthy of trust. These men are governors, athletes, distinguished men, leaders, supervisors of the masses and of districts. They have a share of offices, stipends, or priesthoods. They fall into reversals and criminal charges, betrayed by their own relatives or by females, and they suffer loss of possessions. Later however they recover them because of religious or other unexpected affairs.

Jupiter, Mars, and Mercury cause vigorous, enthusiastic, active men. They receive a salary for public office or military assignment or for doing royal or civic business. But they are unsteady in their livelihood and spendthrift of their goods. They are however intelligent and trustworthy stewards, easily straightening out mistakes and laying on others the criticism originally directed at them. They are maligned and fall into reversals. These stars make some men athletes, prizewinners, and trainers, skilled at many things, fond of travelling and profiting in foreign lands, but failing with their own estates.

Jupiter, Mars, and Venus cause men to have many friends, to be easy to associate with, to be thought worthy of association with and help from the great, to be successful and to progress with the help of women. These stars make some men high-priests, prizewinners, athletes, or supervisors of temples or of the masses. They cater to their own pleasures and at times live unsteadily, subject to ups and downs. These men are blameworthy and indiscriminate about sexual matters, experiencing public exposure and betrayal, grieved with respect to children and slaves, enjoying new associations, and enduring separations from women.

Jupiter, Mercury, and the Sun cause men to be easily successful in business enterprises and to have many friends, to be thought worthy of trusts, honors, stewardships, association with the great, and success. Some men advance from humble origins and are honored. But they let their possessions slip from their grasp; they are easily deceived, and they become poor for some time. They do many things for religious reasons. They are not without a livelihood, but are supported by unexpected sources of high rank.

Jupiter, Mercury, and the Moon make noble, propertied men, shrewd in business, collectors of gifts and sharers in trusts, religious men, intelligent, eloquent, guardians of property and deposits, making their careers amidst documents and accounts. They are lavish, tax-gatherers, stipend holders, with many friends, well-known, trustees, administrators of affairs, generous. These stars also make men athletes, prizewinners, worthy of honors, pictures, and statues. If these stars occur in operative places, they make men discoverers of treasures and overseers of shrines and temples. These men will rebuild, replant, and restore places, and will win eternal fame.

Jupiter, Mercury, and Venus are good, bringing possession of livelihoods and success in business. Men become intelligent, straightforward, generous, sweet, loving their families, cheerful, participants in education and culture, pure, decent, worthy of honor and high rank, associated with the great, and sharing in trusts and stewardships. These men are honored with livelihoods. They foster the young and are fond of education. They are masters of slaves and they rear some and benefit them as if they were their own children. Since they are pious, they know the future from the gods, but they will become unsteady and grief-stricken with respect to wife and children.

Jupiter, Venus, and the Sun make men who are spectacular and glorious, but who are also petty, mentally unstable, and arrogant. Sometimes they are liberal and beneficent, though changeable. At other times they are exalted with the help of another person's fame and possessions, and although coming from humble origins, they become high-priests, prizewinners, leaders, governors, preeminent in public matters, and protectors of the masses. They are thought worthy of honors and gifts and are granted livelihoods. They will however become unnatural and blameworthy in sexual matters. If these stars happen to be rising or in operative places, then these men will be happy with their wives and children.

Jupiter, Venus, and the Moon cause vigorous, famous men, high-priests, prizewinners, overseers of temples and shrines, benefactors, men eager for fame, catering to the pleasures of the masses, of cities, or of villages. These men receive trusts and are thought worthy of honor. They are well spoken of and envied by family and friends, but experience hostility and opposition. With respect to wives and intimate friends, they are unsteady and quarrelsome, living with jealousy and separation and pain, always in suspense. Sometimes they are intimate with relatives, but not even then do they have an undisturbed homelife. They get into partnerships. They will, however, become very spectacular in their manner of life, but they are full of false show, not of the truth.

Venus, the Sun, and the Moon cause famous and vigorous men, those who live with ostentation, those who are malicious and blameworthy, slandered by most people and envied/hated by the great and by their friends. They succeed and gain possessions and are raised high by Fortune, but they are also unsteady with respect to wife and children. Otherwise they are fond of their friends and travel much, finding good fortune in foreign lands.

Venus, Mars, and the Moon make men who are not without resources and not inactive, but who are also fickle and mentally unstable, quixotic, beginning in confusion and putting <no> end to their affairs. They have great plans, are contemptuous, wandering, bold, public, martial, indiscriminate in their use of male and female partners. They are maligned and fall into insulting treatment and trials, changing friendship into enmity because of their criminal attempts, and failing in their livelihood.

Mercury, the Sun, and the Moon make revered and pure men, those who play their part well, stewards, and those who share honors and positions. They are benefactors, participants in the mysteries, troubleshooters, and they put on a great show of possessions. They become bodyguards, chamberlains, and men placed in charge of money, records, and accounts. The speech of such men will be most effective for advice or instruction.

Mercury, the Sun, and Venus make polymaths and men of wide experience. These men are noble, prominent in the arts and sciences, worthy of trusts and positions. They easily regret what has been done, sometimes wavering and moved in all directions, or enjoying changes in their occupations. They have many friends, are well known, succeed through their acquaintance with the great, and are honored with a livelihood and high rank, despite being blameworthy.

Mercury, the Moon, and Venus make good men, easy to live with, straightforward, generous, with a sense of humor, civic-minded, sharers in education and rhythm, ingenious, of wide experience, neat, pure, simple, participating in religious ceremonies, helpful, envied and hated, unstable in their livelihoods, and indiscriminate in their intercourse with men or women, wealthy, and thrifty.

Mercury, Mars, and Venus when configured together bring profit, high rank, occupations. <These stars make men who are> shrewd in giving, receiving, and undertaking other business, who are stewards, wicked and widely experienced men, men who start their careers with documents and training. They are blameworthy, wasting much wealth, generous, wallowing in loans and debts and defaulting, embezzlers of others' money, seducers, deceiving with their charm, wealthy, malignant—but repenting of what they have done.

Mars, the Sun, and the Moon make bold, manly, reckless, vigorous men. They become athletes and soldiers, rulers and governors, and they make their careers through violent, hateful deeds, in laborious crafts, or in work in hard materials. They fall into reverses and into dangerous situations, and suffer hostility and attacks from the great, but if benefics are in aspect, they maintain the basis <of their nativity> unimpaired.

Mars, the Sun, and Venus cause men to have many friends and to be well-known, to be thought worthy of alliances and honors. These men have many resources, love their associates, but are criticized and gossiped about. Their friendships do not last and their accomplishments are fleeting. They desire much, they spend much, they are wrongers of women, and they are very ready to be insolent. They fall into reverses and hostility through their reckless decisions.

Mars, the Sun, and Mercury make men of much experience, inventive in business enterprises. Although careworn and unsuccessful in the goal of their calculations, they prevail unexpectedly. Therefore such men are mentally unstable, reckless, active, hot-tempered; after rushing against their enemies and bringing charges of wrongdoing or damages against them, these men then change their minds. Occasionally they have a cowardly and despicable character. They control their emotions well, play a part, and yield to men whom they should not yield to. For the most part, they have a livelihood subject to ups and downs. On coming into another's control, they curse their own Fortune.

Mars, the Moon, and Mercury make men skillful and ingenious, easily aroused to action and very vigorous, wanting to act quickly, but being remiss, seekers of curious lore, initiates of the mysteries, and partakers of secret knowledge. They are oppressors, violent, insubordinate, covetous, falling into accusations and suits for damages, into trials and dangers, and they experience alarms because of documents and money. However, these stars do make men wealthy and lavish, although failing in their livelihood.

This then is what we have explained with respect to the distinctive characteristics of individual stars as well as several taken together. If other stars share the configuration (being in conjunction or in aspect), the reading of the horoscope will be changed according to the nature of the additional star. However I did not want to continue writing at length about such additional factors, because the old astrologers have expounded them already. The particular effects of the natural influence of each star and sign will be obvious at once to anyone who pays attention. (These have been explained previously in our treatise.) Therefore it will be necessary to determine how each star is configured in relation to the others: is it at an angle or rising? Is it the ruler of a lot, of the Ascendant, or of a triangle? Likewise with the sign in which the star appears: is it of its own or of another sect, and which other signs does it have in aspect? If these things are determined, the predictions will be solidly based. If <stars> fall in inoperative places, the <level of> occupation and of Fortune will be less.

<21. Conception>

Having established all this, now we must speak about conception, putting aside complications and rejecting envy.

There are three factors: minimum, mean, maximum, and the difference between each factor is 15 days. If we add or subtract 15 to or from any factor, the next one will be reached. The minimum factor is 258, which will apply when the Moon just follows the Descendant (in the Place just following the Descendant). The mean factor is 273, which will apply when the Moon is in the Ascendant. The maximum factor is 288, which applies when the Moon is in the Descendant. If we measure the 15 days of difference in the celestial hemisphere from the Ascendant to the Descendant, we find that 2 ½ fall to each sign. Let the Ascendant be Cancer, the Descendant Capricorn:

If the Moon Is:	The Gestation Period Will Be:
Just following the Descendant	258
Aquarius	260 ½
Pisces	263
Aries	265 ½
Taurus	268
Gemini	270 ½
Cancer (Ascendant)	273
Leo	275 ½
Virgo	278
Libra	280 ½
Scorpio	283
Sagittarius	285 ½
Capricorn	288

For example: Nero year 8, Mesori 6/7, hour 11 <of the night>; the Moon in Libra, the Ascendant in Cancer. Since the Moon is at an angle <IC>, the nativity will occur in 280 days 12 hours. We must subtract these days from the 365 days of the year. The result is 84 days 12 hours. Now if we add this 84 to Mesori 6, we come to Phaophi 27, the 23rd hour, which is the time of conception. In other words, if we go from Phaophi 27 to Mesori 6, the total is 280 days.

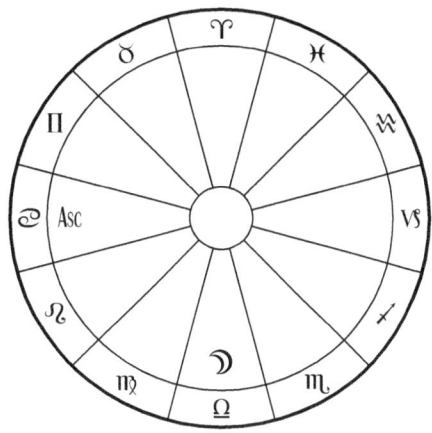

We will now demonstrate this using many methods, all leading straight to the answer. Given the birth date, let us determine the time <from conception> to birth. If the Moon is found to be in the hemisphere above the Earth, calculate the degrees from the Descendant to the Moon's degree-position and assign 2 ½ to each 30° of arc. Then add this sum to the minimum factor (258), and you will find the conception to have been that many days previous. Count this amount back from the birth date, and you will find the date of the conception to be where the count stops.

If you want another method, calculate the degrees from the Moon's degree-position to the Ascendant and assign 2 ½ <days> to each 30°; then subtract this from the mean factor (273). The date of conception will have been that many days previous. Likewise if the Moon is in the hemisphere below the Earth, calculate the degrees from the Ascendant to the Moon, then assign 2 ½ to each 30° division. Summing up, add this to the mean factor (273). The date of conception will have been that many days previous. Or, calculate the degrees from the Moon to the Descendant and figure the total number of days by adding 2 ½ for each 30° division and subtracting the result from 288. The date of conception will have been that many days previous.

For example, so that my readers may understand the determination: Hadrian year 4, Mechir 13/14, hour 1 of the night; the Moon in Scorpio 7°, the Ascendant in Virgo 7°. Since the Moon is found to be in the hemisphere beneath the Earth, I take the degrees from the Ascendant to the Moon; this is 60°. To each 30° I assign 2 ½, for a result of 5 days. I add this to the mean factor (273), and the result is 278. The conception

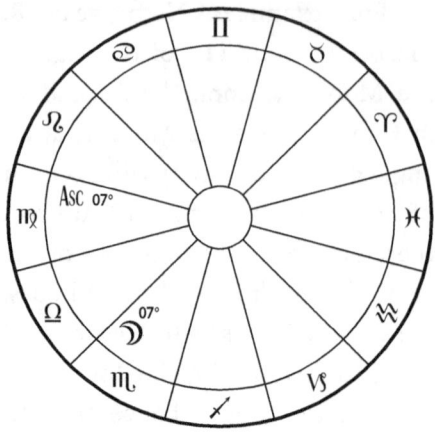

was that many days ago. I count back <278> days from the hour of birth; the conception day is Pachon 11.

Alternatively, I subtract the 5 days of the distance <from the Ascendant to the Moon> from 92, for a result of 87. (The mean factor is 273, which leaves a remainder of 92 when subtracted from 365 days.) If we add 87 to Mechir 14 and count this off from the birth date, we come to Pachon 11.

If you calculate the degrees from the Moon to the Descendant, i.e., Pisces 7°, the total is 120°. Take 2 ½ for each 30°, for a total of 10 days. Now if I subtract this from the maximum factor (288), the result is 278. If you count this amount back from the day of birth and calculate the Moon, you will find it to have been in the Ascendant at the delivery.

If the Moon is in the hemisphere above the Earth, take the distance in degrees from it to the Ascendant, assign 2 ½ to each 30° division, and find the total number of days. If you wish, add 92 to this and count off the sum from the birth date forwards; the date of conception will be where the count stops. Vice-versa, calculate from the date which you determined <to be the date of conception> forward to the date of birth, and you will know the number of days. If the Moon is in the hemisphere beneath the Earth, you will calculate from the Ascendant to the Moon: determining the distance in degrees, assign 2 ½ days to each 30°. Subtract this from 92, and add the result to the birth date. Count from there forwards. That will be the date of conception. Count back from the birth date the amount which you added to the <mean> factor (273).

Another example: Trajan year 17, Mesori 2, hour 11 ½; the Sun in Leo 5°, the Moon in Libra 26°, the Ascendant in Capricorn 24°. Since the Moon is in the hemisphere above the Earth, I take the distance from it to the Ascendant, which is very nearly 96°. To each 30° I assign 2 ½ for a result of 7 ½ days. I add this to 92, and the sum is 99 ½. I count from the birth date forwards and arrive at Athyr 6. Vice-versa <I can count> from Athyr 6 to the birth date as done earlier; the total days are 266. The conception was that number of days previous. If I do not want to add the 7 to 92, I subtract it from 273, for a result of 266. I count this number back from the birth date. Calculating the Moon, I find it in Capricorn, in the Ascendant.

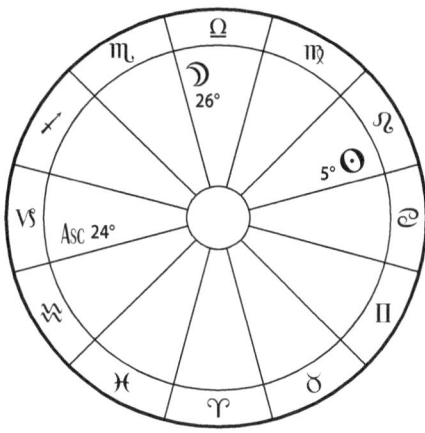

The Moon at the nativity will indicate in which sign the Ascendant of the conception was located. The Moon's degree-position at the nativity will also be the position of the Ascendant at the conception. Other astrologers calculate the Moon by doubling the degree-position of the nativity's Ascendant. Alternatively they take one-fourth of the Sun's degree-position at the birth and consider the sign in trine to the right of that point to be the Ascendant of the conception.

Therefore we will not go astray if we henceforth seek the answers for all nativities using the system given above. Let this be the divinely compelling manner of our future method for solving nativities.

22. Seven-Month Children

We will append another method to determine if the infant spends a full term in the womb, or less—in which case premature death, miscarriages, difficult childbirths, and fatalities, as well as the birth of seven-month children, will occur. The determination is as follows: in each case I note the date (month, day) of the birth in the year prior to the nativity, and I calculate the Moon. I note in which sign it is located. Next I note the date (month, day) of the birth in the year following the nativity (i.e., two years <later>), and again I calculate the Moon. Having done so, I compare its position <then to its position> in the prior year. If I find in both years that the Moons are trine with the Moon's position at the nativity, I forecast that the conception will be carried to term. If in both years the Moons are square with the Moon at the nativity, the native's gestation period will be the minimum factor, 258 days. If the Moon of the preceding year is trine and the Moon of the following year is square, he will be 269 days in the womb. Conversely if the Moon of the preceding year is square and the Moon of the following year is trine, he will be in the womb the same 269 days.

If the Moon of the preceding year is square and the Moon of the following year is turned away, he will have an eight-month gestation period and will be stillborn. Likewise if <the Moon> of the first year is trine and that of the second year is turned away, the infant will not survive. If in the two years the Moons are found to be in no aspect with the Moon at the nativity, the infant will be still-born or will be aborted with danger to the mother. If the Moons of the two years are in opposition <to the Moon of the nativity> and are in harmony, the infant will be of seven-month term. If the Moon of the preceding year is in opposition and the Moon of the following year is trine (i.e., with the Moon at the nativity or with the Ascendant), the infant will be of seven-month term. The same will be true if the Moon is square. If the Moon of the preceding year is square and the Moon of the following year is in opposition, the infant will be of seven-month term. The Sun has the same effect when it is in opposition to the sign in which the new Moon occurred.

The Ancients wrote about this topic, darkly and mysteriously. We have cast light on it.

Book II

The *Anthologies* of Vettius Valens of Antioch: Book II

In the previous treatise we set forth the introductory and educational material, as well as the forecasts for combinations of stars. <We were led to write this> not so much because of any literary rivalry, but as a consequence of our experiences. Now, continuing with our discussion, we will outline the general bases <of nativities> and the distinctions of the Places.

1. The Triangles

When the zodiacal circle is subdivided according to similarities and differences, we find two *sects*, solar and lunar, day and night. The Sun, being fiery, is most related to Aries, Leo, and Sagittarius, and this triangle of the Sun is called "of the day-sect" because it too is fiery by nature. The Sun has attached Jupiter and Saturn to this sect as his co-workers and guardians of the things which he accomplishes: Jupiter as a reflection of the Sun and as his successor to the kingship, a partisan of good, and the bestower of glory and life; Saturn on the other hand as a servant of evil and of downfall, and a depriver of years <of life>. Therefore the Sun is the lord of this triangle for day births; for night births Jupiter succeeds to the throne; Saturn works with both.

Next the Moon, being near the Earth, is allotted the houserulership of Taurus, Virgo, and Capricorn, a triangle earthy in nature and the next in order. It has Venus and Mars as members of the same sect: Venus (as is reasonable) acts as a benefactor and distributes glory and years; Mars acts as the bane of nativities. Therefore for night births the Moon has preeminence; in the second place is Venus; in the third is Mars. For day births Venus will lead; the Moon will operate second; Mars, third.

Next is the airy triangle of Gemini, Libra, and Aquarius. For day births Saturn will rule this; Mercury will operate second; Jupiter, third. For night births Mercury will lead; Saturn will come second; Jupiter, third.

In the same fashion, next is the moist triangle of Cancer, Scorpio, and Pisces. Mars will have the houserulership for night births; in the second place is Venus; in the third the Moon. For day births Venus will lead; after it comes Mars; then the Moon.

Note that Mercury is common and works with the two sects to a special degree to accentuate the good or the bad, and to accentuate the individual characteristics and configurations of each star.

2. The Distinguishing Characteristics of the Triangles, the Houserulers, the Helpers, and the Sects of the Sun and the Moon—for Day or Night Births

An examination of the distinguishing characteristics of the previously mentioned triangles, along with the lofty or mediocre fortune of each person's nativity, will be indicative. For day nativities, it will be necessary to examine the Sun: 1) in which triangle it lies; 2) its predominant houseruler and its helper, viz. whether it is at, following, or preceding an angle, rising or setting, and whether it is in its own signs; 3) which benefic or malefic it has in aspect. Having determined all this, then make the prediction. If <the houseruler> happens to be in the Ascendant or at the Midheaven or is in one of the operative signs, <astrologers> forecast a fortunate and illustrious nativity; if it follows an angle, a nativity of moderate fortune; if it precedes an angle, a base and unfortunate nativity. It is also necessary to see how the Sun itself is situated and which stars it has in aspect. For night nativities it will be necessary to inspect the Moon in a similar fashion and to determine how the predominant houseruler of the triangle and its assistant are configured, as was stated above.

For nativities which are badly situated (whether day or night births), if the predominant houseruler is unfavorably located, but its successor is at an angle or otherwise configured well, the native will experience ups and downs during his early years until the rising time of the sign or until the cyclical return of the chronocrator, but will afterwards be vigorous and effective—except for being unsteady and anxious. If the preceding houseruler is favorably situated and the succeeding one unfavorably, the native will fulfill his promise well at first, but afterwards will be brought low, starting at the time of the rising of the sign in which the succeeding houseruler is unfavorably situated. (We will clarify in more detail the determination of the chronocrator at the appropriate time.) If both houserulers are well situated, good fortune will be enduring and will be remarkable (unless some malefic is opposed or in superior aspect), and the nativity will not take a turn for the worse. Whenever any star is a houseruler and just precedes an angle, it will be negative and a diminisher of fortune: it puts men in the power of others; it brings men into vicissitudes and reduces their rank; it afflicts them with injuries, diseases, and criminal charges, as well as poverty.

Now then, for those born during the day: if the Sun is found in Aries, Leo, or Sagittarius, it is best for it to be at an angle. If it follows an angle, and if the stars of its sect are similarly situated, and if Mars is not in opposition or in square, then <the Sun> will be considered to be indicative of good fortune. If the situation is reversed, the opposite will be the case. If the Sun is found in Taurus, Virgo, or Capricorn (for day births), it will be necessary to investigate first how Venus is configured, second the Moon, and third Mars, and to see what stars they have in aspect. In the same way, if the Sun is in the next triangle, Gemini, Libra, or Aquarius (for day births), it will be necessary to look at Saturn, then Mercury, then Jupiter. The same for the triangle Cancer, Scorpio, and Pisces: if the Sun is there (for day births), it will be necessary to look at Venus, then Mars, then the Moon, to see if they are at angles. Having determined all this, then make the prediction. For night births, it is necessary to look at the Moon in the same manner.

It is best if the stars of the day sect are found at angles in their own triangles or in operative places; the same is true for the stars of the night sect. If they are in other triangles or in the opposite sect, prosperity will be less and will be subject to anxiety. If the houserulers and their helpers are unfavorably situated, it will be necessary to examine the Lot of Fortune and its houseruler. If they are found to be at an angle or just following an angle, with benefics in aspect, then the native will have some good fortune and rank. He will be subject to vicissitudes and reversals on occasion, but he will not be totally at a loss. If even these <the Lot and its houseruler> are badly situated, affairs must be considered mediocre, even harsh: men will find it hard to succeed in their undertakings; they will be in need, poverty-stricken; they will blaspheme the gods. If these places have malefics in aspect, men will be toilers, vagrants, captives, abject, wretched, disabled, and endangered. But if the Lot of Fortune and its houseruler have benefics in aspect—even though they themselves are unfavorably situated—men will get by on others' pity or be adopted by others, and they will lead a respectable life for some time, receiving a share of business, trusts, or gifts. They will not, however, continue their life without disturbance or without criticism.

It will be necessary to look at the aspects of every houseruler and the arrangement of the configurations, to see if they are appropriate or the reverse. If, for example, Saturn is found in opposition or in square for night births, it will bring about reversals, ruin, dangers, injuries, and diseases, as well as sluggishness in enterprises. For day births, Mars causes hot, reckless men, precarious in their activities and in their livelihoods. They experience imprisonment, trials, abuse, cuts, burns, bleeding, and accidents/falls. But if these stars happen to be configured properly, in their own sects, they are actively positive. As a result, these stars are not to be considered malefics in all cases; they can be bestowers of good. Particularly if Saturn (for day births) has a favorable relationship with the houseruler and has Jupiter and the Sun in aspect, it then makes men wealthy, famous, profiting from legacies, lords of estates and slaves, guardians and supervisors of others' affairs. For night births, however, if Saturn is configured well and has a relationship with the houseruler, it will also cause the loss of what was gained, reduction in rank, and infamy. Let the same considerations be true for Mars: for night births it grants leadership, generalship, public commands of the masses; for day births (if Mars is in operative places), it brings about the previously mentioned circumstances, but it then turns them into reversals, fears, and oppositions; it makes leadership subject to factionalism and terror. It brings attacks of enemies and uprisings of the mob, famines and plagues on cities, assaults, fires, dangerous crises.

In the same way, the benefics will take on the character of malefics whenever they are situated badly as houserulers. If they happen to be at angles while their houseruler just precedes an angle, their ability to do good will be weakened. In any type <of forecast/nativity> it will be necessary to examine how the houseruler of the houseruler is situated and what stars it has in aspect. If the overall houseruler is unfavorably situated, but its ruler <=ruler of its sign> is configured well, then the native will have help and a basis of livelihood and rank proportional to the position of the star.

3. The Lot of Fortune and its Houseruler

Since I want to make the topic of good fortune most secure and precise, I am moving on to the Lot of Fortune, the most influential and most potent place. Just as the King has mystically revealed in the beginning of his XIIIth Book: "Next in order, it will be necessary (for day nativities) to count accurately the distance from the Sun to the Moon, then to measure off in the opposite direction an equal distance from the Ascendant, and to inspect the resulting place: which star is its ruler and which star or stars are at this point and all the square or trine asterisms of this place. From this study/combination of the places, make a clear determination of the natives' affairs."

In his book, *The Terms*, Petosiris explains this place in the same way. Others treat this subject in other ways, ways which we will publish when necessary, along with other methods which clarify the topic of good fortune. Now we must speak about the matter at hand.

4. The Star Which Holds the Ascendant or the Lot

If Saturn is allotted the hour or the Lot <of Fortune> and is in the Ascendant, with Mars not in opposition, the native will be fortunate in activities controlled by Saturn. If Jupiter is in aspect, he will be doubly fortunate; if Venus is in aspect, he will be fortunate through the help of women or eunuchs. If Mars is in conjunction or in opposition, the native will suffer disturbance and reversals. If Mercury shares the Ascendant with Saturn, the native will be handicapped in his hearing.

Jupiter, when allotted the hour or the Lot and in the Ascendant, causes men to be very fortunate from youth. If Mars is in configuration (at the same center or in trine), men will advance by means of brilliant campaigns and will win the acquisition of a livelihood. If Saturn is also in aspect, men become exalted; if Venus is in aspect, they become even more exalted. If Mercury is in aspect, men are involved in exchanges.

Mars, when allotted the hour or the Lot and in the Ascendant, urges men toward the military. If Jupiter is in aspect, the native advances in status; if Venus is, he attains an extraordinary status. If Mercury is in conjunction, he will accept a deposit given without witnesses, but will later deny it. If Jupiter is in conjunction, he will acquire much property from many people, but after his death it will all revert to the royal treasury.

Venus, when allotted the hour or the Lot <and in the Ascendant>, indicates great good and makes men far-renowned. If Mercury is in conjunction, it makes musicians. But if, given the preceding configuration, Saturn is in opposition to them or is in a superior aspect, it robs men of what they have.

Mercury, when allotted the hour or the Lot and in the Ascendant, makes men fortunate. If Jupiter is in conjunction or square, men will have control of tribunals and cities. If Saturn is in conjunction as well, the control, honors, goods, and success will be double.

The Sun inheriting the hour or Fortune and in the Ascendant: if Jupiter is in conjunction or square, the native will be fortunate. If Mercury is also in conjunction, he will succeed through his words. If Mars is in conjunction or square along with Jupiter, the native will be great, a master of life and death. If, given the previous configuration, Saturn is square or in opposition, the native will fall into mishaps and penalties.

The Moon, when inheriting the hour or the Lot of Fortune <and in the Ascendant>, makes men great, especially when it is in its own triangle. If Venus is in conjunction or square, the native will be thought worthy of great honor. If Mars is also with the Moon, he will be master of life and death. If Saturn is, he will control many districts. If Jupiter is in conjunction or square, they will be great kings. If none of the above is the case, and if Mercury is configured with the Moon, success will be from words and special aptitudes. If Mars is also in conjunction or square, it makes tyrants and great lords. If Mars is in opposition to the Moon, with no benefics in aspect, the child will be exposed; but if a benefic is in aspect, the exposed child will survive and be reared. Likewise if Mars appears in square or is found in a superior aspect, it entangles the native in wanderings, separations, and vicissitudes. But if Venus is in square at an angle, men will be wronged by women. If Saturn is in conjunction in a lewd sign, men will be pimps, and if Mars is also in the configuration, then men will hire their wives out to others. If Saturn is square with the Moon or is in exact opposition (to the degree), the native will have an interruption of nurture and will be abandoned by his parents. If Mercury is square or in opposition to the Moon, men will be contrary-minded, always in opposition, involved in slanders and accusations from a superior. If, in addition, a malefic is in the aspect or in the configuration, it will bring discredit and condemnation. Jupiter lying exactly opposite the Moon causes sterility and the opposition of superiors.

In general, malefics which behold the luminaries and the Ascendant with no benefics <in aspect> make men short-lived. If the ruler of the Ascendant lies in its proper place or in its own sect, it becomes the bestower of <long> lifespans. If it is configured with the lord of the Lot <of Fortune>, the native becomes full of years and luck. If the ruler happens to be setting, the native becomes short-lived. If a malefic is in conjunction or in superior aspect with the Moon, the infants will not survive.

5. The <XII> Place of the Bad Daimon. Many Configurations

If the malefics happen to be in this place, they will cause great wounds and traumas, especially if they are in their proper face. If the Lot of Fortune is present in this Place and some <star> rules it, there will be no help, not even during transits. They have become enemies from the beginning, from the moment of birth. In the same way, benefics found in this Place will not bestow their benefits. Whenever these three stars fall in this sign (the rulers of the Ascendant, of the Lot, and of Daimon), they make men unfortunate and disgraced, those lacking their daily bread. Many will hold out their hands <for alms>.

6. The <XI> Place of the Good Daimon. Many Configurations. The Hearing and the Beholding Signs Must Also Be Investigated

If the benefics are in the sign of the Good Daimon, located in their proper places and in their proper faces, they make men illustrious and rich from youth—even more so if they are trine from the right with the Lot of Fortune or sextile with the Ascendant. If they are in a listening or beholding sign they provide even more and greater benefits. If one of the benefics appears in opposition to the Good Daimon and its houseruler is also present, these stars bring bigger and better benefits and successes. If malefics are in conjunction with the Good Daimon, they cannot do any evil. It is most efficacious if the houserulers of the Lot, the Ascendant, and the Good Daimon happen to be rising or if most stars are in conjunction or in aspect with these in operative signs; they then make men glorious and extremely wealthy. <If Jupiter is in the Place of the Good Daimon, the native will be fortunate, possess a good income, and have many children. If it is also the ruler of the Lot of Fortune, the native will be rich and blessed. If Mercury is in conjunction with it, the native will be an imperial steward and will be happy in his children.>[1]

<7. The X Place: Midheaven>

Both benefics and malefics rejoice in this place if they have been assigned the Lot, the Ascendant, or Daimon. If any of the <benefics> are in it when rising, or if they have contact with the Moon, tyrants and kings are born, governors of districts, men known by name in many places. The ruler of this Place, if situated favorably, makes vigorous/successful men; if situated unfavorably, it makes feeble/unsuccessful men. If <the ruler> is setting and a malefic is in conjunction or in opposition to this Place, it makes failures, as well as sterile or childless men.

8. The IX Place of the God Sun, just before the Midheaven. The Ninth Place from the Ascendant. It Has Many Configurations

If benefics happen to be in this Place and have been assigned the Ascendant or Fortune, the native will be blessed, reverent, a prophet of the great god; in fact he will be obeyed like a god. If <benefics> are not there, and if Mercury alone is in aspect, the native will be involved in soothsaying; he will expound his craft to the masses.[2] He will become a royal clerk from his middle years.

---

[1] MR: The passage in brackets has been transposed from the end of chapter 8K;9P to its proper place here.

[2] MR: or "…the native will be involved in finance; he will control the masses through his business dealings." (Rhetorius in *CCAG* 8.4, pp. 163–64)

But if malefics are in conjunction and rule the previously mentioned places (the Ascendant and Fortune), or if they are in aspect from the right with the Lot, the native will be a tyrant: he will found some cities; he will sack others; he will pillage many people most wickedly. If Daimon or Fortune happens to be in the <XII> Place of the Bad Daimon, but the houserulers of the Lot and of the Ascendant are in this Place <of the God>, the native will be involved in very many evils, in travel, and will lose whatever he has gained, or he will take refuge in temples because of his desires or pains.

9. The VIII Place of Death. Various Views

Benefics appearing in this place are ineffectual and weak, and they do not bestow their proper benefits. If in addition they rule the Ascendant and the Lot of Fortune, they are even more ineffectual and variable. If malefics are in conjunction and rule the Lot, the native is a vagrant, losing whatever he may have gained. If the Lot falls in this Place and if malefics are in conjunction and are houserulers of the Lot, the native will be poor, unable to clothe himself. If <malefics> also rule the Ascendant, he will be abject his whole life. If the houseruler of the Lot or of the Ascendant is under the rays of the Sun, the native will stretch out his hands to beg. If Mercury alone is in this Sign and is ruler of Intelligence (as Daimon is called), it makes fools, dullards, those handicapped in speech, illiterates. If Fortune <is there>, the native, besides being dull, will also be stupid and poor, especially if <the Lot> is under the Sun's rays. If under these circumstances malefics are also in conjunction, the native will be deaf and dumb. Only the Moon, when its light is waxing, seems to rejoice in this Place.

10. The <VII> Place of the Descendant

Benefics in this Place and ruling the Ascendant or the Lot of Fortune indicate good things for the native: inheritances, sudden acquisition of other property, and benefits from a death. If the benefics are not in their own places, men are less prosperous, but not poverty-stricken. If Mercury alone is in conjunction and in its proper face, the native will make gains in his old age and will be entrusted with cities and the affairs of kings. If malefics are in this Place and rule the Lot or the Ascendant and are in their proper faces, the native's life will be subject to ups and downs, especially in old age, but he will not be in poverty. He will spend the income derived from calumny and wickedness/vituperation. If malefics rule the Lots but are not in their proper face or in their own sect, the native will lead a wretched old age; a few will come into prisons for a time and into decrepitude and disease. If Jupiter is in aspect from the right, men enter temple service because of sickness; they are troubled and suffer from hemorrhages and disease of the genitals or fingers. If Mercury is with Mars in the Setting Sign, men become accomplices in banditry and murder; as a result they perish miserably thereafter. Malefics setting while out of their own signs cause suicides. Benefics make men with much experience and those who are fortunate in old age.

11. The VI Place. The Place of Mars

If benefics happen to be in this Place, the native will lose whatever he possesses; his property will not stay with him. He will suffer loss because of fines when advanced in years. If the Sun is in this Place and rules the Lot of Fortune or the Ascendant, it causes the native to be condemned by the highest authority. If Saturn rules <these places>, the native will be a wanderer, prone to give offense, and he will flee his homeland, barely keeping himself alive. If Jupiter rules the Lot or the Ascendant, the native will lose his property in civil suits. If Venus rules, he will suffer trials and penalties because of a woman. Such men, being disagreeable, are insensible to love. If Mars rules, it causes wounds and diseases in the limb indicated by the sign <where Mars is>, and it makes naked beggars who come to a miserable end. If Mercury rules the Lot or the Ascendant, it makes plotters, thieves, slanderers, and men who are reviled in public. If the Moon is in this Place, the native will be a slave, helpless—unless the rest are in conjunction with the Moon: if the other stars are situated favorably, the native can be free and respectable, even though the Moon is in <the VI Place of> Bad Fortune.

12. The V Place. Many Theorems

If benefics hold the Ascendant or the Lot of Fortune, the native will be great, will lead the masses, and will make laws for them. Venus will be especially gracious if it rules the Ascendant or the Lot. Especially if Venus is in its proper face or in its own place, it makes men wealthy and honored. The same is true for all the stars: if they govern the Ascendant or the Lot, they produce the good that is appropriate to their nature and to Good Fortune. If Mars happens to be situated as specified, men will be rulers of all sorts of places: governors, tyrants, and masters of life and death—not only over lesser men but also over men of high rank. If Saturn is in this Place, men will be masters of estates, flocks, and herds; they will establish towns and villages. If the Sun is in this Place, men will be friends of great lords, associates of kings, governors of temples. If Mercury is in this Place men will be successful through words and worthy of much money. If the Moon is configured well, holds the Lot or the Ascendant, and is in this Place along with its <the Moon's> houseruler, the native will be long-lived, growing old in prosperity. The benefics help greatly while passing through this Place; the malefics cannot do harm.

13. The IV Place—Lower Midheaven

If benefics rule the Ascendant or Fortune, and are in this Place, the native will make his living in temples. If benefics are assigned the Archetypal Lot, and are houserulers at Lower Midheaven, the native will be given revelations by gods and through visions of ghostly shapes. If Mars is here with them and is assigned Fortune and the Ascendant, the native will live a troubled life, disgraced, falling into difficulties, engaged in criminal activity with others, and suffering a violent/self-inflicted death.

It must be observed that this Place implies good repute after death and bequests to heirs. If malefics are in this Place, the native will bequeath his property to whomever he wishes.

14. The III Place. The Place of the Goddess Moon

If the Moon is in this Place, is assigned the Ascendant or the Lot, and is in its proper face, the native will be great and a master of many good things. He will rule a city; he will give orders to many men; he will be obeyed; and he will be master of treasuries. If the Sun should also be in this Place with the Moon when the Moon is just past new, the native will be a priest or priestess of the great goddess and will have an unsurpassable livelihood. If Saturn is here with the Moon, the native will be subject to God's wrath, will be punished, will often come into trials, and will blaspheme the gods many times because of what has happened to him. If Jupiter is with the Moon, the native will be a prophet, fortunate, rich, famous, and will be master of many good things. If Mars is in conjunction with the Moon, he will be successful, but wicked: he will embezzle deposits, will get his living through the murder or robbery of others, and will travel widely. If Mars is appropriately situated in its own faces, the native will be a governor of towns and cities (depending on the character of the nativity), but he will also be unjust, a perjurer, and covetous of others' goods. He will perish suddenly because of the wrath of authority. If Venus in her own places rules the <III> Place of the Goddess and the Lot of Fortune (especially for night births), the native will be rich and well liked by women. Some will be royal governors, rulers of towns, because the goddess <Venus> has been assigned the Lot of Fortune in the House of the Goddess. If Mercury is with the Moon in the Sign of the Goddess and rules the Lot of Fortune or the Ascendant, the native will foretell everyone's future and will share in the mysteries of the gods.

15. The II Place, Called the Gate of Hades. The Place Rising After the Ascendant

In this Place the benefics do no good, the malefics make men sluggish and injured, unable to wade through their lives to the end. If the Lot is in this Place, and if malefics are the houserulers of the Lot or the Ascendant, the native becomes a cemetery guard, living his life outside the city gates. Saturn ruling the Lot of Fortune and in this Place makes dead-souled men, those weak in body and suffering chains/imprisonment for a long time, until the completion of the chronocratorship of the star. Jupiter in this Place causes expenditure of the native's resources until the end so that nothing is left; it brings the gift of children, but not with good fortune. Mars in this Place and houseruler of the Lot and of the Ascendant makes men who are prone to give offence, are subject to penalties, and whose actions are hindered. Some become captives, but are later freed. If Mars (in its own degrees or signs) is in charge of the Lot of Fortune, when the Lot is in this <II> Place, men become jailers, making a livelihood in prisons or a living among the cells. If the Sun is in this Place, and if it is houseruler of the Lot or the Ascendant, and in its own house, <with Mars being in the Ascendant> or in the places of Saturn, the native will lose his sight in the chronocratorship of Mars, will be plundered of his ancestral property, and will become a beggar. If Venus is in this Place and is houseruler of the Lot or the Ascendant, it will bring public, disreputable occupations if Venus happens to be at its morning rising. Mercury in this Place and located under the rays of the Sun makes stupid, illiterate men. If it is also ruler of the Second Fortune (the one called Daimon), it makes men deaf and dumb. If it is rising, men engage in curious arts, attempting what they have not learned <from others>, but still succeeding in their science. If the Moon is in this Place with Saturn in the Ascendant, the opposite happens: the native will suffer from cataracts and glaucoma.

16. Nine Names of the Places

<Name	Significance>
The God <IX>	the father
The Goddess <III>	the mother
The Good Daimon <XI>	children
The Good Fortune <V>	marriage
The Bad Daimon <XII>	diseases
The Bad Fortune <VI>	injuries
The Lot of Fortune and The Ascendant <I>	life and livelihood

Daimon	mental activity
Midheaven <X>=MC	action/occupation
Love	desire
Necessity	enemies

17. The Trine Influences of the Stars on Prosperity or Poverty. The Configurations of Trine, Sextile, and Opposition

Jupiter trine with the Sun indicates great and glorious men. If the Sun is in the Ascendant, the indication applies to the father and to the nativity. If it is at an angle, it applies to the father: it indicates that he is famous, but less so than under the previous configuration. It indicates nothing unusual for the nativity if no other factor improves the outlook. If Saturn is trine with the Sun from the left and the Sun is in the Ascendant, the rank will be higher: such men will own much land, have many estates, and become rich. If Mars is also in aspect along with Jupiter, the configuration indicates tyrants; especially if the Sun is in the Ascendant, such men will control many districts and armies. If Saturn is also in aspect, the native's father will be great, the leader of arms and armies (if indeed the rest of the aspects work towards his greatness), but he will not be a tyrant, warlike, or ferocious.

If Mars is in opposition to the Sun, with Jupiter and Saturn trine with the Sun from the right, the native will lead the masses magnificently and with high rank. If Saturn is in opposition to the Sun (under the stated conditions), the native will be opposed by family and friends, but he will prevail and subdue them. If Saturn and Mars are trine with the Sun, with Jupiter in opposition in its own degrees or signs, the native is imperious and noble. If the configuration is sextile, the forecast is less <spectacular>.

Venus sextile to the Sun in the morning sky indicates that the father and the native will be charming and distinguished. If Venus is configured in Good Daimon or in Good Fortune, the native will be thought worthy (by women) of the purple and of golden ornaments.

Saturn square with the Sun and on the left harms the ancestral property while the native's father is still alive, especially when Saturn is in feminine signs or in opposing degrees. If Saturn is in opposition, the situation is much worse: the native will be overwhelmed by wounds and suffering, and will be betrayed by relatives and clients. If Saturn is on the right, the forecast will be worse. If it should be in the Ascendant or at the Midheaven, the reversals will be less.

Mars square with the Sun is bad for the father and the native. It brings injuries and suffering. Mars in opposition or in afflicted signs or degrees causes injuries to the joints. If Mars is square on the right in the tenth <sign from the

Sun>, worse will happen: in addition to everything else, he will go insane.

Jupiter square with the Sun and in base degrees or signs becomes unpleasant: <this configuration> ruins the star's good influence and turns it to the opposite. But, Jupiter in glorious degrees or signs, and especially at an angle, is productive of rank and wealth. Jupiter in opposition to the Sun is most unpleasant: not only is all of Jupiter's good influence quenched, but the native will feel the anger of superiors and the hostility of the masses. The exact-to-the-degree positions of the square and opposition are harsh.

For night nativities, Mars trine with the Sun, especially when in feminine signs and on the right, indicates great and famous men, masters of life and death—provided that the rest of the aspects in the nativity agree. In addition, if Jupiter is trine to the right, it makes great dynasts, rulers of cities and leaders of the masses. If the nativity is female and Venus is in conjunction, the native will be a queen and will have power over many districts; she will become a benefactor and be unsurpassed. For male or female nativities, if the one star occupies its proper place and the other happens to be in its own triangle, there is no opposition: they become king of kings, provided the one <star> is houseruler and the other is co-houseruler and master of the nativity, and that they both rule the Lot of Fortune and the Ascendant. If they are in masculine signs, fortune will be less, in fact much worse. Sextile configurations have a weaker effect, both for good or for the opposite.

...

For day nativities, if Mars should be square with the Moon while on the left and in another's degrees or signs, it will be the cause of many reversals and afflictions for the mother, as well as reduction in rank. Men will be subject to travel; some become soldiers, toilsome and violent. These things happen, provided that the nativity is not base-born in other respects and that the master of the star, or its helper, or a fellow sect-member are not in places which do not have the Ascendant in aspect. If this condition does obtain <the Ascendant is not in aspect>, men become captives and die by execution. If Mars is in opposition (the other configurations being the same), bad results are stronger and more difficult to avoid. Indeed if it should appear square to the right, men suddenly lose everything. (The difference between square and opposition is great!) If Mars is in Aries <its sign> and the Moon in Cancer <its sign>, the results are quite different and are like those for trine. Likewise if Mars is in Scorpio <its sign>, in opposition to the Moon in Taurus, not only will there be no reversals of fortune, but in fact the stars will produce success and high rank.

For night nativities, Venus trine with the Moon and in feminine signs makes men charming and fortunate. Some rule the masses and are thought worthy of the purple and of golden ornaments—depending on the greatness of the nativity. They become philosophers, artists, scholars, and members of the circle of king's friends. If both <Venus and the Moon> indicate the the birth is "royal," because one is the houseruler and the other the master of the nativity, the configuration is dictatorial: men become king of kings, famous, merry. When sextile with each other, they have a more moderate power. When <the stars> are Good Daimon and Good Fortune, the effects are the same as if they were trine, especially if a tropic or an equinoctial sign lies between; even more so, if the configuration beholds Pisces and Taurus.

Venus square with the Moon makes men successful, charming, and wealthy, all that the trine configuration provides—especially if Venus is in its own sign or degree—but with some ups and downs. What these stars give is easily lost. If the stars are not in their own signs, not in their own sect, or are in contrary degrees, they become the cause of violence, unsteadiness, and infamy due to women or vice. If they are in opposition under these circumstances, worse results.

For day nativities, Mercury as a morning star trine with the Moon makes men inventive, successful, clever, and excitable. If the nativity is quite elevated, it makes secretaries of kings, rulers of cities or districts, scholars, orators, mathematicians. Mercury as an evening star, especially for night births, makes erudite men, philosophers and initiates of the mysteries. If the birth is lofty because of the other stars' <influences>, it makes noble men, those honored by the masses and acquainted with the great and with kings. Mercury does this by being co-ruler with the star which supplies the primary influence.[3] If it is in an inoperative place, it cannot apply any of its own influence. (In general it will be seen of all nativities that any star has the same effects in trine as it does when in conjunction in the same sign.)

Mercury sextile with the Moon has a duller and weaker influence than do the previous configurations. Mercury square makes men keen and shrewd, but this keenness turns to criminality and the men become malicious, slanderers, acting with trickery and violence, inspired by nothing healthy. In addition to the previous <malign> influence, if the two are in opposition, the native is contrary-minded and ungracious in his activities, and so is harmed by what befalls him.

Mercury trine with Saturn, especially if they are in their own triangles, makes royal stewards, procurators, and those who supervise shipping, estates, and similar operations. They become shrewd, intelligent, and single-minded. Mercury and Saturn square with each other make everything dull: they make men sluggish, quarrelsome, and self-willed, slow in action, and feeding off calumny, treachery, trickery, and violence. They also become practically

---

[3] *Marginal note from the manuscripts:* As a helper, it causes these effects.

mute and hard of hearing. Mars in aspect with Saturn or Mercury cancels the previously mentioned handicap in speaking, if they are not in their houses or terms, if they are not exchanging domiciles, if the Moon is not in aspect from the right, if they have no contact with it <the Moon>, and if they are not the overall houserulers or co-houserulers. That's how strong these slight changes are! If they are in opposition, they separate sisters by death.

Mercury in the Ascendant or at the Midheaven makes young men learned, intelligent, educated. They do not, however, get the benefits of their talents, because the gifts of these stars will be frozen by the opposing configuration of the stars. If they are precisely in opposition, to the degree, their effects will reach much further: the native will be handicapped in hearing and in speech; he will take refuge in temples, prophesying or even being mentally distracted.

Mercury trine with Jupiter is indicative of great deeds, especially if Mercury is at morning rising. Men become secretaries of kings, of cities, or of the masses, or they become financial officials. Since Mercury is altogether concerned with occupations and provides the active influence, the native will have a high status and the possession of a livelihood, especially if Mercury is in operative signs. If the stars are sextile, they have the same effects, but to a lesser degree. If they are square and configured well, to some extent they bring possessions and status, but with hatred. If they are configured badly, they bring ruin along with hatred, and the opposition of superiors. If the stars are in opposition, they bring even greater slander, and men are at cross purposes and suffer ups and downs. If the stars are in opposition in the Bad Daimon, men will be crushed by the supreme authority, they will feel the effects of mass insurrections, and they will have few brothers, or will have quarrels with their brothers, children, or relatives.

Mercury trine with Mars or sextile to the right is indicative of quite varied activities: sometimes it makes secretaries, sometimes merchants, translators, mathematicians, lawyers, philosophers—all of them malignant, bitter, intelligent, lying. This star also makes arms instructors and gladiators. If Jupiter is configured with these, especially in operative places, it makes military men, often augurs, sacrificial priests, seers, and those who know more than men should. Mercury square causes even more varied activities than has been mentioned: magi, wanderers, sacrificial priests, doctors, astrologers, demagogues, bankers, counterfeiters, forgers, those making their living by crime, violence, and trickery. Men become thieves, perjurers, atheists, and those who prey on their fellows, are greedy for gain, who are defrauders—in short, those who have nothing admirable in them. As a result, they are involved in many evils and have experience of captivity, exile, and prison. <Mars and

Mercury> cause even worse, especially when they are in inoperative places or degrees. If both are at IC or in the Descendant, or if one is in the Descendant while the other is at IC, they cause murders; the native will be an accomplice and will make his living as a bandit. A few will be fratricides and their final end will be violent, especially if the stars include the Moon in their configuration. They will die violently/as suicides and will lie unburied. If the stars are in four-footed signs, men will be taken by beasts; if in anthropomorphic signs, by bandits; if in solid signs, men will die by falls from heights; if in fiery signs, from fires; if in moist signs, by shipwreck; if in tropic signs, in the arena. The stars do the same things when exchanging domiciles or in conjunction.

If one is houseruler and the other is master, and if Mercury is sextile or in conjunction with Venus, it will make the native intelligent, charming, artistic, fond of games, endowed with a sense of humor; sometimes poets, songwriters, declaimers, actors, mimes; sometimes athletes and victors in sacred games. These stars are productive of quite varied occupations. If the nativity is feminine, the women become musicians, promiscuous, living like prostitutes, of a literary bent, fond of recitations.

...

Venus trine with Saturn makes men severe, humorless, supercilious, rough in love and promiscuous, yet lying with base-born or elderly women, or with prostitutes. These men lie with the wives of their brothers or patrons, with those of their fathers, or with their stepmothers. Their wives sneak off and lie with their husbands' slaves or friends. It is, of course, necessary to note that predictions can change greatly in accord with the changes of sign and degree: the same configuration, even if the stars occur together, can indicate sordid men, those sleeping in their lusts and sometimes promiscuous; but often it can also indicate those who are unaffected by love, who only take enjoyment by themselves. <Venus and Saturn> square are much worse: the effects mentioned for the trine configuration become worse. Men take prostitutes as wives, and they become loathsome and depraved. It is even worse if the configuration is in the Descendant or at IC. The deterioration noted above becomes even worse if Mars in in conjunction, square, or opposition: men then act shamefully and are denounced by everyone. Often because of this they become a subject of scandal, are imprisoned, and meet a bad death. If these stars are in "lurking" signs or degrees, men enjoy impure passions and unnatural pleasures. If these stars are sextile with each other, their effects are the same as those attributed to the trine configuration, but dim and weak. If both are at morning rising in the east, they masculinize women, so that the women not only act like men in their daily life, but they even do the work of men when lying with other women. If these stars are evening stars, they feminize men: sometimes men serve as women when lying with men, but often they lose their sex organs.

Saturn trine with Jupiter indicates a favorable configuration. These stars make men landowners, masters of grainland and vineyards, grainfarmers, constructors of buildings, villages, and towns—but they are austere and supercilious. If the configuration is more exalted, with Mars in aspect from the right,[4] Saturn and Jupiter make men generals, leaders of land and sea forces, and they raise a few men to the kingship or to tyranny. If the configuration happens to be in the triangle of Saturn <Gemini Libra Aquarius>, especially if Jupiter is in Aquarius with Mars turned away, the stars make men humble and fearful, not brilliant in anything or sharing in any office, but rather choosing a retired, rustic life. The variations in occupations occur in accord with the differences of sign and place—but the stars do have the same effects when they are together in operative signs.

Saturn square with Jupiter dulls the good influence of Jupiter, especially if Saturn is on the right and rising. Then men succeed with great difficulty, they are subject to penalties, they make gains only with toil and pain, and they suffer loss in their children: some are childless, others see the deaths of their children. The Place of Brothers is damaging to them: these stars separate close, loving brothers by death and make the other brothers hateful and vicious, especially when the stars are not at the angles. When in opposition, these stars are most harsh and bring misery and setbacks.

Saturn trine with Mars points to those who are insecure in their livelihood and unable to endure hardships. They are stupid but violent in their actions. They either have few children or lose those that are born. These men become captives or are injured. Saturn square <with Mars> is much worse: their children are destroyed, also their brothers; brothers are separated from each other by hatred; they become incorrigible or are injured. They are prone to give offense in their actions and are encompassed by the hostility of great men and are plotted against by them. This configuration falls into great danger: men die violently from attacks of bandits or the enemy, or by shipwreck. A few go into captivity. They are often endangered by fire or sword. If Saturn and Mars are in opposition, they make the previously mentioned influences much stronger. In addition to the above, men become poor, distressed, unlucky; a few become porters, beasts of burden; they have toilsome and despised jobs.

There is, however, much variation in these configurations, not only with respect to the individual characteristics of the signs and degrees, but also with respect to the greatness of the nativity. If Jupiter, the Moon, and the Sun do

---

[4] *Marginal note:* as well as the Sun and Moon.

not behold this configuration, the birth is lowly. If they are in aspect from the right and one is the master of these stars and the other is the houseruler, then the previously mentioned effects happen: quite bad in <the IX Place of> the God and <the III Place of> the Goddess; to a lesser and fainter degree in <the XI Place of> Good Daimon and <the V Place of> Good Fortune; but worse and more intense in <the XII Place of> Bad Daimon, <the VI Place of> Bad Fortune, the Inactive and Shadowy Place. If the nativity is exalted and royal...

Jupiter trine with Mars, if one is the houseruler and the other the master, indicates great men, leaders and dictators, especially when these stars are in their own signs, triangles, or degrees, in operative signs, or when they have exchanged domiciles or terms, especially if they rule the Lot of Fortune or its houseruler. They make great affairs: kings, those in charge of the military (navies or armies), those who rebuild cities or those who destroy them. When sextile, these stars are less strong, just as with the former configurations, but if they are at an angle, they indicate that the evils which are mentioned do not loom over the native but over others. They become bunglers of army and naval battles; they become bandit chiefs, violent leaders, sadists, drinkers of blood. If the nativity is professional, e.g., a notary or a lawyer, the native becomes an informer. If the configuration includes Mercury, and if the Moon has contact with Mars, the situation is quite terrible: such men become worse than wild beasts.

Jupiter square with Mars is strong, if one is in the Ascendant and the other is either at the Midheaven or in <the XI Place of> Good Daimon. This configuration will be stronger than that of trine, especially if a tropic sign is between. (If Jupiter and Mars are in the same sign, they are even stronger.) When square, they have the same effect as when trine, but with dangers and setbacks. When in opposition in inoperative signs, they become harsh. If the rest of the nativity's factors point to leadership for the native, he will fall into great dangers and be betrayed by his relatives and by enemies. If neither star is houseruler or master or co-houseruler, the trine configuration is mediocre. The native becomes a military/government official. If high rank seems to be hinted because of the other stars which are helpers or have the power of helpers, the native will advance in rank. These stars make men rulers of cities and judges on the bench. If the horoscope is military because of the Sun, the Moon, or Saturn, the native becomes a decurion and a centurion, <a commander> in short campaigns and of small cities. If the horoscope is base because of the the Sun, the Moon, and the rest of the stars, or if Mars and Jupiter are trine with them, men become base: slaves of officials, subordinates of governors; they are frequently hunters, gladiators, and weapon makers. These things are indicated by the alteration of the signs' <positions>: if they are at the angles, they cause greatness from youth; if they rise just after an angle, they cause greatness beginning in adulthood; if they rise before an angle, they cause lowliness and degradation.

18. The Lot of Fortune as the Ascendant

Having explained the trine arrangements, I will move on to the Lot of Fortune.[5] First of all it is necessary to determine the Lot of Fortune and to see in what part of the cosmos it is located: at an angle, just following an angle, or just preceding an angle. Likewise look for the ruler of the Lot. If it is in the Ascendant during the day or is in some other operative place, with the Sun, the Moon, or benefics in aspect, it will make the native noble, distinguished, and fortunate. Its effects are more moderate when it is found at the other angles or just following an angle. When it precedes an angle, assume <the nativity to be> stillborn or abandoned—these are the disagreeable places which bring crises and ruin.

In addition, after finding the Place which has been assigned to Fortune, examine the points square with it and the other aspects, just as with the angles in the natal chart. The Lot itself will be equivalent to the Ascendant and will mean "Life;" the tenth place from it will be equivalent to the Midheaven and will mean "Rank;" the seventh will be the Descendant; the fourth IC. The other places will have the same effects as the <original> XII Places. Some astrologers have mystically hypothesized that the astronomical Ascendant and the points square with it are the Cosmic Angles, while the Lot and the points square with it are the Natal Angles, and they have revealed this in their treatises as follows: "When assigning the influence of the Lot among all the multifarious configurations of the angles… neither the tropic nor the solid nor the bicorporeal signs will have the same overall effects. It is therefore necessary to examine the aspects or the conjunctions of the stars relative to the Lot: for example, a benefic in conjunction or in aspect with the Lot will be a sign of good and a giver of property. A destructive star <in conjunction or in aspect> will be responsible for loss of goods and sickness of the body."

19. The Exaltation of the Sun and Moon. Their Effects on Prosperity

We ourselves have found from experience a mystical way of calculating: for day births determine the distance from the Sun at the nativity to Aries, which is the Sun's exaltation (for night births from the Moon to Taurus). <Count this> same distance from the Ascendant and examine the place where the count stops and its ruler. If it is found to be in the Ascendant or at the Midheaven,

---

[5] *Marginal note:* And of Daimon; concerning prosperity.

especially at an angle relative to the Lot, it indicates a royal chart, provided the other stars and procedures point to a basis of greatness for the nativity. In addition, if the nativity is of high rank, and if the exaltation or the houseruler is favorably situated, the native will be exalted even beyond/to leadership, civil or royal office, or other distinguished positions of responsibility. If the basis of the nativity is average, and the ruler of the exaltation or the place itself is favorably situated, the native will be successful in the status to which he has been assigned: a craft, a science, or a talent. The houseruler itself and the sign will point out the type of good fortune to be expected, either from its own nature or from the sign in which it is located. Many times men have fared poorly in early life and have been in distress and gone astray, but later they have become lucky because of other factors.

20. The Lot of Fortune and Daimon. Their Influence on Prosperity and the Outcome of Actions

For the reason mentioned above, the Lot of Fortune and Daimon have great influence on undertakings and their outcomes. The former gives information about matters concerning the body and concerning the work of hands. Daimon and its ruler give information about spiritual and intellectual matters and about the activities of giving and receiving. It will be necessary to examine the places and the signs in which their houserulers are located and to correlate their natures, in order to learn the type of activity and fortune and the quality of activity <to be expected>.

Nativities will be considered glorious, distinguished, and vigorous if they are from the Sun and Moon, and if benefics are in conjunction or incline to these places or houserulers. The nativities from Saturn and Mars are mediocre, inglorious, ruined, or adverse. It is best to find the ruler of Daimon at the Lot of Fortune or at its 10th Place (=Midheaven).[6] If so, then the nativities are illustrious and distinguished. If it is in its proper place or at another angle, the nativities will be as distinguished and vigorous as they can be under the circumstances. If it is turned away from its proper place, just precedes an angle, or has malefics in aspect, it indicates exile and distress abroad. If it is in conjunction with a benefic or has benefics in aspect, the native will live abroad for a long time, having a varied and fluctuating livelihood. If it has a malefic

---

[6] A marginal note from the manuscripts: "So that it is at the Midheaven relative to the Lot. Note that <the author> defines "to be at an angle" as the same or as equivalent to "to be in its proper place." In the same way he makes "to just precede an angle" equivalent to "to not be in its proper place." "Having malefics in aspect" is in the same category as "being turned away," i.e., in the 8th place <relative to the Lot>."

in aspect, the native will become needy, destitute, experiencing trials and imprisonment. Likewise if <the ruler of the Lot or of Daimon> is in opposition to this place, it indicates men who reside abroad and become distressed. Often the goods of such men are not inherited by their own families, but by strangers.

21. The <11th> Place <Relative to the Lot> of Fortune and its Influence on Prosperity

We have found the 11th Place <relative to the Lot> of Fortune to be the Place of Accomplishment, the bestower of property and goods, especially if benefics are in this Place or in aspect. The Sun, Jupiter, and Venus provide gold, silver, jewelry, and very great property, as well as gifts from the great and from kings. They cause men to spend money on the masses for noble purposes and to become benefactors of many people. The Moon and Mercury bring ups and downs of livelihood, bringing changes and sometimes making men liberal and generous, at other times needy and burdened with debts. This happens because of the Moon's waxing and waning, and because Mercury shares qualities of good and bad. Mars takes away what was gained and possessed, causing reductions, thefts, burning, trials, confiscation for public or royal use, or proscriptions and condemnations. If, however, the nativity is in government or otherwise distinguished, then men will become successful due to an <astrological> impulse, from violent and dangerous action, and from theft—provided that the star is in its proper place. Even so, the star will make the occupation risky and will cause losses. Saturn when configured in its proper places makes men rulers of estates and property; if out of place and in the wrong sect it brings disaster, ruin, shipwreck, poverty, and debt.

Saturn with Mercury and Mars forecasts men who are abused by the onslaughts of trials or of criminals, or because of religious or violent matters. Saturn, Mercury, Mars, and Venus forecast men who are wronged by poisons or by females, and who are accused. Saturn, Mars, Mercury, Venus, Jupiter, and the Moon forecast men who benefit from legacies and who profit from shipping, overseas trade, or moist matters. In general, Saturn and Mars at the Midheaven or rising just after the Midheaven and ruling the Lot and the Place of Accomplishment indicate exile.

It is necessary to review the nature of each star and to make predictions according to its specific contribution and property relative to each other star. It is not just the stars in conjunction with the Place of Accomplishment which supply the indications previously mentioned. The sign itself will be influential according to the star's nature, as well as its own.

22. Examples for the Preceding Chapters

For clarification of the previous points, we will use examples, taking first a distinguished nativity:

Sun in Scorpio, Moon in Cancer, Saturn in Aquarius, Jupiter in Sagittarius, Mars in Scorpio, Venus in Libra, Mercury in Scorpio, Ascendant in Libra. Since the birth was at night, I investigate the Moon: this happens to be in Cancer, triangle of Mars. We find Mars rising just after the Ascendant and in its own house <Scorpio>, triangle <Scorpio Pisces Cancer>, and sect <nocturnal>. Then we find Venus sharing rulership with

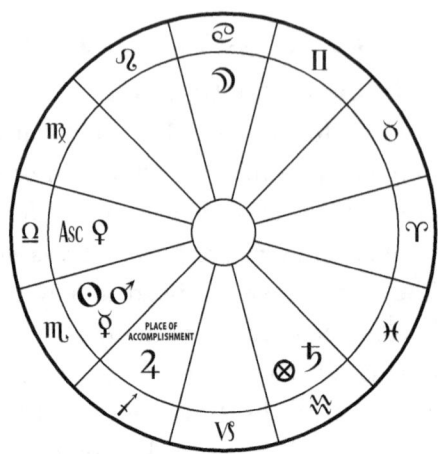

Mars, being in the Ascendant and in its own house <Libra>. Third, we find the Moon at the Midheaven in its own house <Cancer>. It is obvious that the nativity is distinguished, since the houserulers are configured so appropriately. Investigating the Lot of Fortune, I find it in Aquarius; Saturn is there, the ruler <of Aquarius> and in <the V Place of> Good Fortune, in its own house <Aquarius> and triangle <Aquarius Libra Gemini>. Likewise the 11th Place from the Lot of Fortune, i.e., the Place of Accomplishment, is <Sagittarius>, and Jupiter is there. I also found the Exaltation of the Nativity: from the Moon to Taurus is eleven signs, and the same distance from the Ascendant in Libra brings me to Leo, in <the XI Place of> Good Daimon. The Sun is the ruler of this and since it is found to be at the Midheaven with respect to the Lot of Fortune, it made the birth even more illustrious and distinguished.

Another example: Sun, Mercury in Taurus, Moon in Aries, Saturn, Mars, Venus, Ascendant in Cancer, Jupiter in Capricorn, the Lot of Fortune and the Exaltation of the Nativity in Gemini. The native rose from mediocre origins to become a prefect and a governor. Since this was a day

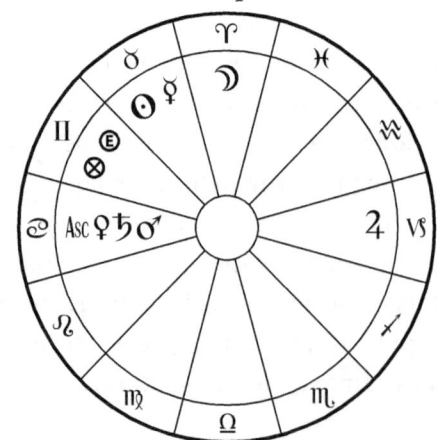

birth, I found the Sun in the triangle of the Moon <Taurus Virgo Capricorn> and its partners, Venus and Mars, at an angle <Ascendant>, the Lot of Fortune and the Exaltation in Gemini, just preceding an angle (hence the beginning of his life was humble), and its ruler <Mercury> in <the XI Place of> Good Daimon.

Another example: Sun, Mars, Venus, Mercury in Aquarius, Moon, Jupiter in Scorpio, Saturn in Aries, Ascendant in Leo. This nativity also went from humble and ordinary fortune to the fortune of a prefect and a wealthy man. Since it was a day birth, we find the Sun in the triangle of Saturn <Aquarius Gemini Libra> with Saturn just preceding an angle <MC>. Therefore his first years were

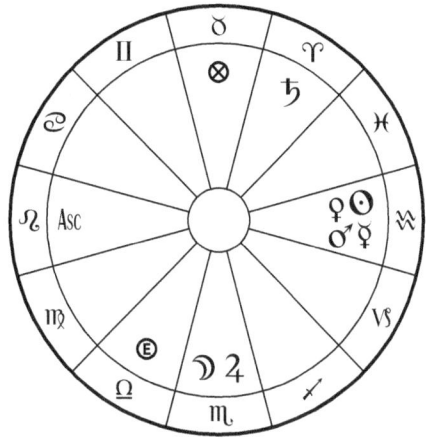

ordinary. Saturn's partner, Mercury, is at an angle <Descendant>. We find the Lot of Fortune in Taurus, the exaltation in Libra, and the ruler of these <Venus> is at the Midheaven relative to the Lot of Fortune and at an angle <Descendant> otherwise <=relative to the Ascendant>.

Another example: Sun, Mercury in Taurus, Moon in Aquarius, Saturn, Venus in Aries, Jupiter in Virgo, Mars in Pisces, Ascendant in Leo. We find the Sun in the triangle of Venus and the Moon <Taurus Virgo Capricorn> with Venus preceding an angle <MC>. So the native's life was at first burdened and lowly, but since the Moon is at an angle <Descendant>, later he came into governmental and advantageous circumstances. Likewise the Lot of

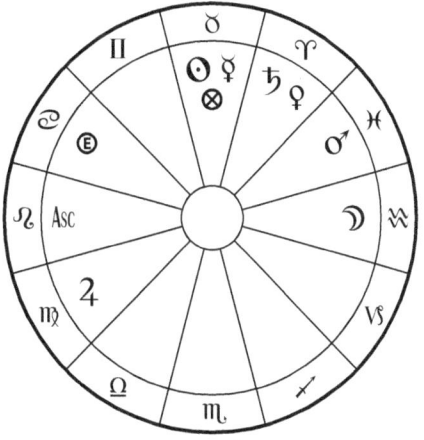

Fortune was found in Taurus, the exaltation in Cancer. The Moon, the ruler of Cancer, was found at the Midheaven relative to the Lot of Fortune; therefore the native came into great fortune and governorship. Mars is found in the Place of Accomplishment, <which gave to him> property from plunder, stealing, and violence, property which after his death was plundered most abominably.

Another example: Sun, Mercury, Saturn, Jupiter in Sagittarius, Moon in Cancer, Mars in Virgo, Venus, Ascendant in Libra. Since this was a night birth, we find the Moon in the triangle of Mars <Cancer Scorpio Pisces>, with Mars itself and the Lot of Fortune and its ruler <Jupiter> preceding angles. Therefore he lived his first years humbly and in poverty; he experienced captivity and servitude and was involved in 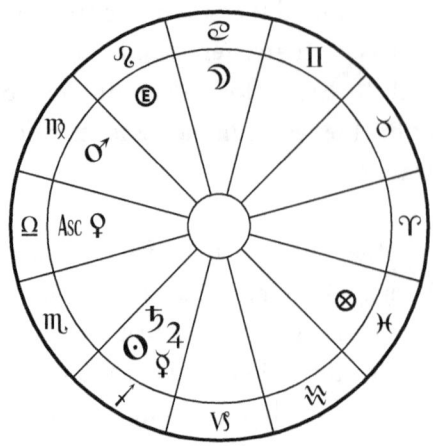 many dangers. But since the stars of the same sect happened to be in operative places, he came into friendships and associations and received positions of royal trust. Since the Exaltation of the Nativity was found in Leo, and its ruler, the Sun, was at the Midheaven relative to the Lot of Fortune, he was thought worthy of the governorship and a position of power.

Another example: Sun, Mercury in Capricorn, Moon, Venus in Sagittarius, Saturn in Scorpio, Jupiter in Libra, Mars in Aquarius, Fortune in Aries, Ascendant in Taurus. This nativity too was at first irregular and mediocre, but later he rose and gained chaplets and a high priesthood. The rulers of the triangle <Taurus Virgo Capricorn> were found to be following an angle <Descendant>, and the third ruler <Mars> of the 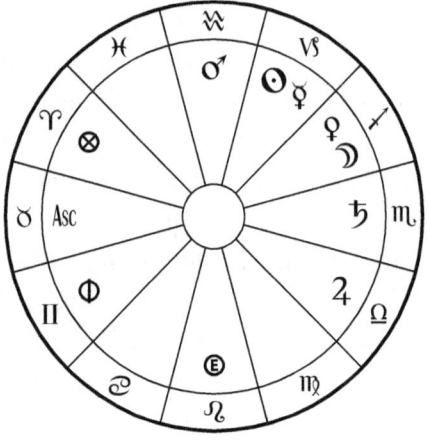 triangle and the ruler of the Lot were at the Midheaven. Likewise the ruler <Sun> of the Exaltation of the Nativity <Leo> was at the Midheaven relative to the Lot of Fortune, as was the ruler <Mercury> of Daimon <Gemini>.

Another example: Sun, Mercury in Cancer, Moon in Taurus, Saturn in Pisces, Jupiter, Mars in Leo, Venus in Virgo, Ascendant in Libra. This nativity too was illustrious and distinguished. The native was entrusted with royal office and was thought worthy of a high priesthood. The ruler <Mars> of the triangle <Cancer Scorpio Pisces> was found with the ruler of Daimon <Jupiter> in

<the XI Place of> Good Daimon and with the Lot of Fortune. The Sun, at the Midheaven, was assigned the Lot. The ruler of the exaltation, the Moon, was at the Midheaven relative to the Lot of Fortune. The Place of Accomplishment was irregular and unstable, sometimes being too full, at other times empty, for Saturn and Venus were in aspect to it <square>.

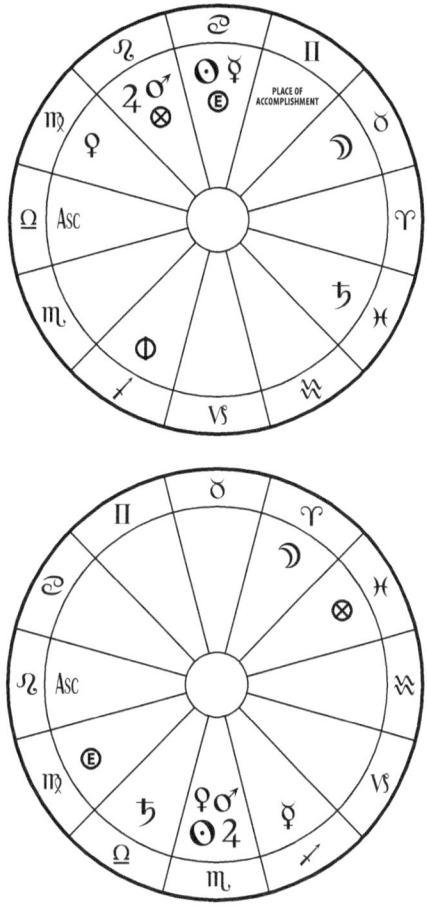

Another example: Sun, Jupiter, Mars, Venus in Scorpio, Saturn in Libra, Moon in Aries, Mercury in Sagittarius, Ascendant in Leo. The ruler of the exaltation, Mercury, was found in Sagittarius, at the Midheaven relative to the Lot of Fortune, and it elevated the nativity with respect to livelihood. Likewise the rulers <Sun Jupiter> of the triangle <of the Sun: Aries Leo Sagittarius> and of the Lot of Fortune were found at IC. This made him miserly, unambitious, and stingy.

Another example: Sun, Mercury in Taurus, Moon in Aquarius, Saturn in Leo, Mars, Venus in Cancer, Jupiter in Virgo, Ascendant in Sagittarius. Since this was a night birth, the rulers, Saturn and Mercury, of the triangle <Gemini Libra Aquarius> just preceded angles <MC Ascendant>. Therefore he had many ups and downs in his early years and lived in debt, although the basis <of the nativity> was good with respect to parents.

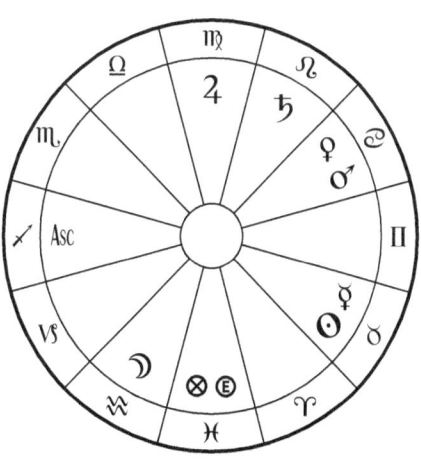

Later he got an inheritance and improved his means by profitable enterprises, and he became ambitious, dominant, and munificent. He was popular with the masses and a friend of kings and governors. He supplied temples and public works and gained perpetual remembrance. The Lot of Fortune and the exaltation were found in Pisces, and its ruler, Jupiter, was at the Midheaven.

Another example: Sun, Mercury in Scorpio, Moon in Aries, Saturn in Virgo, Jupiter in Pisces, Mars in Leo, Venus, Ascendant in Sagittarius. Even when he was a child, the nativity inherited great property. The Place of Accomplishment was in Pisces, with Jupiter in its own house. Venus, the co-ruler of the triangle, the Lot of Fortune, and the exaltation, was exactly in the Ascendant.

Another example: Sun, Mercury in Capricorn, Moon, Saturn in Sagittarius, Jupiter in Cancer, Mars in Virgo, Venus in Aquarius, Ascendant in Libra. The rulers <Jupiter Sun> of the triangle <of the Sun> were found at angles, but in opposition <MC IC>. Therefore the nativity, though well provided for and prosperous at first, was later found to be exiled and needy because of burning and plunder. The ruler of the Lot of Fortune, Mars, was found in the Place of Accomplishment, but preceding an angle <Ascendant> and in aspect with Saturn <square>.

Another example: Sun, Venus, Ascendant in Taurus, Moon in Aquarius, Saturn in Cancer, Jupiter in Libra, Mars, Mercury in Gemini. In his first years, the native had great political prestige, affairs, and positions

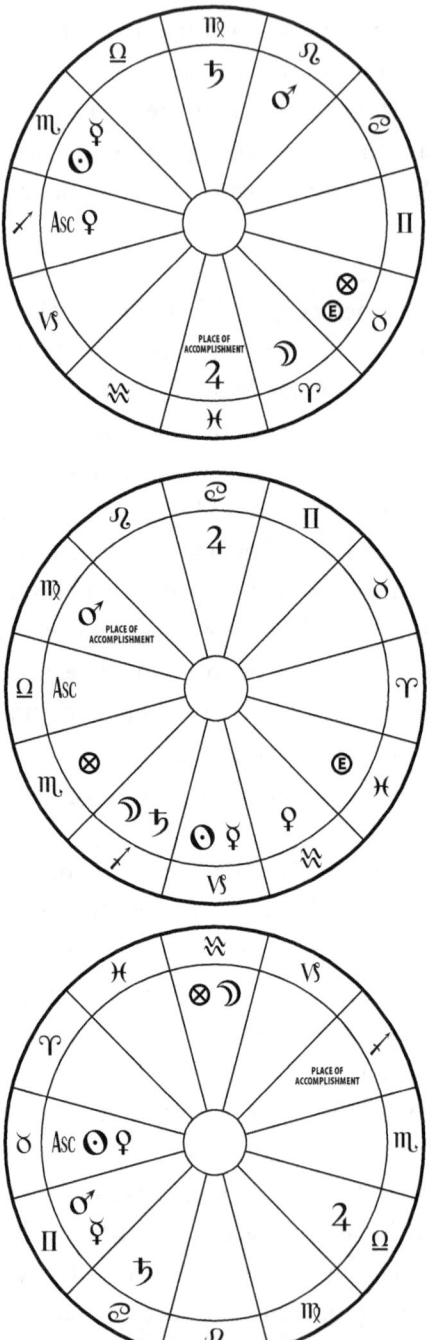

of trust. The rulers <Venus Moon> of the triangle <Taurus Virgo Capricorn> happened to be at angles <Ascendant, MC>. Later his livelihood was ruined and he become a vagabond. Mars and Mercury were in opposition to the Place of Accomplishment and the rulers <Saturn Jupiter> of the Lot and of the Place of Accomplishment preceded angles <IC Descendant>.

Another example: Sun, Mercury in Gemini, Moon in Capricorn, Saturn, Mars in Aquarius, Venus, Ascendant in Cancer, Jupiter in Scorpio. This man, though born a slave, entered a noble family, attained political offices, and enjoyed honors. The rulers <Saturn Mercury> of the triangle of the Sun <Gemini Libra Aquarius> and of the Lot and the exaltation were found in their own domains and in aspect with Jupiter. 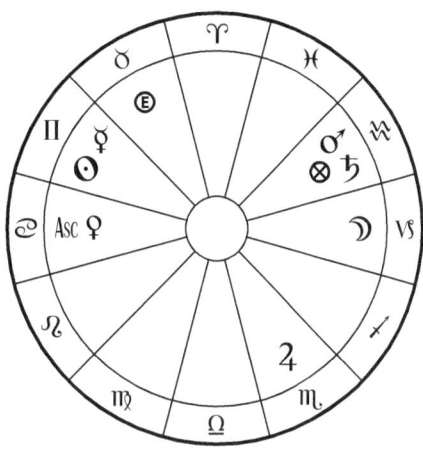 Mars, Saturn, and Mercury were unfavorably situated and so reduced his means and made him financially embarrassed.

Another example: Sun in Aquarius, Moon, Jupiter in Scorpio, Saturn in Cancer, Mars, Venus, Mercury in Capricorn, Ascendant in Pisces. This man was a eunuch, a distinguished priest of the goddess. The ruler <Jupiter> of the Lot happened to be in Scorpio, <the IX Place of> the God. The rulers of the <diurnal> sect, Saturn and Mercury, were found in Good Daimon, but in opposition. Therefore he fell into a great many troubles and losses and quarrels with governors and kings.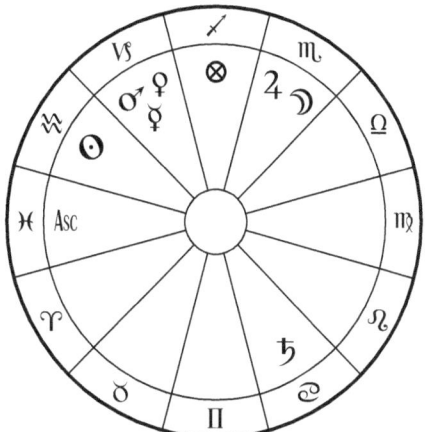

23. Notable and Distinguished Nativities. Also Ignoble and Debased Nativities

I must append the following powerful places in order to clarify the topic of in notable and distinguished nativities. If the Sun and the Moon are in operative signs and are attended by most of the stars which are rising, with no malefics in opposition, they make fortunate and notable nativities of governors and kings. The same is true if their rulers happen to be at an angle. If the sign of the new or full Moon or the ruler of this sign happens to be in the Ascendant or at the Midheaven, the native will be fortunate. If the Sun or the Moon or most of the stars are found at IC, the native will be distinguished and rich, but <the stars> will ruin his life terribly or involve him in hatred, lawsuits, and slander.

Since we wish to make very clear judgements about the Place/topic of prosperity, I will explain it further by citing many proven methods. Each planetary configuration is effective in its own way, but when comparing one with another, you will find that one elevates the native's rank when it is exalted, another utterly overthrows it when it is afflicted. Therefore we append this discussion to reinforce <our teachings about> the previously mentioned pattern of influences, not to abandon them.

So it will be necessary to calculate the effects of the Lot of Daimon in the same way we described for the Lot <of Fortune>. For day births, this Lot is found by determining the distance from the Moon to the Sun (for night births, from the Sun to the Moon), then counting this distance from the Ascendant. Now examine the ruler of the Lot and its place—whatever that happens to be. Do the same for the Lot of Basis: it is found by determining the distance from Fortune to Daimon <for day births> or from Daimon to Fortune <for night births>, then counting that distance from the Ascendant. (The distance will not exceed the number 7 <=7 signs> for night or day births but it is necessary to take the distance from the nearest Lot to the other Lot.) Then determine the place and its houseruler.

Now then, if the houserulers exchange places—i.e., if the ruler of the Lot of Fortune is in the Lot of Basis, the ruler of Basis is in the Lot of Daimon, and the ruler of Daimon is in the place of Fortune—the native is fortunate, royal, noted. If the ruler of Basis, together with the ruler of Daimon, is in the place of Daimon, the native is fortunate and great-hearted. If the rulers of Daimon, of Fortune, and of Basis are in their proper places, in such cases as well the native is fortunate. If Daimon is in conjunction with the Sun and its ruler is rising, the native is fortunate. Likewise if Venus rules Fortune, Daimon, or Basis and is found to be rising and in its proper place, the native is fortunate. If its ruler is in Basis and the Moon is in conjunction with it, the native will be fortunate and distinguished. If its ruler is in Daimon and the Sun is in conjunction with it, the native will be fortunate, distinguished, and dictatorial.

If Mars is found to be in Daimon and in the places of the Moon, with the Moon in conjunction, the nativity is ruling, governing, and distinguished. If Mercury is found in Daimon, rising, and with benefics in aspect in the places of the Moon, the native will gain fortune from letters and education; he will have many friends and be renowned, be thought worthy of honors, gifts, and high rank, and will be called blessed by many. If Jupiter rules Daimon with Mars in superior aspect, the native will not suffer misfortune, but will be vigorous and distinguished. He will, however, meet with reverses, be ruined, and experience arrest and exile. If the ruler is in Daimon and is rising with the Moon, the native will be fortunate, rich, and generous. If the Sun is in Daimon, in its own sect, and with its houseruler in its proper place, the native will be distinguished, elegant, and will have many friends. If it is in another place, the native will be fortunate after the chronocratorship of its adversary.

If the rulers of Daimon and of Fortune are found in the place of Basis, with the houseruler in conjunction, the nativity will be illustrious and renowned. Likewise if the rulers of Basis and of Fortune are found in Daimon, with the houserulers in conjunction, the nativity will be great and fortunate. Men who have the rulers of Fortune and of Daimon at morning rising in their proper places, with the Sun and Moon in aspect, will become famous and distinguished. Associating with kings and priests, they will be thought worthy of gifts and high rank. If Venus (or any one of the other stars) is found to be ruling the Lot <of Fortune> or Daimon along with the Sun and the Moon, and is not in its proper place, but is unfavorably situated, the native will have hard luck and be ineffective in his efforts. If some of them are in their proper places, the native will associate with great men, will be at court, and will receive positions of trust, but in the matter of women he will be grieved and childless.

If the rulers of Fortune and of Accomplishment do not happen to be in their own places, exaltations, triangles, or degrees, although they are at angles or proceeding with their proper motion, then they ruin nativities, especially when malefics are in aspect or in opposition to these places. If benefics happen to be at angles, rising, and proceeding with their proper motion, they make the native illustrious and famous. If the stars just follow an angle, the native lives off his own revenues.

If Accomplishment is afflicted, even though the Lots of Fortune, Daimon, and Basis are favorably situated, men lose their property in the course of their youth. If Fortune is in an unpropitious place and is afflicted, but Accomplishment is favorably situated, then men will become more powerful from youth. If the rulers of Fortune or of Accomplishment happen to be at the lower angles <Descendant IC> or just following them, men will acquire prosperity and reputation in the course of their youth. If malefics are in conjunction with or in opposition to Accomplishment, when this Place is not at an angle, and if they are alien to the nativity and in alien signs and degrees, they then cause destruction of property, even if the Lot of Fortune and its ruler are favorably situated.

Whenever the ruler of Fortune and the ruler of Accomplishment are in opposition, even if they are benefics, they cause property to look like a mirage and to be infirm and at risk. If the rulers are malefics, they bring disaster. If Accomplishment is in opposition to Daimon, they bring failures of enterprises, loss, and damage, if they do not have benefics in conjunction. If the ruler of Accomplishment is in opposition to Accomplishment, it makes wealth useless. If it happens to be malefic, so much the worse. If benefics are retrograde, they do the same thing, and in such circumstances they cause disasters. If Accomplishment is in opposition to the houserulers, especially if they are malefic and not in their own sect, the native comes close to disaster. If Mars is in conjunction or opposition to Accomplishment, the native wastes his substance in pleasures and drink. Likewise if the ruler of Accomplishment is in opposition to it <Mars>, the native is extravagant. The same is true if the ruler of Accomplishment is itself retrograde in motion, not at an angle, or in another's degrees or house.

24. The Lot of Debt

If the Lot of Debt is <badly> situated or if its ruler is square or in opposition to it, with malefics beholding, in opposition, or in superior aspect, this Lot makes nativities debtors. The Lot of Debt is calculated by determining the distance from Mercury to Saturn then counting that same distance from the Ascendant. From the Lots located in this place, or from the stars in conjunction <with Accomplishment>, opposition, or square with this Lot, the fate of the native's property will be obvious. The same conclusions can be drawn from the stars in conjunction with Fortune, with Daimon, with Accomplishment, or from the Lots coinciding with them, and from their rulers. Particularly examine the Lot of Deceit and the Lot of Theft to see if they have some relationship with Accomplishment, Fortune, Daimon, or Life, or any relationship with the rulers of these Lots. It is possible that those <stars> which bring possessions derived from these unwholesome activities, have no relationship <with those places>. If the places just mentioned have no relationship with Accomplishment, Life, Fortune, or Daimon, <the Lot of Debt> ruins the livelihood of the native and his property. If they do have such a relationship, you will find that his property comes from crime, deceit, plots, force, theft, and violence.

25. The Lot of Theft
For day births, the position of the Lot is calculated by determining the distance from Mercury to Mars, then counting the same distance from Saturn; for night births, measure from Mars to Mercury, then from Saturn.

26. The Lot of Deceit
For day births, determine the distance from the Sun to Mars, then count the same distance from the Ascendant; for night births, the opposite <=from Mars to the Sun>. If the rulers of the Lots of Fortune, Accomplishment, or Daimon are located in the Lots of Deceit or Theft, the native will gain his livelihood from violence and crime, or from someone's help. If the rulers of all these Lots are in conjunction, they have the same effect. If the rulers of theft or Deceit are in conjunction either with the Lot of Fortune, Daimon, or Accomplishment, the native's livelihood will be from these same activities. If benefics are in aspect with these places, especially in their proper places or in their own sect, they give the native good moral tone. If malefics are in opposition or square, the interpretation must be carefully considered.

<Ignoble and Debased Nativities>
We must now discuss nativities which are ruined and debased after knowing good fortune. If the Place of Rank and Exaltation has malefics not appropriate to the nativity in opposition, or if its ruler does not have Jupiter in aspect, especially if the luminaries just follow an angle or if the Moon is afflicted, the native's standing and his high position will be ruined. The ruler of the Lot of Fortune, when in opposition to Exaltation or to the ruler of Exaltation, makes the native's standing and high position precarious. Likewise the ruler of Daimon and the Lots <in opposition> to each other are unpleasant and destructive of rank.

If the places of the Lot of Exaltation and the Lot of Standing are in opposition, and if the Lots or their rulers are beheld by malefics, they afflict themselves: the native will become disgraced, ruined, and insulted. If the rulers of the Lot of Fortune, Daimon, or Exaltation are in opposition to the Lot of Standing—either to the Lot itself or to its ruler—or if malefics are in aspect, particularly in superior aspect, to these Lots, the native will be ruined and insulted. The same is true, especially when a malefic is in aspect to the Lot of Standing: it will then bring degradation of livelihood and status on the native, especially when the malefic is at an angle. In such a case it is clearly obvious that evil portends for the native.

The luminaries are ill-omened when in opposition to their exaltations or to the ruler of Exaltation, particularly when the luminaries are afflicted and are not in their own sect, either one or both of them. They then bring infamy and ruin on nativities. If Exaltation is at the Midheaven and a malefic is at IC, the native will succeed in his early years and be honored by many, especially if a benefic is in aspect on the right, but later he will be ruined. If the opposite situation obtains, he will be renowned later, despite having had ill-fortune in his early years. If the places are completely afflicted, they indicate ill-fortune from the native's youth—just as (the opposite case) if benefics are in aspect with the places, good clearly portends, all according to the specific natures and locations of the signs and stars.

Or again: if Daimon is in opposition to Exaltation, it will ruin the nativity. For any nativity, whenever most of the places or their rulers are afflicted, or whenever the new Moon, the full Moon, or the Lot of Standing have the Lots of Justice, Hostility, or Necessity in conjunction, in opposition, or in square, then the nativities meet with great upheavals and are harmed with respect to their standing. If the afflicted places are few, or if only the Place of Exaltation or its ruler is afflicted, the native will end up unsuccessful, obscure, and contemptible. Malefics in opposition or in superior aspect to the Place of Status bring ruin to nativities. If the ruler of Exaltation and the ruler of Status are in opposition, as well as the Lots and their masters, the native is held in contempt. If Jupiter is in conjunction with Exaltation and is at an angle, or if it is the ruler of an angle, it makes men renowned. If it is in the signs of Mars <Scorpio Aries> or in its degrees, or if it happens to be in its own signs <Sagittarius Pisces>, the native will be master of life and death.

As a result, the previously mentioned places and stars, when found in operative signs, make glorious, governing, royal nativities. When found in moderately active signs, they make noble and famous men who take control. When found in signs which just precede an angle, they make wealthy and vigorous men, stewards of others, men thought worthy of positions of trust and responsibility.

27. Examples of the Previously Mentioned Places
Let the Sun, Moon, Jupiter, Mercury be in Leo, Saturn, Ascendant in Libra, Mars in Gemini, Venus in Cancer. This person was fortunate, a leader, dictatorial, possessed of royal fortune, and in solid possession of great property. The Lot of Fortune, Daimon, and Basis were located in the same

sign <Libra>, and Venus, the ruler of these Lots, was at the Midheaven in Cancer. The ruler <Jupiter> of the triangle <Leo Aries Sagittarius> and the ruler <Mercury> of the Exaltation <Gemini> were found in <the XI Place of> Good Daimon and in Accomplishment.

Another example: Sun, Mercury, Venus, Ascendant in Leo, Saturn in Taurus, Jupiter in Sagittarius, Mars in Libra, Moon in Capricorn. This person was a governor, a master of life and death because the stars were found in their own domains.

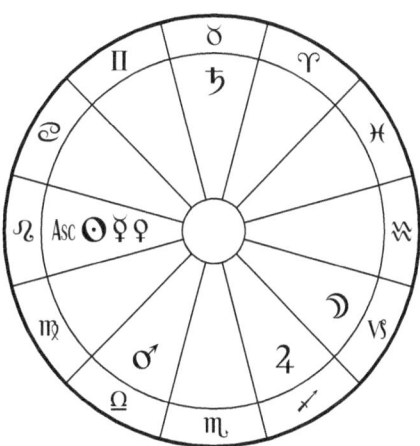

Another example: Sun, Moon, Jupiter, Ascendant in Aries, Saturn, Venus in Aquarius, Mars in Gemini, Mercury in Pisces. This person was commanding and dictatorial because the rulers <Sun Jupiter> of the triangle <Leo Sagittarius Aries> were found to be at an angle and in the Ascendant. The Lot of Fortune, Daimon, and Basis, as well as the Exaltation, were located in the same place <Aries>. The ruler of these, Mars, being unfavorably situated and not in aspect with the <III> Place had the opposite effects, both exile and violent death; for it was the ruler of the new Moon <in Aries>.

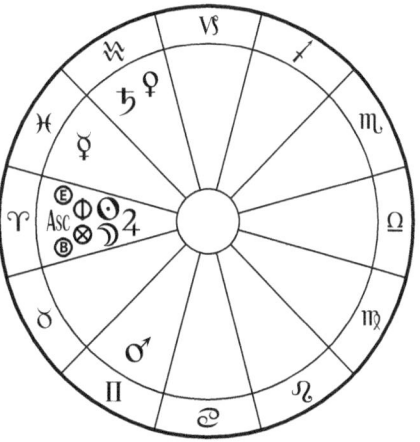

Another example: Sun, Jupiter, Venus in Pisces, Moon in Libra, Mars in Cancer, Mercury in Aquarius, Saturn in Scorpio, Ascendant in Leo. This person was famous and wealthy because the Sun was attended by benefics and was found situated in the Lot of Fortune <Pisces> with its houseruler <Jupiter>. But since the co-rulers of the same sect <Mars Moon> of the triangle <Pisces Cancer Scorpio> were unfavorably situated, and the ruler <Saturn> of Daimon <Capricorn> was turned away, this person was exiled and committed suicide. In addition Mars was in opposition to Accomplishment <Capricorn>, and the ruler <Mercury> of the Exaltation <Virgo> did not have a suitable place, but was afflicted by Saturn, which was in superior aspect.

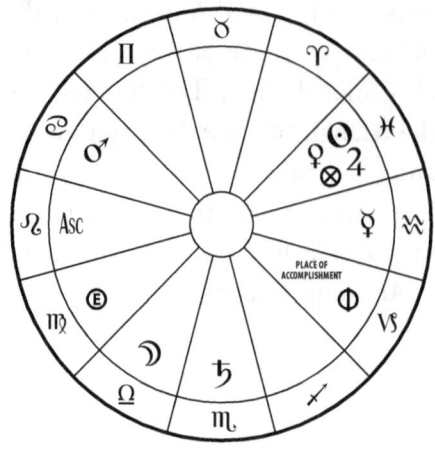

Therefore as I have already said, if most of the configurations or their rulers are found in suitable places, the native will be famous and spectacular in his living. If some <configurations and rulers> are favorably situated, others unfavorably, rank and fortune will be transitory.

28. Propitious and Impropitious Periods. The Length of Life Calculated from the Angles and the Signs Following the Angles

The periods of good or bad fortune, of failure or success, must be determined by using the rising times of each sign or the cyclical period of each star. When investigating the <u>length of life</u>, it is necessary to pay attention to the Ascendant and the Moon, or to the signs in which their rulers are located. With respect to <u>occupation and rank</u>, it is necessary to pay attention to the Lot of Fortune, to Daimon, to the Sun, to the new or full Moons, and to the Exaltation and its ruler. The stars which are in the Ascendant (viz. the most important relationship), begin to rule over the first period of life <=first chronocratorship>. The stars at the Midheaven, at the Descendant, or at IC <rule over the subsequent periods>. If these places happen to be empty, then the stars just following the angles <rule>. If these too are empty, then the stars just preceding the angles <rule>. Even though they are not too strong, they will regulate affairs. (The stars inclining away from <=just preceding> the Ascendant or the Midheaven make the allotment first, then the stars preceding the other angles. They cannot allot their entire rising times or periods, but only an amount proportional to the amount of the sign that they control.) Those stars which are in their proper place and at angles or just following an angle, and which are found to be rising, especially those which have some relationship with the business of the nativity, whatever that may be—whenever they control the previously mentioned places, they allot the rising times of their signs and their own periods, or the rising times and periods of the signs in which their rulers are located.

(Likewise, when investigating the remaining Places and their masters, it is necessary to interpret the chronocratorships (e.g., concerning livelihood, brothers, parents, children, etc.), the harmful and helpful stars, and whatever influence each <star> can produce. We mention this so that we do not write too often about the same matters. Their natures have been explained; we will remind you of them in the rest of this work.)

It is necessary to allot first the minimum period of the ruler <of the sign> and of the star in conjunction, next the rising time of the sign <itself> or of the sign in which its ruler is located. In addition, examine the houserulers of the triangle, as we mentioned above. If both are well situated, the chronocratorship will be noteworthy and beneficial. If the indications are mixed, the results will be the same. If they are badly situated, the nativity will be irregular from beginning to end, involved in griefs and dangers. But if the Lot of Fortune or its ruler is configured in its proper place, it will give the nativity prosperity and a high rank suitable to the <nativity's> basis. If two or more stars happen to be in the same sign, the period of each, distributed consecutively, will be operative, but the effects will result from a mixture of the two or three stars. Likewise the rising time of the sign, distributed consecutively with the period of the star in conjunction (or its ruler), will be operative. If the chronocratorship derived from the rising times and the periods of benefic and malefic stars and signs coincide, then both good and bad together will happen at that particular time.

29. Travel, from Hermippos

The difficult topic of travel has not been treated either by Petosiris or by the learned King in his treatises, except in this fashion: "If a malefic has a phase in this chronocratorship, it will cause travel and vexation for the nativity." This is the truth, but they have nothing more than this to say about the Place of Foreign Lands. The most amazing Abraham has shown us in his books other astrologers' explanations of the Place, as well as his own, since he found and proved additional <secrets/interpretations>, especially concerning expatriate nativities, with the following results: when Mars beholds the setting luminaries or the Lot of Fortune, if that Lot just precedes the Midheaven, or <when Mars

beholds> the Moon or most of the stars at IC, <it causes nativities to travel>. If the ruler of Fortune is found in the Lot or Place of Foreign Lands or in opposition to it, or indeed if Fortune itself is located there in the Lot of Travel, and if Mars is in conjunction with the Lot or beholds that Place, this too causes nativities to travel. The same is true <if Mars beholds> Fortune and Daimon.

30. Travel

The Lot of Foreign Lands is found by determining the distance from Saturn to Mars, then counting that same distance from the Ascendant. These circumstances make changeable nativities. The occasions and the times of travel for such nativities will be evident from the configurations outlined by Abraham. We will add the configurations observed by me personally; let no one reading this criticize us for adopting as our own the work and observations of others—as some do. We testify to the work of these men. Let us return to our subject.

To distribute the operative chronocratorship according to Abraham, i.e., those which are allotted starting with Daimon (for he does allot in this way, starting where the Lot of Daimon is located at birth): first look at the ruler of the sign where the Lot is found; then determine how many years its shortest cycle happens to be and divide that amount among the 12 signs starting from Daimon itself, counting through the signs in order. Next, when that cycle is completed, look at the ruler of the next sign after Daimon, determine how many years its cycle happens to be, and divide this <among the 12 signs>. Do the same in the successive signs, if the nativity has any years of life remaining. If the sign where the chronocratorship happens to be located has a place indicative of travel or the Lot of Travel either <in conjunction>, in opposition, or square, or if the stars (especially malefics not at an angle) which are in the signs that receive the allotment from the original sign, have more years than the <nativity's> basis, then they cause travel.

If the ruler of the sign which has received the allotment is not at an angle, is turned away from the sign, or is a malefic, it causes travel. Even if it is at an angle, it will do the same. If malefics have the allotment and are in the signs or are square with them, they cause travel. If a benefic receives the allotment, but is found in opposition to the nativity, it will cause travel and movement for the native. Again, whenever the rulers of the signs which have the chronocratorship or the distribution happen to be turned away from their signs, or are in opposition or in inferior aspect, or are not at an angle, these signs cause travel. Malefics in opposition, especially when beholding the luminaries in the places of the Sun or Moon, also cause travel. If the ruler of the sign which has the chronocratorship is not at a center, or if it is in opposition to the sign, it makes movement or travel, provided that the Lot of Travel is located in the same place or in opposition or square with it. If it is in its proper place or is found in the squares, it does not cause travel.

Mercury and Venus do not cause distant travel, but rather swift returns. If the two Lots, Fortune and Daimon, fall in the same sign, and if the Lot of Travel is in opposition or square with this sign, and if some malefic is in this place, the native will be involved in travel. Likewise if the Lot of Travel is in opposition to the star which is the chronocrator or which is in conjunction with the Lot of Fortune, and if the two Places, Fortune and Daimon, are in opposition, it is the cause of movement and makes travel for the nativity, especially <if these Lots are> not at centers. Even if they are at angles, or else if the signs which have the allotments also have the Places of Foreign Lands or the Lot <of Travel> in opposition or square, they cause travel for the nativity. Likewise if they are at IC, they make men fond of travel. Again, if the Lot of Travel is located in the Ascendant at the Midheaven or just following the Midheaven—even if the nativity is not naturally inclined to travel or does not have the configurations mentioned previously—it still makes them travel not a lot, but a little, especially if no malefics are in opposition.

If the signs above the Earth have the chronocratorship or its distribution (apart from the XII or the IX Places), they do not cause travel, provided that the Lot does not cause it and that no malefic is in opposition to or conjunction with the sign with no benefics associated. If the signs below the Earth have the chronocratorship, they do cause travel, especially when the Lot of Travel is located in the region below the Earth. If the Lots of Fortune and Travel have malefics in conjunction or opposition, they cause frequent travel. If the ruler of the Lot of Foreign Lands happens to be in opposition to the sign which has the chronocratorship, it will make the nativity travel. If the Lot of Travel and the Lot of Fortune are together at IC, they cause much travel, especially when beheld or controlled by malefics or by a luminary. If it falls in one of the signs which has been assigned either the allotment of the chronocratorship or the monthly period, it causes motion, especially if it has a malefic in opposition or if the luminaries are similarly situated and at the Places above the Earth which precede the angles. If the allotment is less or in opposition, the nativity will have intermittent travel. The stars in superior aspect to the moist signs under the Earth which have the allotment cause travel, especially if these signs have the luminaries or malefics in conjunction.

The configurations under discussion will be particularly influential if the current year <=chronocrator> of the Place has travel for the native or if it produces travelling nativities because of <the nativity's> fundamental nature. Wherever the allotment of the overall chronocratorship or its distribution may be located, the ruler of that sign—whether at an angle or not, provided that no malefic is in opposition...and that the ruler is not in one of the signs of the luminaries, departures will occur. If they have them at or just preceding an angle, they cause foreign departures.

Malefics in conjunction with signs that just precede an angle, or that have the chronocratorship or its distributions, cause travel, and the year has special movement. Whenever the star which has the chronocratorship or the ruler of the Place of Foreign Lands is found to be in the Place or Lot of Foreign Lands, it causes travel, especially if a malefic is square or opposed to the Unlit Place. Likewise if the sign which has the allotment of the chronocratorship is in opposition to the Lot of Travel, especially when it just precedes an angle, it causes travel. If the allotments of the chronocratorship just precede an angle and if the signs do not have <the Lot of Travel?> in opposition or in superior aspect, they do not cause travel; rather the native will nervously anticipate travel and will have unfulfilled intentions to travel. Whenever a benefic is in opposition or in superior aspect with malefics which have the chronocratorships or their allotments, or if the benefic is with <such a malefic> at IC and a travelling "year" occurs, they make delays and obstacles for departures occur.

If Fortune falls in the Place of Foreign Lands, or if the Lots are in opposition, with a malefic in conjunction or opposition, travel occurs, provided that no benefic is joined to any of them or in opposition. If the ruler of Foreign Lands is in opposition to it or to them <?>, with no benefics in aspect, and if Mars is in opposition to the Lot of Fortune or is located in the Lot of Foreign Lands, or is situated in one of them, this makes the native travel extensively. On the other hand, Mars as ruler of both Lots, even though turned away from the "signs" that cause travel or in moist signs, causes traveling nativities. If Mars is turned away from the Lot <of Fortune> or is in the Lot of Foreign Lands, and it is the ruler of neither Lot, it does not cause travel, but it will cause the native to live mostly in his homeland, experiencing only the threat of travel. Likewise if the Lots have benefics in conjunction, they do not make men who are subject to travel, but instead, those who rarely travel.

For any nativity it is possible to find configurations that do not <?> easily bring travel, because most nativities are subject to travel, some constantly and everywhere, others rarely and briefly, because in some <nativities>, the configurations which cause travel are in the majority, in others they are not. Therefore some men become much travelled, others are rarely, only briefly, subject to travel. Concerning those people who have a few configurations indicating travel: if in the original horoscope or in a later recasting, the Lots of Travel and Fortune are located near benefics, they do not cause departures, especially if the year has no impulse toward travel. if the nativity has the configurations I mentioned above, they do cause travel. If the Lot of Travel is turned away from Fortune, especially if one of the Lots has a benefic in conjunction, it will make men spend most of their lives in their homeland, rather than be subject to travel. Mars turned away from the Lot of Foreign Lands causes short trips. The Lot of Fortune does not cause travel if it has benefic stars in conjunction and if they are above the Earth. If the Lot of Fortune is at the Midheaven and is turned away from the Lot of Travel, and if it does not have a malefic or a luminary in opposition, it causes nativities to stay in their homeland rather than to travel. If the two Lots are in conjunction and in the Place just preceding the Midheaven, separated from <Mars> and having no malefic in opposition or conjunction in another sign, the nativity does not readily travel. But if the two Lots have malefics in conjunction or opposition, they cause nativities to be subject to travel, especially when the Lots are in moist signs. The Lot of Fortune, when well situated, having neither malefics in superior aspect nor the luminaries nor the Lot of Travel (especially when Mars is turned away from the two Lots), does not cause travel. Even if the native wants to travel, he does not go. If Jupiter transits these "signs," he prevents departures. The native will have remarkable travels if the year falls just before an angle (Ascendant) and in moist signs, especially if a benefic is not in conjunction (either in transit or at the nativity). If the ruler of the chronocratorship transmits the year to the ruler of the Lot of Travel, especially if a malefic beholds it, or vice-versa if the ruler of the Lot <transmits> the year to the ruler of the chronocratorship, <it causes travel>…

31. The Predecease of Parents, with Examples

Some astrologers have explained the topic of the predecease of parents in one way, others in another way. We have tested these methods and have found the following. Since the Sun indicates the father (as does Saturn in the second rank), the most accurate <procedure>, for night and day births, is to examine <which of these two> stars is associated with the Moon, i.e., beheld by the Moon, in conjunction with the Moon, or in the <Moon's> house or triangle. That star assumes the Father's Place. Venus and the Moon assume the Mother's Place, using the same procedure. So for each nativity it will be necessary to determine which star is beheld by malefics or which star is unfavorably situated, whether Sun, Moon, Venus, or Saturn (although the latter is already the destroyer of the father). If the Sun assumes the Father's Place and is beheld by Mars or Saturn with no benefics in aspect, the forecast of predecease will apply to the father. If the same is true of the Moon or Venus, the forecast will apply to the mother. If both the luminaries or Venus are beheld by malefics, the star unfavorably situated or in another's sect will indicate the predecease.

Another method: the Father's Lot in a masculine sign or its ruler with a malefic in aspect indicates the father's predecease. Likewise the same thing happens with respect to the Mother's Lot, especially if one knows for certain that the father is alive.

Another method: determine the number of days from the rising of Sirius to the birth date. Divide this figure by 12 and count the remainder (less than 12) from the Moon's position, giving one to each sign. If the count stops at a masculine sign, the father will predecease; if at a feminine sign, the mother will predecease. For example, take the nativity cited below, Mechir 13: from the rising of Sirius on Epiphi 25 to Mechir 13 are 203 days. Divide this by 12, and the remainder is 11. Count this from the Moon in Scorpio and stop in Virgo, a feminine sign. Mars is also in that sign. The mother will die first.

An example: Sun, Mercury in Aquarius, Moon in Scorpio, Saturn in Cancer, Jupiter in Libra, Venus in Capricorn, Mars, Ascendant in Virgo. For night births, Saturn is associated with the Moon because it is found in Cancer <same triangle> and is the houseruler of the Sun. Saturn assumes the Father's Lot/Place and was beheld by Jupiter, with Venus [and] Good Daimon. The Moon and Venus, which are beheld by two malefics, indicated the predecease of the mother.

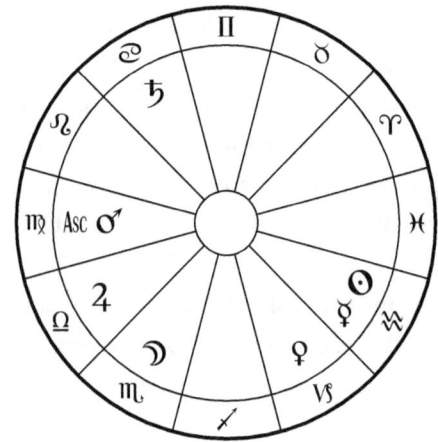

Another method: if the Sun is in superior aspect with the Moon, the mother will predecease; if the Moon is in superior aspect with the Sun, the father will predecease. If neither of these is superior to the other and if they are unconfigured, I examine Saturn and Venus. If these <are unconfigured>, I examine Saturn and the Moon. If the Sun is in superior aspect, but Venus is between, Venus will intercept the superior aspect. Then look to see if Saturn is in inferior aspect with Venus, and if so there will be the premature decease of the father—or the reverse, if Venus is inferior to Saturn. If the star that intercepts the stars of superior aspect has itself a superior influence, the intercepting stars will have the ability to bring about their own effects. (The superior aspecting happens in the same signs or in those in opposition. In general a star which heads for/aims at another <from the right> is in superior aspect to the other; the same is true of a star which has a correspondingly <?> superior power.)

32. [Another Method.] About Parents, from Timaios

Prediction about fathers are done as follows: for day births, the Sun, the sign where the Sun is located, the ruler of the sign where Jupiter is located, and the sign itself which holds Jupiter, all are operative. Predictions about the mother are made as follows: <for night births>, from the Moon's sign (=the sign where the Moon is located) and the houseruler of the Moon; for day births, from Venus and the sign where Venus is located. Whenever these operative stars are found in their own sects, in their own houses, in their own exaltations, with any benefic in superior aspect (or in fact in aspect at all), and when they do not precede an angle or are not afflicted by any malefic in the place where they rejoice, then these stars indicate that the parents' affairs will be famous, distinguished, and illustrious. If the star that should indicate parents' affairs has any malefics in aspect, either by projection of rays or by superior aspect, or if it is found in a place where it does not rejoice, it will indicate lowly and humble parents.

The houserulers, along with the specifically indicative star, will also indicate good or bad concerning parents according to the position and aspect of the other stars. If the star indicative of parents' affairs or its houseruler is unfavorably situated in its place or is afflicted by any harmful aspect—because it is found to be setting under the rays of the Sun, or because it is in <the XII Place of> Bad Daimon, or because the ruler and the afflicted indicative star is not operative in the Place of Parents but is turned away—if this is the case, it will indicate lowly, humble, and base parents. If in addition to being inoperative, these stars are afflicted by having malefics in aspect on the right or in conjunction, this will indicate that the parents are slaves or subjugated people. If however the star indicative of parents just precedes an angle or is afflicted in some other way, but the houseruler is favorably situated and operative… in the Place of Parents, having an indicative star operative in a place not afflicted by any malefic, they indicate harm, punishment, doom, or disaster for the parents. Saturn at the Midheaven and Jupiter at IC indicate the father to be a slave, a subjugated person, or an exile, especially when the Sun is afflicted.

The Lot of the Father is found as follows: for day births determine the distance from the Sun to Saturn and count this distance from the Ascendant. (Some determine the Sun to Jupiter and count from the Ascendant.) For night births, determine the distance from Venus to the Moon and count this distance from the Ascendant. The Lot of Parents is found as follows…

Concerning a stepfather, take the point directly opposite the Lot. If the ruler of the Lot of the Father happens to be at the point in opposition or if the ruler of the point in opposition happens to be at the Lot, this indicates a stepfather. Likewise if the <ruler of> the Lot of the Mother is found in opposition and the ruler of the point in opposition to the Lot of the Mother is found at the Lot of the Mother, this will correspondingly indicate a stepmother.

33. The Loss of Parents

Mars in conjunction with the Sun and square with Saturn causes bereavement. Saturn and Mars configured with Mercury, if Jupiter is not in aspect on the right, likewise make orphans. Saturn setting with Jupiter makes orphans. The Moon in a bicorporeal sign and with Jupiter in aspect indicates children with two fathers. If Venus is in the Ascendant, and if the Moon is at IC, in the house of Mars, and if Jupiter is in unfavorable aspect and out of its own house—this too will make children who have two fathers.

The character of the parents can be determined from the stars which are configured together. Saturn will show them to be surly, envious, depraved, suspicious, foul, involved in secret passions, ugly, spending their money on religious matters, friends of great lords. Jupiter will show them to be lovers of the good, illustrious, generous, frank and open, cheerful. Mars will show them to be bold, hot-tempered, rash, insolent, reckless, restless, risking all, drunkards, toilsome. (Concerning mothers: if Mars as houseruler overpowers the Moon or Venus, it shows the mother to be rough, a whore, troubled acutely by bleeding or consumption, if no benefic in aspect relieves the situation.) Venus in aspect with the luminaries shows the parents to be cheerful, musical, fond of good cheer, affectionate, religious. Mercury shows them to be joiners, sociable and thrifty, sharers in some account or skill, lying most of the time and wronging their inferiors.

<When making this determination about parents> it is necessary to consider the places <of the stars> as well: the Sun in a masculine sign and having a masculine star in aspect shows the father to be noble; in a feminine sign and having the Moon in aspect shows him to be slack and effeminate. The Sun in a feminine sign and having Saturn or Venus in aspect shows the father to be not unharmed and not without a bad reputation. The Moon in a feminine sign and having feminine stars in aspect shows the mother to be dictatorial and wrathful; in a masculine sign and with masculine stars in aspect, it shows the mother to be hot-tempered and uncontrollable; in a feminine sign and having Jupiter in aspect, it shows the mother to be mild and kindly.

34. The Separation of Parents

Mars and Saturn, when intercepting the luminaries or when situated between the <signs> which contain the luminaries, or between their rays, separate parents. Whenever one of the illuminators is in its sect but is unfavorably located, and the other is not in its sect and is malefic relative to the other, this separates parents. Saturn in conjunction with the Sun, if the Moon is estranged, separates parents. If the ruler of the Ascendant is operative, the Ascendant is afflicted, and its co-houseruler is unfavorably situated, the parents will be separated, the native himself will be much disturbed and unfortunate, and his parents' property will be reduced. Parents will be in harmony whenever the luminaries and their houserulers are in harmony with each other. Whenever the houseruler of the Sun is in harmony with the Moon, and the houseruler of the Moon with the Sun, the parents will be in harmony.

When one of the illuminators is not in its own sect, is nullified by a malefic or is in inferior aspect, and is in either conjunction with or opposition to the malefic, then <the parent corresponding to> the luminary which sets first or to the luminary whose place is more unfavorably situated will die first. If the Moon is waxing, and if the nativity is at the full Moon, and if some malefic beholds the first full Moon, and if this full Moon happens in a feminine sign, the mother will die first; if it happens in a masculine sign, the father will die first. If the nativity is at the full, Moon, the next new Moon must be examined: if it happens in a feminine sign with a malefic beholding, then the mother will die first; if in a masculine sign, then the father will die first.

If the Sun is below the Earth, in most cases the father will die abroad. If Jupiter has a malefic in aspect, and if it <Jupiter> just precedes with the malefic just following, this indicates that the father will die abroad. If Saturn is just leaving an angle, and if it is just approaching Mars, and if either of them is in aspect with Jupiter or the Sun, the father will die abroad.

For day births, if the Moon is afflicted above the Earth or just precedes an angle with a malefic approaching, or if Venus is afflicted in the same ways, the mother will die first. If the houseruler of the Sun and the Sun itself do not behold the Ascendant, the father will die abroad. If the Sun is afflicted by a malefic and Jupiter is in inferior aspect, the father will die violently. If only Saturn afflicts the previously mentioned stars, the cause of the violent death will be suffocation, dropsy, fluxes, chills, poisoning, shipwreck, or old matters. If only Mars afflicts them, the cause will be sword slashes, stings, bloody wounds, consumption, miscarriages, burns, or falls. If both malefics afflict the Sun and Jupiter, the violence of the death will be worse in proportion to the natural blending of each star's inclination.

35. Free and Slave Nativities

Differences in birth, i.e., servile and noble nativities, are determined from the phases of the nativity. If the sign of the phase or the ruler of that sign is unfavorably situated or is beheld by malefics, the native will be base. Even if he attains high rank and a position of trust, he will be ruined. If the phase is found at an angle, and its ruler has benefics in aspect, the native will become noble and famous. If the place <of the phase> is in operative signs, but its ruler is unfavorably situated or beheld by malefics, then the native is free-born and begins life well, but he later falls into reversals, servitude, and want. If the ruler is found in operative signs, but the place itself is unfavorably situated, the native will fare very ill in his first years in servile roles and will be unsettled, but later he will live easily, be elevated, and gain freedom, success, and a family <name>, especially if benefics incline. If the place <of the phase> and its ruler are unfavorably situated and both are beheld by malefics, the native will be exposed as an infant, or will become a captive and experience servitude. If under these conditions, benefics come close or are in co-aspect, the native will be released from servitude after the chronocratorships of the malefics and will become a man of property. If the place is guarded by malefics, but its ruler by benefics, the native, although of servile birth, will be raised as a free-born man, or will rise by being adopted or taken in <to be reared>. If the opposite is true, i.e., the place is guarded by benefics and the ruler by malefics, the native, although free-born, will be reduced to slavery or will hand himself over, in middle age, into slavery for lack of food or as a means of gaining a position and occupation.

36. The Eleven Phases of the Moon and The Influence of Their Effects

According to the physicists' reasoning, there are seven phases of the Moon, but we find eleven listed elsewhere:

1. New Moon;
2. First visibility;
3. Next the crescent Moon, 45° from the Sun;
4. Next the quarter Moon at 90°;
5. Next the gibbous Moon at 135°;
6. Next the full Moon at 180°;
7. Next the second gibbous phase when it is 45° from full, i.e., 225° <from the Sun>;
8. Next the second quarter at 270°;
9. Next the second crescent at 315°;
10. Final visibility at 360°;
11. There is another phase as well, when it first begins to wane.

What Each Phase Indicates and What Effects It Has

We will append how the preceding phases are to be taken in casting horoscopes and to which god they belong.

The new Moon is indicative of rank and power, of kingly and despotic dispositions, of all public business concerning cities, of parents, marriages, religion, and of all universal, cosmic matters. The rulers of the new Moon, of the latitude, and of the motion are indicative of the same things.

The first visibility of the Moon (which is also called its "light") and its ruler are indicative of life, occupation, and future wealth; in addition, it strengthens the matters influences by the now Moon. The ruler of the "light" indicates the overall influences in the same way that the monthly cycles and the universal cycles are observed by means of the first visibility. Mercury adds its influence until day 4 of the Moon's motion.

The crescent formation is indicative of nurture and expectations in life, of wives and mothers. Mercury adds its influence until day 8.

The quarter formation is indicative of injuries, diseases, and violent accidents; also of children, status, and good things to come. Venus is configured with the Moon until day 12.

The gibbous phase is indicative of prosperity, future success, travel, and the affinity of relatives. The Sun works with the Moon until day 14.

The full Moon is indicative of fame and infamy, of travel and violent events, of those who fall from pre-eminence as well as those who rise from a humble state, of affinities, passions, political opposition, and the affinity of parents. This phase has the color of the sign in the Descendant.

The first ruler of the waning of the light is indicative of the diminishing of resources, of the chilling of occupations, of those who grow humble and lowly, and of sudden falls. This phase has the same influence as the sign which just follows the Descendant. Mars is its ruler until day 21.

The second gibbous phase is indicative of travel abroad, of great activities, and of prosperity. It has the same influence as <the IX Place of> the God. Jupiter is its ruler to day 25 of the Moon.

The second quarter phase is indicative of old affairs, of chronic diseases, and of children. It has the same influence as… Saturn is its ruler to day 30.

The ruler of the last crescent is indicative of a wife's death, of unemployment or robbery.

Finally, the last visibility is indicative of chains, imprisonment, secrets, condemnation, and infamy.

The preceding was the arrangement of the Moon's phases, their relationships with the five gods and the Sun in the … angles.

<A personal comment>

Since I wished to set out brief explanations of these matters, and since I deprecate all long-winded, mythological mystification, I have published these chapters, most particularly for those who are vitally interested in these matters, those who have spent much time in their studies, and who, because of this, can make an equal contribution from their own insights. I believe that I have persuaded these students, in what I have written and will write, to put aside the hard-to-believe and easily-ridiculed parts of our art, to convict our opponents of folly and mad raving, and to display the immortal foreknowledge which is <now> in danger. Eager scholars, exercised in the mathematical, introductory disciplines by other men, will win the victory-prize of glory with the help of this treatise—although they themselves are not unfamiliar with the mysteries of constructing and arranging astronomical tables (a subject which I did not want to go into and then have to repeat). Even if we seem to be <merely> compiling and explaining the doctrines of the old astrologers, <even> for this we will win the prize of merit from our readers, because of the precision, clarity, and instructiveness of their methods.

Others have employed long-winded, elaborate schemes, and although thinking that they have explained, have really overturned their existing reputation for foreknowledge. Trying to exercise a pure Hellenic style in their writings, they have revealed a thoroughly barbarian mind. One might say that they act like the Sirens, who attracted sailors with their treacherous, but harmonious, voices and with the music of instruments and of baneful song, then destroyed them on the reefs of the deep. This is what some men suffer and have suffered, men who fall in with the sects of those <other astrologers>: beguiled from the start by their spectacular words and their spells, they have become lost in a trackless wilderness, and finding no exit, they perish not only in the depths, but even in a maze. Some who think they have escaped this danger fall into tormenting, soul-wearying agony and come to a bitter end. If someone uses Odysseus' scheme and sails past these "Sirens," he will bequeath <to others> knowledge sanctified by his life, knowledge with which he can live and associate always, enjoying his span of days, while repelling the malignant opinions of his opponents as if by magic. So then, saying farewell to these men, we will reach the glory which lies before us.

37. Injuries and Diseases, with Examples In Each Sign: What Injuries and Diseases are Caused by Aries and the Succeeding Signs

Since the old astrologers have written about the topic of injuries very obscurely, we will lucidly explain it. Some astrologers, with reference to the underlying parts of the body and the mind, for each nativity have <assigned> the limbs starting with the Lot of Fortune and with Daimon, and they make their forecasts concerning injuries and diseases with reference to the proximity of malefics. For example:

Sign	Part Affected	Sign	Part Affected
Lot of Fortune	breast	Sign 7	knees
Sign 2	flanks	Sign 8	calves
Sign 3	belly	Sign 9	feet
Sign 4	groin	Sign 10	head
Sign 5	genitals	Sign 11	face, neck
Sign 6	thighs	Sign 12	arms, shoulders

Diseases are counted from Daimon:

Sign	Part Affected	Sign	Part Affected
Daimon	heart	Sign 7	bladder
Sign 2	stomach	Sign 8	bowels
Sign 3	kidneys, sperm ducts	Sign 9	brain, teeth, ears
Sign 4	colon	Sign 10	gullet
Sign 5	liver	Sign 11	tongue
Sign 6	intestines	Sign 12	stomach

This becomes obvious if one begins with Leo and Cancer, then goes in order, since the Moon <Cancer> is the Fortune of the Universe, and the Sun <Leo> is Mind and Divinity.

That is what the earlier astrologers stated. The following seems more accurate in our experience: Aries is indicative of the head in general, the sensory faculties, and the eyesight. In the point now at issue, Aries causes headaches, dimming of vision, strokes, deafness, blindness, leprosy, lichenous scaliness of the skin, loss of hair, mange, baldness, stupor, festering sores, sudden attacks of panting, arthritic joints, tumors, plus whatever syndromes occur of the sensory faculties, the ears, and the teeth.

Taurus is indicative of the neck, face, gullet, eyebrows, and nose. This sign causes hunchback because of its round-shouldered appearance and lameness because of its bent hoof; also pains and dangerous crises of the eyes and blindness because of the Pleiades. This is a sneaky and degraded sign. It causes fits, excision of the uvula, carbuncles, goiter, choking, as well as injuries, diseases, and pains of the nostrils, falls from high places or from animals, fractures of the limbs, throat tumors, mutilation, sciatica, abscesses.

Gemini is indicative of shoulders, arms, hands, fingers, joints, sinews, strength, courage, change, the birth of women, speech, mouth, blood vessels, the voice. When afflicted, Gemini causes injuries to these parts; it also brings attacks of bandits and enemies accompanied by wounds, cuts, and loss of limbs. It brings jaundice and falls from high places.

Cancer is indicative of the chest, stomach, breasts, spleen, mouth, the hidden parts, the dimming of vision and blindness because of the nebula <in Cancer>. Under this sign the following occur: leprosy, lichenous scaliness of the skin and of the face, strokes, dropsy arising from complaints of the spleen, staggering gait, bilious syndromes, lameness, jaundice, piebald skin, buck teeth, crossed eyes, loss of eyelashes, diseased eyelids, twisted spines, injuries from aquatic animals, birthmarks and moles around the eyes, coughs bringing up blood, jaundice, pleurisy, and lung ailments.

Leo is indicative of the flanks, the loin, the heart, courage, vision, sinews. Under this sign the following occur: lunacy or superstitious terrors, convulsions/wounds caused by violence or vice, or resulting from bravery or asceticism, loss of limbs, amputation, injury to the eyes. It is also the cause of foul odors. It also causes ugliness, amputations, fractures, falls from high places or from animals, bites from wild beasts, and injuries from buildings collapsing and from burns, as well as depression, cancer, and homosexuality.

Virgo is indicative of the belly, the internal organs, and the internal reproductive organs. It causes attacks of passion; with respect to intercourse, it makes people who are either weak, or strong and chaste. (So that we may not seem too lengthy—the injuries and diseases caused by a sign or star are obvious from the nature of the sign and the star.) Virgo causes orthopnoea, hernia, superstitious terrors; in women it causes hysterical syndromes and complaints of the womb.

Libra is indicative of the hips, buttocks, the colon, the genitals, the hind parts. This sign causes paralysis, hernia, rupture, dysentery, dropsy, kidney stones.

Scorpio is indicative of the genitals and the rump. Because of its sting, it causes dimming of vision, blindness, weak eyesight, kidney stones, strangury, recurrent illness, hernia/promiscuity <?>, fistula.

Sagittarius is indicative of the thighs and the groin. Under this sign occur piebald skin with birthmarks, baldness, weak vision, eyestrain or blindness, bad breath, gout. It also causes falls from high places or from beasts, the loss of limbs and injuries from wild animals, and births with extra limbs.

Capricorn is indicative of the knees, the sinews, and internal and external sprains and strains because of its mysterious character. It causes weak vision and blindness because of its spiny vertebrae. It causes insanity, troubles from moist things; also delirium, incestuous women, lesbians and nymphomaniacs, banditry, and vice.

Aquarius is indicative of the legs, calves, sinews, and joints. It causes elephantiasis, jaundice, a sallow color, lameness, dropsy, insanity, castration, fractures, and sometimes strangury.

Pisces is indicative of the feet, the sinews, and the toes. Under it occur arthritis, lichenous scaliness of the skin and leprosy, and people who are on the way down, reviled and suffering many injuries. Pisces causes births with extra limbs, halting speech, deafness, mange, wounds from aquatic beasts, or affliction from moist syndromes.

All this being given, it will be necessary to examine each nativity closely to see in which sign the Lot of Fortune is located, for the nature of the sign will indicate the injury. The ruler of the Lot of Fortune will be particularly indicative, along with the sign in which it is located. Likewise examine Daimon and its ruler to see in which sign they are located, for these will clarify <the nature of> the disease. The stars in the Place of Occupation must be examined by you in the same way. Injuries and diseases will be quite violent if malefics are in conjunction or in aspect with these places or their houserulers. The native will be hale and healthy whenever the places and their rulers are favorably situated and not afflicted.

Each star has its own effect according to its allotted nature: if—to take a hypothetical example—the Lot is in Aries and its ruler, Mars, is also there (since Mars rules Aries and Scorpio), you can foretell an injury to the head and the genitals or the rump. Whatever the star *should* cause, judging from its nature, it *will* cause. Occasionally, if both places are afflicted, injuries and diseases occur, especially when malefics rule or are in aspect.

For example—so that we will not seem to talk in riddles—<take the following nativity>: Sun, Jupiter, Mars in Capricorn, Moon, Ascendant in Leo, Saturn in Taurus, Venus, Mercury in Aquarius, the Lot of Fortune <in Capricorn>, the ruler of Fortune, Saturn, in Taurus. The native was blind on account of the

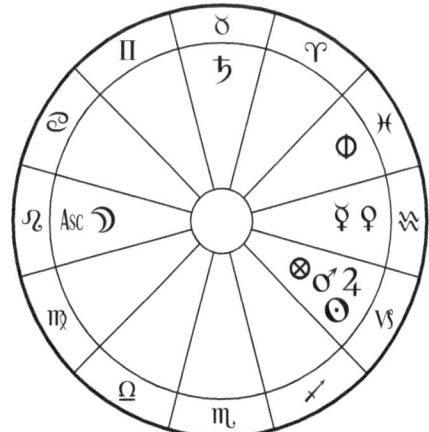

Pleiades and because of the malefic Saturn, and he had unmentionable vices because of both signs <Capricorn Taurus>. In addition, Jupiter, the ruler of Daimon (in Pisces), was found in Capricorn. From these configurations it was clear that he had gout. The Lot and its ruler was sufficient to reveal the disease and the injury.

Another example: Sun, Venus, Mars in Sagittarius, Moon in Libra, Saturn in Gemini, Jupiter in Virgo, Mercury in Scorpio, Ascendant in Capricorn, the Lot in Scorpio.[7] The genitals were injured because the ruler of Scorpio <Mars> was in Sagittarius. The native was bald and blind on account of <Sagittarius'> arrow. Jupiter, the ruler of Daimon <Pisces>, was found in <the IX Place of> the God and caused him to 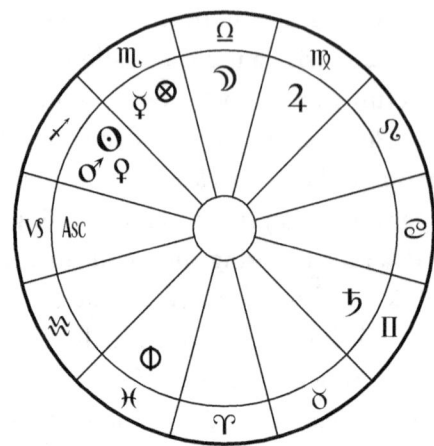 recover his sight with the help of the god. He became a seer.

So we see that benefics unfavorably situated are perverted and lead to infirmities and diseases, while malefics favorably situated cause no infirmities, just temporary and intermittent bouts of illness. If the rulers of the Lot of Fortune or of Daimon happen to be in <the IX Place of> the God or <the III Place of> the Goddess and are intercepted or aspected by malefics, they cause men to be struck dumb, to be raving lunatics, or to be seers. As the Compiler says, and most reasonably too: "If the star which indicates infirmity is in a Potent Place and is beheld by a malefic, the disease which befalls will be incurable and untreatable. If a benefic is in conjunction or in aspect with the Harmful Place, the native will be cured by medicine or by the help of a god." (By "Potent Place" he means the angles and the two <Places> which rise just after <the angles>, especially when the malefics which hold <the rulership> are in these places.) It is necessary to scrutinize accurately the degree-position of the Lots, because often a rough calculation puts the Lot in one sign, but an exact calculation puts it in another. This frequently happens as a result of the positions of the luminaries or of the Ascendant, if they are found either at the beginning or the end of a sign.

Generally speaking, the Sun, the Moon, Saturn, and Mercury, when in

---

[7] CB: The manuscript says that Saturn is in Cancer, but this chart appears several times in the *Anthology*, and in the other instances it is listed as being in Gemini rather than Cancer. Riley noted that this was an error in the text in his translation, so we have put Saturn in the correct sign of Gemini in the text and diagram here.

opposition or when rising just after <another star>, bring injuries to the eyes and onsets of other disease, insanity, or strokes. The Sun rising just after Mars or located in the same sign causes coughing or spitting blood and heart trouble, as well as injuries to the vision. Saturn and Mars at IC either together or alone make men of poor vision and subject to sudden fits, men who see visions of the gods or the dead, men who are initiated into secret, mystic lore. The same stars, if they are in opposition or in superior aspect with the new or full Moon, or if the individually behold the Moon while the Moon is passing out of a given phase, cause lunacy, possession, fits, and can strike men dumb.

For example: Sun, Saturn in Capricorn, Moon in Scorpio, Jupiter in Leo, Mars in Pisces, Venus, Mercury in Aquarius, Ascendant in Virgo, the Lot of Fortune in Scorpio, Daimon in Cancer. Saturn was in opposition to Daimon, which influences the intellectual and spiritual qualities, and Saturn beheld the full Moon, which was the immediately preceding phase. The ruler of the Lot of Fortune <Mars>

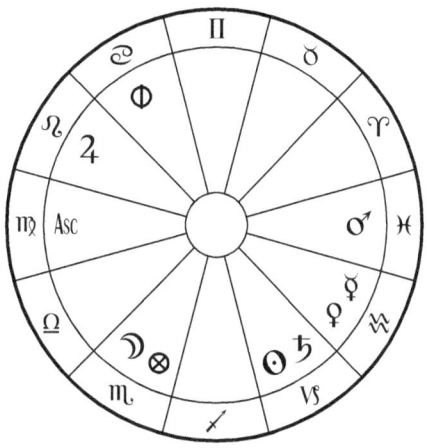

was in opposition to the Ascendant. The native had an injury in the fated places, tender feet, and—most significantly—he was a lunatic.

Another example: Sun in Sagittarius, Moon in Cancer, Saturn in Taurus, Jupiter, Mercury in Scorpio, Mars in Leo, Venus in Capricorn, Ascendant in Aquarius, the Lot of Fortune in Leo <!should be Virgo>. Mars is there, and Saturn in superior aspect. The Sun, found in the places of Jupiter, is indicative of things concerning the groin, thighs, and feet, and it caused infirmity in these parts as well as gout, for the Sun is the ruler of the sinews. Since Saturn was found at IC, the native had visions of the gods and of the dead.

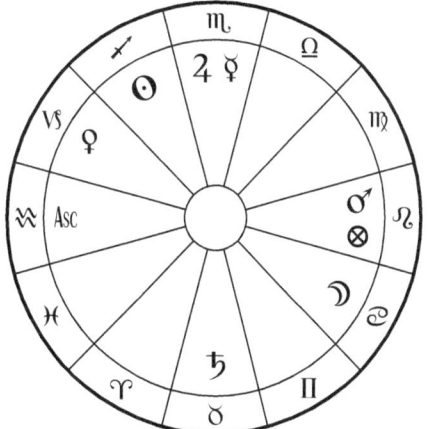

Another example: Sun in Aquarius, Moon in Virgo, Saturn in Taurus, Jupiter, Ascendant in Gemini, Mars in Cancer, Venus in Pisces, Mercury in Capricorn, the Lot of Fortune in Capricorn, Daimon in Scorpio. Malefics were in opposition to the Lots. The native was homosexual and had unmentionable vices, because Capricorn is a lewd sign and its ruler <Saturn> was in Taurus, a pathic sign. Scorpio also indicates this kind of vice.

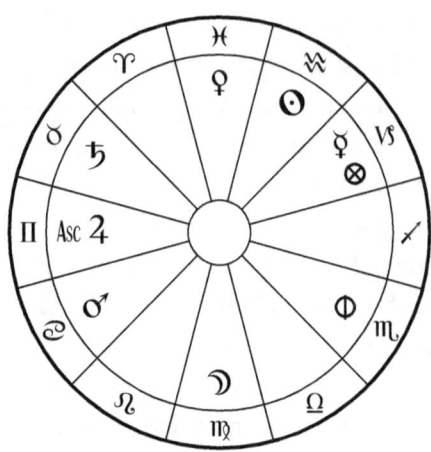

Another example: Sun, Venus in Sagittarius, Moon in Cancer, Saturn in Gemini, Jupiter, Mars in Leo, Mercury in Scorpio, Ascendant in Capricorn, the Lot of Fortune in Leo, Daimon in Gemini. Saturn located in this sign caused him to be castrated. The ruler <of Gemini>, Mercury, was in Scorpio, which indicated the genitals, and the Sun in Sagittarius indicated the region of the groin…

…Malefics entering Daimon or in opposition <to Daimon> cause insanity and possession…

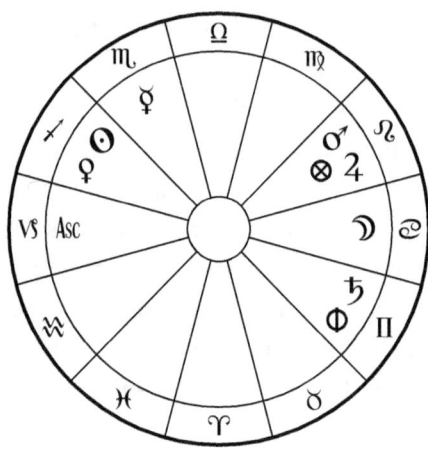

Another example: Sun, Moon, Mercury, Ascendant in Scorpio, Saturn in Leo, Jupiter in Cancer, Mars in Capricorn, Venus in Libra, the Lots in Scorpio. The native was blind because of <Scorpio's> sting. In addition Saturn was in superior aspect to the new Moon <in Scorpio> and to the luminaries, and the ruler <of Scorpio>, Mars, was unfavorably situated.

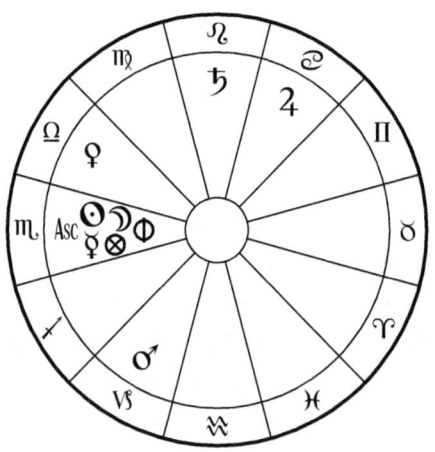

Another example: Sun, Mercury in Taurus, Moon in Aquarius, Saturn, Venus in Aries, Jupiter in Virgo, Mars in Pisces, Ascendant in Leo, the Lot of Fortune in Taurus. Its ruler, Venus, was in Aries with Saturn. The native had mange on the head and leprosy and lichenous scaliness of the skin because the ruler <Mars> of Daimon <in Scorpio> was in Pisces.

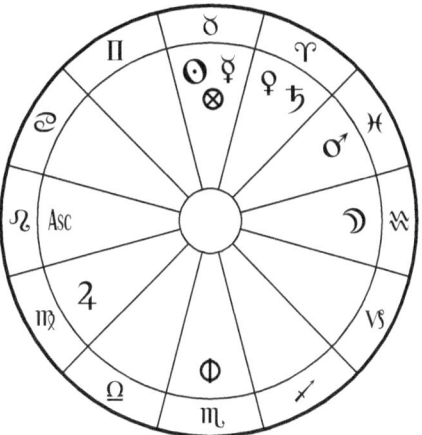

Another example: Sun, Mars in Taurus, Moon in Virgo, Saturn in Sagittarius, Jupiter in Gemini, Mercury, Venus, Ascendant in Aries, the Lot of Fortune in Sagittarius with its ruler <Jupiter> in Gemini. Furthermore Daimon was in Leo and its ruler <Sun> was in Taurus. The native had abnormally short arms.

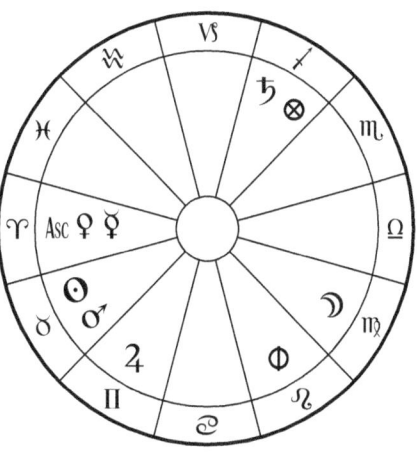

Another example: Sun, Mercury in Aries, Moon in Pisces, Saturn, Ascendant in Aquarius, Mars, Venus in Taurus, Jupiter in Libra, the Lot of Fortune in Pisces, the Lot of Daimon in Capricorn. The native was possessed of a god and insane. The ruler, Jupiter, of the Lot of Fortune was found in Libra, the IX Place of the God, and the ruler of Daimon, Saturn, was in the Ascendant. Venus was found at IC.

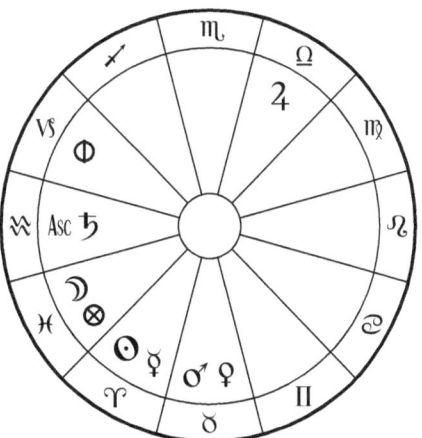

Another example: Sun, Mercury in Leo, Moon in Scorpio, Saturn, Ascendant in Aries, Jupiter in Pisces, Mars, Venus in Virgo, the Lot of Fortune in Capricorn, Daimon in Cancer. The native was a hunchback.

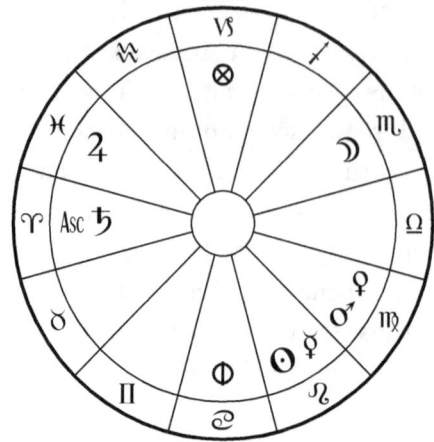

38. Marriage, Wedlock, and Happiness. Various Theorems and Configurations

I have published, with explanations, all the methods which seem from my experience to be true. Now I will explain the Place/topic of Marriage, complicated to be sure, but easily grasped by those who pay attention. Scientifically speaking, the Place of Marriage is considered to be the VII Sign from the Ascendant. It is also necessary to look at the location of Venus, the other stars in <Venus'> sign, as well as its aspects and rulers. If Venus is operative in a tropic or a bicorporeal sign, especially for night births, it makes men oft-married and promiscuous, particularly if Mercury is in conjunction or—even more so—if Mars is in aspect: then the native also rushes into the embrace of boys. If the sign is virile, the native is successful in gaining the object of his passions. If Venus is operative, and its ruler is either setting or in <the XII Place of> Bad Daimon, or if it is a malefic and afflicts Venus, or if it is wretchedly situated, it makes men unlucky in marriages and relationships. If a malefic nullifies Venus or—more particularly—its houseruler by being in aspect <with it>, it will cause deaths, injuries, or other problems to wives. If they are well situated at the nativity, they bring inheritances; if they are badly situated, diseases and pains.

If Saturn beholds the setting Venus, in most cases it makes unmarried, unsociable men. If Venus is in the sign or terms of Saturn, or if Venus has Saturn directly on the line of opposition, with neither Mars nor Jupiter in aspect nor Mercury in conjunction with Venus, the native will be a widow or a virgin. In all cases Saturn, when in opposition to Venus, brings sickly or barren wives—or for wives, brings sickly and sterile husbands. If Saturn is at the Midheaven and is in opposition to Venus, it brings wives who are slaves. If Venus is in the house of Saturn and has Jupiter in aspect, or if Venus is leaving Jupiter and making contact with Saturn, or becoming attached to Saturn, and is beheld by Mars, in these cases the native will lie with his nurse, with the wives of his tutors, with stepmothers, or with uncles and aunts. If the Sun is also in aspect with them or with the Moon, the native will be involved in perversion even more, especially if the Moon is in aspect with them or is aspected by them. Venus in conjunction with Saturn in the Descendant or at IC brings the native a marriage below his station and causes him grief in this marriage. Generally speaking, all those who have Venus in conjunction with Saturn, as a houseruler of Saturn, or in superior aspect with Saturn, and who have Jupiter in aspect with both, are united with prominent or elderly women. If the native is a woman, the same applies to her.

The Moon and Venus at the same angle unite the native with brothers or sisters, especially if Jupiter and Mars are also in aspect. The Moon and Venus square or in opposition make men jealous; Mars in aspect as well intensifies the jealousy. The Moon and Venus trine in their own houses, especially at angles, cause the marriage of relatives; even more so if Mars and Jupiter are in aspect. The Sun in its own house or exaltation and in conjunction with Jupiter and Venus causes marriage with the father's relatives. Venus in its own house or exaltation <or> terms and in conjunction with Mercury and the Moon causes marriage with the mother's relatives. Venus at IC with the Moon, or Venus and the Moon in opposition, particularly with one at the Midheaven, the other at IC, causes marriage with siblings or relatives.

In all cases Saturn in superior aspect, in opposition, or in conjunction with Venus, or as Venus' houseruler, chills or contaminates marriages, especially if Mercury is in aspect. Saturn in aspect with Venus at or just following an angle causes shameless, degrading, rebellious marriages, those involving the low-born or slaves, for whose sake the native is snowed under with trouble, unless some star intercepts and cancels the malign influence. If Jupiter is in aspect, most of the marriage's irregularity will be hidden and there will be no shame; the native will lie with prominent women, with women of high status. He will not have many children; his partners will be barren or conceive only with difficulty, and if they do conceive, they will miscarry. Apply similar reasoning to female nativities.

If Saturn is in aspect with Venus or in Venus' terms, and if Venus itself is configured with Jupiter and Mars, the native will achieve success with the help of children or females and will see prosperity, but he will fail utterly in the end, unless the stars happen to be operative in their own houses or exaltations. If the Moon is struck by Jupiter's rays or if it is configured with Jupiter, and if Saturn is in aspect along with Jupiter, the native will live with a low-born, purchased women. (Saturn harms social standing.)

In this configuration <concerning marriage>, if Venus is in its exaltation and has Jupiter in aspect, the native will become successful and propertied, and will be acknowledged on the part of great men, because of Venus. Again in this arrangement, if Mercury is in the configuration as well, the native will be vigorous, shrewd, intelligent, and charming; he will also be promiscuous and unstable in his marriages. Generally speaking, Jupiter in aspect with Venus from the right, being familiar with Venus, or in agreement to the degree, causes sociable men, those helped by women (or for women, those helped by men). Even if Venus is afflicted, <Jupiter> helps so that not the native is not entirely ruined.

Venus at an angle (especially in the Ascendant or at the Midheaven) and unafflicted by Saturn makes men happy in their marriages. Venus with Jupiter in aspect restrains any malign influence so that no disaster occurs, and it causes affinity and marriage. Venus in <the XII Place of> Bad Daimon, in its own house or exaltation, with Jupiter in superior aspect, or beheld by Jupiter in trine, makes a good marriage, but it will bring the grievous death of a good wife. If Venus and Saturn are in Bad Daimon and Jupiter does not behold them, the native becomes a widower or unhappily married, distressed by death and desertion. If in the preceding configuration (i.e., Venus in Bad Daimon without Jupiter in aspect) a malefic like Mars is in aspect, the native becomes an adulterer or a victim of adultery, a dirty, unlovable man and consequently drawn into difficulties. In all cases, <malefics> in conjunction with or opposition to Venus cause separations, deaths, or grief-producing unions—or even worse, if they afflict the Moon as well.

The Moon setting under the rays of the Sun is not good for marriages. Mars in conjunction with Mercury causes adultery, whoring, lechery; if their sign is tropic or bicorporeal, it causes even worse: the native sins more often, he casts his eyes everywhere but does not attain his desires. Sometimes he lies with people like himself and suffers the terrible things at their hands that he had done <to others>. Even worse happens if Mercury is in aspect with them. (The same happens in the case of feminine nativities.) If Saturn is also in aspect, even more occurs: the native is treated ungratefully even when he is kind to women, so much so that he plots against them as a result of their ill-treatment. Wives also suffer this at the hands of their husbands.

If Mars and Venus are setting under the rays of the Sun, they cause sneaking adulterers and secret sins. If these stars are rising or at angles, the sins are more public. If Mercury is in conjunction and rising with them, the adultery and the public outcry will be rather dangerous. If Jupiter is also in aspect, the native escapes; if not, he will be seized and murdered, if he is fated to this sort of death. If he is not, then he will avoid death by paying a great ransom. If Venus is unfavorably situated with Mars in <the XII Place of> Bad Daimon, and if both of them are operative, not in their own sects, or if they are in the Descendant or in the house of another member of the same sect—for a native with this chart, the ruin will be more terrible, the adultery will be even more hazardous, the outcome will be murderous. If Mars and Venus are in opposition, they still cause the above mentioned effects, but they intensify their influence for divorce, unpleasantness, jealousy, and anger, and they bring in succession even more plots and dangers. Because of their aspect with Mercury, rebellious sins follow. The native is united to slaves and servants, is promiscuous, whores around, and becomes notorious. He is seduced by friends, slaves, and enemies, and is involved in riots and murder by poison.

Jupiter in conjunction or in aspect with Venus causes the above mentioned effects, but they are secret. The native makes progress toward greater property—especially if Jupiter is at morning rising or is at an angle.

Whenever Mars is in aspect with Venus and in harmony with it, the native is united as a result of adultery. Whenever Mercury is in aspect with Venus rising, with Saturn having nothing in common with <them or> the houseruler, the native is joined to a virgin or to a young women. If Mars beholds, this is even more true. If Jupiter beholds, this is positively certain. It is generally true in all cases that Mercury in aspect with Venus involves and unites the native with those who are young and of a lower class. Men and women with this nativity <do the same thing>. If Mars is together or square with Venus, it makes adulterers, lechers, involvement with the base-born, criticism, divorces, and the deaths of mates. It is worse if Saturn is in opposition: this configuration unites the native with elderly or barren women; if Jupiter <is in opposition>, with women of high rank. If Saturn is configured with Jupiter while Jupiter is in conjunction with Venus, the native lies with prominent women or noblewomen. (The same apples to women, but in addition, whenever Mars and Mercury are estranged from Venus, the women are spinsters, marry late in life, and are abstinent and chaste.) If Saturn and Jupiter are in conjunction or trine with Venus, these results are more certain. Those masculine nativities which have Venus rising as a morning star can command women; those which have Venus under the rays of the Sun are commanded by women. The reverse is true for feminine nativities.

Calculate the Marriage Lot as follows: for day births, determine the distance from Jupiter to Venus (for night births, from Venus to Jupiter), then count this distance from the Ascendant. The point in opposition to this Lot is indicative of Adultery. If the ruler of the Marriage Lot is found in opposition, and if the ruler of the Lot of Adultery is in the Marriage Lot, the native will constantly commit adultery, then be reconciled, then having reconciled, be separated, then again rejoin his mate in the course of his adulteries. If the ruler of the Marriage Lot is at morning rising, the native will marry at an early age; if it is at evening rising, he will marry late. If the ruler is operative while setting, the native will have a jealous or an illegal marriage. The ruler of Marriage causes the first marriage, the benefics in harmony with the Marriage-bringer or its ruler also cause marriages, especially if the signs of the stars in aspect or of the Marriage-bringer itself are bicorporeal.

More About Marriage. Examples

<To find the Marriage Lot:> for men determine the distance from the Sun to Venus (for women from the Moon to Mars), then count this distance from the Ascendant. Venus and Mars "depress" both luminaries because the Sun has its exaltation in Aries and its depression in Libra, where it causes the day to become shorter. The Moon has its exaltation in Taurus and its depression in Scorpio, where it causes the cosmic disappearance of light. So, Venus will be the Marriage-bringer for men, Mars the Marriage-bringer for women—generally speaking. For men the Place of Marriage should accord with Daimon; for women it should accord with the Lot of Fortune, because of the conjoining and uniting of the Sun and Moon. <If the Places do accord with the Lots>, the marriage will be judged harmonious and legitimate. If many stars are in conjunction or in aspect with the Marriage-bringer, there will be many marriages. If the stars are linked with the Moon and have Jupiter in aspect, the marriages will be legitimate. If Saturn is in aspect, the marriages will end in death. If Mercury is in aspect without Jupiter, the native will be criticized for marrying a slave. If Jupiter is in aspect with Saturn, a legitimate marriage is indicated—some will even be ennobled by marriage. If in addition these stars are linked to or have some relationship with Venus, the marriage will result from a seduction. If Jupiter is in aspect, the marriage will be legitimate, profitable, and harmonious. If Jupiter is absent, but Saturn, Mercury, and Mars are in aspect, the marriage will be with streetwalking, sterile, degraded, or crippled women. If the Moon is with Venus, whorish and lecherous qualities arise as well as jealousy and quarrels; this sort of union is full of pretense. If the Sun rules the Marriage-bringer and is configured favorably, and if Jupiter is linked with the Moon, the marriage will be legitimate, secure, and respected. If the Moon is beheld by Saturn, the marriage will be with an orphan or under the direction of a guardian. If Venus and Mars are together or are linked with the Moon, the marriage will be with a woman the native has raped or seduced.

If the Moon and Venus are configured with Jupiter and the Sun, with no other stars in aspect, the native will marry once.

For men and women it will be necessary to examine the Lot of Fortune and Daimon, their squares and oppositions, their houserulers and its ruler, to see whether they are benefics or malefics. If they are configured in their own sects, the marriage will be fine and harmonious. If the places and their rulers are in opposition and are espied by malefics, then there will be setbacks, quarrels, jealousy, hostility, and trials concerning the marriage. Occasionally the native will suffer the compulsion of legal penalties. If Saturn is in aspect while all other stars are properly configured, death will separate the mates. If Mercury is the ruler of Daimon, the Moon the ruler of the Marriage-bringer, and both are in conjunction or aspect with each other, the native will marry great ladies or women prominent for their money or rank. If Jupiter is also in some aspect, the union will be profitable and harmonious, but if Saturn or Mars is in aspect, upset, hatred, and separations will occur and damaging accusations will follow. If Jupiter is houseruler, is configured with the Moon, and has Saturn in aspect, the native will unite with his mother or step-mother, but if the Moon has no relationship with the Lot of the Mother, he will unite with elderly women. If Jupiter is the houseruler of Daimon and Venus of the Marriage-bringer, the native unites with sisters or relatives. If Saturn is in aspect, all this will happen secretly; if Mercury and Mars are in aspect, divorces and public exposure will occur. If the Sun is in aspect while Saturn is absent, the marriage will be legitimate and loving, harmonious and profitable. If the Sun is the houseruler, the Moon is the ruler of the Marriage-bringer and configured with the Sun, and Jupiter is in aspect, the marriage will be harmonious, characterized by equality on both sides, legitimate, respected, and illustrious. If the Sun is the houseruler, Venus is the ruler of the Marriage-bringer, and Saturn is in aspect, the native will be criticized for marrying a daughter. If the Marriage-bringer is located with Saturn and <Saturn> or Mars is the ruler of Daimon, the native will remain unmarried. If Saturn is the houseruler of Daimon, and Venus holds the Place of Marriage and is found to be with Mercury and to have Mars in aspect, the native will marry barren women or those of bad reputation. Whenever the Marriage-bringer is away from an angle or is turned away from Daimon, the native marries foreigners or aliens, or gets a wife from abroad—what sort <of wife> will be clear from the nature of the signs and stars.

In the same way, for women it will be necessary to examine the Lot of Fortune and the Marriage-bringer (=from the Moon to Mars) and to interpret their influences. If the Moon rules the Lot <of Fortune>, and if Mercury rules the Marriage-bringer and is in conjunction or aspect with the Moon, the native will unite herself to a slave or a freedman; if Jupiter is in some aspect, this marriage will be legitimized. If under the preceding circumstances Jupiter is in the Place of Children and Saturn is also in aspect, the native will unite herself to a child or some youth in the position of a child. If the Place of Child belongs to Saturn and the Moon itself is in conjunction with Saturn, the native will remain unmarried. If the Moon is houseruler, and if Saturn is the Marriage-bringer and is in conjunction or aspect with the Moon, she will marry, but will hate her husband and live a disorderly life. If the Moon rules the Lot of Fortune and Mars the Marriage-bringer, and if they are in aspect with each other, the marriage will be by force, by kidnapping, or by war and captivity. If Jupiter is also in aspect, later the marriage will be legitimized. If Mars is in opposition to the Moon, with Saturn and the Sun in aspect, the husband will be an acknowledged homosexual. For feminine nativities, if Venus rules the Lot, with the Sun in conjunction and holding the Marriage-bringer and the Father's Lot, and with Saturn in aspect, the native will marry her father. If the Sun rules the Father's Lot, she will marry an older man in the position of a father. If Venus is the houseruler, Mercury holds the Place of Marriage, and Saturn is in aspect with both, the native will be promiscuous and live in brothels—but if Jupiter is also in aspect, she will be purchased and become a loving wife. If Jupiter is not in aspect, she will live shamelessly, in misery. If in the preceding configuration, Venus is found in Pisces or Capricorn, she will also be depraved. If Mars holds Daimon and the Moon holds the Marriage-bringer, the marriage will be by rape. If the two are in opposition and have Saturn or the Sun in aspect, the perpetrator will be recognized and caught. If Venus rules the Marriage-bringer and Mars the Lot of Fortune, the marriage will be the result of seduction. If in addition Saturn is in aspect with Mercury, and Jupiter is absent, the native will be convicted of adultery.

As for the rest of the configurations, whatever has been said of the masculine nativities should be applied to the feminine as well. Even if this exposition seems quite complicated, it will become most clear to these who read <attentively>.

39. Children and Childlessness

The Place of Children, which is figured from Mercury and Venus, must be examined: if afflicted by Saturn and Mars, they cause childlessness or the loss of children, but if helped by Jupiter, they cause fine offspring...

Therefore, it is necessary to examine the houseruler of this Lot of Children, which is found as follows: for male nativities, this Lot is found by determining the distance from Jupiter to Mercury (for female, from Jupiter to Venus), then counting this distance from the Ascendant. If the ruler of the Lot of Children has malefics in aspect, it destroys children; if it has the Givers of Children in aspect, it is indicative of fine offspring.

Petosiris says: "Whenever Jupiter, Venus, and Mercury are not afflicted, they are indicative of fine offspring. When the opposite is true, they cause lamenting and the deaths of children. If the stars that are in aspect with the Givers of Children are in bicorporeal signs, or if <the Givers> themselves are in bicorporeal signs, the number is doubled. Feminine stars in aspect with the Childgiver grant female children; male stars grant male children."

For male nativities: if Jupiter is with Mars as Mars' houseruler or if Mars is Jupiter's houseruler, and if Saturn is in aspect with Venus or is in Venus' house, the configuration is "productive" of childlessness and cuts off those already born.

For female nativities: the Moon in the places of Mercury, and Venus in a masculine sign with Saturn in aspect or as houseruler cause childlessness and destroy those already born. If Jupiter beholds the Moon or Venus, if the Moon is in the places of Mercury, if Saturn is in opposition or at the Midheaven, and if Mars is in aspect with Saturn, the native will bear only one child or be barren. Venus with Jupiter in aspect and afflicted by Saturn causes a difficult childbirth of one infant. If the Moon is also afflicted, the native will be completely childless. Saturn and Mars at the Midheaven, or one at the Midheaven, the other at IC, bring childlessness, unless a benefic is in some aspect.

40. Brothers

The Sun in the Ascendant causes the native to have few or very few brothers. Saturn in the Descendant causes the native to have few or very few brothers. Jupiter, Mercury, and Venus at the angles are the bestowers of brothers, but Saturn in opposition kills the oldest brother. Saturn in conjunction with Mars is destructive of brothers or makes them sickly. Venus and the Moon domiciled in the III Place from the Ascendant, the Place of Brothers, grants sisters, especially if the sign is feminine. If the Sun, Jupiter, and Mercury are in a masculine sign <in the III Place>, they grant brothers. Malefics in aspect with the Place of Brothers, if that Place is unfavorably situated, kill the brothers who have been born or cause the native to have few or no brothers. Benefics in aspect with the Place of Brothers not only grant brothers, but make them prosper. Mars, when operative in the Place of Brothers and favorably situated—especially when it has a benefic in aspect and is beholding the Moon—becomes a Giver of Brothers.

Some astrologers calculate the Place of Brothers in the same manner as the

Lots: for day births, determine the distance from Saturn to Jupiter (for night births the reverse), then count this distance from the Ascendant.

41. Violent Deaths. Examples

The opposition of Sun and Moon is not always bad. Only if an approaching malefic beholds the phase or if the malefic casts its rays while it has some relationship with the luminaries does the opposition become bad. Consequently, even the all-fortunate nativities do not remain lucky to the end; at some place the houserulership of the star becomes badly situated or reversed and causes ill fortune.

Petosiris seems to have defined the place perfectly, even though he spoke in mystic riddles: "The beginning, the end, the controller, and the measurement standard of the whole is the houseruling star of each nativity: it makes clear what kind of person the native will be, what kind of basis his livelihood will have, what his character will be, what sort of body <=health and appearance> he will have, and all the things that will accompany him in life. Without this star nothing, neither occupation nor rank, will come to anyone."

But, how is it possible for a nativity to succeed in everything or, on the other hand, to fail in everything, depending just on the houserulership of just one star? On the contrary, generally one star is found to be ruler of the basis of the nativity (i.e., noble, average, base-born) from its beginning (or that one star activates the influences of the rest). Another star is the ruler of the remaining factors. We see some men fortunate in their livelihood and public standing, adorned with all magnificence, with the apparent houseruler configured appropriately. <We see> these same men, however, to be unfortunate in the wives and children, becoming outrageous and disgusting, polluting their livelihood, and becoming public scandals as if they were unworthy of their excellent beginnings. Some are even ruined later or die violently. Therefore the native is not fortunate in everything nor does everything happen as the consequence of <one> houseruler. Another afflicted houseruler blackens reputations by bringing many crises. We also note that other men have gone from a low and ignoble station to an unsurpassed and unhoped-for condition. We note others who are fortunate in their wives and children, but needy in their livelihood. Still others are prosperous in possessions, but of low rank and sickly. Others are long-lived, but toil-worn and crippled. Some are rich but short-lived or consumptive, and hence unable to profit from their riches. So we say: one star is the Life-giver, another is the ruler of property and of death.

But, someone will say, if the houseruler is unfavorably situated, the native will be short-lived. For that very reason, since it is unfavorably situated, it is of no use for <the houseruler> to grant a prosperous livelihood, nor would it be appropriate for the houseruler to make a subjugated and base-born native illustrious and distinguished later in life. Nor will a well-configured star cause a high-born native, one never entangled in evildoing, to be condemned and to die violently. Instead, the unfavorably situated star creates the lesser man, but the ruler of rank and livelihood, found at an angle and receiving the chronocratorship, renders the man illustrious. If so, then this star which makes the man fortunate, if found at an angle or in operative places, keeps him fortunate during its own chronocratorship. But when the star comes to have another star which causes disease, infirmity, or some other critical affliction in superior aspect or in opposition, then it will yield and its influence will weaken. Many other noteworthy things happen in the life of man, things which come about not through the activity or operation of one houseruler, but through the activity of many.

If anyone researches thoroughly the Places and the houserulers, he will determine quite easily the area in which the nativity is fortunate and the area in which it is unfortunate. Whenever any star that has a relationship with the nativity (i.e., one that controls livelihood, life, injury, disease, occupation, or any of the other areas of concern) is afflicted in one respect, in that respect it will harm the nativity. Indeed, we find that the Compiler does not use <just> one influential houseruler. He says:

"One controls occupations, one the possession of years, one stability and change, one decline;"

or again:

"Observing the positions of the Sun and Moon at conjunction and their separations after full Moon, with respect to the angles and the signs following them, on which the whole <forecast> depends;"

or again:

"When starting to cast a horoscope, one must examine the Descendant, the sign preceding the Descendant, and the sign just following the Descendant, because in these places is found the fated outcome."

He says many other similar things. So it is necessary to consider one place for occupation and rank, another for life, another for injury, disease, and death. Not everything will depend on one houseruler. We act rationally when we make our forecasts after considering many influences.

Later in our treatise we will clarify these points, particularly in <the section on> the distribution of the chronocratorships. Now we will press on to consider violent deaths. When the ruler of the new or full Moon at the nativity is turned away from its sign or is unfavorably situated, with a malefic in aspect, it indicates violent death. In the same way, if Mercury is in opposition to the full Moon and has malefics in aspect, it brings a bad cause of death. If Saturn, Mars, or Mercury are located in the sign <of the Moon> on the fortieth day, they indicate violent death. Likewise malefics in the Descendant or in the sign preceding the Descendant bring violent deaths or the onset of diseases and miserable deaths. The VIII Place from the Ascendant has the same influence on the cause of death; so does the 8th Place from the Lot of Fortune. It is necessary to examine the Lot and its ruler to see in which signs they are located, because the cause of death will be foretold by them: the Moon (which is Fortune), when in conjunction with the Sun in Aries, suffers an eclipse or loss of light in the eighth sign, Scorpio. Therefore Scorpio is called its depression.

We will give a brief tour of each sign in order to make what is said here easily understandable:

Aries is destroyed by Scorpio. Since they are both domiciles of Mars, Mars is a destroyer of itself. Therefore <Aries> causes suicides, those who throw themselves from heights, and those ready for death; accomplices in crime, bandits, and murderers (i.e., those who bring a cause of death on themselves), plus those perishing from animal attacks, from fires, or from collapsing buildings. <It also causes men to die> from animals, bleeding, or attacks

Taurus is destroyed by Sagittarius, i.e., Venus is destroyed by Jupiter. Men born under this configuration die peacefully from luxurious living, from stuffing themselves with food, wine, or sex, or from strokes while asleep or while relaxing. No distressing cause of death will appear, unless some malefic in conjunction or in aspect introduces and indicates a cause of death appropriate to its nature

Gemini is destroyed by Capricorn, i.e., Mercury by Saturn. Some men die violently troubled by black bile, are attacked by painful cramps or are harmed in damp places by beasts or by crawling things. Some are condemned to death, imprisoned, or suffocated. Some are attacked by bandits or the enemy. Some are poisoned—because of the wet quality <of the sign>.

Cancer is destroyed by Aquarius, i.e., the Moon by Saturn. Men perish through dampness or internal complaints, from pains of the spleen and stomach, or from vomiting fluids. They die at sea, on rivers, from chills, from attacks of beasts and crawling things. They perish from elephantiasis, jaundice, lunacy, poisoning, long imprisonment, and other chronic fevers. Women die from pains of the breasts, cancer, infirmities of the genitals or womb, from suffocation, or from abortions.

Leo is destroyed by Pisces, i.e., the Sun by Jupiter. As a result men die from heart attacks and from complaints of the liver. They are at risk in wet places or from moist complaints, falls, the ague, accidents in the baths, and the treachery of women.

Virgo is destroyed by Aries, i.e., Mercury by Mars. They die from treachery and crime. They are attacked by the enemy or by bandits. They perish from burns, collapsing buildings, blindness, imprisonment, the wrath of noblemen, or from captivity, falls from animals or high places, the crushing of limbs, or animal attacks. Females die from collapsed uterus, abortions, hemorrhages, or consumption.

Libra is destroyed by Taurus, i.e., Venus by itself. Therefore men become suicides through poisoned drinks, through snakebite, through self-starvation. They die from excessive intercourse, excision of the uvula, drowning, or they become mutilated, blind, or paralyzed. They are attacked by females or fall from high places or animals.

Scorpio is destroyed by Gemini, i.e., Mars by Mercury. They die by knife cuts to the genitals or the rump, or from strangury, festering sores, choking, crawling things, violence, war, attacks by bandits, assaults of pirates, or because of officials, and by fire, impaling, attacks of beasts and crawling things.

Sagittarius is destroyed by Cancer, i.e., Jupiter by the Moon. They die from disorders of the spleen, liver, stomach, from vomiting fluids or blood, falls from animals, attacks of ravenous beasts, collapsing buildings, shipwreck, wet places. They die from lunacy, blindness, feebleness.

Capricorn is destroyed by Leo, i.e., Saturn by the Sun. They die from heart attacks and fractures and from accidents in the baths or from burns, through the wrath of kings and noblemen, or by impaling, injuries from beasts and animals, or falls from high places.

Aquarius is destroyed by Virgo, i.e., Saturn by Mercury. They die from wasting of the vitals, dropsy, elephantiasis, jaundice, fever, sword slashes, dysentery, and from the treachery of women.

Pisces is destroyed by Libra, i.e., Jupiter by Venus. <They die> from moist complaints, poisoning, painful fluxes or cramps, complaints of the genitals or liver, sciatica, attacks of beasts and crawling things.

So much for the subject of violent death. In addition it will be necessary to take into account the influence of each sign on injuries and diseases so as to make the type of death obvious. Each star in conjunction or aspect will have the effect of adding its influence to the cause of death according to the star's nature. It is necessary to examine how the Places and their rulers are situated and whom they have in aspect (viz. related or unrelated stars), and thus make your determination. Malefics in conjunction with the Places or in aspect with the houserulers bring violent death. Benefics indicate the cause to be distress, injury, disease, or an attack of fever. For example: Gemini is destroyed by Capricorn and Aquarius by Virgo, i.e., Mercury by Saturn and Saturn by Mercury. Now if these stars have the relationship of opposition or square in a nativity, they cause men to have short lives or a wretched death, since the Lifegiver is in opposition to the ruler of Death. If they have no relationship, but simply behold each other without being in their own domiciles, they bring setbacks, trials, exile, and other temporary misfortunes. (Consider the arrangement of Mars and Mercury as having the same effects.) The Old Astrologer wants them to be in opposition when he says: "Let every opposing configuration (=rising and setting) of any star or of the Sun and the Moon cause the native to be subject to the legal process." But I declare that crises concerning rank, livelihood, and death will occur, if the stars have a relationship involving destruction or some other houseruling function.

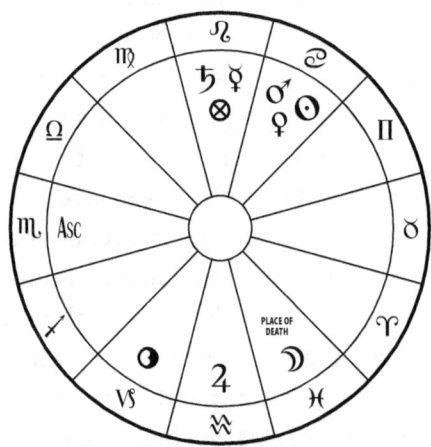

Examples: Sun, Mars, Venus in Cancer, Saturn, Mercury in Leo, Jupiter in Aquarius, Moon in Pisces, Ascendant in Scorpio, the Lot of Fortune in Leo, the <8th> Place of Death in Pisces. The Moon was in this Place, and Saturn was in conjunction with the Lot of Fortune. The ruler <of Leo>, the Sun, was with Mars in Cancer, a wet sign. This person died in the bath, drowned in the water.
Mars was in opposition to the full Moon <Capricorn>, and Saturn, the ruler <of the full Moon>, was turned away. Therefore he died violently.

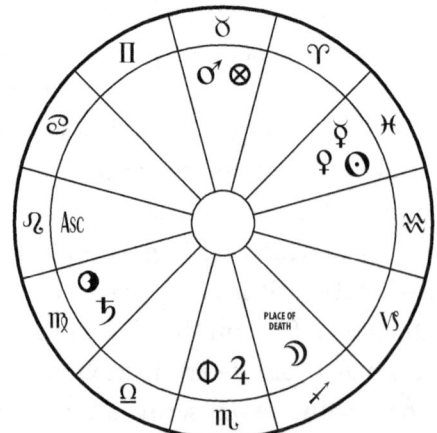

Another example: Sun, Mercury, Venus in Pisces, Saturn in Virgo, Jupiter in Scorpio, Mars in Taurus, Moon in Sagittarius, Ascendant in Leo, the Lot of Fortune in Taurus.[8] Mars was located so that it ruled Daimon <Scorpio> and was in

---

[8] CB: The manuscript says that Jupiter is in Aries, but Pingree corrected this to Jupiter in Scorpio, and we accept his emendation here.

opposition to it. The <8th> Place of Death was in Sagittarius, and the Moon was there and had Saturn in superior aspect in the sign of the full Moon <Virgo>. Likewise Mercury, the ruler of the full Moon, was in opposition <to Virgo and Saturn>. The native was beheaded.

Another example: Sun in Cancer, Moon in Pisces, Saturn, Mars, Mercury in Gemini, Jupiter in Capricorn, Venus in Leo, Ascendant in Libra, the Lot of Fortune in Gemini. In this sign Saturn, Mercury, and Mars attended each other, being destroyers of each other, and they were in aspect with the Moon <square>. Likewise the ruler <Saturn> of the full Moon <Capricorn> was turned away, and Jupiter in the <8th> Place of Death and in opposition to the Sun was not able to help. The native was beheaded.

Another example: Sun, Mercury, Mars, Jupiter, Venus in Capricorn, Moon in Aquarius, Saturn in Taurus, Ascendant in Aries. The native was beheaded.

Another example: Sun, Venus in Aquarius, Moon in Gemini, Saturn in Scorpio, Jupiter in Pisces, Mars in Cancer, Mercury, Ascendant in Capricorn, the Lot of Fortune in Virgo, the <8th> Place of Death in Aries. The rulers <Mars Mercury> of these places were in opposition to each other and in wet signs; furthermore Mars was in the Descendant. The native was roasted while relaxing in the bath.

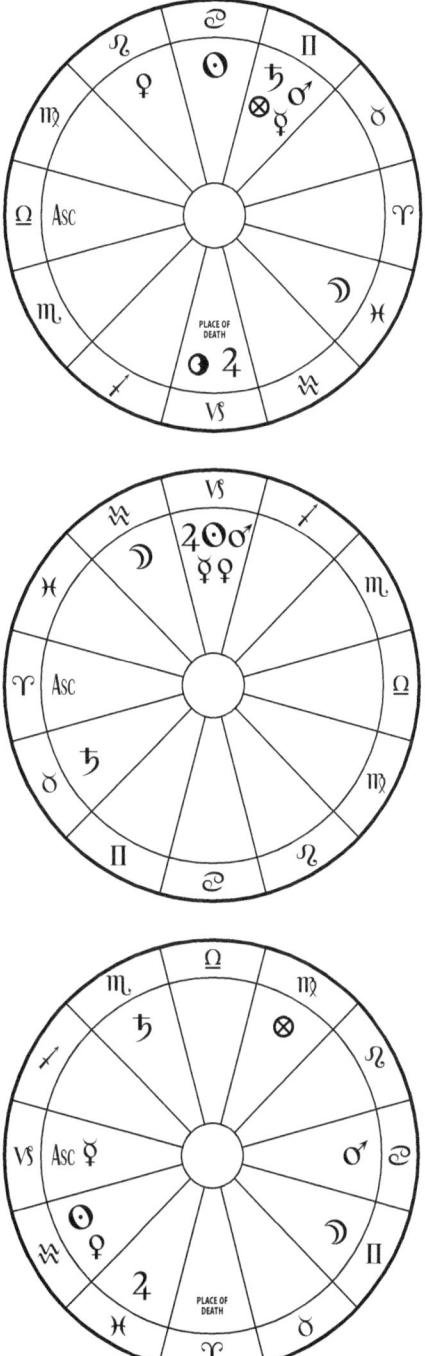

Another example: Sun, Venus in Capricorn, Moon in Cancer, Saturn, Mercury in Sagittarius, Jupiter in Taurus, Mars in Leo, Ascendant in Aquarius, the Lot of Fortune in Leo. Mars was in Leo, a fiery and solar sign, in opposition to the Ascendant. Saturn and Mercury were in superior aspect to the <8th> Place of Death <Pisces>. The native was burned alive.

Another example: Sun in Capricorn, Moon in Libra, Saturn in Taurus, Jupiter in Gemini, Mars, Ascendant in Cancer, Venus in Aquarius, Mercury in Sagittarius, the Lot of Fortune in Libra. The Moon was in Libra and was in inferior aspect to Mars, which was in opposition to the Sun. The <8th> Place of Death was in Taurus, and Saturn was there. The native was thrown to the lions.

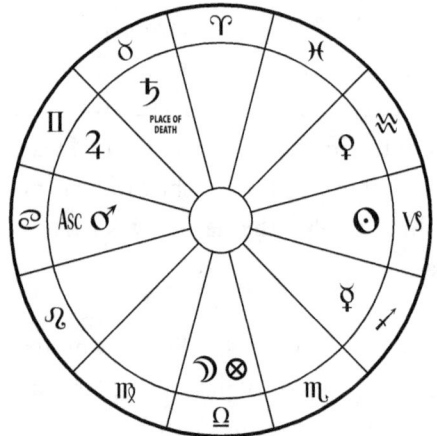

Another example: Sun, Moon, Mercury in Gemini, Saturn in Leo, Jupiter in Pisces, Mars in Cancer, Venus in Taurus, Ascendant in Capricorn. The Lots were also in Capricorn. The ruler <of the Lots>, Saturn, was in the <8th> Place of Death <Leo> and was beheld by Venus. Mars was in opposition to the Ascendant. The native died by poison.

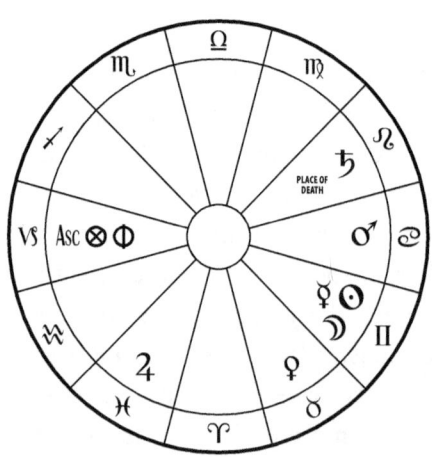

Another example: Sun, Mercury, Ascendant in Taurus, Moon in Pisces, Saturn in Gemini, Jupiter in Aquarius, Mars in Virgo, Venus in Aries, the Lot of Fortune in Pisces. The Moon was in Pisces beheld by Saturn and Mars. The ruler <Moon> of Daimon <Cancer> and the ruler <Mars> of the full Moon <Scorpio> were in opposition. The native drowned in bilge water.

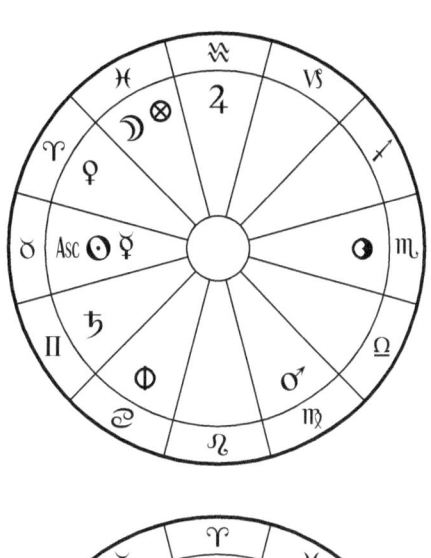

Another example: Sun in Leo, Moon, Mercury in Virgo, Saturn in Gemini, Jupiter in Aries, Mars, Ascendant, Venus in Cancer, the Lot of Fortune in Gemini. Saturn, the ruler <of the 8th Place> of Death was in Gemini and in superior aspect to Mercury, the ruler of the Lot of Fortune, and to the Moon. Furthermore Mars was in opposition to the <8th> Place of Death <Capricorn>. The native hanged himself.

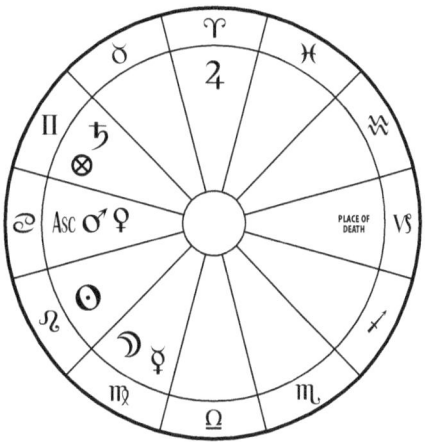

Another example: Sun, Mercury in Aries, Moon, Venus in Pisces, Saturn in Cancer, Jupiter, Mars in Taurus, Ascendant in Scorpio, the Lot of Fortune in Sagittarius. The ruler <Jupiter, of the Lot of Fortune> was in the Descendant with Mars. The <8th> Place of Death was in Cancer. Saturn, the ruler of the full Moon<?>, was turned away and Mars was in opposition to its own house <Scorpio>. The native was thrown to the lions.

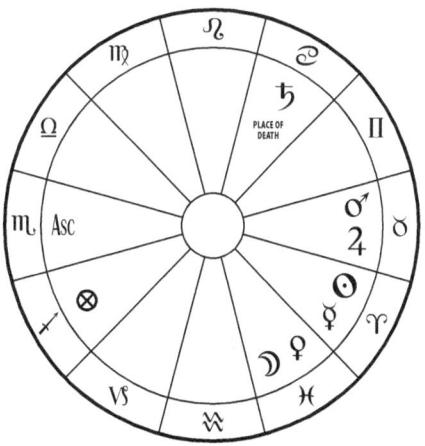

In regard to the configuration of opposition, we have learned that malefics are not harmful in all ways for all nativities. Occasionally they are even benefic, especially for noble nativities, with the caution that <these nativities> are entangled in evils. Such nativities are violent men, living with struggles and involved in wicked, lawless activities. They act illegally; they plunder and rob; they become covetous and insanely arrogant because of the—temporary—blessings of fame. They attribute their own faults to others. Furthermore they despise God and death, because they are themselves masters of life and death. As a result good fortune does not stay with such men throughout their lives, but some fall from glory to a dishonored and lowly life—because of the configuration of opposition. Others die violently. Some suffer what they had inflicted on others, experiencing vengeance and punishment while railing at their previous, vain appearance of glory. When stripped in a moment's time of the possessions which they had swept together after years of toil, care, and violence, they grieve or they unwillingly yield to others. Along with their unsteady fortune, other things follow such men: Nemesis pulling at the reins, envy, plots, treachery, grief, care, bodily exhaustion, so that even if they wished to exchange their useless prosperity for the fortune of the average man, they cannot do so, but must suffer whatever Fate forces on her unwilling victims.

The configuration of opposition can be interpreted in two ways: one way when a star in the Ascendant is in opposition to another; the second when a star is in opposition to its own house, triangle, or exaltation. The rulers of the triangles or the sects will be most malign and most disturbing to livelihoods when they are in opposition to each other.

Book III

The *Anthologies* of Vettius Valens of Antioch: Book III

1. The Control

Various astrologers have handed down various teachings about the basis of the <nativity's> length of life. Since this topic seems quite complicated and complex, we will clarify it using methods proven by our own experience. The first topics of discussion will be "control," "projection of rays," and "houserulership." First let the control with respect to the Sun and the Moon be investigated.

Some give day births to the Sun, night births to the Moon, but I say that the Sun controls night births and the Moon day births, if they happen to be configured advantageously. If both are, assign control to the one which is more appropriately configured in its own sect or triangle. Then the houseruler is found from the terms of the controlling star. If both <the Sun and the Moon> are unfavorably situated, then the term of the degree in the Ascendant or at the Midheaven will fix the houserulership, usually that <star> whose ruler is in an appropriate configuration with the Ascendant.

Let these controlling points be considered as proven by us. The first control: the Sun in Leo, the Moon in Cancer; the luminary in appropriate configuration with the Ascendant or Midheaven will have the control, and the ruler of its term will be houseruler. If both are in the terms of the same star, that star will unquestionably be judged the houseruler.

The second control: if the Sun is in the Ascendant, the Moon in <the XII

Place of the> Bad Daimon, the Sun will have control. If the Sun is in <the XI Place of the> Good Daimon, and the Moon is at the Midheavan, the Sun will have control. If the Sun is in the Descendant while the Moon is in the sign just following the Descendant, the Sun will have control. If the Moon is in the Descendant while the Sun is in the sign just following the Descendant, the Sun will have control. If the Sun just precedes the Midheaven while the Moon is in the Ascendant, the Moon will have control. If the Sun again just precedes the Midheaven while the Moon just follows the Ascendant, the Moon will have control. If the Sun again just precedes the Midheaven while the Moon is also at the Midheaven, the Moon will have control. If the Sun just precedes the Midheaven and the Moon just follows the Midheaven, the Moon will have control. If the Moon precedes the Midheaven while the Sun is at IC, the Sun will have control. If the Moon precedes the Midheaven while the Sun just follows IC, the Sun will have control. If the Sun precedes the overhead angle while the Moon follows IC, the Moon will have control. If the Sun precedes the overhead angle while the Moon is at IC, the Moon will have control. If both luminaries precede the Midheaven, the Ascendant will have control and the ruler if its terms will be considered the houseruler. If the Moon follows the Midheaven while the Sun is in <the IX Place of> the God, the luminary which first sends its rays exactly to the Ascendant's degree-position will have control. If the Sun and the Moon just precede the Ascendant in the XII Place, the Midheaven will have control and the ruler of its terms will be houseruler.

As can be seen, if the nativity is during the day, the luminaries are not dominant if they are above the Earth. The Ascendant will have control and the ruler of its degrees will be the houseruler. For night births, if the luminaries precede IC, the Midheaven will have control. If the Sun just follows IC while the Moon just precedes the Midheaven, the luminary which first sends its rays exactly to the Ascendant will have control. If the Sun and the Moon are in the Descendant, the term of the <preceding> new Moon will have control and the ruler of its degrees will be the houseruler. Similarly if both are in the Ascendant, at the Midheaven, or at IC, the term of the new Moon will have control and the ruler of its terms will be the houseruler. If the luminaries are in the same sign (or in different signs) and in the terms of the same star, infallibly that star will be the houseruler.

If the Sun is found to be in its own depression <Libra>, it will not be the apheta, unless it is exactly in the Ascendant (to the degree). The same is true for the Moon in Scorpio <its depression>. If the Moon is found to be new and to be under the rays of the Sun, it will not be the apheta, unless it too is exactly in the Ascendant.

If the Moon is nearing full and passes out of this phase within the term in the Ascendant, it will be both the apheta and the anaereta, if it passes out of the full-Moon phase on that same day. It will be necessary to examine the number of degrees between this day and the full Moon; having found this number, <you can> forecast the number of years. For example: Ascendant, Moon in Aries 22°. On the same day it passed out of the full-Moon phase at 27° of the same sign. The distance from its position then and the full Moon was 5°, which totals 4 years. The native lived that many years.

Death will occur particularly if a malefic applies its rays and if it is in aspect or opposition to the sign. If a benefic is in the same relation, there will be infirmity and disease instead of death. The rest of the Moon's phases during its connection with <the Sun> are destructive.

It is necessary to consider the control to be certain if the Sun or the Moon is in aspect with the ruler of the terms, and if it is at an angle or in operative degrees. If it is found to be turned away, the nativity is judged to lack a houseruler. If the ruler of the Sun's or the Moon's sign and the ruler of the terms exchange terms, then too will the houserulership be without a controller. It will be necessary to determine if the star that seems to be houseruler is in the Descendant, for if it is, that nativity as well will lack a houseruler.

2. The Significant Degrees of the Angles

First of all, fix the degree-positions of the Ascendant, the Midheaven, and the other angles. Then it is necessary to take the distance in degrees from the Ascendant to IC (moving in the order of the signs), to consider one-third of that total distance to be the "operative" degrees in the configuration of the angles, and to consider the stars in these degrees, whether benefics or malefics, to be powerful. Consider the rest of the degrees in order up to IC, as well as the stars in them, to be "inoperative" and impropitious. The points in opposition to the Ascendant and to the other angles will fall into the same pattern with respect to operative and inoperative degrees and the stars in <the operative degrees> will be powerful. It is therefore obvious that there will not always be 30° at an angle, but sometimes more, sometimes fewer. If in the Ascending and Descending signs there are fewer than 30 powerful degrees, then there will be more than 30° at the Midheaven and IC. If in the Ascending sign and its opposite there are more than 30°, then at the Midheaven and IC there will be fewer.

An example: Ascendant at Pisces 13°, the Midheaven at Sagittarius 22°, IC at Gemini <22°>, Descendant at Virgo 13°. I take the distance from the Ascendant to IC, 99°. One-third of this is 33°. I count this distance from the Ascendant and stop at Aries 16°. These degrees and the stars in them will be powerful; the rest of the degrees from Aries 16° to IC will be inoperative. The points in opposition will have the same effect. Secondly

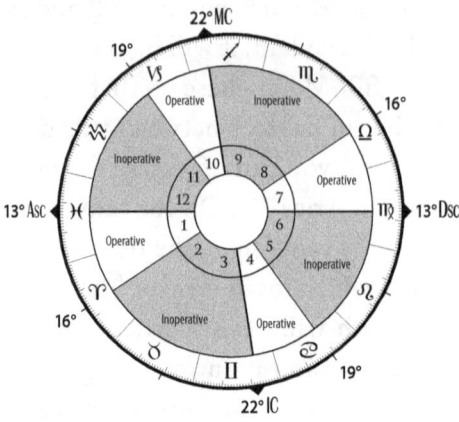

I take the distance from the Midheaven to the Ascendant, 81°. One-third of this is 27°. I count this from the Midheaven and stop at Capricorn 19°. These degrees and those in opposition to them will be operative; the rest will be inoperative. It is necessary to do likewise for other nativities in order to know whether stars are in operative or inoperative degrees.

Now to me the following method seems more scientific: take the distance from the degree in the Ascendant to IC, calculate one-third (as previously stated), then count from the Ascendant in the order of the signs, and consider these degrees and those in opposition to be powerful. Now consider the other <one-third> portion of the degrees to be average, neither completely good or bad, because this region 1) follows the

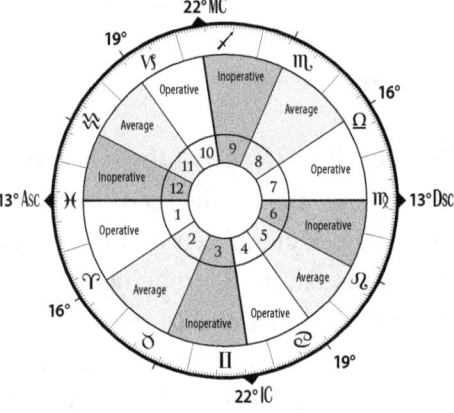

Ascendant, 2) is <the III Place of> the Goddess, 3) is in opposition to <the IX Place of> the God. So then, the first third from the Ascendant will be operative and powerful, the second third will be average, the third third will be crisis-producing and bad. The stars <in these regions> will act in the same way.

It is necessary to calculate likewise from the Midheaven, and to consider the first third of the distance between angles as operative, the second third, following the Midheaven, as of average influence (thus it was called Good Daimon by the ancients), and the last third, up to the Ascendant, as afflicting and inoperative. The Places in opposition to these will have the same force. Orion expounded all this in his book.

3. The Vital Sector

Some astrologers, moved by envy or ignorance, have written elaborately, obscurely, and simple-mindedly about the vital sector. These men have made forecasts by adding, in every case, the rising times of the degrees from the aphetic place to the point square with it. In view of this error, we find it necessary to clarify the method of determining <the length of life>, because we find nativities living longer than the 90° arc, especially nativities in the signs of shorter rising times, even though the Old Astrologer specifically says this is impossible. On the other hand, we see some nativities which do not live this 90° arc, even without the malefics' projection of rays.

Therefore in casting a nativity, it will be necessary to determine if it does or does not have a houseruler, and if the Sun, the Moon, or the Ascendant is the apheta. If the Sun or Moon are in the aphetic place, then it will be necessary to figure the total rising times (in the klima of the nativity) from the position of the apheta to the point square with it. Having found the total time, you can forecast that the native will live as many years. This forecast will be accurate if the houseruler is in its own terms or is configured appropriately, has contact or is in aspect with the apheta, and if no anaereta applies its rays and deducts from the number of years. If the houseruler is not in aspect with the controller, but is otherwise found to be favorably configured (i.e., in the Ascendant, at the Midheaven while rising), it will allot the full span of years. If it is <not at> one of the other angles, it will deduct a portion of the arc proportional to its relationship <with the rest of the horoscope>, but will allot the remainder <as the length of life>.

So, in all cases it will be necessary to figure the number of years allotted by the controller and compare them with the years allotted by the houseruler. The total will be the number of years the native will live. If the years of the houseruler are less than those of the apheta, he will live the years of the houseruler.[1] The houseruler will allot the time—if the nativity has a houseruler—with some deduction of the arc from angle to angle. If the years of the apheta are less than the years of the houseruler, the native will live the number of years allotted by the apheta and the nativity will be judged to lack a houseruler. If the controller is appropriately situated, each one (viz. the apheta and the houseruler) will assign its own period of years.

Some astrologers figure the distance from the houserulers to the angles using <only> the Ascendant and the Descendant. If they are 5 or 6 signs apart, they subtract <an appropriate> amount. I say that one should figure

---

[1] *Marginal note from the manuscripts:* This concerns the horimaea. The controller is one thing, the houseruler is another, and the apheta is another.

the houseruler's distance from all of the four angles, then subtract—if in fact the nativity is found to have a houseruler. For he says: "...If <a star> is found to be at the Midheaven, in <the XI Place of the> Good Daimon, or in some operative place, it will allot the full span of years." So he did not subtract the appropriate amount from <just> the Ascendant or the Descendant position. If neither the Sun nor the Moon are in the aphetic place, but the Ascendant or the Midheaven are, one should not figure the number of years from the aphetic place to the point square with it. <Instead> determine the number of degrees <from the apheta> to the next angle, then forecast the years—unless some anaereta embezzles from the number of years by applying its rays.

An example: let a nativity in the second klima have Gemini 8° as the Ascendant, Aquarius 22° as the Midheaven. Even though the vital sector starts at the Ascendant, its ending point is by no means at the point square with it, Virgo 8°, but at IC, Leo 22°. I can forecast this total of years, unless some anaereta casts its rays. If an anaereta is in Gemini 20°, or in any degree of Cancer, or projects its rays to such a point, the

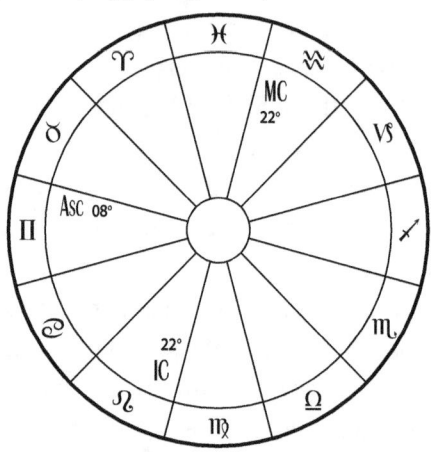

native will live as many years as the number of degrees <=rising times> from the aphetic point to the anaeretic point. In the same way if we make the vital sector begin at the Midheaven, Aquarius 22°, we will not find the sum of years to be the distance from the Midheaven to the point square with it, Taurus 22°, but to Gemini 8° <the Ascendant>. It is obvious that the vital sector can exceed 90° when using the method of signs, but it cannot exceed the distance to an angle.

Occasionally this latter method can be used with the Sun and Moon, in which case they will exceed 90° if they are helped by houserulers, i.e., when they have houserulers in aspect, favorably situated, and able to allot the full span. In the same example: if we start the vital sector at the Descendant, Sagittarius 8°, we will find the end to be at Aquarius 22° <MC>. In each case, after finding the aphetic place, it will be necessary to examine the distance to the next angle, and to make the vital sector extend to that position, if no anaereta intercepts.

Let this further method be regarded as mystically proven in great detail by us: to treat the degree-position of the apheta as <if it were> the Midheaven. With it as the Midheaven, it will be necessary to investigate (using the correct klima) which degree can be in the Ascendant. Having found this, make the vital sector extend to that point. For example: let the aphetic point be at Scorpio 12° in the second klima. If we calculate this as the Ascendant, the vital sector will extend to Aquarius 13°, which is IC. But if, as we just stated, we make this point <Scorpio 12°> Midheaven, we will find in the table of rising times that Capricorn 28° is the Ascendant, and that the vital sector will extend from Scorpio 12° to Capricorn 28°. We will find the same to be true for the rest of the nativities or signs.

Likewise make the anaeretic position the Ascendant (as with the aphetic point) and, while it is the Ascendant, examine which degree of which sign can be the Midheaven. Make the vital sector extend to that position or to the point in opposition. In addition calculate in detail the relationships of the houseruler (as we stated above), and examine the distance to the next angle, the configuration of the horoscope, and the combinations of the stars and the apheta.

An example: let the Ascendant be Sagittarius 18°, the Midheaven Libra 4°, and the houseruler Mercury at <Scorpio> 13°. I calculate the distance from it <Mercury> to the Ascendant as 35°, which equals 2 ⅓ hours. Now since 76 is assigned as the full span of years, I divide this by 12 <hours> and find for each hour, 6 years 4 months. So for the 2 hours we find 12 years 8 months, plus (for the one-third hour) 2 years 1 month 10 days. The total is 14 years 9 months 10 days. I subtract this from 76, and the result is 61 years 2 months 20 days. (It is necessary to calculate in the same way if you subtract from the other angles.)

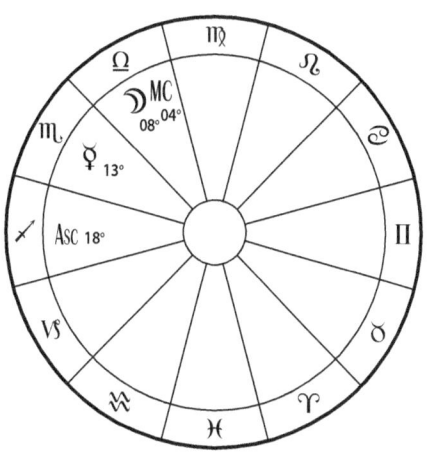

Having established this, now let the Moon be the apheta at Libra 8°. For the remaining 22° <of Libra> I assign 29 years 4 months; for the 30° of Scorpio, 36 years; and for the 17° of Sagittarius, 18 years 1 month 18 days. Added, the total of the vital sector is 83 years 5 months 18 days.[2] Now since the years of the apheta are more than the years of the houseruler, the native will live as many years as the houseruler, Mercury, allots: 61 years 2 months 20 days. If the years of the apheta were less than those of the houseruler and suffered a

---

[2] *Marginal note:* He is not calculating the vital sector and the Midheaven of the Moon according to sphaera recta, but by using the rising times of the signs.

deduction because of a destructive ray, e.g., at 53 years, it would happen that the cited nativity would live only 53 years. If, however, the houseruler is found to be at an angle and rising, or happens to be in operative degrees, even though the vital sector has more years, the houseruler will allot its total span. If the houseruler is favorably located, the destructive stars, even in conjunction or projecting their rays, will no longer shorten the length of life. If the nativity is found to lack a houseruler in the vital sector, it will then be necessary to examine the affiliations of the anaeretic stars or their aspects, whether sextile, trine, square, or opposition.

The anaeretic stars are Saturn, Mars, the Sun, and the Moon coming to a phase. The anaeretic places of each sign are the aphetic terms and the terms of malefics. The anaeretic degrees are considered to be the 3° on each side of the apheta, because each 3° segment either preceding or following has the same effect as a conjunction or equivalent degree-position. As a result, the degree itself <of the apheta> plus the two segments total 7° in all. Malefics projecting rays into this area become anaeretic, while benefics prevent the destruction.

For example: let a nativity have Aries 12° as the Ascendant. This point will be the midpoint <of the segment Aries 9°> to Aries 15°. If a malefic projects rays into the arc from Aries 9° to Aries 15°, it will be destructive in these degrees, not only in the sign of the vital sector, but in the other signs from the apheta to the point square with it. For example: if Aries is the Ascendant, and if Saturn or Mars are found at Taurus 15° or Gemini 15°, and if the vital sector comes to Taurus 12° or 13° or to Gemini 12° or 13° in the sequence of chronocratorships, there will be destructive action.

If the destructive stars are at or just following an angle, they become more active; if they are not at an angle, they are weakened. Let this method be most effective for those at an angle. For example: Aries is the Ascendant as cited above, and Saturn is at Sagittarius 13°, 12° or even 20°. Figured by signs, it just precedes the Midheaven, but since it projects its rays into an angle and into operative places (viz. into Aries, which is trine <with Sagittarius>), it will be considered the anaereta. If, however, Saturn is found in Sagittarius 3° or 7°, it will precede an angle both by degrees and according to signs, and it will not be the anaereta. This happens because an anaereta which projects rays from an angle into inoperative degrees which precede an angle does not become destructive. All this also applies to benefics.

4. The Winds of the Stars, their Exaltations, and their Steps

Having established this, it is necessary to append the winds. First it is necessary to examine the degree in which each star is exalted; from these the determination is made:

Star	Exaltation
Sun	Aries 19°
Moon	Taurus 3°
Jupiter	Cancer 15°
Mars	Capricorn 28°
Saturn	Libra 21°
Mercury	Virgo 15°
Venus	Pisces 27°

Each star has its depression at the point in opposition to its exaltation.

The point square with the exaltation and preceding it is called northern; the point square and following it is called southern. For example: the Sun is exalted in Aries 19°, and the point square with it and preceding is Capricorn 19°. If the Sun is found there, we say it is ascending north and the exaltation is exalted. From Aries 19° to Cancer 19° it is descending north. From Cancer 19° to Libra 19° it is descending south. From Libra 19° to Capricorn 19° it is ascending south.

If we seek the step of the wind, we find it as follows: since each step has 15°, we find the distance of the star from each degree <listed above>, then divide it by 15. For example: the Sun is in Aquarius 22°. I find the distance from Capricorn 19° to Aquarius 22°; this is 33°. I subtract 30° (2 times 15°), which is equivalent to 2 steps, with a remainder of 3°. So the Sun is ascending north in the third step of that wind.

We have given this to use as an example. Note that the northern and southern hemispheres must be calculated when the rest of the winds are determined, as must the wind itself and the step also.

For each nativity it is necessary to note whether the Sun, the Moon, or the Ascendant is the apheta, and which wind it has. Then examine the other stars. If any have the same wind as the apheta, they will be related and associated, especially in their own chronocratorships. In fact they will be stronger and more effective if they are rising, at an angle, proceeding with their proper motion, and in their own sect. If any star has a wind opposite to that of the apheta, it will oppose the apheta and will be malefic, especially at the transmission of the chronocratorship. If the star is setting or proceeding with a retrograde motion, it will be harmful and hazardous. It will not be considered a benefic at all, even if it happens to be at an angle during this period. If any star has a configuration with the apheta which is related in some ways, unrelated in others, it will be variable, not entirely helpful or harmful. If the Ascendant is found to be the apheta, it will be necessary to examine the ruler of the terms, and to note which wind it has and whether it is at an angle, rising, or proceeding with its proper motion, then to compare it with the other stars.

Now some astrologers think that this procedure is useless; I say that it is most scientific and effective. In their astronomical tables, astrologers have worked out this topic in various ways, but they have not brought it to perfection.

5. The Sects of the Stars

It is necessary to examine the sects of the stars: for day births the Sun, Jupiter, and Saturn rejoice above the Earth; for night births, below the Earth. For night births the Moon, Mars, and Venus rejoice above the Earth; for day births below the Earth. Mercury rejoices according to the sect of the houseruler in whose terms the star is located. Consequently for day births, if a nativity is found to have Jupiter, the Sun, or Saturn favorably configured above the Earth, this will be better than having them below the Earth. Likewise <for night births> it is advantageous if the nocturnal stars are found above the Earth. Venus particularly rejoices when in the Ascendant or at the Midheaven; the rest rejoice in the Ascendant or Descendant.

Examples Illustrating the Previous Chapters

An example: Sun in Cancer 29° 30', Moon in Pisces 12°, Saturn in Sagittarius 27° 8', Jupiter in Capricorn 22° 13' <7°?>, Mars in Scorpio 7° 23', Venus in Cancer 28° 13', Mercury in Leo 11° 25', Ascendant in Pisces 17°, the Midheaven in Sagittarius 25°. The nativity was without a houseruler because Venus, the ruler of the terms of the Moon, had already set. The apheta was the Ascendant. Mercury, the ruler of its <Ascendant's> terms, was

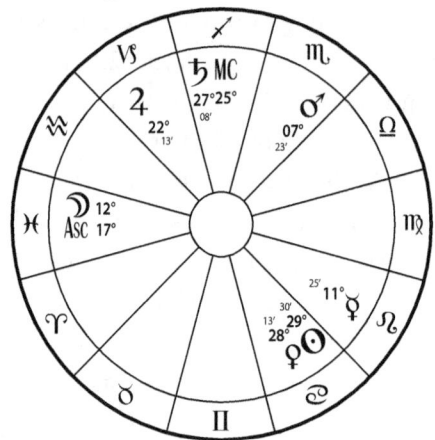

itself found just preceding the Descendant. Thus the vital sector extends from the Ascendant to the point square <Gemini 17°>, and to the projection of rays on the part of Saturn into the point in opposition <to Saturn: Gemini 27°> to Saturn, which is in the terms of a malefic <Saturn>. Mars deflected its diametrically opposite ray because Jupiter was found in an equivalent degree and hindered the anaeretic influence. The native died at age 69, but if Jupiter's trine had not hindered <this malign influence>, he would have lived only 64 years.

Another example: Sun in Pisces 25° 8', Moon in Gemini 16° 53', Saturn in Pisces 1° 25', Jupiter in Sagittarius 24° 18', Mars in Taurus 21° 8', Venus in Aquarius 9°, Mercury in <Aries 12°>, Ascendant in Libra 15°, the Midheaven at Cancer 16°. The luminaries preceded the angles <MC Descendant>, the Ascendant was the apheta in the terms of Jupiter, and Jupiter was unfavorably situated. The nativity lacked a houseruler, and the vital sector was <from the Ascendant> to Scorpio 21°, the point in opposition to Mars. Mars, located in the aphetic terms <of Jupiter> and casting rays into the same terms, was the anaereta. The native died in his 51st year.

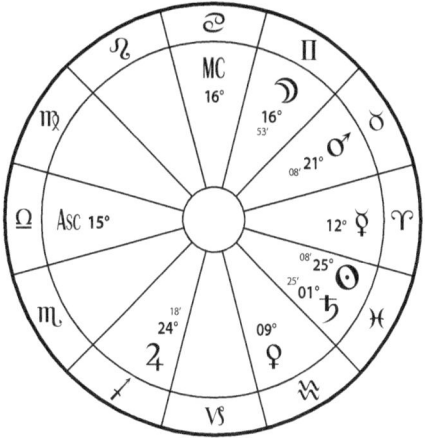

The aphetic terms and the anaeretic terms (i.e., the terms of malefics) are not only those degrees in which the destructive stars are found or into which they cast their rays, but also those where the vital sector is in the beginning of the term <of a malefic>. In addition, it is necessary to calculate not only the chronocratorship of the sign which receives the ray, but also that of the sign which casts the ray, the sign in which the anaereta is found.

...

[Another Method from Critodemus about Hostile Places and Vital Sectors: from the Moon and the Ascendant]

Whenever the Moon is found to be the apheta, one must observe the <contacts> and the points which are sextile, square, and in opposition to the Ascendant with reference to their rising times. These will be considered as effective, especially when they are in signs of the same or equal rising times, signs of the same power, the listening or beholding signs, or the degrees of the antiscia. Likewise if the Ascendant is found to be the apheta, then it will be necessary to examine its distances <=aspects> with respect to the Moon according to rising times. My experience indicates that the fatal degrees and the powerful degrees are those at the Midheaven, those at the Ascendant and the Moon by themselves, and those in opposition <to these points>. If they are at an angle, they have an extraordinary influence.

[Hostile Stars and Critical Places. The First Table of Critodemus[3]

It is necessary to investigate the hostile places and stars, not only with respect to the other stars, but also for the Ascendant, the Sun, and the Moon. When they come into opposition, they indicate critical periods and death. Take Saturn for example: note which god controls the degrees in opposition to the position of Saturn, as given in the table. The native will die when Saturn is there, is square with the Ascendant, or in signs with the same rising time, depending on when the chronocratorships coincide. The same must be done for the other stars, because the rulers of the terms of the degrees in opposition are hostile. These stars indicate destruction when they come to these places or to the places with the same rising times as the Ascendant.

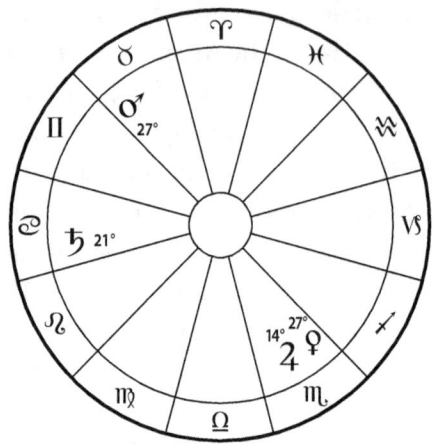

For example: Saturn in Cancer 21°, terms of Venus. The point in opposition is Capricorn 21°, terms of Mars; Mars was in Taurus 27°. The native will die when Saturn is in Virgo, because it was square, as calculated by degrees.

Jupiter in Scorpio 14°, terms of Saturn. Taurus 14° <the point in opposition> is also in the terms of Saturn, and this star does not become hostile to itself. Leo has the same rising time as Scorpio, and Leo 14° is in the terms of the Sun. So Jupiter is the anaereta when it comes to the places of the Sun.

Mars in Taurus 27°, terms of the Sun. The same position in Scorpio <the point in opposition> is also in the terms of the Sun. Since the star does not become hostile to itself, I then investigate Leo 27° or the sign of equal rising time <with Taurus>, which is Gemini according to the hourly intervals. Gemini 27° is in the terms of Venus. The native will die when <Mars> is in Scorpio or <Pisces>, which have the same rising times <as Leo and Taurus>, or in the signs square with them. If anyone calculates Leo 27°, he will find it to be in the terms of Saturn. Saturn was in Cancer. So the native will die when Mars is in Cancer, Sagittarius, or the signs square with them.

Venus in Scorpio 27°, terms of the Sun. The point in opposition is Taurus 27°, terms of the Sun, This star does not become hostile to itself, so I investigate Scorpio 27°, of equal rising time, which is in the terms of Mercury. The native

---

[3] CB: Most of this chapter is in brackets because it is a verbatim copy from *Anthology*, book 8, chapter 9.

will die when Venus is in Virgo, where Mercury was, or in the signs square with it. The same procedure should be followed with respect to Mercury.

In casting horoscopes for patients struck down by illness, it is necessary to examine the places in opposition, the stars in the hostile places, and the stars causing the monthly, daily, and hourly critical periods, with respect to the degree-position/sign of the Moon in which the opposing star is found.]

…

The vital sector will be considered as starting from the Sun, the Moon, or the Ascendant, or from the star found following the Ascendant, then the other <stars> in sequence in order of sign and degree at the nativity, making the determination <of the chronocrators> by the 10 year 9 month system.

6. Winds and Turns

The arrangement some have made of the terms using the seven-zone system, i.e., 8, 7, 6, 5, 4 (and they are not in agreement even as to that) does not seem correct to me. I prefer the arrangement derived from houses, exaltations, and triangles, to wit:

Leo is the house of the **Sun**, Aries is its exaltation, Sagittarius is the <other member if its> triangle. The total is 3, and so in each sign the Sun has 3 terms.

Cancer is the house of the **Moon**, Taurus is its exaltation, Virgo and Capricorn are the <other members if its> triangle. The total is 4, and so in the same way the Moon has 4 terms in each sign.

Capricorn and Aquarius are houses of **Saturn**, Libra is its exaltation, Gemini is the <other member if its> triangle. The total is 4, and so Saturn has 4 terms in each sign.

Sagittarius and Pisces are houses of **Jupiter**, Cancer is its exaltation, Aries and Leo are the <other members if its> triangle. So Jupiter has 5 terms in each sign.

Aries and Scorpio are houses of **Mars**, Capricorn is its exaltation, Pisces and Cancer are the <other members if its> triangle. So Mars has 5 terms in each sign.

Taurus and Libra are houses of **Venus**, Pisces is its exaltation, Virgo and Capricorn are the <other members if its> triangle. So Venus has 5 terms in each sign.

Gemini is a house of **Mercury**, Virgo is its exaltation, Aquarius and Libra are the <other members if its> triangle. The total is 4, so its terms in each sign will be 4.

<The Order of the Terms>

Aries Leo Sagittarius
by day: Sun-3, Jupiter-5, Venus-5, Moon-4, Saturn-4, Mercury-4, Mars-5.
Total 30
by night: Jupiter-5, Sun-3, Moon-4, Venus-5, Mercury-4, Saturn-4, Mars
Total 30.

Taurus Virgo Capricorn
by day: Venus, Moon, Saturn, Mercury, Mars, Sun, Jupiter
by night: Moon, Venus, Mercury, Saturn, Mars, Jupiter, Sun

Gemini Libra Aquarius
by day: Saturn, Mercury, Mars, Sun, Jupiter, Venus, Moon
by night: Mercury, Saturn, Mars, Jupiter, Sun, Moon, Venus

Cancer Scorpio Pisces
by day: Mars, Sun, Jupiter, Venus, Moon, Saturn, Mercury
by night: Mars, Jupiter, Sun, Moon, Venus, Mercury, Saturn

So that you will see the accuracy of this arrangement of terms—you can also recognize it in the nature of the winds. If the Sun is transiting its own terms, with the Moon or the ruler of the Moon's terms in aspect, the physical nature of the star will manifest itself in the wind. For instance: if the Sun traverses its own terms with the Moon in aspect, it will blow westerly. If Venus traverses its own terms, it will blow southerly and dry. If Saturn, it will blow westerly and bring moisture. If Jupiter, it will be northerly and wet. If the Moon, it will be northeasterly. If Venus, southeasterly and there will be shifting winds and storm clouds. If Mercury, there will be westerly and northerly winds, shifting and bringing heavy rains, thunder, and lightning. If any of the stars are in aspect with the Sun and the Moon, it is necessary to watch closely—in addition to the nature of each luminary—which phase the Moon is passing through, i.e., full or new, and in whose terms the phase is located. Then make your forecast with reference to the ruler of the terms and of the stars in those terms or in aspect....

7. From the Books of Valens Concerning the Numerical Lot and the Length of Life. The Same Author on the Topic of Propitious Times, with Examples

There is another numerical method, which King Petosiris has mystically explained, suitable for determining the length of life and the propitious and impropitious times. As a result, whenever we find the controller or the houseruler <configured> appropriately, we will use the method described above for the allotment. If we do not find them to be such, we will use the following method.

It will be necessary to determine if the nativity happened at new or full Moon. If it happened at new Moon, determine the number of degrees from the new Moon to the position of the Moon at the delivery itself, then count this distance from the Ascendant in the order of the signs. The ruler of the term where the count stops will be the houseruler of Life and of the vital sector. If the nativity is at full Moon, it will be necessary to determine the degrees from the Moon's position at the delivery to its position at the next new Moon. Then count this distance from the Ascendant, not in the order of the signs, but in the direction of diurnal motion (towards the Midheaven). The ruler of the term where the count stops will be considered the houseruler. It will be necessary to examine it and the sign where the count stopped to see which <luminary> is more closely related to it, the Sun for masculine <signs>, or the Moon for feminine <signs>. If the sign where the count stopped happens to be related to the Sun when the Sun has control, and if the ruler of the term is also in harmony with the Sun and happens to be favorably configured with the Sun, then it will allot the maximum number of years. If this sign is found to be related (i.e., male, as would be appropriate for the Sun), and if the ruler of the term is opposite the Sun, precedes the Ascendant, or is in ecliptic places, then it will become the anaereta of the chronocratorship, or it will allot the minimum number of years. (The masculine signs belong to the Sun; the feminine to the Moon.)

Consequently it will be necessary to examine how the ruler of the term is configured with respect to the controller and with respect to the ruler of the sign. If it is found to be in its own sign or in operative signs, the length of life will reach its maximum. If it is found to be favorably configured with respect to one, but unsuitably configured with respect to the other, it will allot the mean number of years. If the houseruler of the sign where the count stopped is unsuitably configured with respect to the controller and the operative sign, being either turned away or in <the XII Place of the> Bad Daimon, then the nativity will lack a houseruler. In such a case it will again be necessary to examine the control of the Sun and Moon. If the rulers of the term and of the sign are configured well and harmoniously with the Sun and Moon, then the vital sector will be considered as starting at the degree of the term.

Generally speaking, in this method it will be necessary to examine the houseruler with reference to the influences of the angles, as was demonstrated for the horimaea: it may be rising, setting, at an angle, or not at an angle; it may switch positions with the ruler of its sign or be inharmonious with it.

Use these facts to make your judgement. Likewise <it will be necessary to> look at the rays of the anaeretic stars and to check if the vital sector starts at the beginning of the terms or at the end. It is necessary to consider all of this in order to calculate short- or long-lived nativities—or even the nativities of twins, because often if a malefic term rules the vital sector or if the houseruler is unfavorably situated, the first-born becomes short-lived, but the next-born, if the term or the houseruler changes, becomes long-lived and a foundation for his existence arises. Consequently, a change of one or two degrees often has a very great effect.

An example: Sun in Taurus 25° 18', Moon in Aquarius 7° 10', Saturn in Aries 24°, Jupiter in Taurus 4° 25', Mars in Cancer 22° 53', Venus in Gemini 28° 16', Mercury in Gemini 6°, Ascendant in Capricorn 27°. Since this was a full-Moon nativity, I took the distance from the Moon's

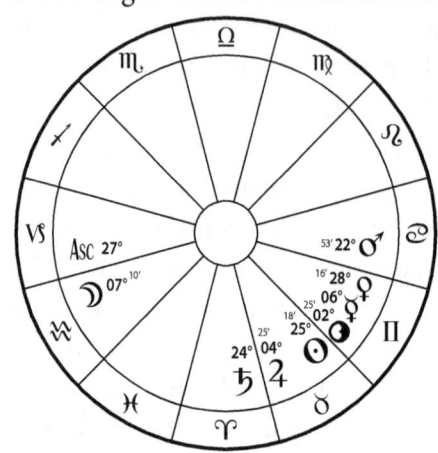

position <at birth> to the next new Moon, which was at Gemini 2° 25'. The distance is 115°. I subtract this from the Ascendant and stop at Libra 2°. The vital sector stretches from this point to the radiation of the malefics. Saturn casts its rays from a point in opposition and Mars from a point square with the same degrees <in Libra> and cause death. Jupiter was turned away; Venus was unfavorably situated and unable to help. The native lived 28 years 9 months.

Another example: Sun in Sagittarius 12° 16', Moon in Sagittarius 17° 24', Saturn in Libra 11° 33', Jupiter in Gemini 19° 11', Mars in Scorpio 4° 20', Venus in Libra 26°, Mercury in Scorpio 27°, Ascendant in Libra 20°. I take the distance from the degree of the new Moon to the Moon's position <at birth>; this is 5°. I count this from the Ascendant and stop at Libra 25°. The vital sector stretched from there

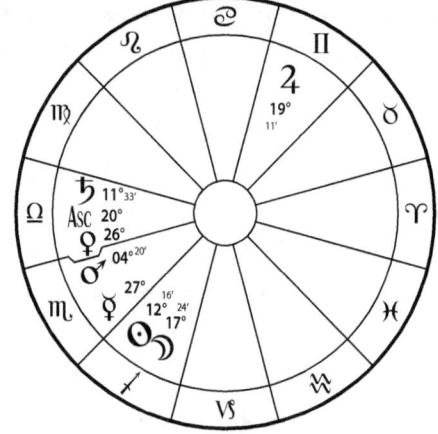

to the position of Mars, Scorpio 5°. The native died in his twelfth year. If this encounter <with Mars> had not happened, he would have lived the years of

Venus, 84.

8. The 7-Day and the 9-Day Methods for the Critical Period

We will now report what the King has revealed about the critical point: take the number of days from the rising of Seth[4] to the date of birth. Divide the total number of days by 52 1/7. Now multiply the <integer> answer of this division by the remainder, and examine the result of this multiplication to see if it is less than the particular number of the critical point. As a sample, let the number of days be 220. I divide 52 1/7 four times <into 220> for a result of 208 4/7 days, with a remainder of 11 3/7...<I multiply 11 3/7 times 4, and the result is 45 5/7.>... We call this the critical 7-day number.

<The King> tells us to examine this number to see if the number of the critical point is less than the number of years. Take the example just cited: if the basis of the nativity's length of life is 47, but the critical point falls in year 45, the native will be destroyed then, since the value of the critical point was less than the years of the basis. <The King> has said that if the 7-day number is a factor of 9, the situation will be inharmonious. For example: this 7-day number <45> contains the factor 5, the result of a division by 9. When this is multiplied by 9, it yields 45. Therefore the 7-day number is a factor of 9. But if the value of the critical point is <not> less than the number of years <of the basis>, and if the previously-mentioned considerations are true, it will not be able to reduce the allotted time. Instead the native will live the assigned period. If the situation is harmonious, the critical point will take precedence over <the number found by> the preceding method.

We claim that the method of multiplying by 5 1/4 and then proceeding using this factor in the same way is more economical than multiplying by 52. Having found the number, one should investigate the 9-day number, to be sure that the 7-day number is not a factor of it.

(Some astrologers do not like to start the year with the rising of Sirius. It is possible to use any given starting point in citing an example, since we see that men begin the year differently in the different latitudes. Still, let us assume that the system in which the calculation starts with the rising of Sirius and proceeds to the birth date is more scientific. Most use this as the beginning of the year. Let this method of determining the 7-day week be the most efficient.)

Some think it proper to investigate the 7-day and the 9-day week for night births, the 9-day week for day births. The results are similar for both methods since the 7-day weeks will be with reference to Mars, the 9-day weeks with reference to Saturn. In either method, they will have an exchange of critical

---

[4] *Marginal note:* The Dog Star <Sirius> in Egyptian.

points. Saturn will be the beginning of the 7-day week because of the Sun and Moon. Mars will be the beginning of the 9-day week. This is because Capricorn and Aquarius (Saturn's houses) are opposite, in the seventh place, to Cancer and Leo <houses of the Sun and Moon>, and Aries <Mars' house> is the ninth sign from Leo, and Cancer is the ninth sign from Scorpio <Mars' house>. But it would be more scientific to derive these from the exaltation of the Moon in Taurus: the beginning of the 7-day week would be Mars, because of Scorpio; the beginning of the 9-day week would be Saturn, because of Capricorn.

An example: the nativity was in Hadrian year 3, Athyr 27 in the Alexandrian calendar.[5] Investigate the subsequent date Antoninus year 17, Phamenoth 11. I take the full years, 35, plus the 3 remaining days in the birth month <Athyr 27 to 30>, plus 2 days for each month from Choiak to Mechir <3 months>. <The total is 44.> With the whole weeks <4 weeks=35 days> subtracted, the remainder is 9. Now add the 11 days of Phamenoth (total 20), plus the 8 intercalary days. The grand total is 28. Let Phamenoth 11 be a critical day in the 7-day week system. According to the sequence of days, Phamenoth falls in Scorpio. Examine which stars are in aspect with this signs and with the Moon.

The 9-day week is found as follows: I multiply the full years by 5 ¼, since each year contains forty 9-day weeks with 5 ¼ days left over. For each month I add 3, since each month has three 9-day weeks with 3 days left over. I total the remaining days until the day in question and I divide by 9 (making sure that the remainder is less than 9.) Now the result will be the number of the critical day, just as in the 7-day week system. It will be necessary to calculate the month and year in the same way.

In the 7-day week system, the critical signs are Aries, Libra, Cancer, Capricorn; in the 9-day week system Taurus, Leo, Scorpio, Aquarius. Common to both systems are Gemini, Sagittarius, Virgo, and Pisces.

---

[5] *Marginal notes:* Athyr 27, Phamenoth 11 in the Alexandrian calendar; November 22, March 27 in the Greek calendar; Tybi 1, Pharmouthi 11 in the Egyptian calendar.

I think this is a recasting of a natal horoscope of Athyr 27, Alexandrian years.

An Alexandrian month has 30 days. If you subtract 28 days (i.e., 4 weeks) from each month, there are 2 days left. So, there are 3 days left of Athyr, 2 days each for Choiak, Tybi, and Mechir (viz. 6 left after subtracting 12 weeks). The total so far is 9 plus 11 days of Phamenoth, for a total of 20. The intervening 35 years make 8 quadrennia, which he calls "intercalary." Total 28. This topic is most clearly presented in Dorotheus' *Epic*, Book V, Chapter 138.

9. The Method of New and Full Moons. Conception with Reference to the Ascending Node. Length of Life, with Examples

I am reminding you of my generosity in supplying proofs for every chapter so that I do not seem to be writing this in order to obfuscate. Now if you rush to the books of the older compilers, be aware that their texts have been adorned with an affected style which can bewilder the minds of their readers and of the ignorant, although their texts have not attained the truth and are enemies of the wise. Wasting the time of many men and leading them astray, these texts have defrauded some of life and have terminally afflicted others.

Let anyone read the so-called *Vision* of Critodemus: how its beginning is so fantastical and how the rest is so marvellous to the unlearned. "Coursing the deep," he says, "and traversing vast wilds, I was deemed worthy by the gods of attaining a safe harbor and a secure anchorage." Then with frightful oaths he expounds his methods and his transmissions. He sanctifies his readers in other ways and displays much bombast throughout the book, such as it is. He indicates that its powers control everything <with its prodigious learning>, but he locks up in infinite verbiage the truth of his teaching. This man should be praised and admired, since he has gone through so much labor and has become a guide for seekers. Indeed, by arranging his material mystically and complexly in tabular form and in connected prose, he has attracted many enthusiasts, some of whom have ignored his useless bombast, have tracked down the relevant chapters with great toil, and have brought praise and credit to the man. Others with a less tenacious spirit have brought criticism to this art.

My exposition will (as I think) be persuasive and educational for my readers, and they will not regret their work. Through the influence of what has been and will be said, I hope to bring back into the fold those who have come to hate their role <as student>.

Since the casting of rays—either houseruling or destructive—has now been set out as previously outlined, I want to share, not to hide, the method for the Numerical Lot and the anaeretic, powerful places, now that I have tested them. First of all, it will be necessary to determine for every nativity whether it has a controller or a houseruler. If it is found to have one, it is necessary to use the previously mentioned terms. If however the nativity is found to be lacking a houseruler or a controller, and is destroyed by no afflicting ray, then it will be necessary to determine the degree of the previous new or full Moon (for night and day births) and to count from the new or full Moon "upward" (=in the direction of diurnal motion) to the Ascendant or to another angle, or (which is more powerful) to the ascending or descending node. Then having noted the number of degrees, count this amount from the Ascendant in the direction of diurnal motion (=toward MC). Where the count stops, calculate the total number of years from the apheta (using the rising times of the native's klima), then make your forecast.

If, for a day birth, the number is excessive, subtract the distance between the new or full Moon and the ascending or descending node from the distance between the angles, i.e., between the Ascendant and the Midheaven, then do your operations in the same manner, counting the remaining degrees from the Ascendant to the Midheaven in the direction of diurnal motion. For night births, take the distance from the new or full Moon to the ascending or descending nodes or a center (in the direction of diurnal motion), then count that distance from the Ascendant in the order of the signs. Calculate the years where the count stops, using the rising times, and make the forecast. If the number is excessive, subtract the distance from the Ascendant to IC, then count the remainder from the Descendant in the order of the signs (i.e., toward the Midheaven). The total, calculated from the rising times, will be the length of life.

In most cases, it is necessary to place the vital sector starting with the Ascendant or with the Descendant at the point to which the ascending or descending node inclines, or to which the new or full Moon inclines, (i.e., whether in the hemisphere above the Earth or towards the one below): if the nativity is at the new Moon, start with the Ascendant; if full Moon, with the Descendant.

If the Ascendant, the ascending node, or the descending node is found in the sign of the new or full Moon, or in the signs in opposition or square with them, then for day births count the total distance from the Ascendant, for night births from the Descendant in the order of the signs. The point square with the ascending node has an anaeretic force—of course, the exact-to-the-degree vital sector which starts at the Sun and Moon and runs to the ascending node and to the points in opposition or square with the node <?>.

Occasionally, when there is a controller or a houseruler, the anaereta coincides with the apheta or the houseruler and strengthens the destructive force. If in such a case the controller is suitably situated, and the apparent houseruler is distributing the chronocratorship, then the vital sector of this horoscope (whether counted in the direction of diurnal motion or in the order of the signs using the total of the rising times) will be considered as characteristic of one who dies at birth or in the womb. The same considerations should be applied when forecasting conception, but the Ascendant at the time of delivery must be observed. The conception itself will be in vain if someone observes the new or full Moon extending to the ascending or descending nodes or to the angles. If the same number of years are found to be granted when you calculate from the delivery and from the conception, then death will indisputably occur.

10. How the Position of the Sun, the Moon, and the Ascendant at the Conception Can Be Accurately Found

We will explain an economical method for finding the latitude. For every nativity, the sign square with the Sun is the sign of the conception. (Occasionally the sign of conception will be trine when the Sun happens to be at the end of its sign, especially in a sign of short rising time; the sign of conception may be sextile for signs of long rising time.) Assume the position of the Moon at the conception to be the same as the position of the Ascendant at the time of the delivery, and from this you can know whether the conception was at new or full Moon.

An example: Sun in Aquarius, Moon in Scorpio, Ascendant in Virgo. At the conception the Sun was in Taurus, the Moon in Virgo. It is clear that the conception was at new Moon, for the Moon (i.e., the Ascendant) had not yet come into opposition to the position of the Sun at the conception. If the Ascendant at the delivery is found to be past its opposition to the Sun at conception, the conception will be at full Moon.

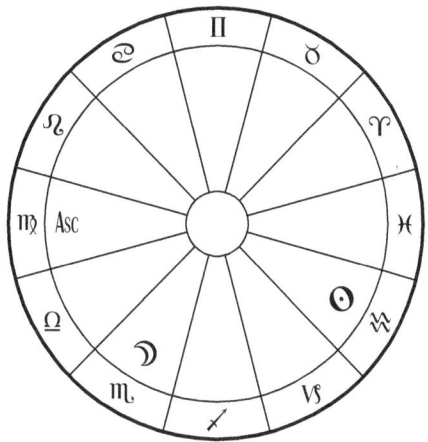

It is necessary to establish the vital sectors for the conception in the same way as was explained for the delivery. In most cases a native whose conception was at new Moon will die at full Moon; one whose conception was at full Moon will die at new Moon.

Another <topic>: having determined in which sign the <preceding> new or full Moon occurred, count the degrees from that point in the order of the signs to the ascending node. Then count the total distance from the Ascendant "downwards" (=in the order of signs) for day births, in the direction of diurnal motion (=towards the Midheaven) for night births. If, however, the ascending node is at the Midheaven, it is necessary to count the distance in degrees from the Midheaven, in the order of the signs towards the Ascendant for day births, in the direction of diurnal motion towards the Descendant for night births. If the ascending node is at the Descendant, count the distance from the Descendant to the Midheaven for day births, to IC for night births. If the ascending node happens to be at IC, then count the distance in degrees in the direction of diurnal motion from IC towards the Ascendant, if the birth is found to be during the day; for night births count toward the Descendant from IC. For example: the ascending node

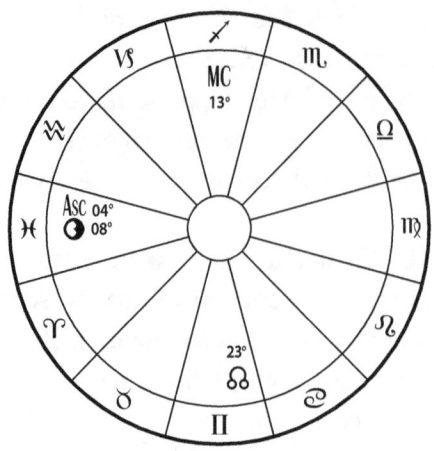

at Gemini 23°, the <preceding> new Moon at Pisces 8°, the Ascendant at Pisces 4°, the Midheaven at Sagittarius 13°. I take the distance from the new Moon to the ascending node; this is 105°. I count this from the Ascendant (since it was a day birth) and stop at Gemini 19°. For the second klima the total is approximately 79 years, <4> months. The native lived that long.

I have explained the systems which I myself have used. I have investigated nativities, observing if two, three, or more of the previously mentioned factors coincide, yielding the same result, and through this investigation I have made infallible forecasts of deaths. As a result it is not without plan, not at random, that I have explained that each method is quite practicable both by itself and when combined with another. If anyone sticks to these methods, he will find a true forecast of the subjects in question to be within his grasp. Now we have written some parts of our work mystically, leaving something to the discrimination and the judgement of our readers. In doing so we have not been led by malice or stupidity, but by our wish to supply the student with point of interest and opportunities for long discussion. For <we know> that if anyone

attains his longed-for goals without being challenged, he considers it a trivial gift, but one who attains them after a toilsome search engages in his activity not only with pleasure but with success.

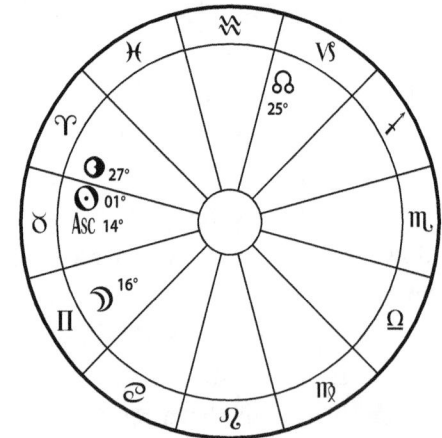

An example: Sun in Taurus 1°, Moon in Gemini 16°, Ascendant in Taurus 14°, the <previous> new Moon in Aries 27°, the ascending node in

Capricorn 25°. I counted in the direction of diurnal motion from the position of the new Moon to the ascending node; the distance is 92°. I counted this distance in the direction of diurnal motion from the degree-position of the Ascendant and came to Aquarius 12°. The 92° total for the klima of Alexandria equals 70 years. The native died in the first month of his seventieth year. The method according to the conception is as follows: since the full Moon <preceding> the conception was at Capricorn 21°...which is close to the year we found previously.

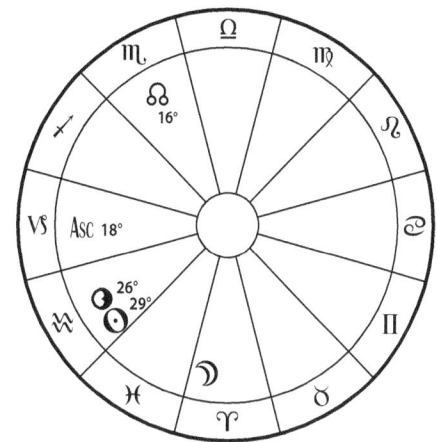

Another example: Sun in Aquarius 29°, Moon in the beginning of Aries, Ascendant in Capricorn 18°, the <preceding> new Moon in Aquarius 26°, the ascending node in Scorpio 16°. I counted the distance from the new Moon in the direction of diurnal motion to the degree-position of the Ascendant; the distance is 38°. I counted this in the order of the signs from the degree-position of the Ascendant. The years total very nearly 33 in the first klima. He lived 32 years 5 months. The place of the conception did not contain the apheta because the full Moon of the conception and the ascending node happened to be at the same degree-position. Therefore he had a dangerous birth and a violent end.

11. The Lot of Fortune and its Relationship to the Topic "Length of Life," with Examples. Included are the Minimum Periods of the Stars

I have found this system for <finding> the length of life to have been elaborated in a very complicated manner by the ancients. After investigation, I have modified their doctrines in view of my experience, and I think <my explanations> will please most <of my readers>. In his thirteenth book, after his preface and his descriptions of the signs, the King introduces the Lot of Fortune <and its derivation> from the Sun, the Moon, and the Ascendant. He considers it to be the greatest, and he mentions it throughout his work, calling it the "Ruling Place." He makes a great mystery of its "forward and reverse": "The Sun, starting in the dawn and declining to his western arc, opens <to us> the vault of the cosmos, as can be seen. When night arrives, the Moon will not always become the Lightbringer, but sometimes it appears in the west, setting, sometimes it stays in the heavens for quite a while, at other times it travels the entire night. As a result, the whole circle <of the zodiac> has rightly been entrusted to the Sun's care."

There are a variety of opinions about this notion. To me it seems best to locate the Lot by determining the distance from the Sun to the Moon, then counting that distance from the Ascendant—for day births. For night births <1> if the Moon is above the Earth, i.e., until the time it sets, determine the distance from it to the Sun, then count that distance from the Ascendant. <2> After the Moon has set, determine the distance from the Sun to it. As for the King's final statement: "The whole circle <of the zodiac> has been entrusted to the Sun's care," this seems correct. It will be necessary to examine the place where the Lot is located, and to consider that place to be the ruler. Then determine in which sign the ruler of the sign <of the Lot> happens to be located. Third, determine that sign's houseruler. From these three places and from their houserulers the native's length of life will be found by using the three factors.

Each star controls its own period:

Saturn	30 years;
Jupiter	12
Mars	15
Sun	19
Venus	8
Mercury	20
Moon	25

Each <sign> also controls its own rising times according to the <nativity's> klima. Accordingly it will be necessary to determine for the <correct> klima whether the Lot is at an angle and operative, or whether it just precedes or follows an angle. Also determine the houserulers of the signs. The Old Astrologer reminds us of this when he says: "Each star, when at an angle, allows the full amount of its times. When not at an angle, it grants its allotment after some deduction from its own numbers." These stars allot the full term of their periods and their rising times when they are favorably situated. The fellow-members of their sects, when in conjunction, in aspect, or in their own signs, add to the allotment, unless both sects in fact join in the allotment. Thus the <Old Astrologer>.

First it is necessary to calculate the numbers: hours, days, months, then years. Then use the three factors, minimum, mean, maximum, adding the first to the second, or the second to the third. It often happens that one place allots the days, another the months, another the years, all according to the differences among the operative signs and the houserulers, or of the baneful influences and setbacks. After allotting the years, they also allot the same number of months to their chronocratorships.

In the distribution <of years> Daimon and the Ascending Place will have the same effects as the Lots whenever the places of the Lots or their rulers are unfavorably situated, particularly when the Lot of Fortune cedes the distribution to Daimon. (Stars can indeed yield to each other; we will show how in a future chapter on the allotment procedure.)

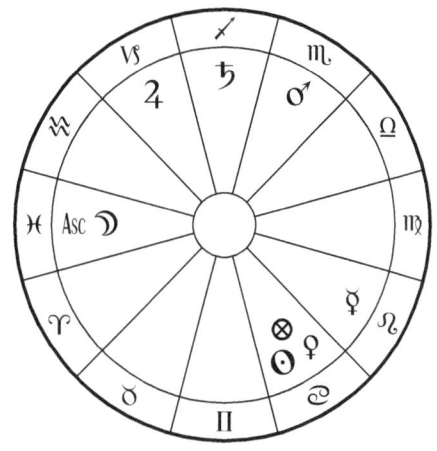

Examples: Sun, Venus in Cancer, Moon, Ascendant in Pisces, Saturn in Sagittarius, Jupiter in Capricorn, Mars in Scorpio, Mercury in Leo, the Lot of Fortune in Cancer which is in Good Daimon <=the V Place of Good Fortune>. The ruler of the Lot <Moon> was found at an angle. I set down the minimum period for the Moon, 25 years, plus the rising time of Cancer in the second klima, 32 years, plus the period of the houseruler of the Moon, Jupiter, 12 years. The total is the same <as in Book III.5>, 69 years. The native died at that age.

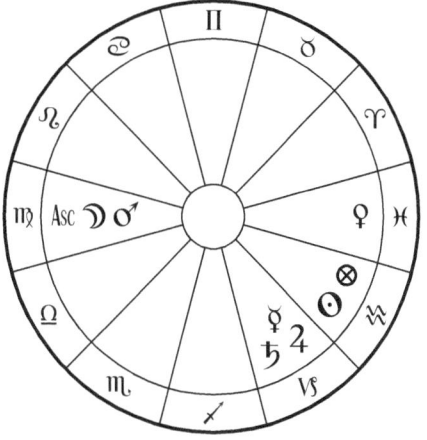

Another example: Sun in Aquarius, Moon, Ascendant in Virgo, also Mars; Saturn, Jupiter, Mercury in Capricorn, Venus in Pisces, the Lot of Fortune in Aquarius just preceding an angle <Descendant>. Its ruler <Saturn> in <the V Place of> Good Fortune, not in its own sect <diurnal; the nativity is nocturnal> allots its own 30 year period plus the same number of months, since it is in its own sign. Jupiter, also in this sign, allotted one year <12 months>. The native died in his 34th year.

For every nativity the rules of procedure laid down previously, the phases, and the degrees, must be observed. <I say this> so that we might not seem to be repeating the same reminders with each new topic. For this reason I consider it necessary to cite sample nativities.

12. Critical Years

Following are the critical point with respect to the Lots, especially if malefics are in conjunction or in aspect with Fortune:

<Position of Malefic	The Critical Years>
in opposition	every 7 years
trine on the right	9
trine on the left	5
square on the right	10
square on the left	4
sextile on the right	11
sextile of the left	3
in the sign preceding the Lot	12
in contact with the Lot	2

Position of the Lot of Fortune	The Critical Years
Aries	every 9 years
Taurus	22
Gemini	20
Cancer	25
Leo	12
Virgo	8
Libra	30
Scorpio	15
Sagittarius	12
Capricorn	8
Aquarius	30
Pisces	15

13. The Mean Years of the Stars

Following are the mean years of the stars:

Saturn	45
Jupiter	49
Mars	42
Venus	46
Mercury	48
Sun	64
Moon	67

The stars allot these years plus their periods or the rising times of their signs whenever they happen to be operative.

Another system of mean years: you will find the mean years by adding the maximum and the minimum periods. For example: the complete period of Saturn is 57 years and the minimum is 30, for a total of 87, half of which is 43 ½. The complete period of Jupiter is 79 and the minimum is 12, for a total of 91, half of which is 45 ½. And so on for the rest of the stars.

Now the rising times of the signs in the *Tables of Rising Times* of Hypsicles are in error if the period <in question> amounts to one or two years…but the King has revealed the rising times only for the first klima.

An example: Sun, Venus, Mercury in Cancer, Moon in Taurus, Saturn in Pisces, Jupiter, Mars in Leo, Ascendant in Virgo. In the first klima the rising time of Virgo is 38 ⅓. Since Mercury, the ruler <of Virgo>, is in Cancer, in <the XI Place of the> Good Daimon, it contributed its rising time, 31 ⅔. The total is 70; the native lived that long.

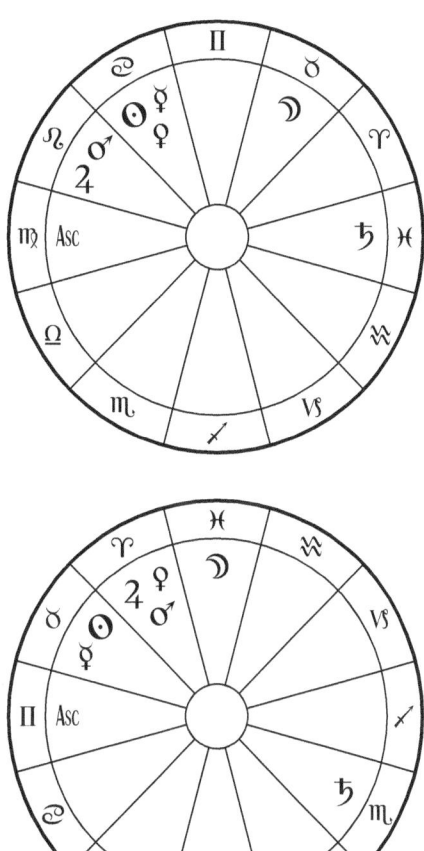

Another example: Sun, Mercury in Taurus, Moon in Pisces, Saturn in Scorpio, Jupiter, Mars, Venus in Aries, Ascendant in Gemini. The rising time <of Gemini> in the second klima is 28. Mercury in Taurus adds its rising time, 24, plus Mars and Venus in Aries, 15. He died in his 67th year.

Another example: the same configuration of stars <as in the preceding horoscope> for a different nativity, except that the Ascendant was in Capricorn, the Lot of Fortune in Pisces. The rising time <of Pisces> in the second klima is 20, plus the period of Jupiter, 12. Since Jupiter is in Aries, we add its rising time, 20, plus the period of Mars, 15. The total is 67. He lived that long.

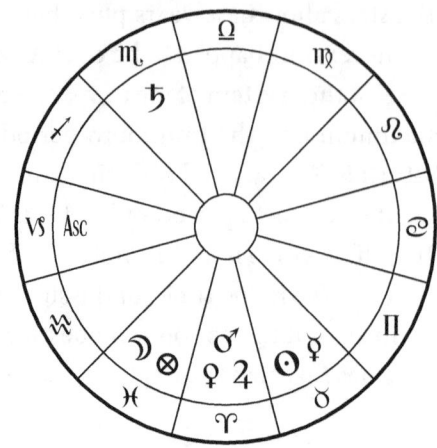

These chapters which I have composed may seem unprofessional because they have been addressed to a youthful audience, my students, in such a way that they might find my introduction to this art comprehensible. In view of this fact, I had wished to revise them for greater accuracy, but I have not had the opportunity because my vision has been troubled and my intellectual capacity has been enfeebled by my deep sorrow for a precious student who has died. May the reader pardon me.

End of the *Anthologies* of Vettius Valens of Antioch, Book III.

Book IV

The *Anthologies* of Vettius Valens of Antioch: Book IV

1. The Distributions of Periods

We believe that we have set forth an appropriate, in fact, magisterial, explanation of the previous <theorems>. We will now reveal a topic investigated by many and hidden from view, namely the distribution of propitious and impropitious times. We must preface our discussion with the distributions which have been proven by our own experience. The primary period is one-fourth of the minimum period, as follows:

Star	Period	One-fourth Period	Days/Year
Saturn	30	7 ½	<85
Jupiter	12	3>	34
Mars	15	3 years 9 months	42 ½
Venus	8	2	22 ⅔
Mercury	20	5	56 ⅔
Sun	19	4 years 9 months	53 ⅚
Moon	25	6 years 3 months	70 ⅚

Altogether, the "fourths" total 32 years 3 months.

2. The Vital Sector

For new-Moon nativities, the <star> located first after the new Moon begins the vital sector, then the other stars as they come in the order of signs. For full-

Moon nativities, the <star> following the full Moon serves the same capacity. It is necessary to examine how the star is configured and which stars are in aspect. Also determine if the other stars that receive <the chronocratorship> are at angles or precede angles, or are rising or setting. Determine the sequence of their transits and their sympathies and antipathies. After the 32 year 3 month period is completed, the second cycle is begun starting with the <next> aphetic star of the one-fourth period.

3. The Distribution of Days

Make the distribution of days as follows: if Saturn is found to be the overall apheta, it assigns 7 ½ years. Now since it is necessary for all the stars to take part in the distribution of this <7 ½ year period>, we will do as follows: multiply the 85 days of Saturn by 7 ½ to get a total of 637 ½. This is the amount Saturn will allot to itself from its 7 ½ years. Now let us find the amount for Jupiter: since it governs 34 days, multiply this 34 by 7 ½ (since Saturn is the apheta), for a total of 255. Jupiter will have this many days of Saturn's chronocratorship. Next in order Venus receives the chronocratorship: since it controls 22 ⅔ days, we will multiply this amount by 7 ½, and we will find the total 170. Venus will control this many days of Saturn's chronocratorship. And so on with each star: if we multiply its days by 7 ½, we will find its allotment <in Saturn's chronocratorship>. If the Moon, on the other hand, controls the vital sector, we multiply each star's days by 6 ¼ <to find its distribution>. Similarly for the rest.

To Find the Days of Each Star

The days of each star are found in this way: double the star's period, then take one-half, then one-third of the period. After adding all these figures together, we will find the days. The period of Saturn is 30 days; I double this for a total of 60. One-half of 30 is 15; I add this to 60 for a total of 75. One-third of 30 is 10; I add this to the 75 for a grand total of 85. Saturn will have this number of days. Likewise for the rest of the stars.

4. The Distribution of the Chronocratorships Starting with the Lot of Fortune and with Daimon

I will now append this truly powerful method: to begin the vital sector with the Lot of Fortune and with Daimon (which signify the Moon and the Sun). Universally speaking, the Moon is fortune, body, and spirit, and when it sends its emanations to us from its position near the Earth, it causes appropriate effects, since it rules our bodily constitution. The Sun is the cosmic mind and divinity. It arouses men's souls to action through its own energy and love-inspiring nature, and it becomes the cause of employment and progress.

So, if we are investigating the chronocratorships with respect to bodily existence, such as critical points of illnesses, hemorrhages, falls, injuries, diseases, and whatever affects the body with respect to strength, enjoyment, pleasure, beauty, or love affairs, then we must begin the vital sector with the Lot of Fortune. Whenever the <first> chronocratorship ends, at that point we calculate the sign, the stars in conjunction or aspect, how the stars are configured with respect to the overall houseruling star of the vital sector's chronocratorships, and whether the rulers of the Lots are at angles or not.

If on the other hand we are investigating employment or rank, then we will begin the chronocratorships with Daimon as the apheta. We will make our determination according to the benefics or malefics in conjunction or aspect with it.

Note that if the Lot of Fortune or its ruler are badly situated, the Lot of Daimon will distribute both the bodily and the active qualities. Likewise Fortune will make the distribution of both qualities if the Lot of Daimon or its ruler is unfavorably situated, and the same is true of the controls and the houserulerships.

Whenever Daimon and Fortune are found in the same sign, we will derive forecasts of bodily constitution from that very sign, but the forecasts of activity from the sign immediately following. In addition we can <use> the same apheta for new or full Moon nativities, since at those times the Lot <of Fortune> and Daimon fall in the same sign, but when we investigate the chronocratorships in such nativities with respect to physical health, we will start the vital sector at that very sign, but the chronocratorship with respect to activity at the one immediately following the Lot. This is particularly true for night births or for those nativities which have the new Moon at IC and as a result have the angles <Ascendant Descendant> square with the Lots. The results of a new Moon are better than those of a full Moon because at a new Moon the Lots are in the Ascendant, at full Moon they are in the Descendant. It also happens that if the luminaries are square with each other, the Lots are in opposition to each other, and under this configuration some astrologers allot the chronocratorships for activities beginning with the signs immediately following <the Lots>. This however does not seem right to me, because <usually> the Lot of Fortune is found at a different place from the Lot of Daimon, although they are at the same place for new and full Moon nativities.

In addition, for male nativities, the vital sector is usually found to begin at Daimon, since these nativities share in activities consisting of discourse, giving and receiving, and trusts. For female nativities it begins at the Lot of Fortune because of their bodily functions. (But even men happen to accomplish things through bodily activities, i.e., handwork, athletics, and bodily motion, and women accomplish things through buying and selling.) Similarly for infant nativities it is necessary to begin the vital sector with the Lot of Fortune until <the time when> the nativity can show evidence for its full development or its occupation. Bodily excellence accompanies these <infant> nativities at birth, i.e., beauty, loveliness, size, elegance, fine proportion, or—which is more usually the case—the opposite: injury, disease, rashes, eruptions, pustules, or congenital defects such as birthmarks and hernias. The active and intellectual qualities come into play later.

For example: assume that the Lot of Fortune or Daimon is located in Aries. The overall houseruler <of Aries> is Mars. Determine if Mars' successors are or are not configured properly. Mars itself allots 15 years first, and from this period it assigns itself 15 months. Next (because of Taurus) it assigns 8 months to Venus, next (because of Gemini) 20 months to Mercury, next (because of Cancer) 25 months to the Moon, next (because of Leo) 19 months to the Sun, next 20 months to Mercury, next 8 months to Venus, next (because of Scorpio) Mars assigns itself 15, next (because of Sagittarius) 12 to Jupiter, next (because of Capricorn) 2 years 3 months to Saturn. Next it assigns to Aquarius the remaining 11 months to fill out the 15 years. Now Venus receives from Mars the overall chronocratorship for 8 years and assigns years to each sign as described. Because of Gemini, Mercury receives 20 years after Venus and assigns the years to each sign. Next is the Moon with its 25 years, then the Sun with its 19. It is necessary to assign the years in the order <of the stars> to whatever date the nativity extends <=lives>.

Now since the circle of the 12 signs has comprised 17 years 7 months, we will allot the remaining time using the signs in opposition: since Gemini allots 20 years, if the vital sector begins there and if 17 years 7 months have been assigned, the remaining 2 years 5 months are allotted beginning with Sagittarius, giving Sagittarius itself 1 year <=12 months>, the rest to Capricorn to complete the 20 years. In a similar manner, if we find the vital sector beginning with Cancer, Leo, Virgo, Capricorn, or Aquarius, after allotting the 17 years 7 months (not counting the intercalary days), we will allot the rest in order, beginning with the sign in opposition.

Some astrologers allot the remaining chronocratorships beginning with the sign in trine, but this does not seem scientific to me. Just as in the universe the four elements are in sympathy with each other, and each becomes alive and grows when linked with another, so in the distribution <it is necessary

to> make the transmission from sign to sign, according to the harmony among them. For instance, since fire and air are upward-trending elements, they mingle with each other. Fire, a dry element, is nourished by the mildness of the air, while on the other hand, fire does not allow the air to take on an icy or dark nature, but renders it warm and mild. In the same way it is logical that Leo, the fiery sign, transmits the period remaining from its chronocratorship to Aquarius, the airy sign, with which it is in sympathy, and in turn, Aquarius transmits its period to Leo.

Another instance: earth, a dry element, is nourished by moisture and gives birth to everything, while water, distilled from the earth and thus born from it, maintains the sympathy <between the two>. So it is logical that Cancer, a moist sign, and Capricorn, an earthy sign, mutually transmit to each other, as do Virgo, an earthy sign, and Pisces. The rest of the signs show the same interchange with the sign in opposition. And so the sequence of distributions is written in the order of zodiacal signs: Aries—fiery, Taurus—earthy, Gemini—airy, Cancer—watery, and the signs trine with these are of the *same* nature. Consequently if we make the connection within the triangles, we will find the nature of the transmitter and the receiver to be the same. No blending will be found, and each element will be overpowered by itself.

If we use the other method, we find that the Sun begins its course at the equinoctial tropic in Aries and makes the days long for one hemicycle. Then, making the connection in Libra, it begins to shorten the days. <The Sun> in Cancer stops the pattern of lengthening days, and when it is in Capricorn, it causes this to happen to the night, making its change in the sign in opposition. Likewise the Moon becomes new, waxes, then in its cycle makes the connection <=full Moon> in the sign in opposition. As a consequence I believe we should use the method described above for making connections.

5. Making Connections. The Mutual Transmissions of the Stars

The connections made will have differing effects because of the nature of the stars: the Sun and Moon when transmitting to Saturn are indicative of setbacks and anxieties, and they bring hostility from the great and threats due to old religious matters, losses, trials, confrontations, suspicions, dubious livelihoods and ranks, ruin, as well as bodily disorders and dangers, shipwrecks, sudden collapses, and very many crises—all this unless a benefic in conjunction or aspect weakens the onset of the crisis. Mercury when transmitting the chronocratorship to Jupiter from Virgo or Gemini brings changes in business and innovations in activities. If the places or Mercury itself are afflicted at the nativity, and if the overall chronocratorship is contrary, the connection which is made will turn affairs to the better and will be indicative of employment. On the other hand, if the places are protected by benefics and are bringing a good chronocratorship, after <one> cycle the connection which is made will be disturbing and harmful. Saturn making the connection from Capricorn and Aquarius to Leo and Cancer indicates that the chronocratorship will be vigorous: it brings matters from darkness into the light, and since it is transmitting the distribution of the chronocrators to the ruling signs, it is most active—depending on the basis of the nativity. It also supplies rank and profits in a way appropriate to the stars in conjunction with it…

6. How Many Years Each Sign Allots. The Maximum Years of Each Star

Aquarius allots 30 years, Capricorn 27. The reason: the Sun rules a maximum period of 120 years, half of which is 60. Half of this, 30, is assigned to Aquarius, the sign in opposition <to Leo, the Sun's sign>. The Moon rules a maximum period of 108 years, half of which is 54. Half of this, 27, is assigned to Capricorn, the sign in opposition <to Cancer, the Moon's sign>. The total for these two signs is 57, which is the maximum period of Saturn.

The rest of the stars take their maximum assignment of years from the Sun and the Moon. The Sun assigns to Jupiter, which is a member of the same sect <diurnal> and which has sympathy with the Sun, being a member of the same triangle <Leo Sagittarius Aries>, half of its 120 years plus the length of its minimum period, 19 years. The total for Jupiter is 79 years. The Moon allots to Jupiter in the same way, because they are both benefics and both are in cosmic sympathy, Jupiter being in Pisces, in the same triangle <as Cancer, the Moon's sign>. The Moon allots half of its 108 years, 54, plus its minimum period, 25. The total is also 79.

The Moon allots to Mars, a member of the same sect <nocturnal> 54 years. The Sun, however, refuses to allot to Mars because of Mars' fiery nature which imitates <the Sun> and because of its malefic ways, and so the task of allotting passes to the next ruler in the triangle <Leo Sagittarius Aries>, Jupiter, and it allots its minimum period, 12 years. The total is now 66 years.

Likewise the Moon allots to Venus, because of its nocturnal sect and because of the sympathy derived from being <exalted in Pisces> in the same triangle <Cancer Pisces Scorpio>, its 54 years, and Saturn allots 30 years, because its exaltation in Libra is opposite Venus'. The total is 84 years.

Mercury gets the maximum period, 57 years, from Saturn, because they are co-houserulers <in the triangle Virgo Capricorn Taurus>, plus the minimum period of the Sun, 19. The total is 76.

7. The Distribution of the Chronocratorships Using the Lot of Fortune and Daimon. The Transits of the Stars and Houserulers. The New and Full Moon, with Examples. Mutual Transmission

This having been established, it will be necessary to examine the transmitter and the receiver of the distribution to see if they are at an angle or are preceding an angle, or if they are in harmony or are contrary. If the distribution, when calculated by sign, is from a place at an angle to another place at an angle, and if at the same time, the houserulers of these places are at angles, in the same sect, and have benefics in aspect, they bring a noble and distinguished chronocratorship. If the *places* are at angles, but their *rulers* precede angles or have malefics in aspect, they indicate that the chronocratorship will be disturbed, subject to ups and downs. If every relevant point is found to be preceding an angle, the chronocratorship will be terrible, bringing charges and penalties; the native will be involved in travels and changes in activities during these periods.

If under these circumstances <the transmitter and the receiver> are benefic or have benefics in aspect, the native will gain profit and attain success in business abroad, but if they are malefic, he will be entangled in disturbances and penalties abroad or be betrayed by foreigners or slaves. (Therefore we say that the points preceding the angles are indicative of foreigners.) If <the transmitter and the receiver> are found at the angles and in their proper places, they indicate delays in certain places <abroad> or residence there: Mercury and Venus cause residence abroad which is not long or extended, since these stars are never far from the Sun. Saturn, Mars, and the Moon indicate that the native will live dangerously abroad on land and sea, wandering or living in alien climes. The Sun indicates a glorious, honored, and amiable native. Jupiter indicates that the native will live abroad comfortably and pleasantly with many friends.

If a star which is controlling the chronocratorship relevant to health is passing through a sign which is not at an angle, or if its ruler is not at an angle and has malefics in aspect, the native will be sickly, subject to bleeding and dangers. If a star which is controlling the chronocratorship <of the matters> governed by Daimon <=occupation> is not at an angle and has a malefic in conjunction or in aspect with the houseruler of its sign, the native will act ineffectively, will be unfortunate, and will be mentally unstable and ruined in his activities and enterprises. If the star controlling such a chronocratorship is found in a fiery sign with malefics in conjunction or in aspect, he will suffer a great nervous breakdown, and will act against his own will, being mentally unstable. If the star is in an airy sign or if the sign or its ruler are afflicted, the native will be distracted and troubled, and will suppose that he is accomplishing something other than what he really is. If the star is in an earthy sign, he will bear the blows of fortune nobly, and will survive most things philosophically because of his endurance. If the star is in a watery sign, the native will have a mind which can be easily reassured, will come into vicissitudes in many affairs, but will manage to succeed and be successful in his dealings.

In many cases predictions about specific activities are to be derived from Daimon and its houseruler. Some men are involved in bodily activities (e.g., handicrafts) or in physical toil (e.g., as porters or in training). Others have activities involving speech, knowledge, or mental effort. To whichever place, Fortune or Daimon, the majority of stars incline, in that place the type of activity will be revealed. It is necessary to take into consideration the activities and the basic character of the nativity (noble, average, fortunate, poverty-stricken, disputed, subject to ups and downs) so that the results of the allotments may be quite obvious. Some stars forecast activities: Mars, Venus, Mercury. Saturn forecasts personal talents, plus whatever happens through moist substances, labor, and legacies. The chronocratorships from Saturn and Mars, with Jupiter not in the configuration, are considered to be base and humble. The chronocratorships are noble and prosperous when derived from the Sun and Moon with benefics in conjunction or in aspect from the right.

If the distribution goes from Daimon to the Midheaven (MC relative to the Lot of Fortune) or to the Lot itself, and if the ruler <of Daimon> is there, with benefics, the Sun, or the Moon in aspect, and if the basis of the nativity is full of glory, the native will come to power and great rank, and will be distinguished, ruling, and prominent in those chronocratorships. He will be called blessed by many because of his prosperity. A distribution which comes at the Ascendant, at the Midheaven, or at the other angles forecasts high rank, but not to the same extent, because the places square with the Lots are most efficacious.

If the transmissions occur as specified, and if the basis of the nativity is found to be average, the native will be involved in occupations and profits; he will be a friend of great men; he will be thought worthy of gifts and offices. He will live happily and successfully in proportion to the level of his occupation, especially if benefics are in conjunction or in aspect. If malefics are in aspect, the influence of the places will be visible in the manner just described, but because of the malefics in aspect, the native will meet with reverses and penalties, and will experience only transitory benefits from the benefics.

Each star is located in the zodiacal circle according to its house. In a similar way, each star becomes associated with another by its configuration at the nativity.

8. A Compelling Example

Consider a sample nativity: Sun, Venus in Cancer, Moon, Ascendant in Pisces, Saturn in Sagittarius, the <preceding> full Moon, Jupiter in Capricorn, Mars in Scorpio, Mercury in Leo, the Lot of Fortune in Leo, Daimon in Scorpio. I am investigating the native's 70th year. I count the chronocratorships relevant to health from Leo <the Lot of Fortune>, first giving Leo 19 years, then Virgo 20, then Libra 8, then Scorpio 15. 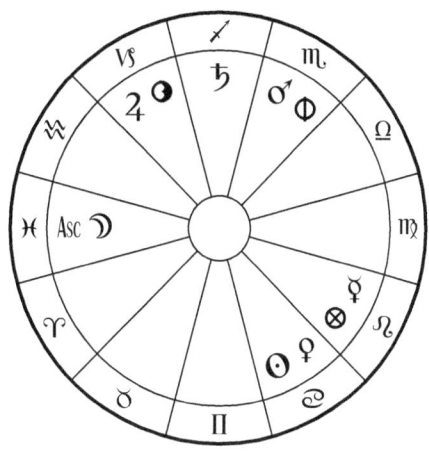 The total is 62 years. In these years he had many critical periods, falls from heights, and broken limbs. I count off the remaining 8 years in Sagittarius, Saturn being there, not in its own sect. In these years he endured shipwrecks and bodily disorders. We learn the cause of the injury from the sign which the ruler of the Lot was found to be traversing: the Lot was in Leo; the ruler of the Lot, the Sun, was found in Cancer. Now Cancer indicates the breast and stomach, and so we say then that the cause of the injury was from Cancer. Now he takes the allotment of years and converts it to 360 days. (After calculating the 5 ¼ days separately, add them to the years.) He gave Sagittarius 1 year, Capricorn 2 years 3 months, Aquarius 2 years 6 months, Pisces 1 year, then Aries the remainder <2 years 3 months> of the 9 years. Mars, the current ruler of the chronocratorship for health, brings death, having received the chronocratorship from Saturn located in Sagittarius: he died diseased in the stomach and afflicted with coughing. The Place of Death was in Pisces, with the Moon there also and Saturn in superior aspect, which caused the dysentery. In addition the ruler of the <preceding> full Moon, Saturn, was turned away and caused the type of violent death. But the injury to the stomach and the cough resulted from the fact that the ruler of the Lot, the Sun, was found in Cancer, and Cancer indicates breast and stomach.

Now I considered the chronocratorships for occupations, beginning with Scorpio <=Daimon>, giving Mars (which was in Scorpio) 15 years, then Sagittarius 12 years, with Saturn in that sign. Until age 27 he was a vagrant, subject to ups and downs. His considerable property was squandered by his guardians, for the <11th> Place of Accomplishment was in Gemini and no benefic was in aspect, but Saturn was in opposition. Next Capricorn received the distribution of 27 years; Jupiter was there, in <the XI Place of the> Good

Daimon, and it was in opposition to and beheld by the Sun and Venus. During this entire chronocratorship he had great success and was entrusted with public and royal affairs. He became a friend of governors and kings and became accordingly rich, but experienced setbacks and ups and downs in the course of time as a result of the malefics which received the allotment or were in aspect. His wealth was transitory because Jupiter was found to be retrograde and in its depression <Capricorn>. Aquarius received the distribution of the chronocratorship <at age 54> after Capricorn, with Mars and Mercury in aspect and the benefics turned away. He ended his career and lost much through misplaced trust: he undertook pledges for relatives and slaves, through whose carelessness and poverty he fell into debt and was found abjectly poor, because the whole basis of the nativity aimed in this direction. Aquarius took 2 years 6 months, then Jupiter 1 year, then Mars 1 year 3 months, then Venus 8 months, then Mercury 1 year 8 months. At that point his affairs went into a great decline. Next the Moon received 2 years 1 month. During this period he seemed to recover some of his pledges and to get the help of friends. Next the Sun received 1 year 7 months in Leo, and Mercury 1 year 8 months in Virgo. Since malefics were in aspect with the Places <Accomplishment Fortune> and with Mercury, he was ruined during this chronocratorship. The Lot of Fortune was found to be preceding an angle <the Descendant>, and the ruler of the triangle of the Moon <Cancer Pisces Scorpio> was Mars. Following Mercury, Venus received 8 months, then Mars 1 years 3 months, then Sagittarius 1 year. This was the end <69 years 4 months>.

9. The Universal Year. The Year with Respect to the Distribution: How Many Days It Has and How It Must Be Calculated

Since the universal year has 365 ¼ days, while the year with respect to the distribution has 360, we subtract the 5 intercalary days and the one-fourth of a day, then we find the number of years. Only then will we make the distribution. (We calculated in this way for the previous nativity.) For example: a person in his 33rd year was born on Tybi 15; we are investigating Mesori 20 of his 33rd year. I multiply 30 years times the 5 <intercalary> days for a total of 150. Now I add 10 <intercalary days> for the two complete years <31, 32> plus one-fourth of 32 (=8) for a total of 168. Next I take the number of days from Tybi 15 to the day in question, Mesori 20 (=215), and I add this amount to 168 for a grand total of 383. From this sum I subtract 360, and the remainder is 23. So the nativity will be in its 33rd full year with respect to the distribution, plus 23 days. I consider this number of years and days when making the distribution of the chronocratorships.

10. The Breakdown into Longer and Shorter Periods: the Years, Months, Days and Hours of Each Star. The Use of These Periods in Nativities

By taking one-twelfth of the year (or of each period) we can discover how many days each star/sign allots. For example: Aries allots 15 years. One-twelfth of 15 years is 15 months. Next one-twelfth of 15 months is 37 ½ days. Next one-twelfth of 37 ½ days is 3 ⅓ hours. <Aries> allots these time-periods during its period of rule. The allotments of the other stars will be found in the same way. If anyone uses this system, he will find the overall, the yearly, and the monthly chronocrators, as well as the daily and hourly chronocrators. We will append the time divisions for each star worked out in detail so as not to confuse our readers:

Star	Years	Months	Days	Days+Hours
Sun	19	19	47 ½	3 days 23 hours
Moon	25	25	62 ½	5 days 5 hours
Saturn	30	30	75	6 days 6 hours
Capricorn	27	27	67 ½	5 days 15 hours
Jupiter	12	12	30	2 days 12 hours
Mars	15	15	37 ½	3 days 3 hours
Venus	8	8	20	1 day 16 hours
Mercury	20	20	50	4 days 4 hours

If we find a nativity it its 50th or 60th year, we begin the zodiacal vital sector of *years* from the Lot of Fortune or from Daimon, assigning to each star its period as far as it applies. Then we assign the months, then the day and hours. If the nativity is an infant's, we begin by assigning the *hours* of the vital sector, then the days and months.

For example: Sun, Mercury in Capricorn, Saturn, Jupiter in Leo, Mars, Venus in Aquarius, Moon in Gemini, Ascendant in Leo, the Lot of Fortune in Pisces, the Lot of Daimon in Capricorn. Let the vital sector start at the Lot of Fortune in Pisces. It is necessary to investigate the fourth year, Mesori 16, including the 5 <intercalary> days of each year. Since 12 <years> for Pisces would

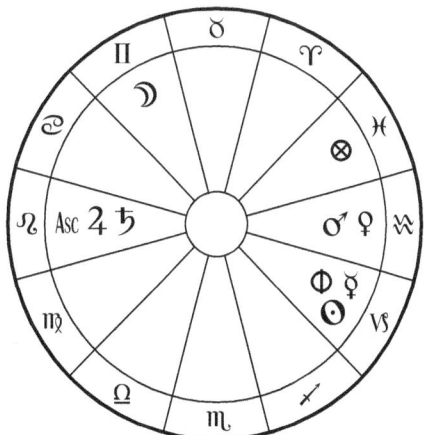

leave no allotment remaining, I have assigned 1 year <=12 months> to Pisces, 1 year 3 month to Aries, 8 months to Taurus. The total so far is 2 years 11 months. Then the allotment passes to Mercury, 1 year 8 months, to total 4 years 7 months. But the nativity has not yet completed this length of time, so let Mercury be the chronocrator for a period of 8 months 15 days, a total of 255 days. It is necessary to allot this amount continuing <to count> in the order of the signs. First Mercury gives to itself (i.e., to Gemini) 50 days, then to Cancer 62 ½ days, then to Leo 47 ½ days, then to Virgo 50 days, then to Libra 20 days. The total so far is 230 days, with 25 remaining. Now Mars will have these 25 days in Scorpio after Venus' days <in Libra>, until the completion of 37 ½ days. Therefore Mars will allot the 25 days proceeding in the order of the signs. First it allots to itself 3 days 3 hours, then to Sagittarius 2 ½ days, then to Capricorn 5 days 15 hours, then to Aquarius 6 days 6 hours, then to Pisces 2 ½ days, then to Aries 3 days 3 hours, and to Taurus the rest <1 day 21 hours> to complete the 25 days. The overall chronocrator is Jupiter <Pisces>; the second is Mercury <Gemini>, receiving the allotment from Jupiter; the third is Mars <Scorpio>, receiving it from Mercury; the fourth is Venus <Taurus>, receiving it from Mars. For the nativity it will be necessary to examine where these stars are located and how they are configured with each other; having done this, then make your forecast.[1]

If the overall chronocrator is found to be a benefic, the Sun, or the Moon, it brings fame and leadership for the nativity, or prominent offices, benefits, and association with the great. In those chronocratorships when a malefic receives the distribution (according to the system of allotment), it brings about bodily infirmity and dangers. If another star which is in opposition to the overall chronocrator or is inappropriately configured at the nativity and in transit receives the days, it brings upset, anxieties, and penalties. If at the nativity the overall chronocrator happens to be unfavorably situated or is beheld by malefics, in the days assigned to those malefics the native will be ruined, fall into danger, or suffer crises. But if, when these malefics receive the chronocratorship, the overall chronocrator is found in operative signs and has benefics in aspect in transit, although embarrassed in livelihood or rank <during the period of the malefic>, the native will <later> live undisturbed.

In distributing the days, when you have completed the whole cycle of days (=528), it is necessary to begin the remaining days starting with the sign in opposition. In the same way for the lesser time-periods, i.e., the days and the hours—after the completion of the cycle of days and hours (=44), count off the remaining days and hours in the order of the signs from the sign in opposition.

---

[1] *Marginal note:* Some astrologers allot the days using the triangles.

11. The Operative Year and the Method of Fractions

After outlining the particular characteristics of the overall chronocrators and those of the shorter time-periods, I must now speak about the operative year and matters associated with it—but first it is necessary to speak a few words about those who have written on these topics. Most have expounded their views on the distribution of the chronocratorships in a very complicated and hateful manner, and they have not taught a valid system. They have fenced in this topic with many devices, and have left their readers a legacy of the greatest error and of futile investigation. Others, carried away in their ignorance by this mass of words, have added false systems and have deceived many. Still others, who saw the power of this science and who laid a foundation, did not add examples, because of their grudging spirit.

We, however, traversed many lands and came to Egypt, where we fell in with avaricious teachers. We paid them money because of our enthusiasm for the work, but we did not come upon the truth. So, choosing an ascetic and independent life, we occupied ourselves with other matters. But this problem of concern to the greatest of the mathematical sciences, viz. the distribution of the overall chronocratorships, drew us back and made our enthusiasm greater, and we came to consider an detailed treatment of the topic a necessity.

Since quarrels have arisen about the general method of distributing—some using the method of following the sequence of terms, others using the minimum periods, others using the dodekatemoria (which total 10 years 9 months), others using the exaltations, all of which methods of distribution falsify the results—I thought it disgraceful to limit forecasts to "year 2" or "year 10" or "year 7," and I thought it best to investigate the chronocratorship for any year or part of a year. As a result, we have spent much time in painful labor, we have considered in painstaking detail the effects of the changing of places, and we have made experiments in close association with those who are eager for such knowledge. Eventually God of his own accord, through his providence, made clear the transmission to a given place, <giving this knowledge> through the help of a learned man. We received this as a basis, we added much labor, and we gained our goal, which we now possess, having ourselves added many useful procedures. For it is from our daily experiences, from the contributions of many men, and from our personal acquaintance with syndromes that we have compiled our divinely-inspired and immortal theorems, and we have shared them without stint, since this topic seems to be the most essential prerequisite for the remaining parts <of astrology>. Without it there neither is nor will be anything; it contains the foreknowledge of the beginning and the end.

I adjure you, my most precious brother, and you, initiates into this mystic art, by the starry vault of heaven and by the twelve-fold circle, by the Sun, the Moon, and the five wandering stars by whom all of life is guided, and by Providence itself and Holy Fate, to preserve these matters in secret and not to share them with the vulgar, but only with those worthy of them and able to preserve and requite them as they deserve. I adjure you to bestow on me, Valens, your guide, eternal and noble fame, particularly since you are aware that I alone ungrudgingly illuminated this part of the truth which had never before been explicated by anyone. Do not put aside my name and attach another's to this compendium. Do not blot out any of what has been or will be written here, with the result of nullifying my readers' efforts and of bringing discredit on me.

May the previously mentioned gods be well-disposed to those who guard these things: may their lives be prosperous, and may the consummation of their plans be as they wish. May the opposite happen to those who foreswear this oath: may the Earth not be passable, the sea not be sailable, may they have no offspring of children, may their minds be blind and fettered, and may they lead shameful and unsuccessful lives. If after death there is a recompense for good or evil deeds, may they suffer the same there also. Therefore, if after learning the doctrines taught here, anyone finds this system mysteriously set forth in another treatise, he must not award praise to that treatise, but he must show gratitude to us as not only the reporter but also the discoverer of many things and the perfecter of the system—for many men receive directions without stint, but give them grudgingly.

Therefore I encourage those who have just met with this compendium, who are just entering the heavenly places, who are surveying for a time the dancing places and the mysteries of the gods, and who are gaining god-like glory—these I urge to lay aside the many schemes of systems and books, to become proficient in the scientific, tabulated theorems of the stars and signs and in the operations which use the tables of visible motions, and to stick to these methods which have already been prescribed. I urge them to observe the position of the stars in degrees when necessary for determinations to the degree, to observe their positions by sign when that level of accuracy is appropriate, so that what is said will have been said truly. (Often I myself have noticed that a star is in one sign with respect to the temporal determination of transits, but in another sign with respect to visible motion, especially if the star is at the beginning or end of a sign. The same variations are possible at stationary points and at opposition to the Sun.) Consequently, it is necessary to make the determination <of the chronocrator> only after first discovering in which signs or degrees the stars—and particularly the Ascendant—are located.

Let us start our exposition from this point: when investigating the current year of a nativity, we divide by 12. Count the remainder from a star which is able <to transmit> to a star which is able to receive. In this way we will discover to what sign the year transmits. What I have said is easy to comprehend but complicated to determine since all the stars, plus the Ascendant, the Sun, and the Moon, can transmit to and receive from each other. Let us take an example so that we may make an intelligent beginning: Sun, Mercury in Aquarius, Moon in Scorpio, Saturn in Cancer, Jupiter in Libra, Venus in Capricorn, Mars, Ascendant in Virgo. We are investigating the 35th year. I divide <35> by 12, for a result of 24, remainder 11. We note which stars are separated by 11 signs: we find 11 signs from the Ascendant and Mars <in Virgo> to Saturn in Cancer; additionally 11 signs from the Moon <in Scorpio> to Mars, or from Venus <in Capricorn> to the Moon. All of these transmissions are effective in the 35th year. Whatever predictive force each star has, it will predict appropriately, good or bad, in the transmissions which we have outlined in the preceding discussion.

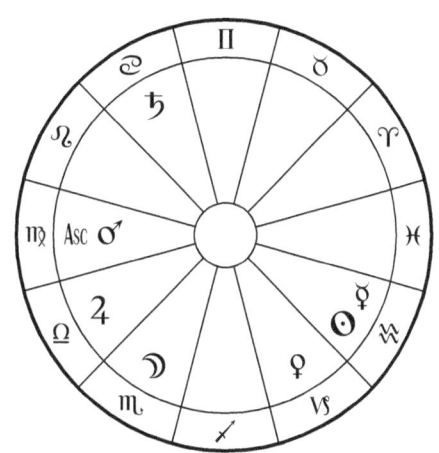

Whenever there are many transmissions, it is necessary to take into account whether benefics or malefics predominate. Award the prize to whichever group does predominate. If neither does, the year should be judged as varied and changeable.

To find the overall influence in any nativity, it will be necessary to count the years from the Sun, the Moon, and the Ascendant, and if the count ends at an empty place, then they <Sun Moon Ascendant> will be transmitting to the rulers of these <empty> signs. These three figures have great influence, whether the transmission is to benefics, to malefics, to the angles or operative places, or to places not at the angles. Next it will be necessary to investigate the transmissions of the other stars: if malefics control the year, but the three aphetas have a benefic effect, then the year will be vigorous and distinguished, after some doubt, anxiety, and annoyance. If no star transmits to another, and if the distribution is to empty places, then it is necessary to note the empty places: especially if any stars are there in transit, they will receive the distribution.

It is also necessary to count from the Lot of Fortune, from Daimon, from Love, and from Necessity, for it is from these points that the critical illnesses, benefactions, and dangers are apprehended.

But it is more scientific to count from the angles, because what is true of the general and cosmic is also found to be true of men. Starting with the rising of Sirius, the year and the four angles rotate through the quadrennium. The years, however, become varied because of the differing configurations, phases, and occasional transits of the stars. Likewise the Sun has four motions (a maximum, a minimum, and two mean motions), and directs its course through the four tropics. There are four astronomical forms of the Moon: new, quarter, full, second quarter. The universe and the Earth itself is composed of the four elements and the four winds <=directions>. If all this is so, then it is necessary for the four angles to be operative in <all> nativities, and it is necessary to count the years from them, and to make judgements from them about the stars at birth and the particular influences of the angles and signs. It is necessary to know ahead of time the universal conjunction <of Sun and Moon>, the rising of Sirius, the Ascendant (if the Ascendant is at a tropic point), and the ruler of Sirius' rising—because this <star> is considered the overall houseruler of the year. (The cyclical rulers are the rulers of the Places. Likewise for each nativity or each later recasting, the ruler of the year is the overall houseruler; the rulers of the new and full Moons are the cyclical houserulers.)

It is necessary to determine if the overall (i.e., universal) ruler is favorably related to the overall ruler of the nativity, or if it is the same. Likewise determine if the universal (i.e., cyclical) rulers are in harmony, or if they are the same. Moreover, the places of the nativity in which eclipses happen (i.e., in operative or inoperative places), plus the risings and phases of the stars, must be noted, because it is from these that distinguished, governing, and royal nativities derive their distinctive differences in occupation and glory; it is from these that great and marvelous forecasts usually come, carrying some to unparalleled fortune, others to a lowly and easily-ruined condition.

(Let no one think we are rambling on and unnecessarily complicating our system. No, we do this for the sake of securely knowing that our determinations will be unassailable for both noble and average nativities.)

In addition, when we investigate the length of life and bodily or mental activities, we count from the Ascendant. On the other hand, when we investigate rank, preeminence, magnificence, the father, great personages, and whatever other matters are usually influenced by the Sun's nature, we will start the year-count with the Sun. For forecasts of dangers to health, diseases, bleeding, or the mother, we will start with the Moon. For forecasts of occupations, livelihood, and work, we will start with the Midheaven. For forecasts of good fortune and success in life, we will start with the Lot of Fortune. For forecasts of mortality, change, or trouble, we will start with the Descendant. For forecasts of estates, possessions, secret matters, legacies, we will start with IC. For forecasts of women, love affairs, associations, or the category "female," we will start with Venus. For forecasts of military or public matters, we will start with Mars. For forecasts of bankruptcy, money or property, secret diseases, or family inheritance, we will start with Saturn. For forecasts of rank, friendship, alliances, and possessions, we will start with Jupiter. For forecasts of associations, slave matters, servile matters, giving and receiving, or written matters, we will start with Mercury.

Then we will proceed as with the single transmissions and receptions: if two or three or more happen to be transmitting and receiving, it is necessary to determine the influence of each star on all those in contact with it. Benefics and malefics will become influential according to the original basis of the nativity. Whatever general configuration <of effects> any given star has when combined with another one which is in aspect or in configuration, those effects will be caused when the star receives from the other or transmits to the other the chronocratorship.

So that our transmission might be seen more clearly and accurately, we will set down some rules and procedures which we may follow to have an easily understood method. First it is necessary to note if the transmission is from an angle to an angle, or from <the XI Place of the> Good Daimon to the Lot of Fortune or to an operative place. If so, the forecast will be for success or fame. On the other hand, note if the transmission is from places that precede angles to angles, or from <the XII Place of the> Bad Daimon to <the XI Place of the> Good Daimon. (The operative and effective signs are the Ascendant, the Midheaven, <the XI Place of the> Good Daimon, <the V Place of> Good Fortune, the Lot of Fortune, Daimon, Love, and Necessity. Signs of moderate activity are <the IX Place of> the God, <the III Place of> the Goddess, and the other two angles. The rest of the signs are mediocre or bad. The influence of a Place is weakened or is strengthened depending on the benefics or malefics which are in conjunction or aspect. <The VI Place of> Bad Fortune, incidentally, seems to be better than <the XII Place of the> Bad Daimon, because of its <Fortune's> position trine with the Midheaven.)

If one transmission is found in a nativity (i.e., if all stars happen to come to one sign) they themselves will transmit zodiacally. The nativity will share whatever overall quality this mixture indicates for it with every star. Say three or four stars are found in one sign, one or two in another: in this case the one in dominant aspect in its degree-position <=to the right> will allot the chronocratorship (i.e., the one with the lowest degree-position of degrees will receive the chronocratorship <first>.) Then the star next in order <will receive>. The same is true for the receivers <?>. Even though the distribution is complicated, if one pays attention he will not go wrong.

The same transmissions are indicated every 12 years. They will, however, not have the same causative influence, but different. Whenever we find a transmission in one cycle, (whether from one or from many), we examine the horoscope recast for that year, particularly the transits of the stars, to see if they have a configuration similar to their configuration at the nativity with respect to the transmitters and receivers, and if they have the same phases with respect to the Sun. If this is found to be true, we say that the results are certain. If the configurations are different and dissimilar, the results will not take place *in toto*: some things will happen overall, others partially. For example: if either Jupiter or Saturn holds the overall chronocratorship and is favorably situated, and if the same star happens to control the chronocratorship in this current period, the native will inherit or will benefit from legacies. If Saturn or Jupiter rules the year in the second or third cycle, but does not hold the overall chronocratorship, the native will not inherit, but will gain something: he will benefit from legacies or some such expectation, or from the selling of possessions, estates, and other property. Likewise in the overall chronocratorship: results will be certain at some point of the 12-year cycle, but not later or earlier—unless the stars reveal the meaning of the forecasts.

Examples: someone has married in the first cycle while in his 34th year. (It is necessary to correlate the results with the time of life.) In the second cycle, the native will give thought to love affairs, a second marriage, or whatever turns the mind to women.

Another person campaigned. The same transmission happening again will lead to success, change, and military matters. If the general basis <of the nativity> happens to be successful, the native will have special success at those times, if benefics are in control. If the nativity is great, the native will be a governor, a procurator, or be one of those in authority. (It is necessary to make the forecasts harmonize with the general tenor of the nativity.)

Another person had children in a certain chronocratorship. When the same transmission happens again (and if his vigor and his time of life permit), the native will have a child or will buy slaves, or he will rear some, treating them as his own children, or he will take thought for another's children.

Another person became a ruler, preeminent among the masses. When the same chronocratorship happens again, and if the basis of the nativity is good, he will receive great and distinguished offices. If the basis is average, the native will associate with rulers or he will have the appearance of rule or preeminence.

Another person is condemned or imprisoned. When the same transmission happens again and if benefics are in aspect, he will be released from confinement or from the lawsuit. If malefics are in aspect, the native will still be at law because of some criminal attempt or malicious accusation, or he will experience even worse.

And so on—whatever can happen in life will happen according to the transmissions, but in a different way because of the overall chronocratorship, the later recasting of horoscopes, the transits and phases of the stars, and the configurations of each star, which are not generally equivalent. If, for example, stars at a particular time are transiting the star which transmitted, received, or was at an angle in the nativity, these stars will contribute an influence from their own natures, whether good or bad, and they will either intensify the outcome or hinder it. We consider results to be certain when the star in transit has the same configuration with the transmitting star as it did at the nativity, or if the transmitting stars and the receiving stars have the same configuration as at the nativity. If the temporal <chronocrators> indicate one thing, but the year and the transits indicate another, the outcomes will be mediocre.

Generally speaking, any star that transmits or receives while setting is ineffective and hindering. If it is found to be a benefic, it provides only the appearance of good. If the three aphetic points (Sun Moon Ascendant) indicate different outcomes, the year will be complex. Often, if the overall chronocrator informs us that the results will be great and noteworthy, although there is no transmission at one aphetic point, then it is necessary to make the vital sector start there <at the overall chronocrator> and to move on to the yearly chronocrator.

Some treatise writers have written mystifyingly about the system just described. Let those, however, who read my treatise remember from the beginning that since no one <else> has worked out any such system before, it was necessary to supply the key by which this transmission method, being very effective, will make forecasts of an astonishing standard for each type of result. If anyone soberly attends to the topics to come in this transmission method, he will continue unshaken <in his craft> through <his use of> the varied theorems of the stars' and signs' influences.

12. The Names of the Twelve Places. The Twelve-Fold Division

Let us begin with

I The Ascendant, life, steering-oar, body, breath.

II Life, the Gate of Hades, shadowy, giving and receiving, association.
III Brothers, travel abroad, kingship, authority, friends, relatives, rents/revenue, slaves.
IV Rank, children, one's own wife and older individuals, activity, city, home, possessions, lodgings, alterations, change of place, dangers, death, confinement, religious matters.
V The Place of Children, friendship, association, slaves, freedmen, the completion of some good deed or benefaction.
VI Slaves, injuries, hostility, disease, sickness.
VII The Descendant, marriage, success, an affair with a woman, friendship, travel.
VIII Death, benefits from the deceased, the Inactive Place, law, sickness.
IX Friendship, travel, benefits from foreigners, God, king, magnates, astrology, oracles, appearances of the gods, mystic and occult matters, associations.
X Occupation, rank, success, children, women, change, innovation in business.
XI Friends, hopes, gifts, children, slaves, freedmen.
XII Foreign lands, hostility, slaves, injuries, dangers, tribunals, disease, death, sickness.

Each Place acts in the way specified, and the nature of the Place in opposition also acts cooperatively. When the transmission of the year has been found, we examine the Place where the transmitter is found and the Place where the receiver is found (using the twelve-Place system described above and the properties of the sign and the Place). The transmission of the stars will have its own causative influence as well, which we will append at the end of <our section> on the distribution.

An example: Saturn or Mars is in the Ascendant and is either transmitting or receiving. We can say that during this year there will be bodily troubles, danger, or bleeding. If these stars are in the VII Place from the Ascendant, there will be a turn to the worse because of a wife, or danger to a wife, or an upsetting crisis because of marriage. If they are in the IX Place from the Ascendant, there will be hazardous travel, trouble abroad, or betrayal at the hands of foreigners. If they are in the XII Place, there will be grief because of slaves or enemy revolts. In other words, the star will activate those matters which each Place influences. If benefics are in these Places, they indicate something good: rank, profits, longed-for purchases, travel. Determinations should also be made by taking into consideration the stars receiving from or in aspect with the Places, noting that the type of influence and the outcome of affairs will be determined by the transmitter, the receiver, and their Places.

It will also be necessary to look at the ruler of the transmitter or of the receiver and the sign in which it is located, because this star too will be influential on the type of effect <to be expected>. The II and the VIII Places from the Ascendant will be considered inactive and fatal. Whenever the transmission or reception is in these Places, the native will benefit from aspects relating to death. Greater benefics will accrue when benefics are in conjunction or aspect. If malefics are in conjunction or aspect, disputatious lawsuits will arise because of a legacy, and the year will be dangerous, calamitous, or impropitious. Occasionally it happens that when only malefics are <in the Places> or are with the Sun, the Moon, or Mercury, the native will be charged with murder or will bring something dangerous on his own head. If in addition Venus is in conjunction or aspect, the native's life will be even more in upheaval because of poisonings, or he will be denounced as a conspirator. Note that the places of Saturn are indicative of death and inheritances, and the transmission to Jupiter forecasts inherited property and benefits from the deceased. If this transmission coincides with the first chronocratorship, without question there will be inheritances and great benefits proportional to the basis of the nativity. If the distribution is in the <II Place>, the Gate of Hades, and if the transmission is from Saturn to the house of Jupiter, there will be an inheritance. If only the transmission occurs, there will be benefits from the deceased—likewise if Saturn and Jupiter are in the same sign and are transmitting or receiving.

If the transmission is from <the XI Place of the> Good Daimon, <the V Place of> Good Fortune, or from the Lot of Fortune, and if benefics are in aspect, there will be inheritances, gifts, or a cause of some good. If the fatal Places transmit to Places which precede the angles or vice-versa, the native will hear of someone's death while abroad or as a result of travel. (The four Places which precede the angles serve as Places of Foreigners and of Slaves.) Likewise in any nativity Gemini and Sagittarius have the same general effect as the Place of Slaves because of their zodiacal position: when Cancer is in the Ascendant, the Place of Slaves falls in these signs. So even when a native has the Place of Slaves in another sign, but has malefics in these <Gemini Sagittarius>, he will experience disturbances and injuries from slaves, even penalties, death, and flight, especially if Saturn is in these Places. If benefics are in these Places, the native will be thought well of <by slaves> and will receive benefits from them, and he himself will be a benefactor of slaves, or will indeed raise some, treating them as his children.

Consider the same to be true for the rest of the Places which precede angles.

13. The Transmission From an Exaltation to an Exaltation

A transmission from an exaltation to an exaltation with benefics in conjunction or aspect is productive of rank and profits, especially if the rulers are in their own places. Similarly a transmission from <the star's> own house to its exaltation or vice-versa with the rulers in aspect indicates vigorous, noteworthy results. A transmission from a depression to a depression indicates a mediocre and variable nativity.

If Saturn and Mars are properly configured and are transmitting to and receiving from their own houses, exaltations, or operative places, they bring great public services and high rank. Saturn provides inheritances, landed property, estates, rents, stewardships, and it brings success in religious undertakings and affairs of ancient lore. Mars controls the governing aspect. If benefics are watching and if the Sun and the Moon are properly configured with them, they bring great and profitable distinction to men. But if benefics are absent and if the luminaries are in opposition or are unfavorably configured, and if Mercury is involved, they bring accusations, reversals, great dangers, plots, riots, and ruin. If the transmission or reception is to or from another star's exaltation, or even to or from its own when it is unfavorably situated, the native will be thrown from high places or from animals, will suffer wounds, bleeding, and dangerous diseases, or be involved in fires and shipwrecks. Even if the nativity is helped and has an allocation of years <left to live>, the native will experience the ruin of his livelihood or rank.

One must observe whether the stars of the night or of the day sect are configured with their sect mates. If they are, they will be more effective for good than the other stars and will be a cause of great good fortune at the times of their own transmissions and transits. If they are not so configured, they will prevent any advancement in rank and will hinder any benefits. Because of this they have been named "malefic," since they are "malefactors" of life, but benefactors in other respects. Even Jupiter and Venus, when found to be setting at the time of transmission or transit, when unsuitably configured, or when unfavorably situated, cause a disturbed period, unsuccessful and full of delays; they are "malefactors" of hopeful expectations or benefits. In addition, they even bring penalties, spiritual torment, and criticism for one's accomplishments.

14. The Phases and Transits of the Stars

For all stars the following general factors must be observed: if they are found to be rising when transmitting or receiving, and to be ruling the year or acting as the overall chronocrator, and if they are rising when they arrive at operative places in their transits, they clearly bring occupation. Their power is aroused then, and each star will cause the results appropriate to its nature. Whatever influence and effects it has at the nativity or whatever the year indicates—in whichever sign it is located, those are the effects it will activate.

If the stars are passed the first stationary point and are found to be retrograde, they delay expectations, actions, profits, and enterprises. In the same way they will be rather weak and thwarting when in opposition to the Sun; they hold out only appearances and hopes. If they are at <or passed> the second stationary point, they cancel any delay and reinstate the same activities. They then bring stability and success in life. If the stars are at their last visibility, they bring obstacles and pains in one's accomplishments, as well as bodily crises, illnesses, and afflictions of the hidden parts. Often they hold out rank and great hopes only to turn them to the worse. If a malefic forecasts something for a nativity and has the year <=is chronocrator>, and if <another> malefic transits the year, it intensifies the evil; if a benefic transits, it brings relief and help. Assume the same is true for benefics.

In any nativity Jupiter has an extraordinary effect. If it transits the year, the points square, or those in opposition, and if the chronocrator is well situated or in operative places, it will bring great public services and high rank, particularly so when it is rising; then it has special power over the stars which seem to control the chronocratorship. If the chronocrator is unfavorably situated while Jupiter is in transit, it will be somewhat weak and unsettled and will delay the public services and high rank. If it is rising, it will relieve or help moderately.

15. The III Place and the IX Place from the Ascendant

The III or the IX Place from the Ascendant, when transmitting or receiving with benefics in those Places, causes travel under favorable circumstances, or occupation and association abroad or with foreigners. If the Place happens to be in a bicorporeal sign, the native will profit or will travel many times. Some men <with a star> in these Places receive messages from God, know the future, and are in charge of sacrifices, prayers, and offerings to God. Others avoid illness, imprisonment, accusation, disease, or danger through the foresight of God, and they bless Him for it. If the nativity's basis is great and if the overall chronocrator is supportive, the native receives gifts from a king, governing responsibilities, or authority, or—having escaped from troubles and crises with royal good fortune—he becomes renowned. Some prepare shrines, temples, and royal images and in so doing win eternal fame.

But if malefics are in conjunction or aspect with these Places, the native is despitefully treated abroad and falls into penalties or poverty. He does not succeed abroad, but is involved in wanderings and danger, and comes to his end cursing his fate as if he were suffering the wrath of God. Some men during these times will deny God's power, will engage in bizarre religious acts or eat unclean food. They will become soothsayers, seers, or prophets, or they will be considered mad. Those endowed with a more lofty fortune or rank will endure disturbances abroad or because of foreigners, as well as scandal, riots, and revolts of mobs or cities, because of which they undergo extraordinary dangers, hostility, and betrayal because of their responsibilities. Sometimes they meet with accusations, are terrorized by the king, and are ruined in rank and livelihood.

16. Nativities of Varying Fortunes

First of all it is necessary to take into account the basis and rank of each nativity and to coordinate the influence of the stars and signs with this basis, so that the forecast for average and for exalted nativities will not be different, not the same. Each star and each sign has an *average* influence for benefit or harm, as well as an *extreme* influence for good or bad, and they are sometimes the cause of great good, sometimes of great evil. So, if we find a distinguished and illustrious nativity <whose basis> is guaranteed by an aspect of benefics in the temporal transmission, but the malefics have the chronocratorship or have come in their transits to the angles or operative places, we say that the nativity will suffer nothing unexpected: the native will put his household completely in disorder, will endure scandal and criticism, and will be disturbed and fearful. If the Sun or the full Moon is afflicted, the native will act unlawfully and violently, will suffer upsets and much-talked-about dangers, as well as revolts of cities and of enemies, because of which he will live assailed by disturbances. For such nativities, it will be necessary to determine the conjunctions and aspects of the benefics in order to see if the causes might go beyond <what is expected>, and might foretell ruin or disgrace. If only the Moon or the Ascendant is afflicted, the high rank of the native will not come to fruition because of his bodily afflictions and sudden illnesses, and it will become painful and grievous to the possessor.

If the basis of the nativity is found to be characteristic of one living an inactive, isolated life, varied and surprising activities during the transmission of the chronocratorships or in the configuring of transits should not be forecast. Furthermore, those who are entirely fortunate will not be harmed by malefics entering operative places, nor will the humble be helped by benefics— all because of the overall predisposition <of the nativity>, which partial influences cannot change. Now there are many nativities which fall from great fortune and rank to low rank, while others rise from mediocre fortune and base descent to prosperity and prominence. <In view of this,> if the nativity is found to be rising to high position judging from the overall situation<?>, and if benefics have the chronocratorship in the detailed configuration of years, brilliant prospects, benefits, and success will follow. If malefics have the chronocratorship, uncertainties, disturbances, and bodily afflictions will follow, but the underlying <favorable> basis will remain unchanged. On the other hand, if the nativity falls to low rank (again judging from the overall basis), even if benefics receive the yearly chronocratorship or are in transit, their influence for good will be quite weak and they will permit malefics to harm the nativity. So, not in every case do benefics have a benefic role nor malefics a malefic role, but they interchange in the detailed configuration of years according to the overall basis of the nativity, becoming benefics <at one time, malefics at another.>

In addition, it is necessary to examine the activities of each nativity to see if it gets its impulse from Mercury, Mars, Venus, or Saturn, or from the Sun, the Moon, or Jupiter, and whether its basis is found to be distinguished. If each star is favorably configured in the transmissions or is coming to a transit, the year will be beneficial and productive of glory in <the star's> type of activity. For example, if Saturn comes into the places of the Sun or the Moon, the native will be harmed in those matters which the Sun, the Moon, or their places naturally indicate. Likewise if the year is with Saturn or comes to it (i.e., where it was located at birth or where it is at the transit), we will make the forecast according to <Saturn's nature>. When the rest of the stars, plus the Sun and the Moon, are in the Leisurely Place and are chronocrators, they become inactive; when in opposition <to the Leisurely Place>, they cause disturbances.

For any nativity, if the year is transmitted from the Sun, the Moon, and the Ascendant and gives any indications, those indications will be unchangeable, whether good or bad: it is good if the transmission goes to Venus, Jupiter, or operative places; it is bad if it goes to Saturn, Mars, or afflicted places; if the transmission goes to both, the nature of the stars and places will indicate what will happen that year. If the three figures <Sun Moon Ascendant> indicate incompatible events, the year will be complicated and subject to ups and downs. It is better if malefics transmit to benefics rather than the reverse. A star transmitting to another star in the same sign (i.e., a houseruler in operative places) brings a vigorous period.

The following procedure seems to be scientific: the apheta of the years should start from each indicative Place. We start from the Midheaven when investigating occupations, from the Place of Marriage when investigating wives, from the Place of Slaves when investigating slaves, and likewise from the Place of Children. If we find that benefics are in conjunction or aspect with the place we come to, or if the sign is operative, we can say that the outcome will have success, profits, and the fulfillment of wishes.

In any configuration it will be necessary to see in which sign the houseruler of the houseruler is located and how it is configured. If the houseruler of the sign is unfavorably situated and indicates some crisis, but its houseruler is favorably situated, relief from this evil will come, as well as partial benefits or a successful outcome of expectations: the native will receive trusts and gifts from the great or from royal personages, if the overall chronocratorship is controlled by the Sun and the Moon or by benefics, and if the distribution is to a good place. The following is particularly <effective> in a nativity: if Jupiter is in superior aspect to Saturn, or is in square, trine, opposition, or conjunction; likewise if Mars is found in trine, square, or in the Place just following the Descendant when Jupiter is at IC—under these conditions the gifts to the native will be very great and most profitable. In the case of those who present gifts to others, who strive for public acclaim, and who spend money on the masses: if Mercury is found to be in aspect with Jupiter and Venus at the nativity, but not with Saturn and Mars, the native will be acclaimed and will share much public repute and honor. If Mercury has Mars in aspect on the right, the native will regret his actions, will experience criticism, upset, and the notoriety of scandal, even if he spends his money lavishly. If Mercury has Saturn in aspect <on the right>, the native will end up a starveling, notorious, endangered. If Mercury also has benefics in aspect, both things will happen. All stellar aspects are powerful, but the aspects of square and opposition are considered especially so. <Aspects> are considered in the signs of equal rising times...

The transmission passing to Taurus and Virgo from those <signs?> indicates that the results will be insecure, subject to delays and lawsuits, and completely ruinous. The transmission to Sagittarius and Capricorn brings mysterious and harmful results because these signs are imperfect.

If the distribution is to be scientifically based, it will be necessary not only to examine the transmissions in the natal chart, but also in charts for *katarchai* and for runaways. Determine the Ascendant, make the chart, then use it in the same way as for nativities.

If Saturn and Mars have a relationship with the Sun and the Moon or with the Ascendant (e.g., opposition, superior aspect, or any other influence for bad)...

Assume, for instance, the nativity of a child is presented for interpretation, a child to whom a forecast for the beginning of an occupation cannot apply. When the transmissions of the stars are found, the results will apply to the father and mother, occasionally to his master, until the time when the native, attaining the age of full development, is subject to the indications <of the forecast>. Forecast for a child only what can apply to him: gifts, legacies, adoption, dislocations, boils, etc. Sometimes surprising forecasts are made for such people, forecasts which become evident from the overall interpretation of the stars. It is also necessary to harmonize forecasts for each indicated period with the age of the native and the customs and laws of the country. If this is done, the operation will be considered irrefutable.

In horoscopes for paired nativities—brothers, man and wife, relatives, other persons linked by friendship—it is necessary to make the forecast for the individual whom the horoscope best fits at the applicable time, and to say that such and such will happen first or second to this individual; then assign the outcome to the other individual in the second place. For example: if the horoscope causes A to benefit from something to do with a death, and causes B to benefit at some time from an inheritance, an inheritance from which A also expects to gain, the gain will not come in the chronocratorship of A, but in the chronocratorship of B, who is expecting the inheritance. (The forecast will be made from the Midheaven.) The same forecast will be realized more quickly for one person, but more slowly for the other, because of travel, a trial, accusation, or some other crisis. The same applies to rank, gifts, buying and selling, association and affinities, travel, and to all other occurrences in life. Therefore events sometimes come to pass sooner or later than expected because of the sympathies and antipathies of nativities. Nature reveals her causative forces through the cycles of the stars just as if she had supplied us with a map, but she brings some things suddenly and unexpectedly, while delaying others and holding them under the power of Necessity, until the star which is the most fitting cause of the matter receives the chronocratorship.

It is necessary to make a comparison between the universal motions and these matters: the Sun moving through the tropic degrees does not always effect the same change of weather, but sometimes it brings the universal fabric to a mild condition before it is expected, and sometimes it passes through the winter tropic with clear weather, but later stirs up heavy squalls and fearsome gusts of wind. Nor does the Moon <always> cause storms corresponding to its visible phases, nor does it <clear> the air after conjunction, but sometimes it storms and shows the effects of its nature before they are expected, and it causes an extraordinary mixture of weather, at other times it partially manifests wintery conditions, but then in that very phase, it brings a clear sky.

Occasionally, when passing out of conjunction, it takes a wintery turn. In a similar fashion the other weather indications and settings of the stars will not <always> have the same results: they will show their phases sometimes early, sometimes late, sometimes not in full measure. These variations will occur according to the risings of the year, the new and full Moons, the eclipses and the quadrennia, the overall and the cyclical houserulers, and with reference to the interchange of periodic transits.

17. The Transmissions of the Stars and the Ascendant. The Results

Continuing this topic, we must append the transmissions of the stars.

<The Distributions of the Sun>

The Sun transmitting to Saturn brings a bad year. It indicates unemployment, setbacks, hostility and rejection, damage from superiors or elders, rebellions of the lower classes, diseases and eye infirmities, ups and downs of livelihood and terrifying upheavals, attacks of subject peoples, the deaths of fathers or of men in the place of fathers. If the transmission is unfavorably situated, it brings convictions and imprisonment.

The Sun transmitting the year to Jupiter indicates a brilliant year: the father's high rank (for those who have a living father), association with superiors, prosperity, gifts, prominent occupations, offices. It brings the begetting of children and marriage (for the unmarried) and brings enterprises to fruition. It brings success and foretells great expectations.

The Sun transmitting to Mars indicates a sickly and hazardous year: danger to the father or to those in the role of a father... For him an effective period<?> and success in business, but with many quarrels, expenses, inopportune penalties, hostility from the great or from fathers, harm from subordinates, cuts, bleeding, loss of blood, troubles of the intellectual faculties, blindness, crises due to hatred, abuse.

The Sun transmitting to Venus indicates a good, affectionate period: it brings associations and friendships, gifts, enjoyment, affections, marriages, childbirths, buying of jewels or slaves. To men of superior rank it brings offices, distinguished rank, a vision of great expectations, and freedom from trouble and every crisis.

The Sun transmitting to Mercury is good, effective, advantageous, associative, beneficent to subordinates, and productive of giving and receiving. If it is beheld by malefics, it brings trials and tribulations, anxiety because of money or documents, the condemnation of slaves and friends, as well as untimely expenses and penalties.

The Sun transmitting to the Moon is vigorous and kindly: it brings acquisition, benefits from males and females, associations, marriages, unions, distinguished births, prosperity and gifts from foreigners or from abroad.

The Sun distributing to itself and being favorably configured brings brilliant prospects and activities: associations with and unexpected benefits from superiors and the great. If the Sun is in conjunction or in aspect with benefics, it brings even greater rank and benefits. If however the birth is at night, the forecast will be less optimistic: disturbed, with hostility, crises, or envious accusations. If a malefic is in conjunction or aspect, it brings reduction of livelihood, ruin of status, hazardous travel, the hostility of or danger to the father, and the disruption of activities.

First of all it is necessary to examine the nature and relationships of the stars: each star in its own sect and favorably configured will show a causative influence depending on the basis of the nativity. The aspects and transits of the other stars will have great power to weaken or postpone a bad influence or to benefit and elevate <the native>. It is better if they are found rising and in operative signs; if they are in the Descendant, or are inappropriately or badly situated and afflicted, they will turn to the worse.

18. The Distributions of the Moon

The Moon distributing to itself is unpleasant: it brings hostility and lawsuits from the great, ups and downs of livelihood, and confrontations with relatives or wives. A malefic in aspect from the right brings bodily weakness and sudden dangers. In such a chronocratorship, it is necessary to examine the sign in which the Moon is located, in order to see if a malefic in transit will cause something worse. If a benefic is in transit, it brings relief from the crisis, but it also brings travel and change of place. At the same time it brings renewed success for the indigent and a cure for their miseries.

The Moon distributing to the Sun brings the waning of livelihood and great expenses. Especially if malefics behold the transmission, the failure of actions and vain hopes are foretold, as well as upheavals, disturbances, domestic disorders, and affairs or marriage with women. For those who have a solidly established rank in life, <this distribution brings> expenditures resulting in purchases or renewed success in business, and advancement or some gifts and benefactions.

The Moon distributing to Saturn brings a complicated and fluctuating year: the sickness or death of the mother (if she is still alive), hostility, disarray in business, changes of place, chilling of activities, bodily dangers, troubles of the hidden parts or of the sensory faculties—especially if the Moon is waning.

If it is waxing, the damage will be less, except that the period will be harmful and grievous.

The Moon distributing to Jupiter indicates a good and productive period, one full of accomplishment and association with the great, rank and offices, benefits and gifts from females. It brings marriage to the unmarried, children to the married, alliances and friendships, or the increase of the mother's livelihood and rank (for those who have a mother living), success in business, and the fulfillment of hopes and expectations.

The Moon transmitting to Mars brings a hard year, especially if the Moon is waxing (for day births): it causes dangers and illness, bleeding, falls, accidents with fire, penalties, domestic disorder, the deaths of or separations from females, hostility, trials, imprisonment, and upheavals of the masses. If the Moon is waning or is approaching new (especially for night births), and since the chronocratorship is passing to the troublesome and active <star>, it forecasts that men will succeed—but only with anxiety and labor.

The Moon distributing to Venus indicates a period which brings success and accomplishment: rank, association, alliances with men and women, and marriage. If the stars are inappropriately situated and are beheld by malefics, they bring about unpleasantness, hatred, expenses, and breaches of promise towards female individuals. Overall, this transmission generally brings jealousy, quarrels, disorders, and hostility towards relatives, family, and friends.

The Moon distributing to Mercury brings an effective and successful period with respect to females and political associations, especially if <the transmission> is configured with benefics; if with malefics, men will endure lawsuits and disturbances because of money, documents, and accounts, and they will suffer great struggles. If Mercury is found situated in its rightful place, they will survive; if not, they will be condemned and will make great expenditures.

19. The Distributions of the Ascendant

The Ascendant transmitting to a malefic brings a very bad period, especially if the transmission is to Saturn (for night births) or to Mars (for day births). It brings bodily dangers, ups and downs of livelihood, anxiety, disturbing crises, falls, and injuries.

The Ascendant transmitting to Jupiter indicates a brilliant and profitable period, high ranks, and distinguished positions. Some are helped and promoted by the great; some escape dangers and crises and their troubles are relieved; others attain freedom.

The Ascendant transmitting to Venus indicates a good, lovely time: associations and affairs with women, buying, good cheer, an escape from evils.

The Ascendant transmitting to the Sun indicates that men will be well received by the great and by superiors, and that the year will be successful. For those of high rank, it brings even higher positions and advancement.

The Ascendant transmitting to the Moon indicates a steady and effective period: help from and associations with women, innovations, occupations, travel with a successful outcome, and (especially if benefics are in aspect) prosperity abroad. If malefics are in aspect, it indicates the opposite—and with disturbances.

The Ascendant transmitting to Mercury indicates an effective, profitable, and successful period. If the transmission is harmed by malefics, the period will be subject to the law and to penalties.

Stars transmitting to the Ascendant show the same results; a forecast will be made of good or bad according to the position of each star, whether appropriate or the opposite.

20. The Distributions of Saturn

Saturn distributing to itself points to trouble and unemployment, hostility from elders or the great, and disgrace. Men will fail in their attempts or, if they do accomplish anything, it will be insecure. If Mercury or Mars beholds Saturn, men will be denounced and have trials because of documents; they will suffer the subversion of matters concerning religion or legacies, will suffer from malignity and tricks, and they will come to an end like those suffering the wrath of God. <If benefics are in aspect,> the results will be milder: <troubles> will come more slowly, mixed with some success.

Saturn transmitting to the Sun brings danger to the father or his death, if he already has some infirmity. It brings an uncertain year: hostility, penalties, lawsuits, troubles of the sense organs, recurrence of disease, meanness on the part of friends and relatives. For day births, if the transmission happens to be favorably configured, men will succeed with wearisome labor and expenditures, or they will profit from deaths.

Saturn distributing to the Moon indicates danger to the mother—if she is still alive; if not, to female individuals. It <brings about> hostilities, separations, damage, criminality, disturbances in business, dangerous movements, bodily weakness, intermittent fevers, internal and nervous disorders, feebleness, dimming of vision, unexpected diseases.

Saturn distributing to Mars indicates a terrible and dangerous year: it brings about illnesses, plots, troubles, dangers, the deaths of family members and suffering or disturbances and lawsuits on behalf of family members, the ingratitude of friends, family upheavals, defense speeches/disputes, fears and hatreds with respect to the great, the deaths of fathers (if they are still alive) or of older individuals, hazardous and profitless travel. If the stars are unfavorably situated, they bring about shipwreck and ruin, diseases and injuries. If they are well configured in operative signs or have benefics in aspect, most of the trouble will be dissipated.

Saturn distributing to Jupiter indicates a fine and effective period: men receive inheritances and legacies. They receive help from older people or from wills. They control estates and property. Some gain profit from moist matters: they own ships, they purchase ships, they demolish and rebuild, they restore old matters and are adorned with a livelihood. If Mars or Mercury are together and in aspect with this distribution, men will endure trials and lawsuits, and will have untimely expenses.

Saturn distributing to Venus indicates those who separate from wives or are wronged by females. Some will see the deaths <of wives> or will be inconstant in their marriages and love affairs. Some will be the victims of plots and will experience poisoning. They suffer internal troubles, are plagued by weakness, chills, attacks of the flux, and endure reversals, lawsuits, and changes in their affairs. If the nativity is of a women, she will live in pain, especially if she is pregnant. She will also have affairs with her husband's friends.

Saturn distributing to Mercury indicates disputes about old or religious matters, about money or accounts, about giving and receiving. It indicates obstacles to accomplishing anything, penalties, betrayals, and hatred. Men will see the deaths of family members, will become accomplices or meddlesome persons during these periods, will be involved in loans and debts, will suffer upheavals because of documents, all according to the proper or improper configuration of these stars in the horoscope. They are most terrible and ruinous when in square or opposition <with each other>; they then bring anxiety and upset instigated by the dead/legacies.

21. The Distributions of Jupiter

Jupiter distributing to itself brings a good and effective period: help from friends, gifts, successful activities, trusts, stewardships, associations with the great, and the begetting of children. If it is beheld by Mars, it brings ups and downs and untimely expenses.

Jupiter distributing to the Sun indicates a brilliant period, full of accomplishment for superior personages: it brings popular success, offices, advancement. It makes men worth of honors, garlands, the offices of governor and general, and indicates the attainment of wealth—all proportional to the <stars'> arrangements and positions in the horoscope. For men of average rank, it indicates employment, escape from evils, freedom, beneficial associations, changes, as well as sympathetic friendships, childbirths, the acquisition of slaves—all this especially when Jupiter is well configured for day births.

Jupiter distributing to Saturn makes movements that can produce good or bad, expenses, domestic distrust. To some it brings deaths, changes of residence or business, unsteady associations, hostility of friends. It makes men fail to succeed in enterprises or to succeed only after delay. It makes men petition and plead <for justice> and to be involved in troubles.

Jupiter distributing to Mars indicates a harmful and disturbing year: it controls hostility from superiors, slanders, condemnations, betrayals, hazardous travel, dangerous diseases, critical periods or deaths of family members, ups and downs in livelihood, expenses. If the nativity is found to be of the public or governing class, and if the configuration is favorable, it brings political ties and advancement, along with expenses, gifts, and promises. These men will live with anxiety and suspicion.

Jupiter distributing to Venus is profitable and full of gain: it brings affectionate associations, gifts, help from or because of women. Men are involved in intimacy, love affairs, and friendships. It brings marriage to the unmarried and conception or childbirth to the married. To noble nativities, it brings the honor of wearing garlands, distinguished rank, state offices, gifts to the masses, great advancement and preeminence, the possession of slaves and ornaments.

Jupiter distributing to Mercury is effective and profitable: it develops business and becomes helpful to those concerned with words, accounts, or documents. It brings friendship with the great, gifts or conveyances, and profits from deposits or treasure troves. As a result men purchase slaves and become elegant. Some advance in rank, especially if the stars are favorably situated. As a rule, however, the native is slandered among the masses and is disturbed, or he endures scandal. Especially if the stars are badly configured or have malefics in opposition, conjunction, or square, the native suffers extraordinary trials and lives in anxiety.

Jupiter distributing to the Moon indicates a successful period full of accomplishment: ties with and help from women and the great, rank, offices, preeminence, escape from dangers, the acquisition of ornaments or slaves, conception or childbirth, affairs with women, gifts, conveyances, and benefits for the mother (if she is still alive). If the configuration is favorable, men will control deposits. It causes men to find treasures and to become wealthy, to bless God, and to escape harm or slavery.

22. The Distributions of Mars

For day births, Mars distributing to itself will be unpleasant and disturbing: it brings hostility, harm, abuse connected with public business, or expenses for the public. So, some are abused or imprisoned by officials or by the wealthy. For night births Mars is not bad: it promotes success and becomes helpful, especially if it is in operative signs, particularly for those who participate in martial affairs or in public or official life.

Mars transmitting to the Sun indicates danger to the father—if he is alive; if not, danger to the one who is like a father. It causes hostility from the great, separations from friends, dangerous diseases, troubles of the sense organs, danger from fires, heights, or animals, bleeding, amputations, and falls. It brings envy, disputes, and risky travels. If <the stars> happen to be in operative signs or have benefics in aspect, they bring employment, benefits, rank, political ties with superiors, but at the same time they bring anxiety, upset, plots, hatred and obstacles in the employment.

Mars distributing to the Moon is hazardous, prone to fail: it causes disorders, confinements, lawsuits, anxieties, hazardous travel, attacks and abuse from foreigners, danger to the mother or to females, battles, separations. It disturbs the masses or the city. It brings weakness, bleeding, falls, relapses of diseases, danger from fire, and shipwreck. Especially if the nativity is during the day, and if the Moon is waxing and unfavorably situated, the previously described effects will become worse: even blindness, wounds, the breaking of bones, troubles and injuries to the eyes. If the stars happen to have benefics in aspect and are in operative places, they cause risky activities and advancement. To females they bring bodily dangers, bleeding and consumption, abortion, and troubles of the generative organs.

Mars distributing to Saturn indicates a terrible and disturbed year: men come into lawsuits and abuse, penalties and breaches of faith; they see dangers to or the deaths and destruction of family members; they are involved in violent disruptive deeds, in harmful or painful travel, in bandit attacks, in illnesses and sudden dangers, revolts of their enemies, injury or grief from slaves. After meeting with imprisonment, anxiety, and the need for defense speeches, they will be treated miserably—unless the stars bring about these crises just to a minor degree, because they are in their proper signs or have benefics in aspect.

Mars distributing to Jupiter indicates a fine and effective year: it brings success, help from and association with the great, good hopes and the fulfillment of wishes. If the native has some connection with the military, he will campaign and be successful. Those of lofty fortune will be distinguished in their governorships and high rank; they will change their position for the better and will be adorned with the prerogatives appropriate to them, even though they had been involved in ups and downs and expenses previously. If the star is in opposition, it is indicative of reversals and penalties.

Mars distributing to Venus indicates hostility with and separation from females, family upheavals, the death of the mother (if she is still alive), or of females, intimacy and whoring, impermanent friendships, and denunciation. Even if the stars have an affinity, men suffer chills <=inactivity> and will be confounded in their <business> affairs. Women live endangered by bleeding and miscarriage.

Mars transmitting to Mercury indicates a disturbed year: it controls dangers, penalties, and disputes because of documents, money, or accounts, crime by magic, loans, debts, legal attacks and defenses. If the stars are in bicorporeal signs, men will display this same behavior towards others and will commit any crime. If the three aphetic points <Sun Moon Ascendant> are preserved, men will survive these effects. If, however, they are badly situated, men will be unsteady in their accomplishments. If they get into lawsuits, they will be defeated, will suffer very great losses, and will be involved in extraordinary crises.

23. The Distributions of Venus

Venus distributing to itself when favorably situated brings friendships and associations, agreements between men and women, gifts, enjoyable intimacies, marriage, family harmony, pleasures, and profits. If the star is found with Saturn or Mars, is beheld by them, or is in inoperative signs, it brings criticism, denunciation, whoring, penalties, breaches of faith, treachery from women, trials, and disorder. Women suffer the same treatment from men.

Venus distributing to the Sun brings a glorious period, full of accomplishment, a period characterized by associations and help from males and females: intimacy, marriage, childbirths, the purchase of ornaments and slaves, or gifts of these same items, high rank for the father (if he is still alive), or sympathy and help from father-like figures—all of this especially if the stars are favorably configured. To those of superior rank it brings the honor of wearing garlands, high-priesthoods, advancement, offices, and gifts to the masses. It brings oracles, association in religious or divine matters, charm, and joy.

Venus distributing to the Moon, when <Venus> is favorably located and configured in auspicious places, indicates a profitable period, full of gain: it decorates men with spectacular livelihoods and bestows on them distinguished ranks—except that <this rank comes> accompanied by envy, jealousy, quarrels, and secret hatred from some men. It usually brings incomplete or partial acquisition and benefits. If Venus is unfavorably configured, it causes injustice and hatred from males and females, and uncertainty and disorder in regard to relatives and friends. Overall, the transmission from Venus to the Moon is basically envious and jealous.

Venus distributing to Saturn indicates an uncertain and damaging period: it brings separations from women, fights, violence, denunciation, injustices even from the mother or from females, the hostility of relatives, disgrace, disputes with older people or associates. It entangles men in gossip and shameful passions, unstable friendships and intimacies. Men are at law with women and endure confrontations. They experience <changes> of place and a chilling of business. They fall into weakness and troubles of the hidden parts or of the sense organs. They are threatened with plots, poison, and recurrent fevers, especially if Mars and Mercury are in aspect.

Venus distributing to Jupiter indicates a good year, full of gain: it brings association with the great, gifts, offices, civic and social magnificence, rank and advancement, marriage and contacts with females, friendships, conception and childbirth, and graciousness in all activities. Even if a man is of mediocre fortune, he will succeed and will gain release from his miseries or from subjugation; he will be thought worthy of trust and honor and will be adorned with the prerogatives appropriate to him.

Venus distributing to Mars indicates an uncertain year: fights and separations from women, bleeding, consumption, the deaths of women or mothers. Men plead cases because of women, and they endure jealousy, hostility, denunciation, gossip, and whoring. They are wronged, are betrayed, and when acting against their real intentions or in pretense, they suffer punishment. Occasionally they think that the breakup of their marriage is what they have prayed for, and they go through with it because of some anticipated good; <but they suffer> scandal in the mouths of everyone.

Venus distributing to Mercury indicates an effective period, full of attainment in the areas of giving, receiving, and trade. For those active in letters or education, it makes friendships, the purchase of ornaments and slaves, alliances and agreements with males and females, ranks and honors, success in business, association in religious matters, trusts consisting of deposits, and the harmony of relatives.

24. The Distributions of Mercury

Mercury distributing to itself is effective and helpful in enterprises and trusts: it causes men who achieve their goals, who are superior to their enemies, who operate as actors or religious figures, who are successful in business, and who gain prosperity from words or accounts. Especially if Mercury is rising, is in operative signs, or is beheld by Jupiter and Venus, it indicates greater trusts and profits. If it is beheld by malefics, it is indicative of anxieties and reversals.

Mercury transmitting the year to the Sun is associative, effective, and full of accomplishment: it brings association with the great, requests, gifts (but with delays and obstacles), stewardships, preeminence, and knowledge of religious matters. It is glorious and beneficial to those involved in letters and education. For the most part, men gain advantage through religion or acting.

Mercury distributing to the Moon indicates an effective year, especially if the Moon happens to be rising and favorably configured and if <both are> in operative places: it brings associations with males and females, profits in business, successes, trusts, achievement of goals, and an understanding with the great. If Mercury is inappropriately situated and is beheld by malefics, it brings trials, expenses, abuse, threats from the great, imprisonment, anxieties, and the <unholy> revealing of mysteries.

Mercury distributing to Saturn indicates a disturbed and dangerous year: it brings the ruin of business, abuse, penalties and trials because of religion, documents, or debts. Men become enfeebled, consumptive, or diseased; they are burdened with bile or attacked with poison. They see the deaths of family members, brothers, or children, and go to court or have disputes about legacies. If these stars are in opposition or square, or are unfavorably situated and beheld by Mars, men contrive something dangerous for themselves; they are involved in shipwrecks or typhoons and live miserably. If the stars are suitably configured, they bring rank and success in business—after expenses and delays. If the stars are turned away, they have a moderately crisis-producing effect.

Mercury distributing to Jupiter is effective and successful: it brings political ties and friendships, success in business, stewardships and the office of prophet, prosperity in letters or accounts. In general, however, men will have bad reputations among the masses, will suffer scandal and anxieties, will be involved in untimely expenditures, will be disordered in regard to family, friends, or relatives, and will suffer struggles for their own health—if not their own, then for others'.

Mercury distributing to Mars is not good: it brings hostility and trials, penalties and crime, forgery, loans, debts, attacks and plunderings, disorder and betrayal, family upheavals. Occasionally men will inflict all this on others: they become bold and active in their assaults; they make their attempts in all directions and contrive assaults; they live in anxiety and upheaval, suspecting crises and anticipating ruin.

Mercury distributing to Venus indicates a good and effective period, lovely with respect to giving and receiving, purchasing and exchanging. It is helpful to those involved in letters, education, or stewardship. Men acquire ties, new friendships and intimacies, and are involved in affairs with males and females. To those standing in high fortune it brings the acquisition of slaves and ornaments, and it makes men successful in their requests, friendships, and advancement, and it makes them beneficent to their own people.

25. The Distributions of the Four Lots

The Lot of Fortune transmitting or receiving in operative places, with benefics in conjunction or aspect, indicates good fortune, advancement, employment, rank, success in business, fulfillment of expectations, and profits from legacies. When it precedes an angle or has malefics in aspect, it provides lower employments or ranks; whatever men accomplish will be impermanent and accompanied by reversals and dangers, trials and abuse.

Daimon transmitting or receiving in operative signs, with benefics in aspect, brings opportunities which accord with one's wishes, discerning and easily accomplished plans, helpful advice/contributions from friends, ties with the great, gifts, and rank. It makes men who succeed in their attempts and who are inflated with much self-esteem. If Daimon is unfavorably situated with malefics in aspect it brings changeable fortunes and emotional anguish, insensibility, cross-purposes. It makes men consider their own mistakes as successes, and makes them lay the blame on others, missing the mark in most respects. As a result such men lose heart; they sometimes contrive danger for themselves, are treated like the insane, and are struck mad.

<The Lot of> Love transmitting or receiving in operative signs, with benefics in conjunction or aspect, brings about moral desires and makes men lovers of the good: some turn to education and physical or artistic training; they are softened by their delight in their hopes and they do not consider their forethought/goal a matter of difficulty<?>. Others are enchanted by love and intimacy with men and women, and they consider <this life> to be good. Mars and Mercury in aspect or in conjunction with this place (especially if they are in their own signs) make homosexuals, men criticized <for affairs> with both sexes, or those who are fond of weapons, hunting, or wrestling. Venus <in aspect or conjunction brings> intimacy with women; men when loved will sometimes love in return.

In the same way each star, when allotted this place <Love>, when in aspect, or when receiving the chronocratorship, will bring about the type of desire appropriate to its nature. In general, if malefics are in conjunction or aspect, desires will result in torment, penalties, and danger. Specifically, if Saturn is in conjunction or aspect with Venus and the Moon, men will have shameful and unnatural loves, will be criticized for affairs with men and women, will suffer under scandal, or (even though repenting) will return to their old practices, overcome by passion. If Jupiter is also in aspect, what happens will be respectable, powerful, or religious. But if Mars and Mercury are in conjunction or aspect, or are receiving the chronocratorship, men will love wicked, criminal deeds: they become forgers, robbers, burglars, gamblers, and have a savage character. If Venus is also in aspect, they become poisoners, lechers, suicides, and so (according to the applicable chronocrator) they are entangled in loans, debts, and villainy, experience imprisonment and trials, and live in danger. This place is strong in many respects, and so pay much attention to it.[2]

<The Lot of> Necessity transmitting or receiving in operative signs, with benefics in conjunction or aspect, brings family ties, associations with the great, and the downfall or deaths of enemies. If malefics are in conjunction, it brings lawsuits, judgements, and expenses. As a result men fail in their goals and live miserably. If the configuration is afflicted, men are condemned or ruined.[3]

These result have been determined for the nativities and chronocratorships of men; they will also apply to nativities of women when the configurations of the transmissions are appropriate and the results described can happen <to women>.

26. The One-fourth <Method> for the Distribution of the Chronocratorships According to the Spheres Upwards—According to Critodemus

Moon - 1   Year - 1
Mercury - 2 Year - 2
Venus - 3   Year - 3
Sun - 4   Year - 4
Mars - 5   Year - 5
Jupiter - 6 Year - 6
Saturn - 7   Year - 7

The total is 28 years.

---

[2] *Marginal note:* The Lot of Love (for day births) is found by determining the distance from the Lot of Fortune to the Lot of Daimon, then counting that distance from the Ascendant; for night births, the reverse.

[3] *Marginal note:* To find it: take the distance from Daimon to Fortune; for night births, the reverse.

The degree-assignment <monomoiria> is done as follows: whatever <star> rules the sign in which the Moon is located, that <star> is taken as the first chronocrator, then the rest in the order of their spheres. For example: the Moon in Libra 6°. Venus is taken first as the ruler <in Libra>, Mercury second, the Moon third, Saturn fourth, Jupiter fifth, Mars sixth. Therefore <Libra 6°> is assigned to Mars. Now Mars is taken first as the ruler of the degree-assignment of the Moon for 5 years, then the stars coming after Mars at the nativity are taken in order. After the 28 years are completed, begin again with the star coming after Mars.[4]

27. Another Method for Years, from Seuthes. The School of Hermeias, Which Starts from the Sun, the Moon, the Ascendant, or the Lot of Fortune

"These are the four Places from which the beginning of the year <=chronocrator> is made: the Sun, the Moon, the Ascendant, or the Lot of Fortune. The choice is made as follows: if the Sun is at an angle, it is necessary to count from it; for night births count from the Moon, if it is at an angle to the degree. If these are inapplicable, count from the Ascendant. If the Lot of Fortune is at an angle, providing the luminaries are inapplicable, make it the beginning of the year. For nativities which have the luminaries approaching the angles, it would be odd to start from <a point> out of its own sect<?>.

"Using our system you will most definitely recognize in which signs the year of the nativity will be operative as it proceeds chronologically. For day births <start counting> from the Sun, if it happens to be in the Ascendant or at the Midheaven; if not, count from the sign in the Ascendant. Then count the year starting with the ruler (at the nativity) of the place where the count stopped. For night births, start counting from the Moon, if it is situated as was described for the Sun, particularly if it is rising and increasing in longitude <=waxing>.† For the two luminaries if it is not full and if it is decreasing in longitude <=waning>, <count> from the node, if it is at an angle alone.†[5] If it is not as described, count from the ruler of the place where you stopped, i.e., when you counted from the Ascendant. If you find the signs at the angles, acting favorably or effectively due to the stars which are in conjunction or which are beholding in the natal chart and in transit, it is clear that the year's results will

---

[4] *Marginal note:* Assign the 10 years 9 months counting from the sun for day births, from the moon for night births. For day births, if the sun is unfavorably situated, start from the moon; for night births start from the sun. If the sun and the moon are both "not dominant," start from the houseruler or any other favorably situated star.

[5] CB: Riley marked this sentence with crosses in his translation to indicate that the sentence is corrupt in the manuscripts and incomprehensible.

be good. If the places are bad, the opposite will result, since the beholding and rising stars provide the active <=beneficial> impulse, while the setting stars provide unemployment and the ruin of what has been done—unless matters happen to be obscure/the chart holds something hidden.

28. The Position of the Month

"You will get the month as follows: <for day births> determine the distance from the Sun at the moment in question to the Sun at the nativity, then count that distance from the sign which has been allotted the year. For night births, determine the distance from the Moon at the moment in question to the Moon at the nativity, then count <that distance> from the sign which has been allotted the year. Observe the sign in which the new Moon occurred, if the nativity was at the new Moon; in the same way observe the sign in which the full Moon occurred if the nativity was at the full Moon. The months will be operative in these signs and will have this point as the beginning: however many days the Moon at the nativity was from the new- or full-Moon position, that same amount will indicate the beginning of the month. If the Moon, for example, was 3 or 5 days from new or full, the beginning of the month will be at that point.

29. The Calculation of the Days

"You will find the days as follows: multiply the completed full years from the nativity by 5 ¼. Then add to the result of this multiplication the days from the birth date to the day you are investigating. If the date is in the Alexandrian calendar, add the intercalary days (i.e., one-fourth of the total years). Then divide this sum by 12. Count the remainder from the sign which has been given control of the month, giving one to each sign. Examine the ruler of the sign where the count stops, and forecast the quality of the day from the stars which behold it.

"Find the hours as follows: count from the sign which has been given control of the day, giving two to each sign, from the hour of birth. Then you will know the good and propitious hours. This method is excellent for the initiation and beginning of any activity. More particularly, you will accurately know the sickly and relapsing <hours> from the Ascendant's relationship to the luminaries and to the other angles of the stars.

"Whatever is necessary for a ready calculation has been declared above; whatever one gains from this brief disclosure, he will make a great contribution to his own welfare, if he has a soul of genius and if he introduces into his inner being the reasoning that man's mind can attain.

"…If you make the progression <=transmission>, use the hourly <factors>

8, 7, 6, 5, 4, or if <you use> the year starting with the Sun or the month (and this is found by determining the distance from the Sun at the time in question to the Moon at the nativity, then counting the same distance from the Ascendant of the year), or as I, Hermeias, have prescribed. It is necessary to make the progression[6] from all the stars to all the other stars according to the rising times of the signs in each klima. For example: for a wife, daughters, or female individuals, calculate from Venus; when forecasting concerning actions or related matters, calculate from Mercury; when forecasting about dangers, death, sickness, or bleeding, calculate from the malefics in aspect with the Ascendant, the Sun, or the Moon. Similarly for the other matters. It is also necessary to note the terms in which the progressions are located, which stars are casting rays, and which stars are transiting the sign of the progression. Likewise note how the transmitter and the receiver relate to the nativity, how they rose, and how they were at the nativity.

"Another method for the year <=chronocrator>. You will get the years as follows: from the Sun, which reveals mental matters; from the Moon, which indicates physical matters and matters about the mother; from the Lot of Fortune. It is necessary to inspect how these relate to each other. If they are benefic and appear harmonious, they indicate a good year; if they are malefic, the opposite. If they are both benefic and malefic, they forecast that the year too will be varied. The so-called Dog-Star year must be used."

30. Propitious and Impropitious Chronocratorships with Reference to the One-Fourth-Part of the Cycle

The distributions of propitious chronocratorships with reference to the fourths:

Star	Period in Years	One-Fourth of Period
Saturn	30	7 ½
Jupiter	12	3
Mars	15	3 years 9 months
Sun	19	4 years 9 months
Venus	8	2
Mercury	20	5
Moon	25	6 years 3 months

Those were the minimum periods; following are the maximum:

Sun	120
Moon	108
Saturn	57

---

[6] *Marginal note:* =vital sector.

Jupiter   79
Mars   66
Venus   82
Mercury   76

<Saturn's> days are as follows:
Saturn   637
Jupiter   255
Mars   318
Sun   403
Venus   169 days 18 hours
Mercury   423 days 18 hours
Moon   531

Jupiter from its 3 years distributes the days:
Itself   102
Mars   127 days 12 hours
Sun   161 days 6 hours
Venus   67 days 12 hours
Mercury   170 days 12 hours
Moon   212 days 6 hours
Saturn   255

Mars from its 3 years 9 months distributes the days:
Itself   159 days 5 hours
Saturn   318
Jupiter   127 ½
Sun   201 days 19 hours
Venus   84 days 18 hours
Mercury   212 days 21 hours
Moon   265 ⅔

The Sun from its 4 years 9 months distributes the days:
Saturn   403
Jupiter   161 days 12 hours
Mars   201 days 20 hours
Sun   255 days 18 hours
Venus   107 days 21 hours
Mercury   269 days 4 hours

Moon   336 days 6 hours

Venus - 2 years:
Saturn   170
Jupiter   68
Mars   85
Sun   107 days 12 hours
Itself   45
Mercury   113 days 12 hours
Moon   141 days 12 hours

Mercury - 5 years:
Saturn   425
Jupiter   170
Mars   212
Sun   269
Venus   113
Itself   283 days 12 hours
Moon   354

The Moon from its 6 years 3 months \<distributes\>:
Saturn   531
Jupiter   212
Mars   265 days 15 hours
Sun   336
Venus   141 days 16 hours
Mercury   354 days
Moon   442

Wherever the year stops, the ruler of the sign gives its period first:
Saturn   85 days
Sun   53 days 20 hours
Mercury   56 days 16 hours
Venus   22 days 16 hours
Jupiter   34 days
Moon   70 days 20 hours
Mars   42 days 12 hours

Another method: the number of terms which a given star has in the 12 signs will be the number of years of that star. For example: the Ascendant in Libra.

The nativity is in its 28th year <=336 months>. Capricorn gives the first 57 to Saturn, then 76 to Mercury, 82 to Venus, 79 to Jupiter, 65 <?> to Mars, 70 <?> to the Moon, and 6 hours to the Sun.

Another distribution: multiply the minimum period of the star by 4, and give 25 to the Moon and 6 hours to the Sun. Saturn will have 120 days because of Capricorn, then Mercury 80, Venus 32, Jupiter 48, Mars 60, the Moon 25, and the Sun 6 hours. Calculate the year from the Ascendant for day or night births. Someone is in his 28th year <with a transmission> from Libra to Capricorn. Saturn is in Libra. The <count of> 28 stops in Leo <sign of the Sun>. Therefore Saturn transmits to the Sun in Libra, and the Sun has the year. This method is approved by Egyptians, Babylonians, and Greeks.

They distinguish the triangles in year 28 as follows: Venus is the ruler of the triangle. From Venus in Cancer, the count stops in Libra. For day births, the ruler of the triangle is Saturn in Libra. Saturn receives the year from Venus. This distribution is at odds.

Book V

Vettius Valens of Antioch, Book V, *The Key*, Which Follows Book IV

1. The Crisis-Producing Place

In the previous books we explained the distributions with worked-out examples. Now in this book we will further clarify other powerful places and the keys which unlock the distributions of the stars.

With this having been established, it is necessary to prove by experience <the effectiveness of> still another place which I will demonstrate most abundantly: this is the Crisis-Producing Place, the place causative of terrors, dangers, and chains. Consequently this place is strong; for day births it is found by determining the distance from Saturn to Mars (for night births, from Mars to Saturn), then measuring the same distance from the Ascendant.[1] It will be necessary to examine the location of this place to see if the sign of a malefic, or malefics themselves, are in conjunction or aspect. If they are, the nativities will be precarious, endangered, and easily destroyed. The nature of each star and sign will cause the particular type <of trouble>. Benefics in conjunction or aspect will cause a lessening of the evil or an escape from crises.

It has seemed best to use the place in this way: if the Sun or Moon is found to be sextile to Saturn or Mars (calculating by signs), the nativity will be at risk and subject to crises, particularly in the similar degrees/within 70° and in the listening signs. This is especially true at the time when one of the stars is

---
[1] *Marginal note:* Others measure the distance from Mercury.

making a transmission into the configuration described above. For example: if the Sun transmits to Saturn or the Moon to Mars, or if Saturn or Mars transmits to the Sun or Moon, and if neither is at the same place, but one is sextile and the other is making the transmission or reception into the configuration described above from a position square, trine, in opposition, or turned away—under these circumstances the nativity will be disturbed, will be involved in defense speeches, imprisonment, custody, or will have suspicions and crises about such matters and will live with a bad conscience. But if a benefic is in conjunction with any of these stars or is in an appropriate aspect, the nativity will have a respite from terrors and dangers or a change to the better, but it will not continue to be undisturbed. If the configuration happens to be afflicted and has no benefic in aspect, the native will be convicted and will come into chains, imprisonment, or custody. If, with this configuration prevailing, the basis of the nativity is found to be great, at that time the native must have a care for his rank and livelihood: he will experience accusation and betrayal; he will defend himself before the authorities or the king—if not himself, then someone else—so that the terror and anguish <of this configuration> might be fulfilled. So great is this Place's power!

The full effects of the crisis (imprisonment and ruin) will come to pass if the overall and the yearly chronocrators take effect at the same time. The distribution using the cyclical chronocratorships will bring terrors and misery. If an infant nativity has this configuration, it will be necessary to forecast anxiety for the father or mother—or for the master, if the nativity is that of a slave. Note that some men, even while infants, come into imprisonment or confinement and spend their lives in such places. If some benefic is in transit or in aspect with this place at such times, a respite or relief from evil will occur; if a malefic is there, worse will occur; if a benefic and a malefic are there, good and bad will occur. In addition, if malefics are found in opposition or square with the Sun or the Moon, they bring anxieties and imprisonment.

If the nativity is found to be helped in some way by an aspect of benefics or by its general basis, with the result that there is no imprisonment, then there will be some figurative type of imprisonment or condemnation: military service, custodianship, debts, loans, to be assigned to convict-duty and to be put in charge of them, or (as often happens to many) to be required to do attendance because of the law or business. Some are fated to have unwanted experiences and to be unable to act as they desire. Some seem to be under the power of others; even though they are free, they are punished by a bad conscience. Some travel abroad or sail, and are held somewhere on an island or in deserted places, or they do service in temples or sacred places. Occasionally they are confined by recurrent diseases or by epilepsy, fits, spells, blindness, the ague, and syndromes such as these. It is necessary to make a careful decision about these places, whether the "confinement" will be only figurative, or will be literal and involve some damaging accusation.

For example: Sun, Jupiter in Scorpio, Moon, Mercury, Venus, Ascendant in Libra, Saturn in Leo, Mars in Virgo.² Both malefics were sextile to the Sun and Moon. If the luminaries had lacked the presence of benefics, it would have been possible to forecast imprisonment. As it was, the configuration was magnificent and noteworthy. The native, a soldier, in his 35th year was in charge of prisoners and a prison. He fell in love with a woman in prison, was troubled by an accusation on her account, had expenses, but avoided the danger. At the same time he captured and bound a fugitive slave.

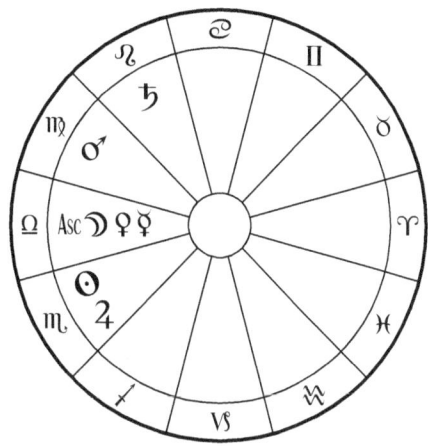

2. The Critical Year. The Ecliptic Places. Initiatives

In order to complete this treatise, it is necessary to continue with the rest of the topics—now the critical year. The critical year is found from the transmission or reception of malefics in relation to the luminaries, the Ascendant, and each other. The general procedure is as follows. In all cases, it is necessary to count off the years from the sign in the Ascendant. If the current year is found to be in the sign of the new or full Moon, or in the sign in square or opposition to the <new or full Moon> sign, the year will be critical and troublesome, especially if (under these circumstances) Saturn is found to be passing through the four places which just precedeed the angles at the nativity. If the basis of the nativity is in accord, death will follow, bodily weakness, bleeding, dangerous diseases, hidden troubles, falls, sudden dangers. Sometimes the critical point affects matters of livelihood and rank, if the bodily state is helped by an aspect of benefics.

---

² CB: Even though the received text says "Mars in Capricorn," and Riley translated it as such, Neugebauer thought this was an error and should instead say "Mars in Virgo" based on the recalculated chart and the fact that the Byzantine symbols for Virgo and Capricorn were very similar. See Neugebauer and Van Hoesen, *Greek Horoscopes*, p. 118. We have changed the text and diagram here to reflect Neugebauer's correction.

In addition, determine the distance from Saturn's position at the nativity to the ruler of the new or full Moon, then count that distance from the Ascendant. When Saturn transits that position or is in opposition or square with that position, death will occur, or a grave crisis to health or business. Likewise the critical year will occur if Saturn is at the ascending or the descending node, or at the points square with these. If someone takes to his bed ill while the Sun is transiting the ascending or descending node or through the points square with them, and if a malefic beholds the Sun, then the bout of disease will be dangerous and hazardous. Indications of the intensity or the danger will occur when the Moon transits the same places (the ascending <or descending> node).

Since the previously mentioned place (i.e., the ecliptic place) is powerful, I offer this advice to my readers, not with the idea that it is possible to appeal the decrees of fate and to act according to one's wishes, but <with the suggestion> that it is possible (I would certainly claim it to be so) for the initiates of this art to weaken the evil to some extent. For God, in his desire that man should foreknow the future, brought this science into the world, a science through which anyone can know his fate in order to bear the good with great contentment and the bad with great steadfastness. Some things which must be guarded against are foreknown because of the conjunctions and aspects of the benefics. Nevertheless even if a benefic is able to do something, a malefic in conjunction or aspect will hinder the good. If either malefics alone or benefics alone are in conjunction or in configuration, with no aspect of the other, then the results will be definite. Accordingly then, the initiates of this art, those wishing to have knowledge of the future, will be helped because they will not be burdened with vain hopes, will not expend grievous midnight toil, will not vainly love the impossible, nor in a like manner will they be carried away by their eagerness to attain what they may expect because of some momentary good fortune. A suddenly appearing good often grieves men as if it were an evil; a suddenly appearing evil causes the greatest misery to those who have not trained their minds in advance.

So as not to be diverted and go into irrelevancies, <let us resume>. It will be necessary to examine the sign in which the ascending node of each nativity is located: note whether it is tropic, solid, bicorporeal, and which star rules it. The effect of the sign will be weakened there. For we often find that stars which normally can have some effect at the nativity or at transits have no effect in these places. If they are at a phase while at the ascending or descending node, they become the causes of evil, especially if they are found to be retrograde or setting. It will also be necessary to examine the current position of the ascending node in the year in question to see which Place of the nativity it is transiting, for in this case too the effects of the sign and its ruler will be weakened. Especially if they are also found to be chronocrators, they can have no effect until the time when they pass out of that place.

Initiatives

With reference to the days under investigation: if the Moon is passing through the current position of the ascending node, or through the points in square or opposition, particularly if it is at the same degree-position, beware of starting anything: do not sail, do not marry, do not have meetings, do not begin anything, do not plant, do not introduce; in short, do not do anything. What has been started will be judged insecure or prone to come to a bad end; it will be something regrettable, incomplete, subject to penalties, grievous, and not lasting. If someone seems to have begun the development of some business in these days, the business will go bankrupt, will be troublesome, subject to penalties, easily ruined, and a stumbling block. Not even benefics which happen to be in these places do anything entirely good. Therefore, even without <consulting> a natal chart, if anyone guards against the current transits of the Moon through the ascending node, he will not make a mistake.

If one finds someone beginning some matter while the Moon is passing through the ecliptic places, he can forecast that the matter will be incomplete, regretted, and subject to penalties. I myself, being as wary of such days as I could be, have cast Initiatives for activities and friendships according to the chronocratorships of the current period, and I have considered the beginnnings to be unexceptionable and easily-attainable. But occasionally I have been in error because of the untimely presence of a friend, an untimely association, or because I began something under duress, and I found the results to be grievous or subject to penalties and delays. Consequently they <Initiatives> must be cast for all beginnings: the sailing of fleets, campaigns, commands, advancement, departures—everything that can come to accomplishment in life. <Without the Initiatives> it is not beneficial to sacrifice to the gods or to dedicate sanctuaries. Prayers will not be fulfilled nor God be worshipped. He will be called lazy and inactive because oath-takers will be perjured and oaths will not be fulfilled. Neither gifts to the masses nor expenditures on buildings will be celebrated or lasting; they will be criticized and will crumble. Neither will the treatment of bodily ills be successful; men will be disease-ridden and incurable, especially if malefics are in aspect with these places or if the Moon is passing through their degree-positions. (If it is only in the same sign, it will be effective in a delayed and dilatory manner; but even so it will bring insecure/unsteady actions.)

3. Critical Signs

The following signs are critical: Aries, Taurus, Cancer, <Leo, Libra,> Scorpio, <Capricorn,> Aquarius. When the years are in these signs, they are dangerous; the month will be evident when the Sun is in them at the transmissions.

The Recasting of a Horoscope with Reference to the Topic of Propitious and Impropitious <Times>

We consider the recasting of horoscopes to be essential because the recasting contributes greatly to the temporal interchange of the chronocrators. Sometimes the recasting increases the strength of the results, sometimes it is indicative of delays in the results. After we calculate precisely the positions of the stars on the birth date in the current year, we will find the Ascendant as follows: while the Sun is still in the natal sign, we examine where the Moon was then and when the Moon will come to the exact same degree where it was at the nativity, and we call that point the Ascendant. If that exact degree is found to be during the day, even though the nativity was nocturnal, we examine the diurnal houserulers, the ruler of the term, and of the Ascendant in order to find their relationships to the stars at the nativity.

4. The Operative Month: For Day Births, From the Current Sun to the Moon at Birth, and the Same Distance from the Ascendant

The King had this opinion about the operative month: determine the distance from the Sun's current position to the Moon's position at birth, then count that distance from the Ascendant. It will be necessary to examine the ruler of the sign where the count stops to see if it is in operative signs, and to make a judgement about the stars in conjunction or in aspect, whether benefic or malefic. (For day births, determine the distance from the Moon's current position to the Sun's position at birth; count that from the Ascendant.)

Some astrologers note the ruler of the degree-position of the new or full Moon and forecast according to that "month." Some consider the following month to be effective: note the configuration which the Moon at the nativity was found to have with the Sun; whenever it has the same configuration with the current Sun, it will determine the month. For example: Sun in Leo 5°, Moon in Libra 26°. The distance from the Sun to the Moon is 81°. When the Moon is the same distance from the Sun in any month, i.e., when it has the same configuration as it had at the nativity, it will indicate the <operative> month.

In my experience, those months in which the distribution of the years occur have seemed to be operative. When the Sun is in those places or at the points in square or opposition to them, it will make a forecast of the results which are indicated for the year or for the transmissions. In the same way Mars, Venus, Mercury, and the Moon, when they are passing through the places mentioned above, will be indicative. We will judge that place to be even more effective in producing results if these stars are passing through a phase while transiting the place. At that time innovations and activities in business will occur. If the sign <?> is passing out of whatever configuration it has, there will be no change or innovation, nor a fulfillment of the expected outcome. However, the Sun passing through these places and arousing the power of the chronocrators is very effective.

The Operative and the Inauspicious Day. This is the Real Distribution of the Days

To find the operative and the inauspicious day, calculate as follows: multiply the full years of the nativity by 5 ¼. Determine the days from the birth date to the day in question. Add this figure to the previous result and divide by 12. Count the remainder from the Ascendant, giving one to each sign. (A few astrologers count from the sign just following the Moon.) We examine the sign where the count stops to see if it is operative or not. It is necessary to note how the Moon and its inclination are configured with respect to the sign. If on the day in question the Moon is in aspect with the sign of its inclination, and if they are in operative signs, the day will be fine, noteworthy, profitable. <If they are in inoperative signs, the day will be average.> If the day and the inclination of the Moon are found in the same sign, results will be even better. If on that day the Moon is turned away from the inclination, but both are in operative signs, the day will be average, not entirely inauspicious. If they are in the other signs, the day will be miserable, hurtful, and dangerous.

It is necessary to examine how the ruler of the day is configured, which stars it has in aspect, and whether it is in the same sign, an operative sign, or a turned-away sign. <It is also necessary to examine> how the stars in transit are situated with respect to the day and its ruler. The quality of the day will be evident from the nature of each sign and star. If a nativity has the day in a given sign, and there is a transit or aspect of a star with that day, the day will be operative for good or bad depending on the stars in conjunction. It is the same as the results indicated by the year: the day will be effective for those results when it comes to the places of the transmissions and receptions and to the points in square or opposition to these places.

An example: Hadrian year 4, Mechir 13, the first hour of the night. I am investigating Antoninus year 20, Phaophi 10. <36 full years multiplied by 5 ¼ gives 189.> There are 243 <days from Mechir 13 to Phaophi 10>, and altogether they total 432. I subtract 360 for a result of 72. I count this from the Ascendant in Virgo and stop at Leo. The day just precedes an angle <Ascendant>. The Sun, the ruler at the nativity, was in opposition to the day (because the Sun at the nativity was in Aquarius), Mars was in transit, and the Moon in Capricorn was turned away. The day was precarious. In addition it was in the <XII> Place having to do with slaves; the native became enraged at a slave.

<It is necessary to note how the day and its ruler are configured together, what stars are in aspect with this place and its ruler, and at what phase they are (i.e., morning or evening rising, whether eastern, western, or acronychal, whether they are at the first or second stationary point, or are proceeding with their proper motions) and whether they are in their houses, triangles, or exaltations.>

...This too is a scientific method: the signs in which the Sun is located foretell the outcome of the month...

5. The Inclinations of the Moon at the First of the Month, Starting with Leo, then the Others Signs in Order

We have had to append the inclinations of the Moon: when the Moon is in conjunction with the Sun in Cancer and has its first visibility in Leo, it inclines towards <Taurus>. Then in Virgo it inclines towards <Aries>, in Libra it inclines towards <Pisces>, in Scorpio it inclines towards <Aquarius>, in Sagittarius it inclines towards Capricorn. It is clear that, when the Moon is passing to the full-Moon phase, it makes its first quarter looking towards the east. It diminishes in its second quarter looking towards the west. When waning in Capricorn it inclines towards Sagittarius, then in Aquarius it inclines towards Scorpio, in Pisces it inclines towards <Libra>, in <Aries> it inclines towards <Virgo>, in Taurus it inclines towards Leo, and in Gemini it inclines towards Cancer. Six signs are towards the east, six towards the west.

Sign of the New Moon	<Current Position of the Moon>	Moon Inclines Towards:
Leo	WAXING:	
	Virgo	Gemini
	Libra	Taurus
	Scorpio	Aries
	Sagittarius	Pisces
	Capricorn	Aquarius

	WANING AFTER FULL MOON:		
	Aquarius	Capricorn	
	Pisces	Sagittarius	
	Aries	Scorpio	
	Taurus	Libra	
	Gemini	Virgo	
	Cancer	Leo	
Virgo	WAXING:		
	Libra	Cancer	
	Scorpio	Gemini	
	Sagittarius	Taurus	
	Capricorn	Aries	
	Aquarius	Pisces	
	WANING AFTER FULL MOON:		
	Pisces	Aquarius	
	Aries	Capricorn	
	Taurus	Sagittarius	
	Gemini	Scorpio	
	Cancer	Libra	
	Leo	Virgo	
Libra	WAXING:		
	Scorpio	Leo	
	Sagittarius	Cancer	
	Capricorn	Gemini	
	Aquarius	Taurus	
	Pisces	Aries	
	WANING AFTER FULL MOON:		
	Aries	Pisces	
	Taurus	Aquarius	
	Gemini	Capricorn	
	Cancer	Sagittarius	
	Leo	Scorpio	
	Virgo	Libra	
Scorpio	WAXING:		
	Sagittarius	Virgo	
	Capricorn	Leo	
	Aquarius	Cancer	
	Pisces	Gemini	

	Aries	Taurus
	WANING AFTER FULL MOON:	
	Taurus	Aries
	Gemini	Pisces
	Cancer	Aquarius
	Leo	Capricorn
	Virgo	Sagittarius
	Libra	Scorpio
Sagittarius	WAXING:	
	Capricorn	Libra
	Aquarius	Virgo
	Pisces	Leo
	Aries	Cancer
	Taurus	Gemini
	WANING AFTER FULL MOON:	
	Gemini	Taurus
	Cancer	Aries
	Leo	Pisces
	Virgo	Aquarius
	Libra	Capricorn
	Scorpio	Sagittarius
Capricorn	WAXING:	
	Aquarius	Scorpio
	Pisces	Libra
	Aries	Virgo
	Taurus	Leo
	Gemini	Cancer
	WANING AFTER FULL MOON:	
	Cancer	Gemini
	Leo	Taurus
	Virgo	Aries
	Libra	Pisces
	Scorpio	Aquarius
	Sagittarius	Capricorn
Aquarius	WAXING:	
	Pisces	Sagittarius
	Aries	Scorpio
	Taurus	Libra

	Gemini	Virgo	
	Cancer	Leo	
	WANING AFTER FULL MOON:		
	Leo	Cancer	
	Virgo	Gemini	
	Libra	Taurus	
	Scorpio	Aries	
	Sagittarius	Pisces	
	Capricorn	Aquarius	
Pisces	**WAXING:**		
	Aries	Capricorn	
	Taurus	Sagittarius	
	Gemini	Scorpio	
	Cancer	Libra	
	Leo	Virgo	
	WANING AFTER FULL MOON:		
	Virgo	Leo	
	Libra	Cancer	
	Scorpio	Gemini	
	Sagittarius	Taurus	
	Capricorn	Aries	
	Aquarius	Pisces	
Aries	**WAXING:**		
	Taurus	Aquarius	
	Gemini	Capricorn	
	Cancer	Sagittarius	
	Leo	Scorpio	
	Virgo	Libra	
	WANING AFTER FULL MOON:		
	Libra	Virgo	
	Scorpio	Leo	
	Sagittarius	Cancer	
	Capricorn	Gemini	
	Aquarius	Taurus	
	Pisces	Aries	
Taurus	**WAXING:**		
	Gemini	Pisces	
	Cancer	Aquarius	

Leo	Capricorn
Virgo	Sagittarius
Libra	Scorpio

WANING AFTER FULL MOON:

Scorpio	Libra
Sagittarius	Virgo
Capricorn	Leo
Aquarius	Cancer
Pisces	Gemini
Aries	Taurus

Gemini

WAXING:

Cancer	Aries
Leo	Pisces
Virgo	Aquarius
Libra	Capricorn
Scorpio	Sagittarius

WANING AFTER FULL MOON:

Sagittarius	Scorpio
Capricorn	Libra
Aquarius	Virgo
Pisces	Leo
Aries	Cancer
Taurus	Gemini

[The following signs are critical: Aries, <Taurus>, Cancer, <Leo>, Libra, Capricorn, Scorpio, Aquarius. The years occurring in these signs are dangerous. The month will be evident when the Sun is in these signs in the transmissions.]

6. The Reason Why the Same Results Do Not Happen at Twelve-Year Intervals. Why Bad Results Happen Although Good Were Expected and Vice-Versa. Why Great Good or Bad Results Happen Even Though the Distribution is Located in Empty Signs

It is necessary to inspect the past, the current, and the future chronocrators and to determine if they are passing from propitious to impropitious, or from malefic to benefic places. <I say this> because often a nativity experiences an anxious period subject to the law and is condemned because of the chronocratorship of malefics. Later, however, when benefics take over and when the overall chronocratorship indicate that the nativity is secure, the nativity experiences a restoration of rank and livelihood through some defenses and the basis of the nativity advances to greater fortune. But whenever the nativity is carried to an inferior overall chronocratorship, and the chronocrators are in accord, then various disputes, accusations, trials, losses, and hatreds are prepared in advance until the nativity meets the crisis which is fated to happen. In the same way, if a cause of good occurs in the sequence of chronocrators, then friendships, associations and ties with the great, stewardships, legacies, and gifts are prepared.

As a result, those who were lowly and weak in their period of crisis are treated as noble, sensible, and charming because of the terms of good fortune. On the other hand, those who are entirely courageous and well educated (at least, according to the basis of the nativity from the beginning) are condemned and are considered coarse, cowardly, and ineffective, and they are oppressed by their inferiors. These men bear their abasement nobly and yield to the laws of Fate. In the case of ruling nativities, we find that when the chronocrators are making the transition in succession with the others, even though the time of rule has not yet been reached, some men attain noteworthy and profitable rank, others tarry in an opposite, ruinous condition. As a result, for some men bad things become good and a source of safety; for others even apparent good later becomes a cause of evil.

Fate has decreed for each person the immutable working out of events, reinforcing this decree with many opportunities for good or bad consequences. Through the use of these opportunities, two self-begotten gods, Hope and Fortune, the assistants of Fate, control man's life and make it possible for him to bear Fate's decrees by using their compulsion and deception. One of the two <Fortune> manifests herself to everyone through the forecasted outcome, proving herself to be good and kind at one time, at another time dark and grim. Fortune raises some high only to cast them down, and degrades others only to raise them to glory. The other of the two <Hope> is neither dark nor bright; she moves everywhere in disguise and in secret, smiling on everyone like a flatterer, and she displays many attractive prospects which cannot be attained. She controls men by deceiving them: these men, even though they were wronged and were enslaved to their desires, still are attracted to her again, and full of Hope, believe that their wishes will be fulfilled. They believe her—only to get what they do not expect. If Hope ever does offer solid prospects to anyone, she immediately abandons him and goes on to others. She seems to be close to everyone, but she stays with no one.

As a result, those ignorant of the prognostic art—or those not willing to engage in it at all—are led away and enslaved to these previously mentioned gods. They endure all blows and suffer punishment along with their pleasures. Some partially attain what they hoped for, their confidence begins to increase, and they await a permanently favorable outcome—not realizing how precarious and slippery are these accidents of Fortune. Others are disappointed in their expectations not just once, but always; they then surrender body and soul to their passions and live shamed and disgraced—or they simply wait, living as slaves to fickle Fortune and deceitful Hope, and they are entirely unable to achieve anything.

But those who have trained themselves in the prognostic art and in the truth keep their minds free and out of bondage; they despise Fortune, do not persist in Hope, do not fear death, and live undisturbed. They have trained their souls to be confident. They do not rejoice excessively at prosperity nor are they depressed by adversity, but they are satisfied with whatever happens. Since they do not have the habit of longing for the impossible, they bear steadfastly the decrees of Fate. They are alien to all pleasure or flattery and stand firm as soldiers of Fate.

It is impossible to overcome with prayers and sacrifices what has been established from the beginning or to gain for oneself something different, something more to one's liking. What has been given will come about even if we do not pray; what is not fated will not happen, even if we do pray. Just as actors on the stage change their masks according to the poets' words and act the characters as they should—sometimes kings, sometimes bandits, sometimes rustics, city people, gods—in the same way we too must act the parts assigned us by Fate and adapt ourselves to the chances of the moment, even if we do not like them. Even if someone refuses,

> "Having become base, he will suffer this anyway."

Now if anyone pays attention to the instructions composed by me and to the overall chronocratorships, he will discover everything in proper order. If he reads over some parts, but does not understand the causative forces and the other explanatory passages, a verdict of both praise and blame together will be pronounced on him. But if he does not attend or obey at all, such a man will be called ignorant and willful by all educated and self-disciplined men.

It is necessary to gain foreknowledge in accordance with Nature, because the same things are not given to and do not suit everyone:

"To one man the god has granted the actions of warfare,
To one to be a dancer, to another the lyre and the singing,
And in the breast of another Zeus of the wide brows establishes
Wisdom, a lordly thing, and many take profit beside him…
    <*Iliad* 13.730–33, trans. Lattimore>

with which the Compiler agrees. Men do not have all thoughts and deeds in common.

We have presented this material to those who dare to speak in praise of this work and to those who have a star-given, scholarly nature. The basis of this study is sacred and august, as befits an art given to men by God so that they might have a share in <His> immortality through this prognostic art. A distinction is made among those who encounter this art: some are true, some insubstantial, some incomprehending. It is like this: several ceramic amphoras receive one crop of expensive wine from one farm. After a time, some of the amphoras give the wine back perfect, filled with flavor and enjoyment for those who entrusted the wine to their keeping. Other amphoras, however, allow the measure of the wine's volume to diminish, are not able to contain the new wine, and allow it to foam over—these amphoras did not alter the flavor or cause the savor of the wine crop to disappear, but they do cheat <the vintner> in both respects, for the taste does not last any time nor does it keep its real nature, but immediately changes. (We can see the same thing occur in other plant growths: from one tree the fruit is sweet and ripe when it is gathered; the fruit from another tree is hard and wild; of another the fruit is bitter and rotten or harmful to its consumers.) Just so are the minds of those who encounter this art: one student does his lessons to the end with eagerness and determination and has pleaure in it. The unscientific and ignorant students get only a taste of the introductory portions, spend no time on these studies because of their lack of diligence, study with no legitimate teachers, and bring the charge of ignorance on themselves and reproaches upon the instructors of this art.

Let us leave this talk of plants and crops and return to the human race and examine it. From two producers, i.e., from the same father and mother, come many children, but all do not have the same nature in their conception or in their affinities with each other. They go through life with the unequal fortune due to the basis of their nativity: some live orderly and respectable lives, add credit to their families, become blessed, construct buildings and temples because of their love of beauty, and are beloved by the masses. Such men leave behind offspring and statues, and while they live, they live in glory; when they die, their fame remains eternal. Other men, because of their vicious character, are hated, not only by their parents and relatives, but also by those who are not kin. They discourage many others from having children. Such men are pursued by Nature and by God, and they suffer just punishment and meet a shameful and a violent end—a fate which I think the opponents of this art will suffer.—

So as to add a conclusion to our comprehensive treatise, we will append the scientific and powerful distributions. Note that occasionally, even when the transmission occurs in empty places in the given 12-year-cycle, noteworthy things happen, and vice-versa, even when benefics alone seem to have the chronocratorship, some cause of evil arises.

An example: Sun, Mercury in Aquarius, Moon in Scorpio, Saturn in Cancer, Jupiter in Libra, Mars in Virgo, Venus in Capricorn, Ascendant in Virgo. From Mars and the Ascendant to Jupiter there are 2 signs, from Jupiter to the Moon 2 signs, and from Venus to Mercury and the Sun 2 signs. So the years, 2, 4, 6, 8, 10 apply to them.

Then from Mars to the Moon are 3 signs, from Saturn to Mars 3, from the Moon to Venus 3. So the years 3, 6, 9, 12, 15 apply to them.

Then we count 4 from Saturn to Jupiter, 4 from Jupiter to Venus, and 4 from the Moon to the Sun and Mercury. So the years 4, 8, 12, 16 apply to them.

Then from Mars and the Ascendant to Venus there are 5 signs, from Jupiter to the Sun and Mercury 5, and from Saturn to the Moon 5. So the years 5, 10, 15, 20 apply to them.

Then again from Mars and the Ascendant to the Sun and Mercury there are 6 signs, and from the Sun and Mercury to Saturn 6. So the years 6, 12, 18, 24, 30 apply to them.

Then from Saturn to Venus there are 7 signs, and <from Venus to Saturn 7.> So the years 7, 14, 21, 28, 35 apply to them.

Next from Saturn to the Sun and Mercury there are 8 signs, and from the Sun and Mercury to Mars and the Ascendant 8. So the years 8, 16, 24, 32, 40 belong to them.

Next from the Sun and Mercury to Jupiter there are 9 signs, from Venus to Mars and the Ascendant 9, and from the Moon to Saturn 9. So the years 9, 18, 27, 36, 45 apply to them.

Next from the Sun and Mercury to the Moon there are 10 signs, from Venus to Jupiter 10, and from Jupiter to Saturn 10. So the years 10, 20, 30, 40, 50 apply to them.

Then from Venus to the Moon there are 11 signs, from the Moon to Mars and the Ascendant 11, and from the Ascendant and Mars to Saturn 11. So the years 11, 22, 33, 44, 55 apply to them.

Then from the Sun and Mercury to Venus there are 12 signs, from the Moon to Jupiter 12, and from Jupiter to Mars and the Ascendant 12. So the years 12, 24, 36, 48, 60 apply to them. One will find <the year> by continuing the enumeration as far as one wishes.

This number is powerful even when doubled because of the nature of the chart. In many nativities the number which is derived as a factor of the 12-year number seems more scientific and effective. Consequently it is necessary to note it <the year of the cycle> first, then divide by 12 and investigate the remainder <=find the number modulo 12>. If it is found to have a transmission, use it even more. If it is not so found, we will have to factor it or the number less than it. An example: if we are investigating year 20, we subtract 12 and investigate the remainder 8, to see if a transmission is there. If none is found, we investigate the places 4 signs apart and use them just like the 8 (for this transmission will be quite influential), or we could investigate those places 2 signs apart, for the factors 8 are 2 and 4. (2×4=8, and 4×2=8) The transmissions will be influential if this is so.

Next the numbers 21 and 19 give information by their being in opposition: if we subtract 12 from 19, 7 is left; and if we multiply 3 times 7, we find 21. For the number 27, the <signs> 3 and 9 signs apart will be influential. If the year 24 is found to have a transmission, I will use it because of the factor 3. The stars which are 13, 25, or 37 signs apart stop at the same sign. If a star is in that sign, it will be transmitting to the <same> sign. If, when the star is there, other stars are in the next sign in order of the signs, it will transmit to them instead. Using the previous nativity as an example: in the 13th and 25th years, Mars transmits to Jupiter and Jupiter to the Moon. If no stars are found in the next sign, the stars transmit the year to themselves.

Now each number seems to be most scientifically used when its own natural interrelationships are taken into account. Therefore in distributing the circles we will most appropriately first use 12, because of the 12 signs, then 7 because of the 7 stars. If no transmission of 12 signs is found where it must happen from these…

But I must add this most scientific explanation: it is necessary to make the vital sector run from every star to the degree-position of the encounter and of the ray-casting <of benefics or malefics>, and to determine the causative force of each star relative to any other star. If the Ascendant, the Sun, or Moon is considered to be the apheta, and any one of these three travels its course through the transitions of the chronocrators, arrives at the rays which are cast by benefics or malefics (or to their degree-positions), and becomes the cause of good or bad, or even brings the end sometimes—if this is so, why can the other stars not effectively act as the apheta or the ray-caster <=anaereta>? Or shall we assign the rulership of the vital sector to these three alone <Ascendant Sun Moon> and ignore the rest as if they were firmly fixed and planted like <mere> signposts. <No>, every star moving in its own course of wind <=direction> will be productive of good or bad.

I am aware of this fact since I have tested it by experience: many times, although I have found no appropriate controller, no houseruling cause, nor seen any influence from another source, great and unexpected occasions of good have arisen. At other times dangerous and fatal circumstances have ensued. I understood these occasions from the vital sector of the stars: when malefics in their degree-motions come to the Ascendant, the Sun, or the Moon, they bring the end; when they come to the Midheaven or the "opportune" places, they bring unemployment and upsetting or dangerous crises. (In their turn, benefics bring rank, preeminence, and profits, if the apheta of the basis of the nativity is found at the Sun, the Moon, or the Ascendant, and at the houseruler.)

Concerning the other types of affairs and the kinds of livelihoods, it is necessary to pay attention to the aphetic points, aspects, and ray-casting of the other stars. For how could Saturn and Mars not produce illness, sudden critical times, the deaths of fathers and mothers, hostility from the great, ruin of rank, dangerous anxieties, and anything else that their nature indicates, when they are at the aphetic degree-position, at the Ascendant, the Sun, or the Moon (providing that the nativity has sufficient years)? How could they <Saturn and Mars> not bring the deaths of wives and other females, hostility from them, trouble, life-crises, rebukes, and shameful passions, when they are in the places and degrees of Venus? How could they not bring trials and abuse because of documents, money, or religious matters, or the deaths of brothers, relatives, and slaves, when they are in the places of Mercury? How could they not bring rank, stewardships, acquisition, childbirth, success, political ties with the great, when they are in the places of Jupiter?

In the same way, each star will be influential according to the power of itself and of those stars which are in conjunction or which are casting rays. If they are in operative signs or at the angles, they will be more definite and positive in their results, less so if they precede the angles. If a star is found to be retrograde, we will make its vital sector run upwards <in the direction of diurnal rotation>, not in the order of signs. Then, having determined at which point its retrograde period ends, we will examine what star is able to cast rays to that point during that chronocratorship. If it is turned away from the presence of any star or angle, it will cast rays from one sign to another sign which is the length of its retrograde period away, and it will be influential for good or bad.

It is necessary to calculate the motions in degrees using the books of the tables of visible motions because the overall basis and the sequence of chronocrators is controlled by these vital sectors. As a result of not knowing that predictions are made using many methods, and since they have devoted themselves to applying one method to every case, most men have knowledge which is nonexistent, ineffective, or careless. Those who have accurately operated with many methods and who have used a scientific system which employs methods appropriate to the nativity possess a careful grasp of the effects of causative influences. Just as men from all climes come to various cities, particularly to the royal city <Alexandria>, many men from all directions, but not all approaching by the same road: some arrive from afar on foot, travelling desert places and rough roads and falling into fearsome dangers; others travel the thoroughfares easily and safely; others come through storms at sea and blasts of winds, often picturing death to themselves—all to attain their goals. No form of contest nor prize for their journey, either short or difficult, is placed before them. Rather each one attains profit, rank, or his particular goal (according to the influence of his current chronocrator), or he becomes involved in crises and is ruined—or even loses his life. On some doom comes slowly. Others expect a swift end, but <gain> unexpected good fortune.

Our situation is as complex: we must attend to our studies and come to the art of forecasting as if we were travelling by many roads. For many thousands of events happen to men, events which cannot be grasped through the use of one method or star, but through the use of many. Knowing that twelve Places are indicative for each nativity and that very many configurations can be derived from these Places and from the nature of the stars, we must observe the position of the angles and the interchange of the Places. Often two Places fall together in one sign, or a presumed angle really just precedes the <true> angle. This also occurs with the events indicated by the Ascendant.

An example: Gemini in the Ascendant, the Midheaven in Aquarius when calculated by degree. This X Place includes the Places relevant to action, to rank, and to children. It also includes the Places of Foreign Lands and of the God, since it is found (when calculated by sign) in the IX Place from the Ascendant, and the transmission operative from places 4 and 5 signs apart acts from it to the Ascendant, while the transmission 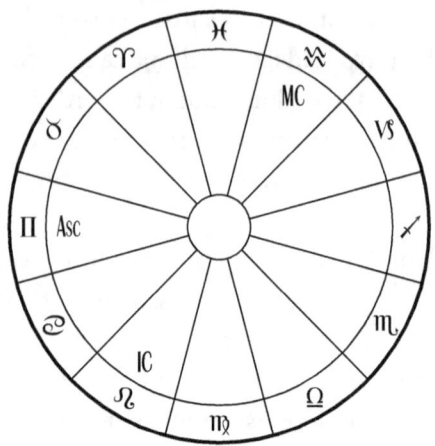 operative from places 9 and 10 signs apart acts from the Ascendant to it. In the same way the sign in opposition to Aquarius (Leo, which is IC) includes the Places relevant to buildings, estates, and parents, and the Places of the Goddess, brothers, and strangers; the transmission from places 3 and 4 signs apart acts from the Ascendant to it, while the transmission from places 10 and 11 signs apart acts from it to the Ascendant. Let the same calculation be made for the other signs, particularly for those of long rising time, because in those signs, the Midheaven would be sextile <to the Ascendant>. In short, if we calculate the Places and the distances between stars by degree <not just by sign>, we will not go astray.

An example: Mars, Ascendant in Virgo, Moon in Scorpio at IC, the Midheaven in Taurus. It is necessary to investigate the 34th year. 34 divided by 12 gives 2, with a remainder of 10. The transmission can go from the Moon to Mars, since they are both at angles <10 signs apart>, and from the Ascendant and Mars to Taurus (i.e., to the Midheaven). During this period the client worked abroad, was a friend of great men, was in mortal danger because of a woman, and suffered cuts and bleeding. Other transmissions 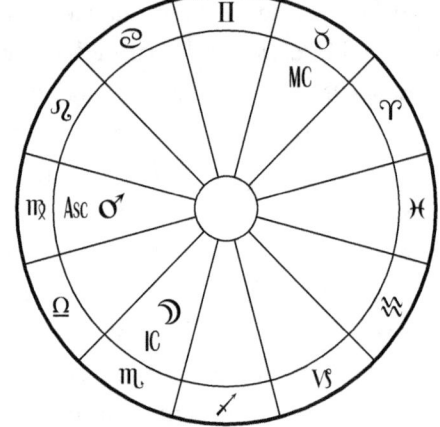 were operative at this time, but they did not reveal the <particular> crisis.

To sum up: often opportunities for bad things arise even when the chronocrator is not under suspicion; on the other hand, great rank and profit follow even if the chronocrator does not seem to promise these things.

Examples of the Preceding Method

We will use these nativities as examples in order to make our system understandable to our readers: Sun, Moon, Venus, Mercury, Ascendant in Scorpio, Saturn in Sagittarius, Jupiter in Capricorn, Mars in Leo. In the 20th year the transmission was from Jupiter in Capricorn to Mars in Leo, which are 8 signs apart. Jupiter in the third sign <from the Ascendant> transmitted to Mars in the tenth sign, the Midheaven. A

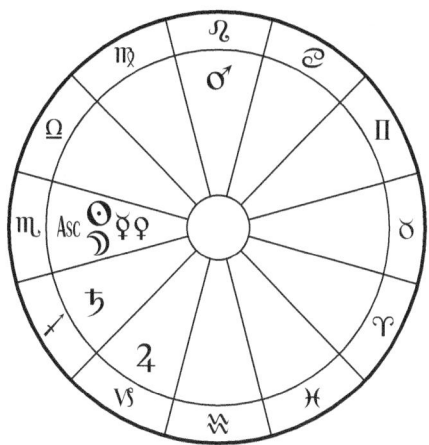

petition for higher rank was submitted to the king but did not succeed, because the transmission from Jupiter to Mars is grievous. The distribution by 4 signs is also strong, from Mars to the Sun, Moon, Ascendant, Mercury, and Venus. He was ill in his 20th year: after falling from an animal he was dragged so badly as to almost lose his eyesight. With regard to a female he suffered gossip, assaults, and a penalty, so that each star had its own effect when it received the chronocratorship from the malefic. In his 23rd year Jupiter transmitted from the Kingly Place (the III and the IX Places from the Ascendant indicate God and king) to the luminaries, Venus, the Ascendant, and Mercury, and they provided him with a powerful ally by means of gifts. Nothing can give a man friendship with kings and the great if the chronocrators are against it.

Another example: Sun in Taurus, Moon, Mercury in Aries, Saturn in Pisces, Jupiter, Mars in Aquarius, Venus in Gemini, Ascendant in Virgo. In his 42nd year he was the heir of a female because the transmission by 6 signs was from the Moon and Mercury in the <VIII> Place of Death, Aries, to Virgo <the Ascendant>, the house of Mercury, and from a sign of exaltation <of the Sun, Aries> to an exaltation <of

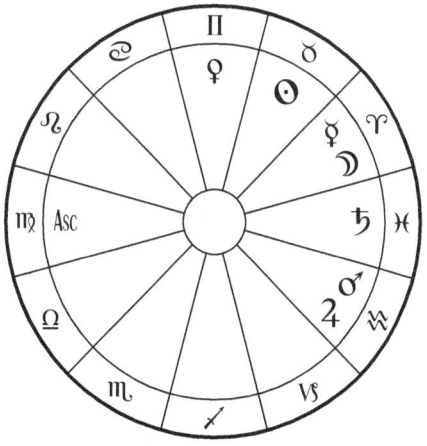

Mercury, Virgo>. In his 45th year he had a distinguished office of public affairs, because Venus at the Midheaven transmitted to Mars, which indicates trouble, and to Jupiter, which indicates high rank. The vital sector was also from the Ascendant to the Sun, and so he was recognized by the king at that time. In the same year he freed his concubines because Jupiter, in the VI Place concerned with slaves, received the chronocratorship from Venus. In his 46th year he had troubles and the disruption of <religious> matters, troubles because of females, and the deaths of two concubines, because the transmission was from Venus to Saturn in the Marriage-bringer <VII Place>, and from the Sun to Mars and Jupiter. He escaped from these disturbances.

Another example: Sun in Taurus, Moon, Venus, Ascendant in Aries, Saturn in Capricorn, Jupiter in Virgo, Mars in Scorpio, Mercury in Gemini. In his 51st year he travelled abroad, and going before the king he won a lawsuit for a high-priesthood on behalf of a friend. The transmission from the Moon, Venus, and the Ascendant was to Mercury in <the III Place of> the Goddess and king. In the same year the death of a child

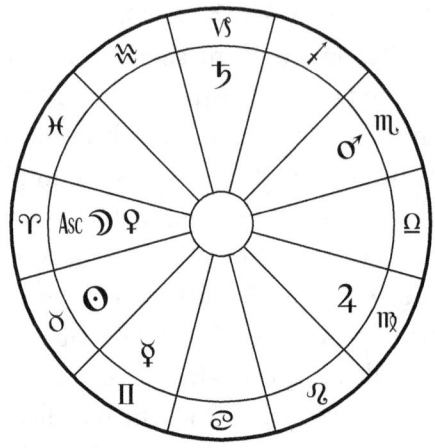

occurred, because Mars in the <VIII> Place of Death transmitted to Saturn in the <X> Place associated with children.

Another example: Sun, Mercury in Scorpio, Moon, Mars in Sagittarius, Saturn in Capricorn, Jupiter in Aquarius, Venus in Virgo, Ascendant in Taurus. The horoscope of the son of the father (whose horoscope immediately preceded) is given for comparison. Using this distribution he comes to his 22nd year in agreement with his father's horoscope. Jupiter made the transmission to the Sun, i.e., to the father, and the trans-

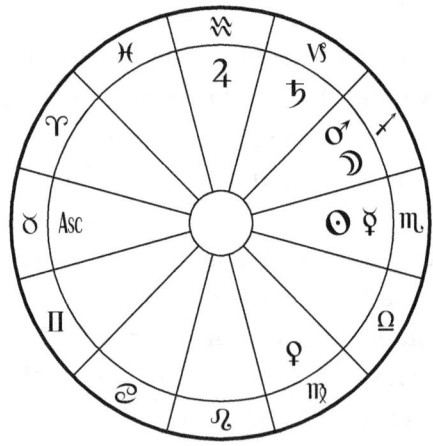

mission from Mars in the <VIII> Place of Death to Venus was the cause of death.

Another example: Sun, Mars, Venus in Leo, Moon in Aquarius, Saturn in Aries, Jupiter in Pisces, Mercury in Cancer, Ascendant in Virgo. In his 24th year he profited from legacies and friends. In his 26th year, marriage and help from a women. In his 29th year he had trouble and disturbances because of the death of someone else's slave and a charge of poisoning, because Saturn made the transmission to the Sun, Mars, and Venus in the <XII> Place associated 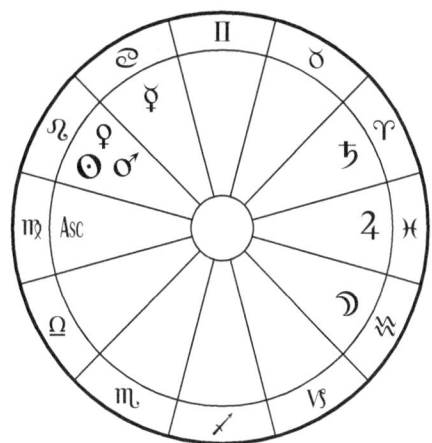 with slaves. He found help through his friendship with the great, both males and females. In his 31st year he travelled, and while abroad he managed pleasantly and profitably at the start, but later he seduced a slave and experienced jealousy and quarrels, because the transmission was from the Sun, Venus, and Mars (in the <XII> Place associated with slaves) to the Moon, and from the Ascendant to Jupiter in the Marriage-bringer <VII Place>. In his 33rd year he was ejected from a ship <?> and condemned to be a slave. Even though convicted, he found kindness because of the transmission from Mercury to Jupiter. The term of imprisonment, however, is made obvious because of the sextile aspect of the Moon with Saturn (as we have previously explained), and because the chronocratorship passed from Mars and the Sun to the Crisis-producing Place <VIII Place>, i.e., to Saturn, causing the conviction. In his 45th year he was released through the influence of great individuals on the grounds of illness; the transmission <by 9 signs> of the previous chronocrator <at age 33> and of this one <age 45> was a mixture of benefic and malefic. But the malefics were retrograde <Saturn>, under the rays of the Sun <Mars>, and becoming dim, and they fell in rather weak Places.

Consequently it will be necessary to examine the transmission of all the stars to see if the transmissions of malefics or of benefics predominate, or if they are mixed. Having done this, make the forecast. We have explained this in our instructions; so as not to seem verbose, we have appended the following condensed horoscopes. The reader can interpret the places and the causative forces by using the explanations which have been or will be given:

Sun, Mercury, Venus in Libra, Saturn in Aquarius, Jupiter, Ascendant in Sagittarius, Mars in Virgo, Moon in Leo. In his 47th year he was the heir of a friend, and in the same year he was separated from his wife because of jealousy and abuse.

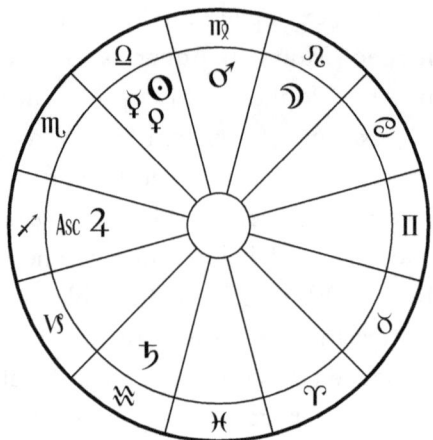

Another example: Sun, Mars in Taurus, Moon, Ascendant in Aries, Saturn in Leo, Jupiter in Cancer, Venus in Pisces, Mercury in Gemini. In his fourth year the death of his father occurred.

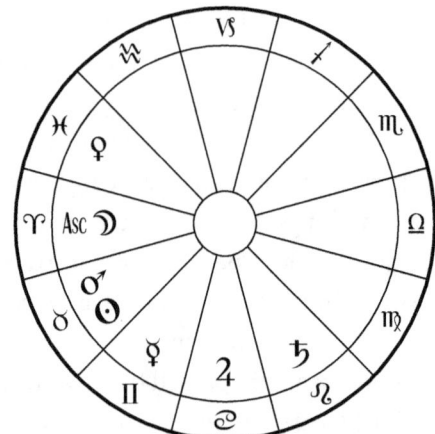

Another example: Sun, Mercury, Saturn in Sagittarius, Moon in Pisces, Mars in Leo, Venus in Capricorn, Ascendant, Jupiter in Taurus. In his 45th year twin children were still-born <?>. In the same year he became a high-priest. In his 51st year a distinguished public office. In his 52nd year the death of a child.

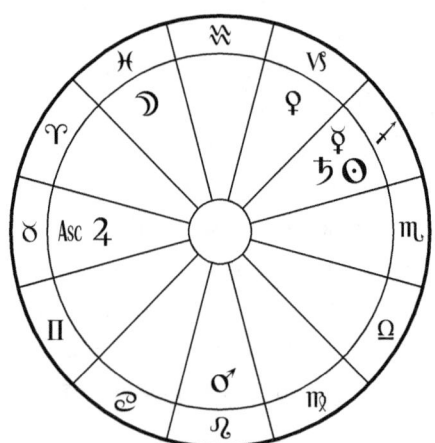

Another example: Sun, Venus in Taurus, Moon in Aries, Saturn in Cancer, Jupiter <in Libra>, Mars in Virgo, Mercury in Gemini, Ascendant in Sagittarius. In his 36th year he had court cases and trouble on behalf of his wife, as well as the hostility of friends.

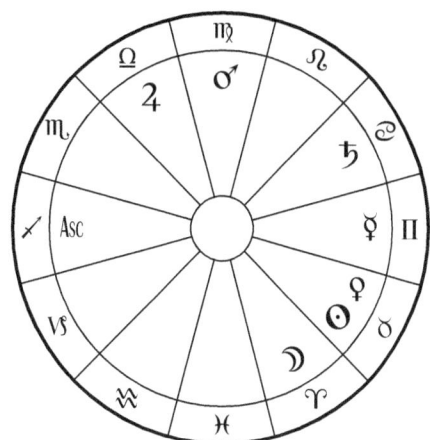

Another example: Sun, Venus in Aquarius, Moon, Jupiter in Sagittarius, Saturn in Leo, Mercury in Capricorn, Mars, Ascendant in Libra. In his 35th year he was in danger of prison because of riot and violence: the Moon was sextile with Mars, and Mars itself had received the year from the Moon and had transmitted it to Saturn. These successive transmissions are grievous and dangerous. But Jupiter was with the Moon and received the

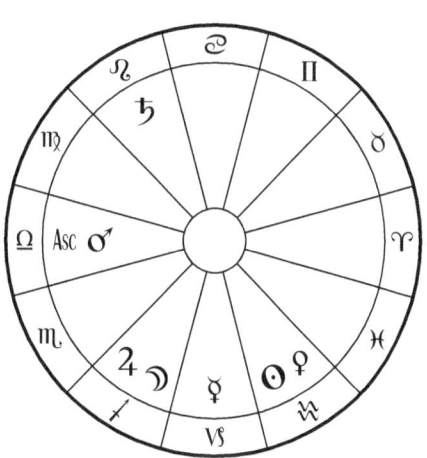

year from the Sun and Venus, who were in the <V> Place associated with friends. Jupiter happened to be in the Place of Travel and caused travel which was voluntary but risky, as well as help from and associations with friends.

Another example: Sun, Mars, Mercury in Scorpio, Saturn in Aries, Moon in Virgo, Jupiter in Taurus, Venus in Libra, Ascendant in Sagittarius. In his 42nd year he experienced troubles, confusion, and scandal because of a woman. In his 44th year the violent death of a slave, a crisis for his father, and an accusation of base descent and of violence. But he got help and gifts from friends. He had

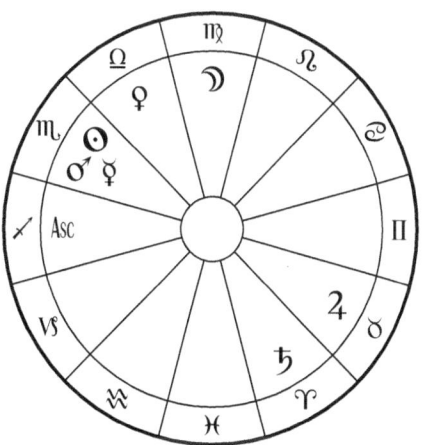

troubles related to documents; he experienced penalties, assaults, and false accusations. He suffered grief because of his slaves and he had problems with his health. We see that each transmission had its own influence, and likewise each Place.

Another example: Sun, Jupiter in Capricorn, Moon, Saturn in Leo, Mars in Pisces, Venus, Ascendant in Scorpio, Mercury in Sagittarius. The Crisis-producing Places were found in Pisces and Scorpio, because Venus was in Scorpio and Mars in Pisces. He was a dancer, and in his 20th year he was taken into custody during a mob uprising. He, however, was defended before the governor by the help of his friends. He was re-

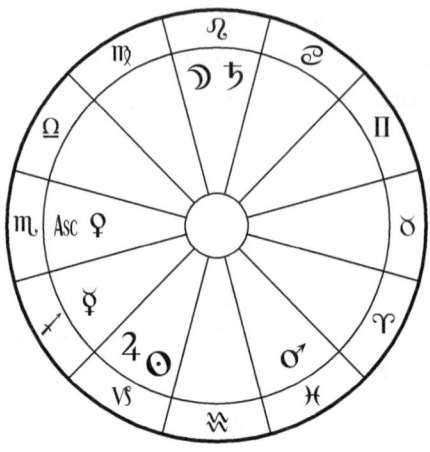

leased through the pleas of the crowd and became even more famous. The transmission of the year was from Saturn and the Moon to Mars and the Crisis-producing Place <by 8 signs>, and from Jupiter and the Sun in the III Place concerned with property to Saturn and the Moon at the Midheaven, in the X Place, a Place associated with occupations. In addition the distribution by 4 signs, i.e., from Saturn and the Moon to Venus and the Ascendant, is indicative of the riot, the quarrelsomeness, and the rivalry throughout the affair, as is the distribution by 4 signs, from Mercury to Mars and the Crisis-producing Place (4 signs). All the stars were operative in his 20th year, and so the nativity was in danger of loss of rank, of condemnation, and of loss of life. Since, however, Venus was found in the Ascendant and <Mars> in the Crisis-producing Place, while Jupiter was with the Sun, the native had a spectacular escape and gained success from this affair. In addition the Lot of Fortune was in Aries and the ruler of the Exaltation of the Nativity, the Sun <in Capricorn>, was at the Midheaven relative to the Lot of Fortune, as was Mars relative to Daimon <in Gemini>. Later in his 32nd year he lost his office, his rank, and his livelihood, and lived in disgrace, since the Lot of Fortune happened to be preceding an angle, and Saturn was at the Midheaven, not in its own sect, and in opposition to the <11th> Place of Accomplishment in Aquarius, Saturn's own house. As a result he caused his own downfall, being arrogant and boastful. Mercury, the ruler of Daimon, the Intellectual Place, was in opposition to itself in Gemini <a house of Mercury>.

Another example: Sun, Moon, in Cancer, Saturn, Jupiter, Mars in Aries, Venus, Mercury, Ascendant in Gemini. In his 20th year both his parents were killed while attending a festival by an attack of bandits, because the transmission was from the Ascendant to the <VIII> Place of Death <Capricorn>. Even more operative was the transmission by 4 signs from Saturn and Mars to the Sun and Moon, which were in the 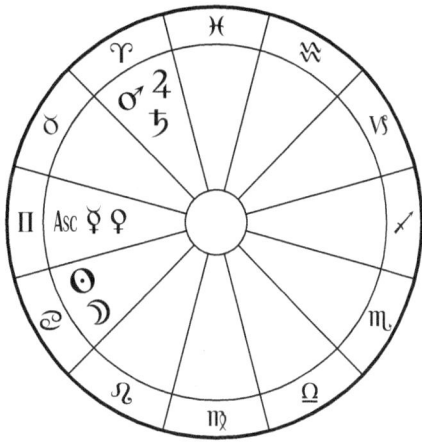 <II> Place associated with death and which indicated the father and mother. The native, however, escaped danger in the uproar, so as to show that the transmission from Jupiter <to the Sun and Moon> was also powerful at the same time.

7. The Aphetic Points/Transmissions

The aphetic points of the years are operative when starting from any star, but the following aphetic points are most effective: for day births the Sun, for night births the Moon, especially when they are at the angles. Next <in effectiveness> is the Ascendant. If the vital sector starting from the Ascendant, the Moon, or the Sun passes to one of the stars in the nativity, then use it for forecasting. If one of the stars in transit has entered this place, then it will be transmitting the chronocratorship. If the sign where the count stops happens to be empty, then count from the position (at the nativity) of the ruler of the sign, and examine in the same way the place found, whether using the nativity or the transiting stars. Then forecast the results of all the places and stars. <In other words,> if the count goes from star to star, use the stars for forecasting; if from a star to an empty sign, use the rulers of the signs.

An example: if the aphetic point goes from the Moon to either Aries or Scorpio, but no stars are in either sign, then count off the same number of years from the position of Mars <ruler of Aries and Scorpio> at the nativity; if the count stops at Saturn, the year will be dangerous and troublesome, plus whatever else the transmissions and the places indicate. The same method holds true for the year starting from the Sun, the Ascendant, or the Lots: each will forecast an appropriate result according to its transmission and reception.

Now if two stars are active in one year, <both transmissions will be effective>, but especially those from the angles, next those from signs which follow the angles, next those from signs which precede the angles. Benefics transmitting or receiving from angles, exaltations, or operative places become the cause of great good and high rank; when transmitting or receiving from signs which follow the angles, they cause moderate good; when transmitting and receiving from signs which precede the angles, they are weak. When transmitting or receiving from <signs> in opposition, they are damaging and troublesome. In the same way malefics acting at the angles are the worst; in signs which follow the angles they are mediocre and bring crises slowly; in signs which precede the angles they are less bad. When acting in opposition they are indicative of reversals and dangers.

Whenever malefics in superior aspect receive the chronocratorship from stars in inferior aspect, they make the bad even worse, even if they are in opposition to benefics and are receiving from them. When trine <with benefics> they make their results more agreeable and mild. The receivers are considered more influential than the transmitters: it is better if a benefic transmits to a benefic than if a malefic transmits to a benefic; it is the worst if a malefic transmits to a malefic. If the vital sector comes to a currently empty sign, but later a star transits this place, that star will be receiving the chronocratorship. A star's influence will be considered very vigorous, whether benefic or malefic, if it is passing through a phase in that sign; if it is transiting, it is weak. If the vital sector comes to an empty sign, the vital sector of the previous year <=chronocratorship> will have the control until another takes effect.

The settings and retrograde periods of the stars will be weak, the risings and stationary points will be vigorous, blending their influences in complex ways. <Forecast> according to the basis of the nativity for the rich, the middle class, the toilers, the poor, and the craftsmen.

Forecasts will be quite definite with respect to actions and critical points when the same stars come into the same configuration they had at the nativity—as the divine Critodemus reminds us. We append his system in the following chart and the accompanying directions:

<	Ar	Ta	Ge	Cn	Le	Vi	Li	Sc	Sa	Cp	Aq	Pi
Ar	1	12	11	10	9	8	7	6	5	4	3	2
Ta	2	1	12	11	10	9	8	7	6	5	4	3
Ge	3	2	1	12	11	10	9	8	7	6	5	4
Cn	4	3	2	1	12	11	10	9	8	7	6	5
Le	5	4	3	2	1	12	11	10	9	8	7	6
Vi	6	5	4	3	2	1	12	11	10	9	8	7
Li	7	6	5	4	3	2	1	12	11	10	9	8
Sc	8	7	6	5	4	3	2	1	12	11	10	9
Sa	9	8	7	6	5	4	3	2	1	12	11	10
Cp	10	9	8	7	6	5	4	3	2	1	12	11
Aq	11	10	9	8	7	6	5	4	3	2	1	12
Pi	12	11	10	9	8	7	6	5	4	3	2	1>

The preceding table is the table of the stars' mutual return to the same intervals and configurations.

For example: Sun, Mars, Mercury, Ascendant in Sagittarius, Moon in Leo, Saturn in Virgo, Jupiter in Scorpio, Venus in Capricorn. The Moon controls the second interval since it is two signs from Saturn. The same is true of the Sun, Mars, Mercury, and the Ascendant with respect to Venus. Saturn, Jupiter, and Venus control the third interval. Saturn controls the fourth and fifth interval. The Moon controls the sixth. The seventh is common to all. Venus controls the eighth. The Sun, Mars, Mercury, and the Ascendant the ninth. Jupiter the tenth and eleventh, and Venus the twelfth. The horoscope is in its 31st year.

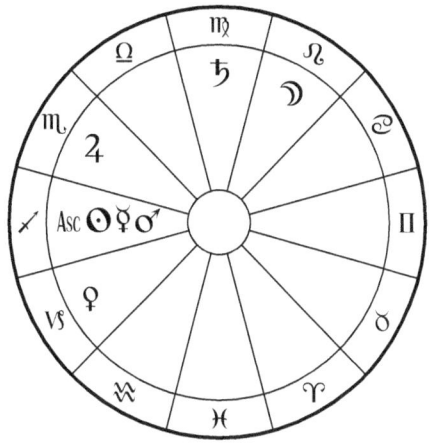

The operative stars and the critical points are found as follows: when calculating the previously mentioned critical points, begin at the third row (=third interval), because the preceding two intervals, the first and the second, are inoperative. (The first is operative to year 12, the second to year 24, the third to year 36, and so on.) It is calculated thus: since the 31st year falls in the eleventh column of the third interval, and since Saturn, Jupiter, and Venus control the third interval at the nativity, investigate the stars in transit at the time in question to see if they transmit to another star or to themselves at a distance of 11 signs. Take the preceding nativity: the stars' positions at the time in question were as follows: Sun, Jupiter, Mercury in Gemini, Saturn in Virgo, Mars, Venus in Taurus, Moon in Pisces. Now the stars controlling the interval of 11 were Saturn, Jupiter, and Venus, and we find at the time in question that Venus has returned to a position 11 signs from the Moon, but that no star has returned to a position 11 signs from Jupiter. Immediately I move to the fourth row. I find 32 in the eighth position. None of the ruling stars are critical in the fourth interval. I move to the fifth interval: the Moon and Saturn are operative in the fifth interval and are found to be returning to each other five signs apart. I move to the sixth interval: no stars are six signs apart. I move to the row of the seventh interval. [The chronocratorship is found to be passing through the fifth interval.] The seventh interval is found to be empty of any star (as mentioned above); Mars and Venus to Saturn <?>. I move to the row of the eighth interval: Venus rules the eighth interval because of the factor 4. It is returning to no star. Then to the critical point of the ninth interval: the Sun, Mars, Mercury, the Ascendant, and Venus rule the ninth interval; 36 is in this row. At a 4-year-interval the Sun, Jupiter, and Mercury are found to be returning to Saturn. Next I move to the tenth interval: the Sun, Mars, Mercury, Jupiter, and the Ascendant rule the tenth; in this row is the number 4; therefore the Sun, Mercury, and Jupiter are found to be transmitting to Saturn.

The chronocrators found by using these intervals will be incontrovertibly active and operative when their rulers at the nativity have the same intervals in their transits at the time in question as they had at the nativity.

8. Another Method For the Critical Years: Critodemus Begins with the Moon

An example: Sun in Aquarius, Moon in Leo, Saturn in Cancer, Jupiter in Gemini, Mars in Scorpio, Venus in Aries, Mercury in Pisces. The 12 years <are derived from> Mars' distance of 4 signs <from the Moon>. The critical year is simple, because 4×4=16. (The squares are *simple*; the rectangular numbers are *composite*.) The 18 for Venus is composite: 2×9. The 2 <is from Leo> to Virgo, but no star is in Virgo, so Venus is 9 signs from the Moon. If there were a star in Virgo, it <Venus> would have returned because of the…

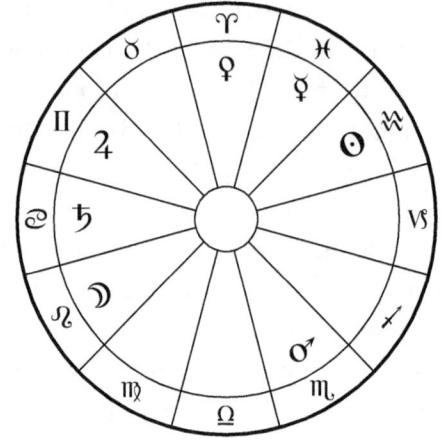

Since 3×6=18, we investigate this figure too. However, no star is in Libra, the third sign <from the Moon>, or in Capricorn, the sixth.

Next 20 is composite, because 4×5=20, and 5×4=20. So Mars in Scorpio <the fourth sign> is operative; no star is in Sagittarius, the fifth sign.

3×7=21: no star is in Libra <the third sign>, but the Sun is in Aquarius <the seventh>. So <the return> is to the Sun.

4×6=24: again Mars is in Scorpio <the fourth sign>, but no star is in Capricorn <the sixth>.

25 is square, a simple number, but no star is in Sagittarius <the fifth sign>.

3×9=27: no star is at the third interval, only Venus in the ninth <Aries>.

28 is composed of 4 (the return to Mars) and 7 (the return to the Sun).

4×10=40 and 5×8=40: this is associated with Mars, because of the 4, and with Mercury because of the 8.

<4×11=> 44: this is associated with Mars and Jupiter. Sometimes several stars return to the same point together, as in the case of 40, because Mars lies in the fourth sign and Mercury in the eighth. If some star had been in the tenth and the fifth signs, they would also have returned together there.

He says that outcomes will be more vigorous and obvious if the number of the year is the same as the number appropriate to the intervals between stars, as follows:

Saturn -3	Jupiter -10
Venus -5	Moon -13
Mars -7	Sun -18
Mercury -8	

If the number and the interval coincide at the same star, the star will be operative in an operative sign. If the year-number does not coincide with any of the intervals applicable to the star, it will be inoperative in an inoperative sign. If one interval is found to be operative, but another interval does not occur in the subsequent years, the initial interval must be used until another is found. Using the preceding horoscope as an example: 28 is associated with Mars and the Sun <4 and 7>. 29 has no interval. 30 has 3, 5, 6, and 10: these signs too are empty. 31 again is not associated with any interval. Therefore Mars and the Sun, operative in the 28th year, control the succeeding years until the 32nd year, when Mars (because of the 4) and Mercury (because of the 8) have mutual returns.

We will append the differences of the critical years according to the chronocratorships of the stars and their mutual returns to each other.

<Year # Critical Points and Results>

1   He will be sickly and anxious.
2   He will be endangered by fluxes and convulsions.
3   A critical point of Saturn; precarious.
5   Of Phosphorus <Venus>; he will be weakened.
6   A second critical point of Saturn.
7   The first critical point of Mars: dangerous, involving fevers, bleeding, wounds, falls, ulceration, sword cuts.
8   The first critical point of Mercury; uncompounded.
9   The first critical point of Jupiter; the third point of Saturn; dangerous. He will be sickly and and burdened with the ague and troubles of the bowels.

10	The second point of Venus. He will be ill because of surfeit.
12	The fourth critical point of Saturn. <He will die> unexpectedly or because of moist matters.
13	The first point of the Moon; a difficult fever or seizures will occur; troubles of the insides or chest.
14	The second point of Mars; dangerous, troublesome.
15	The fifth point of Saturn, the third of Venus; relaxing.
16	The second critical point of Mercury; compounded of cholera, bronchitis, and difficult convalescence.
18	The second point of Jupiter, the sixth of Saturn, the first of the Sun; very grievous.
20	The fourth point of Venus; generally safe; the diseases come from surfeit or exertion.
21	The third point of Mars, the seventh of Saturn; difficult and dangerous.
24	The eighth point of Saturn, the third of Mercury; difficult because of black bile and most syndromes.
25	The fifth point of Venus; compounded.
26	<The second point of the Moon; dangerous.>
27	The third point of Jupiter, the ninth of Saturn; average.
28	The fourth critical point of Mars; precarious.
30	The tenth point of Saturn, the sixth of Venus; generally safe.
32	The fourth point of Mercury; tiring.
33	The 11th point of Saturn; difficult.
35	The fifth point of Mars, the seventh of Venus; dangerous and exposed to treachery.
36	The fourth point of Jupiter, the 12th of Saturn, <the second of the Sun>; grievous and dangerous.
39	The third point of the Moon, the 13th of Saturn; precarious and dangerous.
40	The eighth point of Venus, the fifth of Mercury; not grievous.
42	The sixth point of Mars, the 14th of Saturn; grievous and dangerous.
45	The fifth point of Jupiter, the ninth of Venus, the 15th of Saturn. This critical point is called Stilbon. It is necessary to beware lest some infirmity of the foot occur at this time while Mercury is operative in the nativity, because Mercury brings dangers to the joints, sickness, life-threatening and disgusting syndromes.
48	The sixth point of Mercury, the 16th of Saturn; very grievous and dangerous.
49	The seventh point of Mars; sudden dangers through fevers, bleeding, and violent occurrences.

50	The tenth point of Venus; dangerous.
51	The 17th point of Saturn; it brings diseases, harm, and misfortune.
52	The fourth point of the Moon; not good.
54	The 18th point of Saturn, the sixth of Jupiter, the third of the Sun; grievous and full of danger.
55	The 11th of Venus; not bad.
56	The eighth point of Mars, the seventh of Mercury; painful and bitter.
57	The 19th point of Saturn; the worst.
60	The 20th point of Saturn, the 12th of Venus; precarious.
63	The 21st point of Saturn, the seventh of Jupiter, the ninth of Mars; the "Man-killer," grievous and fatal.
64	<The eighth of Mercury; not especially bad.>
65	<The fifth of the Moon, the 13th of Venus; a combination.>
66	<The 22nd of Saturn…>
69	<The 23rd of Saturn; grievous.>
70	<The tenth of Mars, the 14th of Venus; difficult and grievous.>
72	The 24th point of Saturn, the eighth of Jupiter, the ninth of Mercury, <the fourth of the Sun>; grievous and fatal.
75	The 25th point of Saturn, the 15th of Venus; dangerous.
77	The 11th point of Mars; difficult and fatal.
78	The 26th point of Saturn, the sixth of the Moon; grievous.
80	The 16th point of Venus, the tenth of Mercury; a mixture.
81	The 27th point of Saturn, the ninth of Jupiter; dangerous.
84	The 28th point of Saturn, the 12th of Mars; difficult and malefic.
85	The 17th point of Venus; a combination.
87	The 29th point of Saturn; dangerous.
88	<The eleventh of Mercury…>
90	The 30th point of Saturn, the 18th of Venus, the tenth of Jupiter, <the fifth of the Sun>; grievous.
91	The 13th of Mars, the seventh of the Moon; difficult.
93	The 31st of Saturn; grievous.
95	The 19th point of Venus; not good.
96	The 32nd point of Saturn, <the twelfth of Mercury>; difficult.
98	The 14th point of Mars; grievous.
99	The 33rd point of Saturn, <the eleventh of Jupiter>; average.
100	The 20th point of Venus; not bad.
102	The 34th point of Saturn; grievous.
104	<The eighth of the Moon, the 13th of Mercury; not especially bad.>
105	The 35th point of Saturn, the 21st of Venus, the 15th of Mars; difficult.

108 The 36th point of Saturn, <the twelfth of Jupiter, the sixth of the Sun>; fatal.
110 The 22nd point of Venus; not bad.
111 The 37th point of Saturn; precarious.
112 The 16th point of Mars, the 14th of Mercury; difficult and dire.
114 The 38th point of Saturn; dangerous.
115 The 23rd point of Venus; a combination.
117 The 39th point of Saturn, the ninth of the Moon, the 13th of Jupiter; dangerous.
119 The 17th point of Mars; precarious.
120 The 40th point of Saturn, the 24th of Venus, <the 15th of Mercury>; fatal.

An example: Sun, Jupiter, Mars in Cancer, Moon in Libra, Saturn in Sagittarius, Venus, Mercury in Leo, Ascendant in Gemini. The native died in his 54th year. The cycle was at the 18th critical point of Saturn, the sixth of Jupiter, the third of the Sun, i.e., the mutual returns of these stars. The Sun and Jupiter were found in the death-bringing month, Sagittarius. In addition the Sun, Jupiter, and Mars transmitted the 54th year from the <8th> Place of Death <relative to the Lot of Fortune> to Saturn in Sagittarius. Such a transmission was grievous.

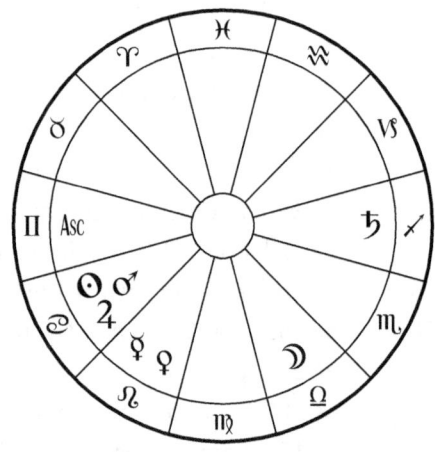

In every nativity it seems right to put the start of the critical points not just at the Moon, but at all of the stars from whose <positions and nature> the fatal times and life-threatening troubles can be determined. If the life-giving chronocrators take effect—this is determined by using these methods—the critical point will occur without any doubt. If the basis of the nativity has a continuation <of life>, but the critical point falls at that time, a crisis will occur with respect to actions and types of livelihoods: loss of rank, ruin, violence, convictions, shipwreck, trials, imprisonment, exile, anxieties, losses, penalties, sudden dangers, threats, robbery, plus whatever crises arise in man's life: injuries, diseases, amputations of the extremities, burns, cuts, illnesses, dangerous plots. If the stars which have critical points and which are mutually returning are found to be in opposition, beheld by malefics, and located out of their own sect at the nativity, they indicate that the period will be precarious and troublesome. But if they are in an appropriate configuration, they weaken the onset of the crisis and make the critical point milder in its effects. The transmissions or receptions from signs of equal rising time must be considered active: from Aries to Pisces, from Taurus to Aquarius, from Gemini to Capricorn, from Cancer to Sagittarius, from Leo to Scorpio, and from Virgo to Libra. The same is true in reverse order.

These facts we have tested with sober reasoning and much careworn toil; we have expounded them with great labor for those who have the necessary intelligence. <We hoped> to be able to equal both in achievement and in fame what the sages of old accomplished when they devoted themselves to this art. But as it is, those who bastardize this science with fancy words and complicated schemes find it easy to persuade not only those who are uninitiated into this art but also those who have something to boast of and who have a great reputation. Their success in persuading comes from the fact that their wizardry and effrontery is hard to grasp. Such men do not consider errors to be setbacks and they are successful in their brazenness, since they do not have blushes as the refutation of their ignorance. Instead they strut the stage like tragic or comic characters, walking in the ways of deceit, not of truth.

But the man who has started with rules and theorems does not wish to bring disrepute on the knowledge which he gained with such difficulty, and so he leans on his experience as on a staff, and he answers slowly and hesitantly, and he is not driven <?> from his purpose, because he considers that a mistake is worthy of exile or death, but that a success is the "toilsome heart of virtue." This <error> occurs with respect to the ignorant or those who do not precisely calculate the year or the hour.<?> So it would be necessary for those wishing to hear with special confidence about the present or the future to judge carefully these men and to praise any of their deeds, so that the prognosticator, having grasped the precise effects of the angles and of the powerful places using specific numbers and a definite system, may forecast the truth.

For often (as I have said) not only have these deceptive men and their spiritual fathers falsified the times and wronged our science; I have learned this from my spiritual ancestors as well. But they do this since they wished in one moment to hear things which are in accord with their desires and are mixed <with honor>, and to be involved with impossible things by means of some wicked magic art. After they have learned from the ignorant and done with enthusiasm what they should not have done, they then enjoy praise and honors, and repay their enemies: they revile honored men, the experienced <astrologers>, on the grounds that they cannot easily make forecasts nor compose treatises in detail. They do not know that the details of each nativity are grasped only with much labor and investigation. Later thay fail in their expectations, and they not only repent and bring censure in a precarious and painful way on their own falsehoods, but they also call this science "unreal" and consider its practitioners as enemies. Thus it happens that this science has been dishonored in the eyes of the public by a few men unworthy of it.

The end of Vettius Valens, Book V.

Book VI

The *Anthologies* of Vettius Valens of Antioch: Book VI

1. Preface

Every art and every craft is pleasing in proportion to the activity and the intelligence of its practitioners, or in proportion to their bodies' fitness or unfitness for the activity in question. As a result, many criticize and mock their neighbors <?> because they do not share the same activities—of course it is impossible and undesirable for everyone to know the same things. Each man believes himself to think and plan better than anyone in that sphere of activity which he has and which he thinks is best. For example, often a man is found to be craftsman-like and systematic in all types of activities, and he is successful even though illiterate. Another man, well educated, is easily deceived like one inexperienced in business and is betrayed by his naiveté and his disorganization. This man in his unhappiness thinks that the possession of an education is useless and considers the ignorant man to be happy.

Such differences are the works of Fate and Fortune, who come quietly, ineffably to men and who, without sense or decency, make some men fortunate, other men wretched. Life, acting with criminal deception, in her course exalts and glorifies men in some respects and leads them to prosperity and preeminence, so that many men become lovers of such things. At other times life pains, wastes, and withers men, and brings them to obscurity, danger, and hatred. Life even turns some to the loathsome arts and sciences, and endows them with hardened and stubborn minds, activities, and fortune.

All this happens and comes to pass mixed with pleasure, satisfaction, and pain, depending on the changes of situation and the recurrent cycles of the chronocrators.

I have written this because I have prided myself on the knowledge bestowed on me from heaven by the Divinity, knowledge which is now dishonored and rejected, even though it is primordial and governs everything in life, and even though without it there neither is nor will be anything. Now even its name seems to be hated, although men before our times prayed for it and blessed themselves by it. I am grieved by this, and I envy the old kings and rulers who devoted themselves to such matters. I am envious because I was not fortunate enough to live in those times which saw such a climate of free and ungrudging speech and inquiry. Their devotion to this science was so enthusiastic and so steadfast that they left the earthly sphere and walked the heavens, associating with the heavenly souls and the divine, holy Minds. Of this Nechepso is a witness when he says:

> I seemed to walk the midnight aether,
> <...>
> and a voice from heaven echoed around me,
> at which the dark robe covered my flesh,
> bringing the gloom of night...

and so on. Who would not consider this knowledge to be superior to any other and to be blessed, since by means of it one can know the Sun's ordered paths which foretell the changing seasons when it enters the tropics in the advances and retardations of its motion; one can know the risings and settings, the days and nights, the seasons' cold or heat, and the weather? It is also possible to know the varying paths of the Moon, its inclinations and departures, its waxing and waning, its heights and its depths, the direction of its winds, its contacts and separations, its eclipses, its near eclipses, and all the rest. From all this it seems possible to understand everything on Earth, in the seas, in heaven, as well as the beginning and end of all events. Likewise for the five other stars, with their motions, their uneven paths, and their varied phases. Although they are called "variable" and "wanderers" <planētai>, they have a fixed nature and return to the same places in regular cycles and periods.

But as it is now, the inquiry into and the rectification of astrological matters has been hindered—or withered—by fear. Man's intentions, rejected and unsupported by rationality, do not remain constant, but jumping from here to there, always return to the original state of oblivion. Even though a man has good intentions and loves wisdom, still he easily becomes hesitant and chooses ignorance rather than the hazards of virtue.

Nevertheless, in all men the drive <towards learning> is strong, even though repressed and pained, and it remains constant. In my case, colorful horse races and the sharp crack of the whip have not carried me away, nor have the rhythmical movements of dancers, the vain charm of flutes, of the Muses, of melodious song, of those things which attract an audience by tricks and jesting delighted me. No, I have not even shared in those harmful, though profitable, actions, those actions of mingled pleasure and pain <=love>, nor have I consorted with those polluted and wretched <prostitutes>. Instead, when I had once discovered this divine and revered knowledge of heavenly bodies, I wished to purify my life too from all evil, from all taint, and to keep my soul immortal. From that time I felt I was associating with divine beings, and I kept my intellect sober, in order to seek truth clearly.

Now I have compiled many amazing things, things which can lead my readers back to the Ancients and their lore. I have repeated these doctrines because the Ancients expounded many methods which are difficult and abstruse. I considered it necessary in this treatise to explain the mystic and secret methods concerning propitious times and the future. In so doing, I hope our science will appear understandable, be supported by the facts, and drive away hostility. It will convert its enemies and show itself to be holy and revered. I do not care if I seem to be speaking repeatedly of the same matters. For I discovered some things and simply appended them to my earlier writings, due to the sudden rush of enthusiasm caused by my discoveries—the compiler was in ecstasy, particularly about these matters, and he felt that he was meeting God face to face. Other matters <I wrote out> in an orderly manner. Consequently, if any envy has intervened to damage our treatise, the substance will be found written out elsewhere in the book.

2. Propitious and Impropitious Times According to the Degree-Intervals and Contacts of the Chronocrators

In the previous books the distribution of the chronocrators which had been roughly calculated by signs alone has been explained. Now we must speak of the intervals and contacts calculated in degrees, a method which I treated only obscurely before. Experience has led me to clarify these matters.

For any nativity it is necessary to determine precisely the stellar chronocrator to the degree, using the treatise, *The Perpetual Tables*. It is necessary to take the distance in degrees from each star to its point of contact (a position expressed in degrees) with another star (as near or as far as one wishes) according to the applicable chronocrator and the sequence of signs. Add the number of degrees and allocate them using the hours, days, months, and years of the star's period.[1] Then forecast the effects of the stars from their natural activity and from the predictive effects of their transmissions to each other at the chronocratorship/time-period which the nativity has reached. If the total number is less than the length of time <reached by the nativity>, examine the magnitude of the difference and forecast that the results will happen after that amount of time. If the total is greater than the time, subtract one factor, then count the remainder from the degree-position of the apheta. See if the rays of the stars incline to that point either at the nativity or in transit. Great and remarkable forecasts are often made when this is done. If a rough distribution <i.e., not by degree> shows nothing, and if the time is different after the factor or the remaining time is determined <?>, then reinterpret the number as a lesser period (i.e., months or days), correlate the factors with the stars' periodic cycles, and count until the time in question.

In addition, these varied aphetic points and contacts between benefics and malefics indicate varied, multifaceted, and easily changed results. For it is possible to see many men who experience many things at one time, since aphetic points or operative places crowd together and mingle at the chronocratorships in question. A few men do not even have an alternation of good and bad, but stay in the same condition. Others are exalted and attain an unsurpassable fortune (according to their basis from the beginning). Although they are even blessed by the public, they come to death or danger. Others are in difficult circumstances, are failures in their livelihood, have no good prospects, and are grieving in vain. Their fortunes however reverse themselves into the same condition, or even gain a greater magnitude. This happens because sometimes a transmission occurs at an eclipse and indicates a great threat, but the threat is diminished by a chronocrator in the arrangement, i.e., by a different transmission of a benefic. In the same way the transmission of a benefic is hindered by some afflicting cause.

The degree-numbers, which are used as factors, remain the same from the beginning and are counted in the cycles as far as the chronocratorship in question extends. As for the propitious, yearly aphetic points, the distributions are found using the suitable number for the same places and stars, and they

---

[1] *Marginal note:* "The distance and contact in degrees: suppose the moon is in Virgo 21° 30', Saturn in Libra 4°. The distance is 12½°. This amount multiplied times the moon's period (25) equals 312½. We consider this figure to be days, months, hours, or years. I say that after 312½ days, the moon transmits to Saturn, and I will make the resulting forecast from the nature of the transmission from the moon to Saturn." - a note in *Marc. gr.* 334, ff. 172–73 (432.26–30P).

show the general tenor of the forecast. But if another <transmission> is entangled with it at the change of chronocrators, affairs become altered and occasions for good and bad arise. Therefore it is necessary to pay sober attention to the numbers: examine the angles and the signs preceding or following the angles to see if the signs are suited to the presence of the stars. Note the risings, the setting, the sects, and (to be brief) whatever we have explained in the preceding books. (We are not speaking to the ignorant or the uninitiated.) It is also necessary to examine the transits at given times, because they have a great effect for overturning or rectifying affairs, particularly when they are passing through operative places or are beholding the ruler of the chronocratorship while in conjunction, in aspect, or in opposition.

It is necessary to take into account not only the degree-position at which the contact occurs, but the 3° on each side of the contact (as we made clear previously), because it will be obvious from these degrees whether the stars' effects will occur early or late—just as with eclipses, one can see the period of totality and the period of separation <to be within this distance>. It is also necessary to see if the transmitter beholds the receiver in an appropriate and operative way. The brief extent of the contact shows what will happen, but it will last only until another contact comes to share in the operation and to weaken that first contact's effects.

He allots to each star the time appended here:
The **Sun** assigns 19 months per sign, 19 days per degree.
The monthly cycle is owned by the **Moon**, and the Moon by nature assigns 2 years 1 month per sign, 25 days per degree.
Saturn assigns 2 years 6 months per sign, 30 days per degree.
Jupiter assigns 1 year per sign, 12 days per degree.
Mars assigns 15 months per sign, 15 days per degree.
Venus assigns 8 months per sign, 8 days per degree.
Mercury assigns 20 months per sign, 20 days per degree.
In this way the zodiac is subdivided by the periods and cycles of each star.

Whenever <an astrologer> makes a vital sector/transmission from one star to another, let him be sure to note the right numbers and which star is transmitting to which, because the numbers are not the same nor are the effects of the transmitters and the receivers the same. For example, if one finds a transmission from Jupiter to Mars, then one from Mars to Jupiter, the numbers for the chronocrators will not be the same because of their differing periods nor will the forecast be the same. (It is better for Mars to transmit to Jupiter than for Jupiter to transmit to Mars.) Whenever vital sectors are charted from every star to every other star, it is necessary to determine and forecast results depending on whether the transmissions of benefics or of malefics predominate.

"But," someone will say, "the chronocrators for twins will be the same, since the same stars are located at the same degree-positions!" I answer that in such nativities, the shift of just the Ascendant alone alters the angles and the fortune and condition of the native, and it occasionally brings his end. Because of these shifts, it is necessary to take into account the distributions with respect to the position of the angles and the stars' aspects with each other, if they are not at the angles with respect to the horizon. In addition, if a star at its current degree-position should have another star in superior (or in any) aspect at a distance equivalent to that between angles, i.e., if the first star were in the Ascendant, the other would be at the Midheaven according to the distance between the signs, (or we could use the distance between any two angles)—in such a case the aspect will be especially vigorous.

In its effect this system <of chronocrators> might be compared to the game of white and black pieces—for life is a game, a pilgrimage, and a festival. Competitive men devise wicked traps for each other, move their pieces along the many straight rows, and put their pieces down in various places when summoning each other to a skirmish. As long as the place happens to be unguarded, the counter moves unchecked according to the will of the player: it flees, stays, pursues, attacks, wins, and loses in turn. If it is surrounded by the opposing pieces as if in a net and finds the straight rows to be blocked, it is intercepted and captured. In this way, of the two players, one finds momentary pleasure and enjoyment for himself, the other momentary mockery and pain—momentary because the one who had been in despair suddenly comes back into the game by means of some stratagem and gives back the burden of despair to the other player, who had just now laid it on him.

The stars' effects should be viewed in the same way: as long as a benefic controls the chronocratorship and no malefic comes into contact, this active, healthy, easy, and successful benefic gives the one who is living through this period the reputation of being fortunate, bold, and intelligent, even if he is a boor. Even if he is unworthy of the happiness bestowed on him by the current situation, he prides himself and rejoices at what he has. He does not attend to the changes of situation, and he causes bitter grief for many men. But when a malefic dominates the chronocratorship, it is impropitious, diseased, impossible to overcome, and full of setbacks, so that the one who is living through this period is said to be helpless and cowardly in the face of evils, in fact wicked, even if he is in truth a worthy man. Such a man, although driven to despair because of the evil of the times, still resists the fickleness of Fortune by the force of his reason, and shows himself to be noble and resourceful. If afflicted benefics control the chronocratorships, both good and bad happen: damage with profit, ill-repute with high rank, ruin, dangerous accusations, fears, easily-cured diseases. As a result, those who are living through this state of mixed pleasure and pain do not come to their ends with either unalloyed bad or unalloyed good.

It is necessary to compare the influences of the transmissions to see which type is more vigorous: if the malefic, then the native will fail in his expectations for good, will feed on vain hopes, and will experience bitter grief; if the benefic, the native will overcome delay, distress, reversals, and expenses, or he will escape from injuries, suffering, and mortal crises combined with fears and dangers. Of necessity he will endure punishment and will consider that very thing an excellent gain <?>. The general tenor of the transmissions must be viewed with respect to the basis of the nativity and the distribution of the overall chronocrators—as was explained previously. It is necessary to determine if the nativity is distinguished, average, exalted, ruined, subject to the law, etc. The stars in the cycles of the chronocrators can assume the causative power which the nativity's foundation has previously indicated.

The long intervals have a slower causative effect; the closer intervals have a more rapid effect. Some stars, traversing the chronocratorship/in their movement at the chronocratorship have similar effects: they are generally operative for a short time in the chronocratorship of a benefic [or a malefic], and they indicate success, trust, profit, blessedness, benefactions, and <honors, but when the interval is greater, or even different> and a malefic receives the chronocratorship instead, the situation changes to one of ruin, disgrace, misfortune, and sudden danger due to accusations and hatred. Occasionally, when another chronocrator takes effect, particularly when a benefic receives the transmission, a restoration of fortune and rank occurs.

It is also necessary to make a determination about the "encounters" with the degree in the Ascendant, because it is from these encounters that the critical, the diseased, the injurious, and the dangerous chronocratorships are discovered, and on the other hand, the healthy, the delightful, the lovely, and the desired times—all according to the presence of benefics or malefics. Through these, the soul becomes undisturbed and strong, feels itself able to do what is best, stretches itself out to the maximum, shows itself a benefactor, and is honored and blessed. The body <=health> is soothed as well.

I suspect that those men whom we mistakenly called good and bad have gained their appellations from these <encounters>. (The scientists <say> they keep their original makeup.) Whenever <the soul> is afflicted, it is ensnared and blinded. It is marked off as much-hated, wicked, and evil, and even crazy and mad, so that it contrives something dangerous for itself. If it is so burdened then it cannot bear to live its whole lifetime to the end, being distraught in its misery, and it separates itself from the body. It then travels with its compelling demon, carried wherever that demon wishes.

3. Why the Ancient Impressed Their Particular Colors on the Five Planets and the Sun and the Moon

We must assay the quality of the stars. We might use painters' colors as a comparison: each color has a certain chromatic or translucent quality, and with this quality the color delights the beholders and is useful for many things. If an incompatible color is mixed with it, it becomes muddied and changed, no longer having its previous nature nor preserving the hue of the color which was mixed in. It cheats the eye of either color, since it has taken on a false, coerced color, one dark and repulsive. On the other hand, the artist occasionally makes a harmonious mixture of colors and creates a lucky and beautiful blending. (Still, the artist depicts man by means of many colors, showing him to be a shadow of reality and truth.)

In just such a way, the stars sometimes preserve their original nature when they are alone, but when one star mixes with another, the individual qualities of their nature are changed. The stars put a halter on men and lead them with pain, degradation, and various combinations of these <forces> to the business of life, in which men are trained in many ways, win the crown of endurance, and become what they were not before.

Wherefore the Ancients were correct in comparing the stars to colors:

Saturn's color is black, since it is the symbol of time. The god is slow, and therefore the Babylonians called it *Phainōn* <Illuminator>, since everything is illuminated in time.

Jupiter's color is brilliant; it is the cause of life and the giver of good.

Mars' color is orange, because the god is fiery, cutting, and consuming. The Egyptians called it *Artēs* <The Hook>, since it is the diminisher of goods and life.

The **Sun's** color is translucent because of the purity and transparency of its light.

Venus' color is changeable in hue, since it rules the desires and extends its control over many things, good and bad. It seems to rule by itself many appropriate and inappropriate occurrences in life. Since it has been allotted the circle which is below the Sun (whose zone is in the middle, dividing the stars), it receives the emanations of the stars above it and of those below it, and brings about various desires and actions.

They make **Mercury's** color pale yellowish-green, like bile. It rules intelligence, discourse, and bitterness, and as a result those born under Mercury are like it in nature and color.

The **Moon's** color is like that of the air. Its course is inconstant and varied, as are the deeds and intentions of those governed by the Moon.

In order not to seem to tell all this twice, the nature of the stars is discussed in Book I.

4. Why Malefics Seem to be More Active than Benefics

Malefics seem stronger than benefics. Just as a drop of black or brown, falling into a container of brightly colored paint, dims the color's beauty, and the large quantity of brilliant color cannot hide the dark stain, however small—so it is with malefics, stars which can attack men and rob them of the things in which they seem to be fortunate: family, livelihood, health, rank, beauty, and whatever is rare. Malefics take away possessions, involve men in crises, injuries, diseases, and they stain nativities. Good men, who think that everyone has the same beliefs as they, so who live naively, trusting and helpful, easily succumb, even if they are not <worthy of such an evil fate>. Still, they are celebrated for their nobility. On the other hand, bad men, who think that everyone is like them, who do not trust even their own people or those whom they should trust, and who are unreasonably greedy, are deprived of their own property, and thus give pleasure to the public. For <Fortune> preserves some men, even though they are unwilling, until the time when it wishes to turn them upside down, pushing some to the heights, and some to their doom. In such cases, many men pray in vain for their lives, yield themselves to trouble, and are grief-stricken at their circumstances. They criticize the tardy arrival of death, and they contrive something against themselves or manage a violent end. Men are by nature mockers of others and criticizers of faults; they rejoice greatly at the troubles and the trials of neighbors, but later repent of their deeds and show themselves as the defenders of others' faults…

Just as with the preconceptions with which anyone makes decisions—they have an appearance of the truth not only to those who believe them but also to many others who are forced by their misconceptions to act in such a way, even if they have differing opinions. It is the same with those who compile astronomical tables: some facile men are considered as able to lead others to the truth; these are men to whom the ignorant are attracted. But the scientists and the precisionists are rejected and condemned either from jealousy or from the crookedness of <their readers'> approach to science. Therefore, it is necessary to test their precision and to stick to the scientific viewpoint, even if approximations are sometimes necessary. Note that even Apollinarius, who calculated the visible motions using the old observations and publications of many returns and spheres, and who met with criticism from many readers, confesses that his calculations were one or two degrees in error. The source of the miscalculation is easily understood—as I myself using the results which have already occurred, have tried to establish the precise degree of a star by noting its natural effects as the Ancient says. As our exposition proceeds, the facts themselves, brought before your very eyes, will clarify what I have said. When the degree is found, then it is possible to make definite forecasts about the future. Determining the precise degree is difficult, but not impossible.

5. Transits

The transits of the stars are considered vigorous when the masters of the chronocratorships transit the Places, or are in opposition or square with them. For instance, when each of those stars which hold the rule and leadership makes a transit in its allotted hour, it acts vigorously to save or to destroy: no man, however great he happens to be in family, livelihood, or rank, can block either its threats or its benefits for anyone. The person will yield to the laws of the occasion until the star abdicates its rule. When the star completes its chronocratorship, it transmits the governance to another and resumes its ineffectiveness for either good or bad. The methods of determining the effects of transmissions, the combinations of interrelated aspects, and the effect of conjunctions have been explained by us previously. These methods must be used, since each star acts in accord with its own nature and the applicable chronocratorship to show the type of result to be expected.

6. The 10-Year, 9-Month Distribution of Propitious and Impropitious Times

I have discovered, tested, and put to use the following distribution, which had been discarded casually, even blindly, because the explanation of it had been puzzling. I append it now so that lovers of beauty may make their nature divine, travelling through many paths to one power of forecasting. They may expect to meet in one place after travelling many straight, as well as many rough, roads.

Let our method be this: for day births make the Sun the apheta (for night births, the Moon), if it is well situated, since (as we have written in *The Controlling Points*) for day and night births the luminary which is well situated must be considered the apheta. If both luminaries are badly situated, the star found to be following the Ascendant will be the first to distribute the chronocratorship, the star just following it will be the second, and so on with the rest.

For instance, let the Sun be the apheta for the distribution of 10 years, 9 months: it will take 10 years, 9 months, and after it the next star in the zodiacal circle at the nativity will take 10 years, 9 months. Assign the yearly chronocrators as long as there are years <of the nativity> to receive them. It is also necessary to incorporate the hourly, daily, and monthly periods of each star in the yearly period, and to include in the forecast the overall master of the chronocratorship, as well as the master of the months, days, and hours. It is necessary to determine the cycles, how long they are and who is receiving the cycle and the week from whom. <I say> this because the chronocratorship, even if it comes back to the same stars, will not be in the same part of the week or of the cycle. One cycle joined to a different cycle in the sequence of chronocratorships will alter the effects of the stars, and a given star at one time may be a cause of good, at another time a cause of bad, all according to the activity and the appropriate or inappropriate position of the transmitter and the receiver.

It is necessary to inspect and examine the current and the future chronocrators and to forecast good if they move towards <=transmit to> benefics—even if a malefic has control for a very short time, because the force of the malefic is dissipated in advance by the benefic action of the receiving star, a star which may provide various impulses: friendship, affinity, associations, success, rank, profits, and the achievement of one's goals. Sometimes a star stains men with mystic, secret, or perilous activities, but later brings about good fortune, with the result that these men enjoy or tolerate what they had previously loathed, and they repent of having wasted in vain so much useless time. In the same way when the chronocratorship of benefics moves to malefics, the malefics turn <the good impulse> to hatred, disgrace, treachery, penalties, danger, and to sudden, unexpected crises and ruin. Because of this, many men regret not having any defenses against their enemies. They have preserved good faith and fellow-feeling, but in vain. Not being able to keep what they wish, they are pained at others' good fortune and are oppressed unwillingly.

Let the following nativity be an example to illustrate our approach concisely: Moon in Pisces 18°, Venus in Aries, Jupiter in Libra, Saturn, Ascendant in Sagittarius, Mars in the beginning of Aquarius, Sun in Aquarius, Mercury in Pisces. The stars were arranged thus, in order in increasing longitude. We are

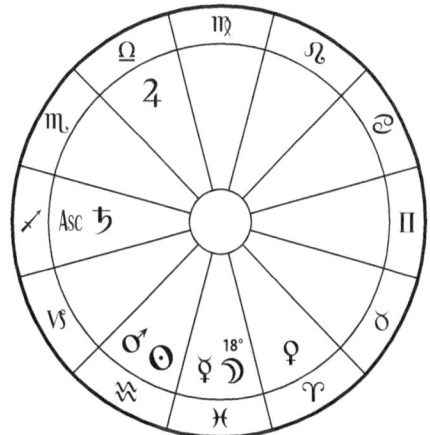

investigating 52 years plus the time to Payni[2] 15 of the 53rd year <=52 years, 4 months, 3 days>. Now in this type of distribution the days and the cycles are calculated using 360-day periods, but the years of a nativity are calculated using 365¼ periods. Therefore I multiply the whole years, 52, by 5¼ for a total of 273. Then from Mechir 12 <the birth date> to Payni 15 there are 124 days. The grand total is 397 days. I subtract one circle <=one year> and the remaining days total 37. Since the birth was at night, the Moon was considered the apheta of the overall chronocratorships. It was at IC, in a feminine sign in a triangle of a sect member <Pisces Cancer Scorpio - the triangle of Venus>, and appropriately situated. So the Moon took 10 years 9 months of the given number of years first, then Venus in Aries 10 years 9 months, then Saturn in Sagittarius 10 years 9 months. So far there have been 4 cycles, or 43 years.

Next follows Mars. Its cycle of 10 years 9 months would make 53 years 9 months total, which is more than the given number of years under investigation. So I resorted to calculating by months, and gave to Mars itself, as the ruler of the cycle, 15 months, adding this to the previous total for the fourth cycle, 43 years. Now the running total is 44 years 3 months. Next, <I give> to the Sun 1 year 7 months, to Mercury 20 months, to the Moon 25 months, to Venus 8 months, and to Jupiter 12 months. So far, the total is is 51 years 3 months. Next Saturn has 30 months to complete Mars' cycle, for a grand total of 53 years 9 months.

But since this figure as well exceeds the given number of years, I count off the days as follows: including the period of Jupiter the total was 51 years 3 months. I took the remaining days of the 52nd year (270) and of the 53rd year (360) and of the 54th year (37). The total is 667, with Saturn receiving from Mars. From this total Saturn gives itself, in the first subsequent cycle, 129 days. Then it transfers the second cycle of a like 129 days to Mars, and that star assigns itself its own days. The Sun takes the third cycle next from Saturn and assigns itself 129 days, then Mercury the fourth, and the Moon the fifth, both assigning themselves 129 days. Twenty-two days remain for the sixth cycle, which belongs to Venus. Venus assigns itself 8 days, then 12 days to Jupiter. The remaining 2 days until the day in question belong to Saturn.

The overall chronocrator of the years was Mars receiving from the Moon. The chronocrator of the months was Saturn receiving from Mars. The chronocrator of the days was Venus receiving the cycle from Saturn. Consequently in the native's 53rd year the grievous death of his wife occurred. Dangerous diseases and fines came on him. In the days under discussion, the native was condemned in a suit on behalf of his wife against a woman about

---

[2] *Marginal note:* "=June".

legacies, about old matters, and he was oppressed by the great and was in nearly mortal danger. He had grief for his own family and for others', so great as to turn to despair. He was entangled in other precarious actions subject to penalties. For Saturn still held the chronocratorship, not in its own sect, being in the Ascendant, and having the Moon (the apheta) and Mercury in inferior aspect <square to the left>. As a result many forgeries accompanied him, as well as lies, deceptions, many expenses, and dangerous diseases.

The Subdistributions of the Preceding System
The third stage subdivision is done as follows:

    I. Saturn rules 2 years 6 months. It will transmit
        a. to itself 6 months, 29 days, 6 ¼ hours.
        b. to Jupiter 2 months, 23 days, 17 ⅓ hours.
        c. to Mars 3 months, 14 days, 15 ⅔ hours.
        d. to the Sun 4 months, 12 days, 13 5/12 hours.
        e. to Venus 1 month, 25 days, 19 ½ hours.
        f. to Mercury 4 months, 19 days, 12 ⅔ hours.
        g. to the Moon 5 months, 24 days, 10 hours.
In this way the 2 years 6 months of Saturn are completed.

    II. Jupiter has 1 year. Jupiter will transmit
        a. to itself 1 month, 3 days, 11 ¾ hours.
        b. to Mars 1 month, 11 days, 20 ⅔ hours.
        c. to the Sun 1 month, 23 days, 20 ½ hours.
        d. to Venus 22 days, 7 ⅚ hours.
        e. to Mercury 1 month, 25 days, 19 ½ hours.
        f. to the Moon 2 months, 9 days, 18 ⅓ hours.
        g. to Saturn 2 months, 23 days, 17 ¼ hours.
    III. Mars has 1 year 3 months. It transmits
        a. to itself 1 month, 22 days, 7 ⅔ hours.
        b. to the Sun 2 months, 6 days, 6 ⅔ hours.
        c. to Venus 27 days, 21 ⅚ hours.
        d. to Mercury 2 months, <9> days, 18 ⅓ hours.
        e. to the Moon 2 months, 27 days, 5 hours.
        f. to Saturn 3 months, 14 days, 15 ⅔ hours.
        g. to Jupiter 1 month, 11 days, 20 ⅔ hours.

IV. The Sun has 1 year 7 months. It transmits
   a. to itself 2 months, 23 days, 22 ¾ hours.
   b. to Venus 1 month, 5 days, 8 ⅓ hours.
   c. to Mercury 2 months, 28 days, 8 ¹¹⁄₁₂ hours.
   d. to the Moon 3 months, 20 days, 11 ¼ hours.
   e. to Saturn 4 months, 12 days, 13 ¼ hours.
   f. to Jupiter 1 month, 23 days, 8 ½ hour.
   g. to Mars 2 months, 6 days, 6 ⅔ hours.

V. Venus rules 8 months. From these it transmits
   a. to itself 14 days, 21 ⅕ hours.
   b. to Mercury 1 month, 7 days, 4 ¼ hours.
   c. to the Moon 1 month, 16 days, 12 ¼ hours.
   d. to Saturn 1 month, 25 days, 19 ½ hours.
   e. to Jupiter 22 days, 7 ⅔ hours.
   f. to Mars 27 days, 21 ¾ hours.
   g. to the Sun 1 month, 5 days, 8 ⅓ hours.

VI. Mercury has 1 year 8 months, from which it transmits
   a. to itself 3 months, 3 days, 9 ½ hours.
   b. to the Moon 3 months, 26 days, 6 ¾ hours.
   c. to Saturn 4 months, 19 days, 12 ¾ hours.
   d. to Jupiter 1 month, 25 days, 19 ½ hours.
   e. to Mars 2 months, 9 days, 18 ⁵⁄₁₂ hours.
   f. to the Sun 2 months, 28 days, 8 ¹¹⁄₁₂ hours.
   g. to Venus 1 month, 7 days, 5 hours.

VII. The Moon rules 2 years, 1 month, of which it assigns
   a. to itself 4 months, 25 days, 8 ¼ hours.
   b. to Saturn 5 months, 24 days, 10 hours.
   c. to Jupiter 2 months, 9 days, 18 ⁵⁄₁₂ hours.
   d. to Mars 2 months, 27 days, 5 hours.
   e. to the Sun 3 months, 20 days, 11 ⅙ hours.
   f. to Venus 1 month, 16 days, 12 ¼ hours.
   g. to Mercury 3 months, 26 days, 6 ¾ hours.

7. To Discover Which Star Controls the Current Days When Using the Preceding System

In addition, if we wish to know which star controls the current days, we will calculate as follows: multiply the years which have passed since birth by 365¼. Get the number of days from the birth date to the date in question, and add it to the previous result. Divide by 129, and note how many cycles there have been. From the answer we cast out the weekly cycles <=divide by 7>, and the remainder of this division (which will be less than seven!) will show which star controls the days.

For example, take the preceding horoscope: multiply the full years, 52, by 365¼. The result is 18,993. There are 123 days from Mechir 12 to the day in question, Payni 15. When this figure is included, the total becomes 19,116. I divide this by 129, and get 149 with 24 days of the next 129-day cycle as a remainder. Next I divide this (i.e., the 149) by 7 (the week-number), and get 21 with 2 cycles remaining. Now since—as was stated above—the Moon was found to be the apheta, I gave the first cycle of the week to the Moon. Venus, the star immediately following the Moon, has the second cycle, 24 days, of which it gives to itself 8 days, then to Jupiter 12 days. The remaining 4 belong to Saturn, the days when the native was condemned.

Alternatively, the attempt could be made to equate the weekly cycles to 49-day periods and to count these from the apheta, giving one to each star. The star at which the count stops will rule the 49-day period and the first cycle of the weeks. Then transmit the cycles to the other stars in order. Take the preceding horoscope as an example: since there were found to be 149 weekly cycles, I subtract three 49-day periods from that <49×3=147>. There are two cycles remaining of the fourth 49-day period. I count these four periods from the Moon, the apheta, and stop at Saturn; so Saturn rules the fourth 49-day period. It assigns the first weekly cycle to itself, the second to Mars, the star immediately following it, which has 24 days. Mars assigns (from this 24) to itself 15 days. The remaining 9 belong to the Sun.

That a Few <Astrologers> Misuse the Aphetic Point in the Preceding System

Most <astrologers> distribute the chronocrators for each nativity using the seven-zone system beginning with Saturn; they put Jupiter, Mars, the Sun, Venus, Mercury, and the Moon following in that order. In the rotation of the chronocrators, they examine the master of the week and of the days using the same system. Such a procedure does not satisfy me, because those who use it find the same chronocrators for most nativities. I prefer (as has been stated) to put the aphetic point at the Sun and Moon, or at the star found to be following the Ascendant, then to allot to the other stars in order, just as they happen to be situated by sign and by degree at the nativity.

8. The Length of Life Found by Using the Full-Moon and the Horoscopic Gnomon

I now have methods for a ready determination of the matters in question thanks to my constant practice and the underlying theorems of my flexible system. Still, the methods for making final decisions and for critically evaluating <horoscopes> needed more time—and time has become short for me. Man's life is but a blink of time, even if he seems to be enjoying a long lifespan, so just like a father who, weighed down by illness at the end of his life, leaves his last brief commandments to his children before the silence of death creeps on him, I have carefully reviewed the collected chapters of my theoretical treatise, and I have noted the important topics. In so doing, I have presented the beginnings of an approach <to this science> to the lovers of beauty.

Now if the mind were long-lived or immortal, any decision would be free of doubt and would be simple—"But the gods know all." Now since the length of life is the most essential topic, it has been treated in many different ways in the preceding books. I came into contact with a man who was boasting of some method, and I discovered (after much trial and error) a complicated method of regular calculations, a system which I myself had previously known to some extent and which now I will explain to everyone because of my zeal, after pruning off all excess verbiage. <We know that> every method when combined with another and tested gives us an exact scientific viewpoint.

Let our method be this: we will use the Light-bringing Moon and the Ascendant. These two, mingling their influences according to the hourly motions which lead to their positions at any given moment and their visible appearance, make the aphetic point and indicate the beginning and the end. They have a mystic power over conception and delivery. Neither Mars nor Saturn will be considered as destroyers nor the benefics as helpers. Instead, when the Moon is found to be the apheta, it is necessary to observe closely its contacts and its sextile, square, and opposition aspects with respect to the Ascendant, particularly when they are in signs of the same or equal rising time, signs of the same power, the listening or beholding signs, or in the antiscia. Similarly if the Ascendant is the apheta, examine its aspects with the Moon using the rising time.

In my experience it seems best to judge those degrees as fatal and those aspects as powerful, i.e., those aspects of the Moon and the Ascendant with each other—also their squares and oppositions, since these aspects have an extraordinary power when at the angles.

Now, many mistakes are constantly being made about the aphetic (or anaeretic) places, and almost anything can present difficulties to this art, since the lack of any proof of its accuracy can give rise to criticism and rejection. Because I have found the truth, I feel it necessary to correct the mistakes. So, when the aphetic points are found to be unrelated to the apparent anaeretic point, it is necessary to examine both degree-numbers using the rising times and to consider the <resulting number> as the length of life—if it does not exceed the maximum period, because rarely will anyone live longer. In addition when a great interval is found between the apheta <and the anaereta>, and when the Moon and the Ascendant are in the same sign, or when (in the case of another aphetic point) the interval between the two does not happen to be found in the signs of long rising time, with the result that the aphetic places are very near each other—in such a case, add the time-periods using the rising times, take half of the sum, and consider that to be the length of life. It is necessary to examine the vital sector in this way, not only in the case of long intervals and signs of long rising times, but also in the case of small intervals and aphetic distances (viz. in the signs of short rising times).

With respect to the determination of the aphetic points of the chronocratorships, the degree-positions of the Moon's phases in each sign, when calculated with reference to the aphetic points and correlated with the time periods corresponding to each interval, indicate the anaeretic point—particularly when the Moon is the apheta. When the Moon is the apheta, it is destroyed by itself. The relevant phases are those of new Moon, full Moon, and the two quarters, each being effective when moving toward the Descendant.

Let no one think we have composed this treatise in too complex and complicated a fashion. It is my favorite occupation to inform my readers of every method of inquiry. It is possible for those readers to train their minds over time in these systems, to discard vulgar notions, and to embark on the exact, scientific way. I have claimed in the preceding books that I have elucidated what was obscurely composed by the Ancients—indeed I have expounded their correct opinions so that I might not seem to be uninformed about their studies. I have also compiled here my own discoveries. If the reader trusts in this information, he will have an unexceptionable explanation <of this art>.

One must observe in which stars' signs or terms the aphetic or anaeretic places occur, because it is from these (i.e., from their natural activity) that crises and deaths can be determined. It is also necessary to examine which star is afflicted or helped by which, which star is in harmony or is not, and what their mutual configurations were at the nativity, at transits, and at the transmissions of the chronocratorships.

Much of our discourse has been to explain the Ascendants by degree and by sign, and the operative degrees, places which have a complicated and complex relationship with the topic "length of life," even if they do not have their mutual points of contact in the same (or nearly the same) degrees or signs—a thing which is rare and wonderful to most men. But in the cosmic revolution, all things are possible, attainable, holy, and true, and become so through thousands of complex paths, which when investigated, will reveal the truth to one who searches not at random but with scientific skill. For the universe itself is not random, and day and night it shows without stint to everyone the good and holy things it contains. When <merely> seen, it is not grasped; but when apprehended with the intelligence, each thing is known to the extent possible for a man. Therefore, what has been seen, known and said is comprehensible, and in fact I have grasped it in my turn. I have ignored who <the discoverers> were, from where they came, and how they made their discoveries. Others have written endless words about such matters. I have interpreted what has been discovered and proven by the observations of the chronocrators, and I have been mystically inspired to compile this treatise, hoping to have laid a strong foundation in my writings, revising them and constantly laboring (though with great pleasure), because the functioning of the cosmic bodies and the discovery of long-sought treasure, a discovery involving new theorems, drives me on.

9. The Determination of the Moon and the Ascendant at the Conception

In every nativity the Moon's position is figured by longitude and latitude. Note where the latitude of the Moon is located at the nativity. The Moon's position at the conception will be the position we have found. For in all nativities, the latitude <of the Moon> at the delivery will be the same as the latitude which the Moon had at the conception. In the fulfillment of time the Moon cannot exceed its own "guidepost." Count back the days, and set the Moon at that <correct> degree, then see where the previous new Moon occurred. Add the days from that point, and you will know at what day and hour the conception occurred and whether the native was an 8- or a 10-month child.

For example, if the Sun at the conception is in Aries and the Moon is 120° past the new-Moon phase, there will be a full-term gestation period of 270 <days> (for this to be the case, it is impossible that the distance exceed 120°, because in this distance the full-term "Ascendant" <?> is completed) and the birth will be in the tenth month. If it does exceed 120°, in every case add the days to the nine months; after summing the total, you will know the date of the conception. In each case search out the degree of the latitude and see when (i.e., in how many days and hours) the Moon will come to the same guidepost. Just like a revolving wheel, it will slow down when coming to its own place.

I have composed this book not artistically as some do, performing an enticing "concerto" in their arrangement of words and their use of meter, charming their listeners with their mythological, mystifying obscurities. Although I have not used fine language, I have experienced much, have expended much toil, and have personally examined and tested what I have compiled. Experience is better and more reliable than mere hearing, because one who hears has only an unreliable and doubtful grasp. One who has had experience, has tried many things, and has remembered them, validates what he has experienced. Men who are naturally malicious, ambitious, and contrary-minded are easily seen to be such and are punished, but their nature cannot be subdued: it can be made mild because of its shame and sorrow when pressure is put upon it, but when it is proven wrong, it becomes angry and bold at this provocation.

One can note this phenomenon particularly among the young: they want to act differently <?>, they hand over to another the control over bad or good, they are carried along willfully and are forced to take the lead <?>, to act in a contrary manner, and to be bold in the face of everything. They become alien to their family and friends; they enjoy the company of their enemies. Since they lead the future with a halter, they despise everyone and rejoice in others' troubles. As a result, evil comes on them, and they pray for dangerous harm <to come> to their enemies <?>. They suffer the reverse and are in pain to no avail; they do not honor the gods nor fear death, but are led by a demon. The end of such men is swift and dangerous, and their life is easily crushed.

It is better for men, as far as possible, to put stiff-necked pride from their minds and to avoid boldness, to strip themselves bare and to surrender themselves to reason. For no one is free; we all are slaves of fate and if we follow her voluntarily, we will live undisturbed and without grief as a whole, having trained our minds to be confident. If someone adopts a false cast of mind and attributes the possibility of acting to himself, he will be refuted by the impossibility of his acting and will be a laughing-stock. Then he will remember these words of the tragic Euripides:

> Lead me, O Zeus, and you, O Fate,
> Wherever you have assigned me to go.
> I will follow even if I hesitate. If I did not wish,
> Having become base, I will suffer this anyway.

In any type of systematic (or even unsystematic) art or talent, or in any other occasion, Nemesis will be the charioteer, holding the balance as in the mythical picture, showing that nothing is done beyond measure. Her wheel is lying at her feet, indicating that what has <happened> is unsteady and insecure, since the wheel is unstable when it rolls by itself. In the same way these men who criticize and boast have an intelligence that always revolves in the same spot, and an inflexible reasoning ability which entangles them in passions. They live in a sweat, not able to attain those things which first they despised, but later wanted, when they had already lost them.

The End of Book VI of the *Anthologies* of Vettius Valens.

Book VII

The *Anthologies* of Vettius Valens of Antioch: Book VII

1. Preface

First of all I must exact an oath from my readers—particularly in regard to this book—that they guard my words as a mystic secret. I have expounded the preceding methods in a complex but logical order, methods which have a great power to attract and to guide men to a love of beauty. <Through these methods> they may extend their range of interests from the lesser matters to the greater, and they might not abandon their quest and, in so doing, bring criticism on us. Now it is best to come to these matters after training oneself in those books which we previously composed. For the distribution <of the chronocratorships> will be considered unassailable and sacred as a result of the <previously made> overall and periodic determinations <of the chronocrators>. For just as a man might climb to a mountain peak, hiking through canyons and winding places with great toil, then come upon a temple with its precious statues of "gold, silver, and ivory" and perhaps of purple. This man would consider his climb to have been of no trouble or toil, and he would worship with gladness, imagining that he is associating with the gods in heaven. Those who follow our directions have this same experience, and I adjure them by the sacred circle of the Sun, by the varied paths of the Moon, by the powers of the other stars, and by the circle of the twelve signs to keep these matters secret, never to share them with the ignorant or the uninitiated, and to remember and to honor the one who inducted them into this art. May it go well for those who keep this oath and may the aforesaid gods grant them what they wish; may the opposite happen to those who foreswear this oath.

2. A Method for Propitious and Impropitious Times and Length of Life, with Respect to the Houseruler, the Rising Times, and the Ascendant

In the previous books we explained the rising times and what effect they have on the distribution of the chronocrators. Now we must add additional clarification. For every nativity, after the stars have been accurately charted, it will be necessary to examine how the houseruler is configured, which stars it has in aspect, whether it is rising or setting, and if it has a proper configuration or is out of its sect. <It is also necessary> to inspect the star which is allied with it, the Lot of Fortune and its ruler, and of course, the status of the nativity.

If the houseruler is found to be at an angle or operative, it will begin the chronocratorship; the rule will then pass to the stars next in order in the order of signs. If these stars are in the same sign, their positions in degrees must be calculated, since the one in the leading position will rule first. It is of primary importance to inspect the Ascending angle and to see how its houseruler is configured: if they happen to be together or appropriately configured in different signs, the houseruler will have a good effect on the length of life and on mental activities. They have a bad effect when setting, in opposition to each other or inappropriately configured, because when the houseruler completes the rising time of the sign in the Ascendant, the rising time of the sign in which it is located, or the period of the star in whose sign it is located, it will abdicate from the chronocratorship; in so doing, it will make the native short-lived, or it will allot months instead of years, days instead of months.

If the ruler of the Ascendant is not in conjunction, but another star is, then the latter star will begin the chronocratorships. If several are in conjunction, they all will share <in the chronocratorship>, with the star closest to rising or most related to the <Ascendant> sign ruling first. Similar forecasts can be made from the nature of the star and of the sign. If they are not found at the angles but are just preceding them, they will rule the chronocratorships briefly, or for as long as they transit a part of the sign (in degrees), and they will fall short of their own numbers and rising times.

After examining the Ascendant, it is necessary to investigate the Midheaven and to determine its ruler; then examine the Descendant and IC in the same way. If <their rulers> are not found at the angles, the rulerships which follow the angles must be examined; if the stars are not in those signs either, the signs which precede the angles must be inspected. (Even if such positions do not possess a great deal of influence over activities and do not allot the maximum length of life, they are nevertheless active.) It is also necessary to take into account the contacts and aspects of the Moon and the ruler of its sign, because if it is found at an angle and has the configuration of a distributor, it will be the first chronocrator. Following it, the stars closer to the angles or passing through a phase will rule. Moreover, rising stars differ from evening stars.

After these matters have been researched accurately, it remains necessary to know the general basis of the nativity, i.e., to what high or low rank it belongs, the harmful and the helpful stars, which star has been assigned the rulership of which place and type of forecast (i.e., activity, rank, wife, children, father, mother, brothers, and whatever else applies to the body, the mind/soul, and the livelihood) so that the result of the distributions might be very clear.

But we have explained these matters in the preceding books. However, the same stars often have mastery over many matters which they bring about in their own times of rule. If they happen to be together at the same time, they make their influences obvious then too. Their times of rule must be determined from the rising times of the signs and from the periods of each star. If the stars are at or following the angles, they allot the total rising time and period of each star. If the period of the star is found to be greater than the rising time of the sign, the star which has the chronocratorship allots its period. If the rising time is greater than the period, we allot the rising time. Occasionally they allot their total years <rising time+period>. If many stars are together, and if the periods of all exceed the length of the rising time, they allot the periods. If the periods are less than the rising time, they allot the rising time. <Not all stars allot their maximum periods>, only those which have some relationship with the allotting sign. Those which have no relationship (e.g., those which precede the angles) allot their minimum period. If a star happens to be in its proper face or is in an appropriate sign, it will allot only the rising time of its sign. The results will come to pass when the rising times or the periods are completed. If the stars are found to precede the angles, they allot neither the full rising time of their signs nor their full periods.

It is necessary to be aware in advance that malefics are not always harmful; they can be helpful and the cause of life and rank. In the same way benefics can bring dangers and harm—all of which can be foreseen through the appropriateness of their configurations or their oppositions. I have come to understand by experience that malefics are really malefic for average or humble nativities: these nativities are involved in all sorts of troubles, and even if the benefics seem to help momentarily, later they take away what was gained and render the native unsuccessful and unfortunate. Sometimes however they do give these men good physical condition, and make them excited by food, indiscriminate or cheerful about sex, and laboring with pleasure.

With respect to lofty nativities, malefics make men active, renowned, successful. Still, even then these stars do not cast off their own nature: these men have a bold, terrifying, dictatorial, greedy, and destructive nature; they desire others' goods and disgrace themselves with lawless and violent deeds; their rank is easily lost and their fortune easily changed. As a result, such men do not direct their offices, their positions of leadership, or their lives in an orderly manner, but they are involved in upheavals and plots, attacks or revolts of enemies and the masses, violence. While they are in office, plagues, famines, crop failures, cataclysms, earthquakes occur—depending on the configuration of each malefic. As a result, such men live wretchedly, suffering what each malefic portends. They are involved in violent or unexpected deaths and pay the penalty <for their crimes>. The fortune of such men becomes a subject of story, and their end is far-famed.

So as to make our explanations concise: the stars, when acting as chronocrators, will cause the results indicated by the configurations which they are found to be making with each other at the nativity, whether good or bad, taking into account the basis of the birth. Moreover, those stars which are in superior aspect or which are opposed to each other are most powerful; those which are in their own or in opportune signs and which rule the chronocratorship are most vigorous and active in producing results. Let the opposition of Saturn and Jupiter be considered productive and beneficial, particularly when these stars are in their own signs, provided that this configuration is not harmed by another afflicting influence. Likewise, the mutual configuration of Jupiter and Mars is good, if it happens to be in appropriate signs. One star in another's sign and having some relationship with it is productive and beneficial during the applicable chronocratorship. Each star will be operative at the end of its maximum period.

3. A Second Method of Distributing the Chronocratorship with Respect to the Rising Times of the Signs and the Periods of the Stars

Since the overall chronocratorships and their mutual relationships have been determined, I will now append the detailed distribution which I derived with much experience and toil. In advance I urge all those who wish to strive for the best, and particularly our followers (or any of those who have the incurable, long-standing disease of scholarship), to go soberly in the matter of methods, and never to forecast carelessly using any system. For often one distribution when it takes effect indicates a good chronocratorship—and indeed it will be good if it controls the chronocratorship by itself. If, however, another chronocratorship of malefics takes effect, it not only turns away the good but becomes a cause of evil. In such a case, even if the chronocratorship of benefics is vigorous in the nativity, the activity and rank will come accompanied by reversals and losses. If the chronocratorship of malefics is strong, unemployment, penalties, and upheavals will occur until the chronocratorship of benefics is operative. Moreover, often a star which is in a given sign, which is completing its own period or the time-interval <=rising time> of the sign, and which is apparently passing out of its time as chronocrator, combines with another star and becomes the cause of a different outcome or continues to keep the nativity in the same condition. In addition, the sextile aspects must be taken into consideration, because they are powerful and beneficial, particularly when they alone are operative. For infant nativities, it is necessary to calculate the chronocratorships of the stars in aspect using first the days, then the years.

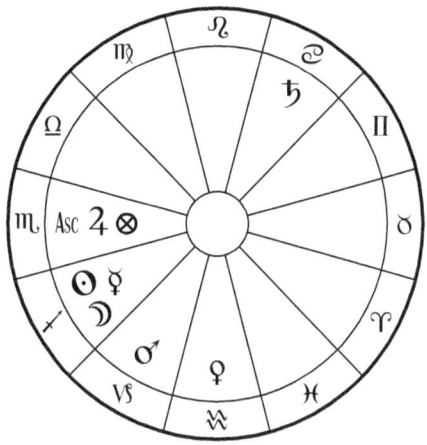

As examples let us append nativities which we have tested with precision in some forecasts and which I had a hand in: Sun, Moon, Mercury in Sagittarius, Saturn in Cancer, Jupiter, Ascendant in Scorpio, Mars in Capricorn, Venus in Aquarius, Lot of Fortune in Scorpio, klima 2. In his 33rd year he was exiled: the rising time <33> of Cancer in which Saturn was located with Mars in opposition. The Moon sextile to Venus indicated treachery from female individuals during the 33rd year. He was also in danger in his 27th year because of Capricorn and in his 30th and 40th years because of bodily illnesses of the eyes and feet: the period of Cancer <=Moon> is 25 and of Mars, which was in opposition, 15. Until his 42nd year the period of Mars and the rising time of Capricorn <27> were also operative, and in this time many crises arose. You see that in such configurations it is necessary to forecast after determining the <degrees>, in order to see if some ray of the benefics may take effect and may remove most of the bad effects.

Another example: Sun, Venus in Libra, Saturn in Aries, Jupiter in Taurus, Mars, Mercury in Virgo, Moon in Sagittarius, Ascendant in Libra, klima 3. In his 39th year he was exiled: the rising time of Aries is 20, and Saturn is there with the Sun (19) in opposition. Both were in opposition to their own exaltations. To be sure, he had critical periods in the previous years, but we observed the 39th year because 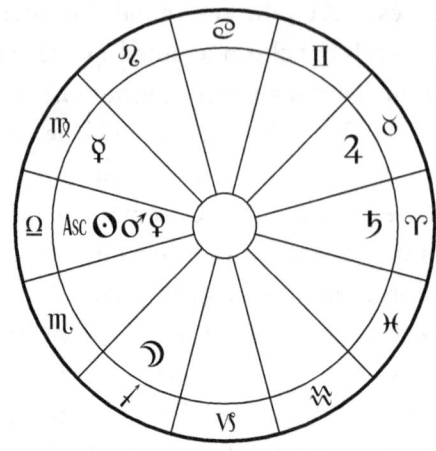 of the comparison with the preceding nativity, which was his brother's. We must marvel at the natural law that brought the chronocratorships to the same results, even though they were born in different klimata.

Another example: Sun, Mercury, Ascendant in Sagittarius, Moon in Cancer, Saturn in Leo, Jupiter in Capricorn, Mars in Aquarius, Venus in Scorpio, klima 2. In his 34th year his wife died because of the 19 of Leo <=Sun> and the 15 of Scorpio <=Mars>, or the 15 of Mars itself, since both malefics hemmed in Venus. In his 36th year he was about to go on trial, being accused before the king on a charge arising from the death of 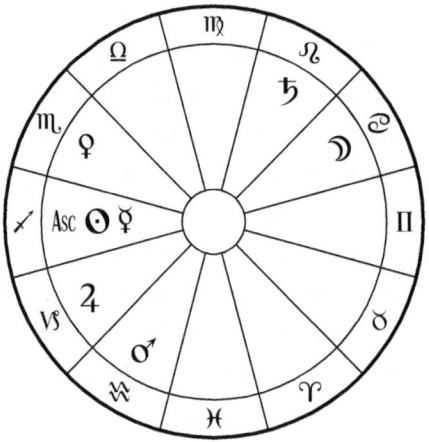 his wife, on the grounds that she had been treacherously murdered, but he fled into exile. For 36 is the rising time of Leo and of Scorpio as well, the location of Venus, in inferior aspect with Saturn. A more kindly chronocratorship was about to occur in his 37th year, because of the 12 of Jupiter and the 25 of the Moon, in opposition <to Jupiter>. Many other factors were operative in the past and the future <chronocratorships>, but I have thought it necessary to set forth only those which I myself know exactly and which I had a hand in.

Another example: Sun, Mars, Venus in Sagittarius, Moon in Libra, Saturn in Gemini, Jupiter in Virgo, Mercury in Scorpio, Ascendant in Capricorn. In his 19th year his father died violently and he himself was blinded by eye trouble. In the same year he travelled abroad and was in danger at sea, because the Sun's period <19> was operative, with Mars in conjunction and Saturn in opposition. In his 20th year he recovered his sight through

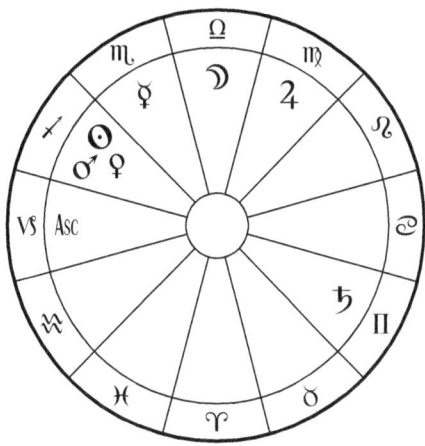

a treatment and an ointment given by an oracle of the god. But Saturn <in Gemini> even then was operative, with Gemini <=Mercury> giving 20, and therefore he suffered many ills. Virgo <=Mercury> also indicated 20, since Jupiter was in that sign. The 20 came from the 12 of Jupiter plus the 8 of Venus square. The chronocratorship belonged to many stars, but the operative ones were powerful. The stars in conjunction or aspect have a weaker influence for helping or harming, but they do have some power, especially when (as we have mentioned before) they are in the sign or the exaltation of, or are trine with, a fellow sect-member. Benefics and malefics had the same effects since they were preceding the angles, but Jupiter was most active since it was in the sign and <the IX Place of> the God and of Foreign Lands. Additionally, they were found in signs of equal rising time or in houses of the same star <Mercury>, and are as effective as if they were in aspect, particularly when the signs are found to be at the angles or operative.

Another example: Sun, Jupiter, Ascendant in Cancer, Moon in Sagittarius, Saturn in Gemini, Mars in Taurus, Venus, Mercury in Leo, klima 3. After serving in a distinguished military post, he was involved in an accusation in his 38th year and lost his rank: the rising time of Taurus, 23, and the period of Mars, 15, were operative for a total of 38. In addition, the sextile configuration of Saturn and Venus

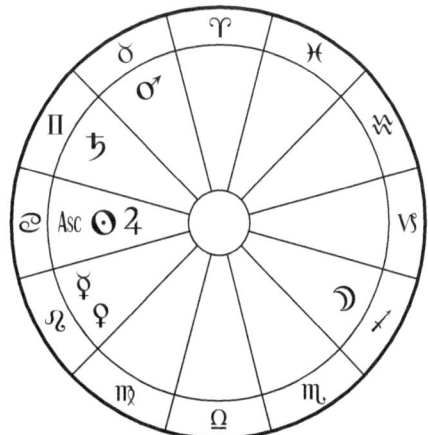

totalled 38. Moreover, from his 37th year he endured enmities and reversals, because the Moon indicated 25 and Sagittarius <=Jupiter> indicated 12 for a total of 37, with Saturn in opposition. On the other hand, Cancer <=Moon> had 25 and Jupiter 12, and as a result he got some small assistance. In his 39th year he was in a lawsuit and was imprisoned with no power to set things straight. For Mercury in Leo allotted 20 plus 19 for the sign <=Sun>, but it was in inferior aspect <sextile to the left> with the star which caused the crisis <Saturn> and hence was weaker. Besides, Saturn was about to begin another period of setbacks: the rising time of Gemini is 28 plus 12 for Sagittarius <=Jupiter>, for a total of 40. During this period the native traveled abroad and was betrayed through documents by a woman; he became debt-ridden and troubled about slaves, some because of alienation, others because of death and penalties. He himself was physically ill. Even though the chronocrators were malefic, some hint of good is about to appear from the benefics, and total loss and degradation will not follow. For friendships and hopes are being sown in advance, and it is through these that the native's troubles are alleviated. In the same way, even if the chronocrators had been benefic, some malefic influence is about to impinge: the friendships change to enmity and the loss of livelihood comes quickly with the loss of standing accompanying it. If the stars in trine, sextile, or some other aspect are operative, and if another aspect does not interpose itself in the succeeding period, the original aspect will predominate. Again, if the same stars later become chronocrators, they will display the same influence on outcomes in the same activities or ranks, predominating until another influence is operative.

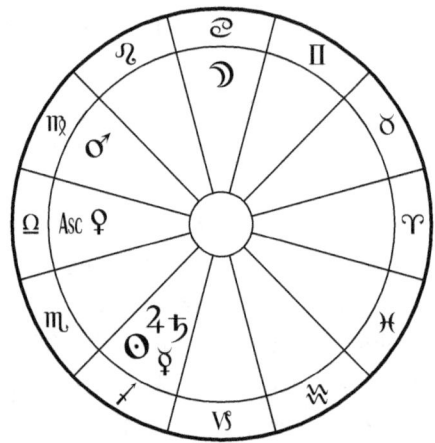

Another example: Sun, Saturn, Jupiter, Mercury in Sagittarius, Moon in Cancer, Mars in Virgo, Venus, Ascendant in Libra, klima 1. In his 69th year he was judged worthy of the governorship and became feared and spectacularly respected. He was blessed by the public but was also hated, was involved in mob uproar and disturbances, and did not complete his term of office. He was overtaken by painful illnesses and death. Operative at the time were the rising time of Libra <Ascendant>, 38;20, and that of Cancer <MC>, 31;40, for a total of 69. The malefics happened to total the same length of time: 30 for Saturn, 19 for the Sun, plus 20 for Mercury total 69, or in addition 38;20 for Virgo <Mars>, 12 for Jupiter, plus 19 for the Sun total 69. All the stars were operative and each of them had its own effects according to its own nature and its place in the natal chart.

That most of the stars—or even all of them—can be actively producing their effects at the same time can be observed from these examples. We find that activities take place throughout the cosmic fabric of the Earth every day and every hour: births, deaths, inheritances, ranks, ruins, injuries, illnesses, etc., whatever good or bad arises in man's life. For the universe, whirling in a sphere and sending the emanations of the stars onto this globe, does nothing vainly or uselessly: every moment it makes many things new in life, things which each person must abide patiently, some at one time, others at another, in order to fulfill the aims of Fate.

Many men have devoted themselves to such matters and have compiled many books and many systems; indeed all of them have left many interminably long accounts for men. A comparison can be made between them and those men who appear to be rich, but who in fact owe much money, and who leave little to their heirs. The heirs are well satisfied at first, although they receive as their own only a little money and have a very brief possession of the great wealth. (The fact of their ignorance casts a great delusion on them.) However, when they have become involved in lawsuits, troubles, and setbacks, because of the <attendant> hatred and anxiety they choose to get rid not only of this useless inheritance, but also of what they had enjoyed having. The same things happens to men who spend much time in the endless mass of treatises: they do not heal their chronic disease <curiosity>, but rather lose their minds, their education, and the profession which they already have.

For my part, I do not wall myself in with a show of words or a pile of books, but I have "embellished" my <treatise> with conciseness and truth. As a result, my heirs enjoy their inheritance without lawsuits and hatred as long as they live, some progressing far in forecasting by means of careful and accurate study. Others who approach it on a part-time or a negligent basis gain little— except that they do gain a higher and a better profit than those who study with great toil the interminable systems of others.

Since I myself have been a finder of treasures—and I have found not only the guarded topics, but have also illuminated the hidden topics—my readers must also be aware that, when delving deeply into them, they have discovered what was mystically hidden in darkness. One who enrolls in my school must also know what basis his own horoscope has, and he must apply himself to forecasting after taking into account his active chronocrators, so that he might gain profit or testimony <?>. (If he applies himself <to forecasting> in the chronocratorship of a malefic, he blames the method when he fails through ignorance or the omission of some place.) Nevertheless, if he searches with accuracy, he will not fail of this gift, and he will be thought worthy of the honor that any of the "Lovers of Time" may show him, depending on the basis of his nativity. Since I have experienced these things in my own life, I have explained them. Wherefore one should not blame me or the forecast for the chronocrators, but one should soldier on bravely and gladly under all circumstances, recognizing the level of one's nativity. It is of no use to live in despair, wishing to equal the fortunes of other men. One must remember:

> Lead me, O Zeus, and you, O Fate,
> Wherever you have assigned me to go.
> I will follow unhesitating. If I did not wish,
> Having become base, I will suffer this anyway.

And this:

> Fate wove with the strand of his birth that day he was born to his mother.
> <Iliad 19.128>

And this:

> But as for Fate, I think that no man has yet escaped it. <Iliad 6.488>

4. A Method for Length of Life with Reference to the Lot of Fortune and its Ruler

I cannot tell whether the Ancients, although knowing the efficacy of forecasting, were driven by envy to hide this art because of their vainglory and because the human mind finds this art difficult; or whether they spoke in such riddles even though they had not, in fact, grasped what Nature had created, had prescribed, and had bestowed abundantly on mankind after sealing it with Fate. Of all the lovely elements of the numerous great creations in the world, none seems to me to have been begrudged by God for man's daily use. God would not have revealed it if He had not wished to provide it for use. In contrast men have revealed this art only as they wished or as they were able. As a result, when I read over their chapter <on the following topic>, I wonder at the crookedness and the obscurity of their thought. But I reveal whatever I have discovered by my experience, and in addition, I do not wish to conceal whatever I have gone on to discover <after writing my previous pages>—this because of the remarkable quality of many forecasts, both good and bad, those happening in a short time or those remaining for a time at a steady state.

Now the following subdistribution will instruct diligent scholars. I have explained it in minute detail since I consider it superior to any other and since I wished to embellish the topic in every way. A general treatment displays a vague outline of details and is easily refuted because of the undisciplined thinking of its students. Let no one shrink away because this chapter is complex, multifaceted, with many rules, but let my reader divinize his nature. For although many <astrologers> have composed many systems, they have put together no solid system.

Now then to the task at hand. The fatal critical points must be determined just as I have directed in my book *The Length of Life*. Now I will clarify this topic more precisely. The chronocratorships are composed of three factors, minimum, mean, maximum. I have found their determination to be as follows: calculate the periods of the stars and the rising times of the signs from the Lot of Fortune and its ruler, first by hours, then by days, months, and years; or calculate hours for some, days for others, months for others, and years for still others; or using the stars at the angles and rising and in their proper configurations, calculate first days, then months, then the periods. For men who are already in the prime of life it is possible to allot periods and rising times; for infant nativities begin with the shortest units.

For example: Sun, Venus in Aquarius, Moon, Jupiter in the beginning of Aries, Saturn in Aries, Mars in Sagittarius, Mercury in Capricorn, Ascendant in Scorpio, Lot of Fortune in Libra, klima 6. The allotting stars are Venus because of Libra, Saturn because Venus is in Aquarius, Mars because Saturn is in Aries. Next I calculated according to periods and rising times, first hours, then days, then months, as follows: I took for Libra

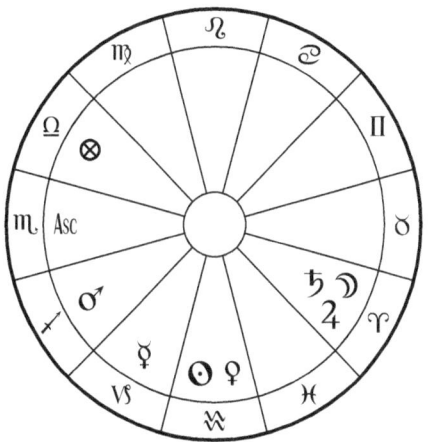

<=Venus> 8 days 8 hours, plus the rising time of Libra (in klima 6) 43 hours. Since Venus is in Aquarius <house of Saturn>, I took 57 hours for Saturn. Since Saturn is in Aries <house of Mars>, I took 15 hours for Mars. The total is 8 days, 123 hours. Now 123 hours equals 5 days 3 hours, and so the grand total is 13 days 3 hours. He lived 13 days 3 hours.

Another example: Sun, Venus, Mercury in Cancer, Moon in Capricorn, Saturn in Scorpio, Jupiter in Aquarius, Mars in Leo, Ascendant in Taurus, Lot of Fortune in Scorpio, its ruler <Mars> in Leo, and <Leo's> ruler <Sun> in Cancer. He lived longer than the hours and the days of the periods of the stars plus the rising times of the signs, and so I calculated the <u>months</u> as the third option. For Mars I took 66 months plus 15, and for the Sun in Cancer <=Moon> I took 25 months. The total is 106 months, which is 8 years, 10 months.

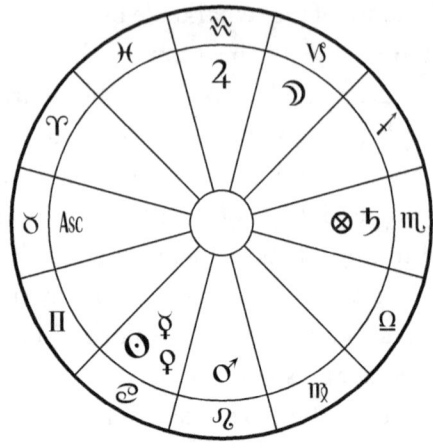

(I submit these nativities as examples; it is also necessary to note the houserulers and the places to see if they are controlled or opposed by malefics or happen to be out of their sects. Follow all the other directions too.)

Another example: Sun, Mercury in Aquarius, Moon in Taurus, Saturn in Sagittarius, Jupiter in Aries, Mars in Capricorn, Venus, Ascendant in Pisces, klima 6, Lot of Fortune in Gemini. I took the months for Mercury <ruler of Gemini> and since Mercury is in Aquarius, I took the rising time for Aquarius, 23 months, plus 33 months for Sagittarius, since Saturn is in Sagittarius. Altogether the months total 132, which is 11 years. He died at that age. We can find the precise number of days and the precisely measured hours by taking 1/12 of the period of each star.

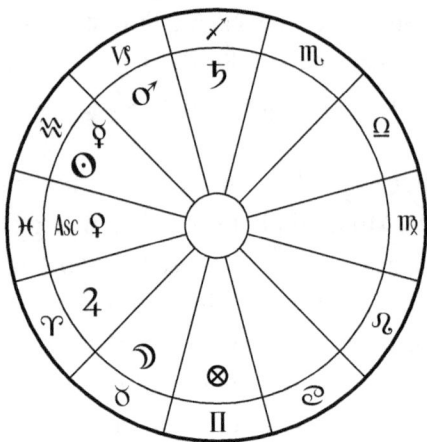

Stars which are appropriately configured with each other and in the same sect can combine their allotments. For example: Sun, Mercury in Cancer, Moon, Mars in Libra, Saturn, Venus in Leo, Jupiter in Sagittarius, Ascendant in Virgo, klima 6, Lot of Fortune in Sagittarius.[1] The ruler of Sagittarius,

---

[1] CB: In the manuscript the Ascendant is said to be in Capricorn, but Neugebauer and Van Hoesen noted (*Greek Horoscopes*, p. 120) that this seems to be incorrect based on the position of the Lot of Fortune, and they suspected that it was a scribal corruption where

Jupiter, was located at the Lot. So it allotted the rising time of Sagittarius, 33 years, plus its own period, 12 years, for a total of 45. Saturn trine with Jupiter added its period, 57 months, to the previous amount for a total of nearly 50 years. He died at that age. If anyone calculates the rising time of Leo, 38 months, plus the period of the Sun, 19 months, he will find the same number of months.

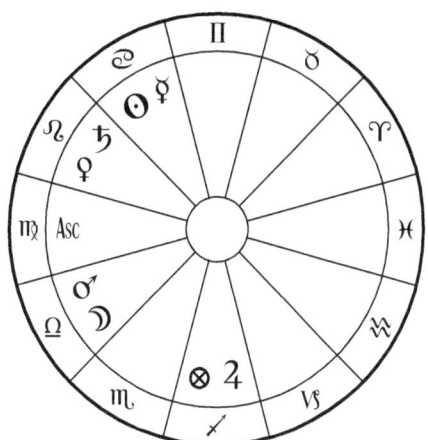

I have submitted these nativities after testing them by personal experience. If anyone wishes to test this method using a mere hearsay nativity, he will not find it to be valid. Note that different critical points are indicated whenever the chronocratorship of a malefic in configuration and in aspect takes control. The same caution applies to the Ascendant and its ruler, whenever the stars happen to be succeeding to or yielding the chronocratorship, if the Lot of Fortune and its ruler are not operative.

5. A Precise Method Concerning Propitious and Impropitious Times with Reference to the Rising Times and the Periods of the Stars

The same procedure must be observed with respect to propitious and impropitious times: after the yearly periods, allot the monthly periods to the operative signs and to their houserulers. Just as when we construct scientific astronomical tables, we use integer numbers and smaller fractions in order to make a solid structure; but we see that the structure is not consistent if the starting point of the numeration is not clearly established. In the same way, one who wishes to go through a nativity accurately must begin with the hours and months, then bring the chronocratorships (in all their variety) up to the transfer of the chronocratorship at the time in question. In so doing we will find that one star is chronocrator according to the rising times, another is chronocrator according to the stars' periods, and that even though the results as a whole seem to be good or bad, in the intervening days and months the opposite may occur, and perhaps the events may seem to happen earlier or

---

the symbols for Capricorn and Virgo were confused because they were so similar in the Byzantine period. I believe that this is correct, and we have changed both the text and the diagram to reflect that the Ascendant should be in Virgo in this chart.

later <than predicted>. Just as a stone hurled against some skillfully-crafted bronze object hits it only momentarily, but its clang echoes for quite some time—in the same way, when the stars are chronocrators, they display their causative effects only briefly, but during the succeeding periods they are active, just like the clang. The configurations of the stars and their aspects with each other (especially the aspects with the Lot of Fortune) are effective in the chronocratorships which are in harmony. (The whole is seen and arises from the aspects of the Lot of Fortune and from its ruler.)

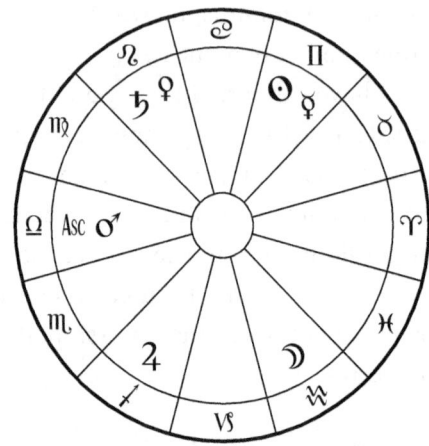

For example: Sun, Mercury in Gemini, Moon in Aquarius, Saturn, Venus in Leo, Jupiter in Sagittarius, Mars, Ascendant in Libra, klima 1. Assume we are investigating the 42nd year. I took the rising time of Libra, 38;20 (which is 38 years 4 months) plus the same number of months, 38 (which is 3 years 2 months). The total is 41 years 6 months. In that year while fleeing from battle, he fell from his horse as the enemy were approaching. Although many were killed and he himself was wounded, he was entangled with the rest of the slain, pretended to be dead, and escaped the danger. He then remained in the enemy's country until his 44th year leading the campaign. To the previous number of years I added 8 months for Venus (because of Libra) and 15 months for Mars because it was there also <in Libra>. In addition, the opposition of Saturn and the Moon was operative at that time. The rising time of Leo, 35, plus 57 months for Saturn, plus 8 months for Venus, plus 25 months for the Moon plus 19 months for Leo <=Sun> together total 44 years, 1 month.

As a result, it is necessary to give the total of rising times or of periods for the length of the nativity, then the months and days, until the forecast is made for the exact period of time. Therefore, one must observe for every nativity the stars in square and in opposition, particularly when malefics are in inappropriate configurations. In such a case, the native will be involved in all kinds of inescapable troubles. Such a man will struggle all his life, wrestling against crises hard to overcome; he will be inclined to slip and come crashing down, and he will easily fail. If malefics behold <the chronocrator>, such a man does not shrink from criticizing the gods; he lives wretchedly, begging for death—but in vain, unless some aspect of the benefics is effective in helping him. Now whenever a benefic is operative with a malefic, the bad influence will be halved and easily remedied. If one or the other is by itself, it indicates that its effects will be definite and complete, because a good effect is hindered and overcome by a malefic, while a bad effect is broken up and soothed by a benefic.

It is necessary to indicate the starting and the ending points of the time periods during which the stars begin to be or cease to be chronocrators, because it is during these periods that the influences will be most powerful. It is also necessary to research the following most accurately: the configurations of the stars, their aspects, if they are alone or together, if they are benefic or malefic, and if the chronocratorship is malefic, mild, or temperate—all this so that the prediction might take these factors into account. Often oppositions or squares of malefics do no harm at all, but instead are beneficial because they are in their proper places, have a benefic in aspect or have a distribution in their own sect.

In these points the ignorant go astray and therefore I must mention these same points so often: it is better to repeat, even to be verbose, and so keep this treatise free from criticism than to present an opportunity for abuse to envious and small-minded persons. These persons are pained by the success of others and revile work that is well done; they cannot follow what is being said nor think critically about what they say. The following story applies to such persons: they say that a young man was critically revising the plays of Euripides. The playwright was standing by and said, "If it is badly written, you write it better." The youth said, "I do not know how to write poetry, but I can revise what has been badly written." Euripides then said, "So then, write something badly and then revise your own composition to make it good."

This preceding system seems to present the easiest introduction, but the goal and the way to the goal is labyrinthine for those who love exact inquiry. If <the student> grasps the beginning (i.e., the distributions) as if it were the guiding thread of Ariadne, comes to the sought-for place, and discovers the final chronocratorship and its results, he will receive great knowledge, in the same way as Theseus discovered the Minotaur.

The stars allot the mean length of the periods which they rule:
The **Sun** has half of 120 years and hence receives 60; its minimum period is 19. The total is 79, half of which is 39 years, 6 months.
The **Moon** receives half of 108, which is 54, plus the minimum period, 25. The total is 79, half of which is 39 years, 6 months. It allots that amount.
Mars has the maximum period, 66, the minimum, 15, for a total of 81, half of which is 40 years 6 months.

Venus has a complete period of 84, a minimum period of 8, for a total of 92, half of which is 46.

Mercury has a maximum period of 76, a minimum of 20, for a total of 96, half of which is 48.

Jupiter has a maximum period of 79, a minimum of 12, for a total of 91, half of which is 45 years 6 months.

<Saturn>...

I think these mean periods are most scientific.

6. A Method Concerning Propitious and Impropitious Times with Reference to One-Half, One-Third, and Two-Thirds of the Rising Times and the Periods of the Stars

We have set out here the systems which we have discovered with long, persevering investigation and which we have confirmed from our study of nativities. Now we append the topic of propitious and impropitious times, about which the King and Petosiris spoke in riddles. Even if this system seems to our readers to be complicated and entangled, these readers may still marvel at the quality of its predictive force and its scientific effectiveness. The procedure of finding <u>one</u> chronocrator among the stars (the procedure characteristic of the other methods) and from this one to predict the future, <and to say> that the same star receiving the chronocratorship in the cycle of time will forecast the same matters, seems to me to be ignorance and error. For one star, according to its own nature, will bring about good or bad in the year <in question>, or in two or three years. We find in one period of time, either months or days, differing results occurring, mixtures of bad and good—we gain confidence that these are the facts, because in a given nativity we find at one time rank, stewardships, accusations, exile; or at another time a distinguished office, grievous pain, and weakness; or similarly a governorship, the possession of a livelihood, and death. We find some men unfortunate in their health, but lucky in their livelihoods, some troubled in their wives and their occupations, but strong and cheerful. So we do not think that these things come from <u>one</u> chronocrator, but from <u>many</u>. And the good that had been indicated is dissipated by the power of malefics, likewise the bad by the power of benefics.

Wherefore the Compiler says some things are unavoidable, other things are not. Unavoidable things occur when malefics happen to be activating something by themselves; avoidable things, when a benefic is involved while the malefics are operating and breaks up their power. When a configuration of a benefic is found in a nativity and that benefic is found to be the chronocrator, the good results will be total, but (as before) if the chronocratorship of malefic aspects is also operative, both good and bad will occur—according to the nature of the stars and signs. In addition of course, the good and bad will come to pass proportionate to the greatness and the basis of the nativity. Just like the general forecasts for infant nativities: if we find that benefics are operative and are beholding the Sun or the Moon and the Ascendant from the right, we then promise length of life, rank, and the support of a livelihood. If malefics are operative, we consider the nativity to be unviable. It is necessary to examine the distribution of chronocrators in the same way: in so far as benefics control, promise great success; if both are mixed, predict a similarly <mixed fortune>; if malefics alone enter into rule as chronocrators, predict dangers, ruin, and the onset of many crises.

So the King says:

"When the chronocratorships are plotted (*i.e., those of the nativity*) and when any are operative (*he means any of the stars*), if some other star comes into aspect or even has contact in the alternation of chronocrators, the chronocratorship must be granted to both stars. For example, if the Moon occupies the degree-position <of the chronocratorship> while some other star is also in the Moon's sign, when the Moon itself makes contact with the other place <=star>, it will control the chronocratorship of the sign, whether it is good or bad, or whether the associated stars are benefic or the opposite. Moreover, if the star of Jupiter happens to be in the aforementioned place, it will be indicative of rank, or of moderate rank plus the possession of a profitable livelihood. (*He is referring to the Lot of Fortune, the point indicative of possessions and benefits. The point concerning rank is a different one.*) If a malefic is also in aspect or has contact with it, evil will come to pass in the chronocratorship of the benefics, as well as good. The time of the star which has attached itself is taken together and calculated with the other's times. Whatever sum is arrived at, forecast that the results will occur toward the end of the periods and rising times. Now every star which is at an angle gives its full period. (*We have explained this in the preceding chapters.*) The allotment of those which are not at the angles is subject to a deduction from their proper factors. (*I think I have explained this matter in my book* The Length of Life.)

"In addition: suppose the Moon controls the aforesaid place and the star of Saturn is also there; the Moon's place (which is also the location of the star of Saturn) is also in the Ascendant. Now the complete period of Saturn is 30 full years, that of the Moon is 30 days. Let the Moon in its present sign be at an angle, let the star of Mars either precede or follow the given sign so that it will make contact with it, and let the star of Saturn have Mars, the Moon itself, or the Sun in aspect. Men <with this horoscope> will be born of lowly parents. Add the chronocratorship of the sign in which the star of Saturn is located and the chronocratorship of Mars; this period will come into vicissitudes or will even cause travel. In the same chronocratorship, it will be the cause of injuries and wounds, particularly to the eyes. If the Moon is waxing, but is not yet at the full Moon, it indicates dimming of vision…and troubles happening to the eyes. Indeed it adds burns…and even cuts in the same places because Mars is in contact with the Light-Bringer and hems it in with its burning heat.

"Next in order, forecast the effects of the star in aspect or in conjunction with the Moon's sign, if one or more happen to be located in the Lot <of Fortune>. Next forecast the stars following the angles, in whatever Place they are located and whichever angle they follow."

We have cited this in his very words because of the following explanation. We have found it to be true by testing and long calculation.

Now if, as we have already said, the chronocratorship of <u>one</u> configuration takes effect at the time in question, when calculated from the total of the rising time of the sign and period of the star, then use the preceding rules. However, when <u>combined</u> chronocratorships are taking effect, attend to what is to be predicted and determine the outcome using the positions of the angles and the stars preceding or following the angles, the positions of the Lots, and of the new and full Moons, considering all of these according to the proper aspects or oppositions of the stars. If the chronocratorships of the aspects are combined, the results will come to pass in one-half, one-third, or two-thirds of the time, provided each one does not hold <the chronocratorship> alone.

It is necessary to investigate the contacts of the Moon: if its configuration with another star is not in the same sign, but is in the next sign, then add the times of both stars (or the rising times of the signs in which they are located) and make the prediction. The consideration of the chronocrators is quite complex, sometimes involving the Moon's path and the Lot, sometimes the angles, sometimes the eastern, western, and other (i.e., when the stars are at a standstill) phases. The chronocrators must be understood as the results of the interaction of malefics and benefics.

…As for my statement about one-half, one-third, or two-thirds of the time: the cut will come at the Place of Injuries if you calculate the distance in degrees. We have also discovered this in our discussion of propitious and impropitious times…

For example: Sun, Moon in Leo, Saturn in Virgo, Jupiter in Pisces, Mars in Sagittarius, Venus in Gemini, Mercury in Cancer, Ascendant in Libra, klima 7. In his 37th year he suffered a lawsuit about an inheritance on account of his wife, from whom he had expected great benefits. He lost the case at the king's court. This time was not altogether injurious except insofar as it disappointed his hopes. The

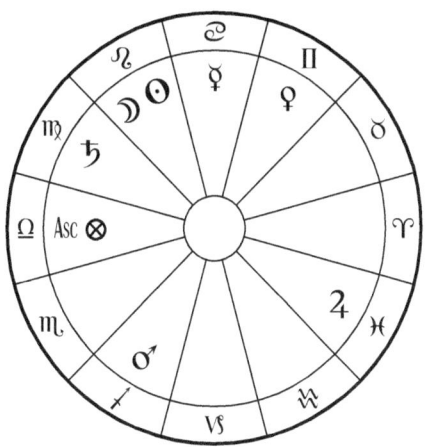

Moon trine with Mars indicated the 37th year: 25 for the Moon plus 12 for Sagittarius <=Jupiter> total 37. Likewise Jupiter and Mercury <trine>: 12 for Jupiter plus 25 for Cancer <=Moon> total 37. Investigating in the way we have explained, we find the opposition of Mars and Venus to be similarly operative in klima 7, as is Saturn, which is square <with both>: 27 for Gemini, 8 for Venus, plus 20 for Virgo <=Mercury> total 55, two-thirds of which is 36 years, 8 months. Pisces <=Saturn> also indicated the same amount, but the malefics were strong. Venus was the ruler of the Lot of Fortune <Libra>. The native had won the same lawsuit in his 35th year, but when it was appealed, he lost. The 35 had good luck because of the rising time of Pisces, 15, and of Gemini <=Mercury>, 20, plus Gemini again, 27 <its rising time> and Venus, 8, for a total of 35. Or 20 for Gemini, and 15 for Mars total of 35. Or 20 for Virgo <=Mercury> plus 15 for Mars total 35. So both benefics and malefics were operative, and since they were in bicorporeal signs, it will be necessary <to use> them several times <in making the forecast>. Now the fact that malefics are in superior aspect and in opposition has great power. Wherefore Petosiris himself said, "The chronocratorships must be understood as the results of the interaction of benefics and malefics."

The horoscope of the wife who lost the lawsuit is as follows: Sun in Cancer, Moon, Saturn, Jupiter in Sagittarius, Mars, Venus, Mercury in Gemini, Ascendant in Capricorn, klima 7. In her 25th year she seemed destined to win her case, for the Moon being with Jupiter and Saturn indicated 25, and the Sun in Cancer <=Moon> also signified 25. In addition, the rest of the stars were operative by combination and 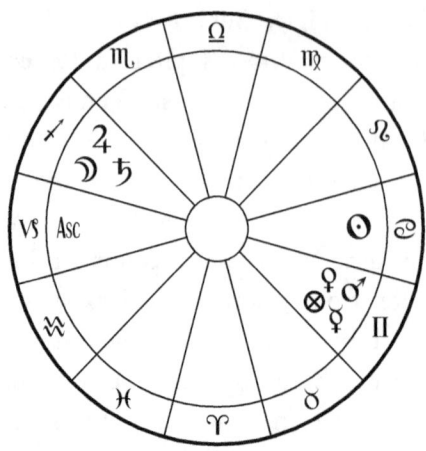 opposition: 30 years for Saturn plus 20 for Mercury in opposition total 50, one-half of which is 25. Or 30 years for Saturn plus 20 for Mercury plus 25 for the Moon total 75, one-third of which is 25. From that time the affair reversed itself: when the appeal was made in her 27th year, she was defeated. The rising time of Gemini <27> was operative, the location of the Lot of Fortune accompanied by Mars and Mercury. Additionally, 25 for the Moon plus 15 for Mars in opposition total 40, two-thirds of which is 26 years, 8 months. Here too the stars happened to be in bicorporeal signs.

Another example: Sun, Mercury, Jupiter in Scorpio, Moon in Taurus, Saturn in Aquarius, Mars in Virgo, Venus in Libra, Ascendant in Leo, klima 2. In his 52nd year he had a very great quarrel and a lawsuit with his sister about property and an inheritance, and he won at the king's court. The configuration of opposition was operative: 25 for the Moon, 12 for Jupiter, 15 for Scorpio <=Mars>, for a total of 52. 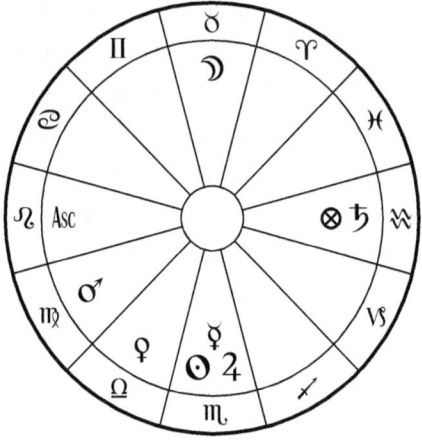 Additionally in klima 2, 36 for Scorpio, 12 for Jupiter, 30 for Saturn (in the sign of the Lot of Fortune) total 78, two-thirds of which is 52. Or again, 24 for Taurus, 24 for Aquarius, plus 30 for Saturn total 78, two-thirds of which is 52. So all the stars except Mars were operative. He was ill at that time, had a narrow escape at sea, and made great expenditures, but the benefics seemed to be in superior aspect to Saturn and were more powerful.

The horoscope of the sister who lost the lawsuit is as follows: Sun, Mercury in Sagittarius, Moon in Cancer, Saturn in Aquarius, Jupiter, Venus in Capricorn, Mars in Scorpio, Ascendant in Gemini, klima 4. The 54th year is indicated by 30 for Saturn plus 24 for Venus, totalling 54. Or again 36 for Scorpio, plus 15 for Mars, which was in the sign of the Lot of Fortune and which was operative, plus 30 for Saturn total 81,

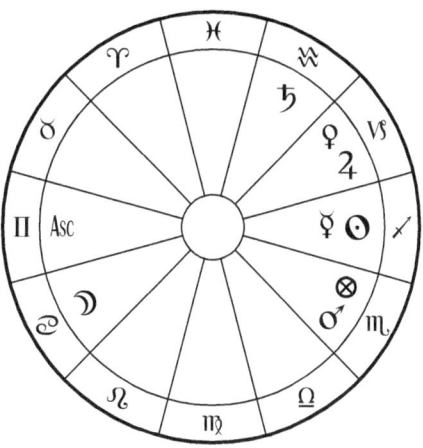

two-thirds of which is 54. The dominant aspect of the malefics was operative. So in her 53rd year she had an apparent and supposed victory through the help of the great, and so she resorted to a lawsuit; this was because the Moon allotted 25 and Capricorn 28 for a total of 53. But in her 54th year she was abandoned by her helpers, for the benefics did not combine to become chronocrators at that time.

Another example: Sun, Moon, in Cancer, Saturn, Jupiter, Mars in Aries, Venus, Mercury, Ascendant in Gemini, klima 1. In his 47th, 48th, and 49th years he was ill, suffered a great flow of blood, and was enfeebled. At the same time he was banished. The 47th year was indicated by 31; 40 for Cancer plus 15 for Mars totalling 46 years, 8 months. The 48th year was indicated by 31;40 for Cancer again, 25 for the

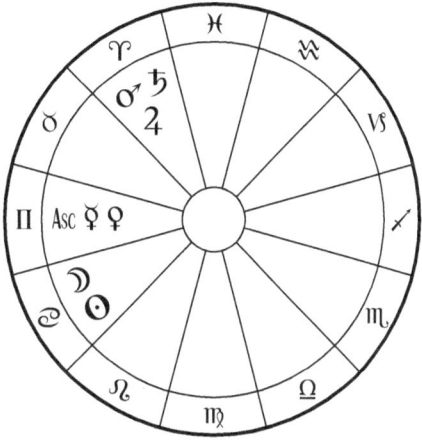

Moon, plus 15 for Mars, for a total of 72, two-thirds of which is 48. Also in the 48th year the rising time of Gemini, 28;20, plus the period of Mercury, 20, were operative, totalling 48 years, 4 months. At that time in his 49th year he found a little charity and support. The Sun and Saturn allotted 19 and 30 for a total of 49. The malefics in superior aspect to the luminaries were the cause of great dangers, and if Jupiter had not been in the configuration, the malefics absolutely would have brought him violent death.

Another example: Sun, Mercury in Capricorn, Moon, Mars, Ascendant in Taurus, Saturn in Scorpio, Jupiter in Cancer, Venus in Pisces, klima 6. In his 30th year he escaped slavery, committed many robberies, avoided capture for a short time, but was caught in the same year. Both sets <of signs> in opposition were operative <Taurus/Scorpio, Cancer/ Capricorn>: they both total 60, one-half of which is 30. Also 28 for Capricorn, 20 for Mercury, plus 12 for Jupiter total 60, one-half of which is 30. Also 30 for Saturn plus 15 for Mars, two-thirds of which is 30. Also 25 for Cancer <=Moon>, 12 for Jupiter, plus 8 for Venus (which is trine) total 45, two-thirds of which is 30. Because of the benefics, he seemed destined to escape danger for a short time and to live comfortably from the takings of his robberies, but because of the malefics, he fell.

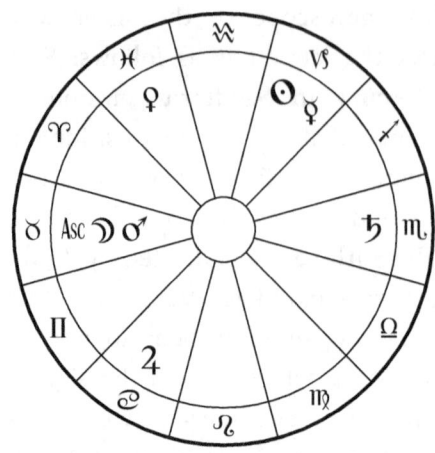

Another example: Sun, Saturn, Mercury in Sagittarius, Moon in Cancer, Jupiter in Taurus, Mars in Leo, Venus in Capricorn, Ascendant in Virgo, klima 2. The native, although of governing rank, fell into the governor's disfavor and was condemned to the mines/ quarries in his 34th year. Mars, together with the Sun, controlled the chronocratorship: 19 for the Sun plus 15 for Mars total 34. In his 36th year, through the help of the great, he was released from confinement as disabled. At that time in his 36th year the rising time of Leo was operative. In addition, 12 for Jupiter in superior aspect <to Scorpio, Mars' house> plus 24 for Taurus also total 36. Also 28 for Capricorn plus 8 for Venus total 36. So the benefics were powerful. In his 39th year trouble arose again because of the pre-existing hostility, and he was exiled to an island/oasis. The stars in Sagittarius controlled this period: 19 for the Sun, 20 for Mercury for a total of 39. Also take two-thirds of 58, which is 38 years, 8 months. (19 for the Sun, 20 for Mercury, plus

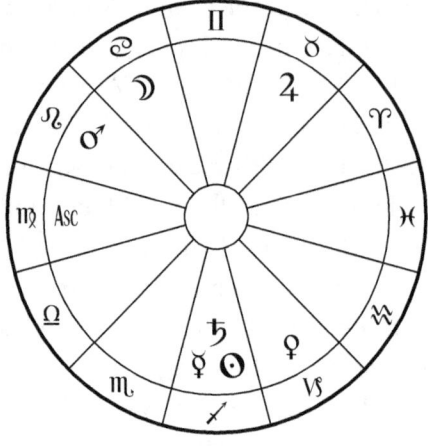

19 for Leo <=Sun>, because Mars is there in trine, total 58. Again for Mars <in Leo=Sun> 19, plus 19 for the Sun, plus 20 for Mercury total 58.) In his 40th year he lived endangered and fell ill. His wife, however, accompanied him with affection, comforted him, and shared her property with him. The 40th year is indicated by the contact of the Moon with Mars (25 for the Moon plus 15 for Mars total 40), and the fact that Jupiter and Venus were trine showed the same, because 12 for Jupiter plus 28 for Venus <=Capricorn> total 40. I myself had a hand in these forecasts.

Another example: Sun, Mercury in Capricorn, Moon, Saturn in Sagittarius, Jupiter in Cancer, Mars in Virgo, Venus in Aquarius, Ascendant in Libra, klima 2. In his 48th year he saw the death of his beloved son, a very great sorrow, and in the same year the death of his mother. Virgo and Libra indicated this because of their equal rising times <40>: 8 years for Libra <=Venus> plus 40 for Virgo total 48. Since Mars was found

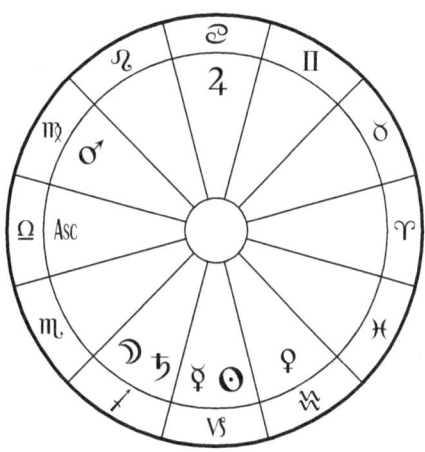

with the Ascendant, it brought grief with respect to the mental/emotional factors. Additionally, 40 for Virgo plus 32 for Sagittarius total 72, two-thirds of which is 48.

Another example: Sun, Mercury, Venus in Leo, Moon in Virgo, Saturn in Libra, Jupiter in Capricorn, Mars in Aries, Ascendant in Cancer, klima 6. From observation I made note of these chronocratorships, and since the nativity was that of an infant, I calculated them as months, not years. At the completion of his eighth month and for part of his ninth, he was subject to convulsions and was almost in danger of dying. The eighth

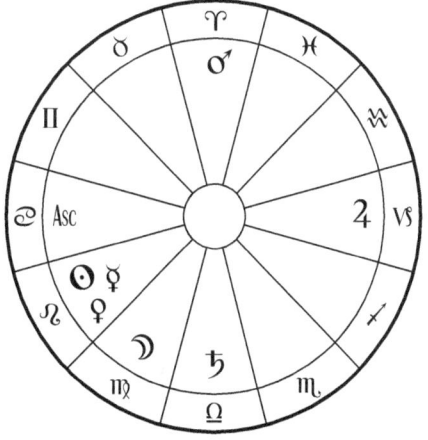

month was indicated by Libra <=Venus>, with Saturn in that sign. Half of the ninth month was indicated by the rising time of Aries, 17, operative until the completion of 8 months, 15 days. Additionally, the rising time of Capricorn was operative to the same effect: one-third of its rising time, 27, is 9; 19 for the Sun plus 8 for Venus total 27, one-third of which is 9. There were indications in the other months which were controlled by malefics: he suffered from boils and eczema in (for example) the 15th, the 17th, the 27th and other months, particularly the 27th. The cause was this: when playing with an animal he fell and was injured in the generative organs. The 27th month was indicated by Mars and the Moon: 15 for Mars plus 25 for the Moon total 40, two-thirds of which is 26 months, 20 days. (I consider Aries and Virgo to be in opposition because <the Moon> was moving toward it <opposition>.) Additionally, 15 for Mars plus 25 for the Ascendant in Cancer <=Moon> total 40, two-thirds of which is 26 months 20 days. But in that month the rising time of Capricorn, 27, was also operative; 15 for Mars plus 12 for Jupiter total 27; or again 19 for the Sun plus 8 for Venus total 27. From this 28th month he lived precariously: the rising time of Libra and the period of Saturn coincided. In his 32nd month he was dangerously ill and was in convulsions: 15 for Mars plus the rising time of Aries, 17 total 32. In his 33rd month he died: the rising time of Cancer equalled this figure. Additionally 25 for Cancer <=Moon> plus 8 for Libra <=Venus> total 33, as does 25 for the Moon plus 8 for Libra. I calculated as if the Moon were in Libra with Saturn, which is permissible because of the equal rising times <of Virgo and Libra>.

Another example: Sun, Mercury in Libra, Moon in Aquarius, Saturn in Pisces, Jupiter in Capricorn, Mars in Aries, Venus in Leo, Ascendant in Cancer, klima 6. The native was rich, but in his 47th year he was exiled, for Saturn was operative at the Midheaven, the IX Place, as was the rising time of Pisces: 30 for Saturn plus 17 for Pisces total 47. In addition the fact that the Sun and Mercury were in opposition to Mars <was operative>: 15 for Mars, 17 for the rising time of Aries, 19 for the Sun, plus 20 for Mercury[2] total 71, two-thirds of which is 47 years, 4 months. In addition the square configuration of Libra and Capricorn <was operative>: 27 for Capricorn plus 20 for Libra total 47. To all appearances, he seemed to be protected all around, but he endured reverses and losses because of a woman.

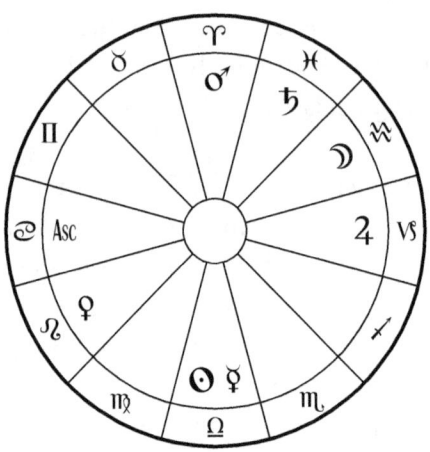

---

[2] *Marginal note:* and 38 for Leo.

It is absolutely necessary to prove the appended topics: Saturn at the Midheaven for night births is indicative of exile <as in the previous nativity>. Mars following the Midheaven for day births forecasts the same. If the ruler of the Midheaven is in aspect to the right with the Midheaven or is operative, then after the exile, there will be recovery and restoration beginning with the chronocratorship indicated by the rising time of the sign or by the cyclical return of the star. The Sun operative at night at IC without a houseruler, or the Moon at the Midheaven, forecasts a precarious nativity. New or quarter Moons with Saturn in square, opposition, or conjunction are indicative of exile. Likewise full or first quarter Moons with Mars in opposition, square, or conjunction indicate great ruins and disaster, dooms that are far-famed in song and story. If they are in solid signs and degrees, the native is laid low once and for all; if they are in bicorporeal signs, often; if in tropic signs, they defame men far and wide; if they are at the angles, the native goes from the greatest good fortune to the greatest bad fortune; if they follow the angles, they make the native suffer and expect changes, one after the other; if they precede the angles, they involve him in downfall, kidnapping or banditry, violence, tortures, and a miserable death. It is hard on a night birth to have the Moon (for a day birth, the Sun) precede an angle. If the malefics are square with the Sun and Moon, the native is dragged into large-scale warfare and uprisings, and he is killed.

In general, Saturn opposed to Mars is not good for either a free man or a slave: ill fortune will extend far. When in square or opposition, these stars make toilsome and troubled men. It is best if such configurations of these stars precede the angles, because if they occur at the angles, they bring death to <good> fortune and danger to occupations and to the whole basis <of the nativity>. If they follow the angles, they cause expected good to turn to the worse, they repress enterprises, and they make fortunes toilsome and wearisome. If they precede the angles, there are complex but understandable changes regarding livelihood for those who are endowed with such a configuration. If, however, benefics are in aspect with the above-mentioned configuration, the bad will be less or can be alleviated.

The same effects occur when they rule the configurations in the distribution of the chronocratorships. Since most stars—indeed all—seem to be chronocrators, the determination of good or bad results will be made from the transits at any given time, particularly when the chronocrator transits operative places and has some connection with the affairs of the nativity. Then it shows results which can be securely forecasted.

<To show> that nature is astonishing and that nothing happens apart from the will of Fate—yea, even those lost in wars, collapses, fires, shipwrecks,

or any other disaster are altogether governed by Fate—I will append a short illustrative example: Sun, Mercury in Leo, Moon in Libra, Saturn in Aries, Jupiter in Taurus, Mars, Venus in Virgo, Ascendant in Capricorn, klima 2. In his 40th year he had a critical point: 25 for the Moon plus 15 for Aries <=Mars> total 40, or 20 for Aries (in opposition <to the Moon>) plus 40 for Libra total 60, two-thirds of which is 40.

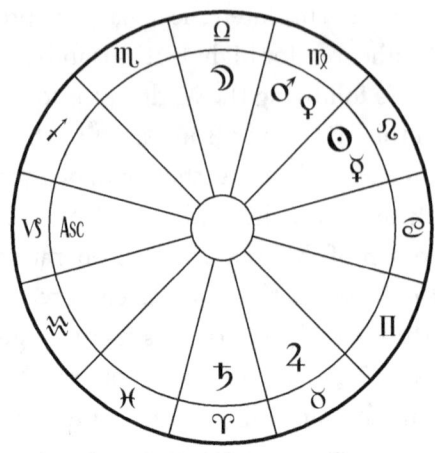

The point was critical by a multiple of two: at the same time I found 28 for Capricorn, the Ascendant, plus 12 for Jupiter trine, for a total of 40; or again 30 for Capricorn <=Saturn>, 22 for Taurus, plus <Venus'> period, 8, for a total of 60, two-thirds of which is 40.

Another example: Sun, Mercury in Aquarius, Moon in Scorpio, Saturn in Cancer, Jupiter in Libra, Venus in Capricorn, Mars, Ascendant in Virgo, klima 7. In his 35th year he had a criticial point: Mars' period, 15 years, and Virgo's <=Mercury's>, 20, were operative for a total of 35. In addition 8 for Venus plus 27, the rising time of Capricorn, total 35. Or again 30 for Saturn, in opposition <to Venus> plus 32;30 for Cancer plus 8

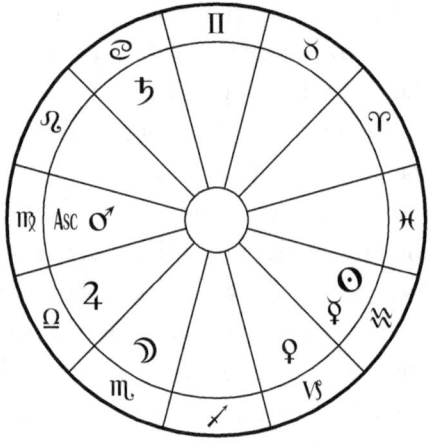

for Venus total 70 years 6 months, one-half of which is 35 years, 3 months. Additionally Jupiter and Saturn shared the chronocratorship, because 42 years 6 months for Libra plus 27 years, 6 months for Cancer totalled 70 years, one-half of which is 35.

Another example: Sun, Mars, Venus in Sagittarius, Moon in Libra, Saturn in Gemini, Jupiter in Virgo, Ascendant, Mercury in Capricorn, klima 6. At age 36½ he had a critical point: 27 years 6 months, plus 8 for Venus, total 35 years 6 months. Add 19 for the Sun (for Gemini), and the total is now 54 years 6 months, two-thirds of which is 36 years 4 months. The benefics also had a share in these matters.

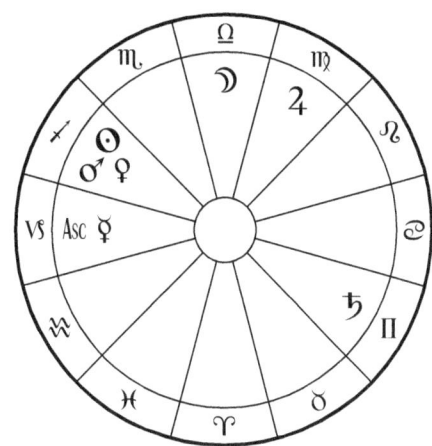

Another example: Sun, Mercury, Venus in Cancer, Moon in Aries, Jupiter, Ascendant in Gemini, Saturn in Libra, Mars in Leo, klima 1. In his 27th year he had a critical point: 19 for the Sun plus 8 for Libra <=Venus> total 27. Additionally 28 years, 4 months for Gemini plus 12 for Jupiter total 40 years 4 months, two-thirds of which is approximately 27. Again 19 for Leo <=Sun>, 31 years, 8 months for Cancer, plus 30 for Saturn total 80 years, 8 months, one-third of which is approximately 27.

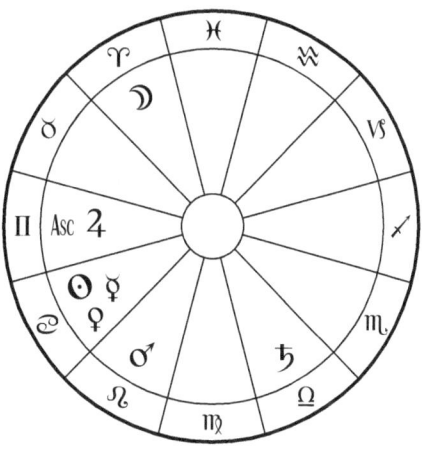

Another example: Sun in Aquarius, Moon in Aries, Saturn in Leo, Jupiter in Sagittarius, Mars in Libra, Venus, Mercury in Capricorn, Ascendant in Pisces, klima 6. In his 33rd year he had a critical point: 25 for the Moon plus 8 for Libra <=Venus> total 33. 30 for Saturn and 19 for the Sun total 49, two-thirds of which is 32 years, 8 months. In addition, the rising time of Sagittarius <MC>, 33, was operative, with Jupiter in that sign.

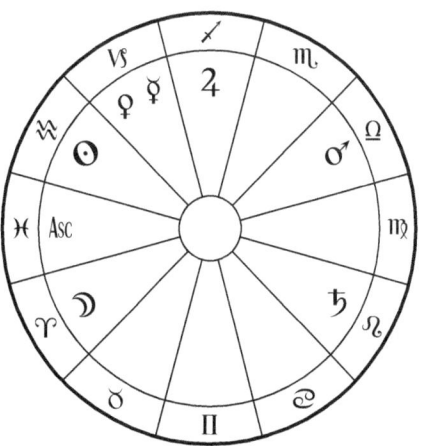

Another example: Sun, Mercury, Venus, Moon in Taurus, Saturn in Sagittarius, Jupiter in Scorpio, Mars in Leo, Ascendant in Pisces, klima 2. In his 22nd year he had a critical point: 19 for Leo <=Sun> plus 25 for the Moon total 44, one-half of which is 22. Additionally 36 for Scorpio plus 8 for Taurus <=Venus> total 44, one-half of which is 22.

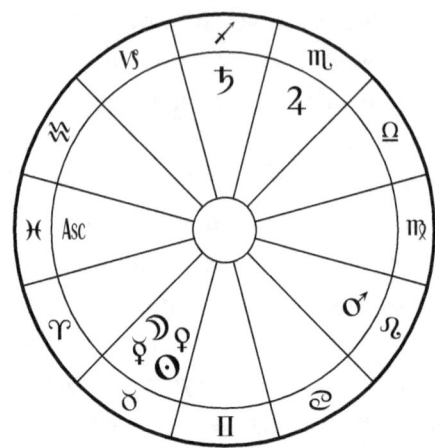

These six men, while on a voyage with many others, encountered a violent storm and, with the rudder swept away, were in danger of drowning as the ship took on water. But because of the direction of the wind and the steersman's management of the sails, they escaped. They encountered other dangers at that time, particularly a roving pirate ship.

As a result, if—as often happens—many or all of the stars are found to be operative at the given period, it is necessary to determine how each one is configured and which star's aspect is the more opportune and powerful, the one causing good or the one causing bad; make that one the guidepost of your forecast. Then forecast according to the others which have a weaker effect, acting through hope, postponement, anxiety, and penalties. Often even when the stars should show an obvious effect, they will be weak because another star prevails, being at a powerful place. If the influences derived from their configurations and signs are equal, then both bad and good will occur. Now often in regard to chronocratorships, unavoidable and vigorous angle-relationships <sextile trine square> are found to have a wide-ranging effect, and even when they seem to be leaving the chronocratorship, they again become powerful and <continue> ruling. As a result, even if another aspect is operative, it will not be vigorous since it is overcome by the previous aspect, particularly when a malefic is influential, being in opposition or in superior aspect.

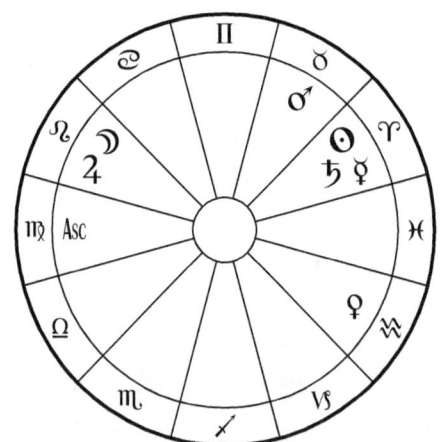

Let us take an example: Sun, Saturn, Mercury in Aries, Moon, Jupiter in Leo, Mars in Taurus, Venus in Aquarius, Ascendant in Virgo, klima 1. In his 18th year he travelled abroad with a distinguished woman because of her friendship and rank, and for futher intimacy and erotic passion: Aquarius <Venus' position> indicated 25 years, and if Venus had been operative alone, it would have applied its benefic influence quickly. But as it was, Mars controlled 25 years also, because of the rising time of Taurus, and in addition the period of the Moon also brought 25, two-thirds of which is 16 years 8 months. If, after the aforesaid chronocratorship, other aspects of benefics had been in agreement, his hopes would have been realized. But as it was, the same stars were again in power, for in his 18th year the female individual died, and he returned home having failed in his hopes and with little benefit: Jupiter allotted 12 and Mars (in superior aspect to Jupiter) 15 for a total of 27, two-thirds of which is 18. In addition, 19 for Leo <=Sun> plus 8 for Taurus <=Venus> total 27, two-thirds of which is 18.

In his 19th year he found profit and success, but had disagreements, mental problems, and enmity with his relatives: Leo (the position of Jupiter and the Moon) indicated 19 <=Sun>. In addition, the Sun itself, in Aries with Saturn, indicated 19. Alternatively, 30 for Aquarius <=Saturn> plus 8 for Taurus <=Venus> total 38, one-half of which is 19. In his 20th year he travelled abroad because of friendship with a woman and looked forward to greater hopes and profits—but he failed in this too when she died: Mars indicated 15 and the Moon 25, for a total of 40, one-half of which is 20. In addition 25 for the rising time of Taurus plus 35 for Leo total 60, one-third of which is 20. And Mercury in Aries with Saturn indicated 20. In his 21st year the same stars were still in control: 19 for Leo <=Sun> plus 8 for Taurus <=Venus> plus 15 for Mars total 42, one-half of which is 21. The rising time of Aries, 21 years, 8 months, plus 20 for Mercury total 41 years 8 months, one-half of which is 20 years, 10 months. In his 22nd year the same stars were still in control: 19 for Leo <=Sun> plus 25 for Taurus total 44, one-half of which is 22. Venus and Mars held the 23rd year: 8 for Venus plus 15 for Mars total 23.

Thus, as often happens, the stars which seem to be configured well, if judged from a broad, overall survey, are really indicative of reversals, since they are counteracted by the power of the chronocrators. For instance: 21 was indicated by 19 for Leo <=Sun> plus 12 for Jupiter in Leo, two-thirds of which is 20 years, 8 months. In addition Jupiter and the Sun trine indicated the same. Therefore he had friendship with a great, royal personage, from whom he expected the right to wear a wreath and a high priesthood. Unquestionably this would have come to pass—<u>if</u> Mars had not been operative and in superior aspect. And since Saturn was in the same sign as the stars which were providing the gift <Sun Mercury>, investigations, delays, expenses, and jealousy attended him. The obstacle to his elevation was not so much Saturn trine with Jupiter, as it was Mars in superior aspect, from a sign of a different sect. The critical point was characterized by illness, bleeding, obstacles to his elevation, the treachery of slaves, attacks, penalties, poverty. Then later the native became successful: an upward trend developed for the following period, and he was put under the simultaneous influence of benefics and malefics. There will be occupations and great expenditures, or there will be independence resulting from previous activity or from some other source, including the help of friends.

The results come to pass after the completion of the rising times of the signs or the periods of the stars, just as the King himself says about a nativity: "The native, while passing through the current chronocratorship of Venus, will be childless, bereft of the necessities of life, and, since he lacks everything, will live like a beggar." Chronocratorships begin to be active when they come to have full control. At that time they prepare (in good forecasts) friendships, associations, profits, fellow-feeling, rank; in bad forecasts, they prepare afflictions and crises.

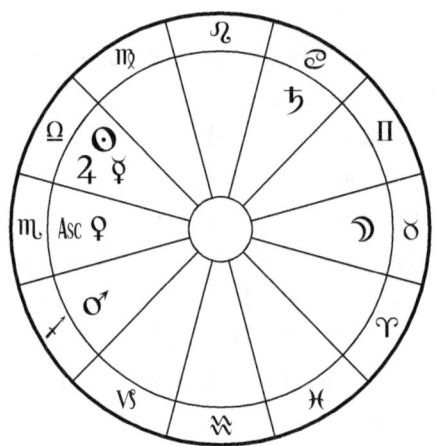

An example: Sun, Jupiter, Mercury in Libra, Moon in Taurus, Saturn in Cancer, Mars in Sagittarius, Venus, Ascendant in Scorpio, klima 2. During his 40th year he was condemned to exile. The 40th year was indicated by the superior aspect of Saturn to Libra: 32 degrees for Cancer plus 8 for Libra <=Venus> total 40. Also the opposition of the Moon to Venus <was operative>: 25 for Taurus <=Moon> plus 15 for Scorpio <=Mars> total 40. Consequently the results were activated through female persons and for the purpose of profit. And again the "contact" of the Moon with Mars <was operative>: 25 for the Moon plus 15 for Mars total 40.

(As the King says: "Let the Moon be in any sign or at an angle, and let the star of Mars be just preceding or just following the Moon in the contiguous sign; then the Moon has 'contact' with it. And so, even if the star is not in the same sign as the Moon, but is found in the adjoining sign, or in the sign in square or in opposition, then consider the contact to be solid. Sum up their periods or the rising times of the signs to forecast the chronocratorship".)

First of all, as we have said before, it is necessary to begin with the overall forecast, then to investigate how the stars are configured, whether these configurations are benefic or bad, in what place they occur, and what this can signify; then investigate the phases of the stars in conjunction or in aspect. Having done this, predict the effects at the allotments. For instance, the aspect of opposition or of square is not always malefic, but is occasionally <benefic>. Just as <this aspect's> influence is changed in the overall forecast by its place, its aspect, its angle, or the nature of another star, in the same way, its influence in the distribution of chronocrators is changed or is strengthened by the current transits of the stars. It is necessary to pay attention to the transits of the stars, so that these directions may prove to be accurate and to have an easily recognizable force.

In order not to seem to be elaborating the same rules over and over, I will append what the King has said about these matters, in his own words.

> "Every star, whether situated in its proper place or square to its place, if it is beneficial or harmful to the nativity...at a similar place it is damaging to the chronocratorships of the nativity. If one is helpful, the other harmful, and both are at their proper places or square with those places, the star which brings gain will make the distribution when it comes to the place of the malefic; the other star will take away what it previously distributed, because when either is situated in square, the one becomes the bestower, the others (since it is in aspect with the giver) exhibits a lessening of the damage."

Again the King says:

> "It is necessary to consider how the star which rules the chronocratorship is located relative to the character of the nativity, and <it is also necessary> to consider the places of control, accomplishment, and harm. The <place> where the stars happen to be located must be considered not only at the beginning of the chronocratorship, but also in the succeeding period, and the transits of the remaining stars must be taken into account, viz. the transits which aspect or sit with the ruler of the period, with Mercury and the Moon factored into the interpretation. For it is possible at the beginning of the period, even though these stars are favorable, that the benefic can be at the Place of Accomplishment or can be making a transit <of the Place> at any given period, and that a malefic can also be in transit. If so, even though the chronocratorship is good, a loss of revenue will occur. Vice-versa, even though the chronocratorship if reversed

<=negative>, if a benefic is in the Place of Accomplishment, and if the malefic is operative with respect to the nativity, for as long as the malefic is chronocrator, during that time the period will be full of accomplishment, with the chronocratorship adverse to nothing. The <malefic> however will show itself by the difficulties and repulsions inherent in it. In either case observe the transits of each star into the sign which most concerns the nativity.

"Carefully examine the motion of the Moon, because whenever it is rising, beheld by Mars or Saturn square to the right of left, one must beware of the transmission—which will be in no way beneficial. If this happens in the chronocratorship of a malefic, e.g., in the chronocratorship of the star of Mars, the native will come into close confinement or be involved with wounds. If the star of Mercury is associated in this chronocratorship, i.e., by being in conjunction with the star of Mars or by being in one of the signs belonging to the star of Mars, it indicates that the assault or imprisonment will occur because of documents. Saturn in aspect or in conjunction <shows it occurs> because of old matters, ancestral matters or the like, or because of an older person. If the star of Venus is chronocrator, and if the star of Mars happens to be in the houses of the star of Venus, <the attack occurs> because of a female person. If the star of Jupiter is chronocrator and if the star of Mars is in the houses of Jupiter, <it occurs> because of royalty or magnates.

"The native obtains great advancement if the star of Jupiter, while being chronocrator, is at the Midheaven or in the Place of Accomplishment with the star of Mars. When Jupiter and Mars are providing the active impulse, it will be necessary to see if the star of Saturn is coming into a transit or opposition, with the result that the chronocratorship of occupations becomes contrary. If the star of Mercury is the ruler, and if the star of Jupiter receives the chronocratorship from Mercury, the native will advance in business and will fare well at those times. If <Mercury> is favorably situated at the nativity, the native will engage in greater activities, proportionate to the distinction of the nativity—for this is changed to that and that is changed to this by differences in the hours of birth.

"If the places appropriate to the nativity seem invalid, judging from the positions of the stars, and if the chronocrator bestows anything (*as we previously said, this is the star which is at the Place of Accomplishment*), despite being profitable, it causes the income to be transitory because of the inappropriate asterisms at the nativity. The things which are granted by the asterisms proper to a nativity remain valid if they are appropriately given at a chronocratorship, i.e., if most of the benefic stars are associated with either one, are in the signs which pertain to the nativity, and are in aspect with the star which rules the chronocratorship at the time of the nativity.

"The star of Saturn coming into the place brings reversals and the chilling of affairs; if it comes into a place of <several> stars in conjunction and if the star of Mars has the Place of Accomplishment while the star of Saturn has the Place of Employments, it brings mortal danger. In every case the star of Saturn in the Sign of Accomplishment must be considered harmful. <It is also harmful> when in opposition to this Place and to the places of the stars of Mars, Venus, and Mercury, depending on its relationship to any of them. The same is true of the star of Mercury when it is in the places of the Moon and in its own signs, while aspected by Mars and Saturn. Likewise for the star of Venus. Every star when suitably located in its signs at the nativity … in the places of the Sun and Moon, and interwoven in the previously mentioned combined relationships. They reveal a similar type of result when the ruler of the chronocrator shares control with the remaining stars which are associated with it.

"In every case the phases of the Moon waxing from new to the quarter must be observed, particularly in the X Sign <=MC> (as was mentioned) and when aspected by malefics. If the stars of Mars and Saturn behold the opposing place at the time of the nativity, with the Moon passing through the ruling places … The Moon is helpful when it is in the place of benefics, if indeed it is discovered to be in the places which are opportune for the nativity."

O Marcus, I have researched and discovered these matters with much ascetic labor, and I have compiled and published these systems. Consequently, I adjure you by the Sun, the Moon, and the orbits of the five stars, by Nature, Providence, and the four elements, not to share this too quickly with any unlearned person nor with any chance acquaintance, but to consider my labor, my longing, and my long devotion to and research of these matters. Estimating this work of years to be worth much money, I have left it to you, for money is easily spent and attracts envy and treachery, but my compositions will bring you a livelihood, fame, honor, pleasure, and profit, if you handle them in an orderly, secure manner (as I have described above), not in a controversial or trivial manner. And considering the exertion to be the same as if you yourself had compiled this—but indeed you did exert yourself when you received this art and when you were selected, giving a worthy recompense. Share this knowledge with those who are capable of it. In so doing, you will glorify both me and my science, and you will benefit yourself and show yourself to be diligent and a lover of beauty.

May your wishes be fulfilled if you keep your oath. I have finished.

The End of Book VII of the *Genethlialogy* of Vettius Valens of Antioch at Daphne.

Book VIII

The *Anthologies* of Vettius Valens of Antioch: Book VIII

1. The Construction of the First Table

The first table from 1° to 6° is constructed as follows: the figure 2 is entered next to Libra 1°

    Libra 1°   2
    Libra 2°   4
    Libra 3°   6
    Libra 4°   8
    Libra 5°   10
    Libra 6°   12

There is a progressive increase of 2.

At Libra 7° this sequence is broken and a factor of 14 is added for a total of 26 to be entered next to Libra 7°:

    Libra 7°   26
    Libra 8°   28
    Libra 9°   30
    Libra 10°   2
    Libra 11°   4
    Libra 12°   6

Here again 14 is added to the sequence for a total of 20 next to Libra 13°:

    Libra 13°   20
    Libra 14°   22

Libra 15° 24
Libra 16° 26
Libra 17° 28
Libra 18° 30

Here again 14 is added to the sequence for a total of 44, from which 30 is subtracted, leaving 14. This figure will be entered next to Libra 19°:

Libra 19° 14
Libra 20° 16
Libra 21° 18
Libra 22° 20
Libra 23° 22
Libra 24° 24

Again 14 is added to the sequence for a total of 38, from which 30 is subtracted, leaving 8. This figure will be entered next to Libra 25°:

Libra 25° 8
Libra 26° 10
Libra 27° 12
Libra 28° 14
Libra 29° 16
Libra 30° 18

So every 6° the sequence will be broken, 14 will be added, then 2 will be added <per degree> in each sign. Therefore Libra will have the figure 2 next to Libra 1° and 18 next to Libra 30°. Leo and Pisces have the same arrangement of figures as Libra.

Next in order Scorpio will have 14 next to Scorpio 1°, 2 will be added to each degree in the series, giving 24 next to Scorpio 6°. Then the sequence is broken, finishing with 30 next to Scorpio 30°. Aries and Virgo will have the same numbers.

In order to explain the construction more briefly so that the table as a whole and its particulars may be remembered, calculate the increments <between signs> as follows: 2 is entered next to Libra 1°. To this figure I add 12 (for the circle of signs) for a total of 14. Scorpio has this figure entered next to Scorpio 1°. Add 12 again to this 14 for a total of 26. Sagittarius has this figure, 26, next to Sagittarius 1°. Going in the order of signs and adding 12, we can find the correct figure to be entered next to the first degree of each sign. By adding 12 <to the figure at 1° of each sign> and by breaking the sequence with the addition of 14, we can construct the entire table. The figure next to Sagittarius 1° will be the same as Taurus 1°; Aquarius 1° will be the same as Cancer 1°; Capricorn 1° will be the same as Gemini 1°. In one respect these pairs will have similar powers and will support each other mutually, but in other respects they will be different because of their different rising times.

This table also has the years tabulated beside the figures and the degrees as an example <of the procedure>. Intelligent students will easily grasp the precise calculations for each klima and for changes in the location <of the nativity>.

2. The Scientific Construction of the Second Table

Having described the organization of the table, we must go on to give the rationale for its construction. The additional factor in the sequence, 14, indicates the "illumination" of the Moon, while the progressive increase of 12 <from sign to sign> indicates the "fingers" of the Sun. Two times 14 equals 28, the Moon's period. So, since 2 is entered next to Libra 1°, we subtract 1;40 from it for a result of 0;20—which is a magnitude of one-third. (This divided into 60 yields 180. I split 180 up into sixtieths for a result of 10,800. I divide this into 540°, i.e., into 1½ circles, and the result is 0;20.) This figure will be placed beside Libra 1°. This 3 becomes 60, which is equivalent to one year.

We bring the remaining years into the calculation as follows, adding 2;20 to each <degree>:

Libra 1°	0;20
Libra 2°	2;40
Libra 3°	5;0
Libra 4°	7;20
Libra 5°	9;40
Libra 6°	12;0

Next we add 14 (the Moon's illumination) in this sequence to the 12, for a result of 26;0. We subtract 1;40 from this and are left with 24;20 to be entered next to Libra 7°. We then revert to the factor 2;20 and place 26;40 next to Libra 8°:

Libra 7°	24;20
Libra 8°	26;40
Libra 9°	29;0
Libra 10°	1;20
Libra 11°	3;40
Libra 12°	6;0

and so on.

At the point where the sequence is broken and at the initial numbers we must subtract 1;40, then continue with the addition factor 2;20. Use this procedure in the same way for the rest of the signs: we will find (for the second table) the figure to be entered next to the first degree of each sign in the same way we found it for the first table.

3. The Fixing of the Degree in the Ascendant with Reference to the Two Appended Tables

First of all, it is necessary to determine the precise position of the Sun in degrees, then to examine the previous new Moon (if it was a new-Moon nativity <=between new and full Moon>). Find when the new Moon occurred—at what hour and what degree of the zodiac. Then add the total number of days and hours from the new Moon to the day and hour of the birth and calculate what fraction this period is of the total time between new and full Moon (i.e., 15 days). Then subtract this from the magnitude of the Sun's degree-position. (This procedure is for day births; for night births subtract from the degree in opposition to the Sun.) Treat the result as a fraction of an hour.

Alternatively, count from the position of the Sun to that of the Moon and take 1/12 of that figure. See what fraction of the 15 days this is. Then subtract this from the magnitude <of the Sun's position>, and consider the remainder to be a fraction of an hour. So, if hour 4 is given, we consider this as 3 hours plus a fraction—not everyone can be born on the stroke of the hour. Because of this fact, twins have much variation in their lives>due to the changes of hours, signs, and sequences, because it happens that one of the twins will be short-lived, or will die immediately at birth, the other may be long-lived, depending on whether the hour does or does not make the connection.

If the Moon is past full, it is necessary to calculate and find the fraction in the same way. When the Sun and Moon are in syzygy, or if the Moon is in the sign of the full Moon and is no more than 2° or 3° from opposition, the hour will be considered full. Its fraction will be the number of degrees the Moon (i.e., at its *phōtismos* <=phase>) is from either new or full, whichever is the case. If the hour is not in accord with the sect/distribution, by moving ahead or back one degree, we can determine the error in the data, particularly for a native who has died. For it is possible from these to find the years of life. For this reason the investigation must not be carried out carelessly; instead the prediction must be made after working with skill and accuracy. It is necessary to determine if the distance from the day and position of the new Moon to the birth date, i.e., to the Moon's position then, must be considered, or from the Sun's position to the Moon's, or from the *phōtismos* (i.e., the point in opposition to the Sun) to the full Moon.

As an example: Sun in Taurus 3°, Moon in Aries 2°. The distance from the Sun to the Moon is 329°, which is 27 lunar days; the distance from the

<previous> new Moon to the Moon's position is 29 days. I count off the days from new to full Moon, 15; there are 14 days <since full Moon>. I multiply this by 12° for a result of 168°. The distance from the point in opposition to the Sun (Scorpio 3°) to the Moon's position is 149°. Now 168° exceeds 149° by 19°. It is necessary to calculate in such a way that the numbers are equal. So the distance <to be considered> will not be from the time and position of the new Moon, but from the position of the current syzygy, i.e., the full Moon. Therefore it is necessary to subtract the apparent excess, 19°, which equals 1½ lunar days, from this amount. So, if we subtract the 1½ days from the 14 days, the result will be 12½, the total from the point in opposition to the Sun to the Moon's position. Since from the Moon's position to the next new Moon there are 32°, which is 2½ lunar days, if we add the 2½ to the 12½, <we find> the 15 days of the cycle <from full to new> will be completed. (The synodic period of the Moon is 29 days; the sidereal period is 27⅓; the anomalistic period is 27½.)

An additional procedure: calculate the distance from the new Moon to the Moon's position <at the nativity>, or from the full Moon to the Moon's position. Then, if the amount is less than 180°, use the indicated method. If it is more than 180°, subtract 180° and determine what fraction of the <Moon's> motion the remainder is. Then multiply this by the hourly magnitude.

Another procedure: alternatively we find the amount by multiplying by 12 the figure entered at the Sun's position (for night births, multiply the figure entered at the point in opposition to the Sun). Then we multiply this figure by the time in hours given for the delivery. After casting out 360, we consider the remainder to be the horoscopic gnomon. Then take the distance according to rising times from the Sun to the Moon and compare it to this first horoscopic gnomon. If the solar gnomon is greater, add a factor to the Ascendant. If it is less, subtract. The factor to be added or subtracted is indicated by the excess of the solar magnitude. The total amount (before the adjustment) will be derived from the addition or subtraction of the hour or fraction of an hour.

4. How to Establish the Hour of Birth for Twins

The following will be the method for twins: if the first twin is said to have been born at the first hour, assume that both were born in the same one-half, one of them in the … quarter, the other in the other quarter, the fourth. It is also possible for both to have been born in the same quarter hour and for one to have followed the other.

If the first is said to have been born at the beginning of hour 2, the second at hour 3, assume that he was born at hour 2 ½.

If he is said to have been born at hour 5, assume he was born at hour 4 ½.

If at hour 7, assume it was hour 6 ½.
If at hour 8, assume it was hour 7 ½.
If at hour 10, assume it was hour 9 ½.
If at hour 11, assume it was hour 10 ½.

If at hour 12, the report is accurate; it is not possible for another interval to be made <between them>.

If the first is said to have been born well into hour 1 and the second at hour 2, it is not possible. The second will have been born at hour 2 ½ or 2 ¾.

If the first is said to have been born at hour 2, the second at hour 3, it is not possible; he was born at hour 3 ½.

If the first is said to have been born at hour 3, the second at hour 4, this is not possible; he was born at hour 3 or hour 4 ½.

...

If the first is said to have been born at hour 6, the second at hour 7, this is not possible; the second was born at hour 6 or 7 ½.

If the first at hour 7, the second at 8, assume that it was 8 ½.

If the first at 8, the second at 9, this is not possible; the second was at hour 8 or 9 ½.

If the first was at hour 9, the second at 10, this is not possible; the second was at hour 9 or 10 ½.

If the first was at 10, the second at 11, assume that the second was born at hour 10, or in the first hour of the night.

It is possible for twins to be born in the same quarter of an hour. The rapid rotation of the hours, bringing with it a change of degrees, makes the possible points of time uncountable. This rapid motion brings great effects from the briefest of intervals, making one twin long-lived; or it can bring small effects from great intervals, making the other twin short-lived. It is necessary then to determine the intervening degrees and to calculate the difference.

5. The Method for Using the Two Appended Tables

The first table is designed for finding the length of life, and it derives its basis and its method of use from the degree of the Ascendant. The length <of the seasonal hour> (for the correct klima) which is entered next to the degree found to be in the Ascendant is multiplied by 12. We then take ⅟₃₀th of this amount, and we say that the degrees entered there allot that same number years and that the hour of death is that number of years away. In the same way, we can take ⅟₆₀th of the result of the multiplication by 12 and calculate that each degree of the sign will allot that many years. If the degree in the Ascendant is at a connection/node, the native will be short-lived.

Entering the table at the degree of the sign in the Ascendant, we see which number is placed next to it. We determine what fraction of 60 this number is; we take the same fraction of the result of the multiplication by 12; and we consider the answer to be the years of life. It is necessary to calculate the figure (=years) entered in the table first as hours, then as days, as months, and as years. In addition, when the number 2 is entered next to the degree in the table, it is necessary to examine one-half of the time which is associated with the degree, according to the difference of klima and sign.

For example: the number 2 is entered next to Libra 1°. Two is ⅟₃₀th of 60. ⅟₃₀th of 180, the magnitude <=total rising time of the arc beginning with> Libra 1°, is 6. This figure (6) is placed next to each degree. If we calculate with this many years <per degree>, the 30° will allot 180 years, an impossible length of life for a person. So if we take ⅟₆₀th of 180, we will get 3 as the amount which 1° <of Libra> will allot. Three times 30° is 90 (or one-half of 180 is 90—which is the same thing): we can say that Libra allots a maximum of 90 years, according to the applicable degree of its magnitude.

Likewise for the rest of the signs: we multiply the magnitude entered next to each degree by 12, then take ⅟₆₀ (or ½) of it to find the minimum or the maximum years. Each degree of each sign has a different time in <the table's> progressive increase, and for this reason the seconds and the minutes of the hours and the rotation of the degrees have great effects.

I have written for those who wish to learn every systematic procedure. Each of the other astrological compilers has worked out his own complex procedures, but has not published his solutions, since each is secretive and begrudging, and neglected his readers. I, however, have investigated with much toil and long experience, and have published <my system>. This seems to be my greatest achievement, to explicate the ideas of others which have been buried in mystery. I myself could have compiled my many procedures using a fog of words, but I did not want to show myself to be like those babblers. It would be laughable to begin speaking against someone without recognizing first my own faults. Therefore if you find me speaking very often about my generosity and openness, please forgive my words. I suffered much, I endured much toil, I was cheated by many men, and I spent money that seemed to me to be inexhaustible because I was persuaded by mountebanks and greedy men. Nevertheless because of my endurance and my love for systematic knowledge, I outlasted them all. If my readers recognize the accuracy of these systems, they will give us praise with delight. Others, because of their stupidity, will envy and malign us, and they may be exalted by the illumination of mystical and secret things, and they will steal some procedures from my compilation.

So on such men I place dire curses, which I think they will suffer.

Let the readers of our collected works, works which explicate all procedures, not say: "This procedure is from the King, this other is from Petosiris, that one is from Critodemus, etc." Instead let them know that these men propounded their art in an obtuse and recondite fashion, and thereby showed that their science lacked a true foundation. We on the other hand supplied solutions, and not only revived this dying art, but also banked glory for ourselves and initiated other worthy men, attracting them not with the lure of money, but by recognizing them to be scholars and enthusiasts. We too have been controlled by this type of Fate.

Now let our discussion return to this topic, length of life. All of the previously outlined methods are accurate and tested in their own system, including the proven and amazing "three-sign" method. It comprises the following: I accurately determine the degree-positions of the Sun and the Moon relative to the degree-position of the Ascendant at the nativity. I enter the table below and I determine (using the method described below) the ending point of the three signs, starting with the Sun's position. Then I go to the sign in the Ascendant and determine in which degree it <the ending point> is located <in the Ascendant sign>, and I make this the solar gnomon.

Next do likewise <for the number> entered at the Moon's sign: apply the degrees of the solar gnomon to it and again see which sign this place belongs to. Looking for that sign in the Ascendant sign, I consider the resulting <degree-position> to be the lunar gnomon.

Next I determine whether the lunar or the solar gnomon is greater: if the Sun's gnomon is greater, the hour requires the addition of the number of signs between them <in the table>; if the Moon's, the subtraction <of the same number>. This position will be the required, scientifically established Ascendant. Therefore let no one be puzzled if the Ascendant is found in a sign different from that which was originally assumed to be the Ascendant. After the addition or subtraction, I note the degree-position of the Ascendant, I enter the table of rising times for the three-sign system, and I investigate how many years are written beside the degree which was found—taking the klima into consideration. Then I make the prediction. If the Sun's, the Moon's, or the Ascendant's position is out of place by one or two degrees, matters must be judged as discordant.

If someone should wish to test this procedure, let him move up one or two degrees and add this to the position of the Sun or Moon (if it seems to be in error), or let him calculate another Ascendant, then continue the operations in the same way. If he does so, he will find the way. It is possible to prove this procedure using nativities of those who have already died. Do not trust <astrologers> who present erroneous, hearsay nativities and who are fated to blunder; instead establish a firm foundation so as not to go wrong.

Of necessity the ray-casting and the conjunctions of the malefics with the Sun, the Moon, and the Ascendant must be taken into account, as well as the houseruling relationships, because it is from these that the factors of the basis <of the nativity> are apprehended.

We calculate the previously mentioned times of the factors for those who die at birth, or who live only a short time, by calculating first the hours, then the days, months, and years. After completing the first factor (the years), we calculate the second and the third in the same way, first hours, then days and months, and we add the result to the first factor. If we find a nativity of a long-lived person in the signs of short rising times, we combine the first or third factor, or the second and the third, or the all four together plus the remaining figures entered next to the degree; then we make the prediction.

Again, to know which of the three factors is dominant, calculate as follows: entering the table at the degree in the Ascendant, I note how many years is written next to the first factor. Then I enter the table at the degree just opposite, and I investigate the number which is written next to the years and months I found. I add this number to the position of the Ascendant in degrees, then I count off from the sign in the Ascendant—or from the Moon if it is at or following an angle. I will look at the rays of the malefics where the count stops to see if they are hindering; if so, it <the ray> will be the anaereta of the cycles. Do the same for the second and third factors.

Alternatively, I will derive the years from the <degrees> of the contact, from the signs, and from the stars, and I will see if the houseruler of "Dissolution" controls the three in any way at all. (The XII Place is "Dissolution.") It is also necessary to examine the critical time-relationships as we have explained them <previously>. If the number falls a little short, part of the span of years will be deducted. Often the critical point will occur early or will bring death after the calculated number of years. One must note in which row of the table the Ascendant is located, whether it has 2, 3, or 4 numbers, and so use all the numbers together for the years. For example, say the position of the Ascendant is Cancer 8°, which indicates the place of Taurus. <Cancer 9°> is also operative in the same row, and so this degree (9°) will control every operation. Likewise, also in Cancer, the degrees from 25° to 28° are in the place of Aquarius. So here 26° and 27° are also operative.

<The table of place equivalences is missing in the manuscripts.>

6. The Computation of the Rising Times and of the Three Factors

The computation of the rising times and of the three factors is done as follows: assume, for example, that the rising time of Aries in klima 2 is 20. I double this figure and get 40. I assign to

    Aries 1°   0;40 (This is 40 minutes.)
    Aries 2°   1;20
    Aries 3°   2;0
    Aries 4°   2;40
    Aries 5°   3;20

and so on to Aries 30°, adding 0;40 to total the 20 years.

Next we fit the second factor, starting from the first degree in a similar way: since Taurus rises in 24, I double that figure and get 48, which I add to the 20 of Aries for a result of

    Taurus 1°   20;48
    Taurus 2°   21;36
    Taurus 3°   22;24
    Taurus 4°   23;12
    Taurus 5°   24;0

and so on to Taurus 30°, adding 0;48 to the 20 <of Aries> and getting a total of 44;0.

We will derive the third factor in a corresponding way, as follows: the first degree of the third factor is

    Gemini 1°   44;56
    Gemini 2°   45;52
    Gemini 3°   46;48
    Gemini 4°   47;44
    Gemini 5°   48;40

and so on to <Gemini> 30°. By successively adding 0;56 we get a total of 72;0.

Do the same for the rest of the signs: apply the rising time of the sign as the first factor, then calculate for each degree to find the total years. Then the second factor is in the next sign, and the third factor is in the third sign, all according to whatever klima is required.

We explained the rising times in Book I; now we are specifying the factors. I think that my exposition was magisterial. It was sufficient, in the case of the rest <of the other applications of the rising times> to leave them unspecified, or when giving sample nativities, to expressly declare not just seven (as some do), but even more causes. (However we must not compare ourselves to men

7. Sample Nativities

For example, consider the following nativity: Nero year 1, Athyr 2, the third hour of the day. The Sun in Scorpio 10°, the Moon in Aquarius 30°, the Ascendant in Sagittarius. I look in the table at 10° of the Sun's position, i.e., in the column under Scorpio, and I find Pisces entered there. I transfer to Pisces the 10° of the Sun's position, and I find Libra entered there. I look <for Libra> in the Ascendant, Sagittarius. I find it at

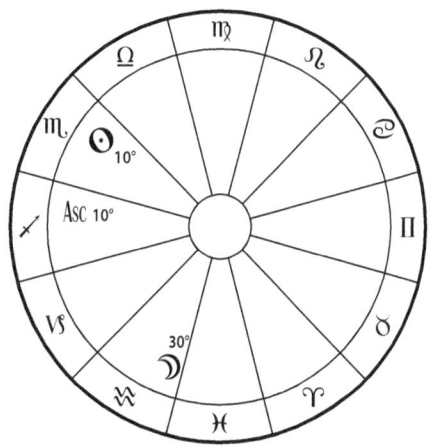

14° and 15°. This will be the <u>solar</u> <u>horoscopic</u> <u>gnomon</u>, and I make a note of it. Next I turn to the Moon's sign, Aquarius, and I see which sign is entered next to 30°. I find Aquarius again. So I transfer to Aquarius the solar gnomon, 14°, which I just discovered, and I find entered at that figure the sign Sagittarius. I investigate this in the sign of the Ascendant, and I find it at 1°, 2° and 3°. This then becomes the <u>lunar</u> <u>gnomon</u>, and it is in the first row <of the table>. The solar gnomon is in the sixth row. Since the solar gnomon is greater, and since there are 4 rows (which equal 4°) intervening <between row one and row six>, I add this amount to the 14° of the previously determined solar gnomon. So now the Ascendant is at Sagittarius 18°. Having found this, I enter the <table of> <u>apogonia</u> <at Sagittarius 18°>, and I find (under klima 6) in the third factor, 73 years. The native died in his 73rd year. Now if the lunar gnomon had been greater, I would have subtracted from the solar gnomon (14°) the addition/subtraction factor (4°). Then the Ascendant would have been at Sagittarius 10°.

Another example: klima 4, Titus year 1, Phamenoth 20/21, Sun in Pisces 29°, Moon in Capricorn 27°, Ascendant in Scorpio. At 29° <in the column> under Pisces, the position of the Sun, is entered Cancer. At Cancer 29° is entered Capricorn. I investigate this sign <Capricorn> in Scorpio, the sign in the Ascendant, and I find it at 4° and 5°. This, then, is the solar horoscopic gnomon, and I make a note of it. Next I go to the Moon's sign,

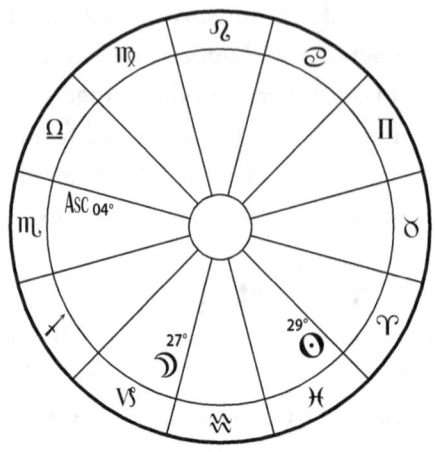

Capricorn, and at 27° I find Aries. I investigate Aries 4° and 5°, the solar gnomon, and in row 2 (at Aries 4° and 5°) I find the sign Capricorn. I investigate this sign in the Ascendant, Scorpio, and I find it at the same position, 4° and 5°, in row 2. So the solar and the lunar gnomons agree, and it is clear that the Ascendant needs no addition or subtraction. I enter the <table of> rising times at 4°, and I find (for klima 4) for the Ascendant, Scorpio, in the third factor, 72;33 years. The native died at age 72½.

Another example: Trajan year 17, klima 2, <Mesori> 17/18, the fourth hour of the night. The Sun in Leo 22°, the Moon in Taurus 14°, the Ascendant in Aries. In the table at Leo 22°, the Sun's position, I find Virgo. At Virgo 22° I find Cancer. This sign, Cancer, I investigate in the Ascendant, Aries, and I find it at 26°. So this will be the solar horoscopic gnomon. In a like manner, since Taurus 14° is the Moon's position, I next enter Taurus and find

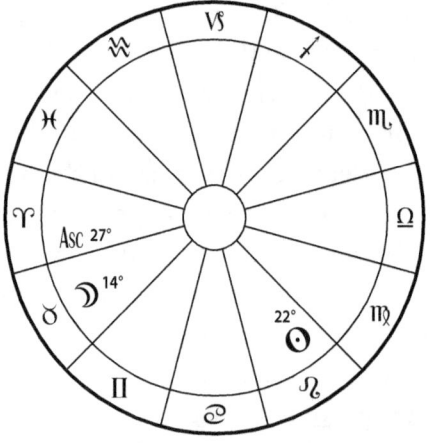

Gemini <at Taurus 14°>, then I transfer the 26° of the solar gnomon to Gemini and find Aquarius entered there <at Gemini 26°>. I investigate <Aquarius> in Aries, the Ascendant, and I find it at Aries 21°. So this is the lunar gnomon. Between it and the solar gnomon is one row, which means 1°. I add this to the previously determined <Ascendant, Aries> 26°, for a total of 27°. The Ascendant will be at Aries 27°. I enter the <table of> rising times for Aries in klima 2, and I find entered at 27°, in the second factor, 42;36 years. The native died in his 42nd year.

Another example: Trajan year 18, Payni 14, the fifth hour of the day, klima 1. The Sun in Gemini 20°, the Moon in Taurus 27°, the Ascendant in Virgo. At <Gemini> 20°, the Sun's position, is entered Cancer; at Cancer 20° is entered Virgo. I investigate Virgo in the Ascendant <Virgo>, and I find it at 1°, 2°, and 3°. This will be the solar gnomon. Next, at <Taurus> 27°, the Moon's position, is entered Aries. I investigate in Aries the solar gnomon (1°, 2°, 3°), and I find there Leo. I look for Leo in Virgo, and I find it at 4° and 5°. <This is the lunar gnomon.> There are no intervening rows, and so the Ascendant is Virgo 1°. I enter <the table of> rising times for klima 1, and I find at Virgo 1°, in the second factor, 39;36 years. The native died in his 40th year.

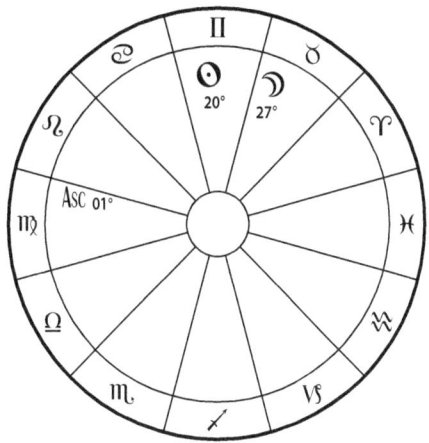

Another example: Hadrian year 12, Athyr 1, the ninth hour of the day, klima 1. The Sun in Scorpio 8°, the Moon in Capricorn 17°, the Ascendant in Pisces. At Scorpio 8° is entered Taurus, at Taurus <8°> is entered Libra. I look for Libra in Pisces, and I find it at Pisces 9° <the solar gnomon>. Next at Capricorn 17°, the lunar position, is entered Taurus. At Taurus 9°, the degree of the solar gnomon, is entered Virgo. In Pisces I find Virgo at Pisces 15° <the lunar gnomon>. There are two intervening rows, which equal 2°. I subtract this from the solar gnomon, 9°, since the lunar gnomon is greater, and the result is <Pisces> 7°. This is the Ascendant in Pisces, and next to it is entered (for klima 1) in the second factor, 26;43 years. The native lived 27 years.

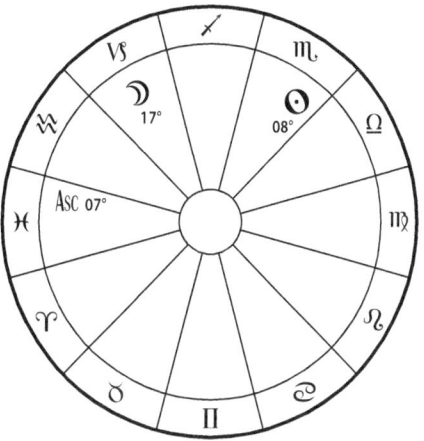

Another example: Vespasian year 1, Epiphi 22, the fifth hour of the day, klima 6. the Sun in Cancer 28°, the Moon in Scorpio 3°, the Ascendant in Libra. At Cancer 28°, the Sun's position, is entered Aquarius; at Aquarius 28° is entered Aquarius again. In Libra I find this <Aquarius> entered at 4°, 5°, 6° <the <u>solar gnomon</u>>. Next at Scorpio 3°, the Moon's position, is entered Scorpio; so in this sign I look at 4° and 5°, the solar gnomon, and I find Capricorn entered there. I find <Capricorn> in Libra at Libra 22° <the <u>lunar gnomon</u>>. Seven rows are found to be intervening between the lunar and the solar gnomons, and I subtract this figure from Libra 4°, for a result of Virgo 27° as the Ascendant. At this position for klima 6, in the second factor, is entered 81 years. The native died in his 81st year.

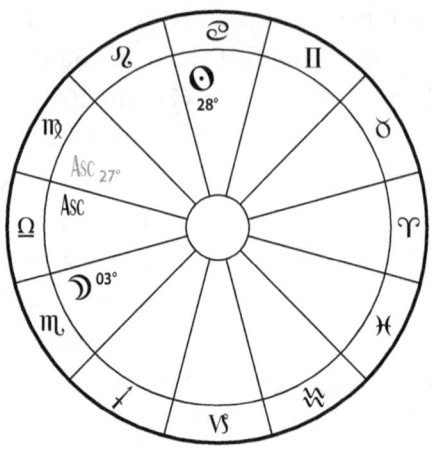

Another example: Trajan year 18, Thoth 14/15, the ninth hour of the night. The Sun in Virgo 22°, the Moon in Aquarius 4°, <the Ascendant in Leo. At Virgo 22°, the Sun's position> is entered Cancer; at Cancer <22° is Sagittarius. I find this sign in Leo at> 1°, 2°, 3°. <Next at Aquarius 4°, the Moon's position,> is entered Sagittarius. This sign likewise I find in Leo, the Ascendant, at the same degrees, 1°, 2° 3°. So Leo 1° is the Ascendant, next to which is entered (for klima 1) one year. The native died in his first year.

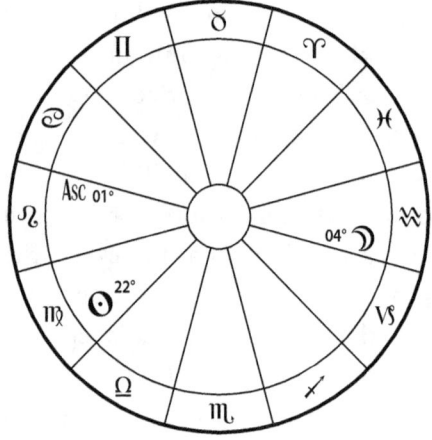

Another example: Antoninus year 5, Tybi 28/29, the eleventh hour of the night. The Sun in Aquarius 6°, the Moon in Taurus 28°, the Ascendant in Capricorn. At Aquarius 6° is entered Virgo, at Virgo <6°> is entered Cancer. I look for this sign in Capricorn, the Ascendant, and I find it at 1° and 2° <the solar gnomon>. At Taurus 28°, the Moon's position, is entered Aries. Transferring to Aries 1° and 2°, I find Leo. Then I find Leo 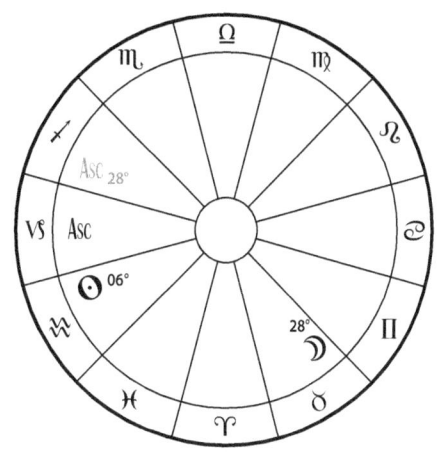 in Capricorn at 10° and 11° <the lunar gnomon>. There are three intervening rows, so I subtract 3° from Capricorn 1° for a result of Sagittarius 28° <as the Ascendant. For klima …, in the first factor, is entered 30+.> (These are months.) The native died in his third year.

Another example: Antoninus year 15, Tybi 12, the first hour of the day. The Sun in Capricorn 20°, the Moon in Gemini 28°, the Ascendant in Capricorn. At Capricorn 20° is entered Libra; at Libra <20°> Pisces, and I find this sign in Capricorn, the Ascendant, at 29° and 30° <the solar gnomon>. Next at Gemini 28°, the Moon's position, I find Aquarius. At Aquarius 29° (the solar gnomon) I again find Aquarius. I find this sign 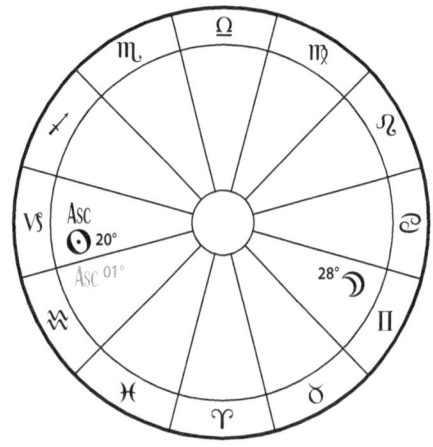 in Capricorn at 23° and 24° <the lunar gnomon>. There are two intervening rows, and I add 2° to Capricorn 28° for a result of Aquarius 1° as the Ascendant. For klima 6, 0;44 years is entered at Aquarius 1°. The native died in his first year.

Another example: Antoninus year 21, Athyr 28/29, the third hour of the night. The Sun in Sagittarius 6°, the Moon in Aquarius 3°, the Ascendant in Cancer. At Sagittarius 6° is entered Cancer. <In Cancer, Aries. In Cancer,> the Ascendant, I found it <Aries> also at 6° <the solar gnomon>. Likewise at Aquarius <3°>, the Moon's position, is entered Cancer; at Cancer 3° is entered Virgo. In Cancer, the Ascendant, I

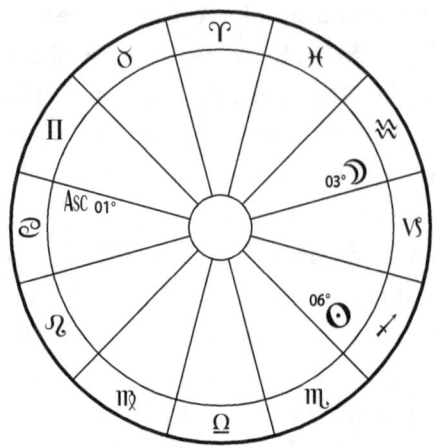

find Virgo at 20° <the lunar gnomon>. There are five intervening rows, and so I subtract 5° from Cancer 6°, for a result of Cancer 1° as the Ascendant. Next to it is entered 1;2. The native lived 1 year.

Another example: klima 6, Trajan year 8, Pharmouthi 26. Most of the sources report the Ascendant as Cancer, since they want the benefics to be at the angles, but we have found from our calculations that the Ascendant was in Gemini. The Sun in Taurus 3°, the Moon in Sagittarius 21°. At Taurus 3°, the Sun's position, is entered Aquarius. At <Aquarius 3° is found...> I found it at Gemini 23°. <At Sagittarius 21°, the Moon's position, is entered... I found

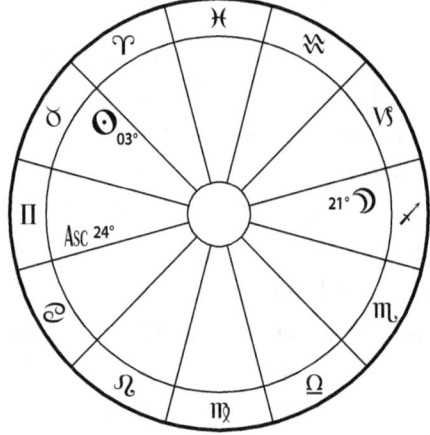

it in> Scorpio. In Gemini I found this sign <Scorpio> at 18° <the lunar gnomon>. I add 1° for the one intervening row to <Gemini> 23° <the solar gnomon>, for a result of Gemini 24°, which is the Ascendant. Entering the table at klima 6, I found 21;55. The native lived 22 years 45 days.

One who pays attention to these collected rules and methods for calculating critical times will not go astray. In the same way that the houserulers, <vital sectors>, or the ray-casting <stars> sometimes produce an increase, sometimes a decrease of years, proportionate to the aspects of the benefics, so this method too can produce an <increase or a decrease>.

There is also the following "further analysis" researched by us with great labor. We will append it with examples.

Hadrian year 9, Phamenoth 28/29, the third hour of the night. The Sun in Aries 6°, the Moon in Aries 30°, the Ascendant in Scorpio. At Aries 6° is entered Sagittarius, at Sagittarius 6° Cancer. I find this sign at Scorpio 22°. This then will be the <u>solar horoscopic gnomon</u>. Consulting the table at <Aries> 30°, the Moon's position, I find Scorpio. In Scorpio I found 22°, the degree number of the solar gnomon, in the same place. So

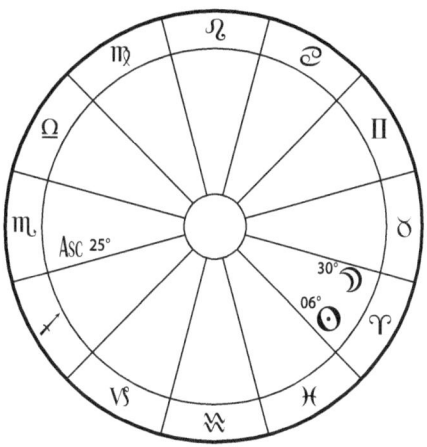

the solar and the lunar gnomons are in accord. So we make our further analysis as follows: I take the remaining degrees of the sign in the Ascendant, 8°, plus the degrees of the Sun, 6°, plus those of the Moon, 30°, for a total of 44°. I count this off from the Moon's sign and the count stops at Taurus 14°, the place of Gemini. I look for this sign <Gemini> in Scorpio, the Ascendant, and I find it at 12°. There are three rows between <Scorpio> 12° and 22°, and so I add 3° to 22°. Scorpio 25° is definitely the Ascendant. At this degree (for klima 6) in the first factor is 31;28 years. The native died in his 31st year. Most <astrologers>, however, avoiding the situation of Mars as a yoke-fellow <Scorpio is a house of Mars>, reported the Ascendant to be Libra.

Another example: Hadrian year 15, Epiphi 16, the third hour of the day. The Sun in Cancer 20°, the Moon in Gemini 25°, the Ascendant in Virgo. At Cancer 20° is entered Virgo, At Virgo <20°> Cancer. I find this sign in <Virgo>, the Ascendant, at 20° <the <u>solar gnomon</u>>. Likewise at <Gemini> 25°, the Moon's position, is entered Aquarius. At Aquarius 20°, the solar gnomon, is found Aries. I find this sign in Virgo at 29° <the

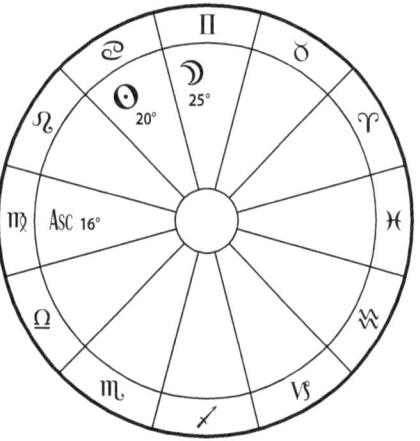

<u>lunar gnomon</u>>. Since the lunar gnomon is greater than the solar, and since there are two intervening rows, I subtract 2° from 20°, for a result of Virgo 18°. We make the further analysis as follows: I take the remaining degrees of Virgo, 12°, plus the degrees of the Sun, 20°, plus those of the Moon, 25°, for a total of

57°. I count this off from the Moon's sign; the count stops at Cancer 27°, which is marked as the place of Aquarius. Looking for Aquarius in Virgo, I find it at 26°. There are <2> rows between 26° and 18°, and I subtract this from 18°. Virgo 16° is the result. For klima 2, the figure 21;20 is entered at Virgo 16°. The native died in his 21st year.

Another example: Nero year 14, Thoth 14/15, the eleventh hour of the night. The Sun in Virgo 25°, the Moon in Aries 10°, the Ascendant in Virgo. At Virgo 25° is entered Capricorn, at Capricorn <25°> is entered Scorpio. I look for this sign in Virgo, and I find it at 11° <the solar gnomon>. Next at Aries 10°, the Moon's position, is entered Virgo; at Virgo 11°, Scorpio. <The lunar and solar gnomons are the same.> I take the remaining 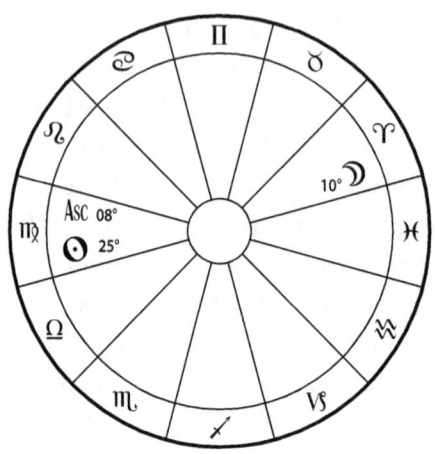 degrees in Virgo, 19°, plus the degrees of the Sun, 25°, plus those of the Moon, 10°, for a total of 54°. I count this off from the Moon's sign, and the count stops at Taurus 24°, at which Cancer is entered. I find this sign <Cancer> at Virgo 20°. There are three rows between <Virgo> 20° and 11°, and I subtract this from 11°, for a result of 8°. The Ascendant was Virgo 8°. Entering the <table of> rising times, I find (for klima 1) in the third factor, the years 86. The native died at that age.

Another example: Trajan year 12, Payni 8, the second hour of the day. The Sun in Gemini 13°, the Moon in Capricorn 4°, the Ascendant in Cancer. At Gemini 13° is entered Libra, at Libra <13°>, Virgo. I find that sign <Virgo> in Cancer, the Ascendant, at 20° <the solar gnomon>. Next at Capricorn 4°, the Moon's position, I find Virgo. At Virgo 20°, the solar gnomon, I find Cancer. I find that sign in the 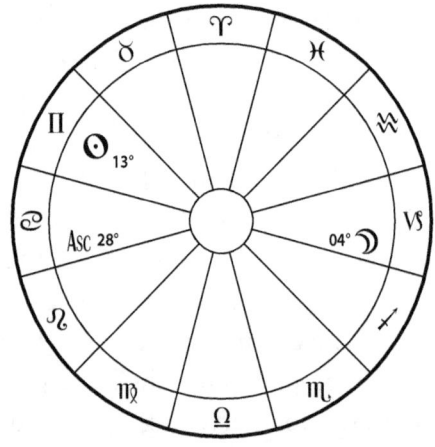 Ascendant at 4°. This is the lunar gnomon. Since the solar gnomon is greater than the lunar, I add the intervening six rows to 20°, for a result of Cancer 26°, which is the <provisional> position of the Ascendant. Next I take the remaining 4° of Cancer, plus the 13° of the Sun, plus the 4° of the Moon, for a total of 21°. I count this off from Capricorn; the count stops at 21° of the same sign. I investigate this position in Capricorn, and I find Libra. I look for Libra in Cancer, and I find it at 18°. There are two rows between this figure and 26°, and I add this again to 26° for a result of Cancer 28° as the Ascendant. That was the further analysis. Entering the table for klima 6, I find 30;25 for the first factor, 67;55 for the second, and 110;28 for the third. We calculate the first factor to be the years, the second and third to be the months; these total approximately 181 months, or 15 years, plus the 30 years of the first factor. Together they total 45 years. The native died in his 45th year. Just as I have said, I calculated first the hours entered beside the factors, then the days, the months, and the years.

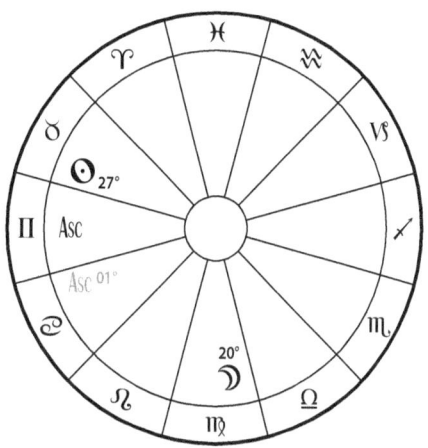

Another example: Domitian year 2, Pachon 20, the first hour. The Sun in Taurus 27°, the Moon in Virgo 20°, the Ascendant in Gemini. At Taurus 27° is entered Aries, at Aries <27°> Cancer. I find that sign in Gemini at 20° <the solar gnomon>. At Virgo 20°, the Moon's position, is entered Cancer, at Cancer 20° (the previously determined solar gnomon) is entered Virgo. I find that sign in Gemini at 4° <the lunar gnomon>. There are six rows between <Gemini> 4° and 20°; so I add 6° to the 20° for a result of Gemini 26°. Next I take the remaining degrees of Gemini, 4°, plus the 27° of the Sun, plus the 20° of the Moon, for a total of 51°. I count this off from the Moon's sign, and the count stops at Libra 21°, in the place of <Cancer?>. I find that sign at Gemini 11°/19°<?>. There are five <!> intervening rows; so I add 5° to Gemini 26°, for a result of Cancer 1° as the Ascendant. For klima 4, I find 71 years for the third factor—and this was his length of life.

Another example: Domitian year 5, Athyr 24, 5½ hours <of the day>. The Sun in Sagittarius 3°, the Moon in Gemini 4°, the Ascendant in Pisces. At Sagittarius <3°> is entered Sagittarius, again at Sagittarius 3°, Sagittarius. I find this sign <Sagittarius> in Pisces at 11° and 12° <the solar gnomon>. Next at Gemini 4°, the Moon's position, is entered Virgo, at Virgo 11° is entered Scorpio. I find this sign in Pisces at 26° <the lunar gnomon>. There are five intervening rows, and I subtract 5° from 11°, for a result of Pisces 6°. Now I take the remaining 24° <of Pisces>, plus the 3° of the Sun, plus the 4° of the Moon, for a total of 31°. I count this off from Gemini, and <the count> stops at Cancer 1°, the place of Scorpio. I find this sign in Pisces again at 26°. Seven rows intervene <between Pisces 6° and 26°>. I subtract this amount <7°> from Pisces 6°, for a result of Aquarius 29°, which is the Ascendant. For klima 4, at Aquarius 29° is entered 22;33 for the first factor and 42;27 for the second, a total of 65. He died in his 65th year.

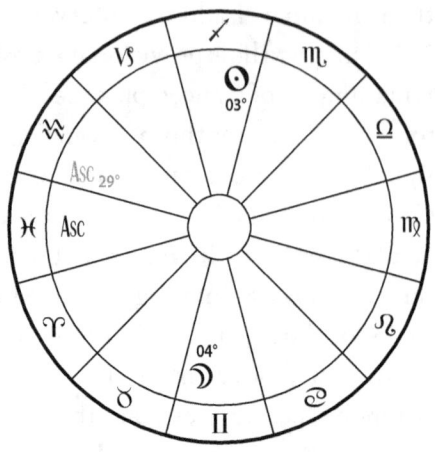

Another example: Titus year 2, Choiak 1, 9½ hours <of the day>. The Sun in Sagittarius 8°, the Moon in Taurus 27°, the Ascendant in Taurus. At Sagittarius 8° is entered Cancer, at Cancer <8°>, Taurus. I find this sign <Taurus> in itself, in the Ascendant, at 1°, 2°, 3° <the solar gnomon>. At Taurus 27°, the Moon's position, is entered Aries; at Aries 1°, 2°, 3° is entered Leo. I find this sign in Taurus at 19° <the lunar gnomon>. There are six intervening rows. I subtract this amount from Taurus 1° for a result of Aries 25°. The remaining degrees of Aries, 5°, plus 8° of the Sun, plus 27° of the Moon total 40°. I count this off from the Moon's sign, and <the count> stops at Gemini 10°, the place of Sagittarius. I find this sign in Aries at 6° and 7°… There are six<?> rows between this position and 25°. I add this to Aries 25°. The Ascendant is Taurus 1°. For the klima of Babylon, 0;48 is entered

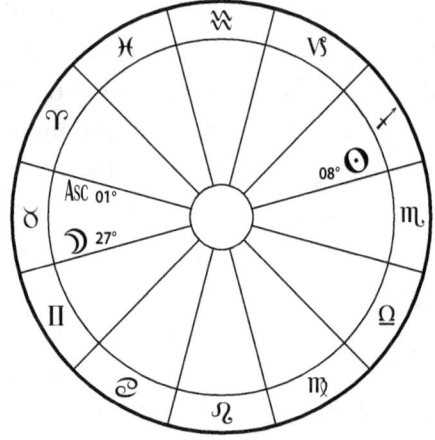

for the first factor, 24;<56> for the second, and 53;4 for the third. I added the three factors to get 78;48. He lived 77;42 years.

Another example: Antoninus year 14, Mechir 23, the ninth hour of the day. The Sun in Pisces 3°, the Moon in Leo 13°, the Ascendant in Cancer. At <Pisces> 3°, the Sun's position, is entered Pisces, <at Pisces 3° is entered Pisces again, and> I find that sign in Cancer at 10° <the solar gnomon>. Likewise at Leo 13°, the Moon's position, is entered Aquarius, at <Aquarius> 10°, Libra. I find this sign in Cancer at 18° <the

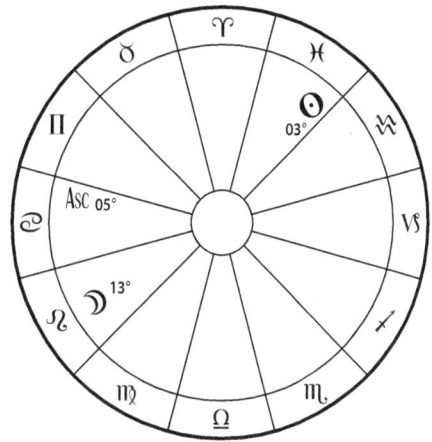

lunar gnomon>. There are two intervening signs; so I subtract 2° from 10° for a result of <Cancer> 8°. I take the remaining degrees of Cancer, 22°, plus 3° for the Sun, plus 13° for the Moon, for a total of 38°. I count this off from the Moon's sign, and the count stops at Virgo 8°, a place of Libra. I find this sign in Cancer at 18°. There are three signs between this position and 8°. I subtract this <3°> from 8°, and the result is Cancer 5° <as the Ascendant>. 5;30 is entered there. He died in his sixth year.

Another example: Hadrian year 5, Pachon 23/24, the tenth hour of the night. <The Ascendant was said to be> in Capricorn, but we found it to be in Aquarius when calculated as follows. The Sun in Taurus 29°, the Moon in Scorpio 15°. At Taurus 29° is entered Scorpio, at Scorpio <29°>, Libra. I find this sign in Aquarius at 10° <the solar gnomon>. Next at <Scorpio> 15°, the Moon's position, is entered Virgo, in Virgo at the previously

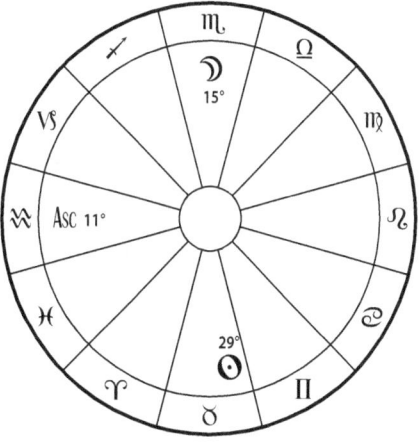

determined solar gnomon, <10°>, is entered Libra. I find this sign in Aquarius at the same degree-position. <The lunar and the solar gnomons are the same.> The remaining degrees in Aquarius, 20°, plus the 29° of the Sun, plus the 15° of the Moon total 64°. I count this off from the Moon's sign and <the count> stops at Capricorn 4°, a place of Virgo. I look for Virgo in Aquarius, the Ascendant, and I find it at 6°. There is one row <between Aquarius 6° and 10°>, and I add this 1° to <Aquarius> 10°, and find the Ascendant to be Aquarius 11°. At this position (for klima 2) is entered 31;25 in the second factor. He died at the end of his 32nd year.

Be aware that the given Ascendant must not be assumed to be correct in every case, particularly for those born at night or during the winter season when the Sun-time can only be estimated because of the cloudiness of the sky. In such cases, evaluate according to the calculated Ascendant and the signs on either side <of it>. If you wish to test the effects of the sign rising just before <the Ascendant>, it will be necessary to subtract from the Moon's position at the calculated time an amount of time correct for the <particular> sign and hour, using the Moon's daily motion. For the sign which follows the Ascendant, add the correct amount to the Moon's position. When done in this way, the analysis will be considered infallible.

An example: Hadrian year 3, Phamenoth 29/30, 1½ hours of the night. The Sun in Aries 7°, the Moon in Pisces 2°, the Ascendant in Scorpio. This sign by itself does not reveal the underlying number of years, but the number is found from the results of the forecast and from the analysis of Sagittarius in Scorpio as follows: at Aries 7° is entered Sagittarius, at Sagittarius 7° is entered Cancer. I investigate this sign <Cancer> in Sagit- 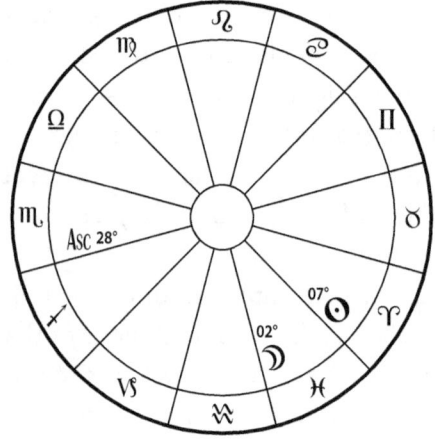 tarius, which must be the Ascendant if the real one is to be determined, clearly at the same degree-position, 6° <same row as 7°>. Next at Pisces 2°, the Moon's position, is entered Pisces; at Pisces 6° is entered Taurus. <I find> this sign in Sagittarius at 12°. There is one intervening row, and I subtract this amount from <Sagittarius> 6°, for a result of Sagittarius 5°. Next I take the remaining degrees in Sagittarius, 25°, plus 7° for the Sun, plus 2° for the Moon, for a total of 34°. This I count off from the Moon's sign, and the count stops at Aries 4°, a place of Capricorn. I find Capricorn in Sagittarius at 24°. There are seven rows between this figure and <Sagittarius> 5°, and I subtract this 7° from Sagittarius 5° for a result of Scorpio 28°, which is the Ascendant. For klima 2 <at Scorpio 28°> is entered as the first factor 33;<36>. He died at the end of his 33rd year.

The preceding detailed analysis being as described, we can find another method occasionally suitable for a few nativities. We will append it, lest anyone become entangled and hence reject this whole procedure. If the luminaries are found in square, in opposition, or in the same sign (i.e., the Moon with the Sun), we calculate as follows: for example, the Sun in Sagittarius 30°, the Moon in Sagittarius 25°, the Ascendant in Virgo. At Sagittarius 30° is entered Aries, at Aries 30°, Scorpio. I find this sign in Virgo at 11°. This is the <u>solar</u> <u>gnomon</u>. Likewise at Sagittarius 25°, the Moon's position, is entered Scorpio. I investigate Scorpio 25° (the same degree-position), and I find there Gemini. I look for <Gemini> in Virgo, and I find it at 26°. This will be the <u>lunar</u> <u>gnomon</u>. There are five rows between this figure and the solar gnomon. I subtract this 5° from <Virgo> 11°, for a result of Virgo 6° as the Ascendant.

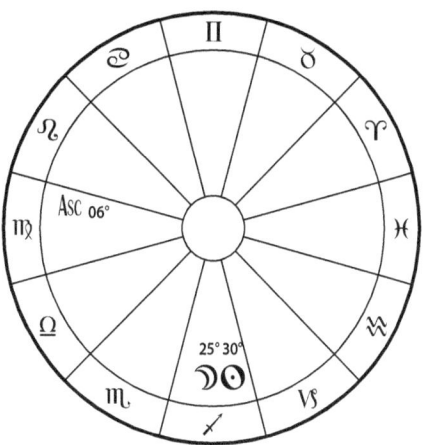

<Another example:> …For klima 7, 71 years is entered there, which was the length of his life.

Another example: the Sun in Sagittarius 3°, the Moon in Sagittarius 7°, the Ascendant in Libra. At Sagittarius 3° is entered Sagittarius, and I find this sign in Libra at 11°. This is the <u>solar</u> <u>gnomon</u>. Likewise at Sagittarius 7°, the Moon's position, is entered Cancer; at Cancer 7° (the same degree-position again) I find Aries. I find this sign in Libra at 18°. This is the <u>lunar</u> <u>gnomon</u>. There are two intervening rows. I subtract this 2° from the solar gnomon, 11°, for a result of <Libra> 9°. So Libra 9° is the Ascendant…

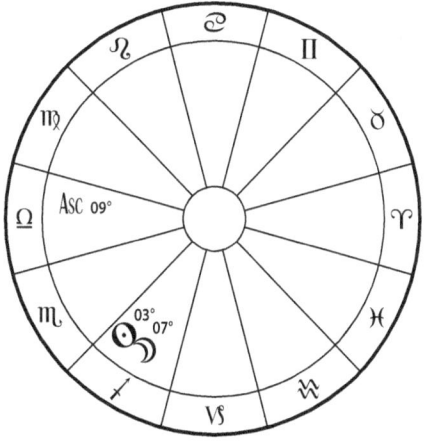

…with the Sun and the Moon together. These hold everything together; they control the phases of the stars whirling, each in its own way, and alternating their effects. But in our system, there are 360° in the circle of the heavens which the Sun, the cosmocrator, gallops over in the course of one year, allotting a fixed time to each person, but changing the types of death. For it is possible to see many men dying in the same year, not all, however, on the same day or hour nor from the same affliction or doom. The Sun traverses one degree in one 24-hour period, but it does not bring the same things to those born during that time period because of the variation of minutes and hours.

In fact, its position, its hours, and its minutes cause a great variation in the addition and subtraction of years, particularly when it comes at the sequence breaks. For example: at Leo 12° is entered 6, a magnitude which indicates 20 years 6 months. At 13° of the same sign, since it is a sequence break, is entered 20, which indicates 75 <!> years. Consider the same to be true for the rest of the signs. As the result of a jump from the lesser to the greater numbers in the sequence, the native may become long-lived, or vice-versa, as a result of a jump from a large to a small number, he may become short-lived. There are sequences which give men an average lifespan, when the number located there is an intermediate value. It is from these considerations that one can make the determination for twins, who are born at very nearly the same hour.

For every nativity the solar and the lunar degree-positions must be closely observed to see if they are coming to a node. (If so, they cause a lack of success in enterprises; even more, they also involve men in violent dooms and afflictions and bring a death that is extraordinary, far-famed, sudden, and unexpected. The diseases of these men are dangerous and incurable.) Consequently, the basis of this method is secure and infallible; the factors however can be in error because of <incorrect> degree-positions of the luminaries and the Ascendant. Therefore the examinations and the calculation must be done with all care and precision, since this science promises nothing casual or ordinary, but rather divinity and immortality.

Since the topic of long- and short-lived men has been raised, we will go on with it because of its strangeness and the disbelief of error. We want our treatise to remain unassailable. Whenever the degree in the Ascendant is found to be in the correct sequential order, (i.e., by the progressive addition of 2°), there will rarely be any error about the length of life. If it is off by one degree, there will not be a great difference in the years. However, when it comes at the break in the sequence or at the 30° point, there is need of much caution because of the extreme variation in the years. For example: at Cancer 27° is entered 104 years; at Cancer 28°, <6> years. So here is a great difference, and one can imagine that someone born at these degrees will live or die more or less time than that indicated for the exact degree.[1] This procedure seems to be

---

[1] This statement is true: the second place with its minutes indicates which are the long-

unbelievable, but the scientific, exact degree of the Sun manifests its influence, allots the fixed number of years, and dulls the persuasiveness of error.

The numbers associated with the 30° segments in the summer hemisphere should be closely observed. In all cases, some men will live the lifespans <indicated there>. But it is <im>possible for very many to live the periods entered in the winter hemisphere, e.g., 91 or 75. It is necessary to calculate from the equinoctial signs, Aries and Libra, the additions and subtractions of the years according to their corresponding magnitudes, and it is necessary to know the number of years for each and every sign. It is not possible for Libra<?> to allot more than 91 years, nor Capricorn more than 75. If some conscienceless <astrologer>, when calculating nativities in this <winter> hemisphere, says the someone lived more than 91 years, right then one can know that he is lying and is willing to use invalid procedures. While convicting himself of ignorance, he is trying to eclipse the truth…

If the factor for the length-of-life is imprecise by <only> a fraction of an hour, but is nearly accurate and is taking effect at the date in question, then an almost fatal critical point and a dangerous crisis will happen, but death will not ensue, because the interval between the years is doubtful and vague. For example, if someone is born at the third hour, it will also be necessary to examine the second and the fourth hour, and their length-of-life factors, to see if they are related to the given hour. (It is also possible for the observation of the Ascendant to have been wrong.) I do not say to consider the hours more distant from the third, such as the seventh, the eighth, the ninth, the tenth, the eleventh, and the twelfth, because the matter will become too elaborate—just the closest. It is necessary to calculate one-half of the years for the degrees following <in the table>, since (as I said) each degree in the table increases its number by a factor of two, and one-half of this figure is calculated as the years. For example: if, when multiplied by 12, its magnitude is 7, then this is one-half of 16, 15, or 14½ years. If the degree in the Ascendant is at the sequence break, this will cause one subtraction of years from the amount, i.e., from 7, 16, 15, or 14½ <?>.

It is necessary to determine the degree-position of the Sun precisely: if it is given in minutes, I subtract a corresponding amount…

…From the observation of the Sun, I find the Ascendant to be at Virgo 1°…

---

lived or short-lived of those nativities born not at the exact degree. - marginal gloss

8. Examples of the Previous Procedure Using Table II

An example: Trajan year 6, Choiak ½, the eighth hour of the night, a conjunction of Sun and Moon at Sagittarius 8° 30'. I take the time from the day and hour of the new Moon to the day and hour of the nativity, which is 7 days 14 hours. This amount is one-half of the period between new and full Moon (15 days). I take one-half of the hourly magnitude entered at Sagittarius 8°, which is 12, for a result of 6. I consider this the "fraction of the hour" figure. I calculate the hours, 9, <for a result of 9×12=108>, and I add this result, plus the fraction of the hour, plus 259;20 for the total rising time <enklima>. I

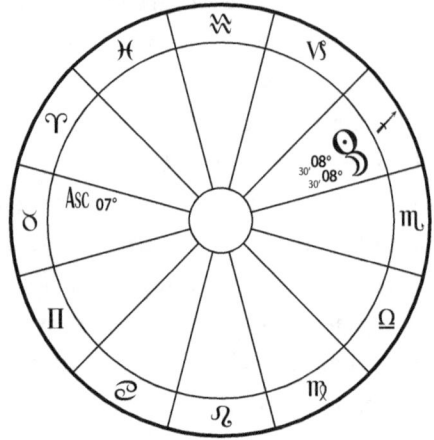

find the total to be 376;20, from which I subtract 360° (i.e., one circle), for a result of 16;20. Making a note of this, I consult the table under the total rising time, and I find entered there at Aries 29°, the hourly magnitude 16;24. Therefore this figure is operative. I add to the 29° another 8° (which I subtract from the Sun's degree-position), and Taurus 7° becomes the Ascendant. Making a note of this, I consult the first table at Taurus 7°, and I find entered there 20. Now 20 is one-third of 60. I use one-third of the magnitude as follows: since the magnitude 16;24 is entered at Aries 29°, the position which indicated the total rising time, I multiply this 16;24 by 12 and get 196;48. I take one-third of this figure and get 65½ years. He died halfway through his 65th year. As for why we subtracted the 8° from the Sun's position, and then added, I will explain that in my next discourse.

The following is a new-Moon nativity, known to me by hearsay. Those who wish to know the reality of this science will do these things: Vespasian year 7, Epiphi 25/26, the <third> hour of the night, klima 3. The Sun in Cancer 27° 43', the Moon in Pisces 12° 52', the <preceding> full Moon was Epiphi 22, the third hour of the day at Capricorn 24°. From the day and hour of the full Moon to the day and hour of the birth

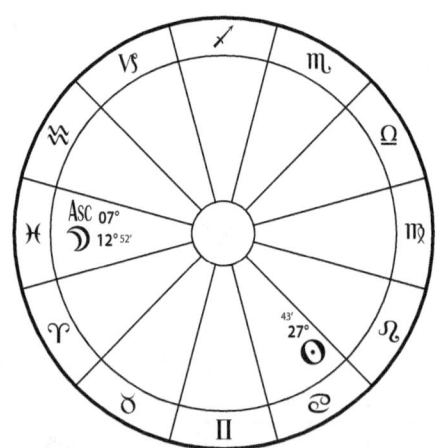

was 3 days 12 hours. This amount is 7⁄30 of the period from full to new Moon (15 days). I subtract these days from the magnitude entered at Capricorn 20°, which is 12;20, and the result is 9;12 <!>. This will be the "fraction of the hour" figure. I calculate the hours, 2, <for a result of 2×12;20=24;40>, and add the fraction of the hours, plus the total rising time, 307, for a total of 340;55. I find this magnitude in the table of total rising times at Aquarius 29°. I add the 8°, and the Ascendant becomes Pisces 7°. Making a note of this, I consult the table at Pisces 7°, and I find 26 entered there, which is 13⁄30 of 60. The hourly magnitude entered at Aquarius 29° was very nearly 13. I multiply this by 12, for a result of 156. Next I take 13⁄30 of this and get 68. He died halfway through his 69th year.

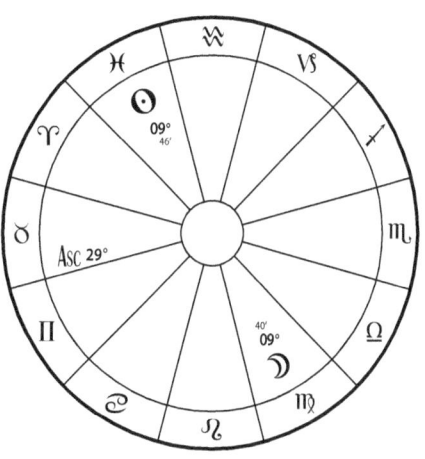

Another example: Hadrian year 18, Phamenoth 2, the fourth hour of the day. The Sun in Pisces 9° 46', the Moon in Virgo 9° 40', the full Moon was about to occur, since the light of the Moon was full. Calculating the fourth hour as the full Moon using the rising times, I put the Ascendant at Taurus 29°. In the table at Taurus 29° is entered 10, which is 1⁄6 of 60. The hourly magnitude of Taurus 29° was 17;27. Twelve times this figure is very nearly 210. I take 1⁄6 of this for a result of 35. He died at 31½ years of age. The last degrees of the chronocratorship suffered a deficiency with respect to the minutes of the Sun, when the degrees are calculated with respect to the factor applicable to each year: 4, 16, 17.

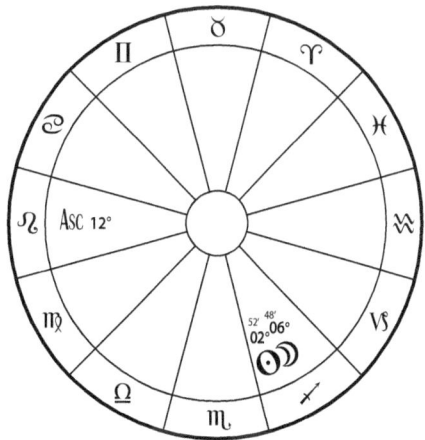

Another example: Antoninus Pius year 15, Athyr 25/26, the end of the ninth hour of the night, klima 6. The Sun in Sagittarius 2° 52', the Moon in Sagittarius 6° 48', the new Moon had just occurred. The distance <between the Moon and the Sun> was not great. When the ninth hour was calculated as the hour of the new Moon, the results were not correct. Calculating the eighth hour as the new Moon, I put the Ascendant at Leo 12°. After the addition of 8°, the figure 4 <?> was found to be entered next to it in the table. This is 1/15 of 60. The hourly magnitude entered at Libra 20° is 15. This amount times 12 yields 180, and 1/15 of this gives 12. He lived that long.

9. The Hostile Places and Stars. The Critical Places With Reference to Table I

It is necessary to examine the hostile places and stars, not only with respect to the other stars, but also with respect to the Ascendant, the Sun, and the Moon. When these come into opposition during their transmissions, they indicate critical points and deaths. Take, for example, Saturn: it is necessary to examine the degrees in opposition to see to which god's term they belong (as entered in the table). The native will die when Saturn is in those degrees, is square <with the Ascendant>, or is in signs of the same rising time, depending on which chronocrator is in effect. The same must be done for the other stars, because the rulers of the terms of the degrees in opposition are hostile. These stars indicate destruction when they come to the places <of the rulers> or to the places of the same rising time as the Ascendant.

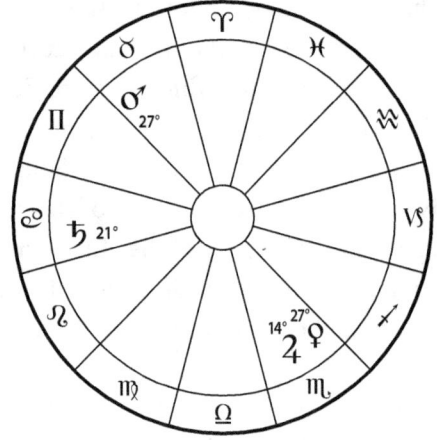

An example: Saturn in Cancer 21°, the terms of Venus. The point in opposition is Capricorn 21°, terms of Mars, which was at Taurus 27°. When Saturn is there, the native will die. He died in Virgo because it was square, when calculated by degrees...

<Jupiter> in Scorpio 14°, the terms of Saturn, and Taurus 14° <the point in opposition> is also the terms of Saturn, and this star is not hostile to itself. Leo has the same rising time as Scorpio, and Leo 14° is in the terms of the Sun. Therefore Jupiter, coming to the places of the Sun or coming to a sign of equal rising time, destroyed the native there.

Mars in Taurus 27°, the terms of the Sun. The same position in Scorpio is in the terms of the Sun, and no star is hostile to itself. So I investigate Leo 27° or the sign of equal rising time, which is Gemini according to the hourly intervals. Gemini 27° is in the terms of Venus. The native will die when Mars is in Scorpio or <Aquarius>, the signs of equal rising time, or when it is in signs square with these. If anyone calculates Leo 27°, he will find it to be in the terms of Saturn. Saturn was in Cancer; so the native will die when Mars is in Cancer, in Sagittarius, or in the signs square with them.

Venus in Scorpio 27°, the terms of the Sun. The point in opposition is Taurus 27°, the terms of the Sun. Now the star is not hostile to itself, and so I investigate Scorpio 27°, the sign of equal rising time, which is in the terms of Mercury. The native will die when Venus is in Virgo, Mercury's position, or in the signs square with it. The same procedure should be followed for Mercury.

In casting horoscopes for patients struck down by illness, it is necessary to examine the <place> in opposition, the stars in the hostile places, and the stars causing the monthly, daily, and hourly critical periods with respect to the degree-position/sign of the Moon in which the opposing star is found.

...

First we must speak about the construction of the table, so that anyone wishing to derive it handily anew might easily determine its structure. You will find the structure of the table line by line to be as follows: multiply 1/60 of the magnitude given for each day by 30, and the result will be the span of life. No star will either add to or subtract from it. This is what I mean: someone supposes that an inscription has been found in the recesses of a temple, an inscription whose progressive increase is 2 for each line. Each line of the inscription is 1/60 of the hourly magnitude of the day, and this figure, multiplied <by 30> gives the length of life. For instance: the beginning is at Thoth <1>. At the first degree is entered 2 (or one-half of 4). The increase is 2 <per degree> until 6°, and when 6° is reached, the number entered there is 12. Then the sequence is broken: at 6°, the breaking of the sequence occurs. The number 14 (which is, of course, the "illumination" of the Moon) is added to the number associated with 6°. At 7° will be 26; at 8°, 28; at 9°, 30.

Now that 30 has been completed, begin again with 2. So at <10° is entered 2>, at 11° is entered 4; at 12° is entered 6. The hexad of 2 has been completed, and again the sequence is broken and 14 is added to 6. The result is 20, to be entered at the 13° row.

They proceed thus, breaking the sequence at each 6° and adding /**307P**/ 14 to the previous number. If somehow in the middle of the procedure the number 30 is reached (as was shown for the second hexad above), we do not add 14, but start again with 2. So the structure from the beginning (i.e., 1°) sets an <upper> limit to the table, 30.

Following is the procedure for knowing the first number of each sign, the basis of which is, is order…

Table I.[2]

degrees		Libra factors	years	months	days		Scorpio factors	years	months	days	degrees
1	Sun	2	6	1	15	Mars	14	39	0		1
2		4	12	3			16	44	5		2
3		6	18	3			18	49	0		3
4		8	24	4			20	55	2		4
5		10	30	3	15		22	60	6		5
6	Mars	12	36	7		<Jupiter>	24	65	0		6
7		26	78	0			8	21	10 [11]		7
8		28	84	0			10	27	2		8
9		30	89	11			12	32	7		9
10		2	6	0			14	38	0		10
11	Jupiter	4	11	9		Saturn	16	43	3		11
12		6	17	1			18	48	7		12
13		20	59	[1]1			2	5	4		13
14		22	64	5	15		4	10	9		14
15		24	70	6			6	16	1		15
16	Saturn	26	76	8		Mercury	8	21	5		16
17		28	81	3			10	26	9		17
18		30	87	4			12	32	0		18
19		14	40	11			26	69	2		19
20		16	46	9			28	74	4		20
21	Mercury	18	51	5		<Venus>	30	79	6		21
22		20	57	11			2	5	3		22
23		22	62	5	15		4	10	6		23
24		24	68	8			6	15	9		24
25		8	22	9			20	52	6		25
26	<Venus>	10	28	5	15	Sun	22	57	0		26
27		12	33	1<1>			24	62	0		27
28		14	39	5			26	67	11		28
29		16	44	10	15		28	72	11		29
30		18	50	4			30	77	7		30

---

[2] Arrowheads < > surround corrections supplied by Pingree. Brackets [ ] surround erroneous readings in the text. The underlined numbers are not in accord with the computations.

de-grees		fac-tors	Sagit-tarius years	months	days		fac-tors	Capri-corn years	months	days	de-grees
1	Jupiter	26	67	6		<Saturn>	8	20	6		1
2		28	72	6			10	25	1		2
3		30	77	<6>			12	30	2		3
4		2	5	2			14	35	1		4
5		4	10 [15]	3	15		16	40	1		5
6	Saturn	6	15	5		<Mercu-ry>	18	45	0		6
7		20	51	2			2	5	0		7
8		22	56	2			4	10	1		8
9		24	61	3	15		6	15	1		9
10		26	66	3			8	20	1		10
11	<Mer-cury>	28	71	4		<Venus>	10	25	1		11
12		30	<7>6	6			12	30 [31]	1		12
13		14	35	7	15		26	65	2		13
14		16	40	7	15		28	70 [73]	3		14
15		18	45	8			30	75	4		15
16	Venus	20	50	9		<Sun>	2	5	0		16
17		22	55	9			4	10	1		17
18		24	60	10			6	15	1		18
19		8	20	10			20	50	4		19
20		10	25	4			22	55	5		20
21	Sun	12	30	5		<Mars>	24	60	6		21
22		14	35	5			26	65	8		22
23		16	40	5	10		28	70	5		23
24		18	45	5	15		30	75	5		24
25		2	5	3			14	35	9		25
26	Mars	4	10	1		<Jupiter>	16	40	6		26
27		6	15	1			18	45	8		27
28		8	20	3			20	50	8		28
29		10	25	2			22	55	9		29
30		12	30	2			24	60	1<1>		30

de-grees		fac-tors	Aquarius years	months	days		fac-tors	Pisces years	months	days	de-grees
1	Mercury	20	50	10		Venus	2	5	4		1
2		22	55	11			4	10	9		2
3		24	61	0			6	16	2		3
4		26	66	2			8	21	7		4
5		28	71	4			10	27	0		5
6	Venus	30	76	6		Sun	12	32	6	10	6
7		14	35	8			26	70	7		7
8		16	40	10			28	75	7		8
9		18	46	1			30	80	2		9
10		20	51	4			2	[8]5	5	15	10
11	Sun	22	56	7		Mars	4	11	0		11
12		24	61	10			6	16	6	15	12
13		8	19	3			20	55	4		13
14		10	25	3			22	61	2		14
15		12	31	1			24	66	10		15
16	Mars	14	36	6		Jupiter	26	72	8		16
17		16	41	9			28	78	2		17
18		18	47	10			30	84	6		18
19		2	5	3			14	39	8		19
20		4	10	6			16	45	4		20
21	Jupiter	6	15	9		Saturn	18	51	2		21
22		8	21	0			20	57	0		22
23		10	26	4			22	62	11		23
24		12	31	9			24	68	11		24
25		26	69	0			8	23	11		25
26	Saturn	28	74	4		Mercury	10	28	11		26
27		30	79	10			12	34	5		27
28		2	5	4			14	40	5		28
29		4	10	8			16	46	8		29
30		6	16	6			18	52	7		30

The Anthology – Book VIII

degrees		factors	Aries years	months	days		factors	Taurus years	months	days	degrees
1	Sun	14	41	1		Venus	26	83	6		1
2		16	47	1			28	90	2		2
3		18	53	2			30	97	0		3
4		20	59	3			2	6	6		4
5		22	65	5			4	13	3		5
6	Venus	24	71	7		<Mercury>	6	19	7		6
7		8	24	0			20	65	0		7
8		10	30	0			22	72	2		8
9		12	36	1			24	78	5		9
10		14	42	2			26	85	4		10
11	Mercury	16	48	4		<Saturn>	28	92	3		11
12		18	54	6			30	99	0		12
13		2	6	1			14	46	3		13
14		4	12	2			16	53	0		14
15		6	18	4			18	59	8		15
16	Saturn	8	24	7		<Jupiter>	20	66	9		16
17		10	30	10			22	73	4		17
18		12	37	9			24	80	0		18
19		26	80	0			8	26	8		19
20		28	87	0			10	33	5		20
21	Jupiter	30	93	6		<Mars>	12	40 [41]	<2>		21
22		2	6	3			14	46	7		22
23		4	12	6			16	53	5		23
24		6	18	11			18	60	7		24
25		20	63	1			2	6	9		25
26	Mars	22	<6>9	8		<Sun>	4	13	6		26
27		24	76	2			6	20	3		27
28		26	82	9			8	27	1		28
29		28	89	5			10	34	0		29
30		30	96	8			12	40	0		30

degrees		factors	Gemini years	months	days		Cancer factors	years	months	days	degrees
1	<Mercury>	8	27	3		<Saturn>	20	69	9		1
2		10	34	1			22	76	8		2
3		12	41	0			24	83	8		3
4		14	47	1<1>			26	90	9		4
5		16	54	10			28	97	9		5
6	<Saturn>	18	61	9	15	<Jupiter>	30	104	10		6
7		2	6	10	15		14	49	0		7
8		4	13	9			16	56	0		8
9		6	20	8			18	63	0		9
10		8	27	7			20	69	11		10
11	<Jupiter>	10	34	6		<Mars>	22	76	6		11
12		12	41	5			24	83	9	5	12
13		26	89	8	15		8	27	11		13
14		28	96	8			10	34	10	15	14
15		30	103	8			12	41	10		15
16	<Mars>	2	6	11		<Sun>	14	48	9		16
17		4	13	10			16	55	9		17
18		6	20	9			18	62	8		18
19		20	69	4			2	6	11		19
20		22	76	3			4	13	3		20
21	<Sun>	24	83	2		<Venus>	6	20	10		21
22		26	90	1	15		8	27	10 [11]		22
23		28	97	0	15		10	34	5		23
24		30	104	2			12	41	8		24
25		14	48	8	[15]		26	90	1	15	25
26	<Venus>	16	55	7	15	<Mercury>	28	97	6		26
27		18	62	7			30	104	0		27
28		20	69	8			2	6	11		28
29		22	76	7			4	13	10		29
30		24	83	7			6	20	10		30

degrees		factors	Leo years	months	days		factors	Virgo years	months	days	degrees
1	Jupiter	2	6	11		Mars	14	46	5		1
2		4	13	10			16	53	8		2
3		6	20	5			18	59	9		3
4		8	27	7			20	66	0		4
5		10	34	6			22	72	6		5
6	Mars	12	41	5		Sun	24	78	11		6
7		26	89	7			8	26	3	15	7
8		28	96	6			10	32	5		8
9		30	103	9			12	39	3		9
10		2	6	10			14	45	7		10
11	Sun	4	13	8		Venus	16	52	0		11
12		6	20	6			18	<58>	<4>		12
13		20	68	4			2	6	3	15	13
14		22	75	1			4	12	5		14
15		24	81	8			6	19	3	15	15
16	Venus	26	88	5		Mercury	8	25	3		16
17		28	95	0			10	31	7		17
18		30	101	7			12	38	11	15	18
19		14	47	4			26	82	4		19
20		16	54	10			28	88	11		20
21	Mercury	18	60	8		Saturn	30	94	8		21
22		20	67	4			2	6	3	15	22
23		22	73	11			4	12	6	20	23
24		24	80	5			6	18	9	7	24
25		8	26	5			20	62	5		25
26	Saturn	10	33	5		<Jupiter>	22	68	5		26
27		12	40	1			24	74	4	15	27
28		14	46	8			26	80	3		28
29		16	52	11			28	86	2		29
30		18	59	10			30	9<2>	<2>		30

Table II.[3]

degrees	factor	Libra fractional part	years	months	factor	Scorpio fractional part	years	months	degrees
1	0	20	1	0	12	20	34	4	1
2	2	40	8	2	14	40	40	3	2
3	5	0	15	3	17	0	48	9	3
4	7	20	22	4	19	20	53	4	4
5	9	40	29	4	21	40	59	4	5
6	12	0	36	3	24	0	65	11	6
7	24	20	73	3	6	20	17	4	7
8	26	40	80	0	8	40	23	8	8
9	29	0	87	9	11	0	29	<11>	9
10	1	20	4	11	13	20	36	0	10
11	3	40	11	9	15	40	42	<5>	11
12	6	0	18	10 [12]	18	0	48	7	12
13	18	20	55	10	0	20	0	11	13
14	20	40	62	6	2	40	7	2	14
15	23	0	69	9	5	0	13	3	15
16	25	20	76	8	7	20	19	7	16
17	27	40	83	8	9	40	25	10	17
18	30	0	90	9	12	0	32	0	18
19	12	20	37	4	24	20	64	9	19
20	14	40	44	11	26	40	70 [72]	10	20
21	17	0	51	6	29	0	76	10	21
22	19	20	58	1	1	20	3	6	22
23	21	40	65	6	3	40	9	8	23
24	24	0	72	3	6	0	15	10	24
25	6	20	19	11	18	20	48	1	25
26	8	40	26	0	20	40	54	1	26
27	11	0	33	0	23	0	60	1	27
28	13	20	40	6	25	20	65	11	28
29	15	40	47	11	27	40	71	11	29
30	18	0	54	4	30	0	78	0	30

[3] Arrowheads < > surround corrections supplied by Pingree. Brackets [ ] surround erroneous readings in the text. The underlined numbers are not in accord with the computations.

The Anthology – Book VIII

degrees	factor	Sagittarius fractional part	years	months	factor	Capricorn fractional part	years	months	degrees
1	24	20	63	1	6	20	16	7	1
2	26	40	69	0	8	40	21	9	2
3	28	0	74	11	11	0	27	6	3
4	1	20	3	1	13	20	33	6	4
5	3	40	9	0	15	40	40	6	5
6	6	0	15	4	18	0	45	0	6
7	18	20	46	11	0	20	0	11	7
8	20	40	51	0	2	40	6	3	8
9	23	0	58	8	5	0	13	11	9
10	25	20	64	7	7	20	18	7	10
11	27	40	70	5	9	40	24	7	11
12	30	0	76	1	12	0	30	[1]1	12
13	12	20	31	0	24	20	61	3	13
14	14	40	37	2	26	40	66	<1>2	14
15	17	0	43	1	29	0	72	3	15
16	19	20	49	7	1	20	3	6	16
17	21	40	55	0	3	40	9	9	17
18	24	0	60	<1>1	6	0	15	0	18
19	6	20	16	1	18	20	46	10	19
20	8	40	21	11	20	40	52	10 [11]	20
21	11	0	27	10	23	0	58	1	21
22	13	20	33	8	25	20	62	2	22
23	15	40	39	3	27	40	70	6	23
24	18	0	46	4	30	0	72	8	24
25	0	20	0	10	12	20	31	3	25
26	2	40	6	8	14	40	37	9	26
27	5	0	12	7	17	0	43	6	27
28	7	20	18	<6>	19	20	49	8	28
29	9	40	24	4	21	40	54	9	29
30	12	0	30 [32]	2	24	0	60	11	30

degrees	factor	Aquarius fractional part	years	months	factor	Pisces fractional part	years	months	degrees
1	18	20	46	7	0	20	0	11	1
2	20	40	52	7	2	40	6	10	2
3	23	0	58	6	5	0	13	9	3
4	25	20	64	6	7	20	19	9	4
5	27	40	70	6	9	40	26	1	5
6	30	0	76	5	12	0	32	6	6
7	12	20	31	2	24	20	66	7	7
8	14	40	37	2	26	40	72	7	8
9	17	0	42	11	29	0	79	0	9
10	19	20	49	7	1	20	3	11	10
11	21	40	55	7	3	40	9	11	11
12	24	0	65	[1]1	6	0	16	6	12
13	6	20	16	9	18	20	48	1	13
14	8	40	22	6	20	40	57	3	14
15	11	0	28	6	23	0	64	2	15
16	13	20	35	6	25	20	70	3	16
17	15	40	40	9	27	40	77	4	17
18	18	0	47	6	30	0	84	4	18
19	0	20	0	[1]1	12	20	35	1	19
20	2	40	6	1	14	40	41	6	20
21	5	0	11	2	17	0	48	2	21
22	7	20	<1>9	3	19	20	55	1	22
23	9	40	25	9	21	40	61	11	23
24	12	0	31	3	24	0	68	11	24
25	24	20	64	1	6	20	18	2	25
26	26	40	70	9	8	40	25	0	26
27	29	0	76	8	11	0	31	11	27
28	1	20	3	0	13	20	38	4	28
29	3	40	9	9	15	40	45	8	29
30	6	0	16	0	18	0	52	8	30

degrees	factor	Aries fractional part	years	months	factor	Taurus fractional part	years	months	degrees
1	12	20	36	1	24	20	78	2	1
2	14	40	42	2	26	40	85	11	2
3	17	0	50 [51]	4	29	0	93	8	3
4	19	20	57	5	1	20	4	4	4
5	21	40	64	6	3	40	11	11	5
6	24	0	71	7	6	0	19	7	6
7	6	20	18	3	18	20	59	7	7
8	8	40	26	0	20	40	67	9	8
9	11	0	33	5	23	0	76	10	9
10	13	20	39	6	25	20	83	4	10
11	15	40	47	5	27	40	91	2	11
12	18	0	54	6	30	0	99	6	12
13	0	20	1	3	12	20	40	9	13
14	2	40	8	1	14	40	48	7	14
15	5	0	15	9	17	0	<5>6	5	15
16	7	20	2<2>	6	19	20	64	2	16
17	9	40	29	4	21	40	72	1	17
18	12	0	37	8	24	0	80	2	18
19	24	20	75	7	6	20	21	2	19
20	26	40	82	6	8	40	27	11	20
21	29	0	90	5	11	0	37	4	21
22	1	20	4	4	13	20	44	8	22
23	3	40	11	4	15	40	52	8	23
24	6	0	18	3	18	0	60	7	24
25	18	20	58	3	0	20	1	1	25
26	20	40	65	2	2	40	9	0	26
27	23	0	73	2	5	0	16	<1>1	27
28	25	20	80	1	7	20	24	10	28
29	27	40	88	4	9	40	32	9	29
30	30	0	96	1	12	0	40	9	30

degrees	factor	Gemini fractional part	years	months	factor	Cancer fractional part	years	months	degrees
1	6	20	21	7	18	20	<63>	11	1
2	8	40	29	6	20	40	<72>	1	2
3	11	0	36	8	23	0	<80>	3	3
4	13	20	45	1	25	20	<88>	4	4
5	15	40	55	1	27	40	<96>	8	5
6	18	0	61	10	30	0	<104>	11	6
7	0	20	1	2	12	20	<43>	1	7
8	2	40	8	6	14	40	<51>	4	8
9	5	0	17	3	17	0	<59>	1	9
10	7	20	22	3	19	20	<67>	7	10
11	9	40	33	4	21	40	<75>	9	11
12	12	0	41	5	24	0	<83>	2	12
13	24	20	84	8	6	20	<22>	[1]1	13
14	26	40	92	2	8	40	<30>	3	14
15	29	0	100	3	11	0	<38>	2	15
16	1	20	4	7	13	20	<46>	6	16
17	3	40	12	8	15	40	<54>	7	17
18	6	0	20	9	18	0	<62>	11	18
19	18	20	63	6	0	20	<1>	7	19
20	20	40	71	8	2	40	<9>	1	20
21	23	0	79	9	5	0	<17>	4	21
22	25	20	81	9	7	20	<25>	4	22
23	27	40	96	1	9	40	<33>	2	23
24	<30>	0	104	2	12	0	<41>	1	24
25	12	20	42	9	24	20	<84>	4	25
26	14	40	51	1	26	40	<92>	3	26
27	17	0	59	2	29	0	<100>	4	27
28	19	20	67	4	1	20	<4>	7	28
29	21	40	75	6	3	40	<12>	8	29
30	24	0	82	8	6	0	<20>	9	30

The Anthology – Book VIII

		Leo				Virgo			
degrees	factor	fractional part	years	months	factor	fractional part	years	months	degrees
1	0	20	1	2	12	20	40 [41]	<1>1	1
2	2	40	9	2	14	40	49	7	2
3	5	0	17	2	17	0	56	1	3
4	7	20	25	3	19	20	63	10	4
5	9	40	33	4	21	40	71	4	5
6	12	0	41	4	24	0	78	11	6
7	24	20	83	10	6	20	20	9	7
8	26	40	91	10	8	40	28	4	8
9	29	0	99	7	11	0	35	11	9
10	1	20	4	7	13	20	43	2	10
11	3	40	12	7	15	40	50	11	11
12	6	0	20	6	18	0	58	4	12
13	18	20	62	8	0	20	1	1	13
14	20	40	70	6	2	40	8	7	14
15	23	0	77	4	5	0	16	1	15
16	25	20	85	2	7	20	23	6	16
17	27	40	93	11	9	40	30	7	17
18	30	0	101	8	12	0	38	7	18
19	12	20	41	9	24	20	77	3	19
20	14	40	49	6	26	40	84	10	20
21	17	0	57	4	29	0	91	7	21
22	19	20	65	[1]1	1	20	4	10	22
23	21	40	72	6	3	40	11	9	23
24	24	0	80	6	6	0	18	9	24
25	6	20	21	3	18	20	57	2	25
26	8	40	28	11	20	40	64	3	26
27	11	0	36	11	23	0	71	4	27
28	13	20	<44>	<5>	25	20	78	4	28
29	15	40	<52>	<2>	27	40	84	4	29
30	18	0	<59>	<9>	30	0	96	3	30

Book IX

The *Anthologies* of Vettius Valens of Antioch: Book IX

1. Preface

Valens sends greetings to Marcus. The information set out by the divine king Nechepso in the beginning of his XIII Book has been exhaustively treated in our previous compilations and in the labors of others. Now I will compile the following material, falling short in no respect. It is obvious that the King made his explanations with mystic intelligence and that he has also been the guide—even for us—in our approach to this art. His willingness to confess, and then to correct, his early errors is a sign of a nobility and wisdom on his part which gave him the intelligence to know when to change his mind. The fact that he despised his kingship and power and devoted himself to these matters <astrology> is a sign of his experience and persuasiveness, qualities which reveal this art's alluring and attractive face to his successors. No necessity for making a living and no trickery caused by greed affected him—as these traits have affected so many nowadays. As a result this man must be taken as a model.

The very wise Critodemus, in the vital work attributed to him, the *Horasis* <Vision>, made such a beginning of great mystery, to wit: "Already having traversed the seas and having crossed great deserts, I was thought worthy by the gods to reach a safe harbor and a secure resting place." Timaeus, Asclation, and many others have said the same. These men were carried away by the beauty of words and by reports of marvels, and they did not produce works which fulfilled their promise, nor were these works complete and lucid, but rather they left their readers in the lurch many times and at all times were warped, begrudging, withdrawn, and deceptive. They never travelled <u>one</u> road, but they piled scheme on scheme and wrote books which could be prosecuted because they are proofs of fraud, not of truth. This Critodemus, although he had inherited a mass of theorems, had developed others himself, and was able to interpret clearly, still obscured the truth because of the appearance of his tables.

I on the other hand in my previously compiled books, have composed an oeuvre which does not consist of vain and empty babble, nor have I included questionable solutions using someone's mere opinion or purely qualitative non-numerical writings. Approaching what seemed to be the truth, he <Critodemus> wandered off into endless inquiry and criticism. One who wishes to write treatises must <proceed> as if wishing nothing else; if he does <have ulterior motives>, he will import error into his work because of his ignorance and spite. Therefore having traversed the sea and having crossed many lands, I have surveyed many climes and nations, have been plunged in long toil and trouble, finally to be thought worthy by God of attaining secure foreknowledge and a safe harbor.

Not everything that men attain is corruptible and burdensome; there is in us some divine, divinely-crafted element. The circumambient air, that incorruptible and all-pervading substance, imbues us with this momentary influx of immortality at appointed and fixed times. Each of us in our daily activity strives to receive or give forth this lifegiving spirit. As the divine Orpheus says:

"Man's soul takes root in the aether."

and

"When we draw in the air, we harvest the divine soul."

and

"The immortal and unaging soul comes from Zeus."

and

"Of all things, the soul is immortal, the body mortal."

Therefore in so far as we posses soul, we move, we associate, we perform, we contrive, we do actions fit for the gods. When our debt <to Fate> soars into the air, our body will lie dead and silent, having given up its spirit in succession to another, an empty artifact of Destiny, perceiving nothing. Its nature then being dissolved, the mortal frame is then examined in its own place.

Now with the help of God, I have discovered these matters which have been treasured up in darkness. For my part, my plan—generous from the start—has been to preserve my exposition as secret and hidden, because of the multitude of the unworthy. But so as not to seem to be an accuser and to fall into greater criticism and to excite accusations from others, I have decided to mystically set forth in this book the chapters necessary for completing the previously outlined topics—not in an arcane and obscure way, but with direct clarity. I can count on the great intelligence of my listeners. I do this so that my heretofore ignorant listeners and those who fight against the Gods may gain faith (with the help of these <chapters>), may become friends of the truth, and may receive this pre-existent and revered science.

2. The Lot of Fortune and Daimon. Their Relationship to the Topics of Propitious and Impropitious Times and of Life

The Lot of Fortune and Daimon have been explained by us in the preceding <volumes>. Now again we will return to them to confirm that these places are powerful and controlling. To make a comparison: just as in the universal rotation, the all-seeing Sun, whirling in its tireless course, galloping through a time of immense eons, leads the dance of the stars in their varied courses back to the same place, then separates them once again. The Sun causes their tropics, their seasons, and their phases, starting where it stopped and stopping where it started. Likewise the Sun charms and arouses the souls of men and becomes the cause of rank, of occupation, and of all success. In a corresponding way the Moon, the Fortune of the universe, waxing and waning under the influence of the Sun's power, goes through phases, causes the variations in the weather, ripens fruits, and becomes a cause of life for men. In the same way in every nativity, the Lots of Fortune and of Daimon must be examined to see from which parts of the universe they emanate. As for their causative force: if these Lots are in operative signs with benefics in aspect, they make nativities propitious, distinguished, and profitable. Particularly if the Lots occur in masculine signs and their rulers are operative in masculine (or feminine) houses and behold the place from the right, they cause the greatest and most glorious nativities, those endowed with unparalleled success and advancing to an unsurpassed fortune. If the Lots are in masculine signs while their rulers are inoperative in feminine signs and have malefics in opposition or in superior aspect, the place is indicative of decline and ruin and is conducive to poverty and crises of every type. It causes men to be confounded by public, infamous, or royal evils; the end of such men is found to be bad.

With reference to lifespans: the two Lots, when calculated with reference to the Sun and Moon and to their distance <from each other> in degrees, and with reference to the Ascendant, the planet under consideration, and its degree-position, will make clear the span of life: they will measure one-half of the distance/interval forward or back, and will either add to the magnitude of the hour or subtract from it, since the two degrees are operative in the sign by necessity, and since the nativity (although being mortal) takes in the lifegiving spirit which is in sympathy with the universe.

These places must be studied religiously, not carelessly, because from these can be seen and apprehended the things which heap on men, after much time and toil, the consequences of the influences of these Lots. Petosiris did not speak irrelevantly about the sympathy of the Sun and Moon in his book *Horoi <Terms>*: "Whether you measure from the Sun to the Moon and take that distance from the Ascendant, or from the Moon to the Sun and do likewise, you will find it <the Lot> located at the same point <!>. The Lot controlling the matter in question is seen there, the Lot with reference to which everything happens and occurs." The King also said in the beginning of his <XIII> Book: "Next in order, it will be necessary to count the distance from the Sun to the Moon, then to measure off an equal distance in the reverse direction (*some count forward*) from the Ascendant, and to inspect the ruling place that has been determined: which star is its ruler and which stars are in that place. From the interpretation of these places make a clear determination of the native's affairs." (His calling the place "ruling" means "powerful," and the next phrase "the whole can be seen" means that it is controlling.) In addition, in the course of his exposition he often speaks strongly in affirmation of this Lot: that if benefics are in conjunction or in aspect, they are indicative of good and givers of property; if malefics, they bring the loss of property and cause bodily wasting, crises, etc.

If the Moon is in a feminine sign at a nativity, this does not bring a good nature to men, but for women born at the same time a <good> basis exists. (This applies to the Sun for those who have the places and their rulers in masculine and feminine signs.) If malefics alone are in conjunction with the places or incline there, they bring burning, shipwreck, falls from high places, injuries to limbs, bleeding and—particularly when they are in solid signs—either disease symptoms or convulsions. Things turn to the worse whenever <malefics> rule the places. We will however explain these matters as we proceed in our exposition, and we will show in varied ways what power is assigned this <Lot> with respect to the propitious times and to the length of life.

Make special note if the Lots are located in Cancer, Leo, Capricorn, or Aquarius, and are aspected by benefics or by their own stars in operative signs. If the nativity has a illustrious basis, then governors, kings, and rulers arise, men having the power over life and death, men who have the king's attention, men thought worthy of gifts and high rank, men successful in their enterprises. Such men are ineffective at first, endure a downtrend in their fortunes and are in despair, but later their fortunes change, and they attain unexpected support, are blessed and called happy by the multitude. Those who are assigned a moderate basis are trusted with royal business, are stewards and superintendents—but are subject to ups and downs and hatred. Some become or are associated with governors; some receive stipends at the royal court or in public offices. They are not however elevated so high in their livelihoods as they are Sunk in inglorious display and in careworn, broken misery.

3. The XII Places and Their Relationship to Propitious and Impropitious Times

These matters were thus arranged according to their cosmic harmony in ancient times. The Egyptians, although they had received them in simple form from antiquity, locked them up with complex and interwoven distinctions, and they used sophistic talk and approaches. Having walled in this art with a myriad of bulwarks and with "bars of unbronzed bolts," they then departed. As a result, those who enter these precincts are like blind men: they wander at random because no gates have been placed there or because they do not chance upon the location of these gates. They have the misfortune of making the same discovery a thousand times. I have knocked down a section of this barrier-gate and have shown the entrance, like a gate, to those who wish it.

Now I return my thoughts to the subject at hand; let this discussion concern the XII Places. Asclepius, beginning with this topic, composed the most; then many Egyptians and Chaldeans did likewise.[1]

The Places starting from the Ascendant are as follows:

I. Life, the basis of years, the psychic spirit—i.e., the Ascendant itself. Relative to the III Place of Brothers this is the Good Daimon and the Place of Children and Friends. Relative to the IV Place of Parents it is the Place of Action. Relative to the VII Place of Women it is the Marriage-bringer. Relative to the V Place of Children it is the IX Place.

II. Livelihood, income from property. Relative to the III Place of Brothers

---

[1] *Marginal note:* The same is true for the Eight-Place system.

it is the Bad Daimon and the Place of Slaves and Enemies and of afflicting crises. Relative to the IV Place of Parents it is the Good Daimon and the Place of Friends. Relative to the V Place of Children it concerns action and rank. Relative to the VII Place of Women it is the Place of Death. If the ruler of the new or full Moon is found in this Place or in the Place in opposition, it indicates exile. The new or full Moon is observed for similar indications.

III. Concerning the life of brothers. Relative to the IV Place of Parents, it concerns enemies and slaves. Relative to the VII Place of Women it is the IX Place [concerning rank, occupation, and childbearing]. It is also the Place of the Goddess, of the Queen, [and of occupation].

IV. The Place concerning the life of parents, concerning religious and secret matters, estates, property, and treasure-troves. Relative to the III Place of Brothers it concerns livelihood. Relative to the VII Place of Women it concerns rank and occupation.

V. The Place concerning the life of children; the Good Fortune. Relative to the III Place of Brothers it is the Place of bastard- and step-brothers, of the Goddess and the Queen. Relative to the VII Place of Women it is the Good Daimon.

VI. Concerning injuries, illness, and afflicting crises. Relative to the IV Place of Parents it concerns brothers. Relative to the III Place of Brothers it concerns step- and suppositious parents. Relative to the VII Place of Women it concerns enemies and slaves.

VII. The Marriage-bringer of a nativity; concerning the life of women. Relative to the III Place of Brothers it concerns children and is the Place of Good Fortune. Relative to the IV Place of Parents it concerns parents, estates, property, treasure-troves, and religious matters.

VIII. Likewise for the nativity this Place concerns death. Relative to the III Place of Brothers it concerns injuries and diseases. Relative to the IV Place of Parents it concerns bastard children. Relative to the VII Place of Women it concerns livelihood.

IX. Concerning Foreign Lands, the God, the King, prophecy, and money matters. Relative to the III Place of Brothers it is the Marriage-bringer. Relative to the IV Place of Parents it concerns injuries, diseases, and afflicting crises. Relative to the VII Place of Women it concerns brothers. Relative to the II Place of Livelihood it concerns death.

X. Concerning occupation and rank. Relative to the VII Place of Women it concerns estates, property, religious undertakings, and the Place of Parents.

XI. The Place of the Good Daimon, the Place concerning friends and desires and acquisition. Relative to the III Place of Brothers it concerns the God, the King, prophecy, and money matters. Relative to the IV Place of Parents it concerns death. Relative to the V Place of Children it is the Marriage-bringer. Relative to the VII Place of Women it concerns step-children.

XII. Concerning enemies, slaves, and afflicting crises. Relative to the III Place of Brothers it concerns occupation and rank. Relative to the IV Place of Parents it concerns travel, the God, the King. Relative to the V Place of Children it concerns death. Relative to the VII Place of Women it concerns injuries and disease.

The precise distinctions between the things indicated by the Places are explained elsewhere. After charting these Places in the order of the zodiac for interpretation, it will be necessary to examine which stars, whether benefic or malefic, are in the Places or are in aspect; which stars' signs they coincide with; and whether these signs are tropic, solid, bicorporeal, moist, dry, lewd, thievish, etc. Likewise determine the rulers of the Places, i.e., which ruler of which sign is in which Place. In the proper determination of chronocrators, determine <u>from</u> which Place <u>to</u> which Place the chronocratorship is passing, and count off the years of each star from each Place. The XII Places, when compared in circular order with each other in this way, will make the results and the type of result obvious.

First of all, it is necessary to calculate the positions of the Places in degrees: count from whatever point has been determined to be the Ascendant until you have completed the 30° of the first Place; this will be the Place of Life. Then proceed until you have completed another 30°, the Place of Livelihood. Continue in the order of signs. Often two Places will fall in one sign and will indicate both qualities according to the number of degrees each one occupies. Likewise examine in which sign the ruler of the sign is and which Place it controls (according to its degree-position in the horoscope). With these procedures, the Place can readily be interpreted. If it is calculated that each Place exactly corresponds to each sign in the chart as a whole (a circumstance which is rare), then the native will be involved in confinement, violence, and entangling affairs.[2]

If the star of Mercury is associated with these chronocrators (i.e., with the sign of the Sun or with the signs belonging to the star of Mars), then this circumstance indicates that the attack or the confinement occurs because of documents. And so on.

---

[2] CB: There is an issue with the manuscript that begins halfway through this sentence, just after "a circumstance which is rare," where the text breaks off and the scribes accidentally copied unrelated natal delineations into the text from book 7, chapter 6 (p. 280). That is why the end of this sentence and the paragraph that follows seem like a non sequitur, because some passages in the manuscript got mixed up.

Be aware of the transits of the stars and their changes of sign at the various chronocratorships, as I have described. It is necessary to calculate as follows: add a number of days to the birth date equivalent to the age (in years) of the native. Then, having first determined the date, whether in the following month or in the birth month itself, cast a horoscope for that day. <See> which star, if any, is in the Ascendant or is coming into conjunction with another star, and whether it is moving from an angle to a point following or preceding an angle, or from a point <following or> preceding an angle to an angle, or whether it was rising at the date of the delivery but is now setting or coming to some unrelated phase, or to something better. You may consider these to be the periodic forecasts.

The following procedure seems valid to me: we add the age in years to the birth date and calculate in which month the new date falls. Then chart the <transits> of the stars of the current year and make the forecast as described. As for the previously explained <previous paragraph> method for the stars: we will not find much change in position for Saturn, Jupiter, and Mars. These stars have an imperceptible motion and stay in the same place. In the latter method <this paragraph> we will find that they come to be in square, trine, and in opposition.

4. A Method Concerning Propitious and Impropitious Times and Lifespans with Respect to the Moon

Through experience I have discovered another aphetic method which uses the zones of the stars. Zoroaster spoke of this method in riddles. Beginning with the Moon we count upwards, giving the following to each star:

9 to the Moon	9 to Mars
9 to Mercury	9 to Jupiter
9 to Venus	9 to Saturn
9 to the Sun	

Now we count in the order of signs until 108 years are completed, the maximum period of the Moon. He proposed this universally as a model, as have the King and many others.

Everyone uses this as described, but I propose to make the following allotment: count off the number of completed years, beginning with the Moon's sign and subtracting first the amount which the Moon controls. Allot the remainder until 9 years are completed. Then give 9 to each sign, proceeding in the order of signs. If the <last> sign does not receive a full 9, from that point give the months to each sign until you arrive at the time in question, noting first the sign which was assigned the 9-year-period during which the starting point of the 9-month-period began. At the point where the count stops, determine (using the previously described system) whether it ends at an active or at a weak spot. If the 12 aphetic points have the same influence, they will bring the maximum period to the life-aspects, and they will indicate vigor in the activity-aspects. Allotting in this way, 9 years to each of the 12 signs, we will complete 108 years. If, having allotted periods to certain signs, we make a second assignment to them, we will find an excess and a deficiency with respect to the stars.

In addition, it is impossible and unseemly for the many nativities that occur at the same time to have one and the same chronocrator. Therefore, the zodiacal aphetic point for each nativity, viz. the Moon, which changes its position in each nativity, causes an extraordinary variation.

As I have said before and must now make clear, it is necessary to examine the star of Jupiter to see if it is in aspect from the right with the Ascendant (to the degree), i.e., whether it casts its rays within its (the Ascendant's) degrees or beyond them. If Jupiter is ahead <of the Ascendant> and is found to have a retrograde configuration, its beneficial effect will be strong because it is being carried towards the position of the Ascendant. If it is behind <the Ascendant, i.e., to the right>, it will be naturally better. If it is turned away from the Ascendant, it is bad. In so far as it beholds any aphetic place or the place of a star or sign at the change of the chronocratorship in question, it must be considered a benefic. Whenever it leaves a sign or degrees in either a direct or a retrograde phase, it becomes malefic and harmful.

It is also necessary to observe the Moon's relationship with the degree-position of the Sun and the angles—i.e whether it is square, trine, or in opposition. Not only that, but also with the intervals of 15° or half the sign's rising times, for then it seems to make a motion/phase. Particularly when it passes through the two nodes in any chronocratorship, the doom will be certain: the determination of the fatal cycle will be made from the lunar and solar degree-positions, just as we have explained using both <the nodes> and the procedure of cycles<?>, or using some other powerful procedure which takes the nodes into account…

5. Critical Times

As is proper, the contacts and unions of the stars, the Sun, and the Moon become very active for good and for bad. It is also necessary to examine the periodic chronocratorships of each star to see if they come into effect in the chronocratorships of benefics or malefics, and what numbers they consist of. For example: the period of **Saturn** is 30 years. I am investigating at what other numbers this 30-year period is operative. I proceed as follows: I begin with 4 and I factor in the next numbers in order: 4 and 5 make 9; then 6 and 7, for a total of 22; next 8, for a total of 30. So the 30-year period is completed by starting with 4. There will be a Saturnian critical point every 4 years, then every 30, its own period.

Jupiter acts as a benefic and brings rank every 3 years: 3 plus 4 plus 5 total 12.
Mars every 4: 4 plus 5 plus 6 total 15.
Venus is found to be unassociated; it will act every 8 years.
Mercury acts every 2 years: 2 plus 3 plus 4 plus 5 plus 6 total 20.
The **Moon** fills three-year-periods: 3 plus 4 plus 5 plus 6 plus 7 total 25.

The **Sun** fills 9-year-periods: 9 plus 10 total 19. The Sun also controls 20-year-periods: this period comprises the unit and the 19 year period, since the Sun travels 1° in a day-and-night period, i.e., in 24 hours it traverses 4 phases, the first from Sunrise to noon, the second from noon to Sunset, the third from Sunset to midnight, the fourth from midnight to Sunrise. If we add the degrees of the phases (first=6 hours, second=12 hours, third=18 hours, fourth=24 hours), the total is 60. In addition, since the Sun allots 120 years as its maximum period (one-half of which is 60), the semicircle <of the Sun> becomes 60. The <astrologer> must make the type of forecast which is operative in accord with the positions of the stars and the configuration and nature of the signs.

6. Horoscopes for Illnesses. The Initiatives

The determination of forecasts when a patient takes to his bed must be made in the following way: determine the number of days from the new Moon <preceding> the nativity to the birth date; divide this by 4. Make a note of the remainder of the division by 4. Now we take the days from the new Moon of the current year to the birth date, and we divide that figure by 4. Note the remainder. As the third step, it is necessary to take the days from the new Moon preceding the illness to the day when the patient took to his bed. Divide this by 4, and compare the remainder with the previous remainders. If the three figures are the same, the time must be judged fatal. If they are different, the danger resulting from the disease, the sickness, or the injury will be escaped.

Through experience we have decided to consider as operative Initiatives not only for the onset of illnesses, but also for the beginning of each and every activity, base or distinguished, elevating or debasing, average—in short, not only actions that happen to men, but also actions caused by men, e.g., the beginnings of buildings and dedications, expeditions, governorships and commands, base and noble enterprises. If I wished to speak about each type of enterprise, my discourse on these matters would become endless. Therefore the horoscope will be cast only for the time of the beginning of the enterprise (i.e., the hour), and for the type of enterprise only (i.e., good or the opposite, enduring or transitory, profitable or damaging).

<I will not be> like some charlatans, who try to predict all activities from one beginning—not only activities but also lifespans—in their attempts to deceive the souls of their clients. It was preferable for <the astrologer> to cast the horoscope and then to begin to interpret it with sober reasoning, taking into account all the relative positions and the angles, not with a multitude of words, but with brevity leading to the truth. Such a man then would appear to be a guide to life, a good advisor, and an unerring prophet of Fate. Some things however happen to these ignorant men, lovers of money: these flatterers bring false delights and dull man's reason; while they have the ethereal soul in their keeping, they snatch it from the heavens and dash it to the Earth. As a result, most <of their clients> suffer grievous harm and gain for themselves foreknowledge with no foundation.

7. The Determination of the Sign and the Degree in the Ascendant

The sign in the Ascendant is found (for day births) by counting the number of the Sun's degree-position from the Sun's sign, giving 1° to each sign. The sign where the count stops is in the Ascendant for the nativity—or the sign corresponding to it, in both the diurnal and nocturnal hemispheres. If the degree is located in the nocturnal hemisphere or if the nativity is diurnal, the sign in opposition or the sign square with it will be in the Ascendant. For night births, count in the same way the degree-position of the Moon from the Moon's sign.

Alternatively: it is necessary to start counting the Sun's dodekatemorion from the sign trine to the left. The sign where the count stops will be the Ascendant—or the corresponding sign.

Alternatively, using a compelling method: in the cases when the Sun is in the sign of the new Moon while the Moon is traversing the sign just following the new-Moon sign, the Ascendant will be in the sign of the new Moon, or in the sign sextile, trine, or opposite, the inclination of the Moon determining which one. When the Moon is with the Sun and at an angle, if the Sun leaves the sign of the new Moon while the Moon is still traversing its first cycle <=phase?>, the Ascendant will be found in the sign square with the Moon or in a sign which is unaspected by the Moon. If <an astrologer> knows whether the birth was day or night, but does not know the hour, he must draw up <a horoscope> with two signs in the Ascendant.

8. Male and Female Nativities; Monstrous or Animal-like Nativities

For any nativity it is necessary to see where the dodekatemorion of the Moon is located. If it and its ruler are in female signs, forecast a female nativity as a rule. If the nativity chances to be male, calculate some addition and subtraction factor for the Ascendant such that the male dodekatemorion can be in the Ascendant when calculated using the rising times. Examine the point in opposition to the dodekatemorion as well: if the dodekatemorion, the point in opposition, or their rulers, fall in a theriomorphic sign, predict a monster or an inviable creature.

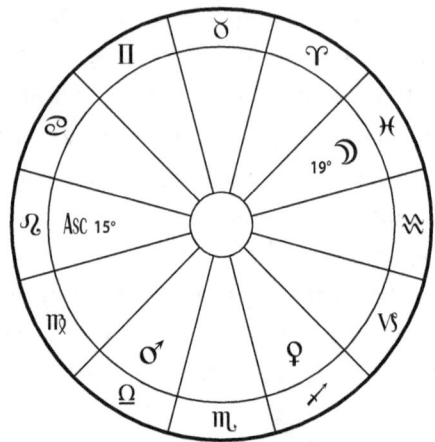

For example: the Moon in Pisces 19°. The dodekatemorion is in Libra, a male, man-like sign, and the nativity was male. The ruler <of Libra>, Venus, was in Sagittarius. The Ascendant requires neither addition nor subtraction since it fell in a man-like sign. I take then the rulers of Libra and Aries, Venus and Mars. Mars was in Virgo, Venus in Sagittarius. After <re->calculating the Ascendant from the table of rising times using the reported Ascendant, I find it to be in Leo 15°. I start counting the dodekatemorion from this point to Mars and Venus, and I will consider the one nearest the degree in the Ascendant (i.e., Leo 15°) to be the ruler of that *monomoiria*: from Leo 15° to Mars in Virgo is a distance of 50 <?>. From 15°, I count two additional dodekatemoria to Scorpio; the result is 56. Venus is in Sagittarius, and if we give a part of the dodekatemorion to Sagittarius, the result will be 12. Therefore this degree-position will be closer to Leo 15°. Since Venus has the closest dodekatemorion, it is necessary to investigate the monomoiria of Venus at Leo 11°, 12°, and 13°, and to consider that to be the Ascendant.

Another procedure: the Sun's position always indicates the length of day and night, depending on which sign it is in. The Ascendant is determined from the hour, the degree is determined from the Ascendant, and the precise degree of the Ascendant is determined from this degree, since they arise, are governed, and are corroborated by each other—particularly for day births. (For night births, it is necessary to take the remaining degrees of the Sun plus the degrees included in order of those attributed to the signs<?>. If some inaccuracy is suspected in the Ascendant's position, it is necessary to enter the table of rising times using the data of the horoscope and to examine the hourly magnitude to see what numerical ratio it has. Then add this to the total rising time, and subtract an amount proportional to the apparent error. The resulting position is to be considered the Ascendant. This exact point will be the standard, because of the differing inclinations of each nativity.

Next the relationship of the *hōrimaia* is mystically made clear: not every nativity has the same eastern <=aphetic> point, nor an equal length of life. Some are extended through a great space, others through two or three signs, others through not <even one> entire sign.

If anyone wishes to foreknow the point of the Ascendant, he can discover it from the degree determined by the methods set forth in the previous book <VIII>. Now let us add some clearer notes to this topic. Determine the number of degrees from the <preceding> new Moon to the Moon's position at the birth. Now double the number. The first number, counted upwards from the new Moon, shows the eastern point <=Ascendant>. The second number, counted in the order of signs from the new Moon shows the western point <=Descendant>. Now it is necessary to take the distance from the eastern point to the western, and to see what fraction of 360° the distance is. The nativity will survive this fraction of time with respect to the maximally allotted time. In a like manner, count off the number of months from the degree-position of the Ascendant, in the order of signs and in the opposite direction with respect to the eastern and western hemispheres.

Another procedure: each of the Lots, by itself, shows the degree-position of the Ascendant. For example, if the Lot of Fortune is located within a sign and if the degree-position of the Moon is known, count the degrees from the Moon to the Sun, then count the resulting number upwards starting from the Lot. The Ascendant will be where the count stops. Daimon will be similarly useful for day and night births: when compared <with the Lot of Fortune it gives the result> by sign; when used with the Sun, <it gives results> to the degree. For day births, count from the Sun to the Moon and take an equal number of degrees upwards from Daimon. For night births, count from the Moon to the Sun and take an equal number in the order of signs from Daimon. (Or from the Sun to the Moon and the same number upwards from Daimon—both procedures will have the result coming at the same point.) This degree-position will be considered operative.

The determination of the <Ascendant> in question using the method at hand will be made from the tables of rising times and of the inclination: by adding to or subtracting from the total rising time the amount by which the length of the hour varies, one can calculate the difference in degrees. Then after adding or subtracting that distance to/from the previously determined operative degree, one must consider the new degree-position to be the Ascendant. Therefore the layout of the XII Houses, which are arranged differently depending on the inclination of the ecliptic in different <geographical areas>, cause an extraordinary variation <in fortune>. Those born in Rome will not have the same lifespan as those born in Babylon, and vice-versa. Sometimes a very small variation is found, sometimes a very great one, sometimes an enormous one. If the difference of a fraction of an hour or of a day has such an effect, why not the same for one klima with respect to another—because of the <different> shadow lengths on the <different parts of the> Earth, as well as the ascents and stations of the Sun relative to the ecliptic? But these matters are difficult of approach to the multitude and are considered madness; to the wise, however, the results of the forecasts are proof of what I have said.

Another procedure: add the degree-positions of the Sun and the Moon. Treat this figure as the *operative gnomon* and the *vital degree*, one active according to the determination made by the directing <sign?>. Then begin with the first degree of the sign that appears to be in the Ascendant, and position the two Lots in such a way that the positions of the Sun and the Moon are <correct>. It is absolutely necessary that two degrees (occasionally three) in any sign be in the Ascendant, whenever the total number of the Sun and the Moon falls in the beginning of a sign or in the middle or at the end. The addition or subtraction occurring at the equinox will show the ratio of the degrees<?>. The same is true for the Sun and the Moon: the Moon passes through a sign in $2\frac{1}{2}$ days. The gnomon, when halved, yields the same ratio.

Nature, sending to us emanations from her immortal elements, creates and fashions piece-by-piece the universal structure of everything, unalterable and invariant. Nature directs the universe without exceeding the bounds of law. She supports the cosmos, awakening and recycling it to immense ages. Sometimes she destroys, expends, and brings to oblivion the tribes of men and beasts, and the kinds of plants and crops; sometimes she begets, nourishes, and rejuvenates others. No earthly thing is everlasting or extremely long-lived, nor is any <totally> destroyed or desolate, thus causing the bereft Earth to assume a formless character. No, the Earth is piloted by the heavenly bodies, glorified by the good things in it, made splendid and transfigured by the different colors, and takes on its lovely shape—for none of the elements is unshapely.

These elements rejuvenate the sea which is exercised by the winds and tides, and because of its needs <?> the elements restore it with streams and springs pouring down out of the Earth. Filled at all times, <the sea> never comes to an end, nor indeed does it flood over beyond its appointed limits. Although spreading widely with its thousand billows, it seems to stand still, although not motionless. The sea nourishes the multitude of fish swimming in its whirls and eddies, and it has made some for whales, some for the use of men, some for food for other fish.

Not even the apparently empty air is to be considered useless and inactive: it is reined in by the winds and alters its direction so quickly that it seems ever-changing. Unperceived by us, it creates our vital spirit with its mildness. By directing the many tribes of winged birds sporting in the air, it provides stimulation and delight at the sight of them...

In such a way each of the elements changes one to the other according to natural law, transforming itself and taking on its own beauty and its own value to make manifest the universal structure. An element that stays in its own form to encroach on the other elements is nothing but useless and harmful. But when blended with another, it creates a temperate state, and when permeating everything, it is not destroyed by anything. In our view, the earth seems to referee the other elements, controlling the universe as its creator.

9. A Method for the Length of Life Using the Apogonia

All of the preceding methods are effective and easily understandable to those who study them, and they result in the same answer, i.e., the same degree-position, but not the same number of years. Consequently those who wish to discover the <correct number of years> must approach the calculation with all eagerness and zeal, because the one who is willing to work gets what he desires.

Toil and constant thought accompany every business, whether good or bad: royal, governing, or ruling affairs; matters of wealth and poverty; and the arts and sciences as well. Moreover, neither pleasure nor enjoyment directs matters in a way that lacks care and grief. Rather these two lead to decline, conceit, and endless mental pain. I have set a table rich in learning and I have invited guests to the banquet. Let those who wish to feast act with the physical assistance of the body, which helps them to use the nourishment not in a greedy or insatiable way, but only in so far as the victuals can provide reasonable pleasure. (What is consumed beyond the bounds of nature usually causes harm.) Now if any of the guests should wish to continue living unharmed, let him eat one or two courses, and he will be happy. To make a comparison: when small scraps of wood come in contact with fire, they make a great, towering blaze which is very overpowering and bright, but which falls in on itself rapidly and becomes dim. The glow of the fire is quenched, and a billowing, thick smoke and a strong, tear-producing stench surrounds the bystanders. A thick haze surrounds those who are farther off. In the same way, if anyone spends some time on one or two of the preceding methods, he will find his goal to be easily grasped, and he will spend his time in pleasure and delight and will enjoy great repute.

If, however, anyone is slow to understand what he reads, yet wishes in one day to run through two or three books, he will not discover the truth. Instead, he will be like a storm-fed river, rolling its burden along, worthless and profitless to the onlookers, and sinking back quickly to its useless state. Nor does a racehorse running in a desert place, outside of a stadium or a battle, win any prizes. If the river carries profitable loads, men will readily leap into it to win the profits, even if the river is swift and dangerous. Or again, a ship running swiftly on course gives great joy to its sailors. The horse who runs with determination delights in the praise <showered on him>, attracts many admirers, wins much attention, and gains prizes by his labor.

It is just so for those who enter these mysteries with keen intelligence: they are worthy of the prize, and they do gain pleasure and profit for themselves. On the other hand, those who enter perfunctorily or rapidly come to jeer at this art, because fate has not granted them ready understanding and immortality. It was not enough for Nature to make it possible for men to know the epicyclic theorems of the stars, with their stations and invariable passages. In addition, Nature fitted everything together by means of this circular motion. As a result, mortals' affairs are destined to be intelligible. An exact knowledge of the things administered or planned <by Nature> on Earth is difficult of attainment by men, e.g., the dimensions of the klimata and nations, the boundaries and the depths of the sea, since this smallest and weakest of creatures (as one must guess until one comes closer) does not have the power of seeing afar. Nevertheless, men can share in immortality and in anticipation can be associates of the Gods through their investigation of the celestial circle, the motions of the stars, the courses of the Sun and the Moon, the subdivisions of the years, months, and hours, the tropics and the variations of weather, the contacts and separations, and because of the resulting foreknowledge.

If indeed it is true as the Poet says:

Meanwhile Kyllenian Hermes was gathering in the souls of the suitors, etc.
<Odyssey 24.1–2>

then obviously this god <Hermes> has a nature partaking of Earth and of heaven, and he conducts the souls of men aloft, around the astral regions of the cosmos, surrounding the souls (particularly of those who are immersed in these matters) with inspired, scientific, intellectual forces. Those wicked men who are blind to these matters not only miss their share of immortality, but even their humanity: they are herded together like brute beasts, they later pay a justly deserved penalty for their greed and their rash reasoning, and they do not escape the law.

It is then perfectly obvious that the gods can attend to men and can supply them with the finest and most respected benefits. Wishing men to keep the laws which they have made, the gods do not nullify the Fates; rather they confirm their effective control of human affairs with unbreakable oaths. For there is among the gods a fearsome and respected oath "By the Styx," an oath which is accompanied by a steady cast of mind and unalterable Necessity. The Poet is a witness to this when he says:

A golden chain reaching down from Heaven, etc. <Iliad 8.19>

The poet portrays Zeus making this threat, a god who can do what he says, but the Poet also mentions that Zeus does nothing to transgress the law nor does he do wrong among the gods. The following verses are said in a mystic fashion, not as some have taken them, when the poet reminds us, in connection with the aristeia of Hector, that as long as Hector's basis of years remained, he was unconquerable, killed many men, advanced beyond the tomb, broke down the gates, and burnt the enclosure:

He raged like destructive fire or like spear-shaking Ares. <Iliad 15.605>

and he seems to be helped by Apollo. But when his doom faced him and his years were fulfilled, he was struck by Achilles and

He went down to death, and Phoebus Apollo forsook him. <Iliad 22.213>

The same is true of Achilles: he filled the plain of Troy with blood and the river Xanthus with corpses. He appeared to battle the gods—all with the support of the gods. Then he was deserted by Athena and killed by Paris, while his goddess mother stood by. In the case of Diomedes and Odysseus too, Athena in sleep made the Trojans drunk so the Rhesus, the Thracian king, might be killed. In so doing Athena glorified Diomedes and Odysseus. Other proofs of this point have been collected and transmitted by many writers.

With respect to those men who have strength of body, who are helped in their effective actions by the chronocrator, and who seem to associate with and stand among the gods, one should infer that even the gods are agents of the Fates: at times they become helpers of men, at other times enemies. For nothing is accomplished among men, for good or for bad, without reason. In addition, Fate is preparing the future by means of agreements, friendships, rank, and existing associations; also through hatreds, injuries, disease, secret and religious matters, death, etc.

All this being given, the discussion of the power of the *apogonia* must begin. Critodemus created the basis, but I myself previously discovered an approach, explained it in other books, and now, having made a more detailed investigation, I will expound it further. I must make clear that the approach to any method at the beginning is as yet incomplete, but when researched at length, it becomes more solid. Now if anyone should debate which is better, the clever and penetrating compiler, or the discoverer of solutions, he would declare (in my opinion) for the discoverer. For a musical organ does not produce praise for its builder, but rather for the person who can skillfully produce a musical tone through the air's action. Likewise every type of instrument making—or the compilation of procedures—which does not have an expert performer of the activity, is considered to be empty, useless, and vain. If someone could distinguish music by modes and recognize their effects, he would provide not only pleasure and delight <to his listeners>, but also profit and fame <for himself>. On the other hand, I have heard of many learned men who depreciate certain compilations because of their obscure and recherché quality—but we should turn our attention to the matter at hand.

In this method, the Sun and the Moon are mutually supportive. (It is not necessary to prove at length their mutual cosmic sympathy and harmony, since these have been discussed previously.) The explanation is complicated and I will outline first the opinions of others.

First it is necessary to determine the Sun's degree-position. Then consult the table of apogonia (under the appropriate klima) and multiply the degree-number entered there by the degree-position of the Sun. Note the result. Next consult the table of rising times at the Sun's degree-position. Multiply the <hourly> magnitude entered there by the time (in hours) of the nativity. Without adding <?>, multiply this number by the result of the previous multiplication, viz. that of the Sun's degree-position times the figure in the table of apogonia expressed in minutes. Divide the resulting total, either 10,000's, 1000's, or 100's, by 30 and note the remainder of the division. See what fraction of 30 this figure is, then add this to or subtract this from the remaining part of the 30 or the magnitude of the Sun's degree-position. Now having found the degree-position, consult the table of apogonia, and make the forecast according to the years entered there, using the three factors.

This method did not seem worth keeping after I made a clearer explanation of it. The error in the figure not only obscures the intention <of the forecast>, but also makes one forget the previously calculated magnitudes. If someone were willing to enumerate erroneously in the second or third step, he would be terribly in error, because such a complication would confuse even me— and I am active and eager in such matters.

For the most part, I did my calculations from the Sun and the Moon, and I acknowledged that the calculation of lifespans and ends is derived from these stars, and I directed my attention to the mystic three-sign system (which I have set forth previously). Thus it is necessary to determine the Sun's and the Moon's hourly motion, expressed in minutes. (I say this frequently so that I will not seem to be in error.) Then count from the Sun to the Moon or from the Moon to the Sun: the same position will be mystically arrived at. Having summed up the total number, divide by 30. Determine what fraction of 30 the remainder (which will be less than 30) is, and take this fraction of the equinoctial times. This fraction of the remainder must also be added to the Sun's degree-position. The result will show the apogonion, i.e., the degree in the Ascendant. Alternatively, add to or subtract from the equinoctial times, depending on the nearest hour.

Every nativity has gnomons at two degree-positions: if we investigate the ratio of the two Lots using the method appended by me, <just as we did> for the Sun and the Moon in their degree motions, it will not be different, but we will find it in the same ratio, not being greater or lesser than the equinox <=30>, because the equinox is the universal gnomon, the commander of the klimata, and the just mediator of day and night.

So, when the degree is found, we enter the table of apogonia and research the years using the first, second, and third factors. If the degree is in a sign of short rising time, but the basis of the nativity is receptive to a number of additional years, it is necessary to add the years of the third factor to itself, then combine the third factor with the first and second. Having done this, make the prediction. Similarly in the signs of long rising times: if this <great> number of years is <not> in effect, calculate the entire factor, then apply the calculated degree-position to the second factor. Alternatively, moving up <in the table>, add the years entered at the degree in the first factor.

The result will be discovered to be quite accurate if the investigator tests it according to the previous account, counts it out, then finds the years which correspond to the apogonia. One method combining with another contributes great certainty. For "one" by itself attains nothing and has a vague and evanescent utility, since it is unsupported and aided by nothing. We see that infants and the very old have a precarious gait, and in the same way the blind make their way leaning on a staff. Moreover nature has not created for men anything useful which is at the same time self-contained and complete: night accompanies day, death life, black white, dry moist, bad good, bitter sweet, etc. Each marches with and is completed by the other. For some it indicates good hopes for life, livelihood, and safety, and brings hope for survival; for others it indicates only despair and a wish for death, because of its afflicting crises and their compulsions.

...

When the Ascendant falls at the beginning of a sign, it is necessary to investigate the preceding sign with respect to the aphetic point. When it falls at the end of a sign, see if the following sign is in agreement. Critodemus has used the Sun in this method also, another procedure which he has not published.

10. A Method for the Length of Life with Reference to the Sun and Moon

Still wishing to prove my generosity as often as possible, I now move on to the topic of the affinity of the Sun and the Moon. When the Sun and the Moon come together, the star which controls (to the degree) their separation will intercept the span of life and the amount <of years>, depending on the ratio of the klima. Whenever one star by itself encircles them (the Sun for day births, the Moon for night births) and destroys the zodiacal interval <between them>, calculate the remaining part of its sign and subtract it from the equinoctial times. Add the solar or lunar degrees to the remaining fraction; then the investigator will find what he seeks, if he looks. Let this procedure apply because of their contact with each other. Generally speaking for night and day births the encircled star will be operative in the previously described way.

In addition, for day births add the remaining degrees of the Sun to those of the Moon (for night births, add the Moon to the Sun) and the same effect will be found. Moreover, I have discovered this: for day births, the Moon is operative from the third hour <of the night> to the third hour of the day, then the Sun from the third hour of the day to the third hour of the following night, and again during the tenth, eleventh, and twelfth hour of the same night. Similarly the Moon controls the tenth, eleventh, and twelfth hours of the day.

In the previous method, we have attempted to proceed using the comparison with the equinox, and we have attempted to add the degrees corresponding to the degree determined <by this method?>, so that the second degree would be operative. The attentive student will test the difference between them.

11. A Method Concerning the Degree in the Ascendant

Since many scholars take delight in all sorts of <astrological> systems, I will append yet another method which has been transmitted by some of my predecessors in a riddling manner. I do this so that scholars can become familiar (through our help) with the systems held in honor by others, can gather together the potentialities of these systems, and can award us eternal fame. It is odious and disagreeable to test others' opinions, especially those which have not been received through written books or compelling dialogues—as Petosiris and the King mystically published books on many subjects. For the compiler knows the beginning and the potential; he then makes the end agree. He intentionally publishes <u>many</u> systems for the initiates and for the ignorant, systems whose power will be easily grasped by attentive students. Some of these have been written out privately, others secretly, and they are despised by their readers since these readers fail to recognize their power. It is as if a man trod on a piece of ground which held a treasure: he does not see what is under his feet, but walks on blindly because of his ignorance. If, however, someone were to inform him of the treasure, he would excavate, would find it, and would feel an extraordinary delight.

In every case it is necessary to take the distance from the Sun's degree-position to the Moon's in the order of the signs using the rising times<?>, and to mark the resulting number of degrees as the solar gnomon. Next consult the table of rising times under the klima of the nativity and see what fraction is entered at the Sun's degree-position. (This is for day births; for night births, look at the point in opposition to the Sun.) Multiply this by 12; then multiply the result by the hour of the day at the delivery. If the result exceeds 360°, subtract 360° and see if the remainder corresponds to the previously determined gnomon. If it does, the hour which was reported will be accurate and should be used. If, however, the remainder greatly exceeds the solar gnomon, subtract from the <reported> Ascendant an amount equal to the excess. (Do this by figuring what fraction the excess is of the <hourly> magnitude, and subtract that.) If the solar gnomon is greater, add to the <reported> Ascendant an amount corresponding to the excess. Then determine the fraction <of the hour> and enter the table of rising times. Continue by calculating the full hours and the fraction. Add the years and note at what degree of the zodiac the *enklima* falls. Consider that point to be the real Ascendant. Thrasyllus used this method, made a scientific beginning, and fashioned a forecast of the end.

12. What Tables Should Be Used; Who Should Be Followed; That Nothing Is In Our Power

I believe I have compiled the powers of the preceding <methods> in a sufficient, even generous, fashion. With this being done, there is something I wish to leave to scholars for their investigation and reflection. I am not speaking now to the uninitiated, but to those who are keen about these matters, so that they too can become aware of this multifarous and complex art, which reaches its peak by means of its many paths, its ins and outs; in so doing, they may seem to associate with the gods. It is clear from what has been and will be said that this art by itself has an everlasting, irrefutable, and eternal foundation. It is also obvious that it is occasionally in error, in view of the weakness of the practitioners of the science and the fact that they are not experienced in the variations from one astronomical table to another. I will omit any mention of those who construct tables of rising times and of the variations in their diagrams and numbers, in the motions of the Sun, the Moon, and the other stars which these astronomical tables show. Even the length of the year has been fixed at different values: Meton the Athenian, Euctemon, and Philip fixed it at 365 $\frac{1}{5}$ $\frac{1}{19}$; Aristarchus of Samos at <365> $\frac{1}{4}$ $\frac{1}{162}$; the Chaldeans at 365 $\frac{1}{4}$ $\frac{1}{207}$; the Babylonians at 365 $\frac{1}{4}$ $\frac{1}{144}$; and many others at various values. If then in the four-year cycle, one day coming around shows the precise degree in the astronomical table of the Sun, why then would it not necessarily be correct to determine the exact degree position <of the Sun> by adding the appropriate motion to the day in question, using whichever year-length one had calculated?

I had reasoned to myself that the previously mentioned men were aware of the power of calculation, but had not discovered the determination of the length of life. If they had researched this, they would certainly have added this missing part to their astronomical tables. So I myself have tried to construct a table of the Sun and Moon using the eclipses: but since time prevented me from bringing this to a conclusion, I was brought to say, along with the King, "Others have beaten these paths, and because of this I omit mention of them." I thought it best to use Hipparchus for the Sun, Soudines, Kidenas, and Apollonius for the Moon, in addition to Apollinarius for both bodies (if one applies the addition-factor of 8°, which I believe to be correct). He however calculated quite well the tables with respect to the observed motions, but he confesses (being mortal) to have erred by one or two degrees. (Absolute accuracy and precision is for the gods alone.) For the rising times they used the *proenklima*, and they calculated the 14 klimata.

First of all, it is necessary to observe with all accuracy the numbers of the Sun, the Moon, and the five stars, with the time's/hour's relationship to them being the referee of their mutual aspects, because it is from this that the Ascendant is known and the XII Places are positioned by degree. If the investigation appears accurate in the way described, it will make the forecasters famous, it pleasantly confirms good and bad for the connoisseurs, and it brings eagerness, encouragement, and belief in the words of those who wish to make such an investigation.

If it were generally true that the rich man never became poor, or that the man who by good fortune has attained the kingship, rule, fame, or any pinnacle whatever always continued secure in his good fortune, or that the strong man continued hale and hearty, or that the man lucky in business never went bankrupt, or that the sea captain never was swamped by waves or sailed off course in his voyages, or that the doctor never was sick, the seer never suffered, or the prophet gained eternal possession of the good which the gods give to men—if all this were true, then the prognostic art would not be useful. Each man would keep what he was allotted, would occupy himself with his portion, and would live his span of years without anticipating anything new. But as it is, all of man's affairs are insecure and unsound. They are seen to be shaky, ready to turn into their opposites: the king becomes a prisoner and a slave; the rich man becomes poor and needy; the strong and powerful man becomes crippled and helpless; and so on. Everything that is beautiful and fine in life, everything concerning health, beauty, fame, and business, changes into something else and gives men the "opportunity" of suffering what they had not suffered before. Rarely does anyone conclude a life free of reproach and care. Most men, according to the basis of their own nativity, experience vicissitudes from day to day in their fortunes.

For this very reason and due to the information derived from my forecasts, I know myself, I know the foundation which my Fate has assigned me, and I know that it is impossible for anyone, contrary to Fate, to become different from what he is. Therefore I have not become a lover of positions of command, rule, or any other prominent rank; or of lavish wealth, of possessions, or of numerous slaves. I have not become a slave of desire, an impious flatterer of the gods and of men, hoping to gain what the Godhead does not want to grant. Just as an intelligent slave of a bad master knows his master's character and his daily behavior, and therefore he does his duties in an orderly manner: he does not contravene the master's orders, and in acting thus, he considers his station to be free from pain and suffering. In this same way, I do not view my service as labored and strained. I have abandoned all vain hopes and thoughts, and I have kept the laws of Fate.

If someone who loves inquiry and who has strengthened his intelligence wishes to learn about what is and what will be from a learned man, he will despise vulgar matters and will become a devotee of those things that suit the foundation <of his nativity>. Transforming himself day by day, he will obliterate any fear of the evil he must suffer. The bad will be blunted and worn away by his contentment, and he will bear voluntarily and in good order the end of his life, acting under his own self-control just as if he were under the command and control of another. If anyone wishes to learn from experience how this can be so, let him compare <this state of mind> with the thoughts of an unlearned man, and let him do the opposite. I mean, if he is poor, let him become rich; if lowly, a commander; if inactive, successful, uncriticized, without grief or care. (For all men are by nature lovers of good things.) If someone attains all this, he will despise Fate. But it is impossible that whatever he wishes to be accomplished should remain unchanged to the end. For that reason it is advantageous for Fortune to be…and to remain unsteady, because men do not bear fortune's favor <indefinitely>. Just like those maddened by stinging gadflies, governed by many masters, and suffering the goads of desires and passions, they pay an appropriate penalty, even though unwilling.

To some simple minds it seems right to say, "Everything is under our own control." Being unable to prove this by experience, they resort to saying that this is partly true: "Some things are under our control, some under Fate's." Going this far, they impudently move on to circular and inappropriate conclusions, saying: "Leaving my house is in my power, as is bathing, going where I wish, carrying on some business, buying, meeting friends" and other matters. Now I declare to these men that the opposite is the case, that not even these trivial matters are under their control. Their very choices go to the contrary because of some unforeseen cause. I myself for example have often wished to do some business or to meet with a friend; having chosen a propitious time for the meeting, I did not attain my goal nor get to where I was going. On the other hand, when I did not desire this, the very thing has happened.[3] For this reason, an intelligent man should follow where God wishes to lead him (for God readies <man's mind> for what he wishes). Or the intelligent man should choose propitious times and after casting an Initiative for the business, taking into account the universal motion, he must examine the forecast resulting from the current stellar positions and the position of the Ascendant.

…

12. Concerning the Nodes
One must be sure to make an addition or subtraction of the years to be

---

[3] *Marginal note:* It would always be necessary for the time to be appropriate for the thing that is about to happen.

assigned according to the zodiacal tables, whenever it is located exactly at the node or within the 6° arc <around the node>. With respect to distinguishing the two systems or methods: if they result in the same number of years, or very nearly the same, then observe if the degrees fall in the same sign. If they are in adjoining signs, they will strengthen the basis of years, <if> the sacred gnomon shifts from day to night or from night to day. By means of these <calculations>, the precise position of the luminaries will be apprehended.

13. A Method for [Propitious and Impropitious] the Length of Life, with Reference to the Sun and the Moon

It occurs to me in connection with the preceding method (i.e., of 27 years) to append the 24 lunar cycles. Whenever this number can apply to a nativity, calculate as previously described. For infant nativities calculate as follows: make the Moon the aphetic point and assign 2 months 15 days to each sign. Proceed to the contact of the Moon or to the signs in trine or square, then to the ray-casting of the malefics,[4] using the ray-casting closest to the total time of the nativity's basis. When the Sun is the aphetic point, assign 30 months to each sign. Carry out the operations as we prescribed when we outlined the precise determination of the Lot, until the chronocratorship receives its total allotment of months and years.

14. Conception and its Relationship to the Topic of the Length of Life

The procedure which we explained previously in the discourse on conception <VI 9> must be applied: consider the Moon's degree-position at the delivery to be the Ascendant at the conception and the Ascendant at the delivery to be the Moon's position at the conception. Determine the length in days of the conception, and calculate with reference to the new and full Moons and the remaining phases. <According to this> method, the Ascendant at the delivery will be in agreement.

15. That It Is Necessary to Establish Accurately the Hour and Fraction of an Hour of the Nativity

Since the Ancient Poet, the wise man devoted to the Muses, has hypothesized two Strifes, one of which is warlike and frightful, delighting in bloodshed, pain, death, battles, hatred, and afflicting crises; the other of which is a hard worker and a lover of beautiful things, peaceful and not unpleasant in her works because she transforms work into pleasure. This god is good, and

---

[4] *Marginal note:* to an angle.

I myself have become her devotee because I wished to gain victory over my malicious opponents by means of my experience and my scholarship. Because of this I was not satisfied to leave the preceding methods as a pledge to future generations of scholars. No, I have found another powerful method, and I have explained it in such a way that those who confirm the accuracy of my generous gifts step by step with all freedom and sacred striving can silence the malignant and blasphemous voices of my enemies. (The anger fed by hatred and pain is, in fact, dying away, especially when the hostile party comes to defeat.) So, by training themselves with all enthusiasm by means of our compilations, our students will turn criticism of this art to praise, knowing that this science brings pleasure and delight, profit and happiness, and intellectual insight beyond <the reach of> most men. But let us turn our thoughts to the matter at hand.

Take the distance in degrees from the <preceding> new or full Moon to the Moon's position at the delivery. Subtract the distance in signs. Treat the remainder as the "fraction" of the Ascendant. Therefore <make> the precise degree-position of the Moon evident. From this the goal of the investigation will be intelligible, since the Sun referees the length of days and hours according to the differences in klima and the changes of season.[5] By itself this "fraction" has the force of an Ascendant.

Alternatively, take the distance in degrees from the new Moon to the Moon's position <at the delivery> according to the rising times. Subtract the distance in signs. Then consider the resulting degree to be the Ascendant. Do the same from the full Moon to the Moon's position, or (as seems better to me) from the Moon's position <at the delivery> to the next new Moon. Taking this distance and subtracting the distance in signs, treat the degree that has been determined as the Ascendant. Complete the total of years by adding or subtracting first the equinoctial times. By adding the two gnomons and dividing by two, you will determine the desired sum according to the real, complex science. (<"Complex" because> the beginning of any type of thing is simple, variable, and hard to understand, but research into it is complicated and difficult.) If the distance is capable of precise determination, this fact indicates that the chronocratorship is uniquely determined.

Wherefore, my dearest Marcus, if you know the numerical tables and the

---

[5] Now even if my statements have received a concise and brief explanation, still the readers should not ignore them and treat them as trivial. They should inquire into them with all care and zeal. In my experience, need, toil, poverty, ambition, self-control, and desire teach most things. We have experienced all of these, and (even if we seem to boast) it has been through these that we have succeeded in attaining the best part of virtue. Some have failed in this, have been scorned, and have faced misfortune. They have gained an empty fame despite their attempts. - *a misplaced fragment*

methods of their composition—and you have proven that you do by word and deed and through the traditions handed down to you by me—and if you apply your natural powers of analysis, and if you make it your goal to carry out your operations with all precision, viz. when you visit the many nations and climes of the world and when you display your talents there, then you will make me worthy of undying fame, and you yourself will be glorified among the people as worthy of this heavenly art. You, having laid a foundation with the abundance of your learning, will attain the status of treatise writer yourself. For you have the nature, the energy, and the self-mastery necessary for this, and you possess the illuminated, mystic initiation into this art, having found the sacred and holy entrance to it. I urge you by the previously mentioned oaths to guard this art and to hide it from the unworthy or the uninitiate, and never to act contentiously against them. For it is better for you to be silent and be defeated, rather than to win victory while showing disrespect for divine matters.

16. A Method for the Length of Life, with Reference to the Sun and the Moon

Although I have already engaged in many contests and have been involved in struggles without number since I was led by my zeal and my ambition to face my rivals, and although I had anticipated the attainment of my investigations and was already putting an end to this treatise, just like a noble athlete in the sacred games, the Olympic contest, still I have reversed my intentions because of the multifaceted operations of nature. The one who brings or lifts these operations into the light of day gains eternal honor and fame. He turns his previous struggles to pleasure and delight. He strengthens his powers and certifies his deeds. He dismisses vain chatter and turns his enemies into friends and associates, however unwilling they may have been. He takes to his bosom many devotees.

Therefore we must return to the cosmocrators, the Sun and the Moon: it is necessary to calculate the rising time and the hourly magnitude of their degree-positions according to the klima of the nativity. Then subtract 360° circles. Treat the remainder as a powerful degree position derived from the equatorial times, and which is the "complement" of the Ascendant. Four degree positions in all are operative, and two of the four remain as potent. Occasionally five places are operative, or perhaps two.

It is necessary to examine the sign in the Ascendant and the signs on both sides. It is from these that the operative degrees allow the chronocrators to be calculated, particularly when there is some error in placing the Ascendant or if one gnomon is used in the Ascending sign, while the other gnomon does not fall in the same sign<?>...The sixteenth degree equals $1\frac{1}{30}$...

It is necessary to take into account the variations due to the klimata, because often a place or a nation which seems to be at the beginning or the end of a "parallel" is really in another area or is divided between two parallels and the time is in error by some addition/subtraction factor. Additionally, as is obvious to those devoted to such matters, they have different astrological attributions. As you can see, this art and its methods are sacred and infallible for those who attend to the details.

17. A Method for the Length of Life with Reference to the Sun and the Moon

This method seems scientifically appropriate: combine the remaining degrees of the Sun and Moon, subtract the distance between them in signs, and treat the remaining degree position as powerful and as the complement of the Ascendant. Consider the remaining <number> in the 30 as the lunar gnomon, using an addition/subtraction factor derived from the equinoctial times. Add the lunar gnomon to the solar, divide by two, and treat the answer as the length of life. Moreover, often the solar gnomon by itself (or the lunar), when the addition/subtraction factor derived from the equinoctial times is used…one-half of the sum of the two [places] indicates the length of life, depending on its temporary or operative states<?>. So it is best to calculate the intervals of degrees and signs using rising times. Moreover, if the gnomon is operative by itself, calculate the times of it alone.

18. The Sign in the Ascendant, and the Required, Scientific Hour of Birth

The appended table is constructed so as to give the sign in the Ascendant and the required, scientific hour of birth. It resembles the roughly accurate table which was constructed (in a puzzling manner) by the King, and which begins with the Sun's position at the conception. I have constructed a precise table, starting with the month Thoth (which is odd because it is month #1), then with Phaophi (which is even because it is month #2), then Athyr (likewise odd), then Choiak (even). Then in sequence it is necessary to examine the remaining signs <=months> one by one. Enter the appended table at the day in question and at the operative month, and we will find for day or night nativities the hour of the birth on that same line.

19. The Lunar Degree-Position with Reference to its Hourly Motion; A Compelling <Method> Which I Have Discovered

I have not wished to hide any of the methods which I have previously worked out, and now I am generously bestowing another scholarly gift on you devotees of such matters, as if you were my children. The tables described below are on two rectangular sheets. As before <end of Book VIII>, they are arranged in equal intervals across the page. The first sheet is the daily motion of the Moon, from the minimum factor of 11 <hours>, going from one square to another in the first row. The same series of intervals is in the bottom row, extending to the 15 hours/squares of the maximum factor. From the top to the bottom are 48 rows. So there is an increase of 5 minutes <per row> from the 11 hours <of the first row> to row 48 <15 hours>, i.e., 4 full hours, the excess <of 15 over 11>. When 60 minutes are completed, there is a red mark to indicate the beginning of another cycle. In this way the motion of the Moon is charted.

The second rectangular table shows the length of the hours for each of the 7 klimata. This one has the numbers for <every> klima arranged from least to greatest, i.e., from 10;30 entered in the first row to 19;30 entered in the outside <?> row. I write each entry in order from 0;30 in the first row to the blank/zero in the bottom row. Therefore, the increase is 5 minutes <per row>. I find the bottom row ending with 15, which indicates one equinoctial hour. And so, continuing from 15 at the bottom, add 5 minutes going up the table to end with 19;30 in the first row.

The horizontal lines separate the two-hour periods, and each pair of hours equals an equinoctial hemisphere <30>. (For night births, calculate using the point opposite <the Moon>.) A double line separates these. The ratio that night length has to day length is the same as that between the lengths of the night-hour and the day-hour: for example 17 to 13. 12 times 17 is 204; 12 times 13 is 156. The total is 360°.

Both tables show the degree-positions of the Moon and its phases, so if we want to know the Moon's degree-positions at a nativity with reference to its hourly motion, this is how we operate. First we must enter the table of klimata, holding the compass with legs apart. At the Sun's degree-position in the night hemisphere<?> and after we have determined the length of the hours, we place one leg of the compass right there. Then we open the compass until the other leg reaches the hour in question <of the night>. The 12 hours of the night are tabulated <to allow this>. If the nativity was during the day, note the extension of the compass legs in the night hemisphere and extend this distance to the hour in question of the day.

Now having measured out the total number of hours in the way described, move the compass to the lunar table. Set one leg of the compass at the figure equal to the motion, then see what degree-position the other leg touches. The degrees will be obvious from the chart of its motion, and these must be added (if the nativity is after Sunset) to the degrees previously determined for the Moon; add the difference due to klima as well. Having added, consider this to be the Moon's degree-position. It is necessary to know the hemispheres accurately, particularly the night hemisphere.

It is also possible to measure off the degrees remaining until Sunset in the day hemisphere and to apply them to the Moon's hemisphere. Treat it as having that distance and being at that degree position. But if we proceed in such a manner, the whole width of the lunar table will not be used, only a part. Therefore use the night procedure.

We will give a clearer explanation by using examples: a nativity on Hadrian year 3, Athyr 30, the fourth hour of the day; the Sun in Scorpio 7°, the Moon in Virgo 30° late in the day. Its motion was 14;15. The length of the day (using day-degrees) was found to be 11 hours 42 minutes. Entering the column of klimata at 11, I find 11;42, and I use this row. Since this is the day hemisphere, I go to the opposite point (i.e., in the night hemisphere) at 18;18 so that 18;18 plus 11;42 might total 30. Now I place one leg of the compass at 18 and I extend it over the other hours of the day, along the line in the row for 11;45. Keeping the compass at this extension, I move to the previously mentioned table of the Moon's motion. For the nativity at hand, it has run 14;15. I enter the table at that point, place one leg on the compass there, and see which square in the whole chart the other leg touches. I find it in the tenth square, around the fourth part. Since each square indicates one degree, I add this amount to what was determined <to be the position> at Sundown, Virgo 30°. The Moon is found to be approximately at Libra 11°. Alternatively, I enter the day hemisphere at 11;42, the <hourly> magnitude of the Sun's degree-position, and I extend the compass to the 8 hours still remaining until Sunset (for this nativity), and the same magnitude <results>...

A Fifth-Century Addition

A Fifth-Century Addition

1. The Length of Life, With Reference to the Tables of Chapter 12. The Determination of the Degree in the Ascendant Using the Two Tables of Valens in Chapter 12

First of all, determine the Sun's degree-position accurately. Then it will be necessary to examine the preceding new or full Moon. See how many days and hours there have been from the preceding new or full Moon, and see what fraction this is of 15 days (the period from new to full Moon or full to new). Having found this fraction, note it separately, and investigate whether it should be added or subtracted in the following way: it is necessary to take the distance from the Sun's degree-position to the Moon's (in the order of signs), with reference to the rising times of the correct klima. Register the total number of degrees as the solar gnomon. Next, again enter the table of the rising times for the correct klima, and examine the hourly magnitude of the Sun's degree-position. (This is for day births; for night births examine the magnitude of the point in opposition to the Sun.) Multiply this by 12, then multiply the result by the hour/time of birth. If the result exceeds 360°, subtract a 360° circle, and see if the result <=the horoscopic gnomon> corresponds to the solar gnomon. If it does, the reported hour will be in agreement with the facts and should be used. If the horoscopic gnomon exceeds the solar gnomon, subtract from the reported hour a fraction of the hourly magnitude of the Sun, which fraction is derived from the period counted from the new or full Moon to the day and hour of the birth (i.e., the calculated fraction of 15 days).

For example: a nativity at the third hour of the day; there are five days from the new or full Moon to the day and hour of the birth, a figure which is one-third of 15 days. The hourly magnitude of the Sun is 16. Subtract one-third from this magnitude, which is then... You make it 2 hours total. In this way you will calculate the Ascendant. If the solar gnomon exceeds <the horoscopic gnomon> then add to the reported hour and make it $3\frac{1}{3}$ hours. In this way you will calculate the Ascendant according to hourly magnitudes and rising times.

Another method: calculate the distance from the new or full Moon to the Moon's present position. If it is less than 180°, multiply it by 12, and see what fraction the result is of 15 days. If it is found to be greater than 180°, subtract 180° and see what fraction the remainder is of the Moon's motion. Deduct this from the hourly magnitude.

Example 2: Diocletian year 147, Tybi 14/15, the third hour of the night, klima 4; the Sun in Capricorn 19° 2'; Moon in Taurus 23° 30'; the <preceding> new Moon in Capricorn 9° 29'. From the new Moon to the day and hour of birth (Tybi 14/15) are 10 days, i.e., two-thirds of one hour.[1] I investigate how many rising times there are <=what the difference is between the hourly magnitudes> from the Sun to the Moon in klima 4,

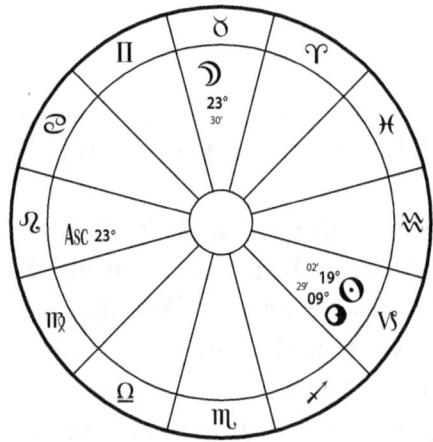

and I find 90 time degrees. I record these 90 time degrees as the <u>solar gnomon</u>. Next I take the hourly magnitude of the point in opposition to the Sun, Cancer 19° (because it was a night birth). Its hourly magnitude is 17;53. I multiply this figure by 12 and find 215. I multiply these 215 time degrees by the 3 hours of the nativity for a total of 645. I subtract a 360° circle for a remainder of 285 time degrees. I record this as the <u>horoscopic gnomon</u>. Now since the horoscopic gnomon exceeds the solar gnomon, the third hour (the time of birth) requires subtraction. So I subtract two-thirds of an hour, because there were 10 days from the new Moon to the day and hour of the birth. Do not calculate using the third hour, but using $2\frac{1}{3}$ hours. Proceed as follows: Sun in Capricorn 19° 2'; the hourly magnitude of Cancer <19°> (because of the night birth) is 17;55. Multiply by $2\frac{1}{3}$ hours for a total of 41;48. Add the rising time of Cancer (93;7) for a grand total of 134;55. With this figure I enter the table for klima 4, and I find the Ascendant to be Leo 23° 0'. With this 23° I enter the table for Leo and

---

[1] *Marginal note:* Rising times from the sun to the moon=21.

I find written there 22 sixtieths, which is ⅓ ¹⁄₃₀ and which equals 73 years 11 months. I investigated the proportional part as follows: the Ascendant in Leo 23°, the hourly magnitude 16;45. I multiplied this by 12 for a result of 201. I multiply this by ⅓ ¹⁄₃₀: ⅓ times 201 gives 67 years; ¹⁄₃₀ times 201 gives 6 ⅔ ¹⁄₃₀ years. The grand total is 73 years ⅔ ¹⁄₃₀ years <73;42>.

Example 3: the reign of Valentinianus, klima of Spain <=4>. The native was killed in his 36th year. Year 135 of Diocletian, Epiphi 8, the beginning of the first hour. The Sun in Cancer 7° 11'; the Moon in Aries 22° 30'; the Ascendant in Cancer 7° 20'. The <preceding> full Moon was at Gemini 18° 40', at the seventh hour of the day on Payni 29. From the full Moon to the day of birth were 7½ days, which is one-half of 15. Since 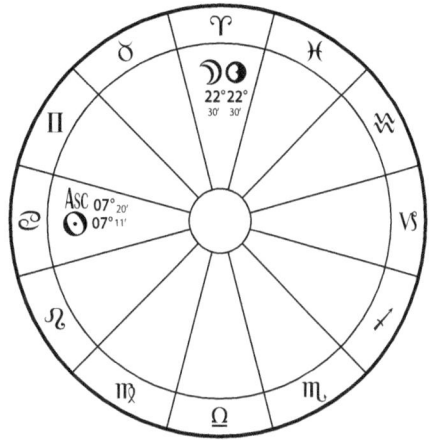 the solar gnomon exceeds the horoscopic gnomon, I add this fraction, ½, to the initial hour of birth, the first hour, and calculate as follows: the hourly magnitude of the Sun <in Cancer 7°> is 18;5, half of which is 9. The rising time of the Sun is 79;7, for a total of 88 time degrees. With this figure I enter the table and I find the Ascendant very nearly at Cancer 14°. I enter the table at this figure, 14°, and I find 34 years 10 months written there, next to the figure 10, which is ⅙ of 60. I now take the hourly magnitude of Cancer 14°, and I find it to be 18;0. Multiplying this figure by 12, I find 216;0 time degrees. One-sixth of this is 36 years, his length of life.

<The next chapters are to be added here>[2]

---

[2] CB: Riley only translated chapters 1, 6, and 7 of the fifth-century addition to Valens' text. He did not translate chapters 2, 3, 4, and 5, so they are omitted here. Chapters 2 and 3 are direct copies of book 3 of the fifth-century astrologer Hephaistion of Thebes, which deal with inceptional astrology. Chapter 4 is about the stars' handing over, or annual profections, and is essentially a list of keywords that have been summarized from book 4 of Valens, chapters 17–18 and 20–24. Chapter 5 is a list of horoscopic data with very brief interpretations, all of which was extracted from book 2 of Valens, chapters 37 and 41. Chapters 6 and 7 Riley translated below.

6. The Terms

Aries	Taurus	Gemini	Cancer
Jup. 6 6	Ven. 8 8	Mer. 6 6	Mars 7 7
Ven. 6 12	Mer. 6 14	Jup. 6 12	Ven. 6 13
Mer. 8 20	Jup. 8 22	Ven. 5 17	Mer. 6 19
Mars 5 25	Sat. 6 28	Mars 7 24	Jup. 7 26
Sat. 5 30	Mars 2 30	Sat. 6 30	Sat. 4 30

Leo	Virgo	Libra	Scorpio
Jup 5 5	Mer. 7 7	Sat. 6 6	Mars 7 7
Ven. 6 11	Ven. 10 17	Mer. 8 14	Ven. 4 11
Sat. 7 18	Jup. 4 21	Jup. 8 22	Mer. 8 19
Mer. 6 24	Mars 7 28	Ven. 6 28	Jup 5 24
Mars 6 30	Sat. 2 30	Mars 2 30	Sat. 6 30

Sagittarius	Capricorn	Aquarius	Pisces
Jup. 12 12	Mer. 7 7	Mer. 7 7	Ven. 12 12
Ven. 5 17	Jup. 7 14	Ven. 6 13	Jup. 4 16
Mer. 4 21	Ven. 8 22	Jup. 7 20	Mer. 3 19
Sat. 5 26	Sat. 4 26	Mars 4 24	Mars 9 28
Mars 4 30	Mars 4 30	Sat. 6 30	Sat. 2 30

7. The Zodiacal Places of the 12 Signs; Their Employment For The Length of Life with Respect to the Minimum, Mean, and Maximum Factors

Most <astrologers> assign the chronocrators for every nativity using the 7-zone system. They begin by giving the rulership first to Saturn, then to Jupiter, to Mars, and to the Sun, after which comes Venus, Mercury, and the Moon. Similarly in the rotation of chronocrators, they examine the ruler of the week and of the days. I do not like this procedure because the same chronocrators are found in most nativities. One should (as was described) put the aphetic point at the Sun or the Moon, or at the star immediately following the Ascendant, then <assign the rulership> in the order that the stars are situated by sign and degree in the particular nativity. A handy way of making the allotment is as follows: reduce the months of each ruler of the 10-year-period <=129 months> to days, and divide them by 129. Multiply the result of this division by the months of each ruler, and you will have the days applicable to each one, viz. the days of the rulership of each star (which were reduced to days and divided by 129). For example, Saturn rules 30 months. Make the distribution to it and to the other stars as follows: take the 900 days <=30 months times 30 days> and divide it by 129. You will find the result of the division will be very nearly 7 <10-year-periods>. Now it is necessary to multiply <by 7> the number of months of each star and to find the days which Saturn will give to itself and to the other stars from its own allotment:

210 to Saturn   56 to Venus
84 to Jupiter   140 to Mercury
105 to Mars   175 to the Moon.
133 to the Sun

When Jupiter is calculated, the result of the distribution of its 360 days <12 months times 30 days> divided by 129 is 2 ½ ⅓. This figure is multiplied by the number of Jupiter's months (and by those of the others) in order to find the days which Jupiter allots to each, as follows:

approximately 7 to Saturn
2 ½ ⅓ <=2 ⅚>to Jupiter
3 ½ to Mars
1 ½ ⅓ to Venus
4 1/12 1/21 to Mercury
5 1/12 1/14 to the Moon
4 ½ to the Sun.

The explanation is quite clear: the ratio

129 days:30 days : : 30 months:210 days <=7 months>
holds <for Saturn>. Do likewise for the rest of the stars.

Now if we investigate the distribution of these very 210 days, again we apply the factor 129. There will be the ratio 129 days to 210 days, and so for Saturn the 210 days will be 1 ⅔ of 129. So if we calculate 1 ⅔ of 30, we will have 50 days for Saturn. 1 ⅔ of Jupiter's 12 will give us 20 days for Jupiter, i.e., the days which Saturn assigns to Jupiter. 1 ⅔ of Mars' 15 gives 25, and so on.

Next let us make a distribution of Saturn's 50 days: as 129 is to 50, so Saturn's 30 will be to some figure, Jupiter's 12 will be <to some figure>; for the others stars, the correct period <will be derived from> 129.

The subdivision to shorter time periods for these stars (when you get down to fractions) becomes difficult. The other method, which distributes the days and the hours to each star according to the ratios of months, is easy and has logic behind it. Take for example Saturn: in the 129 months of the 10-year-period, Saturn is ruler of 30 months. Similarly in any given 129-day-period during the 30 months which it rules, Saturn will be the ruler of 30 days. Again in the 30 days (which equal 720 hours) which it rules, Saturn will be the ruler of 30 hours. As 129 months are to 30 months, so 129 days are to 30 days, and 129 hours are to 30 hours.

For example: let the <aphetic> luminary be the Moon. Let the Moon have the first calculation and the first 10-year-period. Assume that following it in the nativity come Saturn and Jupiter in that order, then Mars, the Sun, Venus, and finally Mercury. Now since the Moon is the aphetic point, it has 25 months, which equal 760 days <25 months times 30 days plus 10 intercalary days>. If the infant is 40 days old, 25 days must be given to the Moon, then the next 15 to Saturn, because Saturn has the days until day 55. We say, "The Moon has transmitted to Saturn." Now if the time in question is more than 55 days, e.g., 60 days, then Jupiter has the days <from 55> to day 67, because it rules 12 days. If the time in question is 70 days, Mars, the next star, must be examined; Mars rules 15. So Mars receiving from Jupiter has the days <from 67> to day 82. If the time in question is more than this, e.g., day 95 (if Venus were the next ruler) then the star following Venus would be ruler, because Venus rules the next 8 days. If the Sun is next, it has the days <from 82> to day 101, because it rules 19 days. If the time in question were day <120> and if Venus were after the Sun, then Venus' days would have passed, because Venus rules to day 109. Consequently Mercury rules <from day 109> to day 129. If the time in question is more than 129 days, the Moon receives control again.

So the completion of 129 days in called a "period." It cycles through the 7 stars, comes back to the first one again, and keeps the same distribution, through the second 129-day period, the third, the fourth, however long it takes to complete the Moon's 760-day period. This 760-day period is completed after the fifth period plus 115 days into the sixth. As a result 14 <additional> days remain in the sixth period, of which Saturn is the ruler, being the lord (following the Moon) of the next 30 months in the monthly periods, and of the next 30 days in the daily periods. So when the Moon has completed its 25 months, Saturn succeeds with its 30 months and gives to itself—not as some say, 210 days=7 months (for why should we apply a distribution of different months, and not a distribution of days derived from the months?) No, it gives itself 30 days, derived from its 30 months, then to Jupiter after it 12 days, then to Mars (if it is the next star) 15 days, then to the Sun (which happens to be next) 19 days, then to Venus 8 (if Venus is next), then to Mercury 20, and finally 25 to the Moon.

Since the first 129-day period is completed, Saturn next after the Moon again receives 30 days of the second 129-day period, then the other 7 stars in order in their correct sequence. After the second period is completed, Saturn will again receive the 30 days first, then the other stars in order until the third period is completed. And so on for the fourth, fifth, sixth, and seventh, until the completion of 30 months, i.e., 910 days. Only 7 days remain after the completion of the seventh period.

Jupiter, the next star after Saturn, then receives 12 monthly time periods. From this period it gives itself the first 12 days, then to Mars, then to the Sun, which is next, then to Venus, then to Mercury, next to the Moon, and finally to Saturn. In the same way Jupiter gives the first 12-day interval of the second period to itself, then distributes to the rest. When the second is completed, the third does not finish but runs for only 107 days. So <in the third period> Jupiter receives the first 12 days again, following Saturn, then Mars next in order receives 15. The Sun receives 19 following Mars, then Venus 8, Mercury 20, and the Moon 25. Finally Saturn receives the final 8 days to complete 107.

After this comes the monthly distribution of Mars, 15 months, which equals 455 days when broken down to the daily distribution. First Mars will have 15 days, then the rest in order. Do likewise for the second and third periods. There will be 68 days left in the fourth period. Of these, Mars receives 15 days first, the Sun 19, Venus 8, Mercury 20, and the Moon the final 6. In all cases, when the year has 6 intercalary days <rather than the usual 5>, add one day to the star which ends <the sequence>; in this case we add one day to the Moon's 6 days.

After the monthly and daily distributions of Mars are completed, the distribution of months from the same 10-year-period passes to the next star, the Sun. It will receive 19 months, which equals 575 days when broken down as before. If the year is a leap year, one more day must be added to the 575. Of this period, the Sun receives 19 days first, then Venus, Mercury, the Moon, next Saturn, Jupiter, and finally Mars. After the first period of 129 days is completed, the Sun again allots itself 19 days, after which the other stars in their order at the nativity receive their days. There are 4 periods. Since there are 59 days left in the fifth period, it is obvious that the Sun receives <the first> 19 days of this period, then Venus 8, then Mercury 20; the Moon receives the remaining 12 (or 13 if a leap year occurred in the 19 months).

Proceed in the same manner, giving the months and the days derived from them to the stars in order, until the first 10-year-period, that of the Moon, is completed. After that, Saturn will receive the second 10-year-period, since it is next in order following the Moon. Saturn will begin the second 10-year-period by giving itself 30 months and 30 days of the 30 months, then the appropriate number of months and days to the next star, and so on until the daily, monthly, and 10-yearly periods of Saturn are completed. Then the next star begins another 10-year-period, with the appropriate number of days and months. From this period it will allot <days and months> in the preceding pattern until the end of the nativity's years.

For example: the lifespan of a nativity is 45 years, 9 months, 25 days. Assume the Sun receives the first 10-year-period, with the Moon following next, then Mars, Mercury, Jupiter, Venus, and finally Saturn. 43 years are four 10-year-periods. The remaining 2 years, 9 months, 25 days belong to the fifth 10-year-period, which is ruled by Jupiter, following the Sun in the fifth place. From its monthly period, Jupiter gives 12 months to itself and 8 months to Venus. 13 months and 25 days remain until the day in question. Saturn, the next star after Venus, has 30 months, of which 13 months, 25 days remain, i.e., 420 days, which Saturn has received from Jupiter. After we break down Saturn's 30 months to 910 days, let us subtract three daily periods of 129 days each (totalling 387 days) from this amount <420 days>. There now remain 33 of the 420. Saturn gives the first 30 days to itself, the final 3 days to the next star, the Sun. So Jupiter is the ruler of the fifth 10-year-period; Saturn is the ruler of the months (succeeding Venus); the Sun is the ruler of the three days (succeeding Saturn), <and its rule would extend> for 16 more days. Consequently there are three distributions: yearly, monthly, daily.

Some <astrologers> make a fourth type, an hourly distribution, by multiplying the days of each star by the 24 hours of the day-and-night period: for example, the 19 days of the Sun become 456 hours. From this amount the Sun assigns:

19 hours to itself   12 to Jupiter
25 to the Moon   8 to Venus
15 to Mars   30 to Saturn
<20> to Mercury

In the second and third 129-hour periods, the Sun distributes in the same way to itself and to the other stars in their order <total 387>. Of the remaining hours of the 456 (i.e., 69), the Sun assigns to itself 19, then 25 to the Moon, 15 to Mars. Mercury is the ruler of the final <10 days> needed to complete the 69 days of the Sun.

We break down the first 3 days <of this 10 day period>, the days which Mercury has received from Saturn (these are the remaining days of the 45 years, 9 months, 25 days) into 72 hours. Mercury grants the first period, 19 hours to the Sun, until the seventh hour of the night. After the Sun, it assigns 25 hours to the Moon, from the eighth hour of the night to the eighth hour of the next night. After the Moon, Mars is ruler of 15 hours, from the ninth hour of the night to the eleventh hour of the day. After Mars, Mercury receives a 13 hour period, from the twelfth hour of the day to the completion of the 72 hours, i.e., to the first hour of the <next> day.

It is necessary to examine the influences in the transmissions: Mars, when operating in the monthly and daily distributions and in the hourly sub-distributions, has the same influence which it has when transmitting to Mercury in the 10-year-period, and it is from these influences that the daily alteration of affairs can be understood. Much indeed <can be learned> from the presiding star and its successor.

After much experience in casting Initiatives, I have found this method of distribution genuine; it has erred not in the slightest with respect to persons or actions. This method, which is found in Valens as well is simple and true, and it does not introduce fractions of months and days, fractions which do not admit of an exact ratio. For it is necessary, if we should wish to subsume everything under the same ratio, to take $\frac{1}{5}$, $\frac{1}{30}$, and $\frac{1}{360}$ of the period of each of the stars, and having done so, to transform the fraction ($\frac{1}{5}$, $\frac{1}{30}$, $\frac{1}{360}$) to a fraction appropriate to the second distribution of each star in order to multiply. (Multiplication is easier than division.) For example: Saturn has 900 days or 30 months. One-fifth of the days is 180 and of the months is 6 (which is also 180 days). The fraction that one day-period is of the other is the same as that of one month-period to the other. Similarly $\frac{1}{30}$ of 900 days is 30 days, and $\frac{1}{30}$ of 30 months is one month, which is also 30 days. Since the number of the days of each star is 30 times the number of months, then clearly $\frac{1}{30}$ of each month is one day, and so $\frac{1}{30}$ of 30 months is 30 days, and $\frac{1}{30}$ of 12 months is 12 days <i.e., for Jupiter>. In general the days of each star have the same number as the months when the months are multiplied by $\frac{1}{30}$.

Now $\frac{1}{5}$ has the same ratio for the days and months of each star:

For Jupiter, $\frac{1}{5}$ of 360 is 72 days; $\frac{1}{5}$ of 12 months is 2 $\frac{1}{3}$ $\frac{1}{15}$ months, which is again 72 days.

For Mars $\frac{1}{5}$ of 450 days <=15 months> is 90 days; $\frac{1}{5}$ of 15 months is 3 months, which is also 90 days.

For the Sun too, $\frac{1}{5}$ of 570 days is 114 days; $\frac{1}{5}$ of 19 months is 3 $\frac{2}{3}$ $\frac{1}{10}$ $\frac{1}{30}$ months, which is again <114 days.

For Venus $\frac{1}{5}$ of 240 days is 48; $\frac{1}{5}$ of 8 months in 1 $\frac{1}{3}$ $\frac{1}{5}$ $\frac{1}{15}$ months, which is also> 48 days.

Likewise for Mercury $\frac{1}{5}$ of 600 days (or 20 months) is 120 days or 4 months; <⅕ of 20 months> is 4 months, again equalling 120 days.

Likewise for the Moon ⅕ of 750 days (25 months) is 150 days (or 5 months).

Since then ⅕ of the days results in the same figure as ⅕ of the months, and ⅕ of the number of months implies ⅕ of each month, which is 6 days, and since the 6 days are 6 times one day, it is clear that when the number of months of each star are multiplied by 6, the same number results as when the number of days are multiplied by ⅕.

So as to understand this more clearly: if we multiply the months of each star by 6, we will get the days of each star. For example:

For Saturn, 6 times 30 <months> gives the same 180 days again.
For Jupiter 6 times 12 <months> gives 72 <days>.
For Mars 6 times 15 gives 90.
For the Sun 6 times 19 gives 114.
For Venus 6 times 8 gives 48.
For Mercury 6 times 20 gives 120.
For the Moon, 6 times 25 gives 150.

Besides this, from 30, without any multiplying, we find the days which have the same number as the months of each star: 30 days are 1/30 of Saturn's 30 months; 12 days are 1/30 of Jupiter's 12 months; and so on.

But taking 1/360 of a number is difficult:
For Saturn 1/360 of 900 is 2 ½.
For Jupiter 1/360 of 360 is 1.
For Mars 1/360 of 450 is 1 ¼.
For the Sun 1/360 of 570 is 1 ½ 1/12.
For Venus 1/360 of 240 is ½ ⅙.
For Mercury 1/360 of 600 is 1 ½ ⅙.
For the Moon 1/360 of 750 is 2 1/12.

Therefore we will transform this fraction, 1/360, to something smaller and easier. Since the number of months is 1/30 of the number of days in those months, the following ratios obtain: 1 to 30, 2 to 60, 3 to 90 and so on, the ratio of the months to the days. Correspondingly, the number of days is 30 times the number of months, so that if I select another fraction for the months instead of 1/30, 30 times the selected fraction will be the fraction of the days. Since the 360 of the days is 30 times the 12 of the months (i.e., 30 times 12=360), if we use 1/12 for each star's months, this will be the same as 1/360 of their days:

So for Saturn ¹⁄₁₂ of the 30 months is 2½, which is the same as ¹⁄₃₆₀ of the 900 days.

For Jupiter ¹⁄₁₂ of its months is 1, which is the same as ¹⁄₃₆₀ of its days. For Mars ¹⁄₁₂ of 15 is 1¼, which is the same as ¹⁄₃₆₀ of its 450 days.

And so on for the rest. Consequently we can use ¹⁄₁₂ of the months instead of ¹⁄₃₆₀ of the days.

We can transform this into the 24 hours of the day-and-night period by multiplying:

For Saturn 2½ times <24> gives 60 hours, which is twice 30, the same number as the months and the days.

For Jupiter 1 times 24 hours <gives 24>, which is twice 12, the number of Jupiter's days and months.

For Mars 1¼ <times 24> gives 30, obviously twice 15, the number of Mars' days and months.

For the Sun 1 ½ ¹⁄₁₂ gives 38, which is twice 19, the same number as the Sun's days and months.

For Venus ⅔ gives 16 hours, twice 8, the same number as Venus' 8 days and months.

For Mercury 1 ½ ⅙ gives 40 hours, twice 20, the same number as Mercury's 20 days and 20 months.

For the Moon 2 ¹⁄₁₂ days gives 50 hours, twice 25, which are the Moon's days and months.

When for each star the number of months are changed to the number of days, ⅕ times ⅙ <times the number of days> shows the number of months; ¹⁄₃₀ is also equal to the number of months. It is therefore obvious that ⅕ <of the days> plus ¹⁄₃₀ <of the days> will be 7 times the same number <of days>. For example: for Saturn, ⅕ of 900 is 180, which is 6 times 30, but ¹⁄₃₀ <of 900> is also equal to 30. 210 is 7 times 30, the number of Saturn's months. For Jupiter, 72 <⅕ of 360> plus 12 <=¹⁄₃₀ of 360> is 84, which is 7 times 12. And so on for the rest.

Since each star is ruler not only of its own recurrent years, but of a number of days equal to seven times the number of months, it is clear that, when it must make a distribution to the seven stars, it gives to each star the same amount it gives to itself, and that there will be no remainder except ¹⁄₆₀<?> which is itself shown to be true since it is double the proper number of the months of each star.

Assume we are to find, using this procedure, which stars control a given time. Let the age be 18 years, 4 months, 13 days. As in the example above, let the Moon control the first 10-year-period of the 220 month total. There are

91 months left for the second 10-year-period. Let Mars be located following the Moon as the ruler of the second 10-year-period. Since this period is not complete, Mars will give itself 15 months; Mercury, the next star, gets 20 months; Jupiter next gets 12; Venus next gets 8; Saturn next gets 30. The Sun receives the remaining 6 months and 13 days, which total 193 days. Since the Sun does not have its complete number of days (because of the given time), it is necessary to break down the partial period, the 193 days. So in this period the Sun gives itself (using this procedure) 163 <?should be 133?>[3] days. Next the Moon, since it cannot receive its complete period of days (175), takes 30 as incomplete and breaks it down to 720 hours (=360 doubled). In this period, it gives itself 25, Mars 15, Mercury 20, Jupiter 12, Venus 8, Saturn 30, the Sun 19. Next after this 129 (doubled) hours, the Moon distributes, beginning with itself, another 129 (doubled), and the remaining 102 <to make 360>. Again beginning with itself it makes the distribution in order, and 22 are left, which Saturn rules, since it rules 30 (doubled). So Mars is the ruler of the second 10-year-period, the Sun is the ruler of the months, the Moon is the ruler of the days, and Saturn is the ruler of 44 hours—because you must restore the 22 (doubled) to the correct number of hours. The distribution will be of months, the subdistribution will be of days, and the sub-subdistribution will be of hours.

The presiding star and the following star will clearly indicate the changes in each day. It is necessary to examine the rulers of the 10-year-period, of the months, and of the days, to see the nature of their transits and configurations. When they are beheld by benefic places and stars, they indicate that the <period> is also benefic; when beheld by malefics, it is malefic.

---

[3] CB: Mark Riley notes that this should be 133, so there is a discrepancy here.

Index

Abraham, xxii, xxiv, 83, 84
Ancients, iii, xiv, xvii, xxi, xxv, xxxii, 48, 122, 141, 231, 236, 245, 258, 293
apheta, xlviii, 120, 121, 123, 123n1, 124, 125, 126, 127, 128, 129, 138, 141, 148, 149, 161, 171, 210, 232, 238, 239, 240, 241, 243, 244, 245
aphetic point, xlviii, li, 123, 124, 125, 148, 165, 181, 210, 219, 232, 243, 244, 245, 332, 333, 337, 344, 349, 358, 360
apogonia, lx, lxn81, lxi, 293, 339, 342, 343, 344
Apollinarius, xxii, xxiin15, 238, 346
Apollonius, xvii, xviii, xxv, lxi, 346
Aristarchus, xxiii, 346
Ascendant, xx, xxi, xxv, xxvi, xxxv, xlv, xlvii, xlviii, xlix, l, liii, liv, lv, lvi, lviin79, lviii, lix, lx, lxi, 9, 17, 18, 19, 20, 21, 25, 44, 45, 46, 47, 48, 50, 52, 53, 54, 55, 56, 57, 58, 59, 60, 61, 63, 66, 67, 70, 71, 72, 73, 74, 75, 76, 78, 79, 80, 81, 82, 84, 85, 87, 88, 89, 90, 91, 97, 98, 99, 100, 101, 102, 104, 105, 106, 109, 110, 112, 114, 115, 116, 117, 118, 119, 120, 121, 122, 123, 124, 125, 126, 127, 128, 129, 130, 131, 133, 134, 138, 139, 140, 141, 142, 143, 145, 146, 149, 154, 155, 157, 161, 162, 163, 165, 166, 167, 169, 170, 171, 172, 174, 176, 177, 181, 185n2, 186, 187, 188, 190, 191, 193, 195, 196, 198, 199, 200, 208, 209, 210, 211, 212, 213, 214, 215, 216, 217, 218, 219, 221, 222, 226, 234, 235, 238, 239, 241, 243, 244, 245, 246, 250, 253, 254, 255, 256, 259, 260, 260n1, 261, 262, 265, 267, 268, 269, 270, 271, 272, 274, 275, 276, 278, 286, 287, 288, 289, 290, 291, 293, 294, 295, 296, 297, 298, 299, 300, 301, 302, 303, 304, 305, 306, 307, 308, 309, 310, 328, 329, 331, 332, 333, 335, 336, 337, 338, 343, 344, 345, 347, 348, 349, 350, 351, 352, 355, 356, 357, 358
  calculation, lv, lvi, lviin79, lix, 17-19
  gnomon 19, 21
Asclation, xxiii, xxvi, 325
Asclepius, xvi, xxiii, xxiiin17, 329
Babylonians, xiiin2, xvii, 191, 236, 346

Bara, Joëlle-Frédérique, viii, xii, xiv, xvn5, xviii, xxxin39, xxxviii, xlivn58, xlivn59, xlvn62, xlvin64, xlvin65, lxiii
brothers, xxxii, xlv, xlviii, 5, 11, 14, 15, 16, 17, 63, 64, 65, 83, 103, 109, 166, 173, 183, 210, 212, 251, 329, 330, 331
calculation, xiii, xiiin2, xiv, xx, xxi, xxii, xxiv, xxxvi, xxxviin48, xxxviii, xxxixn56, lv, lviin79, lix, lixn80, lx, lxii, 21, 26, 28, 31, 43, 98, 135, 187, 212, 238, 244, 266, 285, 298, 306, 339, 343, 346, 349, 360
Chaldeans, 329, 346
children, xliv, xlv, 4, 5, 13, 14, 15, 16, 17, 35, 37, 39, 40, 41, 42, 47, 55, 59, 63, 65, 83, 90, 93, 103, 108, 109, 110, 160, 164, 166, 167, 172, 174, 176, 178, 183, 207, 208, 212, 214, 216, 244, 251, 329, 330, 331, 353
chronocrators, xviii, xix, li, lin77, liii, liv, lv, 131, 152, 157, 159, 165, 171, 194, 198, 199, 204, 205, 210, 211, 213, 222, 226, 230, 231, 233, 234, 235, 239, 243, 246, 249, 250, 252, 256, 257, 258, 262, 263, 265, 266, 269, 273, 277, 279, 331, 351, 358
chronocratorship, xiv, xxii, li, lii, liii, liv, lvi, 33, 59, 77, 82, 83, 84, 85, 86, 87, 92, 111, 126, 129, 130, 133, 138, 143, 148, 149, 150, 151, 152, 153, 154, 155, 156, 158, 163, 164, 165, 167, 169, 170, 171, 172, 173, 175, 176, 184, 185, 188, 194, 204, 206, 208, 211, 213, 214, 215, 219, 220, 221, 223, 232, 233, 234, 235, 238, 239, 240, 241, 245, 249, 250, 251, 252, 253, 254, 255, 258, 259, 261, 262, 263, 264, 265, 266, 267, 270, 271, 273, 274, 276, 277, 278, 279, 280, 281, 309, 331, 332, 333, 334, 349, 350
Compiler, xxii, xxiii, 98, 111, 137, 207, 231, 264, 289, 293, 342, 345
conception, xivn4, xxxvi, xlvii, lvi, lxi, 3, 18, 44, 45, 46, 47, 137, 139, 141, 179, 182, 207, 244, 246, 349, 352
  Ascendant 47, 246-248, 349
  Moon 139, 141, 246-248, 349
  seven-month children, 47, 48
control, xx, 119, 120, 121, 149, 279

controller, xlviii, 110, 121, 123, 123n1, 133, 137, 138, 210
controlling point, 119
critical period, xviii, xx, xlviii, xlix, li, liv, lv, lvi, lxii, 130, 131, 155, 179, 254, 311
critical times, xix, xl, liii, 210, 298, 333
critical years, xx, l, liii, liv, lx, 144, 195, 196, 222, 223
critical day, xlix, l, 136
critical point, xxi, ln73, liv, 135, 144, 149, 195, 220, 221, 222, 223, 224, 226, 227, 259, 261, 274, 275, 276, 278, 291, 307, 310, 334
Critodemus, xvii, xviii, xxiii, xxiiin18, xxvi, xli, liii, 129, 130, 137, 185, 220, 222, 290, 325, 326, 342, 344
death, viii, xv, xviii, xix, xxi, xxvii, xl, xliii, xliv, xlvii, xlviii, lii, liii, liv, 4, 7, 17, 34, 47, 53, 54, 56, 57, 58, 61, 63, 64, 65, 71, 80, 81, 91, 93, 102, 104, 105, 106, 107, 109, 110, 111, 112, 113, 114, 115, 116, 117, 118, 121, 130, 134, 139, 140, 155, 160, 166, 167, 173, 174, 175, 176, 177, 178, 179, 180, 181, 182, 183, 185, 188, 195, 196, 206, 210, 211, 213, 214, 215, 216, 217, 219, 226, 227, 232, 237, 240, 244, 245, 247, 252, 254, 256, 257, 263, 264, 269, 271, 273, 288, 291, 306, 307, 310, 329, 330, 331, 341, 342, 344, 349
degrees, xxi, xxviii, xxviiin35, xxxvi, xxxvii, xxxviin48, xlv, lvii, lviin79, lviii, lix, lx, lxii, 5, 6, 7, 8, 15, 16, 17, 18, 19, 20, 23, 25, 28, 31, 45, 46, 59, 60, 61, 62, 64, 65, 66, 77, 78, 80, 120, 121, 122, 123, 124, 126, 129, 130, 133, 134, 138, 139, 140, 143, 160, 161, 164, 173, 193, 210, 211, 231, 232, 232n1, 233, 238, 244, 245, 246, 250, 253, 266, 273, 278, 285, 286, 288, 289, 290, 291, 296, 299, 300, 301, 302, 303, 304, 306, 307, 309, 310, 312, 313, 314, 315, 316, 317, 318, 319, 320, 321, 322, 323, 328, 331, 333, 334, 336, 337, 338, 344, 345, 346, 347, 349, 350, 351, 352, 353, 354, 355, 356, 357, 358
  feminine, 25
  masculine, 25
  of the Angles, 121
disease, xvin6, xxi, xxviii, xxviiin35, xxxi, xl, xliv, xlvii, liv, 7, 9, 10n2, 16, 38, 51, 52, 56, 57, 59, 93, 94, 95, 96, 97, 98, 99, 102, 111, 112, 113, 114, 121, 149, 150, 155, 162, 163, 166, 168, 169, 174, 177, 178, 179, 180, 183, 195, 196, 197, 224, 225, 226, 235, 237, 240, 241, 257, 306, 328, 330, 331, 334, 342
distribution, xviii, xxn15, li, lii, lv, 84, 85, 86, 111, 143, 147, 148, 150, 151, 152, 153, 154, 155, 156, 158, 159, 161, 164, 166, 167, 172, 174, 175, 176, 177, 178, 180, 181, 182, 184, 188, 191, 193, 194, 198, 208, 213, 214, 218, 231, 232, 234, 235, 238, 239, 240, 249, 250, 251, 252, 259, 263, 265, 273, 279, 286, 358, 359, 360, 361, 362, 363, 365, 366
dodekatemorion, 17, 23, 24, 159, 335, 336
Egyptians, xxvn26, 191, 236, 329
Euctemon, xxiv, xxv, 346
Euripides, xxxiii, 247, 263
exaltation of the nativity > lot of Exaltation
gnomon, xxxix, lix, lx, 19, 20, 244, 287, 290, 293, 294, 295, 296, 297, 298, 299, 300, 301, 302, 303, 305, 338, 343, 345, 349, 350, 351, 352, 355, 356, 357
  horoscopic, 244, 287, 293, 294, 299, 355, 356, 357
  lunar, xxxix, lix, lx, 20, 290, 293, 294, 295, 296, 297, 298, 299, 300, 301, 302, 303, 305, 352
  operative, 338
  solar, xxxix, lix, lx, 20, 287, 290, 293, 294, 295, 296, 297, 298, 299, 300, 301, 302, 303, 305, 345, 352, 355, 356, 357
Greeks, xxiin14, 191
Hephaistion, ix, xx, xxiv, xliv, xlv, xlvii, xlviii, liv
Hermeias, xxiv, xxivn19, xxivn20, xxivn21, xxv, 186, 188
Hermetica, xvi, xvin7
Hermippos, xxiv, 83
Hipparcheion, xxiv, 28
Hipparchus, xvii, xviii, xxiv, xxivn23, xxvi, xlvin64, lxi, 346
horimaia, 123n1, 133, 337
horoscopic gnomon > gnomon, horoscopic
houseruler, xxvi, xlviii, lii, 6, 7, 8, 9, 17, 25, 50, 51, 52, 55, 56, 58, 59, 61, 62, 63, 64, 66, 68, 70, 76, 77, 78, 82, 83, 88, 89, 90, 91, 97, 102, 103, 105, 107, 108, 109, 110, 111, 113, 119, 120, 121, 123, 123n1, 124, 125,

126, 128, 129, 133, 134, 137, 138, 142, 143, 150, 152, 153, 154, 162, 171, 172, 174, 186n4, 198, 210, 250, 260, 261, 273, 291, 298
   in the investigations on the length of life, xlviii, 113, 119, 120, 121, 123, 124, 125, 126, 128, 129, 133, 134, 137, 138, 142, 143, 250, 260
   of the triangle, 50, 51, 83, 152
   of the year, 25, 162
houserulership, 49, 50, 110, 119, 121, 149
   in the investigations on the length of life, 110, 119, 121
   of the triangle, 49, 50
Hypsicles, xxv, xxvn24, 145
Ibn al-Nadīm, xivn3, xxxviii, xxxviiin52
Iliad, xxxiii, xxxiiin43, 207, 258, 341
illnesses, xxx, 96, 98, 131, 149, 162, 169, 170, 176, 177, 180, 210, 215, 226, 244, 253, 256, 257, 278, 311, 330, 334
   Also see disease
inception, 35
initiative, liv, lx, lxiii, 195, 197, 334, 348, 363
injury, xxviii, xxxi, xliv, xlvii, 4, 51, 52, 59, 60, 93, 94, 95, 96, 97, 98, 99, 102, 111, 113, 114, 149, 150, 155, 166, 167, 176, 178, 180, 226, 235, 237, 257, 266, 328, 330, 331, 334, 342
king, xi, xiii, xv, xvii, xxv, xxvii, xxxvii, xxxviii, xxxviiin52, lvi, lxiv, 7, 9, 28, 29, 35, 52, 54, 55, 56, 57, 61, 62, 63, 66, 69, 74, 75, 76, 77, 83, 113, 132, 135, 141, 142, 145, 156, 166, 169, 170, 194, 198, 206, 213, 214, 230, 254, 264, 265, 267, 268, 278, 279, 290, 325, 328, 329, 330, 331, 332, 341, 345, 346, 347, 352
   Nechepso, xvii, xxv, xxvii, xxxiin42, lixn80, 230, 325
Kidenas, xvii, xxv, xxvn25, lxi, 346
Komorowska, Joanna, vii, xi
Kroll, Wilhelm, viii, x, xi, xiv, xivn23, xxivn22, xxvin29, xxviin31, xxxi, xxxin39, xxxin40, xxxviii, xxxviiin54, xxxix, xlivn58, lxiii, lxiv
life, length of, xi, xix, xx, xxi, xxii, xxiii, xxvi, xxviii, xxxviin48, xxxviii, xl, xliii, xlviii, xlix, l, li, lin77, lv, lvi, lvii, lviin79, lviii, lix, lixn80, lx, lxi, lxii, lxiv, 82, 119, 123, 126, 132, 133, 135, 137, 138, 141, 142, 162, 244, 245, 246, 250, 251, 258, 259, 265,

288, 289, 290, 301, 305, 306, 307, 311, 329, 337, 339, 344, 346, 349, 351, 352, 355, 357, 358
   See also: **control**
Lots, xxviii, xlvii, li, lii, liii, lvi, 44, 51, 52, 53, 54, 55, 56, 57, 58, 59, 61, 66, 67, 68, 68n6, 69, 70, 71, 72, 73, 74, 75, 76, 77, 78, 79, 80, 81, 82, 83, 84, 85, 86, 87, 88, 89, 90, 95, 97, 98, 99, 100, 101, 102, 105, 106, 107, 108, 109, 110, 112, 114, 115, 116, 117, 132, 137, 141, 142, 143, 144, 146, 148, 149, 150, 153, 154, 155, 156, 157, 162, 163, 167, 184, 185, 185n2, 186, 188, 218, 219, 226, 250, 253, 258, 259, 260, 260n1, 261, 262, 265, 266, 267, 268, 269, 327, 328, 329, 337, 338, 343, 349
   Adultery, 105, 106
   Basis, 76, 77, 80, 81
   Children 108, 109
   Daimon, xxviii, lii, 54, 55, 56, 59, 60, 67n5, 68, 69, 76, 77, 78, 79, 80, 81, 82, 84, 85, 95, 97, 98, 99, 100, 101, 102, 106, 107, 108, 114, 117, 143, 148, 149, 150, 153, 154, 155, 157, 162, 163, 184, 185n2, 185n3, 218, 327, 337
      and prosperity
   Debt, xlvii, 78
   Deceit, xlvii, 78, 79
   Exaltation, 70, 71, 72 79, 80, 81, 82, 218
   Father, 88, 89, 90, 108
   Foreign Lands, 84, 85, 86, 87
   Fortune, xxviii, xlvii, li, lii, 51, 52, 53, 54, 55, 56, 57, 58, 59, 61, 66, 67, 68, 69, 70, 71, 72, 73, 74, 76, 77, 78, 79, 80, 81, 82, 83, 84, 85, 86, 87, 95, 97, 98, 99, 100, 101, 102, 106, 107, 108, 112, 114, 115, 116, 117, 141, 143, 144, 146, 148, 149, 150, 153, 154, 155, 156, 157, 162, 163, 167, 184, 185n2, 185n3, 186, 188, 218, 226, 253, 258, 259, 260, 260n1, 261, 262, 265, 266, 267, 268, 269, 327, 337
      and prosperity
      as the Ascendant, xlvii, 67
      calculation, xlvii, 52
   Justice, 80
   Hostility, 80
   Marriage, 105, 106
   Marriage for men, 106, 107
   Marriage for women, 106, 107

Mother, 107
Necessity, 60, 80, 162, 163, 185
Numerical Lot, 132, 137
Parents, 89, 90
Rank, xlvii
Standing, 79, 80
Theft, 78, 79
Travel, 84, 85, 86, 87
lunar nodes, xxxvii, xlv, liv, 27, 28, 137, 138, 139, 140, 141, 186, 196, 197, 288, 306, 333, 349
   calculation, 27, 28
Marcus (student of Valens), xviii, 281, 325, 350
marriage, xxi, xxix*n*38, xlviii, liii, 3, 4, 5, 14, 15, 16, 34, 35, 37, 59, 93, 102, 103, 104, 105, 106, 107, 108, 164, 166, 174, 175, 176, 178, 179, 181, 182, 215
Māshā'allāh, xxxviii
Meton, xxiv, xxv, 346
Midheaven, xxi, xxv, xlv, xlviii, 6, 10, 21, 50, 55, 58, 60, 63, 66, 67, 68, 68n6, 69, 70, 71, 72, 73, 74, 76, 80, 81, 82, 83, 85, 87, 89, 102, 103, 104, 109, 119, 120, 121, 122, 123, 124, 125, 125n2, 126, 128, 129, 133, 138, 139, 140, 154, 163, 171, 173, 186, 210, 212, 213, 218, 234, 250, 272, 273, 280
   calculation, 21
Mohammed, xxxviii
monomoirion, 186, 336
Moon, xv, xvi, xvii, xxi, xxiv*n*23, xxv, xxvi, xxxv, xxxvi, xlv, xlvii, xlviii, xlix, l, li, lii, liii, liv, lv, lvi, lvii, lix, lx, lxi, lxii, 3, 6, 7, 9, 11, 15, 17, 18, 19, 20, 23, 24, 25, 26, 27, 28, 29, 31, 33, 34, 35, 36, 37, 38, 39, 40, 41, 42, 43, 44, 45, 46, 47, 48, 49, 50, 51, 52, 54, 55, 56, 57, 58, 59, 61, 62, 63, 64, 65, 66, 67, 68, 69, 70, 71, 72, 73, 74, 75, 76, 77, 79, 80, 81, 82, 84, 87, 88, 89, 90, 91, 92, 93, 95, 97, 98, 99, 100, 101, 102, 103, 104, 106, 107, 108, 109, 110, 111, 112, 113, 114, 115, 116, 117, 119, 120, 121, 123, 124, 125, 125n2, 126, 127, 128, 129, 130, 131, 132, 133, 134, 136, 137, 138, 139, 140, 141, 142, 143, 144, 145, 147, 148, 149, 150, 151, 152, 153, 154, 155, 156, 157, 158, 160, 161, 162, 165, 167, 168, 170, 171, 172, 173, 174, 175, 176, 177, 179, 180, 181, 182, 183, 185, 186, 187, 188, 189, 190, 191, 193, 194, 195, 196, 197, 198, 199, 200, 201, 202, 203, 204, 208, 209, 210, 212, 213, 214, 215, 216, 217, 218, 219, 221, 222, 223, 224, 225, 226, 230, 233, 236, 237, 238, 239, 240, 241, 242, 243, 244, 245, 246, 249, 251, 253, 254, 255, 256, 259, 260, 262, 263, 265, 266, 267, 268, 269, 270, 271, 272, 273, 274, 275, 276, 277, 278, 279, 280, 281, 285, 286, 287, 290, 291, 293, 294, 295, 296, 297, 298, 299, 300, 301, 302, 303, 304, 305, 308, 309, 310, 311, 327, 328, 330, 332, 333, 334, 335, 336, 337, 338, 340, 342, 343, 344, 345, 346, 349, 350, 351, 352, 353, 354, 355, 356, 357, 358, 359, 360, 361, 362, 363, 364, 365, 366
   3rd, 7th, and 40th days, 26, 27
   calculation, lxi, lxii, 352, 353, 354
   full Moon, xlv, li, liii, liv, lvi, 19, 23, 24, 25, 26, 76, 80, 82, 91, 92, 93, 99, 110, 111, 112, 114, 115, 117, 121, 132, 133, 134, 137, 138, 139, 141, 147, 148, 149, 151, 153, 155, 162, 170, 174, 187, 195, 196, 198, 200, 201, 202, 203, 204, 244, 245, 266, 273, 286, 287, 308, 309, 330, 349, 350, 355, 356, 357
   gnomon > gnomon, lunar
   inclinations, liv, 199, 200, 230, 335, 337, 338
   new Moon, xlv, li, liii, liv, lvi, 19, 23, 24, 25, 26, 48, 58, 76, 80, 81, 82, 91, 92, 93, 99, 100, 111, 120, 132, 133, 134, 137, 138, 139, 140, 141, 147, 149, 151, 153, 162, 174, 176, 187, 195, 196, 198, 200, 245, 246, 266, 273, 281, 286, 287, 308, 309, 310, 330, 334, 335, 337, 349, 350, 355, 356
   phases, xlv, li, liii, liv, lvi, lxi, 19, 23, 24, 25, 76, 80, 81, 82, 91, 92, 93, 99, 100, 110, 111, 112, 114, 115, 117, 120, 121, 126, 133, 134, 137, 138, 139, 140, 141, 147, 148, 149, 151, 153, 155, 162, 170, 173, 174, 187, 195, 196, 198, 200, 201, 202, 203, 204, 244, 245, 246, 266, 273, 281, 286, 287, 305, 308, 309, 310, 330, 333, 335, 349, 350, 353, 355, 356, 357
   steps and winds, 28, 126, 127, 128, 132, 230

visibility, 26, 34, 92, 93, 200
nativity, xxi, xxiv, xxvi, xxxvi, xlii, xlvii, xlix, l, li, lii, liii, liv, lv, lvi, lxi, lxii, 3, 15, 16, 17, 21, 23, 25, 27, 28, 29, 31, 32, 33, 34, 36, 37, 38, 43, 45, 47, 48, 49, 50, 51, 52, 58, 60, 61, 62, 64, 65, 66, 67, 68, 69, 70, 71, 72, 73, 74, 76, 77, 78, 79, 80, 83, 84, 85, 86, 87, 88, 91, 92, 95, 97, 102, 103, 104, 105, 108, 109, 110, 111, 114, 118, 119, 120, 121, 122, 123, 124, 125, 126, 127, 128, 129, 131, 133, 134, 135, 136, 137, 138, 139, 140, 142, 143, 146, 147, 148, 149, 150, 151, 152, 154, 155, 156, 157, 158, 161, 162, 163, 164, 165, 167, 168, 169, 170, 171, 172, 173, 175, 178, 179, 180, 185, 186, 187, 188, 191, 193, 194, 195, 196, 198, 199, 200, 204, 205, 207, 209, 210, 211, 213, 218, 219, 220, 221, 222, 224, 226, 227, 228, 231, 232, 234, 235, 237, 239, 240, 243, 245, 246, 250, 251, 252, 253, 254, 258, 259, 260, 261, 262, 264, 265, 271, 273, 278, 279, 280, 281, 285, 286, 287, 290, 291, 292, 293, 305, 306, 307, 308, 327, 328, 329, 330, 333, 334, 335, 336, 337, 342, 343, 345, 347, 348, 349, 351, 353, 354, 356, 358, 360, 361, 362
   male and female, 336, 337, 338, 339
   monstrous or animal-like, 336, 337, 338, 339
Nechepso, xvii, xxv, xxvn26, xxviin31, xxxii, xxxiin42, lixn80, lxiii, lxv, 230, 325
Neugebauer, Otto, ix, xi, xiv, xxvn24, xxxix, lixn80, lxin83, lxiii, lxiv, 195n2, 260n1
nodes > lunar nodes
Odyssey, xxxiiin43, 340
Old Astrologer, 114, 123, 142
operative, xx, xxiv, xlviii, xlix, liv, lvi, 6, 8, 27, 29, 33, 34, 35, 39, 41, 50, 51, 52, 55, 63, 65, 66, 67, 72, 76, 80, 83, 84, 89, 91, 92, 102, 103, 105, 106, 109, 111, 121, 122, 124, 126, 133, 142, 143, 145, 158, 159, 161, 162, 163, 168, 169, 170, 171, 172, 175, 178, 180, 183, 184, 185, 186, 187, 198, 199, 210, 212, 218, 219, 220, 221, 222, 223, 224, 232, 233, 235, 245, 250, 252, 253, 254, 255, 256, 257, 261, 262, 263, 265, 267, 268, 269, 270, 271, 272, 273, 274, 275, 276, 277, 278, 280, 291, 308, 327, 328, 329 , 334, 337, 338, 344, 345, 351, 352
   day, xxiv, liv, 199
   places, 27, 33, 39, 41, 51, 52, 63, 67, 72, 111, 124, 126, 161, 162, 163, 168, 169, 170, 171, 180, 183, 184, 220, 232, 233, 273, 351
   month, liv, lvi, 187, 198, 352
   year, xx, liv, 159
Orion, xxv, 7, 8, 122
Orpheus, xxxiii, 326
parents, xxvi, xlvii, 4, 17, 54, 73, 83, 87, 89, 90, 91, 93, 207, 212, 219, 266, 329, 330, 331
Petosiris, xvii, xxv, xxvn26, xxviin31, xxxii, xxxiin42, lixn80, lxiv, 53, 83, 109, 110, 132, 264, 267, 290, 328, 345
Pingree, David, viii, ix, x, xi, xiiin1, xiv, xivn4, xixn10, xxvn26, xxviin31, xxxin39, xxxvii, xxxviin49, xxxviii, xxxviiin50, xxxviiin53, xxxviiin54, xxxix, xxxixn55, xxxixn57, lxiii, lxv, 114n8, 312n2, 318n3
places, xx, xxi, xxii, xxiii, xxiiin17, xxv, xlvii, xlix, liii, lx, 3, 6, 8, 18, 25, 27, 33, 39, 41, 44, 49, 50, 51, 52, 53, 54, 55, 55n1, 56, 57, 58, 59, 61, 62, 63, 64, 65, 66, 67, 68, 68n6, 69, 70, 71, 72, 73, 74, 75, 76, 77, 78, 79, 80, 81, 82, 83, 84, 85, 86, 87, 88, 89, 90, 91, 92, 93, 97, 98, 99, 101, 102, 104, 105, 106, 107, 108, 109, 110, 111, 112, 113, 114, 115, 116, 117, 120, 122, 123, 124, 126, 129, 130, 131, 133, 136, 137, 141, 142, 143, 145, 149, 151, 152, 153, 154, 155, 156, 159, 160, 161, 162, 163, 165, 166, 167, 168, 169, 170, 171, 172, 173, 174, 176, 180, 181, 183, 184, 185, 186, 187, 193, 194, 195, 196, 197, 198, 199, 200, 204, 208, 209, 210, 211, 212, 213, 214, 215, 217, 218, 219, 220, 226, 227, 230, 232, 233, 234, 238, 244, 245, 246, 251, 255, 257, 258, 260, 263, 265, 266, 272, 273, 276, 279, 280, 281, 290, 291, 293, 299, 300, 301, 302, 303, 304, 306n1, 310, 311, 327, 328, 329, 329n1, 330, 331, 332, 333, 347, 351, 352, 358, 362, 366
   of Accomplishment, 69, 71, 73, 74, 75, 77, 78, 79, 81, 82, 155, 156, 218, 279, 280, 281
   Crisis-Producing, liii, 122, 183, 193, 215, 218
   ecliptic > lunar nodes, 133, 195, 197
   inoperative, 44, 62, 64, 162

names, 54-60, 165-166
operative > operative, places
planetary hours, 24
planets > stars
Philip (astronomer), xxv, 30, 346
predominance > control
projection of rays, 89, 119, 123, 124, 126, 128
prosperity, 4, 51, 58, 60, 67, 67n5, 68, 69, 76, 78, 83, 93, 103, 118, 154, 171, 174, 175, 177, 183, 206, 229
releasing > vital sector
rising times, xxv, xxvi, xlv, xlviii, l, li, lvi, lviii, lix, lixn80, lxn81, 17, 18, 20, 21, 22, 23, 26, 50, 82, 83, 123, 124, 125, 125n2, 129, 130, 138, 139, 142, 143, 145, 146, 172, 188, 212, 227, 244, 245, 250, 251, 252, 253, 254, 255, 256, 259, 260, 261, 262, 264, 265, 266, 267, 268, 269, 270, 271, 272, 273, 274, 275, 277, 278, 285, 287, 289, 290, 291, 292, 293, 294, 295, 300, 308, 309, 310, 311, 333, 336, 337, 338, 342, 343, 345, 346, 350, 351, 352, 355, 356, 356n1, 357
  one-half, lvi, lvii, lviii, 148, 264, 266, 268, 270, 274, 276, 277, 307, 308
  one-third, xxv, 22, 121, 122, 125, 148, 264, 266, 268, 272, 275, 277, 285, 308, 356
  two-thirds, xxv, lvi, lvii, 264, 266, 267, 268, 269, 270, 271, 272, 274, 275, 277, 356
Schmidt, Robert, viii, xii
sect, xlix, 3, 4, 5, 6, 25, 44, 49, 50, 51, 52, 54, 56, 62, 69, 70, 72, 75, 77, 78, 79, 80, 82, 88, 89, 91, 94, 105, 107, 111, 118, 119, 127, 128, 142, 143, 152, 153, 155, 168, 175, 186, 218, 227, 233, 241, 250, 260, 263, 278, 286,
Seuthes, xxiv, xxv, 186
signs, x, xvi, xviii, xx, xxi, xxviii, xxviiin35, xxxvii, xlv, xlvn61, xlvi, xlviii, xlix, l, lii, liii, liv, lv, lvi, lviin79, lviii, lix, lixn80, 6, 7, 8, 9, 10, 11, 12, 17, 18, 19, 20, 21, 22, 23, 25, 26, 27, 28, 29, 30, 31, 32, 33, 34, 35, 37, 43, 44, 47, 48, 50, 52, 54, 55, 56, 57, 58, 59, 60, 61, 62, 63, 64, 65, 66, 67, 68, 69, 70, 76, 78, 80, 81, 82, 83, 84, 85, 86, 87, 88, 89, 90, 91, 92, 93, 94, 95, 96, 97, 98, 98n7, 99, 100, 102, 104, 106, 107, 109, 111, 112, 113, 114, 115, 116, 120, 121, 122, 123, 124, 125, 126, 129, 130, 131, 133, 136, 138, 139, 141, 142, 143, 144, 145, 147, 149, 150, 151, 152, 153, 154, 155, 157, 158, 160, 161, 162, 163, 165, 166, 167, 169, 170, 171, 172, 175, 178, 180, 181, 183, 184, 185, 186, 187, 188, 190, 191, 193, 195, 196, 197, 198, 199, 200, 204, 208, 209, 210, 211, 212, 213, 215, 218, 219, 220, 221, 222, 223, 227, 231, 232, 233, 234, 240, 243, 244, 245, 246, 249, 250, 251, 252, 253, 255, 256, 259, 260, 261, 265, 266, 267, 268, 269, 270, 271, 273, 275, 276, 277, 278, 280, 281, 284, 285, 286, 288, 289, 290, 291, 292, 293, 294, 296, 297, 298, 299, 300, 301, 302, 303, 304, 305, 306, 307, 310, 311, 325, 327, 328, 329, 331, 332, 333, 334, 335, 336, 337, 338, 343, 344, 345, 349, 350, 351, 352, 355, 358
  beholding, 22, 55, 129, 244
  critical, 136, 198, 204
  listening, 22, 55, 129, 193, 244
  years, months, days, and hours, 150, 152
  natures, xx, xxi, xlv, 6-12, 68, 80, 96, 97, 107, 193, 199, 250, 265, 336
Soudines, xvii, xxv, lxi, 346
Sphaerica, xxvi, xxvin27, 8, 9, 11, 12, 13
stars (see also: Moon), xiv, xvi, xx, xxi, xxii, xxiv, xxvi, xxviii, xxviiin35, xxxiii, xxxiv, xxxvi, xxxvii, xxxviin48, xxxviiin52, xliv, xlv, xlvi, xlvin65, xlvii, xlix, l, li, lin77, lii, liii, liv, lv, lvi, lvii, lviin79, lviii, 3, 4, 5, 6, 7, 8, 9, 11, 12, 20, 21, 24, 25, 30, 31, 32, 33, 34, 35, 36, 37, 38, 39, 40, 41, 42, 43, 44, 49, 50, 51, 52, 53, 54, 55, 57, 59, 60, 61, 62, 63, 64, 65, 66, 67, 68, 69, 72, 76, 77, 78, 80, 81, 82, 83, 84, 85, 86, 87, 88, 89, 90, 91, 96, 97, 98, 99, 102, 103, 104, 105, 106, 107, 109, 110, 111, 113, 114, 118, 119, 120, 121, 122, 124, 125, 126, 127, 128, 129, 130, 131, 132, 134, 135n4, 136, 141, 142, 143, 144, 145, 146, 147, 148, 149, 150, 151, 152, 153, 154, 157, 158, 160, 161, 162, 163, 164, 165, 166, 167, 168, 169, 170, 171, 173, 174, 175, 176, 177, 178, 179, 180, 181, 183, 184, 186, 186n4, 187, 188, 190, 191, 193, 194, 196, 198, 199, 200, 209, 210, 211, 212,

213, 215, 218, 219, 220, 221, 222, 223, 226, 230, 231, 232, 233, 234, 235, 236, 237, 238, 239, 240, 242, 243, 245, 249, 250, 251, 252, 253, 255, 256, 257, 259, 260, 261, 262, 263, 264, 265, 266, 268, 270, 273, 276, 277, 278, 279, 280, 281, 291, 298, 305, 310, 311, 327, 328, 329, 331, 332, 333, 334, 340, 343, 344, 346, 357n2, 358, 359, 360, 361, 362, 363, 364, 365, 366

calculations, xxiv, lv, 28-33

colors, xliv, lv, 3, 4, 5, 6, 236-237

combinations, 33-37,
    two stars, xxviii, 33-37, 219
    three stars, xxviii, xlvi, 37-44, 54, 83

configurations, xxxii, xlvii, xlviii, 50, 52, 54, 55, 60, 61, 62, 66, 67, 82, 84, 85, 86, 87, 98, 102, 108, 162, 164, 165, 185, 211, 221, 245, 251, 252, 253, 259, 262, 263, 273, 276, 279, 366

    years, months, days, and hours, 147, 148, 150, 157

    natures, 3-6

    periods, 147, 157

    phases, xlv, liii, liv, 92, 93, 121, 143, 162, 164, 165, 168-169, 173, 174, 230, 245, 266, 279, 281, 305, 327, 334, 349, 353

    steps and winds, 28, 126, 127, 131, 132, 162, 211, 230, 339

    transits, 33, 153-154, 168-169, 238

starter > apheta

terms, xx, xxii*n*15, xxiii, xxviii*n*35, xlv, xlv*n*62, xlviii, xlix, lx, 5, 13, 14, 15, 16, 17, 19, 63, 66, 102, 103, 119, 120, 121, 123, 126, 128, 129, 130, 131, 132, 134, 137, 159, 188, 190, 198, 245, 310, 311, 358

transits, xxiv, li, 25, 33, 54, 87, 132, 148, 153-154, 158, 160, 161, 162, 164, 165, 168, 169, 170, 171, 174, 175, 186, 188, 194, 196, 197, 199, 200, 210, 219, 220, 221, 222, 232, 233, 238, 245, 250, 273, 279, 280, 332, 366

transmissions, xxii, xxiv, xxviii*n*35, li, li*n*77, lii, liii, liv, lv, 87, 127, 137, 151, 152, 153, 154, 159, 161, 163, 164, 165, 166, 167, 168, 169, 170, 171, 172, 173, 174, 175, 176, 177, 180, 181, 182, 183, 184, 185, 187, 191, 194, 195, 198, 199, 204, 208, 209, 212, 213, 214, 215, 217, 218, 219, 220, 221, 222, 226, 227, 232, 232n1, 233, 234, 235, 238, 239, 241, 242, 243, 245, 280, 310, 360, 363

travel, xxii, xxiv, xxvi, xxx, xlvii, liii, 3, 9, 15, 37, 39, 40, 42, 56, 58, 61, 83, 84, 85, 86, 87, 93, 141, 153, 166, 167, 169, 173, 175, 177, 178, 179, 180, 194, 210, 211, 214, 215, 217, 236, 238, 255, 256, 266, 277, 326, 331, 334

triangles, xxviii, xlvii, 44, 49, 50, 51, 54, 61, 62, 65, 66, 70, 71, 72, 73, 74, 75, 77, 81, 82, 83, 87, 88, 118, 119, 131, 151, 152, 156, 158n1, 191, 200, 240

triplicities > triangles

Thrasyllus, xxv, xxvi, 345

Timaeus, 325

twins, 134, 234, 286, 287, 288, 306

Valentinianus III, 357

vital degree, 338

vital sector, xxiii, xxvi, xlviii, xlix, li, li*n*77, lii, liv, lv, lix, 123, 124, 125, 125n2, 126, 128, 129, 131, 133, 134, 138, 139, 147, 148, 149, 150, 157, 165, 188n6, 209, 210, 211, 214, 219, 220, 233, 245, 298

Wālis, xiv, xiv*n*3, xxxviii

Zoroaster, xxvi, 332

www.ingramcontent.com/pod-product-compliance
Lightning Source LLC
Chambersburg PA
CBHW060457010526
44118CB00018B/2440